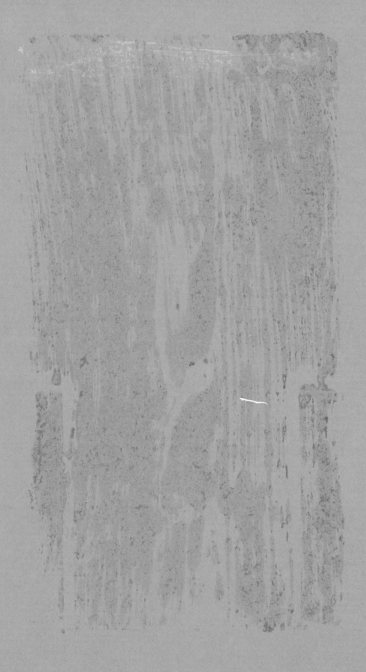

A
Passionate
Prodigality

Letters
to Alan Bird
from Richard Aldington
1949 - 1962

A Passionate Prodigality

Letters to Alan Bird from

RICHARD ALDINGTON

1949-1962

Edited with an Introduction by

MIRIAM J. BENKOVITZ

The New York Public Library
Astor, Lenox and Tilden Foundations

&

Readex Books
A Division of Readex Microprint Corporation

THIS VOLUME IS PRODUCED WITH THE ASSISTANCE OF THE
JUDGE AND MRS SAMUEL D. LEVY MEMORIAL PUBLICATION FUND

FIRST EDITION

Library of Congress Cataloging in Publication Data
Aldington, Richard, 1892–1962.
A passionate prodigality.
Includes index.
1. Aldington, Richard, 1892–1962 — Correspondence.
2. Bird, Alan.
3. Authors — Correspondence, reminiscences, etc.
I. Bird, Alan. II. Title.
PR6001.L4Z543 821'.9'12 [B] 75–23105
ISBN 0–87104–259–2

Distributed by Readex Books
Designed by Marilan Lund
Printed at the Printing Office of The New York Public Library, in
Caledonia types with Bulmer display types, on Warren's Olde Style
paper, in an edition of 1,500 copies.

CONTENTS

Illustrations

(*following page 32*)

Richard Aldington and Alan Bird

To the memory of
John D. Gordan

Introduction

THESE ONE HUNDRED AND FORTY-SEVEN LETTERS which Richard Aldington wrote between 1949 and 1962 to Alan Bird, distinguished educator, writer, and lecturer on literature and art, are one side of a correspondence between two men who never met. In 1948 Bird developed a deep interest in Gérard de Nerval. On holiday in France that year, he had bought and enjoyed a copy of Nerval's poems and stories. When he returned to England and investigated Nerval in the University Library at Cambridge, Bird found Aldington's translation of Nerval's *Aurelia*. Readers were still hampered in 1948 by war-time destruction of books and post-war shortages, so that Bird thought himself fortunate to be able to gratify his interest in Nerval; and in his enthusiasm he wrote to Aldington to express his admiration for the translation and to ask questions about Nerval. Aldington replied on 3 February 1949, suggesting several books for Bird to read. Before the exchange of letters was established, however, Bird took the initiative twice more, once at the end of 1949 by sending a copy of his prize-winning poem *Speed* to Aldington and once in 1950 by congratulating him on his study of D. H. Lawrence, *Portrait of a Genius But. . . .*

By late 1950 Bird had matriculated as a graduate student at Wadham College, Oxford University, and at first the correspondence no doubt seemed another aspect of the intellectual exhilaration and happiness he found there. His undergraduate work was done at Cambridge, where he was a member of Selwyn College and where in June 1950 he had been admitted to the B.A. degree with honors in English. At the invitation of C. M. Bowra, Warden of Wadham, Bird then migrated to Oxford, concentrating on Education. He soon lost his enthusiasm for the theories of Education expounded at the university, but he was highly gratified by his life at Oxford. His own account of "what a delightful place" it could be runs:

> I enjoyed myself so much there even though I could hardly be classed
> as a green undergraduate: winning a prize for a short story (dreadful)
> from dear and kind Neville Coghill, tea with the Cecil family and the
> Nicol Smiths, long conversations with John Masefield, wretched poems
> published, hours and hours of research in the Bodleian and the B.M.,
> music with friends (I'd only just discovered the Winterreise and Dichter-
> liebe), walks in the country, oh! all sorts of pleasures.

As for Aldington, he invariably replied to the numberless letters which came to him — as they come to every author — whatever their source. He liked to discuss literature, and he liked to encourage the critical attitudes of young men. James Reeves, John Atkins, Charles Norman, Edward Nehls,

and many more can attest to that. Besides, a writer wants to be read, and
letters indicating that he has been are welcome. In this instance, when he
had Bird's third letter with its Oxford address, Aldington saw an opportunity
to get help with the book on which he was at work, the biography of T. E.
Lawrence. He asked Bird to cooperate, first in providing material about
Oxford and its eccentricities and then in an examination of the details of
Lawrence's parentage. Although Aldington more than once indicated to Bird
that he would be paid for his research in Aldington's behalf, nothing definite
was offered and no arrangement to pay him was made. Yet, by the time he
left Oxford, Bird was so involved with Aldington's work and Aldington so
relied on Bird for books, suggestions, and verification of facts that the
correspondence was assured. It needed no formal or personal bond in order
to continue. It had developed into an easy, comfortable exchange.

For that reason these letters to Bird are valuable in a consideration of
Richard Aldington. To write to an unknown person whose sympathies can
be taken for granted and whose interests are as iridescent as one's own is
not far from keeping a journal. Of course Aldington practised the ceremonies
of letter-writing. He asked from time to time about Bird's health; he congratulated Bird on coming unscathed through the night of 26 January 1952,
a night of fire and terror in Cairo. He expressed enough interest in Bird's
visit to Spain to reminisce about his own stay in Spain, and he inquired about
Bird's activities at Oxford and Liverpool. But there were few times when
he allowed Bird's opinion to influence the contents of a letter directly. Aldington rebuked Bird for minimizing the near-poverty of John Gawsworth
and Carl Fallas. Aldington corrected Bird's misreading of a statement in
Lawrence of Arabia about Lawrence's *The Mint*, and he bitterly protested
Bird's suggestion that to arraign the University of Oxford for its neglect of
merit and its reward of Wise, the literary forger, was unfair. In these cases,
Aldington spoke his mind briefly and sharply. Then he dismissed the matter
and returned, in the letter in hand, to his usual journal-like spontaneity and
lack of constraint, filling page after page with an account of his own affairs,
his thoughts, and his emotions. That he was sometimes inconsistent and
often extravagant was a part of his ease.

In two respects, the letters may be misleading. First, the difficulties of
getting *Lawrence of Arabia* published in opposition to the maneuvers of
what Aldington called the Lawrence Bureau, a deliberate and organized
effort on the part of Lawrence's influential friends to prevent publication,
and the controversy about the book beset Aldington. But his apparent obsession with the biography, however real, was accentuated by the fact that he

depended on Bird's help and that Lawrence was mutually important in their early correspondence. Second, Aldington's scorn for homosexuality is often shocking, especially more than a decade later when a reasonable view of it at last prevails. Yet, in the midst of a condemnation of "fashionable" homosexuality, he remarked on the need for a "more wholesome outlook . . . neither persecuting . . . nor cultivating."

Nevertheless it is Aldington's discursiveness in these letters and his uninhibited record of the moment — his "passionate prodigality of statement" — which is instructive. They demonstrate what Aldington was in the last thirteen or fourteen years of his life. Day to day living had no greater pleasure for him than good food and drink. He had a discerning taste for provincial French cooking and the wines of France. Even in his last years, when he was often too tired to make much effort, Aldington frequently drove from Maison Sallé into Sancerre for dinner at the restaurant of the Hôtel du Point. More nourishing to him, however, were literature, particularly poetry, and art. He had viewed painting and sculpture in numerous cities and villages, wherever he found them. But his ardor was reserved for literature. Although he disclaimed interest in the novel, his admiration for Dickens was great enough to rank him next to Shakespeare among English writers. As for poetry, Aldington was steeped in it, whether in English or not. In his wide reading, nothing was so absorbing as poetry. When he was close to exhaustion from the Lawrence of Arabia book, Aldington could still "bless whatever gods may be" that he had the "consolation of poetry." Short of writing it, he was as eager to serve its cause as he had been in 1914, when he and H.D. helped Pound foster Imagism. Poetry was at once a joy, a stimulus, and a refuge in a world he sorely distrusted.

Over and over, Aldington showed himself fiercely anti-British, anti-Russian, anti-American, and occasionally anti-French. Richard Aldington was an angry, anguished man; but his rage was directed less at nations than at national leaders. He despised them as hypocrites, and he feared where they might lead. In his eyes every international politician blundered toward war, and war was Aldington's abiding horror. Without reference to his *Images of War* or to *Roads to Glory* and *Death of a Hero*, his attitude is plain in a letter written to Peter Russell in 1952.[1] In it, Aldington recalled in precise detail the circumstances of a leave in 1917 with the mud of France still in his skin and the "louse bites barely healed." He told how, when leave came, because he was "in rags and lousy," he was seized and fumigated and re-

---

[1] Lockwood Memorial Library, State University of New York at Buffalo.

clothed from head to foot "in case England should learn the truth." The posturing and fencing of the United States and Russia, especially in the 1950s, appeared to Aldington to threaten world peace, and he fulminated against both with impartial vigor. The amelioration of his rage at the Soviet Union when the Russians began to reprint his works and to glorify his stand against war may seem expedient, but weighing against that impression is his reluctance to accept Russian attention and his willing faith in the Soviet stance as lover of peace.

Besides, Aldington thought their interest in his work justified. He believed in it. He was confident of his merits as a writer, and he thought he deserved better than he got from English critics and publishers. His absorption in immediate work kept him to a regular, daily schedule almost to the end of his life, but according to these letters he constantly ranged in memory and emotion over the literary figures with whom he had been associated: Ford Madox Ford, Nancy Cunard, Norman Douglas, the Sitwells, Roy Campbell, Wyndham Lewis, and, above all, Eliot, Pound, and D. H. Lawrence. Comparisons were inevitable, and Aldington calmly asserted his place in England's literature.

If his opinion argues a formidable egocentricity, it must be reconciled with Aldington's confiding and affectionate nature. Most obvious in support of this was his dependence on Bird, first in their intellectual pursuits and then, as the years went by, for solace in his isolation. Similarly Aldington accepted without question services prompted by affection from Alister Kershaw. Most telling, however, was Aldington's relation with Catherine, his daughter. On her he lavished his store of love. Nothing was too much for him to offer, even poetry after a long silence, as these verses written for Catherine's birthday attest:

> I was a poet once, but now no longer
>   The vivid words throng burning in my brain;
> Age chills them all; but love for once is stronger
>   And for your sake I feel them burn again.
>
> Scarred from the battle, grim with hopes frustrated,
>   What can I bring your glorious youth but this
> Last feeble murmur of a Muse belated,
>   My love, my anxious care, a father's kiss?
>
> May all your life to come be gay with laughter,
>   May love be true, and all your friends sincere!
> Whatever comes in all the years hereafter,
>   Be sweet, be brave! And there'll be nought to fear.[2]

---

[2] Autograph MS, Humanities Research Center, University of Texas.

But there is no necessity to look outside the letters to Bird for evidence of Aldington's devotion to Catherine. He was proud, amused, and bemused by turns with his daughter; and his greatest delight was to impart to her his cosmopolitanism, his high regard for what endured from the past, often obscurely, in the way of legend, history, and the arts.

While such variety and ease indicate the quality of Aldington's intellect, they make editorial difficulties. They lead to repetition. Wherever possible, repetitious statements have been omitted. A number of other passages have been deleted for one reason or another, some at the request of Aldington's executor. All ellipses in the text of the letters are indicated by three points in square brackets, as [. . .]; they are to be distinguished from Aldington's frequent use of points in a series. His references are so numerous that only the inclusion of a biographical glossary as a part of the index keeps the editorial paraphernalia from outweighing the letters.

Otherwise the editorial problems are negligible. All letters are dated and signed. Now and then there is a lack of continuity between letters owing to the fact that Bird lost a few during a difficult stay in Cairo, and he may have lost one or two others at a later time. No attempt has been made to supply artificial links between letters. The rare errors in spelling and other minor mistakes, usually typographical, have been silently corrected. Informalities in Aldington's usage such as his failure to italicize titles of books have been allowed to stand.

This edition of Aldington's letters was suggested by the late John D. Gordan, then Curator of the Henry W. and Albert A. Berg Collection of English and American Literature in The New York Public Library, to which the letters belong. His successor, Lola L. Szladits, has made every effort to assist in carrying out the original plan of the project. My indebtedness to John Gordan is expressed elsewhere. To Lola Szladits and to the Trustees of The New York Public Library, Astor, Lenox, and Tilden Foundations, I am grateful for access to the Aldington documents. Permission to publish has been granted by Richard Aldington's daughter, Catherine Aldington Guillaume, and his executor, Alister Kershaw. Both have done everything within their power to make this book complete. Alister Kershaw, in addition, has given encouragement and valuable suggestions; he read the typescript in an early stage. Similarly Alan Bird read the typescript and gave me the benefits of his opinion, his vast learning, and his remarkable memory. A. W. Lawrence and Jonathan Cape Ltd granted permission to quote excerpts from books and letters written by T. E. Lawrence. The British Museum allowed me to read the letters from Lawrence to Charlotte Shaw. James Laughlin, acting for the Ezra Pound Literary Property Trust, gave permission to quote Pound's letters. Gladys Brownell and Jacques Temple provided answers to many seemingly unanswerable questions. Mikhail Urnov sent me a copy of his list of works by and about Aldington; it proved to be an invaluable tool. Mary E. Williams helped in too many ways to list here. Both the Humanities Research Center of the University of Texas and the Skidmore College Library have been unfailing in satisfying every request. To their staffs but especially to Mary M. Hirth (now retired) of one and Barbara Smith of the other, I want to record my appreciation. I want to thank Skidmore College for grants which enabled me to have this book typed by Marion Derlick. I wish also to acknowledge other assistance from the University of Basel, M. Benoit, A. Bousselham, the British Broadcasting Corporation, the British Museum, John Byrne, Dorothy M. Butcher, the Registry of Cambridge University, Jonathan Cape Ltd, W. Charlotte, Chatto & Windus Ltd, Alan Clodd, Wm. Collins & Co. Ltd, Condé Nast Publications, Inc, the Slavic and Central European Division of the Library of Congress, Thyra Creyke-Clark, Czechoslovak Television, W. D. Deasey, Mary Jane Devlin, Dilia, Helga B. Doblin, Mojmir Drvota, J. M. Eyles, Keath Fraser, Ralph E. Fulsom, P. N. Furbank, David Garnett, Norman T. Gates, G. Gooden, the Embassy of the Republic of Guinea, the Institute for American Universities of Aix-en-Provence, Thomas J. Jackson, Ann Johnson, Jody Johnson, Laurence Josephs, Sonya P. Karsen, Jean Kempton, Selwyn Kittredge, Phillip Knightley, David V. Koch, Gordon Landsborough, Walter Lowenfels, Harry T. Moore, P. W. Moss, Winifred A. Myers, The New English Library, the Registry of Oxford University, Alison Palmer, Norman Holmes Pearson, Z. Pechold, Gaye Poulton, Evelyn Raphael, Edith Reider, Anthony Rota, Beryl and George Sims, T. C. Skeat, Norah Smallwood, Ludvík Soukup, the Morris Library of Southern Illinois University, the Lockwood Memorial Library of the State University of New York at Buffalo, Rudolf Sturm, Irene Thornley, Arthur Uphill, *Vogue*, the late Herbert Weinstock, Sergius Yakobson, and Marjorie G. Wynne.

MIRIAM J. BENKOVITZ

Saratoga Springs, New York, February 1975

Editor's Note

Richard Aldington (1892–1962) is designated in the notes throughout by the initials RA. The owners of letters and manuscripts quoted or cited in the notes are shown by brief titles in parentheses or, when the format demands it, in square brackets. A key to these follows:

Berg: Henry W. and Albert A. Berg Collection of English and American Literature, The New York Public Library

Buffalo: Lockwood Memorial Library, State University of New York at Buffalo

Texas: Humanities Research Center, University of Texas

The letters which T. E. Lawrence wrote to Charlotte F. Shaw are the property of the British Museum. Other letters unidentified as to ownership are the property of the editor, Miriam J. Benkovitz, who is indicated in the notes as MJB.

The full addresses (abbreviated in the headings of the printed letters) of Aldington's three major places of residence during his correspondence with Bird are given in letters 1, 13, and 131 (see also 133).

THE LETTERS

Richard Aldington to Alan Bird:

But after our death, if people are interested, why shouldn't they know the truth about everyone — and not only about Pepys and Boswell?

Montpellier, 3 July 1955

And the principle that you are not to say anything impolite about the work or character of a writer who has been dead 20 years destroys both honest criticism and honest biography. Why must we be so damned mealy-mouthed?

Montpellier, 15 August 1952

I

3 February 1949   *Villa Aucassin, St Clair, Le Lavandou, Var*

DEAR MR BIRD,

I was very glad to hear from you and to know that you are finding interest in those 19th century writers. One of the curses of professional authorship is that it leaves so little time and energy for leisurely disinterested reading, "art for art's sake" if I may use the wicked words. I rejoice to think that there are yet men to whom it may be possible.

Since I wrote I have looked through J. A. Symonds's In the Key of Blue and Essays Speculative and Suggestive;[1] MacCurdy's Roses of Paestum;[2] two volumes of Dobson; two of William Sharp and three of Gosse — all blank. It occurs to me you might find something of or about Nerval in Gosse's French Profiles[3] which I haven't got. It is true perhaps that, as Yeats always used to declare, Gosse was "merely a correspondent to Parnassus," but he was well read in French. Indeed early in the twenties the T.L.S. paid him the grandiose compliment of asserting that he was "the dean of French letters in England."[4] There is also nothing in any of the books I have read by Frederick Wedmore and Vernon Lee, and nothing of course in Birrell's Obiter Dicta,[5] a grossly over-rated work. Many of those people were in love with an impossibly idealised Hellas and Renaissance Italy, a sort of cultural Avalon. Only selected aspects of France — the Troubadours, the Pleiade and of course the Arthurian romances were allowed by the rules of the game. It is all very delightful after so much social realism and earnest church-going.

I grieve to hear that Cambridge has fallen into righteousness. When I used to make brief visits in the twenties and early thirties it struck me as a cheerful god-less place where life ran high. Isn't it curious that large sections of the British intelligentsia cannot be at ease unless prostrated before an American expatriate. There was Russell Lowell, then Whistler, then Henry James, then Logan Pearsall Smith, now Eliot.[6] The only one who fell by the way was Ezra Pound[7] whom Eliot is now making strenuous though behind the scenes efforts to revive. Well, it is a good idea always to enjoy the elements of comedy which exist even in the grimmest times. I should be very grateful if you would tell me of any discoveries you make in that period, and I shall be glad to pass on anything I find.

Yours sincerely,
RICHARD ALDINGTON

[1] 1893 and 1890.

[2] 1900.

[3] 1905; contains no mention of Nerval.

[4] See London *Times* 15 Feb 1923 p 13 where Mons Abel Chevalley called Gosse one of "the greatest critics and men of letters of our time."

[5] 1884 and 1887.

[6] Lowell, poet and essayist, was minister to Great Britain from 1880 to 1885. The artist James McNeill Whistler moved from Paris to London in 1863. Although James had visited England

[3]

earlier, he began to make his residence there when he moved into 3 Bolton Street, Piccadilly, London, on 12 Dec 1876. T. S. Eliot went from Marburg, Germany, where he was at work on a doctoral dissertation, to England and Merton College, Oxford, in Aug 1914. About RA's statement, Bird wrote, "There was a naughty wilful streak in Aldington which made him perverse in statements of this kind and which I don't think he really believed in himself. He was I'm sure the kindest and gentlest of men in life. But what began as a kind of growling pose sometimes developed into a vein of biting bitterness at his own neglect and the lack of recognition to which he was entitled." (Alan Bird to MJB, Halsall, Ormskirk, Lancashire, 29 Aug 1967.)

[7] In late summer 1908, Pound reached London, where he lived in quarters which RA described as a "really awful slum bedroom in a curious courtyard (down Church Walk) behind St Mary Abbott's" (RA to Peter Russell, Montpellier, 17 Feb 1952 [Buffalo]). Moving later to a flat at 5 Holland Park Chambers, Kensington, Pound remained in England until 1920. By then he had decided that the English had "no brains," and he went to the Continent.

2

20 December 1949   *Le Lavandou*

DEAR MR BIRD,

I have a new Swiss typewriter which prints red and black, and can't forbear showing it off a bit.[1]

It is great fun that you have got the Chancellor's medal, and also a feather in the cap.[2] There is an undue depreciation of such awards, especially among those who are not eligible. Ah, Lucas — I remember his poems, I wrote a silly and rather ungracious review of them.[3] Recently I read his Greek Anthology versions, and thought some of them first-rate. There is one about a sailor in a storm I liked extremely.[4]

How much appreciation of poetry is a matter of local prejudice and unconscious chauvinism. Is not all taste limited by ignorance? Thirty years ago I should have scoffed at anyone who questioned the primacy of Shakespeare and English poets in general. Twenty-five years spent in France and Italy, where there is much poetry of a different kind, (and several years in America where there are so many thousands of bad poets nobody reads the few good ones) have changed my tastes. I still read English poets, but I find my infidelities increase with age. I have a daughter aged 11–12, who arrived in France from Hollywood three years ago.[5] French is now her real language, and she has imbibed the literary prejudices of her instructors. Molière, La Fontaine and Racine are her gods, and indeed when she repeats O mon souverain roi[6] in faultless French (which I shall never achieve) I sympathize. She has very highbrow taste in English — only Lear, Lewis Carroll and one or two others. For the rest — la poésie anglaise n'est pas jolie. So you see, like Pascal's morals, le bon goût is a matter of place rather than intelligence. I gave it up long ago. What amuses me is good, and what bores me is bad, and nuts to highbrows.

Curious you feel Synge is phoney. There again I should have been scandalised in the past. But I re-read Riders to the Sea[7] last summer, and had exactly that sensation of fake. We may be wrong. It may be that Kiltarten English puts one off. As to Yeats — I knew him pretty well from 1912 to 1929.[8] He was much offended by a jest at his expense in a thing I wrote called A Dream in the Luxembourg.[9] He was interesting but either a dupe or a poseur, and as his wife once remarked sotto-voce within my hearing "Willie talking poppycock again." The last of the Quartier Latin bards. He always wore a floppy black tie like Alphonse Daudet and Gordon Craig. Don't you get anything out of his early plays? Mannered but sometimes lovely. I believe his great mistake was in the middle twenties when Ezra persuaded him to imitate what were then more or less les jeunes. He should have stuck to his guns and let their scorn flow over him. One can surely recognize the gifts of one's successors without the weakness of imitating them. All this will sort itself out.

I believe if you were to dig into the critical books of the period 1900–1925 you'd find a lot on the three or four great Russians. An essay on Dostoevsky was as obligatory in 1915 as one on Eliot now; and with rather more justification. Middleton Murry did a pretentious and rather Oxonian work on Dostoevsky,[10] and I think you'll find people like Edward Thomas and Arthur Ransome sacrificed at the shrine. Somewhere or other in one of my stories or novels you will find recorded a saying which I heard at a Chelsea party just after I was demobbed in 1919: "My deah fellow, of course anybody who *is* anybody nowadays admires Dostoevsky." [11] It was a fad and passed. But of course Dostoevsky is a very great writer, and now is a good time to enjoy him on your own.

I'm sure Ezra's really nuts. I came to the conclusion he had paranoia after spending the winter of 1928–29 with him at Rapallo. Any psychiatrist would diagnose it from the peculiar haphazard writing of the Cantos. But then he was a poet, and a paranoiac is not so crazy but that flashes of genius or even more come out. Tasso and Rousseau were both paranoiacs, though unluckily Ezra isn't in their literary class. But he had an awfully tough time in America and in London. He was kind and as a young man very good fun, but such a pretentious bloody ass.[12] In that winter I spoke of an American "musician" called George Antheil came to Rapallo from Berlin, and was closeted with Ezra all day. Next day, meeting Ezra, I said: "Hullo Ezra, where were you yesterday?" "I was with Antheil." Then he paused, blinked and in hushed tones: "Strange that the two greatest minds in Europe should have been thinking on the same lines." And he wasn't funning. Well, I have lived to see one of the two greatest minds incarcerated for a mixture of treason and insanity in Washington, D.C.,[13] and the other running a column of answers to young women's love troubles in a small Hollywood magazine.[14] Sic transit . . .

All good wishes for 1950.

Yours sincerely,
RICHARD ALDINGTON

1 The address and date are in red.

2 For the poem "Speed," printed in pamphlet form by the Cambridge University Press, 1949.

3 For RA's review of F. L. Lucas's *Poems* (1935) see possibly " 'Bradshawism' in Modern Poetry" *Times Literary Supplement* 1 Feb 1936.

4 RA probably refers to "Himself He Could not Save" by Antipater of Sidon in *A Greek Garland; A Selection from the Palatine Anthology: The Greek Text with Translations into English Verse* by F. L. Lucas (1939).

5 Catherine Aldington spent most of the war years with her parents, Netta and RA, in California as suggested by Lawrence Powell, bookman and writer. The Aldingtons returned to Europe by way of Jamaica, arriving in Paris no later than 1 Sept 1946. On that date RA wrote to Pat Covici from Paris: "Well, we made it, after various delays and difficulties. Paris is absolutely intact except for a few bullet holes in walls and shop windows. It is shabby but repairing and repainting." Within the month they were established at 162 Boulevard Montparnasse. But before mid-November 1947 they had left Paris because RA found "conditions unfavourable" for his work. He complained that public libraries were "unheated, neglected,"

and that the Bibliothèque Nationale was "falling down." By 17 Nov 1947 the Aldingtons were at St Clair, Le Lavandou, Var (RA to Pat Covici, St Clair, Le Lavandou, Var 17 Nov 1947).

6 Racine *Esther* Act I Scene iv.

7 First produced at the Abbey Theatre 25 Jan 1904 and published in 1905.

8 RA met Yeats through either Ezra Pound or Harold Monro and immediately thereafter enjoyed numerous evenings in Yeats's bachelor "diggings" in Woburn Place, London.

9 1930. See p 38, where RA quoted from Yeats's *The Shadowy Waters* (1900) lines 148 ff. RA's lines run:

> And we know we should not be like the Romantic poet
> Who found that 'even the bed of love
> Which in the imagination had seemed the giver of all good
> Was no more than a wine-cup in the drinking and as soon finished' —
> Which shows what sort of a clumsy ass he was —

10 *Fyodor Dostoevsky; A Critical Study* (1916).

11 That remark has not been located in RA's fiction or non-fiction.

12 RA's attitude toward Ezra Pound was invariably ambivalent. RA declared about Pound that "pre-1914 . . . no one else at that time seemed to have a more brilliant future." In that period the two men were together often. When futurism was introduced to London in 1910, they invented (with the help of H. D. and Dorothy Shakspear) a suit with trousers of billiard cloth green and blue coat for RA to "wear at Marinetti's lectures on futurist clothing, which we knew was to be drably utilitarian, a single suit fastened by a zipper. M. noticed it and denounced young Passéists in the audience" (RA to Charles Norman, Sury en Vaux, par Sancerre, Cher 5 Nov 1960 [Texas]). Both men were associated with *The Egoist* and *The New Age* and with the Imagist movement. Both were frequently present at T. E. Hulme's "Tuesday evenings" at a house in Frith Street, and in 1912–13 RA and Pound, H. D. and Brigit Patmore met nearly every afternoon for tea at the Grosvenor Gallery in Regent Street. On RA's first trip to Paris, when H. D. and Pound were also there, the three met almost daily. Later RA wrote about Pound that "as a human being he was at his nicest before 1913, when London made him self-conscious and artificial. As a young man he was most charming, full of high spirits and wit, and the soul of generosity" (RA to Peter Russell, St Clair, Le Lavandou, Var 5 Jan 1950 [Buffalo]). But their attitudes and interests began to diverge. According to RA, Pound was adept at "barbed gibes" and he took on the "feuds and dislikes of his cronies, Yeats and Hueffer" (*ibid*). Emphasizing unconsciously his arrogance and own sense of superiority as a devotee of art, Pound, in 1922 gave his version of the events of about 1914: "You and H. D. both stopped progress about the time you ceased to desire perfection.

> You (A.) got an idea that I was a nuisance (as I am) to be did awa with at all cost.

> You (A.) began to back up each other's egoism and consider me as a gaga old adlepate, and to cease to desire castigation.

> Fury at my admiration for Gaudier Brzeska, and modern art, adding to your hatred to my 'apostasy' from the ring of Sappho and Meleager.

> The noble art is so high that one shd. be thankful for my criticism, one shd. be ready to learn from the pastry cooks" (Ezra Pound to RA, Paris [1922] [Texas]).

In 1932, RA satirized Pound as Charlemagne Cox in the short story "Nobody's Baby," published in *Soft Answers* (1932). (See below, letter 29). The real break came, however, in 1940 when, according to RA, Pound told RA that "The Germans were about to sack London and hang Churchill 'on the Gold Exchange.' " In any case RA condemned Pound's "callousness to suffering and a quite vile brutality when his political enemies were concerned" (RA to Charles Norman, Sury en Vaux, par Sancerre, Cher 5 Nov 1960 [Texas]). Yet there was, through the years, another side to their relationship. On 21 June 1920, RA had written from London to Edward Dujardin, the French man of letters, to introduce Pound as "*le plus intelligent des poètes et le plus charmant de mes amis*" (Buffalo). RA submitted with good grace to Ezra's bullying when they joined together in 1922 to establish through contributions an annuity meant to free T. S. Eliot from his clerkship at Lloyds Bank (see below, letter 136 n 4). In 1952, believing Pound was "short of cash," RA was looking for a way to send money to Mrs Pound without offense (RA to Max Wykes-Joyce, Montpellier 29 Jan 1952). And in 1959 RA had this letter from Pound:

Hotel Italia, Rapallo

CHER R/
    amid cumulative fatigue, and much that is gone to muddle, thinking of early friendship and late. This is to say I have for you a lasting affection.

E.P.

25 Ag 59
    Came on some notes of first walking tour in France, amid the rubble a week ago or so

"Quanti dolci pensier"

RA's comment on it runs, "Of course I am personally involved, but I found that infinitely touching, a flash of 'The real Ezra' so long lost under 'the rubble'" (RA to Charles Norman, Sury en Vaux, par Sancerre, Cher 25 Nov 1960 [Texas]). See below, letters 15 and 21.

[13] Pound was committed to St Elizabeth's Hospital on 21 Dec 1945; he remained until 1958, when, on Apr 18, treason charges against him were dropped.

[14] In 1937 Antheil agreed to write a column "Boy Advises Girl" for the Esquire Syndicate. It was discontinued about 1944. Antheil's account in *Bad Boy of Music* (1945) 306, of his participation in the column runs: "Shortly after I had started working for the Esquire Syndicate, its editor, Howard Denby, rejected one column after the other until, at last, I was so weary with the writing of endless new ones (to take their place) that I only too willingly listened to his follow-up offer to continue the column, but with his own staff — but this under my name and under the title I had discovered."

3

12 November 1950   *Le Lavandou*

DEAR MR BIRD,

    It was nice of you to write about the Lawrence book,[1] and equally nice of you to send the letter! The line nowadays is to say or write: "I got awfully worked up over your so-and-so and wrote you a long letter, but then thought I wouldn't bother you with it." An ingenious let-out. Better I think than Henry James's rather flimsy: "You have chosen an excellent subject and treated it with spirit."

    The Bibbles incident doesn't greatly trouble me (I hate dogs) but it *is* nasty to think of any helpless beast, even man, being brutalised.[2] The story is only vouched for by that Dane, Merrild, who wrote his book in Hollywood when he was hard up.[3] But Frieda [4] couldn't deny it, so I had to put it in.

    As to the money — I'm sure you're right to the extent that the mother [5] always nagged about their poverty and hence gave him a feeling of insecurity if he hadn't "a few pounds between me and the world." (The sneer at that didn't come very well from Norman Douglas who happens to hold a life annuity of 500 a year!)[6] But there are other factors. There was a very strong anti-Lawrence faction — for every honest Briton loathes an artist — and the regular method is always to attack the pocket. Render a man penniless and he is helpless, and must knuckle under. Hence the virulent attitude of British law courts if ever they get an artist in their clutches. But there was also a specific and less creditable motive. In an unguarded moment Lawrence made some sort of pact with the Carswells, that they should help each other in poverty, and if either made money by writing, well, they would share. DHL did make a little money by writing; Mrs. C. didn't; hence, as I hint, he always pretended to her that he was poorer than he was during the period 1920–30.[7] There was also some brush-off in Florence before the Ls went to Ceylon etc.[8] In her Savage Pilgrimage, Mrs C. confidently trots out supposed "facts" about his extreme poverty — relying on his letters to her.[9] Without going into details of refutations, which would have involved me with the dreary John Patrick,[10] I corrected as far as possible DHL's own financial notes.

As often happens, there is some truth in both the Pound and Sitwell legends you mention. Ezra *did* "help" other writers, though the help was not always in their best interests, and always seemed to imply all the duties of discipleship in the recipient. The Sitwells certainly helped Willie Walton with money and (I am told) Dylan Thomas. I suspect Edith has done something for Roy Campbell, if I may judge by his super-respectful attitude about her this summer when he was here. Peter Russell, the Pound-essays [11] editor, is a friend of Roy's, and called in here. He has a disagreeable resemblance to Henley in facial appearance. He was not pleased when I told him that he had omitted some of Ezra's oldest friends, e.g.; Carlos Williams.[12] And he waited until some ten days before he went to print before approaching H.D. and myself. Of course you are absolutely right — it is absurd to try to palliate Ezra's custard by appealing to his genuine charitable impulses. It is exactly like the Georgians who, if one ever criticised the writings of any of that enormous clique, instantly riposted: "Oh but he's *such* a nice fellow." [13]

By the way, Campbell has written a most entertaining volume of memoirs, which should take him in a swoop from the highbrow to the intelligent public — IF I have succeeded in getting the book into the hands of a powerful publisher (which Roy is liable to bitch up at the slightest pretext) and IF the said work can be steered through the British law of libel.[14]

The job I am on now needs some real — by which I mean "genuinely documented" — facts about the Oxford of 1890–1920. Hard to come by. There are some chance remarks of Max's.[15] Blackwell, on being appealed to, naturally only dug up some unsold dons from their stores (Godley [16] — not bad; A. L. Smith by his Wife,[17] ridiculous; 55 years at Ox. by G. B. Grundy.)[18] When you are next putting in slips for books at the Bodleian, Brit Mus. or similar large library, get the book out, turn to page 38 and contemplate the effigy of the Rev. George Dooker Grundy,[19] M. A. Oxon., Vicar of Hey, near Oldham, Lancs. (1840–1902) — that was the length of time he was vicar. A more appalling old Bozo it is impossible to imagine — far more awful than those gold masks Schliemann discovered and Flaubert described as "deux affreux bonshommes." Grundy, one sees it all now. What *can* Mrs. G. have been?

Yours sincerely,
RICHARD ALDINGTON

[1] RA's *Portrait of a Genius But . . . (The Life of D. H. Lawrence 1885–1930)* 1950. RA may be thanking Bird for a review which he wrote for *The New Lanka,* a journal published under the editorship of G. L. Cooray in Colombo, Ceylon.

[2] Bibbles was a pet dog of D. H. Lawrence about which he wrote a poem of that name. RA tells in *Portrait of a Genius But . . .* (266–68) how Lawrence beat and kicked "the false dirty bitch" when she strayed away with the "great ranch dogs" who were after her when she had "come sex-alive."

[3] *A Poet and Two Painters* (1938).

[4] Mrs D. H. Lawrence.

[5] That is, D. H. Lawrence's mother, Lydia Beardsall Lawrence.

[6] The quotation, slightly inaccurate, is from Lawrence's introduction to Maurice Magnus's posthumously published *Memoirs of the Foreign Legion* (1924) 24. Norman Douglas objected

to Lawrence's treatment of Magnus in the introduction and replied to it with *D. H. Lawrence and Maurice Magnus* (1924) where (p 31) he quoted the same passage and described its sentiment as a "fine middle-class tradition."

[7] RA *Portrait of a Genius But . . .* 269.

[8] *Ibid* 241.

[9] *Savage Pilgrimage* (1932) 8, 10, 25, *et passim*.

[10] John Patrick Carswell, son of Donald and Catherine Carswell.

[11] *Ezra Pound; A Collection of Essays to be Presented to Ezra Pound on His Sixty-fifth Birthday* had been published in London earlier that year, 1950.

[12] See RA to Peter Russell, St Clair, Le Lavandou, Var 5 Jan 1950: "You have rather overlooked Ezra's real early friends, haven't you? Of course, Ford Heuffer, Fred Manning and Amy Lowell are dead, but Carlos Williams, H. D. and F. S. Flint are still alive, all contributors to Ezra's 1914 [Imagist] anthology" (Buffalo).

[13] The poets (Rupert Brooke, Harold Monro, Ralph Hodgson, James Elroy Flecker, Edmund Blunden, D. H. Lawrence, Isaac Rosenberg, Siegfried Sassoon, and others) whose work appeared in five successive anthologies, each entitled *Georgian Poetry* and all edited between 1912 and 1922 by Sir Edward Marsh. The Georgian poets did not constitute a movement, and their poems had no relationship thematically or structurally.

[14] *Light on a Dark Horse* published by Hollis and Carter in 1951.

[15] Sir Max Beerbohm.

[16] Alfred Dennis Godley *Aspects of Modern Oxford* (1894).

[17] *Arthur Lionel Smith, Master of Balliol, 1916–1924; A Biography and Some Reminiscences* by his wife [Alice Elizabeth Strutt Smith] (1928).

[18] 1945.

[19] Grandfather of G. B. Grundy.

4

24 November 1950   *Le Lavandou*

DEAR MR BIRD,

This is most kind of you. If I accept with gratitude your generous offer of help,[1] it must be understood that this must not involve the waste of one second of your own time for study or any financial outlay. Owing to the complex and (to my naif mind) irrational arrangements of government I cannot have a bank account in England — I suppose for fear I might spend a few pounds in sterling instead of changing them to francs! So if you order any books for me, will you say that the indebtedness will be discharged for me by Heinemann, who will charge to my royalty account. (Heinemann will have to submit the account to the Bank of England specialist, who will charge me income tax on it; whereupon in due course my accountant will intermittently wrangle over ten or fifteen months, with the probable result of getting me charged double tax for impudence to bureaucrats. On sent le progrès.)

The fierce light that beats upon a Throne is crepuscular to that which relentlessly tries to expose the biographer who writes a controversial book; and I believe this will be sufficiently beastly, don't you know, to rouse the Hun in many a patriot who never smelt picric acid. But I don't want to write a caricature of Oxford; I want to be scrupulously fair, while spilling any beans that are spillable, parading available skeletons from cupboards. But every statement MUST BE DOCUMENTED!!!

Here are some of my points of query, especially relevant to the period 1890–1914:

(1) How far was the theology, philosophy and classical scholarship of that epoch derived from Germany, how far original?

(2) Who were the real scholars among the dons?

(3) Who were the brilliant men among the undergraduates? My valuable Grundy proudly lists among his "triumphs" of instruction 23 bureaucrats, 4 Church dignitaries, 1 diplomat (deceased early), 18 dons, 7 public school headmasters, and — hold your breath — an editor of Punch, a part author of "The Nomads of the Balkans" and J. Middleton Murry![2] This, as our old friend Ezra would have remarked, "is a darned clever bunch."

(4) What evidence can be brought to prove that a dislike for women was native to some or many dons and by them to some extent transferred to the youth of Oxford? Who was the don in holy orders who in a sermon passionately besought his hearers not to peril their immortal souls for a pleasure which, he had been credibly informed, lasted only one and three-quarters minutes? [3]

5) Why was it forbidden for boys under 16 to be in men's rooms in College after 10 p. m.[4]

(6) To what extent can it be shown that eccentricity was a feature of College life among the dons? Authentic and striking examples, especially of misogynists?

(7) What is the evidence for the tales that Professor Ruskin habitually spent much of his time in girls' schools and was detected among the adolescent daughters of Dean Liddell to the said Dean's astonishment, he having failed to reach Boar's Hill for a dinner appointment on account of deep snow? And the evidence for the stories that the Rev Campbell Dodgson amused his studious leisure by photographing naked girls of 14 and less? [5] Any other provable histories of mild sexual deviations among these disciples of Chastity and Euphrosyne?

(8) What explanation (if any) is furnished for the immense popularity of ball games (such as e.g. cricket and rugby) among classical scholars, seeing that in the Odyssey ball games are reserved for girls? and that, to the best of my knowledge, no such contests occurred in the Olympic, Nemean, Isthmian etc Games?

(9) Why was self-consciousness so conspicuous in many Oxford men? Was it, as Norman Douglas tells me, the result of masturbation? Or what? Why did so many of them pose?

(10) Was the dons' loathing for publicity and disgust at the thought of writing anything which might be a best-seller sincere? Or sour grapes? If sincere, on what grounds?

I did not mean this to be an examination paper, but it has unconsciously developed on those lines. If you can turn up any books which answer any of these questions do let me have the titles, and I will order them through my book-buyer. If you turn up any such in the cellars of Blackwell et al. grab them.

Yours sincerely,
RICHARD ALDINGTON

[1] That is, help to provide materials for a book on which RA was at work. Bird did not yet know that it was *Lawrence of Arabia: A Biographical Inquiry* (1955).

2 Grundy *Fifty-five Years at Oxford* 237–39.

3 Probably Dean Burgon, Vicar of St Mary's, Oxford.

4 The rule was made by the City of Oxford High School for Boys and not by Oxford University. Apparently this school in a university city, attended by a number of college choristers, found the rule necessary owing to the boys being "led astray." (See H. F. Mathers to Alan Bird, Frinton on Sea, Essex, 17 March 1951 [Berg].)

5 That accusation was made, not against Campbell Dodgson, but against Charles Lutwidge Dodgson, better known as Lewis Carroll.

5

23 *December 1950*   *Le Lavandou*

DEAR MR BIRD,

I wanted to thank you for sending the Oxford Limited book and especially for your very valuable letter, but didn't know where to write as you seemed to be moving about. Now a card comes to me from you at Wadham,¹ so I fire off in that direction, hoping to wing you.

Yes, football rather inferior, but I was thinking of cricket, which surely is a fetish? And squash. An acquaintance of mine, Eton–Balliol, complains pathetically if he can't have his game of squash. But I'm sure you're right in saying that the dons deplored the excessive adulation of les sportifs. A. C. Benson (e.g.) does so in his College Window.² He blames parents. I suggest pathetic eagerness on their part to assure the world that their boy wasn't another Oscar.³ I was ignorant of the Athens bas-reliefs.⁴ Were they perhaps barbarians? At any rate, though I've but a smattering of the classics I don't recollect any reference to ball games. But that may be merely inattentiveness.

Yes, there is a passage about the right of summary arrest of whores in the life of A. L. Smith by his wife.⁵ In those days, a man seen talking to one of these girls was instantly sent down without hope of appeal! But Modern Cambridge has its black spot. I was assured that Empson having just been elected to a Fellowship (at King's, I believe) was deprived of it because the scout moving his (E's) effects reported to the head of the College having found condoms among them. This, if true, must still be in the recollection of many. Mrs Smith, by the way, was pretty broad-minded. She tells her readers that after long reflection she came to think this sin less dreadful than others because there is *love* in it! ⁶ Such innocence is charming in a callous and blasé epoch.

I remember the passage in Praeterita and have been re-reading it — he must have been insane.⁷ I don't know his letters which I ought to have read since I have ventured some opinions in print about J.R.⁸

I am grateful to you for the information you have sent, and do hope you'll find time to send more. Of course it is hard if not impossible to generalise accurately about a large corporate body especially when College life tends to make separate collective organisms within the main one. Incidentally, anything you find about Jesus (Oxon) in the period 1900–14 might be useful.

I was wondering this morning how far a writer on other topics is to be forgiven for ignorance of established scientific fact? Someone sent me a book about the castles of Syria etc. built by the Crusaders. On his first page he speaks of "coral insects" and later on of the descendants of the crusaders "inheriting mixed blood." [9] In reviewing my Lawrence book David Garnett strongly implied that DHL "inherited revivalist tendencies" from a maternal grandfather he had never seen! [10] And Robert Graves attributes someone's supposed aptitude for learning languages to "the inheritance of mixed blood"! [11] I think I must suggest to Alan Lane that he does an eighteenpenny book on genetics.

My Award of the Week goes to a private correspondent in New England, who wrote inside his Xmas card: "Here we are in the same position as England was in 1940. But I know that, like England, we have the guts to face the grim prospect." [12] I have a patriotic friend (English) who keeps framed on a table the editorial on Dunkerque which appeared in the New York Times.[13] I think I'll frame my heroic Boston friend.

Yours sincerely,
RICHARD ALDINGTON

[1] Bird had matriculated as a post-graduate student in education at Wadham College, Oxford, in Oct 1950. See above, Introduction.

[2] See "Games" *From A College Window* (1906) 218–314.

[3] Oscar Wilde.

[4] In the Ashmolean Museum.

[5] P 105.

[6] *Ibid.*

[7] In answer to RA's query about John Ruskin's interest in adolescent girls (see above letter 4), Bird may have called attention to the part of *Praeterita* (1885–89) in which Ruskin tells of his introduction to Rose La Touche and prints her first letter to him. (See Alan Bird to MJB, Halsall, Ormskirk, Lancashire 27 May 1968.)

[8] See for example RA "Introduction" in *The Religion of Beauty; Selections from the Aesthetes* (1950) 10–18.

[9] Robin Fedden *Crusader Castles* (1950) 9 and 42. The second quotation is inaccurate; Fedden wrote of the "mixed strain" of the "offspring of the mixed marriages of the Holy Land."

[10] See *The Observer* 26 Mar 1950, where Garnett's review runs in part, "Aldington should, I think, have linked the 'antithetical self' [of Lawrence, implied by the word 'But' in the title] to the revivalist streak which Lawrence inherited from his maternal grandfather." Garnett goes on to speak of that grandfather, Beardsall, engineer-foreman in a dock-yard, and his relations with William Booth, who formed the organization which evolved into the Salvation Army.

[11] *Lawrence and the Arabs* (1927) 12.

[12] The crucial event for England in 1940 was the evacuation from Dunkerque of some 300,000 troops cut off by the German advance on the Channel ports. 1950 was the year in which the conflict between Communist and non-Communist forces in Korea began. In June the United States, with other member nations of the United Nations, determined to resist the march of Communist troops from North Korea into South Korea or the zone south of the thirty-eighth parallel. In October 1950 Chinese Communist forces joined the North Korean army. By the end of December 1950 the United Nations army, made up predominantly of U. S. troops and under the command of General Douglas MacArthur, was engaged in battle in the air, on the sea and on land, with heavy fighting near the mouth of the Yalu River. The Chinese, whose spokesman was Chou En Lai, Foreign Minister, refused to participate in a "cease-fire parley" and demanded that all foreign troops withdraw from Korea.
  RA's correspondent was probably Leonard Bacon.

[13] The first paragraph of the editorial (1 June 1940) runs: "So long as the English tongue survives, the word Dunkerque will be spoken with reverence. For in that harbor, in such a hell as never blazed on earth before, at the end of a lost battle, the rags and blemishes that have hidden the soul of democracy fell away. There, beaten but unconquered, in shining splendor, she faced the enemy."

6

7 February 1951 *Le Lavandou*

Dear Mr Bird,

The influenza epidemic in England must be really serious — on Monday a letter from one friend saying he had it, yesterday three (!), to-day yours! Five in three days, and I don't think letters from England average more than 20 a week. So far my daughter and I have escaped, but our almost indispensable bonne [1] went down, and I had the pleasure of two weeks housework with only peasant aid. Also, we have had an infernal amount of rain, everything soaked, and the grass slope up to the garage so much a quag that I have the greatest difficulty in docking the wheel-spinning car. Altogether a dreary winter, complicated by the absurd antics of our American friends — dangerous indeed, as you say. I have just written a little story (8000 words) making fun of some of their more obvious failings, which amused the chairman of Heinemann [2] so much he promptly sent copies to English & American editors — with what results I know not, but I must try to send you a copy if it gets printed.[3] I think we all need a little laughter.

Olive oil jumped in two days from 230 to 400 francs a litre, but a very decent wine du pays may still be had at 50 frcs. The mimosa is quite glorious, and the almond trees across the valley look exactly like D. H. L.'s "puffs of pink smoke." I wish I could give you hopes of warm weather moving north, but though the sun is brilliant, there is a pretty cold mistral. I wonder, by the way, what the weather-pundits now say to explain the mistral, which is as much a mystery to me as the Swiss Föhn. After campers and tourists I think the mistral is our worst affliction. Did the English papers report the trial of two fellows who set fire to and burned thousands of acres of pine woods here last August? I don't know whether they were feeble-minded, or communists, or what the Americans call fire-bugs. But they have ruined for a decade that lovely stretch of coast from Cavalaire to Cavalière.[4]

I am now allowed to say that the biographical subject or victim over whom I groan daily is 'Colonel' T. E. 'Lawrence'. (You know his name was really 'Chapman'? [5]) [. . .] It is a most awful job, and I find that (like Lord Allenby) I have a dreadful suspicion that he was all along a good deal of a charlatan.[6] Anything you can find about his Oxford career would be most welcome. Is the head of Jesus a provost, a president, a rector or what? I am told that in Lawrence's day (1907–1910) he happened to be an archaeologist. Who? [7] Do you know if D. G. Hogarth was married? [8] Or was he one of the too numerous 'them'? I fear the national hero was, and that fact is not the least of my embarrassments in dealing with his career, for he kept through life a schoolboy habit of leg-pulling to such an extent that he himself confesses he did not know "where it began and where it ended"! Imagine the difficulties of reconstructing such a life. All information most gratefully accepted. Is there anyone now at the Ashmolean who remembers him? I like Hogarth's historical book on The Penetration of Arabia (takes a don to dare a title like that!) and am trying to get hold of his Wandering Scholar.[9] You may not believe it, but dons do sometimes write extremely well. T. E. Lawrence was not among them.

I am most obliged to you for the Oman book.[10] I find these recollections of sheltered lives quite fascinating, all the more so since the writers have no idea how remote from the ordinary squalid dog-fight of life they are. It will be a misfortune if the miseries of the world curtail still more the opportunities provided by the two universities for the complex life of the irresponsible intelligentsia. I rejoice in them, and wish they could be given back all the privileges of which Mr Gladstone and other traitors unwisely despoiled them. Did you ever read a little portrait of Lucretius Munro by a Cambridge Fellow called Duff? [11] Attached for some eccentric reason to a pre-1914 sixpenny reprint of Munro's translation. Quite a masterpiece of cherry-stone biography.

Under separate cover I send you Albatross reprints of two books.[12] First, they are not supposed to be "introduced into the British Empire." Then, they have been in print for a year or more, and only come on the market this month because the hapless Holroyd-Reece has been struggling with the enormous obstacles and frustrations of I know not how many embattled bureaucracies.

I have got to leave this villa in April. Its owners (the talented impresarios of Comic Cuts and Perrier Water, Sir H. and Lady Harmsworth) say they want it back. I had hoped they were permanently bestowed in America, but probably the drums and tramplings got on their nerves. I have already 3000 books to store, and some of them are of unique literary interest — i.e. signed copies of eminent Victorians, so I must pay to store them. I propose, this done, to pack myself and daughter into our small car and to do a real culture tour of part of France.[13] But it is a nuisance, the leaving.

17 separate Smiths are indexed in A. L.'s biography, but not C. H. But your bit about the theatricals turns up in Grundy,[14] and I'm sure I've read that worms story somewhere — can't place it.[15] Have you read Mallock's New Republic? Superb parodies of Jowett and Ruskin.[16]

Yours sincerely,
RICHARD ALDINGTON

P.S. The Empson Story was told me by an Eton bloke.

[1] Mme Angèle.

[2] Alexander Stewart Frere.

[3] It was not printed.

[4] After raging several days across 5000 acres of pine and brush, the fire was brought under control on 4 Aug 1950.

[5] Thomas Robert Tighe Chapman was in fact the name of T. E. Lawrence's father. At some time shortly before 1885, Thomas changed his name to Thomas Robert Lawrence. See T. E. Lawrence to Charlotte F. Shaw, n.p. 17 Apr 1925: "By the way, what name should I call myself in it [Seven Pillars of Wisdom]? The Lawrence thing hasn't any better foundation than my father's whim." The story of Lawrence's parents had been told as early as 1946 by Leon Broussard in Le Secret du Colonel Lawrence.

[6] After the first meeting between Allenby and Lawrence — "a little bare-footed silk-skirted man offering to hobble the enemy by his preaching if given stores and arms and a fund of two hundred thousand sovereigns to convince and control his converts" — Lawrence said that Allenby "could not make out how much was genuine performance and how much charlatan." About him, Lawrence told Charlotte F. Shaw ([Karachi] 4 Mar 1927): "My campaign & fighting efforts were entirely negligible, in his eyes. All he required of us was a turn-over of native opinion from the Turk to the British: and I took advantage of that need of his, to make him the stepfather of the Arab national movement — a movement which he did not understand & for whose success his instinct had little sympathy. He is a very large, downright and splendid person, & the being publicly yoked with a counter-jumping opportunist like me must often gall him deeply." Yet Allenby participated in the appeal for funds to establish a memorial to Lawrence in St Paul's Cathedral.

[7] Sir John Rhys.

[8] Hogarth married Laura V. Uppleby in 1894; they had one son.

[9] *The Penetration of Arabia; A Record of the Development of Western Knowledge Concerning the Arabian Peninsula* (1904), *A Wandering Scholar* (1925).

[10] Sir Charles Oman *Memories of Victorian Oxford and of Some Early Years* (1941).

[11] Hugh Andrew Johnstone Munro *Translations into Latin and Greek* (with a prefatory note by James Duff Duff) 1906.

[12] *Rejected Guest* and *Soft Answers* (1950).

[13] RA and his wife, Netta, had separated in the previous year (1950). Catherine, their daughter, remained with RA.

[14] Probably p 53, where Grundy speaks of fancy-dress dances at Oxford when men appeared dressed in women's costumes.

[15] A reference to an elderly don of Worcester College, Oxford, named Pottinger, who made a practice of stabbing worms and murmuring, "You haven't got me yet."

[16] In William Hurrell Mallock's *The New Republic; or, Culture, Faith, and Philosophy in an English Country House* (1877) Jowett is parodied in the character Dr Jenkinson and Ruskin in Mr Herbert. Parodies also of Matthew Arnold and Walter Pater are present in Mr Luke and Mr Rose.

7

23 *February 1951*   *Le Lavandou*

DEAR BIRD,

I have lived so long in republics, where one is either formal or fulsomely familiar, that I have dropped out of our more sensible usages. I hope you will allow me to drop the "Mr" and reciprocate.

Thank you indeed for what you tell me about Lawrence. And, before I forget, the Oman book has useful things, particularly that gathering of bloody-minded dons playing the Kriegspeil on Prussian maps of Sadowa! [1] One can't prove it, but it seems possible that their discussions of writers on strategy may have filtered down to the undergraduates of L's time. He claims to have read them all with the absurd addition "like every other undergraduate."

I agree so entirely with you about the dulness of the book I abbreviate as 7 Pills of Wis,[2] and the boredom of the man, and Churchill's awful speech.[3] I wish I hadn't taken on the job. But there is this spur, that I may be able to speak out for myself and some others our opinion of this ridiculous myth. Have a look at Storr's pompous article in the 1950 supplement to the D. N. B.

The note of Polstead Rd [4] is good. Did you notice if the garden still contains the bungalow in which he lived and worked? It was hung for silence sake with "bolton cloth" or "workhouse sheeting," whatever that may be.

Many of Lawrence's friends were homosexuals, but not all. Whatever his *practice*, of which one can naturally know nothing except by his own confession which doesn't exist, his *sympathy* was entirely with homos and against heteros.[5] He had women friends as homos often do, knowing better than a man the little attentions which please women, but sex relations with a woman caused him unfeigned horror and disgust.[6] A year before his death he boasted of his virginity so far as women are concerned.[7] BUT I write under the threat of censorship from Prof A. W. Lawrence and the literary Trustees, who write menacing and truculent letters the moment this topic is hinted at!

Further, there is a mystery and probably a scandal, connected with the father's change of name, and this A.W.L. is said to wish to hush up at all costs. The Chapman name even may be a blind, but rumour from All Souls [8] is that the Lawrence father had two families under different names! Some say he was an Irish baronet.[9] Lionel Curtis is said to be the source of this (and I have also had Geoffrey Faber named) both All Souls, aren't they? Curtis is said to have many unpublished letters and other T.E.L. documents.[10]

It seems certain that T. E. L. had no more right to the name of "Lawrence" than the fact that his father chose to assume it to cover whatever it was he wished to cover. Hence T. E. L.'s embarrassment at the rival fame of D. H. L., his statement that D. H. was "the only Lawrence," and his dropping Lawrence for Ross and Shaw.[11]

The mother, Sarah Lawrence née Maden (according to T. E.'s birth certificate), is still alive. In the book by his "Friends" she gives her birth-date as 1861, but the only discoverable birth certificate of a Sarah Maden is dated 1863. She is said to live in an Oxford nursing home (probably what doctors call "a senile" with horrid cynicism) and must be between 87 and 90.[12] I suppose that while she and A.W.L. live any reference to whatever scandal may be connected with husband and father is libel under our law. (Not in USA though the law is theoretically identical.) No birth certificate of Lawrence's eldest brother [13] can be discovered either as Lawrence or Chapman, though his birth must have been in Dec 1885 or Jan 1886 if he states the truth about himself. The failure may be due to the languid researches of the Somerset House staff. No marriage certificate of Sarah Maden has yet been discovered, but T. E.'s birth certificate registered him as legitimate. Some lawyers say it is impossible to get a false declaration officially recognized; others deny it. The penalty is said to be penal servitude for life! A fearful penalty for the crime of lèse-bureaucracy.

Similar and even more perplexing tangles involve me at every step. Let me give you one very trivial instance, which has taken me some time to work out. In his bungalow at Polstead Rd he had a reproduction of the head of Hypnos which used to be upstairs among classical bronzes at the B.M. — 5th cent B.C., is it? Well, he told V. Richards that he picked it up in an Italian rubbish heap, that the B. M. authorities at one time thought it the original and better than the one they have, but that it was subsequently found to be a copy. Thus he built up his légende. But at the date of his letter he had never been to Italy (confirmed by a note in his own hand on a copy of Crusader Castles) though it is just possible that he might have gone ashore at Messina during his first (1909) voyage to Syria and back. According to Richards, he said his Hypnos was so valuable that he kept it in his cabin bunk and himself slept on deck.[14] Now, pre-1914, reproductions of that bronze were seen by me in that little reproduction shop in Museum St, in the Paris shops and in Naples. It is so common that there is even one over an antique shop in Sunset Boulevard, Hollywood — wondering I suppose what the devil it is doing in that galère. Now it is just conceivable that he might have picked up this copy in the ruins of Messina (though looting was discouraged by the local police, and most stuff surviving must have been collected by 1909) or more likely that the ambiguous "picking up" meant he bought it either in Messina or the Levant. But it is not to me conceivable that the B. M. keepers could have been deceived for a minute by a modern commercial replica of a work in their own possession. I believe they were wrong about that Etruscan tomb (of which I myself was a deluded fan) but to me the whole thing rings false, and is just one example of the innumerable self-important tales he put about, which got repeated and helped to build his reputation. Tell me what you think about this — I give the situation as fully and clearly as I can.

He was a master of arrivisme and literary strategy, able to give points even to our old friend Tom Eliot.[15]

His greatest and most enduring literary admiration was, not for Doughty (whose influence is obvious on the rambling *manner* of 7 Pills, though not on its verbal *style*) but for William Morris, especially those "prose romances,"[16] which in the interests of biographical thoroughness I have read (and think I deserve a minor order for so doing) and can only say that they seem to me about as full as Lawrence, and Doughty at his most pretentiously Elizabethan.[17] By the way what *can* Doughty mean when he says that if a Bedouin Arab heard a man whistling he would think he was "whistering at the jan"? The O.E.D. is not much help with "whistering" nor Doughty's glossary with "jan" though both are entered.[18]

But the whole enterprise is fatiguing and unsatisfactory, with his brother apparently being in a position to censor what I write under threat of refusing permission to quote copyright stuff. The fatigue comes from the enormous verbosity and dullness of most of the documentation, the interminable contradictions and lies. Graves's book is pretty up-stage but for a really comic display of pretentious pomposity Liddell Hart's book wins.[19] I have on order that book of TEL's answers to Hart and Graves,[20] but my usually admirable book-buyer is baffled. I think it must have been a flop, and few copies got into circulation. But, you see, the awful difficulty for the miserable biographer in this case is that the chief witness (i.e. TEL) is himself always and everywhere under suspicion. I suppose, though I don't know, that his feeling against the Cowley Fathers[21] (which I had noticed) was due to the rabid Protestantism of his mother and father, who are said to have been "most religious."[22] But how reconcile that with his disregard for truth (love of truth is surely a Protestant virtue) or in the parents' case with their long life of sexual sin?

You see what extraordinary biographical material is there, if one can only get somewhere near the facts and be allowed to put them down as calmly and without bias as possible.

Thank you very much for the list of Jesus dons and scholars etc. There may be nothing in it, but I notice among the dons a David Leonard Chapman. If Storrs is telling the truth when he says L's father's real name was Chapman (and I repeat this may be a "blind") then the possibility that he was a relative would explain TE's presence there.[23]

Another little point. You know what terrific fuss is made of L's "pioneer work" in tramping on foot round Syria to sketch, measure and photograph the Castles? Well, he needn't have gone on foot, since I learn that his father gave him enough money to hire a mount and escort, but L. "bought a forty pounds camera and *banked the rest*" (V. Richards.)[24] Moreover, in my 12 year old daughter's primer of Le Moyen Age (which obviously is about 40 years old) what do I find but a photograph of Krak des Chevaliers taken from the collections of scale casts of crusader castles in the old Musée du Trocadéro! This was torn down in the 30s (I think) and the present Musée du Chaillot erected instead. I wonder if those casts were not made as long ago as the Third Empire, for Nap III was persona grata with the Sultan,[25] and a man called Rey published several books about 1870 (which I've not seen) on those castles.[26] Would it not be amusing if all these fearful hardships and (publicity) were used to collect data already in a public museum in Paris? [27] Who would be able to tell about this do you think? I know old G. Cohen, prof emeritus of the Sorbonne, who is said to be big stuff on the Moyen age. Perhaps I might ask him. It might make an amusing point.

Yours sincerely,

RICHARD ALDINGTON

[1] Oman's *Memories of Victorian Oxford* 108 has an account of the activities of the University Kriegspiel Club.

[2] T. E. Lawrence *Seven Pillars of Wisdom*, first printed "for security's sake" early in 1922 in five copies of which all were bound, privately printed for subscribers in 1926, and published in 1935. In an unpublished preface composed for the abridgement of *Seven Pillars, Revolt in the Desert* (1927), Lawrence said that the book was "written in 1919, and printed complete at Oxford shortly after. In 1926 it was reprinted for my friends and their friends." See below letter 18 n 21.

[3] Winston Churchill was the chief speaker when the City of Oxford High School for Boys unveiled a memorial to Lawrence on 3 Oct 1936. An account of the proceedings was published at Oxford in 1937.

[4] 2 Polstead Road, Oxford, was the Lawrence family home from 1896 to 1921. After the one term (Trinity 1908) during which T. E. Lawrence lived in his college (Jesus), a two-room bungalow was built in the garden of 2 Polstead Road for his private use.

[5] Colin Simpson and Phillip Knightley, in "The Sheik Who Made Lawrence Love Arabia" *Sunday Times Weekly Review* (16 June 1968) offer evidence of Lawrence's sympathy with homosexuals but an argument against his being a homosexual. See T. E. Lawrence to Charlotte F. Shaw, Clouds Hill 26 Mar 1924 where he wrote of his rape by the Turkish Bey at Deraa: "For fear of being hurt, or rather to earn five minutes respite from a pain which drove me mad, I gave away the only possession we are born into the world with — our bodily integrity. It's an unforgivable matter, an irrecoverable position. . . ." See also Robert Graves's assertion in "T. E. Lawrence and The Riddle of 'S.A.'" *Saturday Review* (15 June 1963) that the flogging Lawrence suffered at Deraa left him permanently impotent. George Bernard Shaw stated that Lawrence had confessed his account of the incident at Deraa to be untrue (see Phillip Knightley and Colin Simpson *The Secret Lives of Lawrence of Arabia* [1969] 214–15). Note that to Mrs Shaw, Lawrence wrote ([Karachi] 14 Apr 1927): "Knowledge of [my mother] will prevent my ever making any woman a mother, & the cause of children."

[6] See T. E. Lawrence to Charlotte F. Shaw, Clouds Hill 26 Mar 1924 where he speaks of himself as "shut off" from the sexual. See also T. E. Lawrence to Charlotte F. Shaw [Cloud Hill] 10 June 1924, which runs in part: "The motive which brings the sexes together is 99% sensual pleasure, & only 1% the desire of children, in men, so far as I can learn. As I told you, I haven't ever been carried away in that sense, so that I'm a bad subject to treat of it. Perhaps the possibility of a child relieves sometime what otherwise must seem an unbearable humiliation to the woman: — for I presume it's unbearable."

[7] No such statement has been found, but Lawrence's virginity is implicit in n 6 above.

[8] T. E. Lawrence was elected Research Fellow of All Souls College, Oxford in Nov 1919 for a period of seven years in order to do research "into the past, present, or future history of Middle East." The annual stipened was about £200. In 1923, although he did not resign the fellowship, he discontinued drawing the stipend.

[9] T. E. Lawrence's father under his real name Chapman had four daughters, all born between 1874 and 1881. He was rightfully the seventh (and last) baronet of that name, the title having been first held by Benjamin Chapman, member of the Irish Parliament, in 1882. See above, letter 6. Under the name Lawrence, T. E.'s father had five sons: M. R. (Bob), T. E., W. G. (Will), Frank, and A. W. (Arnold).

[10] According to Lawrence (T. E. Lawrence to Charlotte F. Shaw [Karachi] 18 Aug 1927) Curtis had letters "for the Tank Corp period [Mar 1923 – Aug 1925] . . . essays in misery, for I felt like Lucifer just before his forced landing at that stage of my career."

11 See T. E. Lawrence to Charlotte F. Shaw, Edinburgh 22 Aug 1926: "You know, as time passes, the number of names for a man ambitious to write, is drawn in. . . . Lawrence was impossible, since there is a very great but very strange man writing book after book as D. H. L. . . . but nobody with any sporting sense of D. H. L.'s fine struggle to say something will make it more difficult for him by using the same name while his fate yet hung balanced: so I took 'Ross' as a yet unreserved name. . . ." He assumed the name in Aug 1922. In Feb 1923 he began to use the name Shaw and shortly before 12 Aug 1927 executed a deed-poll, making Shaw his legal name.

12 For the statement that Sarah Maden was born in 1861 see *T. E. Lawrence by His Friends* ed A. W. Lawrence (1937) 25. According to Lionel Curtis (Curtis to Alan Bird, Hales Croft, Kidington, Oxford 10 Nov 1952 [Berg]), she was in full possession of her faculties in Nov 1952.

13 Dr M. R. Lawrence.

14 *Portrait of T. E. Lawrence* (1926) 23–24; see T. E. Lawrence *Crusader Castles* (2 vols 1936) i 15 (marginal note).

15 Although Eliot replaced RA as assistant editor of *The Egoist* when RA enlisted in the infantry in 1916, the two men did not meet until the following year. RA thought Eliot "attractive and intelligent," and after the war they were on very friendly terms. In 1922, RA, with Ezra Pound, was active in "Bel Esprit," a scheme to endow Eliot with an annuity of £300 in order to free him for poetry's sake from his clerkship in Lloyds Bank (see letters 2 n 12, and 136 n 4). RA introduced Eliot to Bruce Richmond of the *Times Literary Supplement* and thereby secured work for Eliot as a reviewer. They exchanged a number of letters about their hopes and their work, and in 1922 RA served Eliot as an assistant editor of *Criterion*, but neither wholly admired the other's writing. RA, in 1930, said, "It is insane to question Eliot's genius as a poet or his extreme skill as a critic. What can be attacked, and should be, is his expressed and implied attitude to life; and the over-intellectual over-specialized type of poetry he has created as a refuge from life." Furthermore, RA thought Eliot too subservient to such people as Lady Rothermere and Charles Whibley as RA's *Life for Life's Sake* (1941: 217–22) attests. Their friendship did not run smoothly, and according to Eliot he inadvertently hurt RA's feelings "once or twice very deeply indeed." In the mid-twenties they ceased to meet. Then in 1931, in what Eliot called a "cruel and unkind lampoon," RA based the character Jeremy Pratt Sybba of *Stepping Heavenward* on Eliot. In their last years, they renewed their correspondence, and after RA's death, Eliot wrote of him, "I have nothing left but feelings of friendliness and regard" (*Richard Aldington: An Intimate Portrait* [1965] 25).

16 See T. E. Lawrence to Charlotte F. Shaw [Karachi] 23 Mar 1927 about Morris: "Why the man is among the very great! I suppose everybody loves one writer, unreasonably. I'd rather Morris than the world." See also T. E. Lawrence to Charlotte F. Shaw [Karachi] 4 May 1927 which runs in part: "Many of his [Doughty's] adjectives are final, so far as fitness goes, if my judgment is worth anything: and some of these adjectives I've used, because no better ones will ever be found to fill their place. In that sense I've copied Doughty: but I don't like his style, his syntactical style, any more than I like his recondite vocabulary, or his point of view."

17 See T. E. Lawrence to Charlotte F. Shaw [Karachi] 4 May 1927 for a discussion of Doughty's style as Scandinavian rather than Elizabethan "in its syntax (the inversions, the queer verbs, the broken directness) and very eclectic in vocabulary." TEL added about Doughty: "He had less sense of design even than myself: his book is invertebrate, shapeless, horrific: a brickyard rather than a building. So is mine: and my sentences are abrupt, & do not flow, one from the other: . . . ."

18 See Charles Montagu Doughty *Travels in Arabia Deserta* (2 vols 1888) i 556. The *Oxford English Dictionary* defines whistering as whispering; Doughty defines jan as a plural of jin, meaning demon.

19 Robert Graves *Lawrence and the Arabs* (1927) and Liddell Hart '*T. E. Lawrence*': *In Arabia and After* (1934), published in the United States as *Colonel Lawrence: The Man Behind the Legend* (1934).

20 *T. E. Lawrence to His Biographer Robert Graves* and *T. E. Lawrence to His Biographer Liddell Hart* (2 vols 1938), limited to 1000 copies.

21 Popular name for the Society of St John the Evangelist, the Anglican order founded in 1866 by Father Meaux Benson, once vicar at Cowley, near Oxford.

22 T. E. Lawrence to Charlotte F. Shaw [Karachi] 14 Apr 1927.

[23] David Leonard Chapman was not a relative of T. E. Lawrence's. Why Lawrence went to Jesus College can not be determined. Because he was born in Wales, however, he was eligible for a Welsh emolument; he was awarded a Welsh Exhibition for Modern History.

[24] *Portrait of T. E. Lawrence* 53.

[25] Abd-ul-Aziz succeeded his brother as Sultan of Turkey on 25 June 1861; he was deposed in 1876.

[26] See E. G. Rey *L'Architecture militaire des Croisés en Syrie* (1871).

[27] See below, letter 12.

8

15 March 1951   *Le Lavandou*

DEAR BIRD,

Wonderful! That information from Burke and Debrett is exactly what I was looking for. The name of Thomas Robert Chapman is incautiously given away by Storrs in his article on L in the 1950 DNB.[1] It was this that gave me the real clue after months of drawing "Lawrence" blanks at Somerset House and the Irish Records Office in Dublin. All this had to be done through intermediaries, so took time!

If it is not imposing on your good nature, may I have exact transcripts of the entries in Burke and Debrett, together with the necessary titles of both books for my bibliography?

An even more startling bit of evidence entirely linking up with yours came last week from a friend [2] who has been reading and extracting for me the Letters of TEL to Charlotte Shaw (300 of them) just made available in the MSS Dept of the Brit. Mus. If you feel interested, read the Letter (from Karachi evidently) dated 14th April 1927.[3] It fits in exactly with the evidence you found. But how am I going to be able to publish this with TEL's mother and two brothers still alive, and his three sisters or rather half-sisters by Sir Thomas's legal wife? . . .

Here is something that would help — if you can find in Oxford any evidence about the date of those Trocadéro castles-models. I feel sure you're right, that all the information was gathered for Napoleon III and was there in Paris all the time. No need for these melodramatic pilgrimages in the steps of St Paul and Coeur-de-Lion. He could have got all the measurements in Paris![4] But there would have been no advertisement in that.

He was very much against Oman. In those unpublished Shaw letters under date 25/2/28 he calls Oman "a fool: a pompous pretence: a sciolist"!!! Now, I am utterly ignorant of these mediaeval military studies, but in writing a sketch of Wellington I found Oman not only readable but an almost miraculous depot of interesting facts about the Peninsula War.[5] In its way that book seems to me as great as Gibbon and a real triumph for Oxford scholarship. Surely the sciolist was Lawrence? In a letter — I've mislaid the reference in my careless way — he asks for Anatole France, if possible with a translation interleaved and with notes! [6] Is this not a bit baffling in one who was supposed to be reading quantities of Mediaeval French? Graves — a peerless chump in his modest way — says he "read every book in the library of the Oxford Union, the best part of 50,000 volumes" in six years.[7] Allowing 2 Leap Years that gives him 2192 days, and by reading 20 books a day, he would consume 43,840. By the time he got to India his rate had fallen to 3 a day.[8] Have you noticed that Graves by a misprint calls The Wilderness of Zin, the Wilderness of Sin?[9]

Your notes on the Hypnos affair are perfect. I think I shall use this — while pointing out that it is a trifle compared with other tall tales — as a specimen of how the simplest thing is worked up into a tale. I agree with you — it is not credible that the B.M. experts could be deceived for a second by a modern Italian replica of one of their works. I believe they did make a mistake about that Etruscan sepulchre — which vanished to the cellars in pre-war days — but there is a lot of forged Etruscan stuff about — at least two statues in the Metropolitan of New York are forged, I'm convinced. They are labelled "1916" which you'll remember was the year in which the Apollo of Veii was found. But the B.M. would not be mistaken about a classic bronze.

Interesting the fact that there is not a rule forbidding school boys in undergraduate rooms. You will find the original of Garnett's quote in "TEL by his Friends," p. 67.[10] Green, who tells it, was at St John's. Might it be a rule in that College? . . . All this brings up the homosexual problem. Whatever his practice, I can bring much evidence to show that he always jeered at heterosexual practices, and nearly always wrote admiringly, even sentimentally, of male homosexuality. To Mrs Shaw (6/11/28) he wrote: "I've seen lots of man-&-man lovers: very lovely and fortunate some of them were. I take it women can be the same. And if our minds go so, why not our bodies?" This apropos Well of Loneliness.[11] All that stuff in The Mint, the "obscene" conversation of privates and the Sergeant-Major on parade etc.[12] Why is it recorded? Obviously because consciously or unconsciously to do so gratified his genuine loathing for the femaleness of females. He is delighted because the men in their crudity make the female sex organ seem beastly and degraded. Why that extraordinary befouling of poor Queen Alexandra whose real crime was that once she had been a very beautiful woman.[13] Why was he so anxious for Shaw G.B. to write the life of Casement? Would have liked to do it himself if he hadn't been intellectually lazy.[14] He didn't like work, just as his dear father didn't. Read the letter p 134 in which he jeers at Petrie and complains of the hard work. Then turn to p 161 and see how he praises Carchemish as "a place where one eats lotos nearly every day."[15] He was obviously capable of bursts of physical energy and of enduring privations and he worried out his book, but what he most wanted was an easy time such as an old sweat in peace time has. It is the difference between his raids on the Hejaz railway[16] — tip and run — and a six months period without leave in an infantry division on the Western Front . . .

But I weary you. Forgive me. This projected book occupies me so much that I tend to think of little else. I drove over to St Tropez yesterday. They have almost finished rebuilding the ruined parts, and there are actually flats for sale. But of course the tourism boys are doing their best to destroy its charm by making it the luncheon stop-off for all the long-distance bus tours. What they couldn't destroy by bombing they are making odious by mobbing.

Yours sincerely,
RICHARD ALDINGTON

[1] The relevant statement (Supplement to the *DNB* for 1931–40 p 528) runs in part: "His father, Thomas Robert Chapman (who had assumed the name of Lawrence), the younger son of an Anglo-Irish landowning family. . . ."
[2] Denison Deasey.

3 The letter runs in part: "She [Lawrence's mother] was wholly wrapped up in my father, whom she had carried away jealously from his former life and country against great odds: and whom she kept as her trophy of power. . . . My mother, brought up as a child of sin in the Island of Skye by a bible-thinking Presbyterian, then a nurse-maid, then guilty (in her own judgment) of taking my father from his wife."

4 See below, letter 12.

5 Sir Charles Oman A History of the Peninsula War (7 vols 1902–30); see RA The Duke: Being an Account of the Life & Achievements of Arthur Wellesley, 1st Duke of Wellington. . . . (1943).

6 Letters of T. E. Lawrence ed David Garnett (1939) 152.

7 Lawrence and the Arabs 24.

8 Lawrence — or Aircraftsman Shaw — was in India from Jan 1927 until late Feb 1929.

9 Lawrence and the Arabs 39; see Leonard Wooley and T. E. Lawrence, The Wilderness of Zin (1936).

10 That is, that schoolboys were forbidden to visit the rooms of undergraduates and that Lawrence took pleasure in disregarding the rule. See above, letter 4.

11 By Radclyffe Hall (1928). See above, letter 7 n 5.

12 T. E. Lawrence The Mint . . . by 352087 A/c Ross (1955) 50–1, 117–18, et passim.

13 Lawrence's comment on Queen Alexandra (The Mint 185) runs: "When we reached the presence, and I saw the mummied thing, the bird-like head cocked on one side, not artfully but by disease, the red-rimmed eyes, the enamelled face, which the famous smile scissored across all angular and heart-rending: then I nearly ran away in pity. The body should not be kept alive after the lamp of sense has gone out. There were the ghosts of all her lovely airs, the little graces, the once-effective sway and movement of the figure which had been her consolation. Her bony fingers, clashing in the tunnel of their rings, fiddled with albums, penholders, photographs, toys upon the table: and the heart-rending appeal played on us like a hose, more and more terribly." Lawrence explained his motives for writing this passage in a letter to George Bernard Shaw (Karachi, 7 May 1928): "As I worked on it, I was trying to feel intensely sorry for the poor old creature who had been carefully kept alive too long. I was trying to make myself (and anyone else who read it) shake at the horrible onset of age. . . . I was saying to myself 'You'll be like that, too, unless you die sooner than the Queen' . . . . but it wasn't just personal. There were all the hundreds of younger fellows round me in the church, and I was smelling instead the decay of Marlborough House." Shaw had found a "touch of the grinning street-arab" in the passage, and Mrs Shaw called it "cruel."

14 See T. E. Lawrence to Charlotte F. Shaw [Karachi] 26 Aug 1927: "The drama of [Casement's] life was so beautiful: his official duty (consuls are scrubby plain-song things: he made his work great, & won a knighthood early) his early Congo work, his difficult Putumayo work: his political errantry: his life in Germany, his trial & death." Lawrence gave as his reason for not writing the life himself the fact that Casement's diaries, confiscated by the British government, were inaccessible, but he was convinced that Casement "could be made the epitome of all the patriotisms and greeds and lusts and passions of man-imperial" (Letters of T. E. Lawrence 863; T. E. Lawrence to Charlotte F. Shaw [Karachi] 27 Dec 1927). Casement's Black Diaries were first published in 1959.

15 Letters of T. E. Lawrence.

16 Part of a rail system which commenced at Haydarpaṣa, opposite Istanbul, on the Bosphorus and ran by way of Aleppo and Damascus to Medina. For Lawrence's account of raids on the railway in which he participated see Seven Pillars of Wisdom (1935) 198–203, 289–91, 362–70, 416–31, 518–31, 599–604, et passim.

9

17 March 1951   *Le Lavandou*

DEAR BIRD,

I have to write a post-script letter because I forgot yesterday to enclose a Churchillian morsel which you will savour with relish. If you know it already, forgive me. This is W.S.C.'s description of TEL at Paris in 1919:

"The gravity of his demeanour, the precision of his opinions, the range and quality of his conversation all seemed enhanced to a remarkable degree by the splendid Arab head-dress and garb. From amid the flowing draperies his noble features, his perfectly chiselled lips, and flashing eyes loaded with fire and comprehension shone forth." [1] ! ! ! ! !

Dizzy, surely? Those "flashing eyes loaded with fire and comprehension" could have come only from the author — or a follower of the author — of Vivian Grey, Contarini Fleming and Coningsby. [2]

Yours

R. A.

[1] Winston S. Churchill "Lawrence of Arabia" *Great Contemporaries* (1937) 138. See also Churchill in *T. E. Lawrence by His Friends* 195. Both Churchill and Lawrence were in Paris for the Peace Conference from 8 Jan to the end of Aug 1919. Another picture of Lawrence at this time is in Colonel Richard Meinertzhagen's *Middle East Diary* (1917–1956), 1959: "I remember an occasion in the Majestic Hotel in Paris when he ran off with my knobkerry; I chased him, caught him and holding him tight gave him a spanking on the bottom. He made no attempt to resist and told me later that he could easily understand a woman submitting to rape once a strong man hugged her."

[2] *Vivian Grey* (1826–27) was Benjamin Disraeli's (Dizzy's) first novel; it was followed by a number of others which included *Contarini Fleming* (1832) and *Coningsby* (1844).

I O

27 March 1951   *Le Lavandou*

DEAR BIRD,

Your last two letters have brought valuable material, and I feel deeply obliged to you. The Trill Mill stream episode becomes more comprehensible since it was a convoy of canoes. [1] The "Friends" narratives sound as if there were three different "first" explorations. [2] The other Mathers's material is all good. I wonder why he didn't contribute to "Friends"? The canoe upset and rug story is referred to by Mrs. L. but now becomes clear. [3] Also, I am glad to have an explanation of the no boys in College rule. [4]

The Summel anecodotes are excellent. [5] Of course if he has any others and IF it is not an utterly shameless imposition on you, I should be very glad to have them.

According to my friend at the Brit Mus, the Shaw–Shaw correspondence, though verbose and boring, is quite an extraordinary relationship. Her letters are there as well as his. Press marks are C.S. to T.E.S. Additional M/S 45922. T.E.S. to C.S. Additional M/S 45903, 4. The report adds "His hand changes from letter to letter, small and tidy, big and sprawling, always legible, written on any scrap, on the back of Station Orders or hotel paper."!

Among other things he tells her that he doesn't go to the local brothel because he wouldn't know what to do if he did go! [6]

Yes, I have come to that conclusion about his laziness, which was partly an attempt to live up to father's country land-owning prejudices against working and "professionalism."

His mother also was illegitimate (this is libel as she's still alive) and a nurse-maid — that is according to the Shaw–Shaw letters. Her great triumph was to have taken R. T. [Chapman] away from his wife and to have kept him. TEL says his father was a hard rider and hard drinker, careless about money, and she made him a cheeseparing teetotaller! L. says he knew of their relationship when he was "ten" and "didn't care a straw" (it is the clue to his whole life), but only let his mother know when he flew over from Paris on his father's death.[7] They may have had some sort of scene as he evidently didn't attend the funeral. This may have been resentment?

I find him most vindicative against Oman . . . ! Oman says he voted for TEL's All Souls' fellowship. Perhaps they had some quarrel about military matters.[8] Look up the article Guerilla in the 1928 Encyclopaedia, if you want to see Lawrence at his absurdest height of self glorification.[9] He never mentions the Peninsula War. Spite against Oman? As if he would care!

My Paris friend reports that the Crusader Castle models are on display at the Musée de Chaillot, but doesn't say which. He could learn nothing from the attendants, but left a note for the director. Tomorrow I lunch with old Professor Cohen (now Emeritus) of the Sorbonne, whose subject is le moyen age, and I'll ask him. Stupid of me not to have thought of it earlier. It will be very funny if it turns out that these models were there all along, done to scale, so that the fearful deed of endurance, massacre by atrocious Kurds etc, turn out to be unnecessary. . . .

Well, we have had five days of mistral, which entirely prevented the tourists from wearing les short et les bikini. One fine day or rather two and now a cold north wind and clouds, probably rain again tomorrow. We have now been without rain for ten days, but most were disagreeable with mistral. Pre-1939 the peasants here used to blame bad weather on us — c'est à cause du mauvais temps en Angleterre. Now, whispering behind their hands — fear of the Gestapo — they mutter knowingly c'est à cause de leurs expériences. No good pointing out that New Mexico is a long way off.[10]

All my thanks.

Yours sincerely,
RICHARD ALDINGTON

[1] A canoe expedition to explore the underground Oxford Sewer, the Trill Mill stream. H. F. Mathers's account of the incident runs: "The Trill Mill Stream journey was organized by T. E., — I think in the Summer Term of 1909. There were I believe 3 vessels, canadian canoes, and among the party were A. T. P. Williams (now Bishop of Durham), E. F. Hall (now Archdeacon of Totnes), and V. W. Richards (of whom I have lost trace. I believe he and T. E. tried to set up a hand-printing press.) We paddled up past the Gas works and into the side stream which comes down past the Castle Tower, to somewhere near Bennett's laundry where Trill Mill Stream branches off and runs under a brick-arched tunel below Paradise Square, and Rose Place, to come out at the western corner of Christ Church Meadow, where now the War Memorial Gardens join the Broad Walk. Unknown to us, Lawrence had with him a 450 revolver loaded with blank cartridges. These he fired when about half way along. You can imagine the effect in this small tunnel. We arrived safely at Salter's just below Folly Bridge." (H. F. Mathers to Alan Bird, Frinton on Sea, Essex 17 Mar 1951 [Berg]. See also RA, *Lawrence of Arabia* 48–9.)

[2] *T. E. Lawrence by His Friends* 42, 47. A third reference to the Trill Mill stream episode has not been located.

[3] Mathers's account of this episode runs: "T. E. cycled up to my home on Boars Hill early one morning [in the winter of 1908 or 1909] and persuaded me to accompany him in a double, rob-roy canoe to try to get up to Banbury on the Cherwell floods. Progress was so slow that we only reached the Bicester-Oxford road near Gosford in late afternoon where a portage over the road would have been necessary, as the arches of the bridge were almost submerged. So we turned back and started to swoop down the main stream which was running about 5 knots. When we came to a sharp bend where the bank was low, the current ran us bows-first into a

hawthorn bush. We backed out, turned the canoe sideways to paddle hard round the bend, but we hit the same bush, this time sideways, with our bodies. The current carried the canoe under the branches and in we went. T. E. looked a bit helpless, so I went and pulled him to the bank where I hung on to a branch. The current was so fast that I couldn't pull him in, so he climbed hand over hand along my arms, and we got on the bank still up to our knees in water. Then I saw why he was unable to swim. His rug was still tightly wrapped round his legs. As the water cleared from his legs the rug unwrapped itself. Meanwhile the canoe was out of sight downstream. We waded to the L.N.W.R. line not far away and walked along it to the Banbury-Oxford road, and so back to his home . . ." (H. F. Mathers to Alan Bird, Frinton on Sea, Essex 17 Mar 1951 [Berg]. See also RA *Lawrence of Arabia* 48; *T. E. Lawrence by His Friends* 27.)

4 See above, letter 4 n 3.

5 See T. Summel to Alan Bird, Littlemere, nr Oxford 17 Mar 1951 (Berg). See also RA *Lawrence of Arabia* 370.

6 T. E. Lawrence to Charlotte F. Shaw, Cranwell 28 Nov 1925.

7 T. E. Lawrence to Charlotte F. Shaw [Karachi] 14 Apr 1927; see above letter 8.

8 For a possible explanation of Lawrence's vindictiveness toward Oman see a letter to Charlotte F. Shaw [Karachi] 25 Feb 1928, which runs in part: "Sir Charles Oman was one of the film company [which bought rights to *Seven Pillars of Wisdom*]. They wanted to make it historically accurate. So you'd glue peacock feathers to a canvas showing a peacock, I suppose. That wish for accuracy, in a thing that has really happened, is vicious: a sign of something worse than stupidity."

9 The article, included under the general heading "Guerrilla," is entitled "Science of Guerrilla Warfare" and signed T. E. La. It begins by stating that the article is based solely "on the concrete experience of the Arab Revolt against the Turks 1916–1918."

10 A reference to the widely held belief that bad weather in Europe was due to American explosions of the atom bomb, for purposes of testing, in New Mexico.

I I

7 April 1951   *Le Lavandou*

DEAR BIRD,

It is lucky I started making early preparations to leave here. I have now packed ten large cases of books, given away or destroyed a considerable number, and find I still have dealt with only about one half of the accumulation! In pre-1939 days, books could be easily packed and cheaply transported. I now find that it will cost as much to take these books to Hyères for storage as it cost to send about one half that number to America in 1938!

Now that I have packed the "firsts" and signed copies I am getting a man in to pack the rest. Towards the end of the month we shall get into the little car and go adventuring. Of course I shall take with me the essential Lawrence books, my voluminous notes, and the 40,000 words of the first draft. This will have to be entirely re-written owing to the discovery of new information.

Graves is a careless biographer and the article you sent has many little and big errors. A warning to me to go carefully and check much! The S.A. stuff is certainly poppycock.[1] I suspect TEL cooked up this most unlikely feminine interest and foisted it on the naif Graves because of A. T. Wilson's bitter review where, alluding to the fact that the homosexual passages of 7 Pillars are cut out from Revolt,[2] Wilson said:

". . . we must be grateful to be spared, in this edition, more detailed references to a vice to which Semitic races are by no means prone. To most English readers his Epipsychidion on this subject will be incomprehensible, to the re-mainder, unwelcome." [3]

The praise of homosexuality in 7 Pillars is so flagrant, the doing dirt on women so whole-hearted throughout his life, that there can be no doubt where his inter-ests lay. But for the fact that it would take too much space I had thought of quot-ing Doughty's "normal man" description of a handsome young Arab against Lawrence's lip-licking gloats over Daud and Farraj and their "give and take, unspiritual relation, like marriage." (I like that "give and take"!) He ends up by praising them like a sentimental curate for being "so clean"! [4] Clean, of course, because they had nothing to do with women.

But all this will need careful treatment. I wish that for that particular chapter I might hand the typewriter to the late Mr Edward Gibbon, M.P.

Ever so many thanks for sending the Graves article. It is another round of ammunition in hand.

Professor Cohen and his wife are coming over from La Croix tomorrow for lunch with me, and I may have some news of the Trocadero exhibits. Cohen knows the Chaillot director, and wrote to him. But I haven't great hopes of getting accurate information because I don't think Cohen fully grasped what I wanted, and was more interested in arousing my admiration for his extensive relations among influential French than in finding out exactly what information was required. Unfortunately we have only Graves as authority for the Paris visit.[5] Malapropos, I was enchanted to find one of his more ridiculous fans likening his photograph of the Arabs entering Damascus to — a Tintoretto! [6] His literary agent thinks he was, tout court, another Jesus Christ — a very proper attitude in an agent, but hardly cricket.[7] Richards gets into one sentence St Francis, Lincoln, Leonardo, Stonewall Jackson, Stefansson, Odysseus, Sven Hedin and "a Conradian Shakespeare"; and beyond them is still Lawrence! [8] But I think the Tintoretto snapshot is my favourite.

I've got some excellent revelations from the guileless Lowell Thomas which will delight you. You will have noticed that Liddell Hart ignores him, while Graves and Garnett hustle him into a corner as quickly as possible. The fact is that L.T. invented "Lawrence of Arabia" and I have got him to put in writing that TEL collaborated whole-heartedly in both film-lecture and book! [9] He then plaintively writes F. N. Doubleday about "a Mr Lowell Thomas" and excuses himself to Mrs Shaw for "the vulgar reputation" created by L.T.[10] There's no end to it all. If I manage to get it all down I shall have to hide myself in a monastery from the vengeance of outraged Lawrenceites.

I wish I knew how to thank you for the help you have given me, and the stimulus of your letters. I am really most grateful for such accurate and scholarly help.

Yours sincerely,
RICHARD ALDINGTON

[1] "The Heart of a Book *Revolt in the Desert*" *London Magazine* (10 June 1950). Here, for the first time Graves Discussed the S.A. to whom *Seven Pillars of Wisdom* is dedicated with a poem of which the first stanza runs,

> I loved you, so I draw these tides of men into my hands
>   and wrote my will across the sky in stars
> To earn you Freedom, the seven pillared worthy house,
>   that your eyes might be shining for me
>   When we came.

Graves identified S.A. as an unknown woman, a Syrian living in Damascus, and stated that Lawrence associated her romantically with Jehanne, the heroine of Maurice Hewlett's novel *Richard Yea-and-Nay* (1900). In his book on Lawrence, p 80, RA identified S.A. as Sheik Ahmed, nicknamed Dahoum, whom Lawrence first encountered at Carchemish in 1912 and, in 1913, brought to Oxford. Ahmed died of typhus in Damascus in November 1917. (See Knightley and Simpson *Secret Lives of T. E. Lawrence* 160–64, where the same identification is made.) In 1963 Robert Graves attacked RA's identification of S.A. and reaffirmed his own theory. He said again Lawrence had declared that the real S.A. had not died but that he himself had changed (that is, been made impotent by the flogging at Deraa; see above, letter 7 n 5). Graves then identified S.A. with a woman who signed at least one letter to Lawrence, "Jehanne," and whom Lawrence designated as "Son Altesse" or S.A. See "T. E. Lawrence and the Riddle of 'S.A.'" *Saturday Review* (15 June 1963). In 1964 there appeared a pamphlet, *Poems Dedicated to T. E. Lawrence* (privately printed in an edition of 100 copies), whose author associated the *Poems* with Graves's article. The pamphlet is signed "Jehanne."

² *Revolt in the Desert*, an abridgement of *Seven Pillars of Wisdom*, published in 1927, a year after the privately printed *Seven Pillars* was issued.

³ In *Journal of the Central Asian Society* (1927).

⁴ Doughty *Arabia Deserta* I 5, 30–1, 89, 98, *et passim*; Lawrence, *Pillars of Wisdom* 237; see also 508–09.

⁵ Graves *Lawrence and the Arabs* 19.

⁶ Herbert Baker in *T. E. Lawrence by His Friends* 251.

⁷ Raymond Savage in *T. E. Lawrence by His Friends* 393–98.

⁸ Vyvyan Richards *Portrait of T. E. Lawrence, The Lawrence of The Seven Pillars of Wisdom* (1936) 228. Richards's phrase is "a Shakespearian Conrad."

⁹ See RA *Lawrence of Arabia* 108. In Aug 1919 Lowell Thomas opened at Covent Garden with the film-lecture "With Allenby in Palestine and the Conquest of Holy Arabia," a title which he subsequently changed to "With Allenby in Palestine and Lawrence in Arabia." Eventually the lecture was moved to Albert Hall, where it ran until Jan 1920. In his "Foreword" to *With Lawrence in Arabia* (1924) ix, Thomas wrote that in Arabia he "found it impossible to extract much information from Lawrence himself regarding his own achievements." In *T. E. Lawrence by His Friends* 213–14, Thomas stated that when he was writing *With Lawrence in Arabia*, Lawrence "helped." He "regularly . . . worked with me." See also T. E. Lawrence to Charlotte F. Shaw [Karachi] 29 Sept 1927 where Lawrence states that he helped Robert Graves and adds "Lowell Thomas has shown the world what would happen if I refused information."

¹⁰ See *Letters of T. E. Lawrence* 301, where Lawrence says, "You know a Mr. Lowell Thomas made me a kind of matinee idol. . . ." See also T. E. Lawrence to Charlotte F. Shaw, Clouds Hill 19 Mar 1924 where he writes of Thomas as "the American" who made his "vulgar reputation," and then describes Thomas as "a well-intentioned intensely crude & pushful fellow." See also, T. E. Lawrence to Charlotte F. Shaw, Clouds Hill 26 Mar 1924 which says of Thomas, "He's a born vulgarian, who does the best that is in him."

I 2

23 April 1951 *Le Lavandou*

DEAR BIRD,

I lunched with Cohen yesterday and he gave me the enclosed letter. Two photographs were enclosed, one showing the model of Crac with a wall exhibit of photographs, plans, fragments of sculpture and a broken inscription in rather fine mediaeval script; the other shows the two smaller models of Saone. The date 1930 wholly disposes of my theory.¹ The Director says nothing about the Viollet-le-Duc drawings, but then I didn't ask about them. I didn't feel I could ask Cohen to write again. He is 71, in constant pain from his war wound (has to sleep tied in a chair) but has great courage and energy — begins next month a series of ten broadcasts on mediaeval French poetry and its music! [2]

Yours sincerely,
RICHARD ALDINGTON

[1] That is that T. E. Lawrence might have seen models of the crusader castles in Paris's Musée de Chaillot without making the hazardous journey through Syria in 1909. See above, letter 8. The enclosed letter is apparently lost.

[2] See *La Poésie en France au Moyen Age* (1952).

13

10 June 1951   Les Rosiers, Ancien Chemin de Castelnau, Montpellier, Hérault

DEAR BIRD,

The long silence has been due to the move, and the difficulty of settling on a suitable place. I stored the Lavandou stuff and the 3000 books, and pushed off by car on 25th April with the child. We made it half a pleasure trip, and went over much of the Rhone delta, seeing Aix, Lourmarin, Fontaine de Vaucluse, Isle dans la Sorgue (a disappointment), Avignon, Villeneuve, Pont du Gard, Beaucaire, Tarascon, St Rémy, Arles, Nimes, and Aigues Mortes. We then came to Montpellier and finding no accommodation immediately available, went on to Beziers, Carassonne and St Bertrand de Comminges. Fearful weather in the Pyrenees! So for Pentecôte we ran up to see friends in Sancerre [1] by way of Auch, Agen, Périgueux and Bourges, and back by way of Bourganeuf, Cordes, Albi, Villefrance-en-Rouergue. In spite of the war and the inflation France, off the great tourist tracks, is still the pleasantest country for the modest motorist with an eye to the picturesque. The large triangle Irun-Marseille-Fontainebleau was one of my cherished wandering places pre-1938, and I was delighted to find it practically intact and unchanged. Of course, I won't pretend that it has the concentrated art experience of Italy. It hasn't, but Italy is so overpopulated and the barbarians have been over it . . . I believe it was Ruskin who pointed out that for the "Powers" to settle their vulgar differences in Italy was like inviting hooligans to fight it out in the gallery of the Louvre.

Anyway here we are in a pension straight out of Balzac, but with a lovely old garden, not five minutes from the centre of the town. Except for a spasm of building when the 3rd Republic celebrated the centenary of the beginning of the first, nothing much has been added to the place since it was reconstructed after the religious wars. Except for the cathedral there is not a church earlier than the 17th, so there is quite a bit of baroque. There is a chapel of penitents every square yard of which is decorated and painted, with flat painted panels in the ceiling. Unluckily, it is very dark, always has dismal old women gazing at the altar, and a fug which sends me into the air in five minutes. The Musée Fabre is extremely interesting for a local collection, including several Houdons, a Canova and a Pradier, a 17th century bronze miniature replica of the Bernini Apollo and Daphne in the Villa Borghese and some fairly good portrait busts. The pictures include original or at any rate decent school works by Correggio, Bronzino, Veronese, the Carracci (whom I don't despise), Gaspar Poussin, a school of Botticelli, a Guardi, a Primaticcio, several Salvator Rosa. There is a portrait of Baudelaire by Courbet which I never saw reproduced, an absurd Lord Byron by Géricault, and the small original sketch of Goethe in the campagna by Tischbein. Some excellent French pictures.

Now an SOS and a cadge. Has the Bodleian got a copy of Colonel Brémond's La Guerre dans la Héjaz [2] (or some such title)? All my efforts to buy a copy here have failed, and they haven't the inter-library loan system. It is obviously one of the most effective criticisms of Lawrence, from the up-stage efforts of Liddell Hart to score off the author on minute points.[3] Extracts from this would be most welcome. The Foreign Office has a report on the whole affair, but refuse to allow anyone to see it as it is "secret and confidential"! I felt like telling them I hoped it wasn't among the documents carried off by their Mr MacLean and Mr Burgess.[4] But what rot, when the nations are publishing all the 1939–45 stuff, and 14–18 is one with Babylon and Tyre. I have now done nearly 50,000 words of the first draft, but shall be utterly thankful when the job is done and I can stagger back to civilisation. What a phoney! [. . .]

Are you back in Oxford permanently? I forgot to say that the main reason for being here is for the daughter to attend the Lycée, which she is accordingly doing.

Yours sincerely
RICHARD ALDINGTON

[1] George Gribble, English playwright.
[2] Général Edouard Brémond *Le Hedjaz dans la Guerre Mondiale* (1931).
[3] See Liddell Hart *Colonel Lawrence* 91, 93–94, 118, 119 *et passim*.
[4] By 6 June 1951 the British Foreign Office reported two officials, Guy Burgess and Donald Maclean, absent without leave since May 25 and suspended since June 1, but denied knowledge of their whereabouts and continued to do so for several months. Subsequently Burgess's and Maclean's defection to Russia was confirmed.

14

30 June 1951   *Montpellier*

DEAR BIRD,

I write at once to let you know that I have solved the difficulty of Brémond's book. The ever friendly Gustave Cohen used what are known as "Faculty privileges" (in the USA) and got the Bib. Nat. copy which his kindness caused him to post off at once to me. I must be careful of it.

First thing which struck my evil eye was a remark of Général Brémond (himself apparently a genuine Arabisant) that Abdulla spoke only Arabic and Turkish, but Feisal EXCELLENT ENGLISH!!! Now we begin to see why Abdulla was no good and Feisal the chosen one.[1]

Yes, the charm must not be forgotten. I believe myself, though the evidence I bring is only circumstantial and not decisive, that he belonged to the great international trade union of sods. I think this accounts for much of his réclame — remember the case of O.W. and his fugelmen. I think it may in part account for the extreme unwillingness of the RAF to have him — remember Baldwin had to *order* Air-Marshal Swan to accept him.[2]

I still have a long way to go, verifying of facts and sources being complex and wearisome.

I do hope you are right about the Penguin Lawrences.[3] Very little response has come my way, although I slaved myself into a nervous breakdown, trying to get them through the press correctly. I suppose it was cheek, but I silently corrected his misquotations from English poetry and the curious error of Ito the dancer for Foujita — obvious pen-slip. What I long to run a pen through is the paragraph in Studies in American Literature where he refers to Lucretius as an author of the 4th century.[4] I don't give a damn about such slips, but there is a type of "critic" which picks up and exploits such trifles and does do harm. What you tell me about some dons affecting uncontrollable mirth at Lawrence is typical of a certain brand of pedant. Wouldn't they have been doing exactly the same to Blake in 1850?

Well, if you missed the Musée Fabre I missed that chapel in Cerbère. I didn't care for that so-called Côte Vermeille, and got away as quickly as possible. Perpignan is rather pleasant. I wonder if that very fine avenue of gigantic planes is still there. You would certainly find most of the Fabre mediocre, but there are a few good things, and I find much interest in a purely local collection built up by the enthusiasm of three or four men in succeeding generations.[5] I think the worst things are about a dozen diploma pictures presented by the Beaux Arts in germinal, An X, or some such date. Fabre's original collection is interesting as showing the taste of a cultivated amateur painter between about 1790–1820. He lived most of his life in Rome, so had ample opportunities. I suspect many of his pictures are studio copies. The other collection is that of Alfred Bruyas, a French country gentleman, who spent most of his income on buying pictures by contemporary French artists. He abused the occasion, as Whistler would have said, by having his portrait painted too often.

Have you seen a newish (1949) book on Provence by Fernand Benoit?[6] He is Curator of the Musée Arlaten, a place for which I have a special admiration, and his knowledge of Provençal "folk" is what the Daily Mail would call "phenomenal." The survival of beliefs, customs, crafts, tools etc from remote times until living memory is most remarkable. It is the same here in Languedoc. At Saint Guilhem le Desert (about 25 miles from here) a monastery-basilica-village said to have been founded by Charlemagne's cousin, there are most curious survivals. On the eve of Good Friday a procession and the whole village illuminated by little lamps of snail-shells burning olive oil. On mardi gras the married men, preceded by a drummer, hunt the boys and if they catch any duck them unmercifully in the public fountain. What sort of a rite is this? Anti-Chérubin? Do you know the Benedicite of Saint Guilhem:

> "Benedecite de Sant-Guilhem:
> Sèn prou per manjà de qu'abèn,
> E se quancun mai vôu veni
> Que se cope las cambas en cami."

How I wish the publishers would let me write about such things and not condemn me to dreary little buggers like T. E. Lawrence.

I do wish you could manage to snatch a week or two down here and let me run you round in my three monkey-power Fiat to some of these places going up towards and into the Cevennes. (What a duffer R.L.S. was — he saw nothing but his donkey.)[7] Do you know Sommières? And Cordes? And Villefranche-en-Rouergue? Do you know the Goyas at Castres?

My infant phenomenon is much interested in Maurin des Maures,[8] her hero in fact. At lunch just now she remarked: "He lived by himself and so he was an idealist and got into trouble with the gendarmerie." Is this not the history of DHL?

Ever yours
R. A.

[1] Brémond *Le Hedjaz dans la Guerre Mondiale* 72 and n 3.

[2] See Swan's remarks in *Letters of T. E. Lawrence* 363 which run, in part: "I never met him [T. E. Lawrence] until he was brought to me at the Air Ministry and I was ordered to get him into the R.A.F. I disliked the whole business, with its secrecy and subterfuge; I discouraged communication with or from him. I handled all the matters of his entry and movements entirely myself."

[3] RA wrote introductions for the Penguin editions (1950) of the following books by D. H. Lawrence: *Mornings in Mexico; The White Peacock; Sea and Sardinia; Aaron's Rod; Etruscan Places; Kangaroo; The Lost Girl; The Plumed Serpent; Selected Essays; St. Mawr, and the Virgin and the Gypsy; The Woman Who Rode Away, and Other Stories.* RA compiled the *Selected Letters* for which Aldous Huxley wrote the introduction (also Penguin 1950). RA was not associated with another "Penguin Lawrence" issued in 1950, *Selected Poems.* Two more titles by Lawrence with introductions by RA appeared in Penguin editions, *The Rainbow* (1949) and *Women in Love* (1951).

[4] *Studies in Classic American Literature* (1923) 1.

[5] Named Musée Fabre in 1937, when Baron François-Xavier Pascal Fabre bequeathed to the museum, founded in 1825, 330 pictures and *objets d'art*, once the property of the Countess of Albany, whom Fabre had married secretly in Florence. The museum was enlarged by the Collection Valedan and by gifts from Alfred Bruyas and Frédéric Bazille.

[6] *La Provence et le Comtat Venaissin.*

[7] Robert Louis Stevenson *Travels with a Donkey in the Cévennes* (1879).

[8] The hero of the Provençal novel *Maurin des Maures* by Jean Aicard (1908).

15

30 July 1951   *Montpellier*

DEAR BIRD,

You send me very interesting letters, for which in my solitude I am indeed grateful. The copy of Brémond will be useful, and as soon as it arrives I shall return the Bib. Nat. copy.[1]

Recently I have had a renewal of correspondence with Ezra Pound — to whom I hadn't written since in July 1940 he wrote me that Winston Churchill was about to be "hanged on the Gold Exchange" (whatever that may be) by the triumphant Axis. But he asked a small service, and I couldn't go on boycotting an invalid. I enclose his latest letter which, as he is now à la mode in England, may interest you and perhaps some of your confrères at Wadham. How much of it do you understand? "H" means my first wife, H.D., who recently went back to USA and hated it. "W.L." of course is Wyndham Lewis. "F" is Ford Madox Hueffer — I had suggested that he is wholly forgotten as a poet, and perhaps deserves a selection.[2]

Possibly this curious style of writing may have helped to persuade the unimaginative American psychiatrists that Ezra is mad. (I have long thought myself that he is a paranoiac of a rather amiable sort.) But he has been writing letters like that for 25 years. Why? It seems to me that he has adopted the style of the Katzenjammer kids with much skill, because of the influence of James Joyce (Mr Shame's Choice), because of "fear of the cliché" (i.e. of saying anything in a plain, unaffected, straight-forward way), and because of local patriotism, the comic strip and its deformations of language being America's one indisputably successful contribution to world culture. If I remember correctly, Ezra's models, the Katzenjammer Kids,[3] star in the Hearst publications [4] which share and possibly inspired some of Ezra's Anglophobia and Francophobia.

I often used to wonder, in the days of our intimacy, how much Italian poetry Eliot has read. If the Aminta is not a masterpiece of its genre, what is? It seems to me that Fletcher and Milton learned from Aminta [5] and Il Pastor Fido,[6] but I think that Eliot doesn't admire either the Faithful Shepherdess [7] or the Masque presented at Ludlow.[8] Then again some of Tasso's canzoni and sonnets used to seem to me quite perfect in that highly wrought Cinquecento style — not to be read in London on Ash Wednesday, of course, but after a visit to Sant' Onofrio [9] over a flask of Aleatico in late September. And, again, the Gerusalemme [10] — which I admit I have never read through but only in sections — is a masterpiece of the artificial and polished narrative. I personally find Marino's Adone [11] (of which I've read about two-thirds) more interesting, but I suppose if I called it a masterpiece of barocco I should be deeper than ever in the Eliotesque dawghouse. Wasn't it Boileau who talked about "tout le clinquant du Tasse"? These legislators to Parnassus!

I toil on at TELawrence in distress of mind and spirit. I have now finished with the Peace Conference, which had to be scrappy as I couldn't get a verbatim report of the two sessions on Arabia and had to make do with Lloyd George's summary.[12] There is still a weary way to go, with the double certainty that in this enormous confusion of evidence I am bound to make blunders, and that when my task is done A. W. Lawrence may refuse to permit quotation of copyright material and use of photographs. But I think I have uttered this lamentation before. When — I almost wrote "if" — I can complete this task I shall feel as if demobilised a second time.

Nice to think you know and like the santons. My daughter has quite a big collection, and the Christmas crèche of santons is more familiar to her than the Teutonic tree. I don't find any here. There is a very good historical collection in Arles. Tomorrow I am going to take a respite from TEL and not exactly "bathe my hands in the calm twilight of Gothic things" but go and look at the façades of St Gilles and St Trophime, spend an hour in that Mistral museum I love so much, and try to find a ½-bottle of Châteauneuf-du-Pape for lunch. Did you know that when this enormous Rhone hydroelectric plant is complete this year at Bollène they will have enough electric power for 12 huge factories one of which is threatened for Avignon and one for Châteauneuf. Can't they leave us anything? They did Bibbiena's Calendria at Avignon last week,[13] but I couldn't spare the time to go over and see it. I've long meant to read it but never have.

The last photograph I saw of Cocteau in the French press showed him giving an ice-cream to a horse. It wasn't Pegasus.

Yours sincerely,
RICHARD ALDINGTON

---

[1] Bird's autograph note at the top of the letter runs: "I managed to obtain a copy of the Brémond book for A."

Richard Aldington (above)
and Alan Bird

Photographs published
with permission of
Catherine Aldington Guillaume
and Alister Kershaw
and of Alan Bird

2 See below, letter 22 n 3.

3 A comic strip featuring two endlessly mischievous boys, Hans and Fritz, whose speech was strongly Germanic in pronunciation and idiom. Drawn by Rudolph Dirks for Hearst's *Journal*, commencing in 1896 or 1897, the Katzenjammer Kids was based on Wilhelm Busch's Max and Moritz cartoons in Germany.

4 Output of the American news empire founded by William Randolph Hearst, whose name was synonymous with "yellow" journalism and opposition to all internationalism.

5 By Torquato Tasso; completed about 1573.

6 By Battista Guarini; completed about 1590.

7 By John Fletcher; printed about 1610.

8 *Comus* (1637), called a masque but actually a pastoral entertainment written by John Milton to celebrate the Earl of Bridgewater's entry to the presidency of Wales and the Marches; presented 1634.

9 The monastery on Trasteverine Hill (Rome) to which Tasso retreated on 1 Apr 1595 and where he died on 25 Apr 1595.

10 *Gerusalemme Liberata* by Tasso (1576).

11 1623.

12 *The Truth, about The Peace Treaties* (1938).

13 A prose comedy first presented 6 Feb 1513.

16

9 August 1951   *Montpellier*

DEAR BIRD,

My grateful thanks for your notes on the Patch – G.B.S. book.[1] I read it, and lost my notes in the confusion of getting away from Lavandou. Most useful to have these extracts, above all the one about the luxury foods, which will tack on admirably to that absurd anecdote of Henry Williamson's about the haughty hostess who offered him sherry and everything else from soup to grouse, only to be told politely by Mr Shaw that he only liked tea and wads.[2]

I have today finished the draft of the Lowell Thomas chapter which I think is pretty deadly and will, I hope, in time give you a laugh or two. I know Thomas slightly from American days.[3] He is a good speaker, having the gift of the gab werry gallopin — like Mr Jingle — and a rather engagingly naif outlook. I think he doesn't know how TEL double-crossed and betrayed him. But none of these Lawrence claqueurs has read the Letters and other documents — I can prove Storrs hasn't — with the possible exception of Liddell Hart who is surely the world's prize ass.

Do you note that Feisal the son of Ibn Saud is now in the news?[4] Lawrence, by his obstinate refusal to recognise the military ability and strength of character of Ibn Saud, let us in for an endless mess in Arabia, reinforced by his quite senseless Francophobia. If we took Iraq and Palestine and established hegemony over central Arabia, why on earth not keep our word and let the French have northern Syria? Or insist on real independence for the whole area, and get out ourselves while insisting that France get out. . . . .[5]

Why do I bore you with this?

I am sending you two pamphlets which I think may not be in your library. The Museon Arlaten [6] is a poor affair, but may give you some idea of the great interest of the place. There is so much there that in five long visits I haven't by any means exhausted it. If only someone in the last century had thought of making two or three regional museums of country England on ethnographical lines! But I suppose the bishops would have objected and national pride have revolted. Anyway Mistral did a great piece of work there.

The other is a really rare pamphlet, and I have cornered the last copies, at least all in Arles and Montpellier. Did the English newspapers report the recent death of the marquis Folco de Baroncelli, who was the Maître of the Camargue manadiers?[7] Out of sheer beastliness the damned Germans destroyed the Mas du Simbère in which he had lived for many years. I think the mixture of sublime and ridiculous in this pamphlet gives the spirit of the Midi as does the Nacioun Gardiano with its mixed membership of bull-breeders, cow-boys, poets, horsemen, félibres and artists.

Last Sunday I took an Australian friend to see the monument to Le Sanglier,[8] and a passing gardien told us there was to be an abrivado at Le Cailar in half an hour — so we went. A plump of horsemen, each with a "trident," comes galloping in on the white flea-bitten Camargue horses, with a couple of lean black bulls galloping inside. Before lunch one of the bulls is turned out, pawing and snorting, and it is wonderful to see the skill, daring and speed of the village lads as they tease him and just escape over the barrier by inches. The only man hurt was a professional who was careless in trying to put the bull back in his pen, took a toss, and had to grab the horns to avoid being gored.

We had to go on to Arles and couldn't wait for the corrida for cocades in the afternoon. I much prefer the Provençal to the Spanish corrida. Nobody is armed, the bull is not killed, and it is much harder to cut the cocade from the forehead of an enraged bull than to stab it after it has been exhausted by the picadors. The odds are on the bull, and if anyone gets hurt it is the men. The great Sanglier seems never to have lost a cocade, which must be very nearly a record.

Another good thing about the Provençal corrida is that it is still comparatively uncommercial and done as much for the fun of it as a village cricket match. Some of the best corridas are held in extempore rings of farm carts.

Another local sport is the tambourin, a Languedoc variation of longue paume, with Pézenas and Montpellier as its headquarters. It is a fast and very difficult game played solely by amateurs. There is a great match on Sunday at Pézenas which I must try to see.

I got over to Aniane the other day, but couldn't spend much time in the abbey as there was a funeral on. According to a tablet in the church, the monastery was founded by Witiza, a Visigothic officer in Charlemagne's army, who became a monk and reformed the Benedictine order in France. He it was who received Guilhem le Pieux, Ist Duc d'Aquitaine, whose monastery at Gellone (now St Guilhem le Désert) is still comparatively intact.[9] The great church at Aniane was destroyed by the Huguenots (damn them) and rebuilt in 1714 in semi-Jesuit baroque. The monastic buildings, also rebuilt then, are now used as a reformatory! Witiza took the name of Benedict. Do you know anything of him?

Yours sincerely,
RICHARD ALDINGTON

[1] Blanche Patch *Thirty Years with G.B.S.* (1951).

[2] Henry Williamson *Genius of Friendship: 'T. E. Lawrence'* (1941) 10; see RA *Lawrence of Arabia* 362.

[3] RA *Lawrence of Arabia* Part III Chapter 3 p 277–95.

[4] On Aug 7, Emir Feisal, Foreign Minister of Saudi Arabia and second son of King Ibn Saud, had arrived in London for a two-day visit as guest of the British Government.

[5] About Iraq, T. E. Lawrence told Charlotte F. Shaw (ALS, Miranshah, 9 Oct 1928): "That little state owes its beginning to me: though not three people, there or in England, know that!" Feisal (1885–1933), third son of the sherif of Mecca, was made its king in 1921, in accordance with Lawrence's best judgment, and reigned until 1933. He had joined Lawrence in 1916 in the revolt against Turkey and in 1920 had been made King of Syria. The French deposed him that same year, but with British support he won the Iraqi throne. See *The World's Work* (1921); see also *Seven Pillars of Wisdom*, in which Feisal plays a prominent part.

[6] Fernand Benoit, 1945; the second pamphlet was: René Théron *Le Tombeau du "Sanglier"* (1946).

[7] RA refers mistakenly to Folco de Baroncelli-Javon, who died in 1943. Jacques de Baroncelli-Javon had died recently in Paris.

[8] A famous bull of the Camargue, coursed sometimes at Sts-Maries.

[9] Aquitaine became a duchy under a native line of dukes about 670, some twenty years before the birth of Charlemagne. His son Louis the Pious, also called Louis the Debonnaire (778–840), was made first king of Aquitaine in 781. Guilhem or William, first duke of Aquitaine, founded the monastery at St. Guilhem le Désert. From it, the cloisters, chapel, and chapter house were removed to Fort Tryon Park, New York, where they have served as a museum of mediaeval art since 1928. Called The Cloisters, it is a branch of the Metropolitan Museum of Art.

17

23 August 1951   *Montpellier*

DEAR BIRD,

Forgive me for troubling you . . .

I have been going through your letters with the valuable Chapman information before recasting and rewriting my original chapter. In your letter of 2nd April you spoke of sending me the obituary notices of T. R. Chapman. These have never arrived, and it strikes me they may be important in linking Chapman with Lawrence. Are they available?

Going through the pedigree I see no evidence for Lawrence's statement that his family married foreigners. If he is the son of T. R. Chapman, all his female ancestors were Irish or English, unless you exclude Louisa Vansittart.

Le Monde says that following Abdulla's murder,[1] the Iran mess and signs of Soviet action in Iran, the F.O. is abandoning its "Lawrence policy" of support to the Arab League and exclusion of France from the Near East.[2] I wonder if this is true. I am so bored with all these complex and frequently piffling intrigues in and about Arabia that the very word printed anywhere makes an unpleasant impression.

An amusing instance. H'mann sent me an advance copy of a new novel, Eve with Her Basket by Carl Fallas, which, by the way, I liked (I usually loathe novels) for its positive attitude to life and acute observation — there is no story. Well, on a voyage from Genoa to Colombo the author mentions the Red Sea, Arabia, even Akaba — which he seems to know — and each mention made a disagreeable impression though I was liking the book. I knew the author 35 years ago — we were in the ranks together [3] — and I didn't think he had so good a book

in him. If you can snatch time to read it I should value your opinion. I am —
thanks be to whatever gods may be — wholly out of the literary swim here.

Latest local "discovery," La Couvertoirade, a fortified 14th century village of
the Knights Hospitallers of St John, half in ruins, weirdly alone on what the
guidebook calls "le morne plaine du Larzac." A quite marvellous place and so
remote there seems no 19th or 20th century — oxen in yokes moving slowly by,
and cow stables in houses with delicate Renaissance decoration. Few people go
there, and there is no tourist exploitation beyond a little bistro with a terrace
under trees swarming with flies. They give you metal covers to keep the flies out
of the beer or lemonade which is all they have — a few bad postcards.

Yours sincerely,
RICHARD ALDINGTON

1 Abdulla, King of Jordan, was killed on 20 July 1951 as he was entering the Mosque of Omar,
Jerusalem. His killer was an Arab Moslem tailor, Mustafa Ashu, who was also shot dead at once.
2 In 1951 Mohammed Mossadegh, supported by his own Nationalist Front Party and the Communist Tudeh Party, became premier of Iran. At once he nationalized the British-owned oil
industry, an act which resulted in a breach of diplomatic relations between Great Britain and
Iran. The Arab League, formed in 1945 with headquarters at Cairo, was intended to promote
cooperation among Arab States; and in 1951 a treaty for joint defense and economic cooperation, signed in 1952, was under discussion. See "Les Problèmes du Moyen-Orient Londres
Modifierait sa Politique Arabe" Le Monde 22 Aug 1951.
3 RA and Fallas had enlisted together in the infantry in 1916.

18

25 August 1951   *Montpellier*

DEAR BIRD,

I am greatly pleased that you think well of the Museon Arlaten, which is becoming quite an obsession with me! Every time I go there I find new interests and
experience. The place has become — partly through the félibres, of course —
quite a centre of studies of Provence, without the inconveniences of a university
where men of learning and talent have to waste time on ridiculous undergraduates.
The keeper, Fernand Bênoit, has written a number of monographs, on Montmajour and so forth — sold as guides, but solidly done (I found the Sanglier pamphlet there.) If it does not sponsor, it has inspired, a new dictionary Provençal
by Canon X de Fourvières 1 and a "Canto Jouinesso," a collection of Provençal
songs with music — vol I only published so far.2 And many other pleasant things.
What is so valuable is that the learning and the poetry are in touch with the life
of the people. Baroncelli's death is a disaster, for he kept the poets and artists in
actual friendly contact with the gardiens and manadiers and horsemen through
his Nacioun Gardiano.

Bad news yesterday — the last herd of wild horses in Camargue has gone —
there will never be any more — too many rice fields.

I suppose it's too late to attempt any such thing in England. Industrialism will
have destroyed so much, journalists more — and the self-conscious cult of the
gaffer in the pub, and "Granchester," 3 and the old snobbery taken over by branch
secretaries of unions and their hideous flock. But if some millionaire had thought
of it a century ago, what a collection of English "folk" could have been made with

Oxford as its centre. Unluckily they were then so worried about Rome and Evolution that they had no time for anything interesting.

I think that German destruction was part of the "Baedeker raid" psychology and carried out by a small minority of fanatical Nazis with views something like those of the Paris communards of 1870. But — I fear this is treason — the late war to me was on both sides a war on man's heart and mind; in some an intentional, in others unconscious, wish to destroy all that is loosely called "culture." I do not believe it was necessary to bomb the abbey of Monte Cassino or the old towns of Germany or to shell the ruins of Pompeii — I myself heard a G.I. Joe on the USA radio say that he'd gladly give the place for a bo'll of coke and the sooner a bulldozer went over it the better. Joke? No, the bastard meant it, and so did lots of them. One of the Nazis' foulest destructions was the Palazzo Filangieri in Naples, a really charming collection of a princely family with at least 30 first class pictures. The only excuse given was that the Filangieri had always been Liberals!

I am glad the Pound letter was of interest. Of course you are right — it is just that "bits-and-pieces" mind which makes up the Cantos.[4] In his earlier work there are numerous little snatches of real poetry (I think) but hardly any complete and nearly all of them direct imitations of some earlier poet — I once had a copy in which I had pencilled the literary start of most of them before the Lustra [5] twaddle started. In Rapallo he once gave me a lecture on the Cantos — Dante had written the Divine Comedy,[6] Balzac the Human Comedy,[7] and Ezra was writing the — what? Comedy. For the life of me I can't remember. Not the Infernal, surely? The Perfect, perhaps? Something pretty impressive and high-toned. Trouble is, I can only understand two or three cantos which refer to a period of my youth when I saw a lot of Pound, Hueffer, Lewis, Violet Hunt, Gaudier and can catch the apparently meaningless allusions. Otherwise they are Ebrew Greek to me. And I no more intend to waste a moment of passing life on trying to solve these enigmas than on the tedious punning of Finnegans Wake. "Her hips hurrahs and her legs' don'telleries" was mildly rewarding but a little sophomorish, don't you think? [8]

The Wyndham Lewis article is pathetic, but it is courageous and without self-pity.[9] Unlike Pound, he hasn't a trace of the poet in him, but in other respects he is far more gifted. He has no real centre and a weak creative power — otherwise he might have been as splendid a pamphleteer as Shaw and a magnificent novelist. He wasted his powers on denouncing small fry like Godfrey Wynn and the shortcomings of Alec Waugh and the only too obvious weaknesses of Transition and similar small game.[10] On the other hand he tried to score off D. H. Lawrence without having read enough of his books — Mornings in Mexico [11] forms only part of that tremendous prose and poetry autobiography. Lewis' Childermass is one of the most boring books I ever tried to read. On the other hand his early volume of short stories, The Wild Body [12] (isn't it) has some magnificent stuff, and in spite of its inordinate length The Apes of God. The first Blast [13] was very lively, I thought. So often his books like Time and Western Man [14] start admirably and then peter out miserably, because he wrote too fast and exhausted his verve. A very interesting selection might be made from his different books — a W.L. omnibus — but who would dare attempt it? I mean with such a paranoiac to deal with. Personally I find that with the Apes I am bored with the areas where the people are unknown to me, but always amused by those I know. The Rodker–

Ratner piece is too savage [15] (Jew-baiting is detestable anyway) and flipping a mouse with a three-man beetle, but the Sitwell one seems very funny. You must admit that Sachie as Lord Phoebus is irresistible. And Edith squawking in her familiar way all over the premises.[16]

I wonder where Lewis picked up the Bonassus? You remember, Ginger is made to write Osbert: "I don't know what to give you for your birthday, so I am sending you this ridiculous Bonassus." [17] Now, according to the mediaeval Tarasque legend: Erat enim ut pole draco ex genere illius, qui vocatur in libro Job Leviathan, qui absorbebit fluvios et non mirabatur sed habet fiduciam, quod influat Jordanis in os ejus. Venerat enim per mare de Galatia Asiae, generatus a Leviathan, qui serpens aquosus et ferocissimus, et a BONACHO animale. Bonachum animal galatio regio gignit, quod *stercus fluens et urens insectatores suos submonet* (!), quod per spacium ingens velut spiculum dirigit . . .

I doubt if the Sitwells ever took the allusion; anyway, that Bonassus led me into an indiscretion. The first time I went to Monte Gufone [18] I took two friends with me, and after parking the car we missed our way and got into a courtyard instead of to the front door. "What is this?" asked my friend. "Evidently where they keep the ridiculous Bonassus," I replied — and just at that moment Osbert (who must have seen us wandering) emerged from a kind of sally port in a tower. I didn't quite recover all that visit, even when the comic butler presenting a large dish of spaghetti to the first woman guest remarked in sepulchral tones: "The best is at the bottom, Moddom."

There is always in Lewis a tiresome paranoiac suspicion, which shows itself even in trifles. Charles Prentice (late of Chattos) greatly admired him and did all he could to make Lewis a success — the silly chump dumped the Childermass on them. Anyway, Prentice told me that when he was giving Lewis a "new-contract lunch" at Boulestin, he first of all asked Lewis what wine he would like to drink, intending to fit the menu to it. "Champagne" said Lewis, and then seeing Prentice a little surprised and disappointed, added "I'm a bit of a Prussian in my tastes." Asked what he would eat he said: "Grouse," and with a suspicious sideglance, "I suppose you think it's too good for me." These were smart pleasantries, but a mistake. Nobody was less the publisher than Prentice (he was an Oriel man by the way, and detested Shadwell for some reason) and he really respected letters and was ridiculously humble to people he thought real writers. Then he was a most hospitable Scot and a virtuose de la table. Lewis should have let him choose wines and menu in consultation with Boulestin, instead of forcing him to what Prentice thought the barbarity of grouse and champagne, when he had probably been looking forward to some subtle harmony of Hermitage Goutte d'Or and Château Haut Briand. . . . Another bad thing — Lewis could never resist lampooning anyone who gave him money. Not long after I had lent him 50 pounds or so to help him through an illness he sent me the opening of a "story" in which I was ruthlessly caricatured as a squalid commercial popular novelist on the Home Chat level always talking about royalties! I sent it back saying it was one of the best things he had ever written, urging him to finish it and offering to find him a publisher — and no more was heard of it, unless he did eventually publish it somewhere. The thing began in the Gare du Nord, where indeed we had met by accident, on one occasion.

But there is no doubt that he is one of the most brilliantly gifted men of his time both as painter and writer. There are portraits of his which to me are absolutely first class — and damn the experts. If only he had had a small income — Aldous Huxley's 300 a year — he might have done wonderful things both as writer and painter. But he was nearly always pressed for money, had to work too fast and too much. So did D. H. Lawrence.[19] This I think is the real basis for Lewis's bitter attacks on "amateurs" of the Dick Wyndham kind and "champagne bohemia." [20] A fraction of what they wasted would have given him the leisure to work well instead of just hard. He has never really had his due.

I have just finished a chapter on the incredible chi-chi accompanying the writings and production of Seven Pillars, which I take to be a masterly campaign of literary strategy [21] beyond even the powers of T. E. Eliot, who has not yet produced a book fetching (at one time) 500 pounds a copy. (I got only 4 pounds lately for my Ara Vus Prec,[22] which I was told was "worth a fortune.") Lawrence's claim that he "never took a penny" of the Revolt royalties is worthy of him. He took 7000 pounds to pay off debts contracted for that absurd piece of megalomania. What is the difference between taking 7000 pounds to buy an annuity and 7000 to pay off debts contracted in a crazy display of vanity and mistaken belief in his genius as a printer? [23]

Forgive this huge wodge, but as each draft chapter is finished I feel like a tommy who has got a bit nearer his ticket. Roll on the Colonel's death!

Yours sincerely,
RICHARD ALDINGTON

[1] Rodolphe Rieux Xavier de Fourvières. *Lou Pichot, Tresor, Dicionnaire Provençal-Français et Français-Provençal* (1902); a revised edition was issued by a colleague, R. P. Rupert. Bênoit's monograph is *L'Abbaye de Montmajour* (1928).

[2] Marcel Petit *Canto, Jouinesso!; chansonnier provençal* (2 vols 1944 and 1953).

[3] Reference to Rupert Brooke's poem "The Old Vicarage, Grantchester" written in 1912.

[4] See above, letters 2 n 12 and 15. Cantos II, III, and I first appeared, in that order, in the first American edition of *Lustra* (1917). Subsequently one hundred thirteen additional Cantos were published at irregular intervals, the last two appearing in the *Paris Review* (Summer/Fall 1962). The first volume of collected Cantos was *A Draft of XVI Cantos* (1925).

[5] 1916.

[6] Probably started about 1300.

[7] In a *General Preface* (1842) Balzac explained his effort to represent the entire complexity of French society, individuals of every class and every profession, in a series of novels and short stories entitled collectively *La Comédie humaine*. Among the best known novels of *La Comédie humaine* are *Eugénie Grandet* (1833); *Le Père Goriot* (1835); *La Cousine Bette* (1847), and *Le Cousin Pons* (1847).

[8] By James Joyce (1939).

[9] "The Sea-Mists of Winter" *The Listener* (10 May 1951). In that article Lewis explained that, because of his rapidly dimming sight, he must terminate an association with *The Listener* which had commenced in 1946. In 1951, in any case, a revival of interest in Wyndham Lewis had occurred, with a radio version of his *Childermass* (1928) presented that summer on the BBC Third Programme and, earlier in 1951, an extract from *The Apes of God* (1930).

[10] See "The Diabolical Principle" (first published in Lewis's *Enemy, No. 3*, 1927) especially for its attack on *transition*, the periodical published in Paris from 1927 to 1938 except for a suspension between July 1930 and February 1932. Eugene Jolas, helped by his wife, Maria, and Elliott Paul, was its editor. Notable contributions included James Joyce and Gertrude Stein.

[11] 1927.

[12] 1927.

[13] A review edited by Lewis and financed to the extent of £100 by Kate Lechmere. *Blast No. 1* appeared in June 1914. RA was among those who signed the Manifesto of "The Great London Vortex" in *Blast*.

14 1927.

15 See *The Apes of God* 136–37, 143–73, *et passim*.

16 See Part XII "Lord Osmund's Lenten Party" 349–604. Dame Edith Sitwell is satirized as Lady Harriet Finnian Shaw.

17 The "ridiculous Bonassus" was a birthday gift not to Osbert (Lord Osmund) but to Sacheverell (Lord Phoebus). It came from "Cockeye," by whom may be meant the Sitwells' father, Sir George Sitwell called Ginger. See *The Apes of God* 456–57.

18 The Sitwell brothers' home, a Tuscan castle near Florence.

19 See above, letter 3.

20 See "Dick," Part I in *The Apes of God* 27–59.

21 T. E. Lawrence planned *Seven Pillars of Wisdom* no later than 1918, though he said then that he did not want to publish it. (See *Letters of T. E. Lawrence* 296.) By his own statement, he first began to write *Seven Pillars* during the Paris Peace Conference from notes (mainly of impressions) jotted down on the march, strengthened by reports sent to his superiors in Cairo. (See Chapter I of the privately printed Oxford edition; omitted from all other editions.) The book was finished that year (1918) in London, but in Nov 1919 he lost all but the first nine chapters when the MS was stolen from Reading Station. Graves maintains that this first draft of *Seven Pillars* was deliberately lost, that Lawrence was dissatisfied with it and finding it too difficult to burn so many pages in his grate at All Souls College, he left a train at Reading, carrying his MS in a bag, "walked out, dropped the bag in the Thames, and caught the next train" to Oxford. Graves based this belief on a conversation with Lawrence in which they discussed Dante Gabriel Rossetti's attempt to " 'lose' some books in the Thames at Chiswick, forgetting that it was tidal water — longshoremen brought them back next day, muddied but complete." (See Robert Graves's review of RA's *Lawrence of Arabia*, "The Lawrence I Knew" *New Republic* 12 Nov 1955.) In any case, Lawrence promptly began to rewrite and had finished a second version perhaps by the end of Sept 1920; dissatisfied with it, he may have burned this MS in 1922. Meanwhile a third version had been started in London in 1921; it was continued in Jiddah, that year, and finished in London in 1922. Eight copies only were printed by the press of the Oxford *Times* in 1922 at a cost of £175; five were bound and given away. Throughout most of this period, Lawrence received a stipend of about £200 per year from All Souls, Oxford. (See above, letter 7 n 8.) Working sporadically from 1923 to 1926 Lawrence extensively revised the printed text and had this fourth version printed by Manning Pike and C. J. Hodgson as for T. E. Shaw in 1926. According to Lawrence's holograph "History of the Seven Pillars" (Texas), of this printing there were 211 copies of which 127 were subscribed at 30 guineas each, one complete copy was left in sheets, 42 complete and 32 incomplete bound copies were given away by Lawrence — or Shaw — 9 copies were spoiled, and another 22 copies lacking plates, front matter, and appendices were printed for George H. Doran in America for copyright purposes. Mrs George Bernard (Charlotte F.) Shaw read proof. In an unpublished holograph, "*Proposed* Preface to The Seven Pillars" Lawrence wrote, in part: " 'Why did I never think of that way to advertise a play?' said G.B.S. when told that I meant to hold up my book ten years. . . . And so, as I slept, this book advertised itself. The handful of people permitted to read it have praised it, as part-boast of the privilege of seeing it. Its character may even survive publication since honest critics and the crowd run with the current, for a while" (BM). By early 1924, an abridgement made by Edward Garnett existed; the abridgement published in 1927 as *Revolt in the Desert* was made by Lawrence.

22 By T. S. Eliot, 1920.

23 See T. E. Lawrence to Charlotte F. Shaw [Karachi] 24 Feb 1927: "My overdraft was £7000 when I sailed, and now it is less than £4000. The Bank has the deeds of my Chingford land, which has been valued at nearly £4000. So the position is covered, even if Cape & Doran don't roll up another penny of royalty. And the odds are that they will eventually double their advance of £3000. Occasionally I regret my moderation in not putting a little more money into decorating the Seven Pillars." See also Lawrence to Shaw [Karachi] 12 May 1927: "I did inherit some Irish money, & enjoyed it, & made The Seven Pillars out of it"; Lawrence to Shaw, [Karachi] 16 June 1927: "I do not estimate money very much. I've given away a lot, & have been given a lot. The one is as virtuous, or as harmless, as the other. I have no shame either way. Money comes & goes so easily. 'Revolt' will make £20,000 this year. . . . I could help myself to money." Note also Lawrence to Shaw [Karachi], 23 June 1927, where he says of *Revolt in the Desert*, "It has sold 30,000 copies in England, & 120,000 in the States, and so

has earned all the money my bank expects. And I'd rather not make money than make it, for myself or anybody else."

19

3 September 1951   *Montpellier*

DEAR BIRD,

I suspect that article on Provence was partly if not largely derived from Fernand Bênoit's La Provence et le Comtat Venaissin,[1] which is packed with curious learning and customs, all built round the Arlaten. [. . .]

May it be that the silence about T. R. Chapman is due to a wish to avoid scandal? How otherwise could the Times have deprived itself of the customary tribute to a 7th baronet, last of the line? If anything turns up I shall be most grateful. I wish I could find out the origin of TEL's turn from "reading nothing during three years but medieval French and Provençal" to such a violent francophobia. I came somewhere — but have lost the reference — on a hint that it happened pre-1914 in Lebanon. Could some filthy French heterosexual have been lacking in respect to Dahoum? Anyway he prosecuted the feud bitterly, and I suspect (but can't prove) that it was responsible for the sudden outburst of Gourand and the eviction of Feisal from Damascus in 1920.[2] Storrs said Feisal was convinced that if the French attacked him Allenby would come to his aid! [3] Who could have given him that impression? Unfortunately I shall have to leave my paragraph to end with that rhetorical question as I can't pin the responsibility on the Colonel.

Is there anyone in Oxford left who would know about this French-Provençal claim? I looked through the list of his library, which contains no Provençal texts, and a few chansons de geste in translations of modern French "re-writes" (Aucassin et Nicolette of course, but apparently as a Vale Press production)[4] and among them several books which have pre-war dates in his writing and are mentioned in the letters as bought during the French tours. (He is supposed to have lost a lot of books and posted many in bank letter boxes to get rid of them.) Among all the strategists he is supposed to have studied, only Clausewitz is there. No Spanish, no Danish, and no German except Heine, and Faust,[5] though he is supposed to have read all three constantly — his "Marie Grubbe"[6] is in translation. No Arabic, no Italian, and not many classics — a Caesar, a Catullus, several Horace. There is a complete Loeb[7] but it was a gift from Lord Riddell. His Lucian and Longus are in translations, although AWLawrence claims that Lucian influenced him greatly and that TEL possessed a complete set in Greek and Latin.[8] The lack of French mediaeval texts — not a dozen — is surprising if he were such a scholar, but then he may have lost or sold them. Strange that he managed to keep ALL William Morris but then for some weird reason Morris was L's preferred writer! [9] Both specialists in news from nowhere, I suppose. (He had translations of the Moallaka.)[10] His Gryll Grange [11] had never had the pages cut!

Heinemann's say Eve With Her Basket has had some excellent reviews but is not selling.[12]

Adieu, and many thanks for the Arabic quotes from TLS which are valuable.

RICHARD ALDINGTON

[1] 1949; see above, letter 14.

[2] That is, Gourand's twenty-four hour ultimatum handed to Feisal, King of Syria, on 14 July 1920. It demanded acquiescence in the French mandate for Syria, adoption of French as the official language and of French currency as the currency of Syria. The following day the French opened hostilities in two columns — one against Damascus and the other against Aleppo to free the railroad from Ryak to Aleppo in order to supply French troops in Cilicia. By July 22, the French Foreign Office announced that Feisal had accepted Gourand's ultimatum as well as other conditions imposed by the French, Damascus and Aleppo were occupied, and Feisal fled.

[3] *Orientations* (1939) 504; see RA *Lawrence of Arabia* 269.

[4] Vale Press did not produce an *Aucassin et Nicolette*. Lawrence's copy was printed in Vale type by Esther and Lucien Pissarro at their Eragny Press, 1903.

[5] By Johann Wolfgang von Goethe who published the first part of his *Faust* in 1808; it was completed shortly before his death in 1832.

[6] By Jens Peter Jacobsen, translated by Hanna Astrup Larsen, 1917.

[7] The Loeb Classical Library, a series of inexpensive but well produced books which contain on opposite pages original texts and translations of Greek and Latin classics. Founded by James Loeb (1867–1933), who willed its title, rights, and property to Harvard University.

[8] *T. E. Lawrence by His Friends* 585.

[9] See above, letter 7.

[10] *Muallaquat* or *Moallakat*, a celebrated Arab anthology of odes by various poets of the sixth or early seventh centuries compiled by Hammad al Rawiya (d.c. 775). Doubtless Lawrence's translation was the one made by Lady Anne and W. S. Blunt *The Seven Golden Odes of Pagan Arabia* 1903.

[11] By Thomas Love Peacock, 1860 or 1861.

[12] See above, letter 17.

20

11 November 1951   *Montpellier*

DEAR BIRD,

Cohen has got permission for me to examine the archives of the Ministry of War at Vincennes, and it looks as if I shall get the Etrangères too — at least a favourable letter from Schuman's chef de cabinet.[1] So I must go to Paris, and see what I can find to the confusion of the Colonel. I don't expect anything new from La Guerre as Brémond evidently went through the documents carefully — but he may have been under some censorship. It seems to me that the real source of information is more likely to be at Quai d'Orsay. A friend of mine who is very thick with an Inspecteur of the Sureté [2] is trying to get me some access (very hard to get) to their counter-espionage files. (After all, what with Maugham etc. any British author nowadays may be a spy himself.) But if the French have anything against L. as a secret agent in Syria, the evidence will be there.

This comes just in time, as I have the final draft almost done of the first five chapters, 1888–1914, about 30,000 words. I hope to keep the war down to the same amount, and the post-war ditto, making about 100,000 — quite enough on such a topic. Even if the Paris archives draw a blank, I shall have Nelson's consolation.[3]

We have had some most dismal weather here — cloud, rain, wind, and even a nip or two of cold. At the moment the weather is in the comparative quietude of exhaustion, but still sulking. In the last three weeks we haven't had three completely sunny days. The natives express voluble indigation, and blame the Americans.[4] It is some small consolation not to belong to the Most Hated Nation, as was the case until Chamberlain tripped over Dantzig and lost the Empire.[5]

What do you say to Winston in the new and dramatic part (positively his last appearance) as a Labour P. M.? It is surely a record to begin your term of office by decreeing exactly what you have been denouncing the opposition for during 6 years.[6] Observe that he only touches the supplies of his own class — too much afraid of the T.U.C. and the yankee traders to drop on the real waste — fags and pictures. They cost dollars — continental hams and textiles don't. What a mess!

I'll let you know if anything turns up in the Paris archives, but as I am inexperienced in such things I fear being lost in an ocean of papers.

Yours sincerely.

RICHARD ALDINGTON

[1] RA anticipated permission to examine the archives of the Foreign Office (Bureau des Affaires Etrangères) on the Quai d'Orsay. See below, letter 21.

[2] Alister Kershaw and Jacques Delarue.

[3] See Nelson's statement at Trafalgar, "Thank God I have done my duty."

[4] Because of atomic testing; see above, letter 10.

[5] Neville Chamberlain, Britain's prime minister, in an attempt to appease the Axis powers, signed the Munich Pact in Sept 1938, proclaiming "peace in our time." The following year, on September 1, in flagrant violation of the Pact, Hitler's armies annexed Danzig, an act which was the chief direct cause of the Second World War.

[6] When Churchill had assumed office as Prime Minister on 26 Oct 1951, after a Conservative victory, he immediately restricted imports of food after having jeered at the Labor government for their policy of rationing and restricting imports in the interests of national economy.

2 I

23 March 1952   *Montpellier*

DEAR BIRD,

I was very happy indeed to have your letter and to learn that you escaped any serious damage during that unpleasant night in Cairo.[1] Much interested in your notes on the situation. From the "background reading" (as Americans say) I've been doing I had formed the idea that the Wahabis [2] are the only military people left on the Arabian peninsula and Ibn Saud the one ruling personality. But of course he is very old now, and these mushroom empires are created by one personality and are apt to perish with him. The irony of the Egyptian situation is that they owe their prosperity very much to England, and that the departure of British administrators instals native venality and corruption in place of austere integrity. In my opinion the various rebellious subject races don't so much object to British administration as to the British — it is the offensive race-conscious Englander condescending or bullying who makes us unpopular. I could never agree with Osbert Sitwell when he used to maintain that we are a most polite people. Possibly in his class among themselves, but short of the aristocracy the British seem to me (after many years abroad) inferior only to the Americans in offensiveness. And even the Americans often have genuine goodwill and kindliness, which after all are better than their mere ape-ing in polite formulas.

I suppose the hearty methods of the Staff on the canal are the result of the tradition that "the Oriental" respects only a person who inspires fear, and fear is to be inspired by brutality.

The Paris archives were not much good, because in spite of introductions (personal) from Schuman and the Count de Chévingny I could not get direct access to originals after 1906! But I got some "heavy" printed official stuff, with one or two details. Thus, from Capitaine Pisani's original report of a train-wrecking it appears that he and not Lawrence (as stated in 7 Ps.) was fired at by the Turkish officer![3] Also, there is an official American memorandum refusing permission for a US officer to accompany Col. L. in May 1919 on a punitive expedition to the Nedj. This must have been Abdulla's luckless attack on Khurma, in which a night attack wiped out most of his force and Abdulla fled in terror. Luckily for L. his plane crashed in Rome and he was rather badly bashed — otherwise he would have completely lost his grand military reputation.[4] There are some entertaining revelations by St John Philby of the F.O. and I.O. conferences about all this — generals and admirals (all misled by the Arab Bureau reports) assuring Curzon that the Wahabis hadn't a chance against the "British-trained, British-armed" regulars of the Hejaz — Curzon insisting that they must be sure "our man will win"! Then, the disaster, a totally new set of experts sent in by the W.O. and Admiralty, — a voice from the background: "Appears we've backed the wrong horse." Incredible mixture of fatuity and incompetent delay, and this infatuation with L. who was obviously giving the wrong advice.[5]

I have now completed 19 of the 21 chapters, each roughly 7000 words. The last two are rather a bore, as I'm tired, and they must make some attempt at interpretation. I think I have the psychological explanation, but of course it can only be a theory. Hitherto I have confined myself to the search for facts, and the work is heavily documented — up to 100 precise references, author, book, page, in a single chapter. You and many others may feel it has been work wasted. But I believe — or try to believe — that the exposure of a national fraud is worth doing. But I wish I knew someone of scholarly mind with a knowledge of the Middle East who would read the galleys, and put me right on the small slips and errors bound to occur. Do you know anyone? I have been wondering if I dare ask Robin Fedden — whose book on Syria I like very much — he did a Crusader Castles which is a chapter of the book published separately.[6] Suppose in a book of 140,000 words one has ten or fifteen blunders (a modest estimate!) the honourable Times reviewer can easily fill a column with those and give the impression that the whole book is inaccurate.

I continue to receive letters from Pound, and reply because I knew him as far back as 1911 and then life for a sane man imprisoned in what he calls a "buggus" must be dreary. I explained privately to Mrs. P. that my sole object is to try to amuse him. His literary dogmatising leaves me disconcerted, because it is often based on purely personal grounds (i.e. X reviewed P. unfavourably. Y the reverse; therefore X is a rotten writer and Y a genius); or on the partial reading of one book! He much dislikes (e.g.) Norman Douglas because people are beginning to think that the excellence of the old English Review was due as much to N.D. as to Ezra's old friend, Ford Madox Hueffer.[7] Whereupon P. writes me that he had never heard of any work by N.D. except one book, and never heard him mentioned except by me and two women! A strange character, who seems to be a great hero with the neo-fascist young.

Do write when you have leisure.

Yours sincerely,
RICHARD ALDINGTON

1 Angered by the attack of British troops on the Egyptian auxiliary police in Ismailia in order to expel them from the canal zone, the Cairo populace turned Jan 26 into a day of terror by burning, pillaging, and smashing tens of millions of dollars worth of American, French, and British property. Bird, who was a lecturer at Fuad I University, wrote a description of Cairo at this time. It runs in part: "Cairo at the time of which I'm writing . . . was perhaps the most cosmopolitan city in the world. It was a city in which all nationalities and religions mixed on easy and happy terms. It would be possible to lunch at the flat of the cultivated Jewish music adviser to the Egyptian Ministry of Education, to lunch on Meissen, surrounded by Coptic embroideries and with a collection of the world's folk music at an arm's reach — and then to go to tea with a Coptic family educated in Britain, owning vast estates, with servants at their every beck and call, and finally to have dinner on tin plates in the poor suburban dwelling of an Egyptian student, almost suffocated by the white fumes of the aromatic herbs burnt in one's honour — or to wander with students through the Arab quarter, stopping at a kerosine-lit stall for cups of sweet tea or plates of beans. Perhaps one might find oneself surrounded by the noisy dervishes taking part in a circumcision ceremony, be overtaken by an eccentric and loveable English milor in his mini-mini-Italian car (complete with uniformed chauffeur), or get lost in the swirling mob around a tomb or mosque entrance. There was sweetness of life, peculiar, maybe, to Cairo of all Egyptian cities; there was an easy tolerance and serenity; and there was a respect for books, for music, for the theatre (represented by the season of the Comedie française and the Shakespeare performances by students of the English Department of the university, performances which the British Ambassador took care never to attend), and for the many art treasures of Egypt. Thus, in one day I could see stage designs by Dimitri Bouchene (in a house), a painting by Bosch (in a museum), a collection of Coptic dishes and visit the Ottoman tombs outside Cairo. Of course, one could not pretend there was no poverty — then as now on an incredible and enormous scale. One's heart could break at the little boys and girls of five or six begging in the rain at midnight, mute, pathetic, little figures, or nodding over the charcoal fire on which a handful of peanuts or a corn cob slowly roasted. Above them all was the warm clear night sky, lit often enough by the charming calligraphy of Coca Cola in Arabic script. . . .

"Trouble of some kind was frequently in the air at this time. The university frequently closed its door and there were student demonstrations against the presence of the British in the Canal Zone. One day I saw officials at the British Embassy stoking incinerators in the Embassy grounds, a sure sign of expected trouble. Yet at the wedding of the daughter of Fuad Sureg-ed-Din, the Foreign Minister, there was no hint of reproach or of hostility. When I broadcast on Radio Cairo, I was received with charm and courtesy. But disaster was near in January. On the morning of the notorious riots I had gone to have my hair cut in a local barber's shop on the main road running along-side the suburban railway line. Sitting there, shrouded in a white sheet, I looked into the mirror and saw a host of men running down the street, shouting fiercely and hoarsely in Arabic and all of them carrying staves or sickles. They were followed by others with banners, rough-and-ready flags, and others with torches. Many of them had strips of white and green bound round their foreheads, tokens of membership of the Muslim Brotherhood. I was horror-stricken — the more so when I looked at the array of scissors and razors at the disposal of the barber. However, determined to be a presentable corpse if nothing else I waited till I was suitably shorn and groomed and then made my way back to Sharia el Birgas where the flat was situated. Our Italian grocer had begun to put up steel shutters before the door and windows of his shop, the interior of which was crammed with hams, bottles of chianti, cheeses and the other delicious foods unknown in Britain still in the grips of some food rationing and grim shortages. At the flat I found that Professor [M. Bryn] Davis [with whom I was staying] had gone out to lunch with an artistic official of the British Council. I was alone, apart from the old servant and his family. Before long the telephone rang. It was an Egyptian friend connected with the news service who spoke urgently to the effect that I shouldn't go out into the centre of Cairo on any pretext whatsoever. I was grateful. This was an instance — one tends to forget them — of Egyptian kindness and consideration. However, I couldn't resist going on the roof and seeing if there was anything of interest. There was. The Nile Bridges were alive with mobs of people — they were always swarming but now the traffic was one-way and consisted of men pouring into the city. The area around the Kasr-el-Nil Barracks (now demolished and the site occupied by the offices of the Arab Political Agency and the Hilton Hotel) was teeming with crowds. They were not men dressed in suits, not even in the pyjama suits worn by poor Egyptians or by those who found ordinary suits intolerable even in the moderate heat of winter. Instead they were dressed in white galabeyahs, workers from the fields or the suburban factories, now marshalled into violent action. And already I could see smoke rising from the centre of the town. During the late afternoon it was possible to see both smoke and flames. I couldn't go out nor could I do anything effective and resigned myself to writing letters and reading — appropriately enough UNE SAISON EN ENFER. Naturally enough I was worried about the fate of my colleagues but there was nothing to be done. When darkness came about six o'clock there was a lurid red light in the clear Cairene sky.

"About nine o'clock I left the flat and walked into town. At the beginning of the Kasr-el-Nil I was halted by the destruction and the heaps of smouldering rubbish in the streets. In this area were some of the most expensive shops in Cairo. Here were the furriers, the French gown shops, the antique dealers, the picture-galleries, the perfumeries. They had none of them escaped looting and ravaging. Suites of antique (or not so antique) French furniture lay in fragments in the streets: gilded cabriolet legs, swags of velvet and tapestry and broken picture frames lay together in the dirt and filth. The fire engines had begun work and the streets were running with water. Sometimes I was walking over broken bottles, the scents of expensive perfumes and the pungent fumes of medicine rising to my nostrils. Here were crumpled LP records, then new to Cairo as to Europe. Books and papers littered the pavements. Fires burnt in the streets. The St. James Restaurant and the nearby cinema were crackling with fire and heat. Turning back to return to Garden City I was overtaken by a troop carrier. The Egyptian officer in charge asked me in English whether I knew what was going on. Was it true, he asked, that British troops had left the Suez zone and were coming down the Cairo road to safeguard life and property. I had no idea at all. Meantime he asked me to climb into the carrier and come for a trip round the city. I can't describe how that charming city had been devastated and ruined. Restaurants, department stores, shops and cinemas had been looted, pillaged and burnt. Everywhere the sour and sickening smell of smouldering wood and brick. The officer at my side was half-excited at what must have appeared something like warfare and half-ashamed at the horror which had struck his city. Like so many Egyptians he had an innate charm and kindness, but, I wonder, did he not sense that something had been lost that night, something which has never been regained by Egypt. Because, from that night Cairo ceased to be a cosmopolitan city and became an Arab city, not even an Egyptian city, still a remarkable city but a lesser one. Of course, at that time I knew nothing of the loss of life — I could only see the tremendous damage to property. Originally, no doubt, the immediate cause of the riot was the continued presence of British troops in the Canal Zone and, possibly, isolated instances of British brutality, but in effect all foreign property was attacked and damaged. There had been a signal for xenophobic action of an outrageous kind. There had been political manoeuvring by the Waftist and other unseen parties — the Muslim Brotherhood irresponsibly intervening and stoking the fires of revolt. Had some of the ex-Nazi officials in Cairo, war criminals, had a hand in this disaster? Whatever the case, one sensed a loss of self-respect. Such action would, I imagine, be impossible in Cairo today. In retrospect, I had lived through a remarkable day, the full consequences of which are still to be felt. I had seen a terrifying example of a mob run mad and been witness of at least two acts of personal kindness by Egyptians. It is hard to believe that the Egyptian people themselves are capable of such bitter, fruitless and futile hatred. But as the god left Antony, something left Cairo on that sad day. It wasn't just the *douceur* that went but something much more fundamental — tolerance and respect for other religions, other views, other beliefs, for the West to which Egypt fundamentally belongs and, tragically as it turned out, for human life itself." (See Bird to MJB, Halsall, Ormskirk, Lancashire 28 May 1968.)

2 A puritanical reform movement which began in the eighteenth century in Islam under the leadership of Mohammed ibn Abd al-Mahab. The Saud tribe adopted the religion and managed to gain control of most of Arabia. In spite of repeated Ottoman efforts to stamp it out, the Wahabi movement eventually became Saudi Arabia's official religion.

3 See *Seven Pillars of Wisdom* 379, for Lawrence's statement: "A Turkish colonel from the window fired at me with a Mauser pistol, cutting the flesh of my hip." See also RA *Lawrence of Arabia* 202–03.

4 En route by air from Carnin, near Lille, to Cairo in May 1919, Lawrence received a broken collar-bone, broken ribs, and mild concussion when the 0/400 twin-engined plane, a Handley-Page, overturned as Lt Prince, its pilot, attempted to land at Centocelle (Rome) in semi-darkness.

5 See RA *Lawrence of Arabia* 299; *Letters of T. E. Lawrence* 267–68; H. St. John Philby *Arabian Days; An Autobiography* (1948) 178.

6 *Syria, An Historical Appreciation* (1946); see above, letter 5; *Crusader Castles* (1950).

7 Douglas became sub-editor of the *English Review* after Austin Harrison replaced Hueffer (Ford) as editor early in 1910. For a time, Hueffer helped and advised Harrison.

22

20 *April 1952*   *Montpellier*

MY DEAR BIRD,

Please, as always, to have one of your ever interesting letters on my table on returning from the Easter vacances. I loathe public holidays, but am bound through my daughter to school terms and holidays, and she must have a change. We went back to Lavandou. Returning yesterday, we had to use the main Nice–Paris road from Brignolles to St Cannat (via Aix) where we branched off for Arles. I was droning along at a mere 45 m.p.h., and was constantly passed by strings of enormous modern cars, almost all with Paris plates, rushing past at 70–95. Apart from the real danger — imagine a blow-out of a front tire with a line of cars going that speed! — the boredom of it! They treat a car as a private train, instead of a substitute horse which it is good to tie up from time to time and look at something. These people know Paris and/or Nice, Cannes, Cap Ferrat, but know nothing of France. For which I am deeply thankful — Provence and especially Languedoc are still ours.

We gave a lunch to Gustave Cohen, his wife, and a Parisian friend of my daughter, at Jane et Nico (make a note of it) at Lavandou. It is always so striking the respect for learning and literature in France. As soon as Monsieur Nico knew that he was to entertain the great Gustave, he set himself to prepare a real lunch. For a really most modest sum he provided: Hors d'oeuvres of excellent raw ham, oeufs mimosas, black and green olives, anchovies. Then soles meunières which produced murmurs of approval from all concerned, followed by spring chickens roasted on the spit and presented on a sword (I suppose Nico used to be a fencer); asparagus; apfelkucken; and strawberries in a sauce of kirsch and cherry brandy; coffee and Napoleon brandy. As wine he served a delicious Traminer, a Clos Vougeot, and a vintage champagne. All for about 35/= a head. Now if you went in or anyone not known to Nico, he would deny he owned such things; but for "un ami," and "un somité de la France," nothing is too good. I think he probably lost money on the feast. We — at least I — had to fast for 24 hours after. Some day, if you come this way, I must try to arrange something of the sort for you, though, alas, I can present you only as "un somité" of English learning, which is not quite so appealing. But 'twould serve. Think of it.

In return Gustave tried to give me a bouillabaisse — a mistake, because only the fishermen can really make it — but it was well meant. Much drama below stairs. The chauffeur-valet, maddened by the fumes of the bouillabaisse, drank too much pastis, and tried to murder the pretty cuisinière for gazing too lovingly at the garçon–boucher with one of those immense and murderous knives thoughtfully provided in all bourgeois French kitchens. But Alphonse is a bungler — he merely cut his own hand badly. Gustave, who is helplessly nailed to his chair by a foot blown off by a German grenade in 1915, was beautifully unmoved, though of course Alphonse could murder him at any time. He merely remarked that Alphonse should get a better brand of pastis.

I have now nothing to add to the Lawrence book but two foot-notes giving the citations for his C.B. and D.S.O. (they look like H.Q. ration dish-outs to me) and the List of Sources. Your moral support is most valued by me, for if this book gets into print, it will be a national scandal and I shall be even as a burnt offering to the god of Beaverbrook and the god of Rothermere and the god of Churchill — which last I have not spared, and though with no disrespectful comment to our ruler, I think he is displayed as a bull-dust artist of consummate insincerity. First of all, however, the lawyers must come into play; and I am handing the book over to a private company of one or two friends, who have engaged to fight all the battles and to leave me free to go on working. I know from what you say that you have seen through T.E. Lawrence, but the slow piling-up of evidence through chapter after chapter will, I do believe, surprise even you. As to the Lawrence Bureau . . . ! They will of course fight to suppress the book by every possible means,[1] but there are possibilities of handling them. At any rate I get an advance [. . .] and they (the publishers) undertake to fight the battle. I allow them to make any cuts legally necessary. What more could I ask? But America is the important scene, and I think the Russians will leap on it.

Your notes on Egypt most interesting. My remarks on British official integrity were based on a series of articles appearing in France on India, where, according to the writers, many abuses have already appeared which did not exist under H.B.M.'s régime.[2] But of course these compliments may have been meant to bolster French colonial administration.

As to Egypt — why do they not make the Canal an international zone on the lines of the Panama Canal Zone? America does not allow the Panamanians to control the American Canal, why should we hand it over to people who didn't build it, can't maintain it, and couldn't defend it? If it belongs to anyone it belongs to the French, for Dizzy only bought the Khedive's shares.[3] The zone is all desert, so it's being made international under protection of the Western Alliance would hurt nobody.

I get so many letters from Pound now, I could make a regular income by selling them, but he judiciously leaves them unsigned in order to defeat this end. He is a good hearted and kindly fellow au fond, but very silly really.

Ever yours,
RICHARD ALDINGTON

P.S. Your very just denunciation of postscripts causes me a feeling of shame at sending this long one.

In the first place I meant to say that I continue to receive letters from Ezra Pound, in which he exhorts me to perform what I think impossible — namely, to produce a Ford omnibus from the works Ford intended to write or ought to have written but didn't.[4] I can't find anything much except some of the poems and those four war novels, which are good; and tributes from Lawrence and Douglas to Ford as a man who cared about literature and good writing.[5] Doubtless, but that is not the same thing as producing them. Ezra humanises a little, as I refuse to fall into any of his mannerisms of spelling, facetiousness etc. His letters become more rational and less truculent, but he is avid of flattery and most naively shows how he longs for sales' successes and how bitterly he envies all who get them. E.g. Penguin Books and all who are included are indiscriminately referred to as "Slime." He tried to get me to introduce him to the Viking Press, and I had to tell him that the head of the firm is Guinzburg and the chief adviser Huebsch — of a race Ezra has not flattered. Now it is hand-presses, of which I know little or nothing, but I hope to get him a publication if all goes well. But how damned absurd to take up an attitude and write a style which antagonises about 95 per cent of intelligent readers and then belly-ache with fury at not selling like Gone With the Wind [6] or The Dam Busters.[7]

The other item is a first note on my TELawrence book. It comes from a man who was good enough to do some research for me at the Brit. Mus. and before the book goes to press (it is still with lawyers I believe) I wanted him to look over a copy of the script to make sure I had not misinterpreted the evidence he collected.[8] You will like to see his comment:

"I honestly found it fascinating and read on and on until I had finished a first reading. Extraordinary stuff — now at last I see just how much work you must have put in — all those references, checking, checking again. It will surely be the debunk to surpass all debunks. Exit the Colonel. Enter the liar. Some of those stories are side-splitting — the little twirp and the Kurd, the little t. and Kitchener, the little sod and the generals in the map room. And the comment on the crawling flattery of W.B.Y. And the bit about the Turkish 5th Army prisoners. The completeness of the thing is devastating. Not only L., but, by inference, a whole giggle of twirps are demolished."

We must make a big deduction from that since it is the comment of a friend who has some personal interest as he helped with material. On the other hand, it is the reaction of one who had been rather a Lawrence fan, and was somewhat indignant at my casual remarks in letters. I fear the publication will have to be delayed for several reasons, among them the American election. Hopeless to try to get anything read there while they are indulging in that periodic orgy of political D.T.s

R.A.

My motto for the title-page:
"Untruthful! My nephew Algernon? Impossible! He is an Oxonian."

Oscar Wilde [9]

---

1 See below, letters 59 n 15 and 60.

2 The articles on India have not been found.

3 In 1875 the British purchased shares in the Suez Canal belonging to Ismail Pasha (1863–79) who had been granted the title "Khedive" by the Sultan of Turkey.

4 A project which had been under consideration at least since 2 Oct 1951 when RA wrote from Montpellier to Max Wykes-Joyce (with whom Pound had put him in touch) that in the past few years he had "issued Selected Omnibi of Wilde and Pater, and an anthology of Asthetes, in gratitude for pleasure received when they were in vogue some 40 years back" and that he might do something similar for Ford to whom also he was "obliged at a rather later date." RA continued: "Ezra thought a biography, but I can't see more than a biographical – critical preface for Ford, unless there is much unpublished material. A carefully selected Prose and Verse and unpublished letters, if any, might be possible." RA reaffirmed this attitude in a letter dated 31 Oct 1951, also to Wykes-Joyce. And on 19 Dec 1951 he wrote again to say that, although a recent trip to Paris "to burrow (ineffectively) in archives" (see above, letter 21) and a trip to Nice on other business had disturbed his writing, his "consolation" was that he "was able to put down foundations for some sort of Ford reprint or 'tribute'." For a time RA collected Ford's books in order to make a selection but eventually he lost interest owing to the meager enthusiasm generated by re-reading Ford's critical writing (see RA to Max Wykes-Joyce, Montpellier, 1 May 1952) and the difficulty in arranging publication. See below letter 25.

5 See *Phoenix: The Posthumous Papers* of D. H. Lawrence ed Edward D. McDonald (1936) 253; Norman Douglas *Late Harvest* (1947) 45.

6 Margaret Mitchell (1936).

7 Paul Brickhill (1951).

8 Denison Deasey.

9 See *The Importance of Being Earnest* (1895) Act III; Lady Bracknell speaks the lines.

23

3 *July 1952*   *Montpellier*

MY DEAR BIRD,

What a perfectly delightful letter! And how very kind of you to let me share the impressions of your Spanish journey! [1] Your words brought up many half-forgotten memories of my "wanderings in Spain" before that miserable civil war and the Franco tyranny. I think Spain was quieter and more courteous then, but there was always that trouble that a woman could not go out alone (which meant one had to be on perpetual escort duty with one's innamorata of the moment) and the other trouble of that derisive contempt for foreigners which is perhaps universal but most conspicuous in Catholic countries. (Not in Austria, as I remember it.)

The food in Spain must have deteriorated (it has everywhere, even in France) but the best areas used to be the north coast from Santillana westward, Galicia, Seville and Barcelona. In Coruña I found the very best red mullet I have ever had, and Oviedo and places like that offered superb lampreys, partridges, hares etc. But those 10 p. m. dinners, and absurd boccadillos! — yet I liked those Dublin prawns with that light Manzanilla. There was great plenty in Spain in the 1930s. On my first visit in 193? I remember looking at the restaurant displays and saying to my companion: These people have cheaper and more plentiful food than any other European nation because they kept out of the War of 1914 — what will you bet that within ten years they throw it all away over some idiotic quarrel? They did — within 5 years. [2]

How you revive those places! And how ridiculous is the motorist's mind, if it be a mind! One of my vivid memories is the hideous road from Toledo to Aranjuez, which I took under the mistaken impression that it was a short cut. (It was — on the map!) Places I liked for their remoteness — Santillana (wonderful), Santiago da Compostella, Salamanca, Ciudad Rodrigo, Caceres, Trujillo, Merida . . . In those days I was on the track of the Duke's battles, following humbly in Oman's illustrious footsteps (a great book that of his) [3] and picking up crumbs for a popular sketch of Wellington. [4] The power and the glory of our great epoch are so bound up in that war, and anyone who has been through a cadet school can appreciate the consummate skill of the Duke's military positions. Our great man, I think. He said: We've nothing to recommend us but our honesty and reputation for plain dealing — if we lose those, we lose everything. We have.

Do you know the (probably apocryphal story) of the Spanish Infanta visiting the Court of St James in or about 1840 and getting into talk with a little hook-nosed old gentleman wearing nothing by way of orders but the Garter, who filled her with indignant surprise by his remarks, which showed that he had lived en maître at both La Granja and the Madrid Palace — the young Queen had to whisper the Infanta that she was talking to the Duke of Wellington. [5]

Goya — yes! But I like those pictures for tapestries in the style of Bayeux — they used to be in the basement of the Prado, and those innumerable caricatures of the Royal Family. Would E.R. 2 and her subjects tolerate such sardonic humour?

I have little to tell you about the fate of my Lawrence book except to say that it will not appear until after Christmas. [. . .] It takes time, and I assume there will be — or are being — heavy battles with the Lawrence Estate. But we have good lawyers (Joynson Hicks) and I begin to hope. In any case the publishers have indemnified me against any loss on actions for libel or breach of copyright. Obviously they can't exempt me from responsibility for criminal libel, which is what I fear in the case of the old girl, now aged 91.[6] Surely a case of lagging superfluous? Or is that an interested opinion? It would be a great help to me if she would join her baronet in Heaven. I am longing for you to read the book. The one friend who had read it thus far wrote that over certain passages he didn't just smile, but laughed aloud uncontrollably! A pleasing compliment. Have no fear. There is a smiling ferocity which doesn't spare Mr Churchill or any of that whole dishonest gang. You can imagine the drums and tramplings of the Times etc. But they will have some difficulty in explaining away those 1420 precise references to author, book and page. Let me boast, but it is a real exposure. An advance copy shall go to you in due course.

Meanwhile I am turning out a little book of personal recollections of Norman Douglas and Pino Orioli, whom I knew rather well in the 30s, with such letters as happen to have survived the war.[7] I wish you could read the chapter I have just finished, making rather unmerciful fun of Willie King — you will understand why if you have read his Introduction to the 1947 reprint of South Wind.[8]

I have NOT read Ivy Compton-Burnett, and I am going to order her books. It is a great service to have a trustworthy recommendation of books. Agreed a thousand times to all you say of Ford. But I want — for old times' sake — to do either a Ford omnibus (on the lines of my Wilde and Pater) or a Selected Poems. I think it must be the latter. His prose is maddeningly prolix. Dictation. How well I know it! I was his secretary in 1913–14. Another lingerer — still living — I would like you to read is Rachel Annand Taylor. That stupendous Leonardo,[9] and those astonishing Fiammetta sonnets![10]

All hail!
R.A.

[1] Bird had accepted a lectureship at Madrid.

[2] RA's first visit to Spain was in 1933. The Spanish civil war began in 1936.

[3] Sir Charles Oman *History of the Peninsular War* (7 vols 1902–30).

[4] That RA wrote such a sketch is doubtful. No record of it has been found.

[5] The Infanta has not been identified; she may have been a guest at the festivities attendant on the marriage of Queen Victoria and Prince Albert on 10 February 1840.

[6] T. E. Lawrence's mother.

[7] *Pinorman* (1954).

[8] Chapter 6; see particularly p 129–32. The reprint of Douglas's *South Wind* (1917) with King's introduction was published in 1946.

[9] *Leonardo the Florentine* (1927). In a letter to Mrs Taylor dated 2 July 1952 (Berg) RA wrote of "some glorious pages of Leonardo."

[10] *Hours of Fiammetta* (1909) and *End of Fiammetta* (1923).

24

15 August 1952   *Montpellier*

DEAR BIRD,

The B.B.C. has become the national rendezvous of octogenarians — they should issue an anthology From Max to Bertie.[1] But who would have thought the old

man had so much hate in him? One clue to this absurd and rather dishonest outburst is in D. Garnett's very shrewd remark that Lawrence inevitably provoked
the most virulent class hatred existing in England, the impotent hate of the upper
classes for the working people. That extraordinary gift of mimicry (which comes
out in the novels) was allied, as Garnett points out, with a quite merciless disdain
for everything in a man which showed affectation, pose, insincerity, self-consciousness, superciliousness. Nobody but a man so impractical as Russell would have
dreamed of taking Lawrence to a Cambridge College where half the dons would
have qualified as ham actors in a cast of would-be eccentric intellectuals.[2] Of
course Lawrence hated them!

Yet I can't agree with Forster's rather smarmy remarks about Strachey.[3] (And,
by the way the epitaph on him was pronounced by Orioli. When L.S. died I
happened to be in Florence and while praising his undoubted gifts as a writer I
rather tactlessly deplored his habits. "Yes, my dear boy," said Pino, "He was a
bugger, but he was not a bloody bugger." A nice distinction, but valid, I think.)
Anyway why shouldn't Russell say what he feels about Strachey and Lawrence?
And the principle that you are not to say anything impolite about the work or
character of a writer who has been dead 20 years destroys both honest criticism
and honest biography. Why must we be so damned mealy-mouthed?

The objection to Russell here is that he is simply revenging himself for Lawrence's portrait of him. Look up chapter 8 ("Breadalby") of Women in Love,[4]
and see if you can help laughing at Sir Joshua. R. met Lawrence at a time when
much of L's finer self was eclipsed by his passionate worryings about the war.[5]
Under Lawrence's influence Russell wrote one of his best books, Why Men Fight; [6]
under Russell's influence Lawrence made rather an ass of himself.[7] When Russell
was kicked out of his job in the N. Y. City College about 1940 (for motives and
on lines highly discreditable to los yanquis)[8] he sold to a N. Y. bookseller his plan
for the social and political regeneration of England in 1915 (!) with L's comments
and the letters from Lawrence. These were dug up by an American [. . .] Harry
T. Moore, who "specializes" in writing [. . .] on Lawrence.[9] They have never
been published in England. [. . .] Possibly the most absurd of the letters is one
in which Lawrence naively demands that Russell shall bequeath him all his
money — oblivious of the fact that Russell hadn't got any money, wouldn't have
left it to L. if he had, and missing the bus of bardic divination inasmuch as the
tough old earl has outlasted the feeble proletarian by some 30 years or more.[10]

I am much obliged to you for the Sinhalese book on L. which I had not seen.[11]
I don't think it very good, and it only proves (what we knew) that Lawrence
had read the Blavatsky books and picked up a little from them.[12] It is rather a
point with Eastern intellectuals to try to link L. with some Oriental Mysticism.
A Hindu wrote me from Calcutta, very insistent to know how far L. had "studied
the writings of Mr Coomaraswamee" (if that's how you spell it) which so far as
I know L. never opened. A Japanese professor named Megata in Kyoto is even
now trying to persuade me that the Man Who Died is a profound interpretation
of Egyptian mysticism.[13] After Apocalypse,[14] they began barking up the Baby-
lonian tree. Of course, L. was interested in all these things, had read Frazer and
Gilbert Murray and Jane Harrison and John Burnet as well. I wonder how much
the Plumed Serpent [15] stuff is L., how much Blavatsky-tantricism, how much
genuine Mexican. In New Mexico, under the pudic gaze of Auntie Sam, some
weird bloody antics go on under the name of "religion" — blood-sacrifices by

flagellation and so forth. There is no knowing what might have come up in Mexico in the 20s with the hand of the Church lifted. To insist on this, as people do, is to commit the blunder of trying to make Lawrence a thinker instead of an artist, "a great bosher" (as he called himself) instead of a marvellously gifted writer with a quite uniquely sensitive perception of the living world. Possibly Wordsworth is as wonderful as Arnold [16] and the critics say. Compared with Lawrence he is to me limited in experience, not particularly perceptive, and ordinary in expression. Have you seen mangoes growing on the tree? Would Wordsworth ever have hit on or dared Lawrence's exact image "like bull's testicles"? Nobody seems to notice that Lawrence is the English poet of the Mediterranean as it is, and not of Arcadian fantasies based on damp Warwickshire and Dorsetshire meadows. (Browning got some — a little — into that Sorrento poem.) [17] But Lawrence did the English meadows, too, and Australia and the Rockies and Mexico.

As to Orioli's books — my own recollection is that he kept diaries at Douglas's order. The first I saw. It was mostly in Italian, with some English, and was highly indecent in parts. The second was supposed to be written in English, but I never saw it. [. . .] The stories he used to tell so marvellously are ruined in the books by being put into Douglasese. I have, and am reproducing, some of P's letters, as late as 1934, which show conclusively that he couldn't write correct English,[18] and as "his" books are filled with Douglas mannerisms, and they were always together, the inference is fairly obvious.

Ever yours,
RICHARD ALDINGTON

[1] That is, from Beerbohm to Russell. Russell had talked about D. H. Lawrence on the B.B.C. Third Program in July. See *The Listener* 17 July 1952.

[2] D. H. Lawrence visited Bertrand Russell at Trinity College, Cambridge on a week-end, 6–7 Mar 1915. Lawrence described the men he met (including G. H. Hardy, G. E. Moore, J. W. Keynes) as "dead, dead, dead." In a letter to Russell written on 19 Mar 1915, Lawrence said that Cambridge made him "very black and down." He wrote, "I cannot bear its smell of rottenness, marsh-stagnancy. I get a melancholic malaria." See *The Collected Letters of D. H. Lawrence* ed Harry T. Moore (2 vols 1962) I 330.

[3] See E. M. Forster "Portraits from Memory" *The Listener* 24 July 1952, in which he defends Lytton Strachey against an attack made by Bertrand Russell in *The Listener* 17 July 1952.

[4] 1920 p 84–112.

[5] Lady Ottoline Morrel introduced the two men in March 1915 when she took Russell to visit the Lawrences at "Greatham, near Pulborough, in a cottage lent to them by Viola Meynell." According to Lady Ottoline, "From the first these two passionate men took to each other. . . ." See *Ottoline: The Early Memoirs of Lady Ottoline Morrell* ed Robert Gathorne-Hardy (1963) 272–73.

[6] 1917; called *Principles of Social Reconstruction* (1916) in England. The American title was adopted without Russell's consent.

[7] RA may refer to the Lawrence – Russell plans for a joint lectureship, Lawrence to talk on immortality and Russell on ethics, and their eventual quarrels occasioned by a fundamental intellectual difference especially apparent in Lawrence's insistence on "blood-knowledge" and Russell's on "mental consciousness." Lawrence's letters to Russell indicate what Frieda Lawrence described as presumptuousness but what might be called Lawrentian scorn and rage.

[8] In 1940 Russell was invited to join the faculty of the College of the City of New York for the period 1 Feb 1941 to 30 June 1942. When the appointment was publicized, William T. Manning, a Bishop of the Protestant Episcopal Church, denounced it on moral grounds, and a taxpayer's suit against the Municipality of New York was initiated in the name of Mrs Jean Kay of Brooklyn in the New York Supreme Court to vacate Russell's appointment. When the presiding judge John E. McGeehan made public his decision and decried the moral content of Russell's published works, Russell asked to be made a party to the proceedings. Despite appeals, publicity,

and staunch support for Russell from institutions and individuals, the invitation from City College to Russell was withdrawn.

9 *Letters to Bertrand Russell* ed Harry T. Moore (1948).

10 See D. H. Lawrence *Collected Letters* I 432; the letter, written from Portcothan, Cornwall, is dated 19 Feb 1916.

11 Martin Wickramasinghe *The Mysticism of D. H. Lawrence* (1951).

12 *Iris Unveiled* (1877) *The Secret Doctrine* (1888) *The Key to Theosophy* (1889) *The Voice of Silence* (1889).

13 1931. The first part was published as *The Escaped Cock* in 1929.

14 1931.

15 1926.

16 See *Essays in Criticism, Second Series* (1888).

17 Probably "The Englishman in Italy Piano Di Sorrento."

18 See *Pinorman* 166.

25

23 August 1952   *Montpellier*

DEAR BIRD,

Two books of Mrs Taylor should be looked at by everyone, I think. One is a sonnet sequence, The Hours of Fiammetta; and the other her prose book, Leonardo the Florentine.[1] I think them both remarkable, though of course in what is now "period style." She seems to sum up the Aesthetic movement — her sonnets more jewelled than Rossetti's, her prose more astoundingly decorative than Wilde and Pater. A scholar. She is Hon Ll. D; of Aberdeen but never used it. Perhaps it is D. Litt. — I don't remember.[2]

Living apart and getting on with my own little job, I didn't know Russell had gone hysterical about Russia. In practical affairs I think him absurd. And his belligerence in war 2 was an extreme and futile as his pacifism and abuse of America in War I. In those days he was all for Russia and (of course) America was the enemy. In fact, if I remember rightly, he was jugged for writing that the American Army had come to England to do what it did at home — break strikes! [3] It is on a par with Dartingdon,[4] which seems to unfit children for real life altogether, and his theories of perfect marriage which invariably lead to divorce.[5]

While I think of it — do you think you could help me to identify a prose book of Humbert Wolfe's which I need? In Alone Douglas is very bitter about a Jewish gentleman in govt. employ who prevented him from getting a war job in 14–18.[6] Now, in some book of reminiscences Wolfe put out the truth — he was ordered by his chief to tell Douglas that there was no job for him and that if he didn't get out of England at once he would be arrested on the usual Wilde warrant. I have a feeling Wolfe told me this story, but I am also 99% sure he put it in print — and Douglas did not prosecute. I can't remember the title of the book.[7]

Yes, I am sure there is nothing useful to be done about Ford.[8] Have his letters been published? I never saw them. Nor have I seen Ezra's, apart from those he sent me, which are quite enough. Your reaction to his work is that of many intelligent people. How self-centered and ungracious he is! In 1941 in USA I at last completed and published a large anthology Poetry of the English-Speaking World. Before Italy was involved in war I got in touch with E.P. I still have this rude letter in answer to my request for permission to use some of his poems, in which he angrily demanded fees higher than most people. Meanwhile he began yawping over Musso's mike, and the Viking people wanted to cut his poems out. I argued that however much we hated his ridiculous politics, he was a part of American poetry &c. After much difficulty I got my way.[9] In 1946 when H'mann at last got paper to do the job, I found they had simply cut him out. It took a lot of arguing and suffering hints that I was a treacherous agent of the Axis before I got them back.[10] I am sure he knows that, for I know the person who told him — but he took it all for granted, not a word of acknowledgement although in America it had led to my being interviewed by the FBI. Recently he asked for a copy which I sent him (at my expense or Viking's, I forget) and he merely snarled that it was "too big" and refused even to look at it. Of course it is "too big" in the sense that it inevitably reduced him to his true proportions. But I should have thought that an anthology which, without any University prestige, has to date sold nearly 130,000 was worth any poet's while to turn over, if only to see what poems people will buy.

I haven't yet thanked you for the Douglas–Orioli letters.[11] The TLS reviewer (probably Willie King?) is obviously telling the truth [12] — N.D. did re-write Pino's stuff. That the matter is largely Pino's I can swear, for I heard him tell many of the stories before they got into print. Unluckily, Douglas has spoiled them by re-telling them in his style. I enclose with this a Pino letter (which please return) in which you will note his fluency but also his mistakes in English ("abstemy" is a lovely word) and his keeping a diary in English and working at his "C.L.S. book." That was Moving Along,[13] intended to contain among other things a long account of Pino's car trip with Charles Prentice (of Chattos) and myself and Brigit Patmore to Calabria and Sicily.[14] Douglas took several of the episodes and transferred them to Orioli's trips with him! Pino was a great jester and life-source, and meant much more to me than Douglas, who was a spent rocket when I met him in 1931. Also I greatly disliked that sexual mauling of children he indulged in. You will note in Pino's books that Douglas has worked in his own hatred of Lawrence. In fact, Pino was devoted to L. until N.D. gradually worked on him.[15]

Lately I have been sent a MS play about Kiowa Ranch [16] and the doings there, written by a painter called Robert Bartlett, who spent some time there in 1948 and painted an excellent portrait of Frieda. I wonder much what you would think of it. In a sense, I am disqualified by knowing the place fairly well, and such characters in the play as Frieda, Brett and "Angie" (Frieda's Italian). I think it rather good, but I doubt he will ever get it produced.

Returning to N.D. — Low is a pompous ass, who did an edition of Gibbon's *Journals* (good)[17] and a rotten novel.[18] He was a great friend of Prentice, through whom we came to know him. Davis is nobody. I loved Pino's comment to him one year's end when their accounts showed poorly: "What is the good of you being a Jew if you don't make us money?" What indeed.

Adieu. Your delightful letters cheer my solitary days, for all I lack here is the company of a few intelligent English.

Ever yours,
RICHARD ALDINGTON

1 See above, letter 23.

2 LL.D., Aberdeen University, 1943.

[3] For "The German Peace Offer," in *The Tribunal* 3 Jan 1918, Russell was sentenced to six months' imprisonment, which terminated in Sept 1918.

[4] An experimental school which Russell's two older children, John and Kate, attended.

[5] See especially *Marriage and Morals* (1929).

[6] *Alone* (1921) 11–13.

[7] Humbert Wolfe *Portraits by Inference* (1934); see below, letter 27.

[8] See above, letter 22 n 3.

[9] *Viking Book of Poetry of the English-Speaking World* includes Pound's "Δώρια" and "The Return" (p 1153–54). RA removed "Seafarer" when Pound demanded $25 for each of his poems in the anthology and an additional £5.5.0 if the book received English publication.

[10] See *Poetry of the English-Speaking World* (1947) 876–77.

[11] Letters by David M. Low and Irving Davis denying Norman Douglas's extensive participation in the authorship of Orioli's two books *Moving Along* and *Adventures of a Bookseller*. See *Times Literary Supplement* 18 and 25 July 1952.

[12] See "Portrait of Norman Douglas" *Times Literary Supplement* 4 July 1952, a review of Douglas's *Footnote on Capri* (1952).

[13] 1934 (an account of a walking tour in Calabria and Sicily).

[14] A trip which commenced on 26 Feb 1932 and lasted about three weeks.

[15] Marginal note in RA's hand beside this paragraph omitted.

[16] The ranch in New Mexico which Mabel Dodge Luhan gave to Frieda Lawrence in 1924. The Lawrences, with Dorothy Brett, first lived there in May 1924, staying until about mid-October.

[17] 1929.

[18] Low wrote two novels: *Twice Shy* (1933) and *This Sweet Work* (1935).

26

26 August 1952   *Montpellier*

DEAR BIRD,

In a few minutes I must drive to the station to meet friends who will take up my time for some days. I dash off this note to say that at last I have news of the TEL book. The copyright lawyers say that I cannot quote verbatim the Shaw – Shaw [1] letters in the BM without prof L's permission. This is certainly likely to be refused, SO the lawyers advise that if we paraphrase but give the numbered references as at present, AWL can do nothing — on the libel side of those letters he can do nothing because apparently BM Reading Room facilities constitute "publication." This is about 50% of my copyright battle won.

Anyway, Collins are sufficiently optimistic to be taking steps to pay over the balance [. . .] not due until approval of MS.

By the same mail I have a letter from Holroyd-Reece, who has done so much to arrange the Collins agreement and is responsible to them for it. He is quite rhapsodical, and though he limits his letter to literary appreciation, he will obviously support to his utmost the fullest publication possible. He adds cheerfully that I shall "be attacked, and viciously." For that we have been prepared. If I am allowed to quote or paraphrase the evidence, I think only an interested partisan can quarrel with the presentation which is pretty fair.

In much haste,

R.A.

[1] That is the correspondence between T. E. Lawrence — or Shaw — and Charlotte Francis Shaw. A few letters to and from George Bernard Shaw are included.

27

19 September 1952   *Montpellier*

DEAR BIRD,

Many thanks to you for sending the revised version of the Wolfe quotation. I had supposed he was more specific in stating the reason why N.D. was "not a success" (i.e. the decision of the Home Office to force him into exile under threat of prosecution) but I must have received that gloss from some other source.[1] My impression is that Wolfe told me himself, but I can't remember where or when. Must have been in London, but even in the 30s I was usually in such a hurry to get back to the continent that everything was made rapid and hectic, and consequently memories are vague. If I mention this in my little book on N.D. I must be careful to confess the vagueness. Yet I'm as sure that I'm right about the "gloss" as I was about the text.

I have had some annoyance with Collins over the TEL text. Their "Head Editor" sent in a list of enquiries — so many allegations of my supposed errors — whereof about 90% were based either on a total misreading of my words or on the ignorance of the critic. These I have now dealt with, somewhat caustically, and order reigns in Warsaw. But now comes another quandary. Billy Collins is going to US in a few days, and is very anxious to place the book there [. . .]. It seems only fair to allow them any advantage they can get from introducing the book — all American rights are retained by me — [. . .]. Kershaw, who did that bibliography,[2] most generously handles most of these dreary problems for me; but these have had to be referred to me. Well, I am a terribly bad hand at "business," and if I have to consider such problems and then write a decision, it puts me off writing for a couple of days. My original agent, Ralph Pinker, was jugged for embezzling clients' money! Sidelights on that life of "virtual idleness and easy money" which the Inland Revenue as well as the populace attribute to scribblers.

A TEL query. Among other "thrasonical brags" he says he "read all the Manuals of Chivalry." [3] Where are they? Perhaps he merely means the romans in langue d'oil (which I suspect he read in translation, there being several such and hardly any texts in his library) or perhaps Froissart? I am teased with a half-memory that Caxton issued a Boke of Chevalry [4] . . . frm the Frenysshe. Mentioned in Warton,[5] I think, for I can't find it in the Cantab Lit. Hist. I see Caxton did a Book of Curtesye [6] and The Book of Good Manners,[7] so perhaps Lawrence meant them. But are they "manuals of chivalry"? Could one say that of Christine de Pisan even? You will rightly infer from this that I strongly suspect even L's alleged erudition to be largely bogus.

Unicorns! Here is a little puzzle. Here in M'pellier we have an 18th century marble monument to the memory of M. le Maréchal Duc de Castries, our 'voisin', as Castries is only a few miles off and the château still stands — it is where Balzac attempted, but in vain, to seduce the Duchesse de Castries of his day. Now, this monument commemorates the rather obscure battle of Closterkampf (Seven Years War) with two energetically fighting *unicorns*. Why? They could hardly represent such chaste champions as Frederick of Prussia and Mme de Pompadour. Or do they come from the Castries arms?[8] Or what?

Which arose out of Mrs Taylor's Unicorns,[9] and your very just remarks on it. I think it is a type of poem which the Sitwells tried for years to write, without anywhere reaching this virtuosity. Of course Mrs T. is "dated." Even when she began she was a belated member of a dying tradition — like Cotton in the age of Dryden. But I do feel she summed up and concentrated the "Aesthetic Movement" with more ability and "panache" that its leaders in its heyday. There is something attractive, in an age of literary time-serving and venality, to find this pure devotion to an ideal, complete contempt for recognition, and a life of poverty when her talents otherwise applied could have made her comfortable. The other survivor, also in my anthology, is Edward MacCurdy who, I think, has had some little recognition lately for his work on Leonardo.[10] But really! When I think of those two, of Mrs Taylor's real gifts as poet, their scholarship, and then think of all these piffling bootlickers of Eliot and Leavis who lay down the law about literature . . . ! You MUST get Mrs T.'s Leonardo — it is one of the most astonishing tours de force in English, as tirelessly ornate and rhetorical as Gavin Douglas. It is not a biography of Leonardo, really, but a set of extremely decorative and gorgeous tapestries on Italian Renaissance themes. Don't try to read it through — it's like trying to read the Anatomy of Melancholy[11] at a sitting — but read here and there. I am most curious to have your opinion. The book ought to have been reprinted for this Leonardo anniversary. France, by the way, has issued a Leonardo stamp — I suppose on the strength of the residence in Amboise.[12] Also I want to know what you feel about Mrs T.'s Fiammetta sonnets. [. . .]

Ever yours,
RICHARD ALDINGTON

[1] Wolfe *Portraits by Inference* 160–61; see above, letter 25. See also *Pinorman* 58, 147–48.

[2] See Alister Kershaw *A Bibliography of the Works of Richard Aldington from 1915 to 1948* (London 1950).

[3] See *T. E. Lawrence to His Biographer Liddell Hart* 50, where Lawrence is reported as saying he had read "nearly every manual of chivalry"; see also RA *Lawrence of Arabia* 120.

[4] Possibly *The Order of Chivalry* (1484) or Christine de Pisan's *Fayttes of Armes and of Chyvalrye*, which Caxton translated and issued in 1489.

[5] Thomas Warton *History of English Poetry* (3 vols 1774, 1778, 1781).

[6] 1476.

[7] 1487.

[8] That is, The Fountain of the Unicorns by d'Antoine, which is designed without regard for the Castries' arms; they show no unicorns.

[9] See the poem "The Unicorns" in *Rose and Vine* (1909) 144, which begins:

> In lands like faded arras-broideries
> These dead green skies are veiled with golden trees,
> With golden trees, from whose frail branches young
> Star-tangled jasmine in great ropes is hung, —

[10] *Leonardo da Vinci* (Great Masters Series) 1904; *Leonardo da Vinci's Note Books* (1906); *Thoughts of Leonardo* (1907); *The Mind of Leonardo da Vinci* (1928); *Leonardo da Vinci, The Artist* (1933); *The Note Books of Leonardo da Vinci* (2 vols 1938).

[11] By Robert Burton (1621).

[12] At the invitation of Francis I in the last years of Leonardo's life.

28

8 October 1952   *Montpellier*

DEAR BIRD,

My friend Alister Kershaw has spent several days here, reporting at length on the situation with the TEL book. It seems to be longer than I thought, for the finished typescript runs to 660 pages, about 500 of print. Collins make no objection, but as it had to be done by one private secretary the thing took time. Copyright lawyer has now finished and reports that the TEL Trust cannot prevent my quoting any of the passages I have used from printed books, but that I must paraphrase from the Shaw – Shaw unpublished letters at the BM and refer the reader to the press mark. That is a green light, for I was most modest in what I took from the letters of S – S, and can easily paraphrase.

The libel lawyer is now two-thirds through, and, to my surprise and joy, says only a few minor alterations are needed so far. As the adultery – bastardy business comes in my first chapter and is the one essential thing which the law of libel might have suppressed, I am considerably elated. If there is anything in the war and post-war sections which is libellous it can only be a trifle, which re-wording can deal with. The homosexual chapter is done cautiously, and in any case involves no living person — Farraj and Daud having joined Hafiz and Abu Nawas.[1] [. . .]If the book is really to be effective there must be nothing dailymaily about it. I think it is a fearful mistake to increase the early sale by pandering to low tastes while offending what one might call the upper mental class which eventually decides on every book.

The question has again come up of having the script read before publication by experts. Kershaw and I agree that both a military and a scholarly adviser are needed. For the soldier we have decided to ask N. N. E. Bray (Indian Army) who was not one of the Lawrence bureau. If he is dead or unwilling, I suppose we must ask Sir Hubert Young. I am venturing to ask if you would consent to be the scholar reader, picking me up on any blunders, particularly about the Middle East.[2] I don't of course mean that you should verify my 1500 references (which would take weeks) but merely to point out anything which seems to you wrong or which offers an opportunity for hostile reviewers, who love to pick on such details. If you would agree, I would arrange with Collins for what is delicately referred to in America as "a suidable honorarium." I do hope you will consent, for I know you share my point of view about L. and are able to point out my errors. I think Kershaw will be writing to you.

What do you think of the new A. Huxley?[3] Doubtless I am getting gaga and out of touch with the new thought of Los Angeles, but I must confess I am finding the book a bore and very slow going. I do wish Huxley had remained worldly and amusing, instead of godding about southern California in this unfrisky way.

I am lunching with Professor Cohen to-morrow, and will get his views on "Manuals of chivalry." I feel sure you are right in thinking they don't exist. I have done a fair amount of reading in mediaeval French, constantly had lists of books from Honoré Champion, always look at any mediaeval text in bookshops, and have never seen any mention of such "manuals." So I think my phrase "whatever they may be" should stand.[4] I've looked through the books of Jeanroy, Cohen etc.

which I happen to have, and see no such "manuals" in their texts or bibliographies. I suppose he meant chansons de geste, of which he possessed about a dozen, mostly in English translations! I think you will like my analysis of the 1200 books he actually possessed, given out as a selection of the world's essential masterpieces, whereas in fact it consists of survivors of his undergraduate books, gifts from contemporary writers, and new books sent him by Mrs Shaw.[5] Another of the innumerable humbugs. He had 27 books of DHLawrence, more than any other author — I think very likely because they were published under his name! [6]

I look forward to hearing your views on Mrs Taylor's Leonardo. I have Dunbar,[7] and though it is good I think it rates far below the Leonardo. In vain have I laboured to find a publisher for her million words book on the French Renaissance [8] — I hope she doesn't burn it in disgust. Yale with its billions offered merely to issue "selections." I don't see why they can't do it in three vols, and drop the 5000 or 6000 dollars involved. Of course, if she were an American . . .

I once met L. P. Smith chez a Philadelphia cousin of his, but it was on a leave period in 1917 when I wasn't feeling much amused by his type of person. Afterward I read that autobiography of his and liked it very much.[9]

We have had some lovely golden days here, but the wind has turned north again. Still, at 5 p. m. I am sitting without jacket or waistcoat with French windows wide open, so it can't be very cold.

Ever yours,

RICHARD ALDINGTON

[1] See RA *Lawrence of Arabia* 331–39. Farraj and Daud were members of T. E. Lawrence's body guard. See also *Seven Pillars* 237, where Lawrence describes both and remarks on their relationship.

[2] Bray was the expert; Bird read the typescript as a personal service to RA. See below, letter 29; above, Introduction.

[3] *The Devils of Loudon.*

[4] RA *Lawrence of Arabia* 120.

[5] RA *Lawrence of Arabia* 380–81.

[6] On 22 Aug 1926 T. E. Lawrence wrote to Charlotte F. Shaw about D. H. Lawrence: "I can smell the genius in him: excess of genius makes his last book [possibly a reference to *The Plumed Serpent*] sickening: and perhaps some day the genius will burst through the darkness of his prose and take the world by the throat. He is very violent, . . . violent and dark, with a darkness which only grows deeper as he writes on. The revelation of his greatness, if it comes, will be because the public will grow able to see through his dark thinking . . . because the public begins to be dark-thoughted themselves. D.H.L. can't make himself clear: he can't use the idiom of you & me. So often you find men like that, & sometimes the world grows up to them and salutes them as Kings-before-their-time . . . and sometimes nobody ever bothers about them at all, afterwards."

[7] *Dunbar and His Period* (1931).

[8] Although *Renaissance France* (1949) is listed in Mrs Taylor's entry in *Who Is Who* and *Who Was Who*, the book was not published.

[9] Logan Pearsall Smith *Trivia* (1902); *More Trivia* (1921); and *Unforgotten Years* (1938).

29

19 October 1952 [1]   *Montpellier*

DEAR BIRD,

It is a great relief and support to me to know that you will read the TEL for me. You will find the thing has been carefully documented, but there are all the unconscious slips or omissions of ignorance to guard against. Only Ezra Pound and Eliot are omniscient. I don't know whether the thing should come to you in typescript or in galley proof. Would you greatly object to galleys? You can't read them at an arm chair, but the advantage would be that much time would be saved, because you could make corrections direct on the proof. Collins and my friends Kershaw and Holroyd-Reece have dawdled away too much time in pre-liminaries, and I am pressing for action. Collins, unhappily, is in America (pub-lishers always go away when they're wanted) and I don't think the script can go to the printers until he returns. One trouble is that not enough typescripts were made, but that can't be helped now.

Kershaw is trying to discover the whereabouts of Major Bray (he may be no longer with us) but I want the supervision of an officer present at the Arabian scuffle as an additional ward against that imbecile, Liddel Hart.

Gustave says there *are* some "manuals of chivalry" and advised me to read his "Histoire de la Chevalerie en France au Moyen Age." [2] I couldn't find a copy on sale here, so have ordered from Paris; and will report when I get the book. I am not at all sure that he understood what I meant. We were talking in English, and he has had such a fearful amount of pain and misfortune of late that the effort tired him and he didn't always catch what I meant. But he loves to be treated as entirely bi-lingual, which he isn't. His latest misfortune is that the little daughter of his servants at La Croix, of whom Gustave was very fond, has just died of polio. He has been forced to give up the gallant pretence of wearing a boot, and appeared with his foot in an enormous surgical bandage. I should have thought that if 35 years ago the surgeons had amputated he might have been spared all this incessant pain. I do admire that man's gallantry and the enthusiasm which keeps him read-ing, writing, and radio-ing at 73. It is a contrast to another friend of mine, an American, who at 68 (3 years after normal retirement age) is sunk in profound melancholy, if not despair, because he has been retired from his post of Dean of Faculty.[3] He complains that his successor will not carry on his work! But did he carry on *his* predecessor's, I wonder? I doubt it. In fact I know he didn't, for he spent years preaching a philosophical myth of "the developing God," a mixture of Bergson and H. G. Wells with a most extensive knowledge of belles lettres. I can't see where the grumble lies, except at the "ineluctable" (James Joyce brought that in, I think) passage of time.

Did I tell you Pound sent me the reprint of his "Kulchur," which irritates me so much that I have thrown it away. He is an ass in a china shop. The fatuous omniscience, hectoring manner, snap judgments, and absurd blunders, defeat his supposed object of "selling kulchur" though I should not exclude the possibility that he wrote to draw attention to himself. I cannot see that either kulchur or culture or anything whatever is achieved by the idiotic remark that Handel is "dull." He isn't.[4]

Elsewhere he remarks that the editor of Beddoes omits Landor from the list of poets writing after Shelley's death, and adds sneeringly: "What an England!" Now, after all, Gosse wasn't England; and looking again over the Beddoes note as reproduced in Kit-Kats [5] I think Gosse only wrote "poets" instead of "romantic poets." Such a book-worm was certainly not ignorant of Landor or unappreciative.

I shut the book for ever when in a volume which glorifies Musso and Hitler (and denounces Churchill as a warmonger) I came on the priceless sentence: "No decent man tortures prisoners"! [6] I think it quite possible that he imagines the massacres of the Jews, Dachau, Buchenwald etc. are all "British propaganda." Let him. But why do Eliot and his friends and numerous "young" crack up Ezra so much? The fact is that language has ceased to have meaning, and Kulchur proves it. Well, I am glad that 20 years ago I published my portraits of Cibber and Charlemagne Cox in Soft Answers.[7]

Strangely enough, my copy of Mrs Taylor's Hours of Fiametta was bequeathed me by May Sinclair, and has in it some insulting comments in Pound's handwriting! I shouldn't wonder if her book survives his dislike. I am very pleased that you are reading the Leonardo with appreciation. Of course, I think a reader's pleasure in the book depends on the approach. A mistake to read it as a biography, "pure and simple," i.e. "story of a life." I think of it as a suite of gorgeous word tapestries — like the unicorn series — on the theme of Leonardo and the Renaissance. As a mere effort of virtuosity, the maintaining impeccably a very high standard of superb gorgeous prose, I think it unique in English. De Quincey is more colloquial and patchy, and Donne is too wormy for me. Perhaps Jeremy Taylor? Anyway, I am convinced that she left all the "aesthetes" toiling in the dusty rear of her rowing boat, as that great American stylist, H. James, remarked on another occasion. I think the book has to be taken in bits at a time. As you say it is "rich," like foie gras or Xmas pudding — one can't eat much at a time. But it is all incomparably good. Another thing — so far as I can discover there is but one, very trifling, misprint in the whole big book. Is it not disgraceful that ALL her work is out of print in England, that nobody will take her French Renaissance,[8] and that she was contemptuously pushed off the Spectator on some change of editorship? What is the matter with "intellectual England"? Under the sway of the B.B.C. literary sectarianism and snobbery have become intolerable. What am I to think of a literary London which greets John Arlott enthusiastically and refuses even to hear of Mrs Taylor? One reviewer of my Rel. of Beauty referred to her as "a kind of Walter Pater in petticoats." There were others, all contemptuous. It is not surprising that she is a recluse, and rather a tart old lady when run to earth. I sent some young friends of mine along to see her, and she was for a time charming to them, but they were a *little* distressed by the unvarying sharpness of her comments on everyone else.[9] They began to feel that in their absence and the presence of others *they* came in for their share of Scottish vitriol. But I don't blame her. A life utterly devoted to literature and the arts and the most high-minded standards of writing has been received with neglect and derision. My clumsy little attempts to do her justice only succeeded in adding my enemies to hers. But I am pretty certain she will survive all that trash turned out by Faber & Faber and New Directions. If not, criticism is a farce, and literature a branch of la haute couture.

Talking of which . . . "Kulchur" sent me to Donner's Beddoes [10] (of which seemingly from his letter E.P. had never heard) and while feeling great respect for D's learning and editorship, I wish when you are next in the Bodleian you would get permission of the Keeper to put up a notice:

"Never begin a paragraph or a sentence with a genitive."

Does any really good English writer ever begin: "Of the . . . "? It certainly is pompier now. Gibbon almost always *ends* with a genitive, but that is another matter. From which I infer that a man of very high culture, as Donner obviously is, does not necessarily know how to write good English — one of the rarest attainments. If you grant that an ornate and highly allusive prose *may* be used appropriately in writing of the Italian Renaissance, then surely Mrs Taylor's prose is on a very high level indeed? Or am I grown gaga with age and provincial through living away from Bloomsbury?

By the way, you must know Willie King — is he still at the Brit Mus? In any case, what, if anything, was his speciality? Was he in the Print Room or where? [11] I used to think he and Waley were the two most offensive freaks in London, though of course Waley is a genuine Sinalogue, and I daresay King was good at whatever he was good at. I have forgotten. He is Douglas's literary executor, and I may have a dust-up with him in my little book,[12] but I like to give the devil his due.

Apologies for this over-long letter, and forgive me for adding that in looking over Gosse I came upon his note on Fluctuations of Taste.[13] Although he makes no attempt to approfondir, I think he states the problem clearly and brings some startling examples. That of Sully-Prudhomme is remarkable. I recollect somewhere about 1913 persuading myself (in obedience of course to the vogue) that there is something particularly iniquitous about Sully-Prudhomme which I am bound to say I now fail to discover. Likewise Tennyson. In 1912–13 I thought Tennyson horrible and shunned anyone so depraved as to admire this degraded rhetorician; and now I get a good deal of (modified) pleasure from the pre-Idylls work.[14] Why must we in youth be such fanatic imbeciles? I suppose it is the conspiracy of jeunes "killing the king" as detailed by Frazer at somewhat unnecessary length. "Scientific" criticism is self-evidently bunk, and Richards was born to prove it. But is there any standard of taste, any real thread across the centuries, any positive standard? In fact was I so wrong when in the introduction to a Pater omnibus I suggested that "all art tends to the condition of journalism"?[15] I remember "musing" (as the stylists say) in the enormous ruin of what the archaeologists then said had been the library of Augustus in the Forum — about 1912 — and trying to imagine all the libraries which must have existed in the Empire before the Xtians and the barbarians got going. Where are they now? Only a few scholars regret them, and it is still impossible to get money for a thorough and competent excavation of Herculaneum. No allocation from Lend-Lease or Marshall Aid has ever gone to it. In the last war we got a curtain-raiser or rather pre-view of what is going to happen to our "kulchur" — pulped to make a Beaverbrook holiday.[16] Where is the Roman de la Rose? [17]

With all my thanks to you for undertaking that dreary task of correcting my blunders.

Ever yours,
RICHARD ALDINGTON

1 Bird has written on the upper left corner of this letter: "letters in between were probably lost while I was lecturing in Cairo." (See above, letter 21 n 1.)

2 1949.

3 Harry Slonimsky of the Jewish Institute of Religion .

4 RA doubtless refers to New Directions's edition (1952) of *Guide to Kulchur*, first published by Faber & Faber Limited in 1938.

5 P 31–32 in the 1897 edition published by Charles Scribner, New York; *Kit-Kats* was first published in 1896.

6 *Guide to Kulchur* (1952) 255.

7 That is, caricatures of Eliot (see above, letter 7 n 15) in "Stepping Heavenward" (first published separately, 1931) and Pound in "Nobody's Baby" (see above, letter 2 n 7). Both stories are in *Soft Answers*.

8 See above, letter 28.

9 Denison Deasey and Alister Kershaw.

10 H. W. Donner *Thomas Lovell Beddoes: The Making of a Poet* (1935).

11 King was Keeper of Ceramics; see below, letter 31.

12 *Pinorman.*

13 Published as the preface to *Some Diversions of a Man of Letters* (1919) 3–12.

14 That is, work published before 1859.

15 See "Introduction" to Walter Pater, *Selected Works* (1948) 19, where RA wrote: "Without it ['divine moderation'] there is always the chance that the republic of art and letters may collapse into totalitarian regimes labelled Journalism or Politics."

16 RA refers to the plea made during the war of 1939–45 that books be surrendered for pulping toward the war effort. The result was real loss to libraries and scholars, especially since many books in various libraries including a number in the British Museum were destroyed by bombing and could not be replaced. Meanwhile Beaverbrook and his press went ahead with the war news.

17 French poem of two parts, the first written about 1237 by Guillaume de Loris and the second about 1275–80 by Jeun de Meun.

30

23 October 1952   *Montpellier*

DEAR BIRD,

I am now working on the absurd and tedious little job of paraphrasing (back at school!) in my own words all passages derived from the B. M. Shaw – Shaw letters; I must give the information as my own idea, not as quoted from Lawrence, but give the B.M. references in notes! Is there any law in the world so piffling as ours? Really!

Here is another damned vexation . . . Let me interject that to my slight dismay I find that Collins's lawyers are Joynson, Hicks & Co; who presumably will not have relished my remarks about their distinguished founder in Portrait of a Genius But . . . ! [1] However, they seem to have been "decent," (mustn't grumble, you know), but Collins was premature in writing me that the libel objections were "minor." One is very much the reverse — they say I have not proved that Thomas Robert Lawrence is the same person as Thomas Robert Tighe Chapman!

Presumably, when Hogarth out of the blue wrote to TEL at the R.A.F. barracks to ask what he should say in his Enc. Brit. article on L. of A., Lawrence laughed maniacally and rushed to the squadron library, saying: "I shall now look up a family of Irish baronets to whom I can attach myself, and pull the leg of old Hoggers and everyone else by this knavishly brilliant device." Whereupon he discovered the Chapman family, and wrote to Hogarth the letter which is the basis of H's most inaccurate article. Incidentally, I ask you as a scholar, what do you think of the fact that in 1925 Lawrence did not know that the D.N.B. contains only defunct persons? He thought at first Hogarth's request was for the D.N.B. and not for Enc. Britt! [2] Cf. his statement that in his history studies "he never used an index"! [3] Like Marie Antoinette, I appeal to every literary worker.

Well, what is to be done about this legal swash, which hamstrings the whole book? Before proceeding, let me say that Jix have discovered that the mother is not Sarah Maden (as stated in TEL's birth certificate) but Sarah Junner, as stated in AWL's. [4] (Wouldn't he be pleased to know we have that!) Or rather, the only discoverable Sarah Maden was b. 1863, whereas "S. Lawrence" (note how they hide their Xtian names) says 1861. Storrs (DNB) says L's mother's father was "a Sunderland engineer." And lo! the indefatigable Jix have unearthed the birth certificate of Sarah Junner, b. August 1861 at Sunderland (!), father a "shipwright journeyman," romantically turned to "engineer" by Sir Phoney Storrs.

Now, my dear friend, do try to think of some way in which we can find legal proof that Sir TRC was Mr TRL. We are seeking (a) Death certificate of Mrs TRC; (2) Birth certificate of first "Lawrence" child, Dr L. the China missionary! (3) The marriage certificate of Sarah Junner and Thomas Robert Lawrence. But these can be only negative evidence. I have suggested that someone stroll into the offices of Debrett or Burke, and ask how they know that Sir T. R. Chapman died 9/4/19. Officially he is still going strong at the age of 106. Where is his death certificate? Trouble is so many records were destroyed by the burning of the Four Courts. I have suggested (a) Wills of TRL and Sir TRC — easily found as they died on the same day!; (b) Income tax returns, Ireland and England; (c) Photostats of the original declarations of birth of Chapman children and Lawrence children.[5] This must be signed by person declaring, but do the Irish records exist? When I registered my daughter I naively produced as a matter of course my marriage certificate. Apparently old Chapman got away with it without producing one. Would you discreetly ask of any papas in your district if they were asked to produce marriage certificates when formally acknowledging the product of their licensed libidinousness? There is definitely a false declaration in TEL's birth certificate, as Mom is given as Sarah Maden, not Junner. Where does the Maden come from? I suggest the "Bible-thinking Presbyterian" (Shaw – Shaw letters, so don't quote!) who brought the child up in Skye?[6] But why?

Jix says that all the evidence I bring is derived (apart from birth and death certificates) from TEL, and that I have so convincingly proved TEL a liar that his evidence can't be accepted! Whaddyer know?

One of the gems from the Shaw – Shaw letters which has been snatched from me is TEL's admission that Mom was nursemaid to the Chapman daughters.[7] Can't you see it! The old squire accustomed to use his droits de seigneur on all females of the establishment suddenly falling into the bed of a ferociously strong-willed Covenanter or lamb of the Wee Free Kirk o' Scotland, and captive to her — well, I won't say "spear and bow" — triumphantly carried off from his lawful wife and four wailing daughters by this siren of the Hebrides. Positively we should have Fiona Macleod to write a "keen" over it all.

But surely this goddam thing can be dealt with somehow? Do you know Lionel Curtis, gaga Fellow of All Souls? Could you artfully pick his brains, without giving away anything?[8] Remember, the fact that Lionel "knows for a fact" that Tel was a bastard is not evidence. We want documents, facts.

Having just re-read the script with a good deal of honest mirth, I am longing for you to see it.

Ever yours,
RICHARD ALDINGTON

[1] The Right Honourable Sir William Joynson-Hicks, Home Secretary when the sale of *Lady Chatterley's Lover* (1928) was restricted, when the manuscripts of *Pansies* (1929) and the introduction to *The Paintings of D. H. Lawrence* (1929) were seized, and when thirteen of Lawrence's paintings were removed from the exhibition held at the Warren Galleries in the summer of 1929 and the exhibition was closed. See *Portrait of a Genius But . . .* 340–42.

[2] See Lawrence's letter to Hogarth in *Letters of T. E. Lawrence* 491–92.

3 See *Seven Pillars* 7.

4 See above, letter 7.

5 Bird cooperated with RA's suggestions by attempting to secure signatures of Thomas Robert Lawrence and of Sir Thomas Robert Tighe Chapman for comparison and by seeking information from Burke's *Peerage*, Burke's *Landed Gentry*, the Public Record Office of Ireland, the Genealogical Office (Dublin Castle), H. M. Land Registry, the University Registry of Oxford University and the Assistant Registrar's Office of Trinity College, Dublin. Letters from all these and others in response to Bird's inquiries are a part of the Berg Collection.

6 See T. E. Lawrence to Charlotte F. Shaw [Karachi] 14 Apr 1927; see also above, letters 7 and 8.

7 T. E. Lawrence to Charlotte F. Shaw [Karachi] 14 Apr 1927.

8 In answer to Bird's inquiries Curtis replied in a letter dated 10 Nov 1952 (Berg). It runs in part: "'T. E. L. gave me a detailed account of his parentage, which does not agree with your statement. I frequently see his mother who is in full possession of her faculties.'"

3 I

30 October 1952   *Montpellier*

DEAR BIRD,

The nicest tale I know about Tennyson's mother is in that preposterous book of Hallam's. Old Mrs T. was one of those sensitive lachrymose old ladies, always shedding unnecessary tears, whereupon Alfred would always says cheerfully: "Dam your eyes, mother, dam your eyes." [1] It makes Alfred very sympathetic, don't you think?

I have been spending wretched days with typewriter, scissors and paste, paraphrasing and pasting in. And now have to repeat it on the duplicate script! I also had to paste out a number of repetitions. As to the legal evidence on Chapman – Lawrence, I can do no more. By written understanding I am exempted from all legal troubles, except that of course I agree to make any cuts required by law. This extra legal proof required is due to some very Victorian decisions of judges who "set their faces like flint" against any evidence "tending to bastardise a child once recognised as legitimate." What chicanery it all is! [. . .] I think the will's the thing. TEL (in those Shaw letters you haven't seen) definitely says he inherited "some of the Irish money." [2] I should think from what is let drop that he got about 5000 or rather more. 4000 he put into that Chingford land,[3] and wasted the rest on lordly gestures of aristocratic patronage to Doughty, Graves and Kennington.[4] While he was doing that, or very shortly afterwards, he represents himself in the opening of The Mint as broke, his clothes worn, his shoe burst out, and himself hanging about the Duke of York's monument to cadge for meals from fellows going to their clubs! [5] I've only been able to hint at this, as I'm not allowed to quote from the Mint. Isn't it clear from all these prohibitions that there is a Family Skeleton? [. . .]

Last week H.D. sent me a letter from a woman (aet. 60) an American friend of hers who has lately visited Pound.[6] It left me gasping — this utterly egotistic, utterly shallow description of her "trip," down to soft-boiled eggs and the TV set at 25 cents in the motel, the horrifying glimpses of America gone mad, and the picture of Pound and his wife in the asylum "campus" sitting on "aluminum morris chairs" (shades of Wm Morris!) with their friends on park benches opposite, talking violent anti-Semitism, Ezra eating egg rolls dipped in sauce brought him by a Chinese girl student who was obviously, though a Catholic, having an affair with the professor who brought her, and who was enigmatically consoled by Ezra because she has to study Anglo-Saxon and resented it . . . ! What a picture, what a world!

Which reminds me that I get disquieting letters from American friends — one who knew pre-war Germany well says the "atmosphere" is only too similar to that just preceding Hitler. There are actually concentration camps, in readiness I suppose, for nothing is said about anyone being in them. (I don't know if the State of Emergency proclaimed by Truman automatically suspends Habeas Corpus — if not, obviously the camps must be empty.) But if America is like this under Truman, *what* would it be under Eisenhower – Taft! I try to keep out of politics, but I do feel that if Stevenson loses this election it will be a case of God help us all. What can be expected from a party like the Republicans, where the Duke of Bedford would be considered suspiciously radical by the all-powerful Taft faction? The loss of world hegemony by the comparatively sane and decent English – French group may turn out an appalling tragedy. Let's hope Adlai wins.

Willy King — of course — keramics! [7]

Ever yours,
RICHARD ALDINGTON

[1] Hallam, Lord Tennyson *Alfred Lord Tennyson, a Memoir* (2 vols 1897) I 265.

[2] T. E. Lawrence to Charlotte F. Shaw [Karachi] 12 May 1927 runs in part: "I did inherit some Irish money, & enjoyed it, & made The Seven Pillars out of it." Bird had seen the letters and made notes from them.

[3] Land in Essex owned by T. E. Lawrence.

[4] When the manuscript of Doughty's poem *The Dawn in Britain* was purchased by the British Museum in 1922, Lawrence may have contributed most of the purchase price, £400. David Garnett thought he did. Lawrence lent money to Graves when he was threatened with action in bankruptcy owing to his failure in an "attempt to start a grocery-shop." Lawrence's help to Kennington was apparently the commission to illustrate *Seven Pillars*.

[5] *The Mint* 13–14.

[6] Mrs Viola Jordan. See also a letter from H.D. to Winifred Bryher, 24 Oct 1952, which runs in part, "Nothing special but long account of E from Viola which I think RA would like to see, as he writes Dorothy and seems concerned for her" (Yale).

[7] See above, letter 29.

32

13 November 1952 *Montpellier*

DEAR BIRD,

Many thanks for yours of the 8th. It is — if you will pardon the mixed metaphors of a distracted man — a crumb of comfort in my cup of woe. I am brooding over an immense epistle from Joynson Hicks who says I have libelled (1) Ma Lawrence, as to five counts; (2) Professor Lawrence and his brother; (3) Liddell Hart; (4) Lowell Thomas 14 times; (5) Graves 18 times; (6) Sir John Rhys; (7) D. G. Hogarth! I have pointed out plaintively that Rhys and Hogarth died long ago. You will be glad to learn that Jix by inference advance the principle that to convict a man of a misstatement in a biography is libel. I wish I'd known that earlier.

The kind of rot advanced is this. In the Shaw–Shaw letters Lawrence says of his mother that she was "brought up as a child of sin in the Hebrides." [1] (I am not allowed to quote those letters, but never mind.) I took the words to mean that she was brought up as a child of *original* sin, i.e. as a damned Calvinist, if you see what I mean. The combustible imaginations of Jix and Collins [. . .] twist this 10-word quote from her son into an assertion by *me* that Mom herself was a bastard!

What does one do with such cretins?

Howsomedever (as the rural novels say, though in all my English country years I never heard it once) I have airmailed a revised script to New York [. . .]. This libel – blackmail rot doesn't function in N. Y. State (or where would American journalism be?) and so I propose to issue as full a text as possible in USA and insist that all translations are made from it — and let the English go. I can't bother with their mealy-mouthed hypocrisies. [. . .]

What amuses me is that Jix and Collins both coolly assume that the English edition is the *only* one, whereas to me it has always been secondary to the USA and no more important than the Italian or Mexican edition. I am not an English author, I am a cosmopolitan author. My Italian royalties last year were just double my English royalties, and over 50% of the English royalties were marked "export"! It is a curious position — to be read everywhere but in one's own country.

The information from the Registrar of Baronetage is interesting — another person who says T. R. Chapman died on the same day as T. R. Lawrence! But, alas, the onus of proof of the Chapman – Lawrence story is on me. I cannot challenge Prof Lawrence to produce his mother's marriage certificate. He can refuse to do so, and challenge me to prove she wasn't married. That can only be done if I can legally prove that TRC was TRL and legally prove that Lady C. was alive until 8/4/19. As I don't know what constitutes legal proof as apart from common sense I am stumped. Note the delicious irony of Jix to Collins: "The most important thing, at the moment, is to get Mr Aldington's evidence, to justify the illegitimacy story, *which is the whole essence of the book*." Now that evidence occupies part of Chaps 1 and 2 and is referred to once or twice more in a book of 160,000 words. Moreover, all the evidence is fairly lucidly summarised in my first chapter, and they know perfectly well I haven't any more or I should have quoted it.

Let me give you a specimen of what Jix asserts is a libel on Graves:

" 'Lawrence's knowledge must be pretty extensive. In six years he read every book in the library of the Oxford Union — the best part of 50,000 volumes probably. His father used to get him the books while he was at school and afterwards he always borrowed six volumes a day in his father's name and his own. For three years he read day and night on a hearthrug, which was a mattress so that he could fall asleep as he read. Often he spent eighteen hours a day reading, and at last got so good at it that he could tear the heart out of the most formidable book in half an hour.' (R. Graves: Lawrence and the Arabs, pp 24, 25.)

"Unfortunately for this story, by the rules of the Oxford Union — at any rate as they stand today — only resident members of the University are allowed to borrow books, so Lawrence's father could not have taken them out himself or had them taken out in his name. Moreover, 6 books a day for 6 years doesn't make more than 7000; to read 50,000 books he would have had to perform the impossible feat of reading 25 a day for 2000 days — and what about going to school and lectures?"

That is libel! Am I showing a Wyndham Lewis persecution mania if I confess to a suspicion that Jix are trying to hamstring a book which exposes a national scandal? As a matter of fact I go on to exculpate Graves wholly from any responsibility for the statement, pointing out that Lawrence not only gave him the story but read and passed every line of G's book. And Graves is libelled! What about the truth? Jix ordered me to "tone down" my "vindictive" statements about Graves. Can you tell me what there is to "tone down" and where the "vindictive" comes in?

It is useless to argue with such people, and I want to get on with my Douglas and Orioli book. I think the only course is to tell Collins they can cut whatever they please but write nothing in, and get copies of the American edition for my friends.

Evers yours,
RICHARD ALDINGTON

[1] T. E. Lawrence to Charlotte F. Shaw [Karachi] 14 Apr 1927.

33

15 November 1952   *Montpellier*

DEAR BIRD,

Could you let me have the original of the letter from the Registrar of Baronetage? I see that I shall have to prepare a dossier on this Lawrence – Chapman business. Unfortunately, all my notes are with Kershaw in Paris — he was to have an interview with Collins to explain the situation, but though he can make it clear to common sense I doubt if he can do so to Law. (Can I?)

It strikes me that I should also enquire after the will of William Chapman (b. 1811) the father of Thomas Robert, and also of the Bart who immediately preceded T.R. — and I find I haven't recorded his name in my text.[1] Also the will of the 5th Bart, Sir Montague Richard Chapman, who died childless in 1907. But these wills, I suppose, were proved in Ireland, and may have been destroyed during the "troubles." [2]

But if T. R. Chapman – Lawrence inherited under the will of his father and/or his immediate predecessor then he must be named in those wills. Question is, did he — could he — do a Jekyll and Hyde, be Lawrence in Oxford and Chapman for legal purposes in Dublin? Surely a dangerous game, and a situation destructive of all peace of mind.

The Registrar's letter, if it does not legally prove, informs us that Lady Chapman was alive in 1924. Consequently T. R. Chapman – Lawrence (unless bigamously) could not have married Sarah Junner. All search for their (T.R.C.'s and Sarah's) marriage certificate has drawn blank. As Lady C. was married in 1873, she must have been an old woman in 1924, i.e. supposing her only 21 at the time of marriage, she would then be 72. But apparently her successful rival still persists at the age of 91. It would help a good deal if she would join the majority. Will you emulate the singular habit of Lord Kitchener, who (according to Liddell Hart) had "the Oriental habit of keeping his ear to the ground" and play the Orientalist to Oxford for any rumours of the old lady's decease? That would leave me only the professor and the missionary to deal with on that front.[3] [. . .]

This dismal situation in Africa has surely been largely provoked by Malan's imitation of Jim Crow laws.[4] Incidently, it throws a new light on the Boer War, and gives some weight to what I often heard from heroes of that epoch, i.e. that it was only British victory which saved the Hottentots and Basutos from extermination by the Bible-reading Boers. In the matter of Tunisia and Morocco I can't help noting that American enthusiasm for their "independence" coincides with French discoveries of petrol in both countries and the near completion of the great hydro-electric dams in Morocco — built entirely by French engineers and, I think, with French money. These would be "nationalised" on the lines discovered by the backers of Mossadegh, and eventually find their way into the clutches of American big business. I think this self-determination of small nations may be overdone. Until French occupation north Africa was a haunt of pirates and slave-dealers for centuries. When the French occupied Tunis in 1880 there was not one bridge remaining and only about 10 kilometres of discernable road. The enormous olive groves are entirely due to the French. If these countries and such areas as Burma, Eritreia, Syria and even Argentina are allowed to lapse into a state of bad government and even barbarism, the world will be permanently impoverished. So far as American "idealism" goes, the French have exactly the same right to be in Morocco and Tunis as the Americans have to be in Texas, New Mexico, Arizona, Colorado and California — the very names show they were taken by force from the Mexicans, who form an oppressed minority. In Yuma, Ariz. (where huge bill boards advertise snappy marriages by the competing Sheriff and Parsons, including the hire of costume, "dignified service" and hotel accommodation) Mexicans, Indians and Negroes keep wholly together and never mix with whites. From Uvalde, Tex. right to the Atlantic, in the states of Louisiana, Mississippi, Georgia, Florida, N. and S. Carolina, Virginia, I have myself seen countless times the notice in "diners" — "Colored Custom Not Solicited." What right have such people to criticise the French and English? Of course I think the Wog and Gippo attitude of the second rate Britisher and (especially) his female have done us enormous harm. No doubt the traders were even worse.

Ever yours,

RICHARD ALDINGTON

1 Benjamin Rupert Chapman (d 1914).
2 Bird secured copies of these wills in 1953.
3 That is, T. E. Lawrence's two surviving brothers.
4 RA refers to the advocacy of apartheid and white supremacy during the ministry of Malan in the Union of South Africa.

34

22 November 1952   *Montpellier*

DEAR BIRD,

Ever so many thanks for the Baronetage letter, which has an official look anyway. [. . .] I have been re-reading the law of libel, and it seems to me that almost any slightly critical statement will be "defamatory" in English law, and as the law presumes that "publication" implies that the writer intended malice and that it has damaged the plaintiff . . . ! I don't think people realise how the law of libel and law of "obscenity" have been carefully warped during the last 150 years to act as a hidden censorship of books. (I got one in on Jix in a report when I think will please you . . . "D. H. Lawrence, whom we all now know to have been the greatest English writer of this century.")[1]

There is only one way of dealing with this — American. [. . .] But consider the advantages of American publication. A serial, if I can get it, will be seen by tens of millions instead of tens of thousands and paid for proportionately. My Wellington[2] sold 25,000 in USA. It is not wildly optimistic to hope for 50,000 for a rich story of Briddish 'ristocratic degenracy. [. . .] May these not be counting chickens! — for many "ifs" are involved. The Professor and his English lawyer will first have difficulty in raising the dollars to fight an action in USA, and they will probably be unaware of the fact that in USA the law of libel is not Federal but State, and as nearly all the big newspapers and publishers function from N.Y. the law of libel has moved in exactly the opposite direction to that of England. The last thing they would do is rubber stamp the decision of an English court. [. . .] Therefore, I think my plan must be to refuse battle in England pro tem, [. . .] and (the gods being favourable) suddenly confront them [. . .] with the fait accompli of an American edition. What can they do? I am in France and can't be extradited for libel. Further, with an American edition published I can negotiate translations and other foreign rights with a great advantage. [. . .]

Meanwhile I am trying to get hold of a copy of the script to send you. I could send you my own original, but it has many ink write-ins and many alterations have since been made. I don't think Chapman and Junner married bigamously. There were too many people in the know, and his wife might have been vindictive. Do you know Lionel Curtis of All Souls? [. . .] If you care to look up the TEShaw – Charlotte Shaw letters in the B.M. you will discover that the reason Sarah Junner doesn't live with her sons is that they can't bear her! Or so TE says in one of his letters. One of his main reasons for joining up was that she couldn't follow him to a barrack room! I've sent a copy of that letter to Jix who were most indignant at my saying that Momma had disgusted TE with Jesus — his own words![3] What a mess. [. . .]

I've read Hickey[4] and a splendidly pompous Life of Lord Wellesley,[5] but missed Valentia.[6] He sounds very nice. I so much like these (alas extinct) English and Irish who had some originality of character and dared to be it. Salt and Belzoni I had come across in reading of Egyptian archaeology — early days. I once thought of doing an essay on Belzoni, but realised I didn't know enough. Your story of Valentia and Botany reminds me of a courteous and deserved rebuke I got from the Professor of Botany at Coimbra in 1931. I had heard much of Coimbra's botanic garden and, having seen the marvellous plantations of trees at Bussaco (the Duke[7] took me there, of course) I promised myself a great treat. Well, the Professor took me round himself, most civil, explained, and I was very happy and interested. As we parted I congratulated him on having such a magnificent and valuable garden. "Yes," he said, "But you haven't seen one plant or tree you couldn't have seen at Kew!" I must say I felt a tripper and an intruder. [. . .]

I am laid up with bronchitis — your letter a great consolation.

Ever yours,
RICHARD ALDINGTON

1 See above, letter 30 n 1; see below, letter 67 n 7.

2 *The Duke, Being an Account of the Life & Achievements of Arthur Wellesley, 1st Duke of Wellington* (1943).

3 T. E. Lawrence to Charlotte F. Shaw [Karachi] 14 Apr 1927; see T. E. Lawrence to Charlotte F. Shaw [Karachi] 18 Aug 1927, 8 May 1928.

4 Thomas Hickey *East Indian Chronologist* [2 parts 1801–02].

5 There are several.

6 George, Viscount Valentia [and H. Salt] *Voyages and Travels to India, Ceylon, The Red Sea, Abyssinia, and Egypt* (3 vols 1809).

7 That is, work on the Duke of Wellington.

35

9 *December 1952*   *Montpellier*

MY DEAR BIRD,

Your letters are always a great pleasure, and the talk by Toynbee you send is another.[1] It is really intelligent. *Of course* he is right about Russia and — well, I wish you had read my book on TEL for you will now be persuaded that my remarks on Eastern nationalism and its stimulation by the Lawrence faction were added after reading Toynbee! Lawrence, as you say, was unimportant, but he was the tool of a Foreign Office clique so powerful that they apparently defied even Curzon. When Lowell Thomas made Lawrence a journalistic hero that F.O. set backed it. One of the points made in my book is this. Lowell Thomas in his blundering American way lets us know that before he brought his film-lecture to England he (jokingly) insisted he must meet George V and be given Covent Garden to lecture in. *Both conditions were met.* How? Why? Could the obscure impresario, Barton, by himself have got Covent Garden and, O altitudo!, have persuaded the King to give a private interview to a Yankee showman? There is much more behind this TELawrence fraud than I can either discover or prove. But I am sure he was the tool of Foreign Office faction, who have done enormous harm in the Middle East both to us and to the natives. But I am too ignorant to deal with the problem, and can only hope that it will be taken up by more competent writers. [. . .]

Of course I should go to London and confront them. But even here I have been near the undertaker with bronchities, and London in a winter like this might be fatal. If it were not that America is no place for educating a child I should be somewhere south of Sarasota, the one place in the last 25 years where I have passed two winters without even a sneeze.[2] Florida! that was really a paradise. And do you know what happened? The war department planted a camp of 15,000 of the vilest town Americans who soon sowed vulgarity and syphilis over a land which in 1941 was an unspoiled as when Columbus didn't discover the American mainland. [. . .]

I am not counting on any American dollars from the Lawrence book — what I wrote was a glimpse of possibilities. At the moment I am working daily on a short book (which perhaps I mentioned) of personal recollections of Norman Douglas, Pino Orioli, and their and my publisher Charles Prentice of Chattos — all dead.[3] This of course has no vulgar appeal like the TEL book, but I think we might get off 500 copies to friends.

Malapropos — my friend Kershaw, who has been most kind in helping with these Collins people, express-lettered me this morning urging me to reply mildly to Collins's last letter. I answered him (express) in the words of the great Algernon Charles,[4] that I had been perfectly courteous and merely remarked that he (Collins) was grinning and girning like a Barbary ape from a perch of his own finding and fouling.

And again malapropos — I wonder if Oxford has preserved any recollection of Charles Prentice? He was an Oriel man and a classic, and for some reason I never discovered hated Shadwell so much that he (Prentice) absolutely refused either to read Pater or to hear a word in his favour![5] I never found out why. Anyway, Prentice was a wonderful person, and I'm trying to give some indication of his quality in this little book. He had a tragic end. After making Chattos easily the best publishers in England Prentice sold out at about 40 (on inheriting from his wealthy Scotch father) and transported himself to Greece where the American ambassador,[6] also a Grecian, was a crony of his. Somewhere round Sparta I think Charles picked up a mysterious illness, and the London quacks quite literally did everything expensive from taking out all his teeth to cutting his appendix. It turned out to be a simple dysentery after Harley St had robbed him of thousands. Next, he did what only a very innocent and great-hearted man would have done — he allowed himself to be vamped by the wife of his younger brother, who of course hadn't a quarter of Charles's money, and bolted with her, in spite of my advice to fuck her and say nothing about it. Then came the war, and the best publisher in England had to avoid conscription by working for Alan Lane! By God. Then that woman dragged him through every black market, got him and herself arrested and expelled from Ireland, and finally killed him by insisting on a man with a weak heart going to Kenya. None of this will come into my book, for I deal only with the happy days. What a tragedy. But for that vamp Charles would still be living and telling me what a bad writer Pater is. He was the only really educated publisher I knew. And such a good man. I once persuaded a Parisian friend of mine, a chef, to give Charles his private speciality of roast duck and chopped mushroom sauce. This was on his way to Greece. When he came through Paris on his way back I asked if he had liked that dinner, and he said, "Why, yes, Richard, more than once when dining on tough goat and sour bread I thought of that mushroom sauce." [. . .]

I read George Barker, and note that in BBC England "enigmas" rhymes with "stars" and "give" with "disbelieve",[7] also that doggerel is for reasons of "anarchy" now called poetry. Talking of which, I have now infuriated many cultured friends because they cannot guess what 19th century author wrote the line:

"Spell-bound within the clustering cyclades."[8]

I tried it on E. Pound, knowing of course that he would be stumped, and that he had forgotten he had cribbed it with "Came Beauty barefoot from the Cyclades." I had betted myself ten dollars he would quote himself, and he did! Was not our friend Voltaire right when he said les imbeciles nous sont donnés pour nos menus plaisirs?

I have twice read the article on Salt with much pleasure.[9] Those were our real spacious days — would they might come again! May I keep the paper a little longer, for I want to make some notes before returning it, in case I ever have the cheek to write on Belzoni. Have you ever been to the Hans Sloan (or is it Soane)

Museum where that marvellous Egyptian sarcophagous is?[10] I think it better than any in the B.M. or Louvre, most beautiful. Seti Ist. It is so beautiful, and nobody ever went there, at least in pre-1938 days. After which I know nothing of Angleterre, except the old song everyone is now singing here with the refrain: "Et merde a la Reine d'Angleterre!"

Ever yours,
RICHARD ALDINGTON

[1] Probably "Turning Point in the Cold War?" published in *International Affairs* (Oct 1950).

[2] RA was at Jamay Beach, Nokomis, Florida from 6 Mar 1941 to shortly after 23 May 1941 and again from about 1 Aug 1941 to the end of Aug 1942.

[3] *Pinorman.*

[4] That is, Algernon Charles Swinburne.

[5] Shadwell, Provost of Oriel College, edited Pater's *Green Studies* (1895), *Miscellaneous Studies* (1895) and others.

[6] Lincoln MacVeagh.

[7] See "Letter to a Young Poet" stanzas 4 and 10.

[8] Byron; see below, letter 36.

[9] A pamphlet by M. Bryn-Davis, privately printed in the 30s.

[10] Sir John Soane purchased from Salt, in 1824, the alabaster sarcophagus which Belzoni found in 1817 in the sepulchre of Seti I. The British Museum had refused the sarcophagus; it is now a principal exhibit of the Soane Museum. Sir Hans Sloane (1660–1753) was a British physician and naturalist.

36

26 December 1952   *M'pellier*

DEAR BIRD,

Your letter of the 19TH, para first, very exciting. Strangely enough, my friend Kershaw had suggested that TRChapman might have been a member of the University — this to account for the stories of 50,000 books. I rather brushed this off on the theory (a) that TRC was only a fox-hunting squireen (though this was not incompatible with an Oxford career in the 1860s!) and (b) that if he had been an Oxonian he would hardly have transported self, concubine and bastards thither, where at any time he risked being identified by someone who knew him as TRC and knew that his wife was alive. But if he really took books from the Union Library as TRC it thickens the plot and shows the extraordinary impudence of the family. I await the letter from the Steward with the utmost interest and impatience. If TRC was at Oxford, then, as he was born in 1846, his residence would be — at the extreme — between 1863 and 1870. Are there alphabetical lists of undergraduates for each year covering the whole University or are they arranged by Colleges? It would be staggering if you found that the old man has been to Jesus![1] But is it possible that any Oxford authorities of the period 1890–1910 would have connived at such turpitude? In fact, Miss Sarah Junner (as I prefer pro tem to call Mrs TRLawrence) says they moved to Oxford in Sept 1896. If we take 1865 as a sort of basic year for TRC's residence, then surely only 30 years later there would have been people in Oxford who remembered him?

This Library evidence may be important, for the whole book is held up on the question of legal proof that TRL was TRC. If we can prove that TRL signed for books as TRC we are at least a step forward.[2]

I think myself that Ireland is the place, and I should much like to know if proven Wills were destroyed in Yeats's troubles. If not, there would be much interest in these wills: all post-elopement:

(a) Sir Benjamin James C. Died 1888.
(b) William C. of South Hall, Delvin, father of TRC, who died 1889.
(c) Sir Montague Richard of Killua who died 1907.
(d) Sir Benjamin Rupert who died 22 March 1914, and was succeeded by Thomas Robert Tighe; 7th and last Bart.[3]

Some one or more of these must have willed TRC the "Irish money" Lawrence speaks of,[4] and also must have deprived him of Killua and South Hall. At any rate after TRC's death Killua was occupied by his sister, Caroline Margaret, who in 1894 married Sir Montague Richard, 5th Bart. As we know from the Baronetage people Edith Sarah Chapman [5] was alive as late as 1924, and living at South Hall,[6] the residence of her deceased father-in-law William C.

I am finishing my Douglas–Orioli–Prentice book,[7] and now learn from Douglas's literary executor (who is K. Macpherson, as you said) that Norman left instructions that he did not wish his letters to be published! This means that I shall have to paraphrase the information and cancel my proposed reproduction of a facsimile letter. However, I have a scrap of mediaeval German in Norman's handwriting, and they can't stop me reproducing that. The Nibelungen Lied is, I believe, out of copyright and there is no copyright in handwriting. Macpherson is taking his position very seriously, and seems to think he has the right (I quote) "to revise and censor" any book written on N.D., and is proposing to do this to a book by Nancy Cunard.[8] I have not told him, but he has no more right to do such a thing than the Archbishop or a tinker's mate. If he has written authority from N.D. to prohibit letters he may do so, but he can't stop me, for instance, giving, as my own, information from the letters I have. He can also forbid quotes from N's copyright books but only if they are of a certain length. "Reasonable citation for purposes of comment" is permitted without formal concurrence of heirs and executors. Jix seems to have given me his clearance on all my TEL quotes which are numerous but brief. I hold myself that 7 Ps is not copyright. The original edition broke the law in having no printer's name, and sending no copies to the B.M. and Bodleian. It is therefore as much in the public domain as Ulysses and Lady C. The book TEL by his Friends,[9] which I have quoted extensively, is also out of control of the Lawrence Estate. Their clever agent,[10] to get more money for the Lawrence charities (whatever they may be — AWL?)[11] persuaded the writers to give their work for nothing. You cannot transfer a copyright without a consideration, so the copyright remains vested in the authors.

The "Spell-bound within the clustering Cyclades" is a catch, which nobody I have asked has yet eluded. It is from Byron's Corsair! [12] Pound guessed Lascelles Abercrombie!

I had a different version of that Aldous [13] story from Prentice. No Swinnerton came in. The two first Aldous's were published by Charles without Spalding seeing them. S. then read a flaming attack somewhere, and read the 3rd book — came roaring into the office in a fury next day, and Charles and Raymond had a week's misery calming him down. Did Swinnerton read for Chattos? [14]

In haste, and looking for the news from the Union Library,

Ever yours,
RICHARD ALDINGTON

[1] The University Registry, Oxford, has no record of anyone named T. R. Chapman as a member of the University after 1715.

[2] T. R. Lawrence was known to the librarians of the Library, Oxford Union Society, by no name other than Lawrence. He was a member of the Society from 1901 to 1919.

[3] The wills of all these members of the Chapman family except the last, Thomas Robert Tighe Chapman, are on file in the Public Record Office of Ireland.

[4] See above, letter 31 n 2.

[5] Wife of Sir Thomas Robert Tighe Chapman, 7th Bart.

[6] At Delvin, County Westmeath, Ireland.

[7] *Pinorman.*

[8] *Grand Man: Memories of Norman Douglas* (1954).

[9] 1937.

[10] Raymond Savage.

[11] See "Preface" 6. "AWL" is Arnold Lawrence, T.E.'s younger brother.

[12] Canto iii, line 62.

[13] Aldous Huxley.

[14] Huxley's first two books, *The Burning Wheel* (1916) and *The Defeat of Youth* (1918), were published by Blackwell. Chatto & Windus published the next three: *Limbo* and *Leda* (both 1920) and *Crome Yellow* (1921). Prentice, Raymond, and Spalding were associated with Chatto & Windus, for whom Frank Swinnerton read.

37

12 January 1953   *Montpellier*

DEAR BIRD,

It is indeed disappointing that this clinching legal evidence seems always just to elude us. I still think that Oxford is a promising hunting ground, and there must be some document giving TRC the right to take out books. Did you not tell me that a friend of yours said the books were taken out in the name of Chapman? If so, (1) the Library could testify that TR Lawrence was known to him as TRChapman, and (2) the Library must have his signature. [. . .]

John Holroyd-Reece, 24 Old Buildings, Lincolns Inn, was supposed to be taking up the quest for Collins and me, and I was hoping he would carry out my suggestion of getting in touch with you to join forces. It is obvious that you can make enquiries without causing suspicion, and as an ex-don get much more attention.[1] Holroyd-Reece is not a barrister but the publisher of Albatross Continental books. He was a yeomanry officer on Barrow's staff and saw that horror at Deraa.

I am suggesting to Alister Kershaw, who is dealing with the business side of all this for me, that he send you my original script which he has. I am hoping to go ahead with the American edition, and I can't do that until I have your corrections. In this script the references are included in the text, but in the book will be collected (with an identifying number to each) at the end of each chapter. The script has a good many pen alterations and may be troublesome to read, I fear, but in spite of the fact that all quotes from the Shaw – Shaw letters have had to be paraphrased, it is substantially the same as the final text. If you will be so kind as to make your notes on separate sheets, quoting always page of the script, I can use them for the American proofs. And if Holroyd-Reece appeals to you I do beg you will give him the assistance you have so generously given me.

My Douglas – Orioli book went off to Heinemann on Tuesday. Frere, who knew them both well, wrote a very pleasant letter of acknowledgement, but was going to take the script to the country over the week-end. I fear very much there will be another battle of libel and copyright there. You are quite right — it is not Willie King but Kenneth MacPherson —[2]

> "Fairshon swore a feud
> Against the clan M'Tavish . . ."

and he will do his damndest to stop my using N.D.'s letters and quotes from his books. [. . .]

I wish you could manage to run down here some time. It's a humble sort of place, but we keep body and soul together — they gave me a very decent bottle of 1937 Macon at lunch today.

I know nothing of Maundy Gregory.

Quite wonderful not to have the worry of a book on hand. I have plunged into Italian again, reading Burckhardt and J. A. Symonds, and looking up the originals they quote whenever I have them. Talking of which! — do you know ANY *book-seller* who is likely to have texts of Italian humanists and Latin poets? I had a very nice collection, and like a complete cretin, sold them about 1930, to get freedom from two tons of books, which I should have stored. I particularly want either the Toscanus [3] or Gherus [4] anthologies — Deliciae Poetarum Italorum — or that magnificent 11 vols collection published in Florence early 18th century,[5] forget the exact title. Pino once offered it me for two pounds (gold) and I refused — triple idiot!

I must to the post — have not been out since Tuesday when I caught a slight chill but fought it off.

Adieu!

RICHARD ALDINGTON

1 Bird was never a don at Oxford, a fact which he was careful to tell RA. See Alan Bird to MJB, Halsall, Ormskirk, Lancashire, 18 Nov 1972.

2 That is, Norman Douglas's literary executor.

3 Joannes Matthaeus Toscannus *Carmina illustrium poetarum Italorum* (1576).

4 Ranutius Gherus *Delitiae C.C. Italorum poetarum, hijus superiorisque aevi illustrium* (1608).

5 *Carmina illustrium poetarum Italorum* collected and edited by Giovanni Gaetano Bottari (1719–26).

38

29 January 1953   *Montpellier*

DEAR BIRD,

I have friends in the pension, and must be brief.

Have you received the copy of my original script of TEL? It is the only one available, and I am most anxious to have your comments and corrections, to have on hand for correcting the proofs. It is possible that the final version differs verbally from that sent you, but all facts are the same, and it is those — especially on the mid-East — which need attention. I must alter the part about the Union Library in view of what you turned up. It is very singular that the old man joined the library when TEL was only 9, considering that TEL says somewhere his father never opened a book.[1] If they were as poor as TEL says how could they afford 10 guineas for such an unremunerative not to say unChristian diversion as reading? TRL left 17,800 pounds — all to Sarah. She must have divided it into four equal shares or at any rate have given TEL his quarter, since he clearly had between 4000 and 5000 soon after demobilisation.

Kershaw — who sent you the script — is among those here and says Holroyd-Reece and Jix are confident they will find the missing piece of evidence. They are searching now for a TRTChapman signature and I think their first enquiry is for the register of marriages in Westmeath. They have found out the parish, and if the Protestant church still exists and has its register, there you are. They have had copies of several wills, but nothing has turned up. They (Jix) express surprise that Louisa Vansittart C. (TRTC's mother) seemingly left no will. But she died in 1877, before the Married Women's Property Act of 1882, and therefore perhaps could not make a will. TRTC's money may still have come to him from her through a Marriage Settlement, and seemingly there is no way to get hold of this. [. . .]

No passport was needed for Europe pre-1914. I myself spent the first 6 months of 1913 travelling in Italy and had no "papers" but letters and visiting cards. No trouble at all. Between wars, at least in 1922, about the time when Sarah went to Palestine and then to China, one got a passport without birth certificate. I am sure of this, for I never saw my birth certificate until last year when I had to produce it to get a passport for my daughter — to prove that she is the British-born child of a ditto father! A maniacal cousin of mine who studies our genealogy had at that moment sent me a copy of the will of a Richard Aldington (said by her to be our ancestor) who died about 1540 — I thought of adding that as an additional proof that we are not mitteleuropean refugee Jews. So I fear there is no hope in the passport line. *Now* of course S. Lawrence would have to prove her identity, but not then. I seem to recollect that my wife got a passport about 1938 without being asked for any document beyond the usual form.

Apparently MacPherson could have stopped me from using my letters from N.D. The material letters belong to me but the copyright belongs to the N.D. Estate, and N.D. left instructions that no letters may be issued without MacPherson's permission. Luckily he is trying to persuade Heinemann to issue a silly "Tribute," and Frere who is very clever got his consent to my using the letters, but I have to let him read them. I have now asked Frere what we must do about the less important problem of letters from Orioli and Prentice. If Davis is executor I have a slight hold because Pino pinched (and probably sold) the script of my novel, The Colonel's Daughter,[2] for which I have a receipt somewhere! [. . .]

All the things you say about TEL seem to indicate that we see very much eye to eye on that topic. I have been trying to get hold of Bray, but nothing has yet reached me. As he was actually in what little fighting there was, he might be useful. Of course TEL did not plan Akaba — you will find all the evidence I could bring together in the chapter on that instructive little episode in the career of a hero.[3] The book you have in mind is probably Antonius, The Arab Awakening.[4] It is weakened by being so obviously pro-Arab propaganda. [. . .]

In view of TEL's propaganda about how important he was to the French and his hint that they "probably" stole the version of 7 Ps. which he "lost" at Reading,[5] you will be amused to know that apart from a routine report to the Guerre by one of Brémond's subordinates, NOTHING on Lawrence exists in the French archives. If there was a Sureté dossier it is no longer there, for M. Delarue [6] looked for it himself, but added that the Germans destroyed many dossiers. I don't see why they should destroy TEL unless he was marked as pederast — which is highly likely.

Tragedy! The chef has flu!

Adieu,

RICHARD ALDINGTON

[1] See above letter 36 n 2; see also, T. E. Lawrence to Charlotte F. Shaw [Karachi] 14 Apr 1927.

[2] 1931.

[3] See RA *Lawrence of Arabia* 186–87, 190–93.

[4] George Antonius *The Arab Awakening; The Story of the Arab National Movement* (1938).

[5] See RA *Lawrence of Arabia* 315; Graves *Lawrence and the Arabs* 406; Liddell Hart *Colonel Lawrence* 325. Also see above, letter 18 n 21.

[6] A member of the Sureté who was a friend of Alister Kershaw.

39

4 February 1953   *Montpellier*

DEAR BIRD,

[. . .] I think this discovery of Montague Robert Junner's birth certificate important.[1] We had searched everywhere and failed to find it because we looked under *Lawrence!* The identification of the two Montagu Roberts — Chapman and Lawrence — is not so difficult. First we have the fact that in the will of Caroline Chapman [2] (d. 1911) a sum of about 20,000 was bequeathed to Thomas Robert Chapman and one of the trustees was Charles Athill Stanuell, who was also an executor and trustee under the Will of Thomas Robert Lawrence. Second, the Will of Thomas Robert Lawrence gives the name of his eldest son as Montague Robert — surely impossible as a coincidence? Especially since in TEL by his Friends M. Robert Lawrence says he was born 2 yrs and 8 months before TEL. 2.8 before Aug 1888 brings us to *December 1885!* *Another* coincidence, m' lud and gentlemen of the Jury? I think you've found it. But I think Jix and Holroyd-Reece should also get photostats of the original declarations of birth of the 4 daughters of TRTC and his wife, and of William George and "Frank" (Qu Francis?) Lawrence killed in 1915.[3] These should give plenty of signatures and show the similarity of his methods in true and false declarations. Note he cannot abandon the petty snobbery of "gentleman" even when safety counselled its danger. Note also that we have in this certificate a third family name for Sarah — in this case Lawrence or Laurence (spelling immaterial) which is also suggestive. I think that document on top of the others plus the signatures cooks the Lawrence goose no matter how hostile the Court might be. You can have one or two coincidences — you can't have a score.

Odd fact — although "Will" and "Frank" were both killed in 1915, the Will of 1917 includes Will as a beneficiary!

The will was witnessed by Ernest Barker of New College, who conceivably might have been an old friend and have been the recommender to the Union Library — but was he a Fellow in 1897? [4] Not worth looking up.

It is most kind of you to be reading my script, especially since it is so mangled by write-ins. I much want to hear if you think I have been unfair to TE anywhere and if you think any of the little jokes misplaced. I felt that a subject so arid entitled the author to a grin or two, but there has been criticism of both these points. It is suggested I under-rate TEL as archaeologist, but how can one rate an archaeologist whose sole contribution to the science is $2\frac{1}{2}$ chapters in the Wilderness of Zin,[5] those chiefly topographical? The lazy little bastard (literally!) never troubled to write any paper on Carchemish. True, there are his gifts to the Ashmolean, but are they claimed as his discoveries? The only other evidence is Woolley's rather damaging recollections. As a soldier he has been grotesquely overrated, and I think I have listed any action he really did take, but much of his time was spent with his theatrical costumier in Cairo dressing for the part. And I think I've leaned back to praise his writing. Certainly I think 7 Ps. immensely over-praised, for it is strained, insincere and rhetorical throughout; and in my opinion The Mint is dull. I heard lately that an American publisher has refused it as unlikely to sell! I'm sure it won't, even in England. It irritated me by beginning with a palpable lie. He represents himself as starved for 6 months, having lived on meals cadged by hanging outside Clubs, so much so that the M.O. notices his emaciation. Also his boot has split at the welt. Up to within a few weeks before enlistment he had been receiving 1200 a year from the Col. Office, had received at least 4000 under his father's will, owned a 200-guineas motor bike, an expensive gold wrist watch, and at least 1000 books, plus 200 a year from All Souls! If such a person had starved for 6 months he is either a liar or a bloody idiot who ought to have been incarcerated.

Your letter cheered me immensely — and the chef is back in the front line again!

Adieu,
RICHARD

[1] That is, T. E. Lawrence's presumed older brother Bob.
[2] That is, T. E. Lawrence's presumed aunt.
[3] Younger brothers of T. E. Lawrence.
[4] Yes.
[5] See above, letter 8 n 9.

40

11 February 1953   *Montpellier*

DEAR BIRD,

You are the kindest and most generous of men! The information in your notes will be of the greatest service, and save me from that tripping-up-with-trifles which is the speciality of such journals as the famous Suppresio-Veri-Suggestio-Falsi, alias The London *Times*. [. . .] I have phone calls and letters, all suggesting that your miraculous discovery of the Montague Robert Chapman – Lawrence – Maden – Junner certificate is the clincher.[1] How can I ever thank you? You must come down here, and let me try to amuse you with Romanesque, Mistral, the Camargue, and so forth.

Your comments are perfect. I cannot tell you how glad I am to take informed criticism. What I object to is criticism, so-called, which is simply ignorance and malice, or the fault-finding of a piqued genius — [. . .]

What I am longing to read is the "reaction" of that pompous fraud Liddell Hart. The Times has made him such an authority that in to-day's Figaro he is cited as the Man Who Knew Rommell Best! [2] Do I wrong him if I ask where and when he heard the guns begin to roll? In the script you have, I think I call him a-penny-a-Maginot-liner, which (alas!) Jix has vetoed.

All I ask is a free ring and no favour. I'll take correction from any man who knows better than I do. But The Times has repeatedly published insulting and inaccurate letters denigrating me, and contemptuously refused to publish my rejoinders. I had a knock-out for old Edie Sitwell, and What Price Jones [3] wouldn't publish it! Why? Need I ask?

Every hen is busy with her own tail feathers, as DHL rightly reminds us, but I believe this Lawrence book is much more than a mere biography — it is the showing up and repudiation of a whole phase of our national life with Winston at the head. True, *he* is a hero, but . . . Our life as a nation must *not* be based on lies and liars, on slick "policies." We must have the truth. And I am deeply grateful to you for all you have done and are doing to help me tell it.

Roy! More anon. He is a bull-fighter, and is there not a Chinese proverb that to seek the sacred personage of the Emperor in a low tea house is hypocrisy? [4]

Ever yours,
RICHARD ALDINGTON

P.S. When you return script, please send it to me here, not to Kershaw.

1 See above, letters 7, 30, 33 and 36.
2 "Liddel Hart L'Anglais Qui Connait Le Mieux Rommel." The article is part of a discussion of *Carnets de Rommel* (1953).
3 That is Alan Payan Pryce-Jones, editor of *Times Literary Supplement*, 1948–59.
4 This paragraph is a response to a comment from Bird on Roy Campbell's defense of Spain's fascists. RA implies that nothing better can be expected from a bull-fighter. For RA's real regard for Campbell, see below, letter 130.

4 I

12 February 1953   *Montpellier*

DEAR BIRD,

I have been going over your notes this morning, and must tell you how grateful I am for the care with which you have read the book and your scholarly comments. I wish you could have had the final script, but the first Collins blunder was to take 3 months typing the book in only 2 copies, though I had asked for 4, however faint. Consequently, I have been forced to send you an uncorrected copy. I am almost certain most of those repetitions were cut out of the final script, but in any event I shall keep your notes by me when on the proofs — if these sluggards ever produce them. You must remember that a chapter which you read in ten minutes probably took three weeks to write. Consequently, it is very easy atfer a lapse of ten or twelve weeks to feel one must recall the reader's attention to a matter so important as that of L's writing parts of those biographies himself — a fact which Jix (who must be a personal friend of Liddell Hart) virtually denied until I shut him up with the evidence.[1] There has been a hidden battle going on, I am sure, behind the Collins–Jix scene, and only the appearance of the noble Holroyd-Reece on the scene got things started. I believe — but can't prove — that Jix plus someone in Collins's office are trying to sabotage the book in the interests of Hart.[2] He, you will note, comes forth as the great authority on Rommel (another phoney?) and Collins have made a packet out of Rommel's book.[3] The plain fact is that but for you and Holroyd-Reece the legal evidence would never have been found. Even so Collins have not yet started to set. It would do no good for me to come to London. I am impatient and quick-tempered, and as vain as most authors are, and there would only be a futile row. So I have to do the best I can via my friends. H.-R. and Alister Kershaw, who is supposed to see Collins this week and insist on immediate action. [. . .] Moreover, I want the Pinorman to come out after the TEL. Apropos — did I tell you I have permission from Macpherson to use N.D.'s letters?

I am still not clear about the part played by that thesis in winning honours for TEL. I have had to send Reece my copy of "TEL by his Friends" as he couldn't find one in London, but my memory is that Ernest Barker (evidently a close friend, as he witnessed TRLawrence's will) said that for that particular year or period men were allowed to submit a thesis in addition to the usual papers, and even if the papers were below par (as L's seem to have been) the thesis still might give honours.[4] Do you think we could get this cleared up? I did not repeat, (I think) — or did I? — because I don't altogether believe Graves's story that the Tutor and the Examiners gave a dinner celebration to Lawrence on his success.[5] It seems to me as absurd as the statement that there was nobody in Oxford at that time competent to review and mark L's thesis! [6]

I am very much puzzled by the discrepancy between the 1876 and 1879 dates, since I got the 1879 from Sayce's own Reminiscences, page 162:

"The result was a letter in the Academy (August 16, 1879) on 'The Origin of Early Art in Asia Minor' in which I formulated *for the first time* what is now one of the commonplaces of archaeology, and prophesied that the hieroglyphs attached to the Pseudo-Sesostris, which I hoped to examine shortly, would prove to be 'not Egyptian but Hittite.' "

True, on page 161 he speaks vaguely of having written "one or two papers on the subject" (i.e. Hittites) but he doesn't say he read or published them, and the phrase "for the first time" led me to think the Academy letter was the first statement. Which do you think is correct? [7]

I am anxious not to be unjust to Hogarth. I did not like him encouraging Lawrence to sneer at Petrie, who after all was a great figure in scientific field archaeology. Byzantine – Greek Dawkins told me that the real tyrant was Lady Petrie, who made the camp eat up all the tins of sardines before they were allowed to touch bully beef, and so forth. Petrie made everyone work as hard as he did, and that obviously would not suit the Bart's son from Westmeath. Then Hogarth's article on Egypt in the Wandering Scholar seemed to me full of absurd prejudices unworthy of a scholar. Finally, the fact that Gertrude Bell told the Carchemish camp that their methods were "pre-historic" compared with the Germans, and the fact that Hogarth evidently was always instructing Lawrence to buy "antikas" with no archaeological history from the natives suggested that he was the old type of museum-collector-archaeologist, not the scientific excavator like Woolley.[8] But

I discovered recently that he was with Grenfell and Hunt during the first year at Oxyrhynchus.[9] True, he wasn't there when they made the great discoveries, but if he selected the site and laid down the procedure to be followed, he obviously deserves all credit for it. Did you not tell me that there is no article on him in the DNB?[10] There is a fulsome and uninformative article in the Enc. Britt., "one of the greatest scholars and linguists of modern times" or words to that effect — so fulsome I suspect Lawrence wrote it. Anyway, the point is that I don't want either to do Hogarth an injustice or expose myself to the retort that he did so-and-so. In his Penetration of Arabia, he disclaims knowledge of Arabic.[11] Is this a piece of coquetry?

I am truly astonished to find that the word "frequented" is now used in a derogatory sense. There is no hint of this in the Shorter O.E.D., which is the only dictionary I have. I used the word in its basic sense, which is simply that of "resorting to." Lately I gave great offence by using "notorious" in its basic sense of "well known," without any implication of judgment one way or the other. I suppose that the newspapers continually pervert the language, and I miss these things owing to a 20 years absence and a plentiful lack of knowledge of English journalism. When on the very rare occasions that I go to Nice or Cannes and see such productions as the Daily Express, Sunday Despatch and so forth displayed in all their horror, I wonder if my countrymen know how such filthy publications misrepresent them to the outside world. Did you happen to see the Daily Mail Coronation Preview number? It was almost entirely made up of War, Factories, Money and Snobbery — a little Sport, and virtually nothing of art and science (except war-factory science) literature and religion, music and all the activities which lift us a little above the cannibals.

But of course the "frequented" shall be changed. I just didn't know it had any uncomplimentary implication.

What do you advise about the blazers? I think that L. wore them out of swank, and the fact that Hart makes such a point of the cricket-football association (in order to jeer at Petrie) surely justifies my taking the shorts-cum-blazer turn-out in the same sense?[12]

Garnett, I think, misled me about the date of L. and Newcombe "going on ahead."[13] I'm glad to have this put right. I think Garnett was conscientious and worked hard, but though he once or twice suspects his hero, he hastily puts it aside. When I told him I was going to undertake a life of TEL he wrote a letter in which rudeness contended with alarm. I wonder how much those Lawrence legend-makers knew they were fraudulent? Probably not at all — self-deception is so easy.

I think Storrs gives April 1914 as the date of Abdulla's visit to Cairo.[14]

I wrote so hurriedly yesterday that I don't remember if I told you I have got Macpherson's permission to print the Douglas letters, on the easy condition that I make an acknowledgement that they are published only "by special permission." Douglas wrote very indiscreet and indecent letters, which ought not to be published — couldn't be because they are often libellous.

Your later notes are eagerly awaited, especially on the Middle East section where ignorance may have betrayed me into blunders.

Ever yours,
RICHARD ALDINGTON

[1] See T. E. Lawrence to Charlotte F. Shaw [Karachi] 29 July 1927: "Graves sent his typescript, or the first ⅓ of it, and I had promised him to do what I could for him." See also T. E. Lawrence to Charlotte F. Shaw [Karachi] 3 Aug 1927: "Robert Graves has been sending me his book, by sections. . . . I correct little, excise little: add less." See also Graves's statement, "Lawrence read and passed every word of the book, though he asked me to put a sentence in my introduction making it seem that he had not" (*T. E. Lawrence to His Biographer Robert Graves* 1938 59.) See also, T. E. Lawrence to Charlotte F. Shaw [Karachi] 18 Aug 1927: "This book of Graves may be useful to me, in underlining errors of Lowell Thomas, and in unsaying some of the things which the Press have said, I've tried to use him, in that way. . . . Reading it [Graves's book] has been a misery for me. Every page of RG's own held inaccuracies. I corrected it till I was sick: and let as much more rip." See T. E. Lawrence to Patrick Knowles, Karachi, Jan 1928, where Lawrence writes of being "undressed in public" by Graves's "very kind" book. See also *T. E. Lawrence to His Biographer Liddell Hart* (1938) where, in the foreword, p iii, Liddell Hart wrote about his book *T. E. Lawrence: In Arabia and After:* "During its preparation he gave me the most generous help in the way of suggestign sources, answering questions, and commenting profusely on the successive drafts, as well as providing much light on himself in letters and conversations. But, at his wish, I refrained in my preface from disclosing the full extent of his help, lest the acknowledgment which I wished to make might be a cause of embarrassment to him in his relations with authority." See Liddell Hart "Preface" *Colonel Lawrence* vi and RA *Lawrence of Arabia* 108–09.

[2] RA was correct as far as "sabotage" was concerned, but it had not yet developed very far, and it came from sources outside Collins's office. See below, letters 59 n 15 and 60.

[3] *The Rommel Papers* ed B. A. Liddell Hart 1950.

[4] Barker (see *T. E. Lawrence by His Friends* 59–64) did not make this statement, and it has not been located elsewhere. Lawrence's thesis was submitted in the first year in which a written thesis in the Final History School was acceptable toward a degree (See Barker 61; E. T. Leeds 50–51, in *T. E. Lawrence by His Friends.*)

[5] Graves *Lawrence and The Arabs* 20.

[6] Richards *Portrait of T. E. Lawrence* . . . 55.

[7] See RA *Lawrence of Arabia* 76 and note, where RA solves the puzzle by recording a paper read by Sayce in 1876, one which he had obviously forgot. Sayce, in the preface to his *Reminiscences* (1923) comments on the fact that his memory is "no longer what it was in younger years."

[8] *Ibid* 77, 84–85; see also David G. Hogarth *A Wandering Scholar in The Levant* 153–78.

[9] Ancient ruined town of Egypt on the site of the present day Belmesa. A Greek colony during the Ptolemaic dynasty and later a Christian monastic city, Oxyrhynchus contained more than 20,000 monks and nuns. It was first excavated in 1896–97 and again in 1905–06 when important Greek papyri were discovered.

[10] Hogarth is listed in *DNB.*

[11] That statement has not been found in Hogarth's *The Penetration of Arabia* or *A Wandering Scholar.*

[12] See RA *Lawrence of Arabia* 85; Liddell Hart *Colonel Lawrence* 10.

[13] See RA *Lawrence of Arabia* 126, where the date of Lawrence's commission and entry in the British Army and his dispatch with Colonel S. F. Newcombe to Cairo are discussed. See also *Letters of T. E. Lawrence* 189.

[14] *Orientations* (1939) 156.

42

23 February 1953   *Montpellier*

DEAR BIRD,

C'en est fait, as the heroines of Racine say. Perhaps my letters have indicated that of late I have been in poor health. Anyway, a few days ago symptoms became so disagreeable that unwillingly — but my daughter was frightened — I called in a specialist in diagnosis. (Amusing but in Montpellier with its memories of Rabelais and Molière, the doctor at once friendly when he saw Mistral — which he quoted — on my bedside table.) Anyway, it is confirmed, my right lung is permanently infected with bronchitis, every cold will probably be bronchitis k.t.l. Moreover, as a result of overwork, sitting too long at desk, nervous irritation over Collins and the rest, my digestion is upset, and he suspects some displacement of organs . . . Forgive my dwelling on so disgusting a subject, but this will excuse the delay in answering your last letters. TEL has his revenge! Anyway, no operation is threatened. I am to wear a belt and be observed. O wearisome condition of humanity!

Talking of change in the meaning of words, how about these phrases which caught my eye in a letter of Jowett, March 1863:

". . . my name (which is getting notorious)"

". . . the kindness and support of friends and *pupils* . . ."

I think I have cleared up — at least to myself — the "joining" Jesus Coll. It is of course Army. We speak of an officer "joining" or "rejoining" his unit from cadet school, depot, detachment, leave. But I should have said "entered" J.C. I have not yet solved the "frequented," but I shall work out some periphrase. How much has the degradation of language been deliberate, how much the unforseen result of universal elementary education, yellow newspapers, advertising, propaganda, demagogues, dictators? My own observations so far as America goes lead me to think it is deliberate. What we mean by "culture" has no more drafty, more dangerous and more despicable enemy than Americanism. As to Russianism I can't speak, for I know nothing about it, but I suspect that Russia and America are simply head and tail of the same coin. Each secretly admires and wants to imitate the other. The Russians want America's technology, industry and wealth; Americans want Russia's autocracy and control of satellites. (Can't spell!) The occasional furious insulting of France or England in the US press is mainly due to the fact that they will not blindly accept and admire Americanism as the Italians seem to do — though I am told there is resistance even there. Had you realised that the much-trumpeted performance of Porgy and Bess in Paris [1] is due to the fact that Frenchmen will not any more frequent night-clubs with American Negro jazz bands, but insist on Cuban and S. American mambas and rhumbas?

Before I was shot into bed by this last upset I had an interesting (to me) experience here. You must know that the Musée Fabre has lately given an exhibition of Bourdelle (we now have some contemporary Italians, not much good) and a small papeterie had pinned up a photograph of Bourdelle's Beethoven. Just underneath was an ordinary picture post-card of the Louvre Antinöus. It was the most startling lesson in values I ever received. I can't tell you how the vulgarity, meaningless emphasis and "expression" of the Bourdelle were exposed by the strength, distinction and nobility of the Antinöus. Yet Beethoven was an infinitely greater person than the Bithynian slave, and the age of Hadrian was the very twilight of Hellenic art. In trying to give his "impression" of Beethoven as an "âme sombre" and a "génie puissant" Bourdelle makes him look like a sulky nigger in a Bernini wig. Whereas Antinöus suddenly seemed worth all the Christs and gentlemen who have ever been painted or sculpted — but this is nonsense. The experience made a great impression on me, and I thought about it much afterwards, without however being able to say anything to the point.

At last we have real spring with soft airs as well as blue skies. When are you coming this way? There are some interesting environs, and the place is not expensive.

To-morrow my friend and representative, Kershaw, is having a solemn interview — complete with stenographer! — with Collins in Paris; and I shall indeed be relieved if all this nonsensical delay is ended. I suspect much occult pressure on Collins from outside as well as sabotage from his own office. Liddell Hart, I am told, is an intimate friend of C's foremost "literary" adviser. And until Holroyd-Reece arrived in London, Jix was obviously trying to kill the book by raising every possible objection. If I have not lost it I shall someday show you Jix's first list of "libels" on Graves, Hart and Thomas, whereby the slightest criticism of them or exposure of their misstatements was assumed to be a mere gratuitous expression of my uninstructed opinion and hence a libel. When I urged that my book contained a rather careful list of the evidence on which my text was based they replied that they did not happen to own a large library of T. E. Lawrence books! I think this gives some measure of the abuse and mistreatment I must expect if ever a reasonably complete version of the book gets published in England. I think the reaction will be violent, unscrupulous, and both immediate and successful, until time vindicates the essential truth of what I've said. I think most of the press will be hostile, not to say venemous, and as I have dared the law of libel in publishing I can hardly call on it myself. Holroyd-Reece — dear fellow! — hopes for serialisation in one of the dailies. He even wrote lately that he was "80% sure" of it. Wait! The moment they see what is involved they'll throw him into the gutter as the pub-chucker threw Lionel Johnson. I think H.-R. hasn't quite seen how the "patriot press" is shown in an unhappy light . . .

I am as ever self-centred, for which forgive me. This letter has been achieved by a simple misreading of doctor's orders — instead of one glass of champagne I took two.

Ever yours,
RICHARD ALDINGTON

[1] George Gershwin's *Porgy and Bess* with a libretto by Du Bose Heyward opened at the Empire Théâtre, Paris, on 16 Feb 1953 for a three weeks' run. Le Vern Hutcherson and Leontyne Price sang the leading rôles.

43

15 March 1953   *Montpellier*

DEAR BIRD,

I have been unwell again, and owing to the hiatus and an uncertain memory I am not sure how far you are informed. If I repeat, forgive me.

First, though, let me thank you for your notes which will be very useful. Would you mind letting me have Author's name, title, publisher's name and date of the Aubrey Herbert, Kiernan and other books cited; since I shall probably tack on this information either at the end of a paragraph or in a footnote. And of course I must give proper references.[1]

There seems at last a great improvement in the Collins situation. Collins himself spent three days in Paris with my friend Kershaw going over problems in detail. With the lawyers' instructions in hand they seem to have agreed on a final text, though I suppose this will again have to be read and passed. Collins will publish the whole Chapman – Lawrence story (after very understandable hesitations) since Counsel (I know not his name) says we now have full legal proof. I don't myself think that necessarily protects him from Lawrence attack — they might know they would lose their case in the High Court and yet ask for and obtain a temporary injunction, in order to stop the first sale of the book, which it would do. Booksellers and public are so made, that an injuncted book very seldom picks up even when freed. To counter this Collins agrees wholly with me that a serial is essential. He does not share your doubts about it, and his one uncertainty seems to have been which Robber Baron should be approached. Shall he babble with the brook or slobber in the mere?[2] I think it may be the mere, for Holroyd-Reece had already approached his Lordship through a cousin, and reports that he was electrified with the idea. But they also want American serialisation, which will be harder.[3] Book publication in USA has already been secured with Knopf[4] [. . .] Publication is set for autumn, August if possible, which doesn't give the Americans much time. I haven't heard that the serialisation is clinched, but hope to hear this week. So Spenser's port after stormy seas heaves in sight,[5] though I still have the toil and bother of the proof-correction. And of course there will be usual fusses about photographs, maps, blurb, jacket and so forth.

Apropos, the cuttings from the boys' book on TEL reached me[6] — did I acknowledge? The "Prince of Mecca" caption under the portrait in 1927 is interesting. Did he know? He must have given permission for the photograph, though it might have been a L. Thomas or rather Chase production.[7] The Medina caption is funny without being vulgar; and the text of that page is obviously based on Thomas's book. It is another little piece of evidence showing how the Lawrence legend was built on Thomas, who was either a willing dupe or a cunning knave — he can take his choice.

Curious what can be done with propaganda. The Pound cutting you send fits in with the remarks of a young English bookseller who called in here and was full of reverence and belligerence for Pound.[8] I wonder how much Eliot is behind all this strange reversal of opinion, for after TEL I consider Eliot the biggest fraud and cleverest literary strategist and self-advertiser of this century. It is interesting to note how the English intellectuals have allowed themselves to be cowed by a series of American dictators, from Russell Lowell to Berenson and Eliot. If any man wishes to have his enjoyment of painting destroyed I recommend him to read those pedantic and futile works of Berenson . . .

This seems all at the moment, and, as I am still rather feeble, I think I shall crawl back to bed and go on re-reading Imaginary Conversations.[9] What a pity Landor wrote English as if it were a great dead language and dressed up so many historical characters en Romain. What could be more absurd than his Richard 1st, which I read last night. But I want to re-read him entire and find my collected edition has gone. I have only fragments. What is the best edition? Do you think Blackwell could get it? Or were they all pulped in the war? And do please let me know if you come on any Italian neo-Latins — what a fool I was to let my collection go! Perhaps Davis, successor of Davis and Orioli,[10] might have some? But he always had big ideas of prices.

Au revoir. I shall try to write more coherently when I feel better. I am going to St Clair with my daughter for Easter, and hope the change of scene and cuisine will benefit. I think of going to Paris in July.

Ever yours,

RICHARD ALDINGTON

[1] Perhaps Aubrey Herbert's *Mons, Anzac, and Kut* (1919); it is not listed. The book by R. H. Kiernan is *Lawrence of Arabia* published by Harrap in 1935.

[2] That is, Beaverbrook or Rothermere; see below, letter 45.

[3] The only serializations were in Australia where an abbreviated version ran in *Argus* and in France where the "Lowell Thomas Chapter" and other extracts appeared in *Figaro littéraire*. See below letter 60.

[4] Alfred A. Knopf, Inc did not publish.

[5] See *The Faërie Queene* I ix 60:

> Sleepe after toyle, port after stormie seas,
> Ease after warre, death after life, does greatly please.

[6] Lowell J. Thomas *Boys' Life of Colonel Lawrence* (1927).

[7] The photographer Harry A. Chase, who accompanied Lowell Thomas on his mission to prepare an historical record of the first World War and who made most of the photographs in Thomas's *With Lawrence in Arabia* (1924).

[8] George F. Sims.

[9] By Walter Savage Landor (1824–29).

[10] London booksellers.

44

4 September 1953   *Montpellier*

MY DEAR BIRD,

I just hadn't the courage to write you, only to tell you of more delays and misunderstandings with Collins. Of course, I ought to have gone to London long ago, but I shrink from a journey to England. Inevitably I pick up the "germs" of a cold on the Channel boat, and as I have chronic bronchitis that means three weeks in bed and "ordered south" at once.

Any way, when the "evidence" for the bastardy was at last complete, we had months of hair-splitting about "libel," in which our law is a disgrace, amounting to a suppression of free speech. I know the E. M. Forster enquiry is supposed to rectify this,[1] but their recommendations will never become law. The law as it stands is far too lucrative, and people don't understand that lawyers are a closer and more greedy corporation than any Trade Union and more powerful. They will no more allow the law of libel to be changed than they will allow our complicated and wasteful system of Statute law and precedents to be codified.

Well! after all the libel recommendations had been attended to, Collins was just about to send the book to press when he discovered that the person supposed to be dealing with "permissions" had done nothing about it. The matter is not clear to me but Collins hinted that he had learned privately that one publisher was going to refuse. This must, I think, be Cape. Anyway, the book went back to Jix, who advised on what could be quoted and what must be paraphrased to meet the copyright law.

Early in July (I by this time being nearly frantic with impatience) Collins announced that the book was ready for press, but he wouldn't send it then, as the employees of his Glasgow printing works would be on holiday from 18th July to 4th August. And on the 5th down came the strikes, cutting me off completely until a trickle of letters started on the 26th.[2] On the 31st I had a letter from Glasgow saying two sets of proofs up to galley 99A had been sent off. Yesterday, I got galleys 42–99A, and found that Collins's people had wholly disregarded my requests, entreaties, to send them in packets with open ends, registered, and Customs-declared. They were registered, but heavily sealed and with declaration! How that second packet slipped through I don't know. But the other one must be in the Customs and may sit there for weeks.

Well, I open the packet, and the first thing I see is that Collins have coolly disregarded the title on which we agreed after discussion, and have set up their own suggestion which I rejected as cheap.[3] Moreover, the result of cuts for libel and cuts and paraphrases for copyright is a disaster. I can only say that for some hours yesterday I thought the only way out was to wash my hands of the whole thing and tell them to print their text without my name. Among omissions which seem to me the limit is of those four lines of Winston's describing L's beauty at the Peace Conference.[4] True, the lines make W.S.C. look an ass, but he published them himself, and how the quote can be libellous or a breach of copyright I fail to see. Again, Wavell's lines about Erzerum from the Enc. Brit. have been clumsily paraphrased (but so poorly that they become a mere plagiarism) and as the quotation marks are left, an accurate quotation becomes an inaccurate one![5] This has been done continually, giving the hostile reviewer of the Bureau the perfect opening: "Mr A. makes a great pretence of giving authority, but he cannot quote the simplest words accurately. For instance. . . ." And you can get a milliard to one Messrs Collins would never write in to explain that the law insisted on it, and the honest English newspaper would never publish a correcting letter from me. One more thing — they have altered or cut out *all* the references to L's collaboration with Hart and Graves![6] Why? Because Jix, knowing nothing of the evidence, told them to look in the H and G books, and to cut the references unless those books acknowledged collaboration! As if they would! I have written at least five letters imploring them to borrow from Faber's the two vols of TEL to his biogs, G. and H., where they will find the collaboration fully acknowledged.[7] But no! It is too much trouble, and what does it matter anyway? It won't sell any more copies. So cut it, and nuts to the author.

It is an ironic thought but possibly the only English publisher who might have seen the need for completeness and accuracy and might have taken trouble to ensure it is — the Oxford University Press!

Meanwhile, what does A. do? I really don't know. Tentatively I have restored some of the passages, but no doubt they will come out again. I have thought that I might get a full text in USA, but on the other hand Knopf might reasonably be afraid to issue matter which a British lawyer has held to be either libellous or a breach of copyright. Holroyd-Reece did vaguely promise a complete continental edition, but I doubt it would be too expensive nowadays, since the excised passages are not allegedly obscene.

On top of this Heinemann's solicitors have made slash after slash in my book on Norman Douglas on grounds of what seems to me the utmost carping and frivolity.

I am so sick of the whole dishonest business that I'd like to go into the organ-grinder business and play O sole mio all day long under their beastly windows. Every book of mine which has had a chance of success, from Death of a Hero [8] onward, has been cut and slashed on these legal pretexts, with the sole exception of the life of D. H. Lawrence — it being apparently a maxim of English law that D.H.L. and his friends are such blackguards they cannot be libelled.

With which moral I drop my theorbo.

Ever yours,
RICHARD ALDINGTON

[1] RA may refer to the Committee of the Law of Defamation of which Forster was one of twelve members. The committee was established in 1939 by the Lord Chancellor with Lord Porter as chairman; it first met on 4 May 1939.

[2] The postal workers and wine growers of France led the protest against the warning which the French government gave on Aug 4 that it would not yield to special interests in its attempts at financial stability and the reorganization of government departments. The next day, Aug 5, the Socialist Workers Force, supported by Catholic and Communist-led groups called out on strike all employees of the French government in postal, telephone, and telegraph services. By Aug 6 the strike had spread to virtually all public services and nationalized industries. On that day, too, the wine-growers barricaded the highways in the south of France for six hours.

[3] The title used is the title agreed on; Collins's substitution has not been determined.

[4] The lines which had been excised and were not restored run: "From amid the flowing draperies his noble features, his perfectly chiselled lips, and flashing eyes loaded with fire and comprehension shone forth. He looked what he was, one of the nation's greatest princes." (T. E. Lawrence by His Friends 195). See RA Lawrence of Arabia 258.

[5] RA Lawrence of Arabia 133. The quotation was restored and is an accurate one.

[6] These were restored; see RA Lawrence of Arabia 18, 108–09 et passim.

[7] See T. E. Lawrence to His Biographer Robert Graves 45, 47, 48–57, 60–127 et passim; T. E. Lawrence to His Biographer Liddell Hart iii, 24–233. See above, letter 41 n 1.

[8] 1929. Harry Babou and Jack Kahane published in Paris in 1930 an authorized, unexpurgated edition limited to 300 copies.

45

9 October 1953   *Montpellier*

MY DEAR BIRD,

I am by *no* means yet out of the quagmire of this damned Lawrence book. True, England is now settled. We have a text which depresses me and which I hope you'll never read. Some of the paraphrases composed by Jix and Collins are to me incomprehensible (what for instance is a "dog's body" applied to a company clerk and orderly man?) and these I have altered — winning thereby a reproach that it will "take three weeks" to make the alterations. The rest I have had to leave. Most of my little jokes are deleted, innocuous clichés have been substituted for phrases which tried to be precise, and so forth. Worst of all, as I have pointed out, the paraphrases are often so inexact that they may prove to be more dangerous than the quotations they displace, i.e. the offended Lawrence bureau can say I have misquoted.[1] (When of course the misquotations have been imposed by Jix!) Well, anyway, tant bien que mal, there is an agreed London text, and it is due for certain 1st Feb. Rothermere, as I expected (and Collins say they also) turned it down but very courteously [2] — où la vertu va-t-elle se nicher? BUT Collins's publicity man [3] thinks he can get a serialisation to start on publication day, thereby avoiding the newspaper boycott of any exclusive pre-publication serial. What he plans, where, and what may be paid, I have no idea; but he seemed extremely confident. But as a publicity man is in a sense a confidence trick man, is not being confident a part of his stock in trade? I must just leave it. I can't myself see that it is anything but a second serial, and therefore not worth £1000. [. . .]

I don't blame Collins over this. True, they have been dilatory but then publishers usually are except in the case of pure journalism which must be issued at once or not at all. I think Jix frightened the life out of them, by finding I had libelled about a dozen people as well as having the horrid story of the bastardy. By the way, as the birth certificates seem to prove that the old mother's real name was "Junner" what do you say to the title: "Junner of Arabia, a Chap of the Old Block"? Collins unaccountably demur.

All this has given me nervous indigestion, and I think I shall nip off in the car next week for a run round Languedoc and Gascony. I want to look over Saint-Sernin in Toulouse, and at the fragments of sculpture in the cloisters of the Augustinians which are said to be very early and interesting. Do you know them? Before the civil war there was some very early and impressive Xtian sculpture (including an affreux bonhomme of Christos Kosmokrator) at the Collegiata in Santillana. There is obviously a close relationship between south-west France and north-east Spain. I have asked my friend Kershaw to come with me, suggesting we meet at Loches, which I have never seen (poor Lodovico!)⁴ and which is said to have a very good regional restaurant. If he can't come, I must go alone. Collins say they can't send page proofs before the end of the month, and I must have a change.

Many thanks for the catalogue. The Toscano you noted is certainly the compiler of the Deliciae poetarum Italorum ⁵ I once had, but this is not the book. These prices seem high. True, we have nothing of the same quality here except in ancient law and theology which doesn't interest me. But last week I picked up the Latin translation of Strabo made by Guarino da Verona, in 2 vols 12mo, Lyon, apud Gabrielem Coterium, 1557. The frontispiece is mended and trimmed, but the books are otherwise sound, and cost only 400 francs. At the same time for only 100 francs I got Scaliger's edition of Caesar, Toulouse 1716 ⁶ — someone having made off with my Caesar.

Your reading on Salt and Belzoni sounds fascinating. Of course they were the type who made us what we were; but what can be done now in a time of visas and currency restrictions? Did you see that recently the "Council of Europe" (or whatever) issued a few European passports — limited to judges and bureaucrats! The unconscious humour of this quite escapes them.

The summer heats here are over (alas!), we have had September rains just in time to save us from a water famine, and now we are in the sunny October days, a little too cool today as there is a mistral. On Sunday I hope to run over to Martigues to look at those (alleged) Phocaean ruins at St Blaise — there is said to be a "mur grec" of 700 metres. I imagine Ensérune near Béziers is more authentic and more interesting — I have seen photographs of interesting Greek vases from there. It was destroyed by the Romans B.C. 118. The Phocaean wall at St Blaise is said to be c. 4th cent. B.C.

I do hope all is well with you. When are you coming to the Midi?

Ever yours,
RICHARD ALDINGTON

[1] Reviewers commented on other aspects of RA's book on Lawrence. For example, David Garnett (*The New Statesman and Nation* 5 Feb 1955), Robert Graves (*New Republic* 21 Mar 1955), Harold Nicolson (*The Observer* 30 Jan 1955), and Ronald Storrs (*The Listener*, 3 Feb 1955) made no mention of inaccurate quotations.

[2] See above, letter 43.

[3] Politzer.

[4] Sforza, Duke of Milan, who died in 1508 at Loche in Martelet, a part of the dungeon of the royal lodge, built by Charles VII of France.

[5] See above, letter 37 n 3.

[6] J. J. Scaliger *C. J. Caesaris que exstant, ex impera viri docti [J. J. Scaliger] accuratissima recognitione*, first published in 1606. Neither the British Museum nor The New York Public Library catalogues list a Toulouse 1716 edition.

46

11 October 1953   *Montpellier*

Dear Bird,

I am very glad you mentioned that Rothenstein version of the gold dagger, for I think I ought to deal with it.[1] This is so very much the kind of thing which the superior person on the Times (for instance) trots out as a refutation and impresses the ignorant. The version I give is that of Sir Hubert Young, who was Indian Army and with the most Christian Colonel after Akaba.[2] He gives us what was obviously L's original version — the dagger was presented by Hussein and the gold was "melted sovereigns." Now by "sovereigns" I understand English sovereigns and I think most people do. I suggest that after returning to England Lawrence discovered that melting down English sovereigns is a misdemeanour, and also found that taxpayers resented such a use being made of their money. He therefore invented the "captured Turkish" sovereigns. (What an ingenious liar — one can't but admire the infinite resources of his cunning!) A simple-simon like Rothenstein of course took this at its face value. But the giver shifts now from Hussein to Feisal, for the obvious reason that Hussein could not possibly have "captured" a sixpence. The "only gift" is obviously untrue, for the Colonel forgot at that moment "the wedding garment" given by Feisal near Rabegh, the "racing camels" and if I mistake not "an embroidered saddle." In any event where did these T£150 come from? Feisal was only out personally on one expedition, and that was a failure. Is anyone so naif as to believe that the Knights of the Black Tent came to him and presented him with T£150 of their loot? That's a tale for the camel marines. I have emended my text thus:

"King Hussein and Feisal were privileged to melt down some of the war-subsidy sovereigns received from the British tax-payer or captured from the enemy to honour their uncrowned rival etc." An asterisk at "enemy" and the foot-note: "The dagger is said to have been made from '150 captured Turkish sovereigns', but the main source of the Hashemites' gold was the lavish British subsidy. Where were the 'Turkish sovereigns' captured? And by whom?"[3]

I think this deals with the Rothenstein version, and at the same time indicates plainly enough that IF the dagger was made from melted sovereigns their source was British. There is no evidence for it, but I strongly suspect the dagger came from the Hashemite wardrobe or treasury, and the "melted sovereigns" story was dreamed up by Lawrence to cover the melting of English sovereigns entrusted to him for his gold-trimmed head-dress. I think L. may very well have been smuggled into Mecca unknown to Hussein,[4] for I understand that by that time (1917–18) this was not so difficult or dangerous as in earlier times. The only danger was that Hussein as a religious ruler would be much offended if he learned of it. Whether Lawrence really visited the goldsmith making the dagger [5] is a query I must leave to some future Sir Thomas Browne. It seems unlikely, for L's Arabic was obviously not good enough for him to talk to the man without betraying the fact that he was a foreigner, and obviously the man would have gossiped. L's minute description of the exact locality where the man's shop was to be found suggests the usual Lawrence lie with a circumstance.

But what a remarkable character! I doubt if English history provides a similar impostor since Perkin Warbeck and Lambert Simnel, and they weren't successful. Falstaff and Bobadil are exposed. It is impossible for me to estimate how far my book will carry conviction to a people who have been saturated with Lawrence Bureau propaganda for 35 years. It will be interesting to learn what individual (not newspaper) "reactions" are. You, I think, had already suspected him. Kershaw fought very hard but had to yield after I personally had put some of the evidence to him. Holroyd-Reece, who was on Barrow's staff, was soon convinced and thinks I have made L. more "human and interesting" than before. Deasey, who did a lot of research for me, was pro-Lawrence at first, gradually convinced himself as he examined the evidence he helped collect, and in the end down here accused me of "pulling punches" in the homosexual chapter! [6] It is true I have played that down, but I think rightly — it must carry conviction to any sane person, and there was every reason not to push it as a prosecuting advocate would do. There is a rather important person in Collins named Smith who was furious when he read the book, tried to trip me up in a long report which I had no difficulty in showing was based on ignorance and prejudice, but who is still so pro-Lawrence he "fears" (i.e. hopes!) "something will turn up" to discredit me! This has evidently been a hostile and slowing-down force in the Collins office. Luckily Collins himself read the book (which I believe he doesn't do as a rule!) from curiosity, and was not only convinced but enthusiastic. It is really his enthusiasm and pertinacity which have got the thing out. Joynson Hicks were undoubtedly and contemptuously sure I was wrong — at first. When Collins and Holroyd-Reece made them look at the evidence (which like good lawyers they had neglected to do!) they gradually became convinced. What helped to tip the scale was your discovery of that birth certificate of Robert Montagu "Lawrence" in Dublin. The Knopfs obviously disbelieve it. Personally I expect much more hostility and abuse and attempts to shoot me down than you seem to. But 40 years experience of the British literary press has convinced me that their "fair play" doesn't exist. That book would be strangled in its cradle if it hadn't behind it the richest publisher in London. You would have been staggered to hear their "publicity" man [7] here coolly arranging with me who is to review it and who, if possible, staved off! Whether he will succeed is another matter. He may have been bluffing to me. Nous verrons. He thinks Sir William Haley "very important" and was pleased and also much astonished to know that Haley is an old friend of mine.

Adieu!

RICHARD ALDINGTON

[1] That is, that Lawrence found in Mecca "The one craftsman" who could make his famous golden dagger from 150 Turkish sovereigns which he had captured, the only gift he accepted from Feisal. See William Rothenstein *Man and Memories . . . 1900–1922* (1932) 367; *Since Fifty: Men and Memories . . . 1922–1938* (1940) 284.

[2] Sir Hubert Young *The Independent Arab* (1933) 155.

[3] See RA *Lawrence of Arabia* 223.

[4] See *Letters of T. E. Lawrence* 423.

[5] Gasein, "an old Nejdi goldsmith" whose shop was "in the third little turning to the left off the main bazaar" of Mecca. See *Letters of T. E. Lawrence* 519.

[6] RA *Lawrence of Arabia* Part 3 Chapter Six 331–39.

[7] Politzer.

47

15 October 1953   *Montpellier*

MY DEAR BIRD,

I am nicely hoist with my own petard. You know I sometimes amuse myself by sending my friends quotations from well-known poems and asking them to name the author? Well, a man called 'Fulsom' who is a graduate of that great seat of learning, the North-West Missouri State College, is carrying on the great German tradition of digging up unimportant documents to illustrate uninteresting questions. This savant is "doing," he says, "modern poetry from 1912 to 1920," and unaccountably pushing outside his epoch has discovered an article I wrote and published in 1925 on the subject of Elizabethan–Jacobean–Caroline dramatic blank verse and its tendency to break away from the rocking-horse iamb into rhythmic speech which might almost be called free verse.[1] In support of this proposition I quote the following lines without specifying author or play:

> Whither, whither,
> Thou fleeting coward life? Bubble of time,
> Nature's shame, stay a little, stay, till I
> Have look'd myself into revenge and star'd
> This traitor to be a carcass first!
> It will not be —
> The crown,
> The crown, too,
> Now is lost, for ever lost.
> O! ambition's but *ignis fatuus,*
> I see, misleading fond mortality,
> That hurries us about, and sets us down
> Just where we first begun.

Now, it would be humiliating to have to write to this savant and confess I've forgotten where those lines come from! But I'm hanged if I can think. At that time (1925) I had a considerable collection of Tudor – Stuart dramatists, of whom I've kept only the more important. I have an idea the passage may be from one of Suckling's tragedies, possibly Aglaura,[2] but as I haven't looked at it for 30 years I can't remember. On the other hand it might be Davenant or some more minor person I read carelessly and happened to find that passage. Can you trace it for me without too much trouble? I think Aglaura is the place, but I'm uncertain. It is not Fletcher or Massinger, for I had already mentioned them in the article, and

I have been through all Ford and the Mermaid Middleton and Decker, Webster and Tourneur, and the Mermaid Otway. I haven't a Shirley.

How a stupid thing like this teases one!

I have a note from my publisher friend in London who has learned that Collins have given Putnams a 10-day option on the TEL, and that both Doubleday and Rinehart are keen if Putnams fail. Now try to believe that the London publishers don't know each others' business!

Forgive me for troubling you again so soon.

Ever

RICHARD ALDINGTON

P.S. Raining heavily here since Monday morning — rivers over-flowing, roads and villages flooded. When will the heavens learn that "meden agan" of which the philosophers boast?

1 See "A Note on Free Verse" in *The Chapbook* (1925). Fulsom, a graduate of Tulsa University, was at work on a doctoral dissertation for a degree from Northwestern University.

2 1637. Act V scene 1 lines 58–70. Although RA replied to Fulsom's query in a letter dated 23 Oct 1953 (see below, letter 48), Fulsom eventually discarded from his dissertation the lines from *Aglaura*.

48

23 October 1953   *Montpellier*

DEAR BIRD,

Many thanks indeed for verifying (should I say "chegging"?) the Aglaura quotation.[1] I too noticed the similarity to the early Chapman during his Marlowe days. And, by the bye, what an extraordinary piece of absurdity The Blind Beggar of Alexandria [2] is, and how flagrant the cribs from the great Christopher! Yet it is said to have been successful when played. I should much like to see it. I have passed on the Aglaura information to Mr Fulsom, and trust it may aid his graduate work.

I think myself that the heavy university writing, dreary "research" and 100% Americanism all come from the same source — Germany. There are 30,000,000 people of German descent in the USA, and they are determined to gain control of the country, and eliminate the New England and Dutch influence. For many years these Germans have sneered at and depreciated everything English, and Menckenism [3] for example (which English people take quite innocently) had a purely racial and political motive. The idea was to separate as far as possible American English from English English. Well, they've got the first German president,[4] and they are now busy bringing out books to prove that the wicked English and French made war on Hitler, and the wicked (Dutch) Roosevelt dragged USA after them — having virtually arranged Pearl Harbor. A recent one run by the Fascists over here (and eagerly taken up by the German-Americans) is that Winston Churchill (known as Weinstein, because he's really a Jew!) intentionally ruined France (a) by "declaring war on Germany," (b) by "betraying" France at Dunkerque and barbarously sinking her fleet at Ora, and (c) by ruining the towns with fiendish aêrial bombardments. This German American crowd are in close sympathy if not touch with McCarthy, and of course Adenauer — whom I grievously suspect of wanting a guerre de revanche. It is a great mistake to think McCarthy is unpopular in America — he has an immense following, and is in the running for next president unless America comes to its senses.

There must be an immense amount of stuff about TEL which I haven't touched. I quite over-looked that passage in Good-Bye to All That,[5] but Graves is a dreadfully bad witness. The diamond is a new one to me, and sounds like an ad hoc invention of TEL to account for his wasting so much money on Kennington, "that splendid pavement artist." By the way, Jix have cut that from my text as "libellous," though I showed them it is quoted from old Herbert Read who printed it long ago. Incidentally, I suspect Jix of protecting various people, especially Churchill. I have insisted on, and I think secured the restoration of WSC's idiotically rhetorical and fulsome praise of TEL in the Ercles vein of Disraeli.[6] But they have now cut the whole of that carefully arranged set of post mortem opinions on Lawrence and thereby ruined the end of the book. The excuse is this — they come, as do many of my quotations from "Friends," which is a Cape book. So are several other essential Laurentiana. Well, Collins has heard on very good authority that Cape, in consultation no doubt with Savage and Professor Lawrence, proposed to refuse point blank permission to quote from any book he publishes. Now, the law has never decided how far a writer, particularly a biographer, may quote from copyright books on his subject without prosecution for breach of copyright. A certain latitude apparently is conceded on grounds of public interest, just as I, merely as TEL's biographer, am apparently privileged to publish the Chapman story, while you would not be!!! The problem here has been to eliminate many quotations from Cape's book, and to paraphrase the information. This has been done in Jix's office, with disastrous results from a literary point of view. But is it not strange that English law makes it so easy for TEL and his friends to circulate their lies, and so hard for me to expose them? Collins want to run a "slogan" — "Exposure of Greatest Hoax in History," and Jix refuses to sanction the word "exposure." I can't see why. [. . .]

Yes, Manning was a friend of TEL, but after I ceased to know him. Manning became impossible through dipsomania, but my break with him was due to intense irritation with him. He had taken money to do a book on Sir William White, a Director of Naval Construction, and partly from drunkenness and partly TEL indolence couldn't finish it. He begged me to do it, and needing the money for a trip to Italy I unwisely consented.[7] After I had done the work and he had sent it in he did not pay and left letters unanswered. Under legal suasion Manning eventually coughed up. I look on him as a suitable "Friend" for TEL!

That Guiana plot [8] was hatched in Washington and the Trieste imbroglio [9] is probably due to the wisdom of Mrs Luce.

Ever yours,
RICHARD ALDINGTON

[1] See above, letter 47.

[2] 1598.

[3] An attitude named for H. L. Mencken, who attacked American complacency and bourgeois customs as "boobism." Mencken's great work was the monumental The American Language (1919).

[4] Dwight David Eisenhower was elected to the presidency in 1952.

[5] 1929. See p 372 where Graves states that Lawrence had bought Augustus John's portrait of Feisal "with the diamond which he had worn as a mark of honour in his Arab head-dress."

[6] It was not restored. See RA Lawrence of Arabia 258; see above, letter 9.

7 *The Life of Sir William White* (1923). The amount paid to RA can not be determined.

8 On 20 Oct 1953, Great Britain had issued a White Paper explaining a political crisis in British Guiana which led to the presence of British troops in Georgetown and the dismissal of six elected ministers, headed by Dr Cheddi B. Jagan as Prime Minister (all members of the People's Progressive Party). Great Britain charged that the deposed ministers had Communist ties abroad, that they had planned a Communist regime and, to prepare for it, had plotted arson against business property and the residences of Europeans and government officials and had planned economic damage. Evidence, in recent years, has suggested that the CIA, the intelligence agency of the United States, was involved in Britain's act.

9 The continuing quarrel between Yugoslavia and Italy about Trieste and the Istrian coastal strip, together a free state under UN protectorate since 1947, was particularly heated in Oct 1953. In 1954, Italy was awarded the city and environs, and Yugoslavia received the coastal strip and retained use of the port.

49

8 *November 1953*   *Montpellier*

MY DEAR BIRD,

I haven't anything but bad news of the TEL book. [. . .] Collins send along a list of about 25 brief passages which they want deleted because they are "jibes at Lawrence and his friends." (As a plain fact many of them reflect neither on Lawrence nor his friends but on the English upper class society which Lord Samuel has just described as like Sodom and Gomorrah, amid immense applause!)[1] The first two were not mine at all. They are Lawrence's own words in the Shaw letters, paraphrased by me and given as my opinion in accordance with the orders of Collins's lawyers. And I am now accused of putting them out as "jibes!" One is L's saying that his parents ought not to have married,[2] and the other his description of Oman as a fool, a pompous pretence and a sciolist.[3] These I have refused to cut on the grounds that it is suppressing the truth.

I'm afraid this leaves me in a hole, and I don't quite know what to do. Nor do I know when the book will be published. And with that attitude it seems probable that the first threat of action from the Lawrences will see Collins cave in, apologise and withdraw the book. There is simply no way by which an author can fight if the publisher withdraws. And that will be really a disaster and a discredit for me. One up to TEL. Even in his ashes live his wonted fires!

If you do go to London between now and Xmas I hope you will see Politzer, I wish very much you could see Collins and above all his "editor" F. T. Smith. [. . .]

I have just discovered that Hogarth was with Evans in Crete and wrote an article on Myceaean Civilization for the extra vols of the 9th Britannica. I am trying to get this into the text in case it is published. I can't understand why there isn't an article on D.G.H. in the DNB.[4] Another mildly surprising discovery is that Arab Bureaus are originally French. As far back as the 2nd Empire the French had them in Algeria as part of their system of government.

Au revoir,
R.A.

1 In a lecture commemorating the Hibbert Trust Centenary.

2 The statement was not eliminated; see T. E. Lawrence to Charlotte F. Shaw [Karachi] 14 Apr 1927.

3 The statement was eliminated. See T. E. Lawrence to Charlotte F. Shaw [Karachi] 25 Feb 1928. See also above, letter 8.

4 See above, letter 41 n 10; below, letter 50.

5o

MY DEAR BIRD,

Alas! It is not just Collins's views of America that I have to deal with, but the opinions of the American publishers. The Viking Press say that I write "as a prosecuting attorney, not as an impartial biographer." Harcourt Brace say I write with "extreme bias and obvious prejudice" — or so Collins reports. Further, he says his Canadian manager is troubled by my "unfairness" to L. which will "seriously harm" sales in Canada. The two senior salesmen of Collins make the same report. I have agreed to 25 of the 27 new cuts demanded, but Collins has relapsed into silence, which means as usual that his staff are doing nothing and wasting time. It may be that they are waiting for old Mrs Junner to die. I can't help thinking that she has a good case for damages, however right I might be; but of course these subsidised hags become centenarians.

There is better news from Paris. As might have been anticipated they rejoice in it, but the terms are not very lucrative. 150,000 advance on book rights, with serial guaranteed in the Figaro Littéraire at another 200,00. Of course the author goes halves with the translator.[1] My friend Kershaw who is negotiating this for me in Paris saw their contract book, and is convinced that the advance is 50,000 higher than they have paid for any English book, the royalty 1% higher. This is all right so far as it goes, but I am urging serialisation in a daily. True, I suppose 50% of the book-buyers of France see the Fig. Litt., but such a book needs to reach the *casual* reader if it is to be a big sucess, and only a daily does that. The publishers argue that too big a serial réclame (if exclusive) takes the gilt off the gingerbread (people read the serial and not the book) and so much offends the other newspapers that except in the case of a Churchill they neglect the book deliberately. I believe it is true that the huge sums paid to such masters of modern prose as Churchill, Eisenhower and the Duke of Windsor are almost all for serial rights. [. . .]

I am now about to take up Italy, but in spite of Trieste have less hope there than in Paris. If the Italians loath England and Lawrence they also detest France, and my book contains no tribute to those heroic troops who won the 1st war for us at Caporetto.[2]

After I wrote you, I looked up my L. notes and found your letter telling me that Hogarth is in the DNB. I think if the addition is made about his working with Evans at Gnossos and that he was so far recognised as an authority that he was invited to write on Mycenaean Civilisation for the Enc. Britt., I have done enough.[3] The article is wholly out of date, and it is natural I should disregard H.'s books on Ionia &c., to concentrate on his writings about Arabia.

Apropos Lawrence's boast of his "ten years study of history" and the fact that his thesis and 7 Pils have almost no dates, how about Flinders Petrie's "chronology is the back-bone of history?" Add that to his assertion that in his studies he "never used an index."[4]

Thank you, I got the Aglaura confirmation, and apologise for not having acknowledged. I sent it off air-mail to the American savant, who has not however replied. I suspect the letter was an attempt to "catch me out" plus the hope of a dollar or two for the autographed letter. I have been appealed to by people who described themselves as "brother authors" for light on some particular topic, only to find the letters a few weeks or months later in a bookseller's catalogue.

I could not bear the trash coming over my daughter's radio on the 11th, so (like another Lawrence) "jumped" into my "racing" 4 CV, and wandered round about 200 kilms of Languedoc. It is the only unspoiled bit of Western Europe left, full of picturesque sites, nooks, ruins. But of course the Ministère de Tourisme is doing all he can to ruin it. But 'twill last my time. Luckily it is far from Paris and the politicians have richer prey nearer at hand. I came on a village called La Jasse de Bertrand, not far from Alès. Now a jasse is a sheepfold or place for ewes to bring forth, derived from the Provençal "se jassa" to bring forth. I wonder who Bertrand was? Not, I fear Bertrand de Born. But can you not see some post office bureaucrat in Paris deciding that the name is inconveniently long and meaningless, and "in the interests of efficiency" must be changed to Delattre de Tassignyville? The *swine* have changed the age-old Place des Hommes in Arles to Place du Forum! The "pay off" is that the local archaeologists say it wasn't the Forum; that was the present Place de la République!

Lately I have come across the only really good English book on Old Provence by (Sir) Theodore Cook (2 vols 1905) who was a Fellow of your own College.[5] What a relief to find a scholar after wading through tourists and sciolists! He is excellent on the Roman remains and also knew Mistral.

I wish these damned publishers would get that Lawrence OUT and leave me free to trot on with my little barrow.

Try to see Politzer — it might be a great help. In any case write to him.

Yours,
RICHARD ALDINGTON

P.S. I mourn the loss of Czechoslovakia. I used to sell up to 50,000 there.[6] [. . .]

[1] RA explained in an autograph note in the margin: "I mean the translator gets the same royalty & advance."

[2] Where the Austrians routed the Italians in 1917.

[3] RA *Lawrence of Arabia* 75

[4] See *Seven Pillars of Wisdom* 7; RA *Lawrence of Arabia* 47.

[5] *Old Provence*.

[6] At least five of RA's novels were translated into Czechoslovakian and published in Prague: *Death of a Hero* (two editions), *All Men Are Enemies, Women Must Work, Very Heaven,* and *The Romance of Casanova.*

5 1

14 November 1953   *Montpellier*

MY DEAR BIRD,

SOS!

By a sheer accident I was led last night to turn up my pre-1939 Guides to the B.M. Egyptian Rooms, and what do I find?

CARCHEMISH. Report on the Excavations at Djerabis on behalf of the British Museum, conducted by C. Leonard Woolley, M. A. *and* T. E. *Lawrence B.A.*

Part I. Introductory by D.G. Hogarth M.A., F.B.A. With frontispiece and 27 plates. 1914. 4to. 15s.

ditto . . . . Part II. 1921. 21. 10s.

A later guide dates Part II as 1922, which raises a faint hope that it never happened. But, as I have been sceptical of L's archaeological attainments, this must be investigated. (It is still not too late to add a footnote.) Do you know any one in the Bodleian or The B. M. Reading Room who could investigate quickly and intelligently and answer these questions.

1. If Hogarth has a preface to Part I what does he say about Lawrence?

2. In Part 2 is there a chapter or chapters signed by L? If so about what?

3. Does Woolley say anything about L's contributions either to finds or the book?

4. Any acknowledgement of his work as photographer? [1]

If I omit all reference to this it gives a handle to the Lawrence Bureau. It makes me uneasy to think that my usually most careful bibliographer overlooked this. What else may he have missed? I begin to think he never went carefully through the B.M. catalogue.[2]

There is a book on Douglas out, called "Norman Douglas: A pictorial record" by Constantine FitzGibbon.[3] Now nobody in England was even called Constantine FitzGibbon except in a novel. In the 1930s Chattos re-issued Gibbon's Journal edited by David Low,[4] who was introduced to our Florentine circle by Charles Prentice. I bet anything he is the man. [. . .]

In haste,
R.A.

[1] Part I, 1914, p 12 records the fact that C. L. Woolley, with the help of T. E. Lawrence, "directed the excavations. . . ." An account of local tradition with respect to the Kala'at district, as told to Lawrence, appears on p 24. His contributions either as to finds or to the book are not acknowledged and his work as photographer is not mentioned. Part II, published in 1921, contains no writing by Lawrence. He is named on the title page and in the "Preface" (p [iii]) as having assisted in the excavations on the site of Carchemish.

[2] Deasey.

[3] 1953.

[4] 1929.

52

23 November 1953   *Montpellier*

MY DEAR BIRD,

Your letter arrived on Saturday morning and by the same post from London a copy of Vol 1 of the Carchemish. From these I soon concocted a 12-line footnote containing the information you supplied, and ending up with the sage remark — à la Palisse — that Hogarth and Woolley may have used some of L's notes, and some or many of the photographs may be by Lawrence or his pupil.[1]

I looked at the sculptured slabs with some interest. Probably they are the very same ones which Woolley charged L. to make notes of as they were unearthed. When W. turned up the records he found nothing but some of the future Colonel's witty jests. And then Hogarth recording as archaeological science some gossip about the modern tribes derived from a person or persons unnamed by the veracious Lawrence . . . !

The book was printed at Oxford which I suppose is what Graves meant.[2] I ought to have remembered he spoke of it, but the book is such a mess and so much of it a mere summary of Revolt that I worked on my notes.[3] I must remember, by the bye, to take out of the final proofs my blunder about there being no DNB on Hogarth.

Did I tell you Collins have discovered that 200,000 copies of Lowell Thomas's book have been sold in England amid universal applause? What were the figures in America! I shall be lucky if one-tenth that number purchase an attempt to get at the facts; and you can bear witness to the immense difficulties of getting them published.

I wonder why the Custot book figures in TEL's bibliography? My impression is that I did the translation, and he merely wrote (a very poor) blurb for the jacket. Of course he pretended to Cape that it was a parody. The fact is that L. tried to translate — and couldn't. (I believe he burned his attempts with the inevitable blow-torch.) Cape applied to Richmond (TLS) and R. recommended me. The book contains numerous names of sea creatures which are not in any dictionary, and this completely baffled the learned Colonel. The solution, as you will have already guessed, was simple. I took down to the country a dozen French and English scientific books from the London library, found the scientific Latin names in the French books and looked them up in the English books.[4] I think Box salpa was the only one which finally defeated me, but I got most or all the others, did the book in three weeks, and had two cheerful months in Italy on the proceeds.

I was all at sea about Constantine FitzGibbon. He is actually a relative of Mrs N.D. and nothing to do with David Low.[5]

The withdrawal from the Canal, if true, seems rather good news, for it saves England 50 millions a year[6] If the Americans want to use the Canal for their own purposes let them guard it. Otherwise I don't see why it should not be internationally owned. The only too possible American slump is the real danger. The immense debt to European Payments left by the late government has only been partly paid off, is still near 700 millions of dollars (of account) and last month began to rise again. I believe there are still immense war debts due by us to Egypt and India, and yet with all the glories of victory we seem unable to collect anything substantial from Italy, Germany and Japan, who are capturing English trade everywhere. They have little or no taxes to pay for war reparations while America has practically ruined England and France by her exigences. France has Indo-China and has had for 7 years, we have Malaya and other minor troubles. Meanwhile, under American approval our ex-enemies recover and prosper! I really think a bad American slump might sink us — or save us if some government would take up the twin problems of international solvency and reducing the price of British exports to a competitive level.

Yesterday my daughter and I invited out an English girl who has come as a student to the University here. (Why do parents insist on sending quite uneducated and unintellectual girls to impede the work of universities?) We went to Nimes, Avignon, Tarascon, Arles, and for the first and only time in my experience ran into fog! It was a nice introduction for an English visitor. Luckily the lunch at Avignon was a success.

We are still quarrelling with American publishers about "the advance," but the French have leaped at it. In fact they have leaped too hard for I have had to restrain Amiot [7] from the absurd false step of turning it into French propaganda by getting a preface from — of all people — Weygand. However, I learned on Saturday that they abandon Weygand, and will not have an introducer without my permission. If they must have one, I think perhaps Duhamel — not as a writer but as secretary of the Académie. He is not a chauvinist, and a more respectable (and useless) introducer could hardly be imagined.[8]

Ever yours,

R.A.

[1] In fact RA added a paragraph to the text; see *Lawrence of Arabia* 104–05.
[2] Graves *Lawrence and the Arabs* 26.
[3] See T. E. Lawrence to Charlotte F. Shaw [Karachi] 12 Aug 1927, where he says of Graves's book: "It contains the whole of Revolt in The Desert, slightly paraphrased, and put into briefer, simpler language. . . ."
[4] Pierre Custot *Sturly* tr from the French by Richard Aldington, published 1924 by Jonathan Cape Ltd. See RA *Life for Life's Sake* (1941) 267–8.
[5] See above, letter 51.
[6] Although troubled negotiations were under way in 1953, only on 27 July 1954 was an agreement reached to end Great Britain's 72-year occupation of the Suez Canal Zone. The agreement provided for troop withdrawal within 20 months after the pact was signed.
[7] Editions Amiot-Dumont, Paris, who published RA's book on Lawrence under the title *Lawrence L'Imposteur: T. E. Lawrence, the Legend and the Man* (1954).
[8] The book was published without an introduction.

53

18 December 1953   *Montpellier*

MY DEAR BIRD,

I think there is a better explanation of poor Virginia Woolf's suicide,[1] though of course that Bloomsbury – Nation set of her husband [2] was enough to send anyone nuts. Her father, Leslie Stephen, married Thackeray's younger daughter,[3] and you'll remember that Mrs T.[4] went mad on board ship and tried to drown herself. Her type of madness was one not infrequent among Victorian ladies, brought on by pregnancies following after too short an interval. In Mrs T.'s case it was particularly obvious since one of the symptoms was raging lunacy whenever her darling hubby came near the poor girl. She was calm though obviously nuts when he was away. That is what is called "the tragedy of poor dear Thackeray's life," but damn it! what about Mrs T.? Thackeray and Addison are among my bêtes noirs — real British philistines. Addison sending for his son in law to "see how a Xtian can die" — he should have said a half-reformed-by-fright drunkard — nauseates me. And Thackeray's denunciation of "snobs" (by which he meant "outsiders") is maddening in one who was a snob des snobs. Do you remember the scene between Colonel Newcombe and the Hindoo in the opening of The Newcombes? [5] But it is all through his work. Cruikshank's Comic Almanac has the text for the two whole years supplied by William Makepie-or-penny. One shows how wrong it is for a lower class family to inherit money. The other devotes itself to peals of laughter at an officer in the Army who was the son of a shoemaker — and hence a "snob," a coward and a villain.[6] I met Virginia once, and didn't much care for her, though a first meeting is no criterion. But she had that awful Cambridge–Bloomsbury self-consciousness which reduces me to silence. You can say anything you like against Oxford but (apart from the Colonel) I have never come across an Oxonian as detestable as that Strachey &c crowd in the 1920s. Unless indeed Waley is an Oxonian? [7] I think not. His offensive manners on the few occasions I met him were pure Cantab. Leavis was a hanger-on of that crowd. I am glad his silly Scrutiny is dead.[8] Only sorry the demise has not spread further.

You will think me very cantankerous and up-stage when I tell you I found very soon that I didn't want to re-read Landor, though I used to admire him greatly. I think it may be because he tends to write English as if he were writing a dead language. This may be all right, but after editing a reprint of Pater [9] I found I had gone off that type of writing.

I don't know when the Place des Hommes was changed to Place du Forum. What date is your guide? Mistral always speaks of it as Place des Hommes. I do wish these cheating little governments would leave the old names alone. Think of the horror of Paris, where now one descends from the métro at the Franklin D. Roosevelt, and soon finds oneself in the Avenue des Etats Unis, and in the "red" arondissements everywhere is called Stalingrad.

Yes, what a mess Bermuda,[10] and what colossally dangerous fools these Americans are. Mr Eisenhower (here pronounced 'Is-no-where') Mr Dulles and Mr Dean are a triple set of triple idiots. I really think there was a chance of peace if Churchill's original Locarno had been explained by him and promptly followed up. The fact is that Russia is terrified of the USA (beyond what is needed) and quite rightly resentful of the American "leadership" which simply means dollar world hegemony. (I was in USA when all that was put over to the Americans.) What Russia needs is a serious world guarantee against American aggression and further encirclement. I don't know what you think about re-arming Germany. It gives me the shivers, after their behaviour in the first half of this century, and I don't wonder it frightens the Russians as well as the French. The attacks on France over their hesitation to ratify are most unfair. Their original proposal of a European defence force included guarantees and occupation troops from England and America, both of whom are sliding out, leaving the French no option but a pact with Russia. I'd do it myself like a shot if I were running France, and England and America kept up their devious tricks. However, I suppose all this is treason, and you will laugh at me.

I am in for more trouble, having agreed to let a small English press issue 300 copies or so of a lecture on Pound and Eliot I gave at Columbia about 15 years ago.[11] On the basis of Jix's idiotic views the lecture contains about three libels to a paragraph. We must wait and see what happens, but on their records I hardly think those two can bring libel actions for sharp literary criticism however much it "brings them into ridicule and contempt," which it most certainly does.

Collins are still fussing, and the American lawyers are worse than Jix! If you wish me anything for 1954 wish me a good riddance of Colonel Lawrence, C.B., D.S.O., B.A. You know Somerset House refuse to allow us to reproduce the old man's signature. And now Who's Who are trying to sneak out of that letter.[12] Also, Collins say that everything at all derogatory to Churchill *must* be cut! I wish on the strength of your glimpse into all this you would do a nice little essay on Free Speech in Our Time.

You remember DHL's comment on Xmas? "About time someone else got born." So, all good wishes for 1954.

Yours ever
R.A.

1 By drowning, in 1941.

2 Leonard Woolf.

3 Harriet Marian Thackeray.

4 Isabelle Shaw Thackeray.

5 1853–55.

6 "Stubbs's Calendar, or the Fatal Boots" (1839); "Barber Cox, and the Cutting of his Comb" (later called "Cox's Diary") (1840).

7 Waley was a member of King's College, Cambridge.

8 *Scrutiny* ran from 1932 to 1953.

9 Walter Pater *Selected Works* ed by Richard Aldington, with an introduction (1948).

10 Conference of Western Big-Three Leaders met in Bermuda Dec 4–8.

11 *Ezra Pound & T. S. Eliot: A Lecture* published by The Peacocks Press in 1954. For it RA wrote an "Author's Note" dated Christmas 1953.

12 See the letter from the office of *Who's Who* (A. & C. Black, Ltd, publishers) directed to Bird on 13 Jan 1953, a time when he was attempting to help RA establish the identity of T. R. Lawrence as T. R. T. Chapman. The letter (Berg) denies knowledge of the source of information regarding the death of Sir T. R. T. Chapman, Bt., and refers Bird to Chapman's unmarried daughters living in Dublin.

54

6 January 1954   *Montpellier*

MY DEAR BIRD,

We have had a strike of postal sorters here, which has caused great confusion and delay. Your card was 16 days en route, and nothing has come from America except a few airmail letters.

Certainly, if you are able to get us permission to use the T. R. Lawrence signature at the Oxford Union it will be most welcome. Jix are against it, but Collins's people and I myself feel that the different signatures if reproduced will carry conviction to people who will not follow the argument. Apparently Jix has now cut out all the evidence for the bastardy — leaving it merely as my assertion! It seems madness to me or else merely a lawyer's little plot for a juicy libel suit. Their view seems to be: Don't tell the enemy what we know until we get into Court. Whereas, of course, my idea has always been that we should be perfectly straightforward, put all our cards on the table, and say: How can you deny this? The letters from the American lawyer are even more idiotic. I still haven't had page proofs, and don't know what further cuts have been made. The book is so watered down that, in strict confidence, I am thinking of offering the Russians the original unexpurgated text. They will steal the book anyway, as they have others of mine, so I might as well make the gesture.[1]

Talking of "stealing" — you will be amused to know that the Sureté walked into Brentano's Paris shop at the height of the Xmas trade, sealed their files and gave them a summons for selling the Viking Portable Voltaire,[2] which contains my translations of some of his letters and the whole of my Candide without my name (!),[3] without permission and without payment. When I complained they sent me a miserable 100 dollars via a secretary — by "they" I mean Viking. Now they've got a piracy action to think over. I did not know until my lawyer in Paris got going that it is a "delit" (a misdemeanour?) and therefore goes to the criminal court with someone representing me as "partie civile" to claim damages in addition to whatever fine they have to pay. [. . .]

Of course the cheque for 100 dollars was never presented for payment.

Do you know any book which would give reliable information about the Hippolytus myth and sanctuaries? According to Pausanias, H. was buried in Athens and in Troezene and also became the constellation the Charioteer [4] — rather like Mary Magdalene who is buried at Vézelay and St Maximin and also went to heaven. These respectable miracles tend to repeat themselves.

I have not read Belzoni's narrative,[5] though I've read a good deal about him. Either in his Nollekens or Book for a Rainy Day that B.M. Print Room Smith states that he actually saw Belzoni performing at Bartholemew Fair.[6] I wonder if he did?

This re-arming of Germany makes me very uneasy, and I quite agree with the late Duff Cooper that the only difference between Germans today and Germans of the 1930s is that they now have two defeats to avenge. There is something appalling in this alliance of the Vatican, American Irish and American Germans for a guerre de révanche and (incidentally) the wiping out of Protestant England. I think Churchill has done us much harm and liquidated his own Empire by his pro-American obsession. He should go to the Lords as Prince Vortigern II (since we are living on historical reminiscences) and let some more realistic person take over. You can't run the modern world with the 21st Lancers. (And apropos, what is behind this sudden quarrel of the Egyptians and Turks?)[7] For cool cheek I think the Americans take the biscuit — having intrigued and bullied us out of India on the grounds that the British army oppressed the natives, the yanks now propose to send their army to take over Pakistan.[8] As for "argument from strength" — the Americans were in no hurry to do anything about peace until they found the Russians had the H bomb! But in spite of the war-mongers I think the withdrawal of 2 US divisions from Corea is a good sign and I don't mind their cutting down in Europe. I am quite convinced that the Russians for a long time thought the yanks were going to attack them, and are only beginning to realise that the yanks were genuinely scared of *them*! America from all I hear must be a mad house. [. . .] I should think Auden must wish he had kept his nationality. Does he ever come to England?

I don't think Pound could do anything about libel, but I'm not so sure of Eliot. When Chatto's did Stepping Heavenward as a Dolphin, Faber rang up Charles Prentice (publishers behind the author's back!) and tried to persuade him to withdraw it. When Prentice (being a good friend of mine) refused F. hinted at action for libel, to which Prentice had the perfect reply that 1000 copies had been issued by Orioli [9] a year before and Eliot had not complained . . .

Rather a shock . . . I have just received (owing to these delays) a Xmas card addressed by my old friend Leonard Bacon who died a few days ago.[10] It is a weird sensation to receive a message from the dead in this way. The Herald-Tribune didn't say what he died of and I have only a cable from his daughter, whose promised letter has not arrived; but he had a coronary thrombosis last year, so I suppose it was that again. Did you ever read Leonard's poem in my anthology? [11] I like it except for the weak ending.

Ever yours,
RICHARD ALDINGTON

P.S. Do you expect to see Politzer soon? I arranged to go to London but some-how they cancelled the arrangements I made.

[1] Among RA's books published in Russia were *Death of a Hero, The Colonel's Daughter, All Men Are Enemies, Women Must Work, Very Heaven, Artifex,* and *Life for Life's Sake;* see below, letters 114, 129, 131, and 138. Russia usually pays royalties in roubles which must be spent in the Soviet Union.

[2] 1949.

[3] See *The Portable Voltaire* 229–328 for RA's translation of *Candide,* first published in 1927 as one of the Broadway Translations (George Routledge and Sons Ltd); his translation of a correspondence between Voltaire and Frederic The Great appeared the same year in the same series. For RA's translation of letters used in *The Portable Voltaire,* see p 439–67. See also RA to Pat Covici, Villa Aucassin, St Clair, Le Lavandou, Var, 11 Feb 1950 where RA discusses other uses of his translation of Voltaire's *Candide*: "In 1927 I published with Routledge a new translation of Voltaire's Candide. At the time I was told there was no interest in such a book in U.S., and reluctantly allowed it to be published from sheets by Dutton, thereby losing U.S. copyright. Since then it has been used for an illustrated edition by Lane — sheets to Dodd, Mead; an illustrated edition by Nonesuch paid for by the French govt in 1939. An illustrated edition by Rockwell Kent was issued by (I think) Random House, who at first merely took my book, and eventually paid I think about 250 dollars for an edition of 3000 at 10 dollars each! It has since been pirated in America (among others by Pilot Press) and without even my name! I have found it everywhere. Since 1947 I have re-acquired (under out-of-print clause) all world rights, *except American,* from Routledge. Now the pirates have to pause a bit. Recently, the University of Connecticut had to apply to me for permission to sell in Canada; and I made them pay. Now, if you please, we have Doubleday, who wrote to Heinemann in the belief that the rights were theirs. D's quite take for granted that they have a right to use the book in America without payment, and negligently ask for clearance in English-language rights throughout the world. I asked Frere for help about this, but he is away or bored, and doesn't answer. What Doubleday's want is to publish a cut down version of my book in some catchpenny 3 vols summary of world literature, of which you may have heard. Now, Doubleday are a rich firm and I am a poor man. They have treated me pretty shabbily. . . ."

[4] Pausanias's *Description of Greece.* What edition and whether in Greek or English has not been determined.

[5] 1820.

[6] For the reference to Belzoni see John Thomas Smith *Book for a Rainy Day; or, Recollections of the Events of the Last Sixty-Six Years* (1845) 174–76; see also n, p 176–79. Smith's *Nollekens and His Times* (2 vols) was published in 1828.

[7] On 4 Jan 1954 the Egyptian government stripped the Turkish ambassador Tugay of diplomatic immunity and expelled him for anti-Egyptian acts in a dispute over seizure of the property of Turks in Egypt related to the former Egyptian royal family.

[8] For several months the United States had been discussing military aid to Pakistan; on Jan 5 the aid was declared conditional on a defense pact among Pakistan, Turkey, and Iran.

[9] Both editions published in 1931; see above, letter 29 n 7.

[10] 1 Jan 1954.

[11] "Chorus from a Tragedy" in *The Viking Book of Poetry* 1162–63.

55

11 January 1954   *Montpellier*

MY DEAR BIRD,

If the contents of this letter bore you, take no notice! An inbite of ayenwit [3] has long been pestering me about poems which ought to have been in that anthology [2] and were left out through carelessness or ignorance or prejudice. Now, with wages and materials unlikely to drop, the revision and reprinting of such a book is impossible without an equally impossible subsidy. I imagine, though I don't know, that the type has been distributed, and that when the two or three thousand copies remaining in England and America are sold, that will be the end, and Q³ will reign supreme once more. I should like everyone who bought the book to have this appendix, but even if it were possible to track down the 130,000 owners I couldn't afford to give away that number. The only solution seems a limited edition by one of the small "Presses" in the hope that people — a few of them — in time will get them. The additions can only be non-copyright work, for one can't pay any fees on such a book; and the work ought to be really up to permanent national standard. I don't want to include anything which has appeared in The Religion of Beauty, which is a period anthology, though I think perhaps such things as Rossetti's Blessed Damosel, Morris's Pomona and a sonnet of Mrs Taylor's (but that is copyright!) ought to be in.⁴ If you have any suggestions or come across anything in reading will you let me know? ⁵

Here are those I have tentatively typed out for consideration — some of them, I think, certs.

(1) "When the nytégalé singes" (Anon. 14th C.) for its lyrical merits and because of that nice tale of Giraldus about the monk who got into trouble with his bishop for singing "Suete lemman, dhine ore" instead of Dominus vobiscum. A cert.

(2) The passage from the Squire of Low Degree detailing all the delights the King proposed when the lady was pining. Much of it is catalogue but there are nice bits, e.g.:

> "When you come home your menie among
> You shall have revels, dances and song.
> Little children, great and small,
> Shall sing as doth the nightingale . . ."

I felt there ought to be one specimen of the metrical romances. In preference to this would you recommend perhaps something from Sir Gawayne and The Green Knight? If I use the Squire passage I shall have to try to find out what those exotic wines really were. The glosses are useless.

(3) Anon 15th C. the description of the pilgrims on the Channel passage (an essential part of our fair island story) which is cited by Coulton in his Mediaeval Panorama.⁶ Where is the whole to be found?

(4) Spenser's sonnet "Coming to kiss her lips . . ." which I think is prettier than one or two of those I have.

(5) Marston's song "The hour of sweety night decays apace." Doubtful. I don't like "sweety," but the song improves.

(6) Anon 17th C. "Love will find out the way." This was left out by accident. A cert.

(7) Anon late 17th C. Three first stanzas of "Riding to London, on Dunstable way," which is nice and folky. The last two stanzas are too bawdy and quite spoil it. A cert.

(8) Four stanzas from Cotton's "My Caelia, sweetest Caelia, fell . . ." Some people thought I had too much Cotton anyway. What do you think? My own view is that he isn't enough admired. A cert.

(9) Lord Peterborough's "Chloe" ("I said to my heart . . .") though I suspect the charm of stanza one is due to the reminiscence of Dryden's:

> "What's all this love they put into our parts?
> 'Tis but the pit-a-pat of two young hearts."

I quote from memory. I wish Chloe's wit wasn't "genteel."

(10) Isaac Watts's Day of Judgement. These sapphics may perhaps fill a classical scholar with horror, but I don't know enough to be offended. The thing is our Protestant Dies irae, I think.

(11) David Lewis's "While malice, Pope, denies thy page."

(12) Samuel Wesley's "While Butler, needy wretch! was still alive . . ."

(13 Tom Moore's witty Epitaph on a Tuft Hunter. It was a bad miss.

(14) It was suggested that I stinted Clare in limiting him to one poem. The only thing I can find to add is "Love lives beyond the tomb" . . . and I'm not nuts on it. What do you think?

(15) The London Poetry Review (I think) threw away the entire work on the ground that Darley is the most important poet of the 19th cent (!) and I have only those Sirens.[7] I rather boggle at Darley's too pretty Elizabethanisms and can't find any passage or passages in the long poems — I must look again. Doubtfully I have got "It is not beauty I demand" . . . I feel a lot of it is just as false rhetoric as the 18th century people.

(16) R. Browning's spit in the eye to old Fitz for writing "Thank God, Mrs Browning is dead"! There's something to be said for Fitz's view but it ought not to have been printed while R.B. or even Pip [8] were alive.

(17) E. Bronte's "Cold in the earth." A cert. Can't understand why I left it out.

I've sent to London for a Chalmers [9] to go through those vols again, and I'm toiling through the Oxford Wordsworth [10] with many a groan. Pedestrian tours are excellent, but why make pedestrian poems of them?

Ought I to have any more ballads?

The final proofs of TEL (Collins promise) leave Glasgow by air tomorrow 12th.

Ever yours,
R.A.

[1] Remorse of conscience. See *Ayenbite of Inwit*, a prose translation made about 1340 of a French moral treatise.

[2] *Viking Book of Poetry of the English-Speaking World* and *Poetry of the English-Speaking World*.

[3] Sir Arthur Thomas Quiller-Couch who edited *Oxford Book of English Verse* (1900).

[4] See *The Religion of Beauty; Selections from the Aesthetes* with an Introduction by Richard Aldington (1950) 48, 99, 345–48.

[5] RA was at work on an anthology which he eventually abandoned when Heinemann convinced him of the impracticality of publishing it.

[6] 1938; see p 325–26 of the American edition, 1944, for the poem beginning:

> "When may leve alle gamys,
>   That saylen to seynt Jamys!
> Ffor many a man hit gramys,
>   When they begyn to sayle.
> Ffor when they have taken the sea
> At Sandwyche, or at Wynchlysee
> At Brystow, or where that hit bee,
>   Theyr hertes begyn to fayle."

7 "Siren Chorus" in *Viking Book of Poetry* 794.

8 RA may mean Browning's son, but he was usually called not Pip but Pen. See *The Life and Letters of Edward Fitzgerald* ed Aldus Wright (3 vols 1889) I 280–81 for old Fitz's remark: "Mrs. Browning's death is rather a relief to me I must say. No more Aurora Leighs thank God! A woman of real Genius I know but what is the upshot of it all? She and her Sex had better mind the Kitchen and their Children; and perhaps the Poor. Except in such things as little Novels, they only devote themselves to what Men do much better, leaving that which Men do worse or not at all." Browning's "spit in the eye," published in the *Athenaeum* 13 July 1889, runs,

> "I chanced upon a new book yesterday . . .
> — and learned therby
> That you FitzGerald, whom by ear and eye
>   She never knew, 'Thanked God my wife was dead.'
> Ay, dead! and were yourself alive, good Fitz,
> How to return you Thanks would task my wits.
>   Kicking you seems the common lot of curs —
> While more appropriate greeting lends you grace:
> Surely to spit there glorifies your face —
>   Spitting from lips once sanctified by Hers."

9 *The Works of the English Poets from Chaucer to Cowper* . . . ed Alexander Chalmers (21 vols 1810).

10 *Poetical Works* ed E. de Selincourt (5 vols 1940–47).

56

19 February 1954   *Montpellier*

MY DEAR BIRD,

The "news" was apparently sold to the Evening Standard [1] by a man who is supposed to be an old friend and whose family I have been helping to feed for years by sending food parcels from America.[2] By way of a marked coin I sent him a bit about Andrew Macphail (hardly an author to be known to a Fleet St journalist, especially since his book was published in 1929)[3] and Macphail two days later appeared in the E.S. After that I received a letter from the wife, which rang false to my prejudiced ears, containing a quite uncalled for disclaimer of any "leakage." "We see nobody &c." But they have a telephone. Well, others have been "obleeged by hunger" to do sad things, and of course it is not 100% certain. Is it not strange that so long post-mortem TEL has the power to do such mischiefs? I can never trust that fellow again.

There has been a good deal of "brouha-ha" in England, USA and France, rather disconcertingly, for it is using up valuable publicity too soon. I hear from my friend Kershaw that Newsweek had a long piece,[4] and that Paris-Match meditates another. It is a great dilemma. These papers are so powerful. I could not afford to displease Newsweek by refusing an interview. Luckily the reporter sent was an ex-diplomat (just fired for being a "Communist" — he was in fact a rather right-wing Liberal from our point of view) and he quite literally had never heard of TELawrence! I keep telling Collins that America has forgotten him, but they won't believe it. None of them goes to US except Collins, who circulates among publishers and their friends, who *of course* are in touch with such things; but I have lived 8 years in America and know that Lawrence is forgotten except by the cultured few in the East. People don't realise how utterly isolationist most of America is, and how not just ignorant of England and Europe, but utterly without interest they are. I published that Wellington book in US as "The Duke," [5] and a very nice fellow — a professor of English just transferred to his intense joy from Oklahoma University to City College, N. Y. State, — told me in all seriousness that he doubted whether any student of Oklahoma State University would know what a Duke is. I am sure he was telling the truth, for at a soi-disant literary party in Los Angeles, an alleged poet congratulated me on the skill with which I had treated the love episode of Wellington and Lady Hamilton.

I am sick of the book, and want it behind me, feel like Falstaff before the battle — not that I care about the Lawrence Bureau, but I suspect Collins will rat if there is trouble. Liddell Hart, Collins say, has been importuning Churchill, Storrs, Amery and Lloyd to reverse themselves on Egypt. He has been ticked off by Lord Lloyd; and I think Amery honest — the other two are pretty slippery.

Henry Williamson, in true Bureau style, writes suggesting a radio debate between me and Lowell Thomas! In other words I, who have always refused to go on the air, am to meet an American expert in double-talk and bull-dust on the medium he abuses daily! Merci. But you see how careful I must be. The newspapers, of course, want to see a dog-fight; and I am not going to fight.

My views on 7 Ps. were obviously supplied to the Statesman [6] by Collins, who believe or affect to believe that it is a masterpiece. They are much annoyed that I gave Newsweek my real opinion,[7] and ask me angrily if I have forgotten that Churchill wrote if L. had done nothing else his "fame would last" on that book.[8] I turned a deaf ear, though I wanted to say I think Churchill had better construct a valid apology for his own prose before he promises immortality to that of another.

I put all this aside as much as possible, and work at the anthology which, in allusion to Miss Brougham's rather disappointing work, I call provisionally Milke from Olde Cowes.[9] I've rather changed the scope, and the idea now is to make it a full volume of second choices — not necessarily inferior things, but things which were kept out either by space (lack of) or ignorance or the fact that one must not put in too much of one poet at a time. I think it can run to another 1000 pages and the two vols would thus in small compass get a good deal of the cream of English poetry. Of course I would like to do something which won't disgust those who read poetry constantly and even (perhaps too hopefully) the scholars, but the audience I have in mind are the young, particularly the impecunious young, and in fact poorish people everywhere who just can't afford expensive books and haven't time for much reading in public libraries. Heinemann cut the price on the first vol [10] so that I got 3d a volume out of 15/-, raised now to 6d as we have passed 20,000 and are nearly 30,000. I doubt if costs are lower now than in 1946, but I would like to get this down to 10/6, and try to make some arrangement whereby it could be paid for a 1/- a week. Perhaps that is not practical, but it is absurd that books have to be published at prices which can only be met by public libraries and institutions and by a few wealthy, who "haven't time" to read. Did I ever tell you that long ago, when C. P. Snow was still a don at Christ's (Cantab) he and I put to the Syndics a scheme for a real Corpus of British Poets and another of British Poetical Dramatists. The answer was: "An admirable idea and a thing which ought to be done — will you subsidise it?" Meant to be funny, I suppose. Yet it ought to be done, just as Herculaneum ought to be excavated — did you see the photo of the bronze pig in Journal of Roman Studies? [11]

I am waiting telephone calls and cables over this damned book — America now. I want to write more to you about the poems, and will do so. What you said is most helpful. Another mind, another taste, always are stimulating. I have marked down as a cert, Lord Oxford's (Vere) "The labouring man, that tills the fertile soil."

Yours,
RICHARD ALDINGTON

1 Nothing related to this statement has been found in the *Evening Standard.*
2 The friend and his family have not been identified.
3 *Three Persons.*
4 "Lawrence: lies or legends?" *Newsweek* 15 Feb 1954.
5 1943.
6 See "London Diary" in the issue of 6 Feb 1954.
7 RA described *Seven Pillars* as "an incredibly boring book — filled with unimportant men shooting unimportant holes through unimportant water towers, and putting unimportant charges of dynamite under unimportant railroad ties."
8 Churchill declared that *Seven Pillars* "ranks with the greatest books ever written in the English language." See *T. E. Lawrence by His Friends* 199.
9 A parody on the title of Eleanor Brougham's *Corn from Olde Fieldes* (1918).
10 That is, *Poetry of the English-Speaking World.*
11 The photo has not been found.

57

24 February 1954   *Montpellier*

DEAR BIRD,

Your mention of Cowper brings up one of the problems of this new project. I have a coolness for pedestrian verse. If I were American I should say I am "allergic" to it. Cowper, Crabbe and Wordsworth, not to mention the 18th century people of the Akenside – Shenstone sort, simply don't interest me. They have bits, but such an intolerable deal of slush to one poor halfpennyworth of poetry. I have been trying once more to re-read Wordsworth, and can't! I bought a first edition of the Excursion 1 in the hope that it would help me along, but it didn't. Yet I suppose I must try to pick out some more Wordsworth anthology pieces not too reminiscent of "A Mr Wilkinson, a clergyman." 2

I suppose I shall put in Cowper's Poplar Field,3 though I greatly dislike that tum-ti-tum rhythm — it is only tolerable in parody: "Oh, why should our dull retrospective addresses . . ." though not exactly the same, is what I mean. A much better poem I think is the set of Sapphics, influenced I suppose by Watts, written in "Delirium." 4 They are painful, perhaps too painful, but well written and a weird psychological document. Also the subject is a variation on the monotony of English poetry, which is apt to run too much on Love, Death and Landscape.

Have you access to a variorum or at any rate modern Ben Jonson — I have only Barry Cornwall's (Moxon) edition of 1838. From Underwoods (No 40, An Elegy) I want to quote the lines beginning "Fair friend, 'tis true . . ." omitting the last two stanzas. I find difficulty in scanning lines 3 and 4 of stanza 3:

"It little wants of love, but pain,
Your beautie takes my sense,
And lest you should that price disdain
My thoughts, too, feel the influence." 5

I don't quite know what that means, and the metre seems to change. If there is not a better reading I think I must omit that stanza too. Then it makes quite a nice lyric.

It is very interesting to see which poets yield a second harvest, and which do not. I have been carefully through Herbert of Cherbury, and find absolutely nothing to add. On the other hand I easily got 18 more lovely ones from Herrick, though I doubt if another 5 could be added of the same quality. Out of over 1200, he has about 50 real poems! Fletcher's plays yield absolutely nothing more in songs — I bagged the lot first time. Campion has furnished 7 more, and I think there might be others, though I don't agree with some of the other anthology choices. Ault, though obviously a careful textual scholar, strikes me as having poor taste; and his Elizabethans would be immensely improved by dropping the weakest 10%.[6] But I think he is unquestionably right about the text of Beaumont's (?) Westminster Abbey, and my text like everyone else's is wrong. That last line is obviously corrupt, and Ault's version makes it good sense.[7] Though he doesn't say so I think the opening of Beaumont on the Beauteous Young Gentlewoman (my anthol. p 235) is corrupt.[8] It doesn't make grammar or sense.

Tucker Brooke cuts from his otherwise excellent Marlowe[9] the three poems labelled Ignoto. Of course he had to, because of the gros mot in poem 2. The first one is a regular sonnet; the other two are sonetti caudati of 16 lines, and as the indecencies occur in the extra couplets they may have been added. Anyway I think the first one ("I love thee not for sacred chastity, Who loves for that? . . .") is a real poem, oddly Shakespearean, and the other two are not so good. I propose to use the first one. There are later lyric expansions of this theme — if indeed the poem is contemporary with Marlowe. You'll find it at the end of Bullen's edition.[10] After the Ovid translations there is nothing surprising in the slap-dash erotic cynicism of poems 2 and 3, but I think they pass the invisible and almost theological line dividing erotic poetry from indecency. It is of course a matter of prejudice and taste. I think a poet may be as "free" as he chooses if he has real intellect and passion too (Donne) or as voluptuous as he wishes (Carew's Rapture[11] and Randolph) but directly you get the knowing man-about-town note of Dryden and his enormous following, the poetry vanishes — at least for me. The Muse may go naked but not wear Rue de la Paix undies. Of course one mustn't be prudish — Lady Mary Wortley Montagu on the lover with chicken and champagne is excellent. I want to try to get in that couplet which Locker records in a footnote of hers. Some peer sent her a very pompous set of didactic verses which she summarised:

"Be sober in your dress and in your diet;
In short, my dearie, kiss me and be quiet."

Which told him where he got off.

I have been through Hunt's Restoration dramatists[12] and have marked a number of their songs as "possibles," but they are so hollow and unpoetic after the Tudor – Stuarts. That Civil War was a misfortune, and I can never see why the inland towns should not have paid Ship Money for national defence. I suppose the argument was that it was used to buy immoral pictures from Rubens and van Dyck and to stage masques by Inigo Jones. I'm always glad that Cromwell taxed them five times as much.

AWLawrence seems to be threatening proceedings, and Collins has got the American edition into a complete tangle. There is nothing much I can do but sit back and suffer fools as glady as my impatience allows. It would not surprise me if Collins backed down if the Lawrences bluster hard enough. I do regret having sacrificed my tranquillity and mediocrity to this unwelcome fracas. I try to forget it in the poets.

Yours sincerely,
RICHARD ALDINGTON

1 1814.

2 The source of this quotation — if it is one — has not been found. RA doubtless means that he prefers Wordsworth's poetry written before 1808, since his reference here is to the Reverend Joseph Wilkinson in whose book of drawings, *Select Views in Cumberland, Westmoreland, and Lancashire* (1810), appeared anonymously Wordsworth's prose *Guide*, originally titled "A Description of the Scenery of the Lakes." RA particularly disliked Wordsworth's *Excursion* (1814) and his poems of topographical accuracy.

3 The first stanza runs:

> The poplars are fell'd, farewell to the shade,
> And the whispering sound of the cool colonnade;
> The winds play no longer and sing in the leaves,
> Nor Ouse on his bosom their image receives.

4 The lines written in 1763 and beginning,

> Hatred and vengeance, my eternal portion
> Scarce can endure delay of execution,
> Wait with impatient readiness to seize my
> Soul in a moment.

5 Jonson's miscellaneous poems were grouped under the headings "Epigrams, Forest, and The Underwood." The latter was first printed in the Folio of 1640–41 as part of the third volume. The verses here quoted, according to the Oxford *Ben Jonson* ed C. H. Herford and Percy and Evelyn Simpson (1947), are part of an untitled poem numbered 80 in "The Underwood" and written by Sidney Godolphin. The text is accurate.

6 *Elizabethan Lyrics* . . . chosen, edited and arranged by Norman Ault (1949).

7 See *Elizabethan Lyrics* ed Ault 493 and *Viking Book of Poetry* 301. Ault attributes the poem to William Basse.

8 RA's page reference is to the English edition; see *Viking Book of Poetry* 300.

9 *The Works of Christopher Marlowe* ed C. I. Tucker Brooke . . . (1910).

10 *The Works of Christopher Marlowe* ed Arthur Henry Bullen (3 vols 1885) III 246–47.

11 First published in *Poems* (1640).

12 RA may refer to *Dramatic Works of Wycherley, Congreve, Vanbrugh, and Farquhar* with biographical and critical notices by Leigh Hunt (1849).

58

20 March 1954   *Montpellier*

MY DEAR BIRD,

The veracious Colonel and the vexations he has brought me are far from being disposed of. Collins have completely fluffed the American sale, and it looks to me as if the book will either not appear there or only in sheets. [. . .] The annoying "extra" is that I had a contract [1] [. . .] Meanwhile, they doodle on — I think intentionally — finding each week something to query, and the book has not gone to press. Storrs went to them, and after being shown the references to himself, had to admit they are true and fair.[2] He tried to get two sentences altered, but as they are based on his own printed statement I have refused. I have agreed to cut out the reference to his being prominent in securing the St Paul's memorial, although I am sure he boasts of it somewhere.[3] This modesty struck me as significant.

Yesterday Amiot sent me the French translation, and there was another blow. They have given it to one of the underpaid, illiterate women who undertake to translate English books.[4] I spent three hours or more on the first chapter which is full of blunders. It would take me a month to put the thing right — so I bunked it back with a rather sharp letter. Among the pearls offered was the strange distortion that the archaeological discoveries in Crete were due to "William Morriss," whose Kelmscott Press disappeared from the text as unworthy of the attention of cultured Parisians. It is vexatious, but in my experience the French have such a contempt for our literature that many of their translations are bad. When I wrote for the Times L. S. I tried to effect an improvement by reviewing translations of English standard authors and pointing out the blunders. I think they're worse now than then. My Wellington was translated by Jacques Valette who writes on English literature for the Mercure and is professor of English at the Sorbonne. The translation was very poor and perfunctory, filled with misprints, and such blunders as "maréchal des logis" for "Field Marshal!"[5] I expect it was done by one of his pupils.

I still work on at the anthology, and bless whatever gods may be that I still have the consolation of poetry in all this confusion and disappointment. Yes, I do like the "Western wind" fragment (it is in the anthology)[6] and do agree about those little wafts of song which come so touchingly across the centuries. "You and I and Amyas" and the land of Irelonde one. I incline to think some of the ballads owe their vogue to just such scraps. Every Scottish person sings the verse about Lizzie Lindsay and the verse about the four Marys, while not one in ten thousand knows the full ballads.

It is very kind indeed of you to send me transcripts of the Clare and Allingham, and I should much like the Sir Gawain extract and anything else which strikes you. The Clare is a "doubtful" because I am not sure that this time I shall include anything on the deaths of children. It is so facile an appeal to the emotions that the true poetic value is lost, much as the literary value of a hymn is mixed up with religious associations. If I do use any deaths of children, I must have Pearl and the very touching poems of Eugene Lee-Hamilton [7] and Roden Noel.[8] The best poem of Allingham's I have discovered is that given on page 106 of The Religion of Beauty, entitled Twilight Voices. As it is almost unknown (not in any anthology known to me and not in the Muses Library edition of Irish poets)[9] I am going to use it again, as also that Pomona poem of W. Morris. I don't know why people scorned the Religion of Beauty, as it has a lot of nice things and cost only 12/6. Of course it is much cut down. Heinemann said the sales would not bear copyright fees in excess of a certain figure, which cut out a lot of things, and then non-copyright stuff had to be dropped to lessen the number of pages. I had a full bibliography, and indexes, all of which had to go. I offered to scrap my Introduction, on which they remarked sarcastically that it is the only saleable item in the book! A lot of work went into the book which was treated with contempt by the English editors, who either ignored it or gave it to illiterates to make fun of. Yet it sells quite steadily a few hundred copies annually — too few.

This present anthology is a lot of work, and I'm rather old and tired, but it is fascinating, and much more interesting than the first one. There many poems were self-selecting — I had to have them. With all these out of the way, the second choices reveal aspects of poets I didn't myself know, one of which is that some poets have no second choices to offer! Herbert of Cherbury is one, as you noted. Strange to say, I can't find much more in Donne — but I gave a big wodge.

Something must be wrong with me for I fail wholly to share Grigson's enthusiasm for Clare's mad poems.[10] Indeed I find them rather gruesome and repulsive. Now, there is sublimity in the madness of Smart, and great pathos in that Stricken Deer poem of Cowper,[11] but I cannot respond to the rather senile lewdness of a poor bughouse patient who thinks he's Lord Byron. Ugh! Now, you must tell me where I'm wrong, for the things Grigson tells me to admire kindle no answering spark.

I am supposed to be doing Heinemann a little book on Mistral,[12] but can't get on somehow — I think because I don't know Provençal or Mistral's work well enough. It is subtler than one could think. I like Mistral. He was a real man and not just a city slicker and word contortionist. I must go over to Maillane again and refresh myself to the shrine — still much as he left the House. I like the feel of it — unpretentious but full of peace and happiness, things which are strangely unfashionable in these days of H bombs and class warfare.

Ever yours,
RICHARD ALDINGTON

1 With Duell, Sloan and Pearce. The contract was cancelled by mutual agreement, and Collins was allowed to negotiate American sale.

2 See RA *Lawrence of Arabia* 123, 126, 127, 157, 158, 159, *et passim*.

3 Storrs was not a member of the committee which arranged the Lawrence memorial in St Paul's Cathedral.

4 *Lawrence of Arabia* was translated into French by Gilberte Marchegay, Jacques Rambaud, and Jean Rosenthal.

5 Printed in Belgium for Nicholson & Watson (1948).

6 *Viking Book of Poetry* 66.

7 *Mimma Bella* (1909).

8 *A Little Child's Monument* (1881).

9 *Irish Poets of the Nineteenth Century* ed Geoffrey Taylor (1951).

10 *Poems of John Clare's Madness* ed Geoffrey Grigson (1949).

11 The lines beginning "I was a stricken deer, that left the herd" are in *The Task* Book III.

12 *Introduction to Mistral* (1956).

59

26 April 1954   *Montpellier*

MY DEAR BIRD,

A signed copy of Pinorman will soon be on its way to you, delayed only by the fact that I have to buy wrapping paper, and have a ludicrous "resistance" to doing up parcels. Also registration in a French P.O. is a bloody chore. But it shall be done.

Yes, I was worried about the Americans and Viet-nam.[1] I wish people could be made to realise that all this NATO and European Army truck is a German-American plot for a guerre de révanche. Every White Russian I know says that if we re-arm Germany, the Russians will attack at once. I think it's madness to put modern arms in the hands of those people. And the utter inconsistency of it all! 12–13 years ago Russia was saving civilisation at Leningrad, Stalingrad &c., and

the Japs and Germs were the enemies of all time. Great is the power of German –
American – Irish big business to have made such a change. I talked all this last
month to the Brit chaplain from the Consul-General's place in Marseille, and
doubtless am now on Mr Eden's list of suspected persons. But France will save
us — you see. But I'm nine million per cent with you over this.

It is really kind of you to say nice things about the Religion of Beauty, on which
I worked hard, and on which H'mann have (cheerfully) dropped money. A little
help from the gentlemen of the press might have got it going, but there was a
wall of denial and a yelp of derision. We knock off a few 100s a year, but more are
needed.

Of course, you are right about anthol I.[2] But, my dear friend, remember that
this and the one I'm on and even the R. of B. were and are not intended for scholars,
but for — may I put it without offence? — the upper strata of Johnson's general
readers.[3] These books are for the people. If they bring any new readers to poetry
they have succeeded. This new one is a real adventure, and as so many of the
"musts" are disposed of, there is a great chance. In confidence — I am not using
any Americans or Colonials or living poets. It is too much of a bore to have to
fight their vanity and cliques. English poetry is so rich, so beautiful, there will
easily be another 1000 pages without calling on the rear-guard.

Were I the Pharisee of the N.T. I would thank God that my love of poetry,
particularly English poetry, grows as I grow older. It is an immense pleasure, an
inexhaustible compensation. I lately had a Chalmers sent me, having stupidly lost
or sold the copy I had since 1910.[4] What fun! And what a pity they hadn't more
sense of poetry!

Can you tell me if the Bishop Corbet poems in Chalmers are complete. It seems
to me that Chalmers *selected,* here and elsewhere (e.g. Cotton) and I love old
Corbet.[5] But apart from Rewards and Fairies [6] he is hard to quote. That journey
of his — gathering the College rents? in imitation of Horace to Brindisi, is delightful.[7] I long to quote a passage from it. If you know of a fuller edition of Corbet,
do tell me, and I'll put my sleuth hounds on its trail. I have just acquired (for a
song) Lord Somebody's — forget his name though I was told — edition of Saintsbury's Carolines.[8] Pages uncut throughout.

I have absurd dreams — of the English Anthology at Penguin price, of a Corpus
Poetarum Brittanorum. Why not the latter? Books on India paper, similar to the
Pléiade classics here, each complete, all related — EVERYTHING included
from Beowulf to Herbert Read. I believe it could be done for the cost of a tenth
of an atom bomb. I have in mind a more intelligent Loeb too. Could there not be
collaboration — a scholar and a writer? Look at Edmonds — a good scholar, but
a writer!! Holy Mother of God. I have to dig into the Greek with a dictionary to
discover his meaning.[9]

And bugger the Bible.

That Dobell poem is lovely, but I fear it is too long.[10] What do you say, do you
veto Keith of Ravelston? [11] I left it out of No. 1. Have you ever found anything
in Alexander Smith? I don't. [. . .]

I am so glad you like Morris. I go further than you. His E. Paradise [12] is one of
50 books "at my bedside," and I willingly re-read in the night watches. But one
can't represent narrative or dramatic poetry in an anthology. No mistake it is
worse than extracts too many and too long — as in the Auden and Pearson attempt

to kill my anthol in USA.[13] They killed themselves, by giving 80 or 90 pages of Chaucer, per esempio. One must always consider the audience, always remember that the hope is to seduce readers to poetry, not bore them with echoes of one's Middle English course. Life, life, life! The people. Kitty of Col-raine.[14] That's what I'm looking for. What did the people feel? Here is a specimen, which is not going into my text, but into the introduction:

> "In Egypt's land, upon the banks of Nile (Qu: Noile)
> King Pharaoh's daughter went to bathe in style:
> She tuk her dip, then walked into the land,
> And to dry her royal pelt she ran along the strand.
> A bulrush tripped her, whereupon she saw
> A smiling babby in a wad of straw.
> She tuk it up, and said, with accents mild,
> Tare an' agers, girls, which av yez owns the child?"

Find a better if you can. Do you know the tale of the High Church but eccentric Anglo-Catholic who was told to provide a hymn for the Vigil of St Lawrence — and gave the canons and choir "The Night before Larry was Stretched." What a nice man. What happened to him?

Sir W.S.C. has written Collins behind my back a letter designed to stop my book.[15] If he or L. Hart dares to publish it I can give the international press a memo which shows him up. Too mild! It exposes W.S.C. and his lies! Alas, I fight alone; but better perhaps.

All good wishes, all thanks, and more soon,   RICHARD ALDINGTON

1 In early April Vice-President Nixon was threatening to send troops to aid the French at the Battle of Dienbienphu. Although Secretary of State John Foster Dulles, in a talk delivered in late March to the Overseas Press Club of America, had spoken of the threat to the free world if the Communists dominated Indo-China (Viet Nam) and South East Asia and declared that the United States would not tolerate conquest of that area, he now expressed doubt about sending troops to Dienbienphu. That was in spite of the fact that, as was made known about Apr 25, the French had requested direct, large-scale intervention by United States aircraft manned by American crews.

2 That is, *The Viking Book of Poetry.*

3 Samuel Johnson referred to the "common reader."

4 See above, letter 55 n 9.

5 The poems of Bishop Corbet in Chalmers *English Poets* v 561–86 are a selection. For the poems of Charles Cotton in Chalmers see vi 703–70.

6 "A Proper New Ballad, Intituled The Faerye's Farewell" in Chalmers *English Poets* v 582–83.

7 "Iter Boreale" in Chalmers, *English Poets* v 577–81; RA probably refers to Horace's Fifth Satire, which describes a journey to Brindisium.

8 *Caroline Poets* (3 vols 1906–21).

9 Probably a reference to *Characters of Theophrastus newly edited and translated by John Maxwell Edmonds . . .* (Loeb Classical Library, Greek Authors) 1946.

10 "Orphan's Song."

11 The refrain of a ballad by Dobell.

12 *Earthly Paradise* (1868–70).

13 *Poets of the English Language* eds W. H. Auden and Norman Holmes Pearson (5 vols 1950).

14 A poem attributed sometimes to Charles Dawson Shanly and sometimes to Edward Lysaght. Its first stanza runs:

> As beautiful Kitty one morning was tripping,
>   With a pitcher of milk, from the fair of Coleraine,
> When she saw me she stumbled, the pitcher down tumbled,
>   And all the sweet buttermilk watered the plain.

[15] Churchill's letter was part of a campaign led by Basil Liddell Hart and Eric Kennington to prevent publication of RA's *Lawrence of Arabia.* The two men had been active at least since the appearance of the article "Lawrence: Lies or Legends" in *Newsweek* for 15 Feb 1954 (see above, letter 56.) Kennington was particularly vehement, maintaining that RA's exposition of Lawrence's illegitimacy would even endanger Mrs Lawrence's life (she was 92); he insisted that Collins must censor the book. Meanwhile, Liddell Hart, acting for the Lawrence trustees, had asked to see a set of proofs. His request was refused, at first, and then, possibly by agreement with W. A. P. Collins reached on 5 Mar 1954, Raymond Politzer, Collins's publicity manager, delivered proofs to Liddell Hart. Almost at once, he was asked to return them, but a part never got back to Collins, and some galleys with Liddell Hart's autograph corrections are at the Humanities Research Center, University of Texas. In March, Robert Graves joined the battle with these suggestions: that someone punch RA, that they attempt to "get him on copyright," or that he and Liddell Hart try to stop RA with a suit for libel in their own names, since he had made them out as fools to have believed in Lawrence. But legal opinion secured from two highly reputable firms, Field Roscoe and Co. and Kennedy, Ponsonby and Prideaux, stated that the book could not be legally stopped and advised a libel suit against author and publisher after publication to expose the erroneous quality of RA's book. Then Liddell Hart attacked W. A. P. Collins, accusing him of anti-British, even treasonable, sentiments. Liddell Hart also wrote to Amery, First Lord of the Admiralty in 1922, and Churchill, asking them to deny the truth of certain statements about Lawrence attributed to them in RA's book; that is, that Lawrence's contention that he had been offered the post of High Commissioner for Egypt in 1922 was questionable. The replies from both Churchill (that may be the letter referred to here; see below, letter 60) and Amery were equivocal, but Liddell Hart still persisted in calling the book dishonest. Then Pat Knowles, who had lived as Lawrence's neighbour at Clouds Hill, sent Churchill a petition to the Queen, hoping to instigate a Royal Commission. Still others began to agitate against publication: Celandine Kennington, Lady Hardinge, Lady Astor, Sir Lewis Namier, and of course T. E. Lawrence's brother, A. W. Lawrence. Collins, who had planned to publish 24 May 1954, postponed publication twice so that RA's book did not appear until the book had been "toned down," Mark Bonham Carter had re-examined Collins's legal position and visited RA in France. Publication came on 31 Jan 1955, nearly three years after he delivered the typescript to Collins. The French edition, first scheduled for October, was published on 2 Nov 1954 although it was not distributed for sale until the next day. See RA to Bob Lyle, Montpellier 3 Nov 1954 (Berg).

60

30 April 1954   *Montpellier*

MY DEAR BIRD,

May I once again impose on you by an appeal to your knowledge? In that curious miscellany published 1640 and again 1653 under the title of Francis Beaumont's poems there exists a deboshed Cavalier poem called The Vertue of Sack beginning "Fetch me Ben Johnson's scull, and fill't with sack . . ." It is amusing and a variation in the often monotony of English poetic themes (Love, Grief and Landscape) and I want to use it. Obviously it is not Beaumont. Must I give as Anon. or are there any modern theories of its authorship? It might be Randolph or Brome or even Herrick.[1] [. . .]

Is there a complete Corbet available? I like the old boy, but I quoted Rewards and Fairies in VOL I;[2] and am hard put to it to find things which are not too topical and allusive. Is The Country Life certainly his? Chalmers suggests Herrick, but Massingham gives it as Corbet and he is a careful editor.[3] I am tempted by the Iter Boreale, but it is so allusive. The portrait of the inn-keeper giving out cicerone information about Richard and Richmond at Bosworth is first rate, and typical of that kind of information throughout the ages — I suppose Herodotus got it in Egypt and Cicero in Greece. Then Corbet's Elegies on Lord William Howard and Lady Haddington who died of small-pox simply cry for recognition — what a delightful whimsey (and in a divine!) to make satires of funeral elegies! [4] With a few judicious cuts I might use both. What do you think? Bishops were brighter in those days. [. . .]

Do you admire that Phoenix and the Turtle poem at the end of the Passionate Pilgrim? [5] There was a time when Eliot and Murry whooped it up as Shakespeare's greatest achievement!! I don't like it and I don't think it is Shakespeare's unless he wrote it as a parody of Donne. "For these dead birds sigh a prayer" is particularly funny to anyone who has lived recently in America and cannot avoid hearing their slang use of "birds."

The American press is running a story that owing to Churchill's letter the TEL is postponed. C's letter is a scandalous piece of Lawrence Bureau trickery, and I have sent an exposure to the Washington Post which may or may not use it. But the delay is partly due to the sabotage from within Collins's office (a man called Smith) and partly to a flare-up of lawyers' wrangling at the last moment over the contract. Collins object to a clause which my solicitor thinks essential.[6] I don't know what it is (!) but Kershaw has flown to London from Paris and wires me that he is making "encouraging progress" and is meeting W. Collins personally to-day. Collins himself has always seemed most friendly, but Smith (his chief of staff) [. . .] is a great friend of Liddell Hart to whom (if the press may be credited) he showed the whole of my book without permission.[7] (More Lawrence Bureau tactics!) [. . .]

Over here the Figaro Littéraire (as I may have told you) have possibly seriously damaged my world's serial rights by publishing the whole of the Lowell Thomas chapter and other extracts.[8] It is the typical French "fuite" such as occurs at all international conferences. They have no sense of honour in these matters. Neither have the Americans.

Have you read Miss Cunard's diatribe about me in the pages of *Time & Tide*? [9] Of course, all that tribe who were building up Douglas as a dear old man and "perfect darling" are somewhat thwarted by the facts I produce. Miss C. has a book in the press on just those lines, and I fear it may now look rather silly.[10] I haven't any recent letters from London since the strike tied up the postal sorting in Paris (which paralyses everything) and as that small union is nearly all P.C. they may stay out until Monday — damn them. This is an obvious political strike, and doesn't help in the least to deal with the innumerable profiteers and cheaters of France. Anyway, Heinemann's last letter was much more cheerful than the earlier ones about Pinorman, for Frere says: "All the signs now are that we shall do very well with it." I should like something more definite, a few figures. People write and condole with me about H'mann publishing on the 15th, altering the date from the 20th at the last moment. This was done on purpose. The London corps of reviewers are anti-me almost to a man, and the device was to get the book to the public before the reviewers could solidily pooh-pooh it. Too late now. The dishonesty of the Sunday Times review must be seen to be believed.[11] The English proverb "Honesty is the best policy" often seems to mean that the Englishman is honest if it *is* the best policy — but only in that event!

Ever yours,

RICHARD ALDINGTON

[1] J. A. N. Bennett and H. R. Trevor Roper in *The Poems of Richard Corbet* (1955) attribute the poem to Herrick.

[2] "From 'The Fairies' Farewell'" in *The Viking Book of Poetry* . . . 289.

[3] See "The Country Life" in Chalmers *The English Poets* v 583 and n 1; "Country Dreams" in *A Treasury of Seventeenth Century English Verse* ed H. J. Massingham (1926) 42–43. Massingham's anthology was first published in 1919.

[4] "An Elegie on the late Lord William Howard, Baron of Effingham" and "An Elegie upon the Death of Lady Haddington, Wife of John Ramsay Viscount Haddington, who dyed of the Small-pox" in Chalmers *The English Poets* v 567 and 574.

[5] Anthology of poems by various authors but attributed on the title page to Shakespeare (1599).

[6] Probably the omission from the contract of the normal libel warranty and indemnity.

[7] Politzer, Collins's publicity manager had allowed Liddell Hart to see the proofs. See above, letter 59 n 15.

[8] See "Lawrence d'Arabie fut-il un produit de la publicité?" in the issue of 17 Apr 1954. In the same issue on subsequent pages, were two additional headings: "Une Légende Menacée" and "'Who's Who' et publicité." See above letter 43.

[9] "'Bonbons' of Gall" in the issue of 17 Apr 1954.

[10] *Grand Man: Memories of Norman Douglas* (1954).

[11] A review by John Russell in the issue of 18 Apr 1954.

61

10 May 1954   *Montpellier*

MY DEAR BIRD,

I am getting on rapidly with the anthology. I hope that later on I can persuade you to come down here and go over it of an evening with a wine flask. I have definitely included one of Corbet's elegies, and hesitate over the second — the one of the lady who dies of smallpox. I suppose I could leave them out but the lines about her poor pock-marked breasts being like "cullenders" rather baffle me.[1] I feel very much tempted by the Iter Boreale.[2]

This morning I put in 10 excerpts from Trivia and that Toilette Eclogue [3] which is pure Beardsley, and selon moi worth 100 times more than all Beardsley. I have made and stuck up a litle note reminding myself that the 18ième is TOWN, and to look for country in it is stupid.

By selection I have found an Isaac Watts can be made, not as grand as the Dies Irae,[4] but magnificent. He is a great poet.

I'm giving Chloris on the snow as Anon. I'm afraid I have too many Anons. But what a great poet they were! And I've decided to be daring and omit the Phoenix and the Turtle.[5] I had a corespondence about it with Eliot in the early 1920s. I remember that Middleton lecture — a pure piece of arrivisme.[6] He was most anxious to get the Elizabethan Society (or whatever it was) friendly to him, and whooped up Middleton in consequence. M. is good, I think, in his realistic comedies which give us that sense of England in its honest homely days.

The reviews of Pinorman are funny, aren't they? The crime is that I have (1) told the truth, (2) spiked the guns of the GrandOldMan attack,[7] (3) defended Lawrence from this disgusting Magnus conspiracy. I am sure — on the basis of what Pino said — that it was an offended millionaire who paid for the writing of that Magnus pamphlet! [8]

My friend Bill Dibben has a card signed "Pinorman" which I gave him — vide TLS which denies the name.[9]

Of course, what I did for the Lawrence books [10] and for Douglas (e.g. the Tomlinson)[11] was purely out of friendship. I never received a penny. Frere in commenting says: "A pretty good publisher's agent you've turned out to be!"

I have a lovely letter of defence from Frieda Lawrence for Time & Tide.[12] This I am sending to Frere for him to decide; in some ways it is better to ignore these ignorant comments. The TLS is the worst. I wonder if it is Low or Willie King? [13]

That "But" of N.D. is quite right. He said it was due to reading Thucydides at school, and giving too much attention to "ou monon" and "alla kai." But was he right? Of course his German Gymnasium made him a scholar among the Compton Mackenzies and Willie Kings.

What a lot of 18th century drears there are in Chalmers! But what of Byrom? He sounds human, but is so hard to select. The piece on St George or St Gregory [14] is fun, but an article rather than a poem. Do you vote for or against the Finn versus Sutton duel? [15] It is certainly pure English. It makes me think of Hazlitt's boxers, and that wonderful story in Borrow of the little ex-champion knocking the block off the bullying stage-coachmen. I should like to put in the Finn – Sutton fight to the honour of our countrymen in those great days.

Ever yours,
RICHARD ALDINGTON

1 Lady Haddington; see above, letter 60 n 4.

2 See above, letter 59 n 7.

3 "The Toilette; A Town Eclogue" and *Trivia* by John Gay (1716).

4 Bird had urged RA to include Isaac Watts in his anthology. Watts translated this great — perhaps the greatest — mediaeval hymn attributed to Thomas of Celano.

5 Attributed to Shakespeare; included in 1601 in Robert Chalmer's *Love's Martyr*. See above, letter 60.

6 See T. S. Eliot, "Thomas Middleton" in *TLS* 30 Jun 1927.

7 See above, letter 60 n 10.

8 Norman Douglas *D. H. Lawrence and Maurice Magnus* (1924); see also RA *Pinorman* 171–84.

9 "Group Portrait" *TLS* 7 May 1954.

10 RA contributed introductions to or edited (or both) these books by D. H. Lawrence: *Apocalypse* (1932); *Last Poems* (1932); *Selected Poems* (1934); *The Spirit of Place; An Anthology Compiled from the Prose of D. H. Lawrence* (1935); *Mornings in Mexico* (1950); *The White Peacock* (1950); *Selected Letters of D. H. Lawrence* (1950); and eleven Penguin books.

11 Henry Major Tomlinson *Norman Douglas* (1931).

12 The letter was a rebuttal of Nancy Cunard's review of *Pinorman* in *Time and Tide* (see above letter 60); *Time and Tide* did not publish. For a partial text see *Frieda Lawrence: The Memoirs and Correspondence* ed E. W. Tedlock, Jr (1964) 373 n 6. The letter intended for *Time and Tide* was one of five which Mrs Lawrence wrote about *Pinorman*, the other four being addressed to RA. The first of these, dated 29 Mar 1954, is printed in *Frieda Lawrence: The Memoirs and Correspondence* 373–75. All five letters are included in a booklet conceived in July 1954 by Roy Campbell, who enlisted the help of Rob Lyle. He offered to finance the booklet and acted as its editor. It was called "What Next? or, Black Douglas and White Ladyship [alluding to Nancy Cunard's *Black Man and White Ladyship* (1931)], Being an Herpatology of Literary London [alluding to Norman Douglas' "On the Herpatology of The Grand Duchy of Baden" in several issues of *The Zoologist* (1891–92)]. RA took an active and eager part in plans for the plaquette, its production, and sale. It was meant to start with an introduction by Lyle and to include the letters from Frieda Lawrence, an essay by Roy Campbell, a postscript by RA and "*some!* Grim Faerie Tails!" These last consisted of

"exhibits," letters or various published reviews by Miss Cunard, Compton Mackenzie, D. M. Low, Graham Greene, and others. RA wanted to add a letter from Somerset Maugham, but no one succeeded in getting his permission. The publishers, The Forty-Five Press, had galleys when, in November, the printers called the book libellous and refused to continue with it. RA suggested printing outside the British Isles and distributing from France, but by 2 Jan 1955 the project was abandoned. See RA to Rob Lyle, Montpellier 21 Jan 1955; see also RA to Rob Lyle, Montpellier 26 July, 6, 7, 10, 12, 15, 17, 18, and 20 Sept 1954 *et al* (Berg). Only one complete set of galleys (Alan Clodd) and one incomplete set partially pasted up (MJB) are known to exist.

13 King: Low's review of *Pinorman* appeared in *The Listener* 20 May 1954.

14 "On the Patron of England" *Miscellaneous Poems* 2 vols 1773 i 100–04; see Chalmers *The English Poets* xv 203–04.

15 John Byrom's "Extempore Verses Upon a Tryal of Skill between the Two Great Masters of Defence, Messrs Figg and Sutton" published in his *Miscellaneous Poems* i 43–48, see Chalmers *The English Poets* xv 193.

62

25 May 1954   *Montpellier*

MY DEAR BIRD,

   I have come across another book by Sir Theodore Cook, who I discover was Scholar, and not Fellow, of Wadham as I thought. It is not so good as his Provence, but on the whole a most readable work of the travel – history – art kind based on the Touraine Châteaux.[1] (What a pity they are so near Paris and so ruthlessly exploited for tourisme.) Probably it was unavoidable, but I think a fault in the book is that it dwells too much on the crimes of the Valois [2] etc. We should object, I think, to an equivalent book which dwelt too much on the murder of Edward II, the amours and agressions of Edward III and his sons [3] (the harrying of Langue-doc by the Black Prince is still remembered here, I'm told),[4] the murders of Prince Edward and Richard II, and so forth. The more so since, though very fine work was produced in that England, Cook's subject took him among magnificent build-ings. I think he doesn't quite do justice to the taste and splendour of the Valois despite their crimes. I'd forgive Victoria a crime or two if she had really done for culture a fraction of what was done by these wicked people! And I wonder if he's quite fair to the Italianate school of French painters? Possibly it's my bad taste, but I must say I was a little shocked at Clive Bell's fearful contempt for the Fon-tainebleau "murals." Are they as bad as all that?

   Putting these aside as one reader's personal quirks, I think the book an excellent one. It seems strange that a man who did such good work only 60 years ago should seemingly be forgotten. I had never heard of him, until these books turned up. Or is that "the want of my ignorance," as they say? Is he remembered at Wadham? He evidently kept in touch with his College, for he dates his preface from Oxford, and reproduces a print of Chambord and an alleged Mary Stuart from the College Library. This is the kind of work produced by men of an older Oxford which doesn't seem likely to be repeated. It is free from controversy and fads, scholarly without pedantry, "popular" in a sense without that abominable flattery of bour-geois conceit so common in modern American books. Even if such a book were now written, no commercial publisher could afford to produce it. I notice people are very apt to grumble at the publishers and their choice of books and the prices they charge. They forget that the great advances in wages in the printing, paper-making, binding and distributing trades have immensely increased publishers' expenses; and though authors' royalties have been reduced, it doesn't compensate. The result is that a publisher hesitates over a book which will not sell at least 5000, and public taste being what it is such books are of low quality as a rule. The result is you have either works which can be classed as "educational" and used in classes, or popular and low-grade stuff. The only way out is a sudden improvement in public taste — and that seems unlikely. I have by me a letter from a friend who makes a very handsome income by adapting films for people with an adolescent mentality, and similar books. "I wish they weren't so profitable" he says, and goes on to say that he has now been able to buy a small publishing business. This has failed because it went on trying to publish real books. My friend probably will make a lot of money by using it to distribute what he admits is trash. Do you realise that if D.H. Lawrence were 25 to-day he probably couldn't get published at all? His first editions never exceeded 2000, and in England he never got more than 100 pounds advance. It was America which saved him, and that because for some mysterious reason (which he himself could not explain) he now and then wrote a story which fitted the Saturday Evening Post or some such thing.[5] They would reject 9 stories in turn, and then suddenly give him 1000 (gold) dollars for one which did not seem any different. On the other hand we mustn't forget that even in the period 1875–1900 many good books were neglected. But then I think the Aesthetic Movement intentionally put a barrier between itself and the public, just as the highbrows do to-day.

The new public wants to get its reading cheap — witness the success of the Penguins. But they have been living mostly on the production of the pre-war period, and their greatest successes have been detective story writers. They have done unexpectedly well with the translations, but those come under "educational" again. Even if not read in schools, they are read by people who hope to educate themselves . . .

All this out of Cook's Touraine! Is he in the DNB? He must be.[6]

The trend of Penguins in the next 5 years will be worth watching. (In confidence, I know Lane wants to get out, but that is partly a question of age.) I suspect they have now mopped up practically all meritorious books which the public had missed. Not many such can now be produced. (A year or so back they were frantically searching for biographies — and look how many have been published.) I feel myself that they will either go out of business or turn to this "adolescent mind trash" as my friend candidly calls his own work. What do you think? You are closer to the arena than I.

They do these things better in France? Do they! I have lately met a man who has in the press a book on DHL in that series of modern writers which has had such a success.[7] He had never seen my Life, did not know L. is buried in New Mexico, and had never heard of "Phoenix!"[8] The French cavalier treatment of our literature does annoy me. They are supercilious enough if we publish some shallow book on a French topic — they might at least examine the material before dogmatising on a writer as important as DHL. People just don't read. After laying down the law about Douglas, Frieda adds a P.S. "Had he read Gregorovius?"[9] What next!

Yours sincerely,
RICHARD ALDINGTON

¹ *Old Touraine, The Life and History of the Famous Chateaux of France* (1898).

² French dynasty which ruled in direct line from 1328 to 1498.

³ Edward III's sons included among others Edward the Black Prince, and John of Gaunt.

⁴ In the Hundred Years War.

⁵ *A Bibliography of D. H. Lawrence* by Warren Roberts (1963) lists no publications in the *Saturday Evening Post*. There are entries for *Atlantic Monthly, Vanity Fair, New York Times Magazine, Dial,* and others.

⁶ He is not.

⁷ *Biblio* lists no monograph in French on D. H. Lawrence published between 1954 and 1956. In that period three translations with prefaces were issued: *Le renard* translated by L. A. Delieutraz and with a preface by John Charpentier (Collection de La Petite Ourse) (1956) for La Guilde du Livre; *Le serpent à plumes* translated by Denise Clairouin and with a preface by René Lalou (1956) for Le Club des Libraires de France and La Guilde du Livre; and *L'amant de lady Chatterley* translated by F. Roger-Cornaz and with a preface by André Malraux (n.d.) for Le Club du Meilleur Livre. That RA refers here to Frédéric-Jacques Temple, whose monograph on Lawrence appeared in 1960, is almost impossible, owing to Temple's wide reading in English literature and his extensive knowledge of it. See below, letters 98, 138.

⁸ This may refer to a poem first published in *Last Poems* ed by RA and Giuseppe Orioli (1932); to a drawing made by Lawrence and published in *Son of Woman* by John Middleton Murry (1931); or to *Phoenix The Posthumous Papers of D. H. Lawrence* ed Edward D. McDonald (1936). The phoenix was Lawrence's talisman.

⁹ In a letter written from Port Isabel, Texas, on 29 Mar 1954 and possibly used as a covering letter for the one intended for *Time and Tide* (see above, letter 61 and n 12). See Frieda Lawrence *The Letters and Correspondence* 373–74. Gregorovius wrote a *History of Rome in the Middle Ages* and a *Life of the Emperor Hadrian*.

63

28 May 1954   *Montpellier*

MY DEAR BIRD,

I have been sitting in a café in the Place Chabaneau — can you imagine the local historian being so honoured among us?¹ — reading a very interesting long article by André Billy on Edmond de Goncourt and his woes over the publication of the Journal.² The abuse he received! I felt quite ashamed that Pinorman has not had more instead of less. And then I found your delightful letter here and one from Houghton Mifflin in Boston saying they look forward to reading it. I doubt they'll accept it. The very word "pederasty" gives the average American fits, and in Boston the habit is to pretend that it is a calumny of filthy-minded Europeans — the thing doesn't exist! But there is a second chance. A Berkeley professor,³ who has written on Lawrence and is now doing a study of Sinclair Lewis, received proofs of Pinorman from Frieda Lawrence. Thinking to do me a good turn he sent it to a firm of publishers in N.Y.⁴ Unluckily, it is not professional etiquette to have a script out with more than one publisher, and I've had to air-mail Mifflin to explain. Americans always construe — or misconstrue — an action by an Englishman in the worst sense. But I think this prompt explanation will avert any charge of double-dealing. The N.Y. firm in question are small beer, and the question is whether I should let them have the book. But as that may be the only alternative to non-publication, with consequent loss of copyright and inevitable piracy, I suppose I must accept. I fear they are pornographers as they are trying to get out a complete Lady Chatterley.⁵ Neither Lawrence nor Frieda nor anyone else has been able to explain to me why he stuck those "words" in his ideal love story. Of course, they sold it; but that wasn't the reason. He wanted to fight for them, which seems idiotic to me. No one man controls the meaning of words — they are controlled by the mass of our countrymen and by usage. I suppose I'm stupid about this, but I told Lawrence (though I fought for the book and risked legal trouble by circulating it for him) that I thought it was a blunder. Frieda of course always wants to get it filmed — which is charming in an old lady nearly 80.

I feel sure the TLS was King,[6] and I really don't mind it a bit, though I wrote a note pulling Haley's leg. I used to know him when he was Sell on the Man. Ev. News — not a very good critic.[7] And not very observant. Some time in the 30s I remarked — à peu près — "In the 19th century the word "Freedom" rallied all mankind; now it won't bring a dozen geese across the road." He waded into me for this offence to Manchester Liberalism, but I still think I'm right. Now King was mocked in my book,[8] I hope and believe with good humour and not spitefully, and his review sounded like a cry of anguish. Suppose I am wrong about Hitler (though what I said came from the Times itself!) what has that to do with Douglas? True, they were both Austrians.

I do wish Norman had written on Greece, though I fear his Greek may have been a little rusty. I am the merest smatterer, so couldn't judge. There is that one excellent essay, you know, in Three of Them.[9] What is so hypocritical about these "protests of friends" is that Douglas made no secret of his habits, boasted of them in fact. He more than once told me he had a syphilitic throat and invited me to inspect it, opening his mouth wide! Not being a doctor, I can't say if it was an idle boast. If you have not read Looking Back,[10] I do beg you'll read it. The book is good, and if you read with Pinorman in mind you'll find his own words confirming what I say. Now either King – Low & Co have not read the book, or they are completely dishonest.

If I've mentioned it before, forgive. One of them has written a review so libellous it has been rejected.

I am in a state of great nerves because my solicitor still is haggling over that TEL contract, and I don't like the world to think it is held up because of Hart. I have just sent a pungent express letter which I hope may settle the affair. In my experience solicitors are fatal to author – publisher relations. They insist on treating what is essentially a partnership as a contest between a Gas Company and the Board of Trade.

I also may have told you that the Félibrige have made me a Soci,[11] and my daughter and I are invited to the centenary celebrations at Avignon and Chateauneuf du Pape. I also hope to see the château at "Font-Segugno" but I don't know if we'll have time. The banquet at Avignon sounds Homeric. It is also very expensive for the Midi. Pamben, for once in a lifetime. The Mistral book advances but slowly.[12] I am terribly handicapped by Madame Mistral's embargo on the Letters. This, I am told sotto-voce, is because she was jealous of his love affairs. Maitre Julian, a Félibre and avocat à la Cour de Lyon, told me that Louise Colet collected him as well as Flaubert and all the rest. C'était une Muse qui couchait avec tous les écrivains de la France, said he. Again — rather unlike a barrister in our own country! Frédéric Mistral's neveu sent me a charming letter from Maillane. I shall have to try to earn all this gloire.

You are most kind to send the Middle English things, and I shall brood over them. It is the eternal problem which you evoke. Either one includes poems or extracts in a form of the language which baffles and annoys the unprepared reader, or one has to give them in what is virtually a translation. A few of the earliest poems I give intact, including the swart smiths swinking who annoyed the poet so much. The others, including the Lackpenny, I have frankly translated.

Really I am ashamed that I didn't have Watts in my first collection. He is a real poet, and by judicious cutting one can show his genius. I was a fool and an ignoramus to miss him. Now I hope to make amends. Since you vote for it, I shall include Byrom's contest of the Finn and Sutton heroes which has been on my possible list for a long time. I almost copied it out yesterday! It shall go in tomorrow. One of the things I am trying to do is to give poems which illustrate the life of the people. We have too many artificial love poems and "upper class" poems, and the Finn and Sutton go in nicely. In "pastoral" I have tried to give the genuine country poetry (e.g. Drayton and Browne) while cutting out all the false pastoral stuff. I am also giving the "townee" stuff which utters a perfectly genuine preference of London to the country.

Will you forgive me if I make another appeal to your knowledge and kindness? On page 109 of Lyra Elegantiarum,[13] poem CXLVI is entitled "On a Woman of Fashion" and is attributed to Tickell. I can't find it in the Chalmers' Tickell, and it is not — so far as I know — in the excellent Oxford 18th Century.[14] It reads to me like an extract from a longer poem. The use of the word "macaroni" suggests to me a later epoch than Tickell's. Now Locker was a charming man — do you like his Confessions as much as I do? [15] — but he was a bit wobbly on attributions. (He gives Carew one of Herrick's.)[16] I should like to include this Woman of Fashion, but I want a more solid editor than Locker and a more reliable text. Can you help?

Was Locker quite fair when he laughed at Wordsworth for rhyming "boy" with "thigh," i.e. Cumbrian "thoi?"

I think it too risky to give the Country Life to Corbet, though I see Massingham does.[17] I have included the Elegy on the nobleman, and am still pondering the Iter. I think I may give it entire, and defend it on the ground that it is "the life of the people of England." By the way, I have that amusing poem of the 15th century pilgrims being sick at sea — surely an essential episode in our fair island story? [18] What do you think of Garrick's "Come, cheer up, my lads?" It was still sung in camp concerts in 1916, and you know one of the Colonels or Brigadiers at Albuera sang it as he led his men and himself to death. I've got Oman here but I'm too lazy to look up the exact name — anyway, you'll know it.[19] Surely that poem is part of our life?

Coming back to Douglas — that "dearie" was in no sense "pansy." He was a most masculine pederast. The only similar one I ever knew was a General in the old Royal Flying Corps, whom I have seen in London pubs with most dreadful little tapettes. I am attacked by one of the crowd for calling Douglas "insolent" because he intruded, unasked, one of his slum children into my car. This is worded by my critic to look as if I acted in such a way because I scorned Douglas's act of charity to "a slum child." [20] Now, I didn't stress the thing, but . . . I had with me the woman who for 17 years has been my wife and is the mother of my daughter, and this child of Douglas's had to be stopped from publicly undoing his fly buttons! In Latin countries, as you know, outrage à la pudeur publique is a very serious offence, and this made us accessories. Luckily no one in the restaurant saw. But, a sinner myself, I still think I have a right to resent that without being pilloried as one who would have cast the first stone! The spectacle of Norman as the woman taken in adultery is too much. It arrideth me, as Lamb says.

Forgive this garrulous letter, but yours cheered me much.

Ever yours,
RICHARD ALDINGTON

1 Place Chabaneau was named for a late nineteenth-century authority on romance languages and the history of Languedoc.

2 *Les Frères Goncourt, la vie littéraire à Paris pendant la seconde moieté du xix siècle* (1954). The Goncourt journal was published 1887–96.

3 Mark Schorer, who had reviewed *The Later D. H. Lawrence* (1952) in *New Republic* 7 Apr 1952. His *Sinclair Lewis* was published in 1961.

4 Grove Press.

5 Grove Press published the first authorized unexpurgated American edition of *Lady Chatterley's Lover* in 1959 with an introduction by Schorer.

6 RA was correct; see above, letter 61 n 9.

7 As a young man, Sir William Haley wrote literary articles under the name Joseph Sell.

8 See *Pinorman* 120–30, 132–33, 152–53.

9 "One Day" in *Three of Them* (1930) 3–51; the essay was published separately at Nancy Cunard's Hours Press in 1929.

10 1933.

11 In May 1954 Roy Campbell and RA were elected honorary members of the society founded at Font-Ségugne by Frédéric Mistral and others for the purpose of perpetuating the language and folk arts of Provence.

12 *Introduction to Mistral.*

13 Edited by Frederick Locker (1867).

14 1926.

15 RA probably means *My Confidences* (1896).

16 Both poems XXV and XXVII in Locker's anthology are almost identical with poems by Herrick, "Mistress Elizabeth Wheeler, under the name of the lost Shepherdess" and "The Primrose."

17 See above, letter 60.

18 See above, letter 54.

19 "Heart of Oak," sung in *Harlequin's Invasion* (1759).

20 *Pinorman* 112.

64

14 June 1954   *Montpellier*

MY DEAR BIRD,

I send you an article from a local review given me by a Montpellerain named Temple, who says he is descended from an English émigré [. . .] and who for some exquisite reason has translated and is publishing at his expense my obsolete pamphlet on DHL written in 1926 [1] and about 30 or more of my forgotten poems.[2]

What do you make of this story of Elizabeth Medora Leigh and her troubles?[3] Here I have only Byron's Poems, Tom Moore's Life[4] and a selection of letters. I suppose the modern Lives and (possibly) the modern complete Letters and Journals deal with the topic. I brought the thing on myself by saying to Temple I had read somewhere that *Ada* Byron died at St Affrique, but that I looked there in vain for any memorial to her.[5]

Byron seemingly re-met Augusta [6] early in July 1813, and their amours coupables (if they really occurred) must have started then. If E.M.L. was 34 in 1848, she was born in 1814; and the name Medora points to the same year, as Lara was published in Jan. 1814.[7] But what possible evidence can there be that the girl was Byron's daughter? In a letter before Allegra's [8] death, Byron mentions that he has another illegitimate child, but that might have been the mysterious son celebrated in Hours of Idleness.[9] It is true, however, that he left all the money he could dispose of, not to Ada, but to Augusta and her children with complex legal directions about providing for the children. If I have not misunderstood the legal jargon of the Will, Medora was entitled to an income even during her mother's lifetime. Who was Trevanion?

The remarks about alcoholism seems to me damned nonsense. Byron sometimes got drunk, like other gem'men of his time, but he starved and soda-water'd so often, and seems to have been so temperate in the Ravenna – Pisa [10] period that he can't possibly be called alcoholic. And was anything ever so silly as tracing Elie Taillerfer's debauches to the non-existent vice of a problematic wicked grandfather? If he drank the poisonous muck they sell here as wine, no wonder he finished up in the hospital at Sète — the great centre for the distribution of falsified wines. Half the "Beaune" sold in England is manufactured there by adding per bottle a tablespoonful of genuine Beaune to the remainder of a bottle of inferior Corbières from Rousillon.

Did I bore you with the tale that the BBC say they intend to broadcast my Alcestis on the 3rd Programme, July 4th and July 7th? [11] If by chance they do, and in an idle moment you hear any of it, I'd like to know how the thing is done. I dread those pseudo-genteel BBC voices. The only merit of the translation is that the English is straightforward and not Biblical poetical (in the Loeb style) and that the version is fairly accurate.

Last week I also recorded here for the BBC personal reminiscences of DHL. I was asked to talk 10 minutes — forgot to look at my watch before starting, guessed, and found I had babbled for 13. I suppose they can cut. I should have tried it at home by the clock, but I hate rehearsing — it spoils for me all the spontaneity of the talk. I hope they use this, for I had a cut at Russell [12] — which doubtless *they* will cut. What a nation of sportsmen our editors are. They will publish all sorts of blackguardings of an author, and downright falsities, and then refuse to print an answer — not that it is wise to answer. We need a law such as there is in France. If any journal criticises an author, he has by law the right to exactly the same space to reply; and so on, always giving the last word to the author. Is that not an indication of the difference between the two countries?

I am in a mood of damning the world in general, having about 4000 pounds in various sums due from various countries, and not being able to get a cent either because of "Exchange control" or negligence. I haven't heard from Houghton Mifflin about Pinorman, and Heinemann have raised some futile objection about the anthology — in order to comply with the moronic booksellers who (it seems) now insist that books must belong to "a recognisable category"! They objected to Pinorman as not being a "regular biography"(!) and now H'mann urge me to make it an anthology of "light verse," of which they are confident they can sell 10,000. No doubt they are right.The Religion of Beauty hasn't sold 4000.

I am also still damning Collins [and] lawyers [. . .] I have before me a letter to Kershaw from my solicitor, dated 27th May, which says:

"If Mr Aldington accepts the documents in the form in which they stand he has only to let me know, and I will have fair copies prepared for signature, which will only take a couple days or so, and send to him . . ." [13]

My express "yes" must have been in London on the 29th. 16 days have elapsed, and I have heard not a word more. Is it not enough to exasperate one? The same letter said that IF we could "complete" at once Collins and Putnam (in US) would have simultaneous publication on the 4th Oct. I simply don't understand it, for Collins lose by these delays, though not as much as I.

On top of which we have had gloomy weather, with not a skirr of one cicada. My daughter and I went to the agapes of the Felibres, whereof more later if I happen to remember them. But try to enlighten me about Medora Leigh.

Yours ever,
RICHARD ALDINGTON

[1] *D. H. Lawrence, An Indiscretion* (1927).

[2] The book was not published.

[3] Elizabeth Medora Leigh, reputedly Byron's child by his half-sister Augusta, allowed herself at age fifteen in 1829 to be seduced by Henry Trevanion, husband of her sister (or half-sister) Georgiana Leigh. Medora's child died in infancy. In 1832, however, Trevanion and Medora eloped to Normandy, where they lived as Mr and Mrs Aubin. Eventually she broke with Trevanion only to rejoin him when she found herself pregnant again. This child, like the first, was a daughter, Marie. More than five years later, representing herself as Byron's child, Medora appealed to John Cam Hobhouse, an intimate of Byron, for financial help with the excuse that she was starving. Lady Byron and her daughter Ada, Countess of Lovelace, attempted to help Medora but both ended by rejecting her. She began a liaison with a French soldier Jean Louis Taillefer, by whom she had a son. After Taillefer left the army, he married Medora, legitimatising their son and Marie, Medora's second child by Trevanion.

[4] *Life and Journals of Lord Byron* (2 vols 1930).

[5] Marie Byron Leigh Taillefer died at St Affrique; see below, letter 66.

[6] Byron's half-sister, Augusta Byron, who had married Lt-Col George Leigh in 1807.

[7] By Byron; published later than January in 1814. Medora is the name of a character in Byron's *The Corsair* (1814) to which *Lara* was advertised as a sequel.

[8] Byron's daughter (1817–22) by Claire Clairmont, Mary Shelley's half-sister.

[9] 1807. That Byron had a son has not been proved, though a "Major Byron," 1844, attempted to establish himself as Byron's son by a Countess de Luna, reputedly loved and abandoned during Byron's visit to Spain in 1809. This was not, however, the supposititious son to whom RA referred. Doubtless he had in mind Byron's poem "To My Son," first published in Thomas Moore's *Life and Journals of Lord Byron* i 104 and subsequently reprinted in later issues of *Hours of Idleness*, a title used to include all Byron's juvenilia. Byron's mention of a son in his letters has not been located.

[10] 1816–1818.

[11] That is, RA's translation (1930). It was adapted for radio and produced by Raymond Raikes with music by John Hotchkis. The cast included Deryck Guyler, George Hagan, Denys Blakelock, Sulwen Morgan, Mary Wimbush, Godfrey Kenton, Cyril Shaps, Carleton Hobbs, Peter Claughton, and the members of the chorus.

[12] See above, letter 24.

[13] Documents whereby the book about T. E. Lawrence was assigned to a trust, of which RA's daughter was the beneficiary and Alister Kershaw the trustee.

65

MY DEAR BIRD,

Delighted to have your letter.

My news is that at last I have received the voluminous and incomprehensible legal documents [1] [. . .]

Roy Campbell has written an amusing but outrageous letter to the Times about Pinorman.[2] I have received a long anonymous communication explaining Douglas on astrological grounds — or should I say, "airs"! [3] Copies of these shall come to you as soon as I have time to copy them. What a strange world we live in! Are you not surprised by the violence of the reaction to Pinorman? Are homosexuals *so* sacred in England? Surely not! And yet . . . ? [. . .]

I think that Richard Tickell must be the solution to the problem.[4] Locker is very careless in his editing — as indeed becomes a gentleman and a bibliophile. If you can track down the real text, I shall be most grateful. I draw to an end now. My latest entry is those two wonderful pieces of G.K.S. "In the Backs" and "On the King's Parade." [5] I suppose they are well known? The only word I can think of for them is the over-worn "formidable." I think "And vain Methuselah's unusual years" is one of the great lines of modern poetry! [6]

My Columbia University lecture on Pound – Eliot [7] is held up by the usual binder's bastardry — they pass over the small orders for the big. God knows when it will be out. How hateful these beastly little capitalists are.

Talking of which, should we not arm ourselves á la Charlotte Corday for Messieurs Churchill and Eden? Methinks they have caved in like cowards, and sold us and peace down the river.[8] Well, I expected as much when I heard that they had obeyed Their Master's Voice. Can't you get a caricaturist to draw Churchill and Eden, as a pug and a Mexican hairless dog, listening obsequiously to a blaring old-fashioned phono with the mug of Eisenhower — may Allah reject him! What bastards. There is a chance of peace, and it has to be sabotaged to please American milliardaires and their dividends.

I fear Alcestis will be a misery. But if you can manage to listen for a few minutes, I'd like to know how — in spite of the BBC voices — it comes over. My idea was to make a version which modern voices could speak, whatever violence is done to the perfect beauty of the original. It was a violent reaction against the pseudo-Bible – Shakespear Loeb versions. I think it is fairly accurate. Be as brutal as you feel — I want to know. The version was "done" pre-1939 by various societies — Cambridge University among them.[9] I had hoped to do others on the same lines, but had no encouragement to speak of, and it is ghastly hard work for someone whose Greek is as rusty as mine.

Prentice certainly went around Greece with the American Ambassador, an ex-publisher, Lincoln Macveagh, in the 1930s. Norman's contacts were certainly with the British School. I think the point is that he spent his money and energy on boys, and he found classical learning had progressed far beyond the Karlsruhe Gymnasium of 1886. One of his really dirty tricks is to hint, in a way that anyone with a faint knowledge of Greek studies instantly grasps, that he had an affair with

Jane Harrison. It may be so — but what a "gentleman" to boast of it! And how surprising — to him! — that she cut him on the Channel steamer! Now just ask yourself — Lawrence ran away with another man's wife, whom he married, and stuck to for life, for which crime he has been crucified — but did he ever do anything dirty like that, trying to make people believe he had had J.H. and then sneering at her! Talk of gentlemen and cads! Isn't that caddish?

I have some letters of Prentice describing his travels in Greece — and the horrors of retzinato — but, as he admits, he was usually too tired to write much. He had to leave it until too late. He was over 45, and not up to long journeys on mule-back, followed by scanty meals and buggy beds.

Hodders have a book in the press which I have read in proof, and like. It is a — very belated — account of a subaltern's experiences in March 1918 disaster.[10] Read only touched the fringe.[11] This tries to give the full story. Its defect to my humble intelligence is this — the first part describes the life of a battalion which had been coddled to softness, if the author is right; and the soldiers were there, not to fight the enemy, but to love one another. If that was the 5th Army, no wonder they got licked! I have harsh memories of the discipline in the 3rd Army. I also remember that we held the line until the recoil of the 5th made us retreat; and in September I saw with amazement the interminable series of German graves in front of our front line. Battalion after battalion after battalion under one huge cross: 21.3.18.; and the Colonel, his officers and men buried all together. I never before understood why we got that licking. Now I know. The 5th Army weren't soldiers — they were a Salvation Army of mutual admirers. You shall have an advance copy of the book. It is a sort of Georgian Poetry war.

We have had super-heat and thunder galore. Now fresh and sunny and pleasant. My daughter is on the rack of her Brevet — sort of Oxford Local — and miserable accordingly. She goes to the guillotine on Thursday, but I have arranged for her to give a dinner tonight to some friends and — as Pino says — "so forget the terrible time"!

Yours
RICHARD ALDINGTON

[1] See above, letter 64.

[2] The *Times* did not publish. Campbell also pepared a long letter for the booklet compiled by Rob Lyle in answer to the detractors of *Pinorman*. See above, letter 61 n 12.

[3] The letter runs in part: "I suppose you think astrology is nonsense, but when you tell us that Norman Douglas was born on December 8th you have given the clue to his character. He was born under the sign of Sagittarius, and both homosexuality and selfishness are typical Sagittarian traits. André Gide was of this House. I have been a boy-lover for 20 years and soon discovered that the only way to avoid trouble was to throw the onus of making the advances on to the boys. I am friendly with them, and if they want anything further, it's up to them. Well, I can tell you this, that if a Sagittarian boy enters the milieu, I know at once that a fierce homosexual adventure is on the cards. . . . Sagittarian selfishness is evident all along the line. Look at Spinoza's ethics — the very handbook of selfishness, or at Samuel Butler's or Beethoven's opinions. It is due to the fact that the Sagittarius is so masculine that he likes to stand alone. He has no understanding of the claims of friendship — the Sagittarian boy never has a circle of friends — and if you draw him into a union he will try to turn it to his own advantage — like Stalin in Lenin's circle, for instance." This letter was also included in the booklet defending *Pinorman*.

[4] That is, the problem as to who wrote "On a Woman of Fashion"; see above, letter 63.

[5] The only poem with either of these titles which could be traced is "In the Backs" by Frances Cornford, first published in *The Distaff Muse; An Anthology of Poetry Written by Women* (1949). G. K. S. has not been identified.

6 The line has not been traced.

7 *Ezra Pound and T. S. Eliot, A Lecture* (1954). Part of a lecture series delivered about 1938.

8 On June 29, after talks between Eisenhower and Churchill and Eden, which commenced on June 26 in Washington, the United States and Great Britain announced their agreement to draft plans for a Southeast Asian defensive alliance, dependent on France's new premier's making peace with the Communist-led rebels of Vietnam, Laos, and Cambodia.

9 By the Amateur Dramatic Club.

10 Carl Fallas *Saint Mary's Village through the Eyes of an Unknown Soldier Who Lived On* (1954).

11 Herbert Read *The Innocent Eye* (1933).

66

20 July 1954   *Montpellier*

MY DEAR BIRD,

The fatal day of M. Mendés-France! Nothing yet signed, but the radio sounds hopeful.[1] We all long for peace here, I can tell you, and the quelling of these arrogant Americans, with their "leadership" — as usual, leading in the rear when there is something to be done! If this succeeds, note it has been achieved by France and England with the positive hostility of America which has been forced to come in at the tail end. Note also it happens in Geneva, not in N. Y. State. The "United" Nations cease for the first time to be a rubber stamp for USA. You haven't lived in America, and can't know the vindictive hatred for "Eurrup" outside the old original States, nor the strength of the German – Italian – Irish coalition which is all for war with Russia. That China Lobby is a most sinister thing with huge interests behind it.

You realise why the French now oppose the European Army which they first suggested? [2] They meant England to come in whole-heartedly and make it a Third Force, mediating between the two Barbarians. England half-ratted, and allowed the Americans to twist it into another move in their encirclement of Russia. This South-East Asia "Defense" (!) Pact is another.[3] Why does England so meekly acquiesce in such obvious aggression?

But I shall be relieved when this agreement is signed. It's a real step towards peace.

There is a point about Marie Byron Leigh Taillefer which has been misreported. She could not possibly have been Ada Leigh or a Protestant, since the Departmental archives register her as having died a nun in the region of St Affrique. Ada Leigh must be another daughter of Augusta.[4] The whole English bunch seem to have cut off from Elizabeth Medora when she married. The "retired soldier" is a delicious piece of British snobbery! Taillefer was an officer's batman, and a peasant. But he gave Elizabeth and Marie a home, and allowed Marie to use his name. I think it probable the Lovelaces were very happy to see the last of Elizabeth!

We hear you have a poor summer. It is not really hot here — 75° instead of the usual 95° — and we have had more rain than usual. The Midi Libre pointed out gravely that this July we've had 27 millimètres. You can infer how drowned we are! However, the fruit is late, and there is a little mildew in the grapes (magnified by the newspapers into an economic disaster!) but I can forecast the vintage for you in this Department and its neighbours — too much poor wine and too little good, sold by the vignerons at 25–30 frcs the litre, and by the restaurants at 200–250. Et vive la bagatelle!

Strange that there are no records of Theodore Cook. I thought the Colleges kept some memoranda of their alumni, especially when they achieved distinction? It seems impossible that a scholar and writer and sportsman should so soon be quite forgotten. But of course the two wars punched terrific gaps in cultural tradition. The ignorance of young English appals me but then I suppose old codgers always are appalled by the young. I must turn my friend Dibben on to Cook — it was he who found those rare books for me. Although in no sense a scholar — he can't even read French — he has a remarkable knowledge of the bye-ways of our own literature, especially poetry, a strange hobby in the Deputy-Chief Traffic Manager of what used to be the G.W.R.!

Thank you for your too generous note on the Alcestis production.[5] It seems to have fallen completely flat, for only one other friend has even mentioned it, and the B.B.C. have forwarded no mail. As far as the reviewers and their somewhat sheep-like readers are concerned, I seem to reverse the Queen's prerogative, and am not able to do anything right! But I am glad the B.B.C. did not over-poeticise. It is a strange play — we have to remember we are in fairy-land with Herakles as clown – hero. What I always wonder is how Admetus was able even to look Alcestis in the eye again, still less how he could play the noble husband. Euripides was surely a feminist here!

The delay in the TEL is really quite maddening. I learned from the solicitor that the *six* legal documents involved must be signed and released at intervals "of a few days"![6] [. . .] Unless they hurry up, we [RA and his daughter] shall have a less care-free holiday. I have everything arranged, but with extra dollars I could have taken her about more and provided a more chic toilette de plage. You have no idea how much these scanty bathing suits, shorts &c. made in the beau style now cost. Alas! I do.

Have I mentioned that I am at work on a little book to be called "Who *was* Frédéric Mistral?"[7] Oh, it's a poor thing and a bit cheap, you may say, but an attempt to give the visiting English a few hints about the less frequented places of Provence and Languedoc, linking the places with Mistral and the other poets. I am taking Mistral's life and books as the theme, but embroidering with places and the other poets. Do you know our 18th century Montpellérain, l'Abbe Favre, author of the Siege de Cadaroussa?[8] Very amusing, almost the only burlesque poem I really like.

The anthology is done. Will it ever appear in this age of high living and low thinking? Heinemann are not exactly warm about it.

Ever yours,

RICHARD ALDINGTON

1 On the following day, 21 July 1954, in Geneva, representatives of France and the Communist Vietminh forces signed armistice agreements, thus bringing to a halt fighting in Vietnam and Laos.

2 An attitude expressed in the Paris Pacts, 1954, which implemented Western European Union, ended Allied military occupation, and recognized the sovereignty of the Federal Republic of West Germany, who were permitted to rearm and enter NATO.

3 Southeast Asia Treaty Organization signed Sept 1954 at Manila by Australia, France, Great Britain, New Zealand, Pakistan, Phillipines, Thailand, and U.S.A.

4 No record of an Ada Leigh has been found.

5 Presented July 4 and 7; see above, letters 64 and 65.

6 See above, letters 64 and 65.

7 See above, letters 58 and 63.

8 1858 (first separate publication).

67

13 August 1954   *A Daou,[1] Le Lavandou, Var*

MY DEAR BIRD,

Your account of the visit to Quebec and Montreal is very interesting.[2] Although I was so long in USA I never visited Canada, because of the liberal nature of American immigration laws. If we had once crossed a frontier we should not have been allowed in again without going on the quota for a second time — which is usually refused! I have driven along the banks of the St Lawrence in upper N. Y. State, in the evening with vast areas of violet shadow beyond the river — wonderful. But Canadians are yankees, and have nothing in common with us. Even in the West Indies I noticed that any criticism of England at once gained their approbation, no matter how absurd or violent the criticism, whereas a hint against the USA had them bristling.

I wonder how much poverty there is in the USA now. In the years between 1934 and the full employment of the war it was still staggeringly common. What it must have been before F.D.R. I hesitate to guess. As late as 1937 there were still huge gangs of men working on unneeded highways, and such absurd "boondoggling" jobs as cataloging ALL the names on graves in the cemeteries of Connecticut!

It is the West which is still interesting, outside such places as Los Angeles. Once you cross the Mississippi, you are comparatively free from the crass industrialism, in country sparsely inhabited. Texas huge and open, though infested with chauvinist Germans. There were oases in Florida, too, but I'm told they're swamped under the muddy waves of vulgarity.

I shall ask Temple to clarify this Marie situation, and to try to get me the date of her death. I have not seen those departmental archives myself, and am going only on what I am told — not a very safe basis.

Yours is the first indication I have had that the B.B.C. are doing Alcestis again.[3] It is quite unexpected. They wrote recently offering a very inadequate fee for permission to copy the recordings for (a) broadcasting in the Colonies, (b) performances on H.M.'s ships. I replied that it seemed rather hard on the poor sailors who would doubtless prefer something more modern with girls in it, but that of course they might reproduce. The particular meanness of the British Government towards writers is shown in all these transactions — no fault of the B.B.C., of course. For two Alcestis broadcasts of 70 minutes each they paid just under 40 pounds after deduction of tax at 9/– in every pound. (Does the Aga Khan pay that on his English investments?) Moreover, as you know the Govt. helps itself to a monstrous share of the license money before any goes to the B.B.C.

It seems A. W. Lawrence has been threatening action (legal) and has dragged in Namier — why? My solicitor and Kershaw are having a grand meeting with Collins and their lawyers (today, I think, or Monday) and are going to say plainly that Collins must either stop "stalling" and fix a publication date or lose their option on the book and the 4500 they have paid. I see their difficulty better than Kershaw or the lawyer. It is quite easy with an English judge to get an injunction against a book when the pretence of libel is obviously frivolous or inadequate. The main purpose of a British Judge is to procure litigation and fees for his junior confrères. But though publisher and author eventually win their case, the book has been off the market for weeks, perhaps months, costs are terrific, and book-sellers are so frightened that they won't re-order. The trouble — I don't know what it is — seems to be in Chapter I (obviously the Chapman scandal) and in the last chapter. What that may be I can't imagine. Perhaps there is some refer-ence to the Colonel's dislike for his mother, which is based, as you know on his letter to Mrs Shaw,[4] which Jix won't let me quote verbatim. I had to give it as my opinion! I said at the time that this seemed to me both dishonest and inviting litigation.

Did you see that a man called Lord Russell (not the great Bertie) has resigned his official post in order to publish a book the government disapproves![5] And do you know that Frere (of Heinemann) is to be brought up at Bow Street for publi-cation of an alleged obscene work, which in fact was warmly recommended to him by that blameless Ethiopian, Morgan Forster, O.M.?[6] We are back in the days of Jix.[7]

You can hardly conceive how pleasant it is to re-live the thoroughly wholesome life of Mistral and the rustic if unimportant Félibres, after the morass of lies, pre-tentiousness and intrigue of Lawrence. Really TEL represents the very worst side of upper-class England, though I think some of his most unpleasant features are Irish. They have no equals in underhand intrigue.

Yes, the settlements are a great relief. If it were not for American fanaticism there would be an excellent chance for a general settlement which might last 50 years. But that indifference to world affairs you noticed in Canada is even more widespread in America; and to get the money for re-armament &c a terrific propa-ganda bogey had to be created — the Communist Terror Conquering the World. Truman and all Washington lost their heads when the yank divisions ran away from the Chinese.[8] Eisenhower, I think, is not a bad fellow, but how can he con-jure down this Bogey, and deal with the insane chauvinism of the Generals and the Big Money Boys? I think our line should be to pay lip service to America, get rid of Churchill toot sweet!, not commit ourselves one inch more, try to wiggle out of what we are committed to, and make a separate peace. We are all in a lather here over the European Army. I send you a typical article;[9] which I doubt would be copied in England except perhaps by the Guardian or the Tribune.

Ever yours,
RICHARD ALDINGTON

1 RA was on holiday chez Mons Clerc, A Daou.
2 Bird had lectured at McGill University in Montreal.
3 *Alcestis* was not repeated again; see above, letters 64, 65, and 66.
4 See T. E. Lawrence to Charlotte F. Shaw [Karachi] 18 Aug 1927 and 8 May 1928; Miranshah 10 July 1928.
5 *Scourge of The Swastika: A Short History of the Nazi War Crimes* (1954) by Edward Frederick Langley Russell, Lord Russell of Liverpool. He resigned as Assistant Judge Advocate General, a post he had held since 1951.
6 On 8 Oct 1954 William Heinemann Ltd, Alexander Stewart Frere, chairman of Heinemann, and Walter Baxter, the author, were committed for trial charged with publishing an obscene libel in *The Image and the Search*. When the case was brought to trial at the Old Bailey, the jury was unable to reach a verdict, and the presiding judge directed a retrial. On Nov 30 a second jury disagreed on the verdict. At a third hearing at the Old Bailey, a verdict of not guilty was returned. Frere wrote a brief account of the trials in a letter to *The Times* (3 Dec

1954). RA called Forster an Ethiopian in reference to Jeremiah XIII, 23: "Can the Ethiopian change his skin, or the leopard his spots?"

[7] That is, William Joynson Hicks, who as Home Secretary was instrumental in the seizure of typescripts and paintings by D. H. Lawrence. See above, letter 30 n 1; below, letter 133 n 7. Usually RA uses "Jix" to designate Lancelot William Joynson-Hicks.

[8] RA refers to the Korean War.

[9] The article has not been identified.

68

9 *September 1954*   *Montpellier*

MY DEAR BIRD,

I am grieved to hear that you have been down already with a winter malady while I here have my chronic bronchitis entirely quiescent under a genial sun, with the cicadas still chirring away by night and the owls (strangely known as grands-ducs) hooting merrily at night. It was England's climate which made England great — there was nothing for it but to go out and found a world Empire! But I am appalled at the thought of what people may suffer this winter. Let us hope that it will be mild. It can be. I remember that in the 1930s I had to spend several weeks in London for some reason, and hardly needed an overcoat, although it was in Dec – Jan. Those were the days when the Chief Customs Officer in Dover was a great fan of mine, and the various peers and plutocrats on the Channel boat could scarcely believe their ears when the loud speaker at Calais chanted: "Mr Aldington's car off first!" I think that's my only claim to la gloire. But oh! the bliss of getting back on a bad pavé road, with a smell of fresh croissants, garlic and drains, and a bistrot Au Rendezvous des Alliés! I meant to tell you — recently in a very remote hamlet about 40 miles inland from here I saw a faded sign on a little tumbledown inn: Ici on loge à pied et à cheval. I could have wept.

Yes, I have been under a very great strain over this TEL book, for it is important financially, and still more my reputation is at stake, particularly since the Pinorman affair — which last by the way was "arranged" by Miss Cunard [1] who evidently doesn't know the English law of Conspiracy! I have found much comfort in your always interesting and kindly letters, and I think you are one of the very few friends who have realised the strain. It is a ray of real hope to get by to-day's post a letter from Collins saying:

"I have sent Kershaw today the FINAL list of corrections which I hope you also will find very small. And then I will never trouble you again! I discussed them with Kershaw in Paris, and I don't think he was too appalled."

Of course, it is not quite as sweet as that sounds. Collins's directors have been at loggerheads, and pressure of an extreme nature was brought to bear on them by Prof Lawrence, Liddell Hart, Storrs, Namier and — Winston Churchill, who did not disdain to suggest a lie, — all trying to force Collins to suppress the book.[2] If these alterations are reasonable, that coalition is defeated, for I shall accept. Remain the Americans, who seemingly are more suggestible. They are restive about Lowell Thomas who, in my opinion, is a contemptible phoney and a bigger liar than Lawrence. I'll let you know all news.

Later. Since writing this I have decided that it might be a good idea to go to Paris and try to fix up the definitive text with Kershaw. We can telephone London in case of doubt. So I have wired Mrs Kershaw to ask if she can put us up for a few days — as she has often invited us — and await reply. I think the change might be good, and Catherine should see a little of jeune fille's Paris. I shall go by car. It is cheaper than a train, ever so much nicer, and by taking the Auverge-Centre route one can find quite cheap inns of a reasonable sort.

I'm sorry to hear about J. O' London,[3] following the others. I thought of it as a stepping stone for all those very numerous people who are groping for something above the mere money-making rags. It is such a damned shame that the *people* are so badly provided for "culturally" — to use an odious word. That is one aspect of the Félibres which I like, they are so truly "democratic" in the genuine sense. At the centenary banquet in Avignon we had Daladier and the Archbishop[4] and a prominent barrister (Maître Julian of Lyons) mixed in with clerks and farmers and peasants and shopkeepers and cow-boys with just the one bond of poetry, Provence, the old traditions, and not a trace of condescension on the one hand or servility on the other. There was none of the Edith Sitwell, old-lady-of-the-Manor patronising of "Mr Smith, the bootblack poet." Apart from Daladier and the prelate, the only rank recognised was that as Félibre — from Capoulié through Majoral to Soci, i.e. poetic merit or seniority. Finally I like it that in Provence the greatest insult is to say very politely: Sir, I fear you are impolite.

Yes, of course, journalism by pictures. Can't you see it in the USA, where the comic strips are all important? If you watch the average American you will often see that on buying a paper he glances vaguely at the headlines, and then is absorbed by the "comics." On Sunday mornings there is a 15 or 20 minutes broadcast telling people what the comics are for that day. I think people in Europe don't realise what a danger the Americans are to our culture in that they have debased the minds of many of their own people, and now are doing it to ours. The Universities are part of it. Columbia, for instance, takes no care of its English poetry and drama, and undergraduates scribble freely on margins or underline or write sneers. At Columbia for instance I found that several odd volumes had disappeared from the sets of Bullen's Elizabethan Dramatists,[5] and the librarian coolly "guessed" that "some of the boys" had stolen them — "only fer fun." When I asked how he proposed to replace them, he merely grinned and shrugged. In some ways I think America a nearer danger than USSR.

All good wishes,
RICHARD ALDINGTON

The head of the B.M. Reading Room[6] has most kindly offered to look up facts for me within the limits imposed by his small staff. I mean to ask what he can tell about Theodore Cook. It is a shame he should be forgotten.

My friend Temple here has been made director of the local radio, and I haven't seen him since. I shall try to prod him along useful lines. He is a strong DHLawrenceite.

1 RA refers to what he called a "concerted attempt to discredit" *Pinorman*. He attributed it to Nancy Cunard, whom he described as the *"pimpante* cheerlaeder of this little gang" which attacked *Pinorman*, because of her letter of April 1954 to William Heinemann Ltd, publishers of *Pinorman*. It runs: "It is astonishing that a reputable publishing firm such as yourselves should bring out the gross travesty of Norman Douglas and Orioli by Richard Aldington, entitled *Pinorman*. As you must be aware, there would be a strong case for libel here, among all the other misrepresentations, if Norman Douglas were alive. All the friends of Norman Douglas will, I am sure, be as ready as I am to co-operate in whatever form of collective pro-

test may be judged the most suitable." Elsewhere she referred to "preposterous slanders, incomprehension, wilfull misrepresentation" in *Pinorman* and described it as a "labor of hatred." (See Nancy Cunard to Walter Lowenfels, Toulouse 15 Nov [1954] and Bedford 14 Jan 1955.) Nancy Cunard's review of the book in *Time and Tide* (see above, letter 60 n 9) and those of others such as Compton Mackenzie and David Low confirmed Aldington's opinion. For his plan to retaliate see above, letter 61 n 12.

2 See above, letters 59 n 15 and 60.

3 *John O'London* discontinued publication 10 Sept 1954.

4 Monseigneur de Llobet, originally from Perpignan and once secretary of the celebrated Cardinal de Cabrières.

5 *The English Dramatists* ed Arthur Henry Bullen 14 vols (1885–87).

6 Noel Farquharson Sharp.

69

7 *October 1954*   *Montpellier*

MY DEAR BIRD,

There is nobody here who really understands English literature, so that I naturally think of you. How do you scan Paradise Lost, Bk 8. line 216:

"Imbued, bring to their sweetness no satiety."? According to the sense and punctuation "imbued" should belong to the line before:

"Though pleasant, but thy words with Grace Divine" But that only shifts the problem, for one of the two lines (to my ear) has two syllables too many. One is surely not intended to pronounce "satiety" as "sa'tie"?

Now will you look up Carlyle's 1827 essay on Goethe, read the first paragraph carefully, and tell me if you don't think it slap-dash journalese? True, it was first published as a review (which it isn't), but he published it in book form (or was it collected posthumously?) and in that case should have revised.[1] The defect to me is not that of a mannerism or eccentricity, but of sheer incompetent writing and rather vulgar English. He was at least 30 at the time.

Which brings me to Matthew Arnold, who shocks me by stating somewhere that Carlyle was the greatest living English writer in his day. I don't believe it. I think Carlyle a bad influence — look how he made a fool of Ruskin![2] It only goes to show how much we are all afraid of the pulpit. A man has only to display moral earnestness and to affect authority, and we instantly say he is a great writer. Even Arnold tends to preach, I feel, instead of discussing. He is a much better *writer* than Pater (who appears to have had no natural talent whatsoever as a writer) but Pater as *critic* is more civilised.

Arnold's poetry is a very different thing, and to me his two elegies[3] still seem virtually flawless. And there are many of his other poems which are infinitely attractive, and grow on one with time. But he had no dramatic and very little narrative power. Sorhab and Rustum[4] strikes me as too Homeric by half — an interesting demonstration that the Homeric manner does not suit modern English. Indeed, I incline to the heresy that Homer was a mistake. Verse is the wrong form for any continuous narrative, and stanzas quite ridiculous. The fountain-head of true narrative is Herodotus, not Homer. If Homer ever existed in the form of "Lays of Ancient Greece," no doubt they went very well — one at a time — after dinner to the accompaniment of the minstrel's harp. But an "epic" is really a monstrosity. It is only the amazing beauty of style of Virgil and — in a very different way — Milton which makes us think otherwise. Ariosto is much more lively, but even his skipping stanzas become tedious. I can't read more than a canto at a time, and it is a mystery to me how Symonds was able to read Marino's 40,000 lines of "Adone" in two days.[5] I see the beauty of extracts, but none of these writers could tell a story. Chaucer could, but he had the slow mediaeval rhythm.

I daresay this is all dreadful nonsense, and I will avoid the good confrère's natural transition of saying: That of course brings up Wyndham Lewis. I too have much admired those portraits of his, and have felt indignant at the way self-appointed art "critics" have brushed them aside in favour of work which seems to me plain charlatanism. John, Lewis and Dali have always seemed to me naturally gifted artists, who would have done much finer work in a less hostile and stupid environment. Some of those early Dalis — drawings — are equal to the old Masters, and he has to make a mountebank of himself to support his wife and himself! Disgusting. These foul governments waste milliards on every kind of corruption and folly (in which I include Unesco!) and won't spare 1000 a year for men of genius like Lewis and Dali. I wonder how much Lewis's blindness is psychological, as Joyce's was said to be? Lewis's books leave me torn between admiration and impatience. They usually begin with splendid energy and felicity, only to peter out as he grows tired of his theme and hurries to be done with it. He was driven of course by the necessity to earn his living. If he could have had a little leisure and respite, the chance to write half as much, I believe he would have written more than twice as well. Some of his asperity and contempt must be due, I think, to his indignation at seeing preferred to him by the public and highly paid other writers who were immeasureably his inferiors intellectually and artistically. Another fault of his as a creative writer is taking some whimsical notion and elaborating it to absurdity. You will find one or two examples — well-written though — in the earliest numbers of the English Review.

If there is ever another period of well-fed leisure I think the critics of that time will look back on the writers of this age in much the same spirit of contemptuous pity that the Victorians looked back on the Grub Street of the age of young Johnson. The highly-paid writers of the last 40 years have not been the best, and those honoured are not the best. Gold medals and O.Ms. for Audens and Eliots — calumny and even persecution for Lawrences and Aldous Huxleys. The later Huxley is a drivelling pervert, in my opinion, but up till Eyeless in Gaza [6] he was almost the best we had. They should have given him the Nobel. Douglas was never given his due. Apropos, I suppose all this nonsense about him stems from an artless remark of Coleridge's to the effect that a good writer must be a good man? [7] It is a labour of Sisyphus to make Douglas a good man! Did I tell you Maugham wrote me: "All you say about Norman and Pino is true"?

Yesterday I signed the Spanish-American contract for TEL, and whatever Collins do we publish in France on Nov 2nd — All Souls day! Absit omen. I'll get you a copy. There are some cuts (to spare the impatience of the frivolous Gaul) but many passages now cut from the English version. What do people say about the prosecution of my old friend, A. S. Frere? They must see it as a Beaverbrook humbug. Why does Maxwell-Fyfe lend himself to such malicious Tartufferie?

Adieu! Ever yours,
RICHARD ALDINGTON

[1] Carlyle's first two essays on Goethe appeared in *Foreign Review* in 1828: "Goethe's Helena" (April) and "Goethe" (July). Both were collected in *Miscellanies* (1839) 143–93 and 194–255. RA probably refers to "Goethe's Helena."

[2] Possibly in Ruskin's view that salvation was available in a return to mediaeval conditions and dictatorial rule by a just man.

[3] "Thyrsis" (1867) and possibly "The Scholar Gypsy" (1853).

[4] 1853.

[5] 1623.

[6] 1936. See also RA to John Atkins, Montpellier 26 June 1957: "He [Aldous Huxley] is certainly the best essayist we have, and his early novels were very amusing indeed" (Texas).

[7] RA may refer to Coleridge's remark in *Biographia Literaria* (1817) that a good poet must also be a profound philosopher.

70

14 November 1954   *Montpellier*

MY DEAR BIRD,

What you say about Milton interests me greatly. I have never been able to agree with the Pound – Eliot depreciation of him — (since abandoned by Eliot) or with the over-valuing by the English Universities. I think he was potentially a very great poet indeed, but that he was happiest when English-inspired. I believe he was definitely spoiled by "highbrowism" — "knowing too damned much" as DHL defined it. From my smattering of Italian and neo-Latin Renaissance poets I should say they gave him some beauties but many faults. There are magnificent passages in Paradise Lost [1] but it seems to me a travesty of Christianity or even of Judaism. What his sect was I have no idea. Possibly he was the only Miltonian? The whole subject has been distorted by political and nationalist prejudices. But of course I really know nothing about it. The intellectual tragedy of our time is that so much is known and that so very few know it. The lowbrow despises a knowledge beyond his grasp; the highbrow over-values himself for that little knowledge which is a dangerous thing. You don't find the really great men despising anyone for lack of learning. I think of something they said to me in the Hollywood studio when I failed to succeed there: "Never over-estimate the knowledge of the people, but never under-value their intelligence." I think the opposite of that is the mistake of all highbrowism.

St Mawr [2] has been over-praised by Leavis, and wildly denounced by Middleton Murry for personal reasons. Very few books of DHL's are fully comprehensible unless one knows the personal circumstances; for, like Goethe's, nearly all DHL's "creative" writing is a projection of his own life. His opera omnia are huge autobiography embroidered. Towards the end of 1923 Frieda suddenly got one of her almost animal yearnings for her children — when they were in Mexico and DHL wanted to get on with the Plumed Serpent! [3] They had a fearful row and she insisted on going to England, whither most reluctantly he followed her — in the middle of winter! and of course went down flop with a "cold." He suspected Frieda of an intrigue with Murry. There was that ghastly scene at the Café Royal.[4] And there was the rankling fury of his combats with Mabel Luhan, for Americans and especially American women are incomparably gifted for ill-bred offensiveness. It was a period when DHL was maddened with hate — "hate" of Frieda who had dragged him away from his book, hate of Murry who he thought had betrayed him, hate of Mabel who had insulted him and thus was holding him away from completing his American – Mexican phase, hatred of "England" which repelled and disliked him, and hatred of "America" because it was against his England. (You've got to live in America to know how much they hate England and long to see it humiliated by them, which they have done, damn their eyes!) He was in a paroxysm of hate — one or two of those anti-Murry stories (Smile, The Border Line, Jimmy and the Desperate Women)[5] are almost insane in their hatred.

St Mawr belongs to this phase, which to me is a painful and regrettable one. You will find in Brett's book an account of how vindictively DHL felt when he was writing St Mawr, where Mrs Witt is Mabel, Rico is a projection of Murry in terms of Jan Juta, and Frieda is satirised in her and in Louise.[6] Strangely enough although the last part of the story has those magnificent Rocky Mountain pages, the early part is not well written. It has mannerisms. In the first edition he had "curious" or "curiously" dozens of times, and cut them or changed them when I pointed it out in 1926. St Mawr is an expression of the powerfully disagreeable side of DHL, though of course it has his genius and is redeemed by the superb ending.

You will forgive my arrogance if I say that I think a man like Leavis is as incapable of understanding DHLawrence's real genius and beauty as most of his countrymen. He has even less chance as he is a self-important highbrow.

Alarums and excursions on my front. The French TEL is out, but alas! "done" by illiterate translators who have made a fearful mess, while the publisher (without asking me) has given it the stupid title of Lawrence l'Imposteur. There was a steal of some of the stories under guise of a review on Radio Paris, and a friend of TEL's got out a pre-publication-day review![7] Otherwise it seems so far to have attracted little attention. Unfortunately, as you so rightly point out, reviewers don't read books — they report the gossip of the town and praise their friends.

From Collins I hear that the book is now printing in Glasgow. Let us hope this is true. It would be fallacious to have any hope that it will be favourably or even fairly treated. Lawrence's friends are powerful — extending to Downing St — and have worked to secure key reviews and create prejudice. In any case, with none of Lawrence's genius I am rather in his state of British literary Ishmael. I belong to none of the powerful cliques — sodomites, communists, reviewers, Civil servants, university men — yet have had the impudence to earn my living and freedom abroad by writing for 30 years. Yet my writing is not utter trash and flatters nobody. As Aldous Huxley (a fellow victim) said years ago — they will forgive you if you make 1000 a year by writing trash, and they will forgive you if you write decently and make nothing, but if you write decently and make 1000 a year *that* is the unforgiveable sin which must be revenged. The journalists make up for their flatteries of the conformists by abusing any independent who lacks influential friends and large capital. I don't even know one English writer who would stand up for me. Maugham, for instance, knew perfectly well that all I say in Pinorman is true; but he won't allow himself to be quoted — *that* might involve controversy and lose the support of some reviewers. So he contents himself with writing me a private letter (NOT to be quoted!) in which he says he knows all I say is true, and invites me to dinner!! Honour is satisfied. So I think I can safely promise you that if (for a change) Collins keep their word and publish me in

January, you will read some choice abuse and curious distortion of truth some ten to fourteen weeks hence.

I hope you escaped the latest floods we read of?

Yours,
RICHARD ALDINGTON

[1] 1667.

[2] 1925.

[3] 1926.

[4] In Feb 1924 the Lawrences were hosts at a farewell dinner, a "Last Supper" at the Café Royal. The guests were Murry, S. S. Koteliansky, Dorothy Brett, Mary Canaan, the Carswells, and Mark Gertler. The dinner ended when Lawrence collapsed, very ill from too much drink, and Murry and Koteliansky took him away. During the evening Murry said to Lawrence, "I love you, Lorenzo, but I won't promise not to betray you." Afterward Lawrence wrote to Murry reminding him of "that charming dinner" at the Café Royal, repeating Murry's remark, and then adding, "Well, you CAN'T betray me, and that's all there is to that. Ergo, just leave off loving me. Let's wipe off all that Judas – Jesus slime."

[5] In *The Woman Who Rode Away and Other Stories* (1928); all three had had prior periodical publication.

[6] *Lawrence and Brett, A Friendship* (1933); see p 128 where Brett states that she has "begun to type a new story" by Lawrence, *St Mawr*. Lawrence was often in RA's thoughts at this time; commencing in 1952 he carried on a correspondence with Edward Nehls, who was at work on his *D. H. Lawrence: A Composite Biography* (3 vols 1957–59).

[7] The review has not been found. Even RA did not know where it had appeared, having seen only "torn out sheets." See RA to Rob Lyle, Montpellier 12 Nov 1954 (Berg). *Lawrence l'Imposteur* appeared on 3 Nov 1954.

7I

4 December 1954   *Montpellier*

MY DEAR BIRD,

Many thanks for your cutting, about Frere — the first news of this re-trial I have had.[1] I *cannot* read the contemporary English papers, remembering the grand old England that was — they are humiliating. I am glad Frere has been able to escape. But I have a grudge against him. He published this dubious book (I am told that the author is the usual "homo" and that the experiences of his "heroine" with men are really his own!) and rejected scornfully Carl Fallas's war book, St Mary's Village.[2] This book has been highly praised by many people, is selling steadily, and Churchill has awarded it 300 pounds from some fund the P.M. controls! This last news I have from Mrs Fallas, and it may be confidential. Anyway, Frere has lately taken in "young and vigorous" literary advisers, who have rejected Fallas's book and my anthology, and damned nearly got old Frere jugged!

I don't trust E. M. Forster.[3] It is a libel to write it even to you, but he really belongs with that same disgusting crowd who disgrace our country.

I enclose a cutting about my TEL here. You will see it was partly suggested or "documented" from London. But after a slow start, the book is beginning to attract serious attention. I am in touch with a French family of high standing (among others) who formulate a sensational charge against TEL which I am investigating. I have been on the radio here, in my Frensshe of Stratforde-atte-Bowe; and apparently must do so again.[4] Radio-Paris asked for a "débat." I refused to undertake a merely extempore discussion in a language which is not mine with people who are violently pro-Lawrence, have not studied the evidence, and are clearly being prompted from London. I have replied that I must have written questions and a guarantee they would not be changed; and will record my answers at the Radio station here under a similar guarantee.[5] I hear from Amiot-Dumont [6] this morning that they think those conditions will be met — which surprises me.

The Monde review was reviewed by the Times as news in a loathly hypocritical "let's-all-be-broadminded-give-the-fellow-a-fair-trial-and-shoot-him" style which is more disgusting than frank hostility.[7] As to the abuse etc coming in January, I am prepared for it. A compensation is that Collins say their advance orders are so heavy their entire staff will be occupied for two *weeks* from the 3rd Jan in packing and despatching. Review copies go out on the 31/12/54. The cuts are fewer than you fear. The end has gone, but it is preserved in the French edition and I will send you a copy as soon as I have time to correct it for you. Such stupid blunders, which all the Lawrence experts reviewing have so far failed to detect!

Will you return the Monde cutting? I am sorry, but I may need it for the "débat." There have been other enormously long reviews but nothing to the purpose. The high-brows so far have entirely boycotted me. Only the common newspapers and weeklies have reviewed.

Ever yours,
RICHARD ALDINGTON

1 See above, letter 67 n 6.
2 See above, letter 65.
3 See Forster's "The Law and Obscenity" in *The Listener* 11 Nov 1954, a letter prompted by attention in England to the legal question of obscenity. Frere's trial was a sympton. Forster addressed another, later letter (23 Dec 1954) to *The Listener* on the same subject.
4 RA was interviewed by Jacques Temple on his program "Littérature" broadcast from Montpellier.
5 Radio-Paris or, properly, Radiodiffusion Française broadcast a program, 45 minutes in length, devoted to RA's book on Lawrence. RA did not participate; Alister Kershaw spoke for him.
6 RA's French publisher.
7 See "French Criticisms of T. E. Lawrence, Old Memories Stirred by New Book" *Times* 27 Nov 1954. See also Jean Béraud-Villars, "La Legende du roi non couronné d'Arabie L'affaire Lawrence," *Le Monde* 26 Nov 1954.

72

11 December 1954   *Montpellier*

MY DEAR BIRD,

Fearful drums and tramplings going on at the girls' Lycée here. The Science mistress (it is said) called up a pupil to sniff a harmless gas which turned out to be chlorine, and the child is asthmatic! Such is the hardness of the youthful heart, my daughter hopes the mistress will be fired. It is apparently one of those cases where a Ministry of Education blunders. This young Science mistress has very high degrees, but no ability as a teacher while she has been given a class consisting half of girls who have done a year's chemistry or physics and half of girls who have done nothing in either subject to date. All this apparently because of some stupid rule which insists on one or two years at a Lycée before a University Lectureship is awarded. I fear a promising career may be broken, for parents have votes, and there is a belligerent Parents Association here on the American pattern. I belong, but never attend. Having lived through several chlorine gas attacks I don't understand how even a test-tube of chlorine gas did not make itself known to the whole class. But perhaps the German concentration was stronger.

This TEL affair, following the publication of the French translation, is becoming a sinister farce. The reviews here beat even our dear home-land in stupidity, bad faith, credulity and malice. I think it will give you a good English laugh to know that I have had to write to Le Monde in *defence* of the gallant Colonel! I am informed that TEL plotted and nearly carried out the assassination of Georges Picot. I am informed that a Frenchman who tried to stop the Gourand – Feisal row in Damascus [1] was nearly assassinated by his own countrymen. I am informed by a professor at the Collège de France and by Somerset Maugham that Lawrence committed suicide because Scotland Yard had a warrant for his arrest. I am informed that my description of Lawrence's entrance into Jerusalem is "inaccurate," [2] though all I do is to quote the contradictory versions of Lord Wavell and the Official War History and leave judgment to the reader. I receive not only reviews but letters about the book giving ex cathedra opinions — and the writers obviously haven't looked at the book. One of these is a "Professeur des Sciences" in the University of Bordeaux. "From what a height of bliss have we fallen," as Lucretius remarks. I really thought professors of Science read a document before incriminating the author.

What will it be in England? Frankly and perhaps fatuously I don't and can't think the reaction will be as silly. Someone will read the book and try to report it. Or will he? The Americans are still coughing violently over Lowell Thomas. I wish the Benedictine Maurists still existed here. I should like to join them and work on that colossal History of French Literature.[3] With half a dozen other students in monk's cowls, released from all worldly cares and ambitions, how much could be achieved. When I was working in the Library of the University of California (dreadful place) I used to take down a volume of that great Benedictine work and read a few lines before going on to my hideous doom. You would be staggered if you realised how poverty-stricken in English poetry the great American libraries are. In order to make my anthology I had to petition MacLeish (then Librarian of Congress) for permission to call on ALL the libraries of the 48 states. The (American) Encyclopaedia Britannica paid me very handsomely to compile (a still unpublished) anthology of European poetry in translation.[4] I was ashamed of the result, for America simply does not possess the books I asked for, every one of which must be in the B.M. and the Bodleian. "Trust not the Frank" said Byron. In matters of culture, especially poetry, "trust not the Yank."

Yes, Milton. What a problem. A very great poet indeed but somehow overlaid by a gigantic learning. I forget Arnold's exact words, but you will remember what he says about the danger to a poet of knowing too much. (He should know — wonderful and lovely as he is both as poet and prosateur.) What offends me in Paradise Lost (I think) is his bringing Jesus into it. That is such a lovely and heart-breaking story and told so inimitably in the Gospels. But he drags it into a Baroque pseudo-epic based on Judaism, Gnosticism, and I know not what weird heresies of Alexandria and Rotterdam. It is a profanation. Jesus in a Byzantine or Sicilian mosaic as Kosmokrator is perfectly acceptable — in Milton (to me) repulsive.

If I may boast, I scored the other day off an English highbrow who (to put me in my place) sneered at biography. I said: "I must disagree — the four greatest and most influential books in Europe are biographies." He fell into the trap, and demanded their names. "Matthew, Mark, Luke and John." I hope that may earn me a drop of water.

I am so glad you dislike Bunyan. I have resented him since childhood Sunday afternoons when all other books were forbidden. Surely he represents the dissidence of dissent at its most unpleasant, and Macaulay was at his worst in praising him. Allegory makes even the Faery Queen [5] a place of quicksands — but the Pilgrim's Progress [6] a slough of despond. But how many names it suggests for Churchill! Mr Boasting-both-Ways. Mr Falsest-Hour. Mr Yankee-Poodle. Lord Blenheim-Turnip. One could go on for hours. Are there none of the knaves who eat of England's table who will rid us of this pestilent knave? (I suppose that is treason? Let's hope so.)

I don't like Scott Fitzgerald.

Do you note my old friend Michael Arlen is in London? Much better than Fitzgerald, but the English highbrows hate him because he saved 100,000 pounds.

Ever yours,
RICHARD ALDINGTON

P.S. Your floods sound very unpleasant.[7] None here, bright sunshine, but the Rhone valley is said to be flooded. I am reading the complete unexpurgated Lockhart's life of Scott.[8] A wonderful book — in most ways better than Bozzy.[9] How much I dislike Fanny Burney — such ill-bred self-consciousness and rusticity.

[1] See RA *Lawrence of Arabia* 266.

[2] RA *Lawrence of Arabia* 212–13.

[3] *Histoire littéraire de la France* (12 vols 1733–63); sixteen additional volumes were published 1814–81.

[4] See below, letters 133, 134, 135, and 136.

[5] By Edmund Spenser (1590, 1596).

[6] 1678.

[7] On 11 Dec 1954 there was widespread flooding reported in the twelve Southern English counties. Sea walls at Fleetwood, on the west coast of England, had had to be reinforced, and a wide gap torn in the wall there had been closed only after hundreds of volunteers had worked long hours.

[8] 1838.

[9] That is, than James Boswell's *Life of Samuel Johnson* (1791).

73

15 December 1954 *Montpellier*

MY DEAR BIRD,

Herewith a cutting from les Nouvelles Littéraires,[1] which I discovered only yesterday. It is the first and only one I have seen which is both friendly and competent — René Lalou is a good and honest writer. What a pity he was not given the space other writers have had. From his opening paragraph I infer (perhaps wrongly) that the editor of the N.L. refused more space because of the (admittedly) cheap-jack title. Of course these literary papers everywhere are preoccupied with local gossip — at this moment the election of Giono to the Goncourt,[2] and various prize-winners. Interesting to note that even the most philistine newspapers here have front-page headlines on such events, while on the very same day the Daily Mail had a letter from some yahoo sneering at "art nonsense."

Apropos Churchill I also enclose a remarkable outburst from a French journalist who seems to have been much offended by some remarks of the Bishop of Leeds [3] quoted by and doubtless envenomed also by the Daily Mail. It is strange how the French cling to that story of Cambronne.[4] He not only utterly denied the story in the French Senate, but he was in fact taken prisoner at Waterloo as one can easily prove by turning up the Duke's despatch, where he mentions that Lobau and Cambronne were waiting as prisoners at his H.Q. when he came back from the battlefield. Like "Up Guards and at 'em!" and "My country, how I love my country," and Washington and the cherry-tree and how many more "historical" anecdotes, these flourish by being disproved. Which lends some weight to the veracious Colonel's contention that "History isn't made up of truth, so why worry?" [5] The answer to that is that one should not *deliberately* add to the lies and confuse the record, as he so unscrupulously did. But I think he will always have adherents. Did you ever read the singular case of Elizabeth Canning, temp. George II? Her case was phoney and she was obviously lying from the start, but the mob beseiged the Old Bailey and threatened to lynch anyone who gave evidence against her. The jury found her alleged oppressors and ravishers guilty, and there was another riot (I believe) when the Judge insisted on a King's Pardon for one of them. Even after the re-trial, when Canning was convicted of perjury and sentenced to deportation to America (apt place of punishment!) her adherents persisted she was innocent and raised money to make her independent! What next!

Talking of that, I have just received a most interesting long letter from a Detective-Inspector of the Sureté in Paris! [6] He has studied my text with evident care and writes to congratulate me on a smart piece of professional work certain to secure a conviction. But he is most intelligent in his remarks and evidently a man of wide reading and genuine culture, as so often happens in France. From his own experience he assures me he has found "women and pederasts" are almost invariably "illogical and elusive" in their evidence, which is certainly the case with Lawrence. The problem to me, however, is not that peculiar mixture of insolence and lying so typical of pederasts (think of Wilde!) but the fact that stories so improbable were believed by so many people in England, and still are, so that I and not Lawrence at the moment pass as the liar!

In confidence I got a glimpse of the peculiar English ambivalent attitude to pederasts in August. I was discussing the book with Bonham-Carter and Kershaw, and B.-C. brought up the question of how the press got hold of the story of TEL being at Farnborough [7] just at the silly season and giving Lawrence's own explanation that he wanted peace and was writing a book. I pointed out that as Sir Oliver Swann is categoric that the leakage was from the Colonial office, as Eddie Marsh was then Churchill's secretary at the C.O., and also a personal friend of Lawrence who in a letter not long before had told Marsh the tale, I thought the evidence pointed to him as the source of a newspaper story L. wanted published without giving it out himself. The story of the officer who knew him in Arabia and sold the news for £30 is too silly for anyone to believe but the Lawrence Bureau.

Bonham-Carter listened attentively, smiled and said: "Well, of course *he* would do anything for men." Rather wistfully and affectionately! Yet the same people can be quite ferocious in other cases, e.g. Wilde and Casement. Nobody, by the bye, seems to have seen yet the significance of L's continually urging Shaw to write on Casement and Shaw's continual refusal! Lawrence wanted his substitute father to write a defence of another Anglo-Irish pederast adventurer.

Vheels vithin vheels, as Mr Weller so wisely remarked.

I am sorry you formed so low an opinion of Fallas's St Mary's Village.[8] You surely cannot have read it, but go on some hostile review? I thought myself it was an excellent and moving account of the March '18 battle, with the sole fault that the author is a little mealy-mouthed and too apt to see good in everyone. I believe in a more realistic attitude, but apart from that it is an astonishing feat of observation and memory, and the characterisation of the soldiers is first rate. It is to a slight extent a refusal to accept the truth, which naturally appeals to Churchill who has lived on bunk. I am told that the Australian Official War History [9] shows Churchill up savagely. He was sending "finest Hour" cables of congratulation to New Zealanders fighting for their lives against appalling odds! "V" for Humbug!

Dick Church tells me John O'London [10] was killed because the owners found they could make more money by using that 4 tons of paper and printing-press to produce "comics." A fine comment on our culture. Another one is the Catalogue of remaindered books from the débâcle of that M.P. jailed for forgery — forget his name.[11] Judging from this list the blame lies with the philistine public who made him bankrupt when he was trying to publish contemporary books not all proletarian twaddle. It must be a blow for Grigson. The whole of his Crown Poets series and two of his own books.[12] I am sorry for him.

Ever yours
RICHARD ALDINGTON

[1] A review of *Lawrence L'Imposteur* in the issue of 9 Dec 1954.

[2] The Goncourt Academy, founded by Edmond de Goncourt, awards an annual prize for fiction. Jean Giono's *Voyage en Italie* (1953) received the prize in 1954.

[3] John Carmel Heenan.

[4] The story is that, at the battle of Waterloo, Cambronne commanded a division of the Old Guard. His division was almost annihilated. Surrounded by his enemies and summoned to surrender, Cambronne heroically replied, "The Guard dies; it does not yield."

[5] As cited by Lowell Thomas in *T. E. Lawrence by His Friends* 214. See also Lawrence to George Bernard Shaw [Karachi] 7 May 1928 where he describes *Seven Pillars* as "an effort to make history an imaginative thing" and calls it a "try at dramatising reality."

[6] Jacques Delarue.

[7] RAF station.

[8] See above, letter 65.

[9] RA is mistaken; see *The Australian Army at War, An Official Record of Service in Two Hemispheres, 1939–1944* (1944).

[10] See above, letter 68.

[11] Captain Peter Baker, member of Parliament for Norfolk South and head of the publishing firm Gray Walls at 7 Crown Passage, Pall Mall. On Dec 15 he was already serving a seven-year sentence for forging the names of Sir Bernard Docker and Sir John Mann to bills of exchange in an attempt to save a flimsy financial empire. The next day, Dec 16, Baker was expelled from the House of Commons.

[12] RA may refer to Grigson's editions of *Poems* by Coleridge, *Poems* by George Crabbe, and *Selected Poems* by Dryden, all published by Gray Walls Press. Apparently no books by Grigson, published by Gray Wall, were still in print in 1954.

74

6 January 1955   *Montpellier*

MY DEAR BIRD,

My daughter and I are just back from Florence, where we spent a very cheerful time with kind friends in a villa just below San Minato al Monte.[1] I bring back a mixed grill of feelings and observations. Briefly, I feel that Italy has saved her body and lost her soul. The régime is simply a humble satellite of the USA, even to the extent of disfiguring the roads and landscape with the innumerable commercial advertisements which alone save the travelling American from the shameful ennui of having to look, listen and think. The fleecing of the motorist in Italy is fantastic — they are encouraged by the Ministero del Tourismo to cheat the traveller. And after all, I am not a novice — I have known l'Italia for 40 years and can speak Italian. Ma chè.

The Italian Riviera is quite spoiled, except for a very few nooks. Pisa is rebuilt, but the Campo Santo is a complete wreck. The destruction in Florence is dreadful, and the rebuilt streets as dreary as Genoa. Much remains in the churches and galleries, though the Uffizi is entirely re-made and re-hung to make it as ugly as the National Gallery and as stupid as Berenson. The Tribuna is a parody. The churches are intact — there was of course a political motive on both sides for not antagonising the Catholics. The two high spots for me were seeing once more that lovely tomb of Leonardo Bruni by Rossellino in Santa Croce, and — unexpected — the marble plaque to E.B.B.[2] still with the phrase about her linking England to Italy in "un anello d'oro." I thought the Germans would have had that down, but perhaps they didn't read Italian. I was told the Italians still keep flowers on her grave — nice, if true.

Nothing of the Florence of Pinorman remains — all our restaurants gone, except Fusi which has become Silli! (What next?) I drove out to San Gemignano, far less damaged than the lying American press led me to think in 1944; and to Montegufoni,[3] looking sadly neglected and shabby. The Florentines insist that poor Osbert has cancer. I hope this is not true? [4] We stopped at Certaldo, but so little is left, and Boccaccio has gone.[5] None of the places in the Val d'Elsa and Val d'Arno were as damaged as the journalists reported — but then they are paid to lie sensationally. So long as the slaves are amused and prevented from thinking, that is all that matters.

It is interesting to see the result of modern politics in a place such as Florence. The poor student, artist, wanderer, poet, musician can no longer exist, and is utterly unwanted. Only the really rich can afford the place, so we should be back in the 18th century if the rich to-day happened to be cultivated. In the "best" restaurants you see the most horrible faces and bad manners. One house-agent alone in Florence has 50 villas for sale. They are picked up by Americans for a few thousand dollars, soon abandoned, and the old servants who have depended for generations on Italian or English families brutally thrown out. An American woman last year bought the finest of those towers at S. Gemignano, paid for it in "real" dollars, then within a week got bored, went "home" and has not been heard of since!

The threat of the railway strike, cutting right across my publication, is a worry. At the same time, we have here in France a ca'canny strike of Customs people (so no parcels), a strike of letter-sorters, and a ca'canny strike [6] of post office railway workers. Yours is the only letter from England delivered here to me this year, though I know others should be here, and parcels. Que voulez-vous? We have made the servants our masters, and it is the nemesis of 19th century exploitation. Dickens's Scrooges and Gradgrinds have only too naturally produced la revanche. I hope the beneficiaries will live to enjoy their Russian or American masters, for this flimsy pretence of Western European democracy can't last. England is so obviously in queer street financially, and even the comparative prosperity of France seems to me phoney. It is done by constant inflation and printing paper money. Someday the piper will have to be paid, and woe unto Churchills and Atlees! I really think Bevan, though I hate him, is the only one with a clear view. Nous sommes foutus. If you start moving and talking to people, you can see it.

The American Xmas tree has been imposed on Italy, to the destruction of their poor efforts at re-afforestation. It is on a par with all their stupidities and destructions. American officials — I can state on personal knowledge — are working frantically for a war, a preventive war, with Russia! Where do we come in? Why, we take the bombs and the brunt, and America comes in at the end — as usual — and wins. I wish we could get rid of Winston and all his pro-American crowd, and get people who can think for humanity as well as for us.

The French reviews have been mixed pickles, the longest and most "important" being all by friends of the Colonel and documented from London. Before this curtain of strikes came down I had evidence of the abuse-campaign in London. People with a bad conscience and a bad cause, can and must play foul. I think they will win, for I have no belief in human nature. Magna est veritas et prelavabit is about the biggest lie ever told.

I am trying to find out if there is any record of the TEL warrant. No hope from England of course. But I hope to get aid from a friend in the Sûreté — when, as and if postal communication is restored.

My daughter is in high indignation against her French professeur, who told her to study du Bellay and Rabelais over the holidays, and then set a three hour paper on Ronsard. "What did you do?" I asked. "I wrote an essay which would have applied to the Emperor Napoleon!" I look forward to reading this. What a farce education is — and yet, it is something that these children hear of civilised men.

Will this reach you before the curtain finally descends?

Ever yours,
RICHARD ALDINGTON

1 The friends have not been identified.
2 Elizabeth Barrett Browning.
3 The home of the Sitwells near Florence.
4 It was not.
5 Boccaccio was partly educated at Certaldo, where a statue of him stood before World War II.
6 A slow-down.

75

MY DEAR BIRD,

Did I send you a cutting from Les Nouvelles Littéraires with a short note by René Lalou?[1] If by any chance you still have it, will you at once put it in an envelope and send it to Mark Bonham-Carter, 14 St James's Place, S.W.I. Forgive me for troubling you. I sent my other copy to my friend Alister Kershaw. . . . Lalou was kind, and Collins think they might quote him in their puffs, though who in England will know that he is one of the best and most respectable critics in France? Recently there was a second long notice in Combat,[2] rather vindictive to TEL, I thought, as it dwelt heavily upon the bastard and homosexual aspects. However, the author also accuses me of having "plucked the feathers" from DHLawrence, and perceives much "rancour" in my TEL. He goes on to say that I must evidently be "mesquin" to discover so many "mesquineries." Clearly, he has never read Boswell with attention or he would know that Dr Johnson long ago exploded that fallacy with his celebrated dictum: "Who drives fat oxen must himself be fat."

I had the British Press on the telephone again yesterday. You may have seen that the Spectator published an offensive paragraph about me and menaced a review of the French TEL — from which they quoted some of the translator's blunders which they generously attributed to me. However, Mark Bonham-Carter got on to them, and stopped it.[3] But the line indicating how to steal my news without paying me was evidently too much for the integrity of the Sunday Chronicle which is said to have published eight scurrilously virtuous columns with large headlines denouncing me.[4] This I have not seen, and the journal will not be among your reading. The Sunday Express rang up, professionally most interested in the dimensions of the main headline, and hopeful of stealing a little more news. I referred the speaker — who astoundingly gave the honoured name of Sydney Smith[5] — to Collins. It struck me as rather characteristic of our epoch that this usurper proposed to write a long article on this complicated topic without having read the book either in French or English. As he got me on to the telephone by a trick, he can no doubt publish any fantasies as an "interview." And what can I do?

I wonder if people realise the great abuses of the press and the utterly unscrupulous way in which completely false statements are attributed to people who happen to be in the news? Here at least they are compelled by law to publish a contradiction, especially in the case of a review. Catch England doing authors that justice. Recently they caught a tartar here — Maître Ribert, bâtonnier of the Paris bar to whom wholly imaginary motives were imputed when he offered his resignation. Look at the hideous way in which the world press persecutes and libels Princess Margaret, and the Americans even the Queen's Majesty!

Do you know, I think R. Catholicism is more of a menace now than in Borrow's time? Then we were on top of the world, and the Pope's legions had lost the most active part of the Occident. Now, by the crafty policy of abandoning the old highly-cultured countries where criticism is well-informed and often unanswerable and by concentrating on the new, raw, wealthy countries, they have made great advances. In Australia the R.C.s are very powerful, not very far from the majority they require to install the Jesuits and take Australia out of the Empire. Much the same is true of USA, and people in England don't seem to realise that McCarthyism [6] is extreme Catholicism — a sort of ballon d'essai. They are the only sect rapidly increasing in USA, and the only sect which has any considerable number of converts in the Orient. I am surprised to learn how many there are among the Viets. The Spanish War regained control of Spain, and Ireland like "a bastinadoed elephant" lies at the Pope's feet. Roosevelt in his stupid way unconditionally supported them, and in his ignorance announced that the R.C.s would distribute supplies to the almost wholly Protestant town of Berlin. They are certainly more cock-a-whoop here than under La Troisième. Note that the Pope's confessor is a Jesuit. People don't realise that the Jesuits had a double line of action and propaganda in the 18th century, which has been prolonged in ours. On the one hand, in those countries which were governed by absolute monarchs they inculcated the doctrines of divine right of kings and passive obedience and strove at all costs to capture the monarch. It was their capture of James II which convulsed England and led to the Revolution of 1688.[7] The "dictators" of this century have proclaimed doctrines often taken over from the Jesuits. On the other hand, the Jesuits also tried to destroy the Protestant limited monarchies by pushing doctrines of equality and extreme democracy. I saw a letter in the USA from a Jesuit in which he boasted of the success of this policy. And I noticed here during the confusion of the National Assembly there were several Jesuit members all pressing extreme left doctrines, apparently without ecclesiastical censure. I daresay much of the propaganda has perished and what has survived cannot often be definitely marked as Jesuit — they like to work through literary tools, as they did e.g. through Belloc and Chesterton. But if there were some don with the old leisure and the old learning, what an admirable life task it would be to track down, study, analyse and report the direct and indirect Jesuit propaganda issued openly or clandestinely, chiefly in Holland, England and perhaps the American colonies in the 17th and 18th centuries. Apropos — can you recommend any really scholarly and impartial history of the Society of Jesus? I should like to read it. The Jesuits seem to me a rather sinister preview of the modern Marxists — fanatics without scruple and with the appalling ambition of dominating all men. The Jesuits kept God as a convenient puppet to hide the fact that their real object of worship was the Society. The Communists have achieved the hideous victory of fabricating a religion without God and without the infinite tenderness of Buddhism.

    Excuse garrulity!

Ever yours
RICHARD ALDINGTON

[1] See above, letter 73.

[2] See Jean-Jacques Mayoux "Le Colonel Lawrence et sa legénde" in the issue of 30 Dec 1954.

[3] The offensive paragraph has not been found. *The Spectator* of 4 Feb 1955 published H. M. Champness's favorable review of RA's book on Lawrence, referring to both the French and English editions.

[4] See James Mayo "Desert Hero Debunked" in the *Sunday Chronicle* 9 Jan 1955; a sub-heading runs: "Lawrence of Arabia Sensation."

[5] RA alludes to the eighteenth-century divine who, with Jeffrey and Brougham, founded the *Edinburgh Review* in 1802.

[6] Vicious and unscrupulous attacks, led by Joseph R. McCarthy (1908–57), U. S. Senator from Wisconsin (1947–57), on those whom he accused as Communists, fellow-travelers, or garden-variety subversives.

[7] The "Glorious Revolution" of 1688 erupted at the birth of James Edward, son of James II, a possible Catholic heir to the throne of England.

76

1 February 1955   *Montpellier*

MY DEAR BIRD,

Thank you for your warm-hearted letter which gave me much pleasure.

Standing like a dwarf on the shoulder of the colossal Colonel I am receiving some of his publicity. I have had single interviews in the past, but I did not know how tiring it is to have them in series, especially on the telephone. I have lost count, but I have now been interviewed — in some cases by repeated calls from Paris or London — by D. Express,[1] Paris-Match [2] (most fatiguing), France-Soir [3] (on Francophobia and pederasty — found myself defending!), D. Mail,[4] E. Standard,[5] Illustrated [6] (whole day with photos), E. News,[7] United Press. There are others but I've forgotten. Is the U.P. American? If not, the yanks have completely boycotted! [8] Can they continue? [. . .]

Do you realise that the "glib showman" quoted by Nicolson was really about Lowell Thomas! [9] [. . .]

You will not have seen that The Herald,[10] Daily Mirror [11] and Express [12] are wholly on my side. Virtually speaking, the press divides on class lines — popular papers for, upper class against. This is natural. Lawrence was a "governing class" hero imposed on the people, not chosen by them — as an evil Saint might come from the Vatican, whereas the enduring Saints are made or even invented by the people. There is one saint of Marseille (not Marius!) whom the Church has denounced as spurious for centuries, yet the people still cherish him — he is really a primitive local rain-making deity. On the whole I think I prefer to be with the people than with the (British) governing class.

I hear from Maugham that Osbert has not got cancer, but something nearly as distressing though luckily not painful. It is Parkinson's disease. If you don't know it (I didn't) it is in the Britannica. Most humiliating.

The Paris-Match correspondent, who spoke English very well, was most hopeful about international affairs. He says that Eisenhower has got the better of the war faction and China lobby, at any rate for the time being; and that we have the paradox of Washington and Moscow actually working together to cool off the respective Chinese factions. Russell of course is gaga, but the US government is most skilful in its use of the newspapers to distract attention from what the Govt is really doing. Let Russell yawp of the end of the world, while Washington makes peace. Certainly, the French papers I see are unperturbed.

Yes Italy in the days of Symonds! [13] There was a case of hereditary wealth (not excessive) well used, in spite of the fact that the conflict in Symonds between his homosexual tendencies and his conscience brought him to the verge of insanity. Although in the end he succumbed, he never seemingly gave pain to wife and daughters, and was a rather noble character I think. At any rate, he more than repaid his privileged life by what he wrote of his travels in southern Europe and his travels in literature. To me his books are still readable, especially his "culture" books on Greek literature, Italian literature and Greek Italian travel.[14] I like his courage. He was one of the first if not the first to point out that Michelangelo is not always as great an architect as he was sculptor and painter.

I always ramble off on reveries when writing to you! I think the day goes well on the TEL front. Anyway the 23,000 [books sold] is official, and that means the public will form their own opinion. So far my most kindly critics have been detectives, lawyers and dons!

By the way, look in the D. Mail for Rowse of All Souls, accusing me of being anti-don, anti-Oxford, and anti-British! The D. Mail is I think printing my reply.[15] I do not wish to involve you at all, so I did *not* say that my best and most effective helper in research was an Oxford don! [16]

Yours sincerely,
RICHARD ALDINGTON

P.S. I met a Magdalen man in Florence who was insistent that the Magdalen white blazer is worn only by the second Eight. I suggested that perhaps about 1910 this might have been represented by Lawrence in his canoe, but he wouldn't hear of it.

1 "Why I Decided to Debunk a Hero. Richard Aldington Talks to Sydney Smith" *Daily Express* 28 Jan 1955.
2 Paragraph in the weekly feature "elles et eux" *Paris Match* 27 Nov – 4 Dec 1954.
3 Roger Giron "L'Homme le plus mysterieux d'autre guerre, Lawrence d'Arabie, idole des Anglais, fut-il un imposteur? L'historien Richard Aldington a écrit un gros livre pour le démontrer" *France Soir* 7 Jan 1955.
4 A. L. Rowse "The Battle over Lawrence of Arabia: Richard Aldington Defends His Book" *Daily Mail* 1 Feb 1955.
5 "The Big Lie is not Proved, Randolph Churchill finds Lawrence a Liar" *Evening Standard* 31 Jan 1955.
6 Richard Aldington "Why I Debunked the Lawrence Legend" *Illustrated* 5 Feb 1955.
7 John Connell "The Man who Loathes Lawrence, a Protest" *Evening News* 31 Jan 1955.
8 On Feb 4 the New York *Times* carried an article written by Peter D. Whitney "Lawrence of Arabia Book Creates Literary Storm."
9 Nicolson wrote, "Aldington dismisses his [T. E. Lawrence's] . . . writing as 'the clever patter and pictures of a glib showman untroubled by the majesty of truth.'" (See Harold Nicolson "The Lawrence Legend" *The Observer* 30 Jan 1955.) RA uses similar phrases in his *Lawrence of Arabia* (see pp 287, 290) to describe Thomas's writing; the exact statement quoted by Nicolson has not been found.
10 Deryck Winterton "Lawrence of Arabia, Now a Book Debunks Him" *Daily Herald* 28 Jan 1955.
11 Charles Curren "Hero or Fake" *Daily Mirror* 27 Jan 1955.
12 See above, this letter n 1.
13 Because of ill-health Symonds lived in Davos from about 1860 to the year of his death, 1893; but he usually spent his summers in Italy, often with his friend Horatio Brown at Venice.
14 Such as *Studies of the Greek Poets* (1873); *Sketches in Italy and Greece* (1874); and translations from Greek poets and from the sonnets of Michelangelo and Campanella (1878).
15 See A. L. Rowse "Legend or only a Lie" *Daily Mail* 31 Jan 1955; RA's reply appeared in the issue of 1 Feb 1955; see below, letter 77.
16 See above letter 37 n 1.

77

7 February 1955 *Montpellier*

MY DEAR BIRD,

Tenella Kaillinike!

In spite of the terrific Bureau counter-attack, in which they mobilised the ban and arrière-ban down to Naomi Mitcheson and invented a story that TEL was about to marry but had his balls clawed off by the Turks, they have failed. [. . .]

Two Generals from Allenby's staff have written Collins in full support.[1] One Colonel from ditto returns book on account of the insults to Allenby and Buxton and the infamous suggestion that Our National Hero wrote in praise of a sexual habit I still maintain is unEnglish.[2]

Interesting about Rowse. Did you ever meet Shepperd (if that is the spelling) of King's, Cambridge? I was taken to see him in the 1920s, and was amazed that a great University could tolerate, let alone honour, such a "type." You evidently didn't see my counter-blast to Rowse in the D. Mail. I'll send it to you as soon as I get a duplicate. Or you could look it up in D.M. of 1/2/55. They gave the honours of the editorial page with a banner headline, and I think Oxford will be laughing at Professor Rowse. He thought I was in America and couldn't hit back. One of his accusations was that I wrote a book to depreciate D. H. Lawrence!

I am ignorant of the Xenophon news.[3] What is it? Has an American discovered the bones of the 10,000 in the ruins of the Ark on Mount Ararat?

Balzac — tell me how you get on.[4] I have the lovely Pléiade edition here,[5] dip into it, am at times almost fanaticised by his genius, then repelled by his verbosity and pretention. You know my theory that just as tea makes old maids chirp too much, so excessive strong coffee made the divine Honoré go on too long.

I still think Flaubert's Education Sentimentale [6] the one novel (apart from Don Quixote)[7] we of the West have to put up against the great Russians.

The strain of continuous interviews last week was heavy, and I blessed the sabbath rest. Since I did not jump on my racing camel and dash away from reporters at 100 miles a day or assault a press photographer, I hope they'll now leave me alone. The Amerians started to come in on Saturday, but as most of them haven't heard of TEL that will die down. The scandal there is Lowell Thomas. I have just copied out and sent Morris Ernst (the N.Y. lawyer) an extract from the TV broadcast with Muggeridge ruthlessly cross-examining Storrs.[8] What is Mr Thomas going to do?

I am very sorry to hear of your cough. I have my daughter down with "flu," and last night I was reading Evelyn's Diary [9] and noting the appalling "rheums" he contracted. Ours is a sad climate. I find Montpellier and Southern Florida the only parts of the earth where I avoid annual bronchitis — and I've had it so often and so badly that I can't afford many more attacks. Curious, that in the 18th century Montpellier was so famous for "bronchs" and is now neglected. It pays sometimes to read old books. I owe Montpellier to that, and also the discovery of Brantôme [10] (circa 1930) now alas! frequented by yanks, but still a perfect little place.

I think the enclosed from Roy Campbell will cheer you.[11] Our common friend Rob Lyle wrote me in all seriousness that Roy was a great friend of Storrs and intended to send him a letter which would influence him to take my part. I can't imagine a more tactful proceeding!

Forgive the crass insistence on sales — but the Bureau attack was meant to kill the book from that point of view. Abraham Lincoln was right.

Ever yours, get well, we are on the verge of spring here already,

RICHARD ALDINGTON

1 General Sir George Barrow and possibly Major-General Lord Burnham or Brigadier-General Jellicoe.

2 See RA *Lawrence of Arabia* 194–97, 203–5, 279–80, 333–36 *et passim*. The colonel has not been identified.

3 The reference can not be explained.

4 Bird had set himself to read Balzac's complete works. He had in mind a radio dramatization or serialization of the novels for BBC. Eventually the plan was abandoned.

5 1935–37.

6 1869.

7 Cervantes, 1605.

8 BBC's "Panorama" on 26 Jan 1955.

9 1818; more extensive editions appeared in 1879 and 1906.

10 Where RA wrote *All Men Are Enemies* (1933); he gives a brief account of his stay at Brantôme in *Life for Life's Sake* (1941) 382–84.

11 The extract from Campbell, according to RA, was "received 4/2/55." It runs: "I wrote Ronald Storrs a longish letter (to which I've had no reply yet) to thank him for an edition de luxe Virgil: and say, 'I understand from the papers that you are going to speak about that ghastly little pederast T. E. Lawrence, the greatest fraud in British History. Give it to him! Don't worry about Public Opinion! etc. etc. You will be cleaning out an Augean stable and Posterity will take your side!' As for me I am sending the dirty little sod, and any who defend him, down to posterity with a pair of banderillas in his fat feminine fanny that will last him longer than his Seven Mountains of Balderdash — in what promises to be the best satire I've yet written."

78

21 February 1955   *Montpellier*

MY DEAR BIRD,

[. . .] The English press is incredible. The Telegraph published a Cape sneer against me because Lawrence wrote a blurb for Custot's Sturly which I translated (I had "probably" never heard of it.) Now, Lawrence failed to translate Sturly, and so did some other unknown person, because they didn't know how to get at the technical French words. Bruce Richmond wrote me Lawrence failed, would I do it? I did it and successfully since Custot invited me to stay with him at Monaco and work there at the Oceanographic centre.[1] How characteristic of the Bureau. They sneer at the man who could and successfully did do the job at which the great Lawrence failed! You can't learn French by scattering sovereigns off a camel.

I saw Sheppard snubbed by an undergraduate. In his affected pansy way Sheppard said that "the highest achievement of humanity was to write Greek verse." Slight pause, and an undergraduate remarked artlessly: "Greek verse? I always thought it was a recreation of country parsons!"

Eric Kennington is to be slapped down by a letter from a friend who had read the Shaw – Shaw letters, which Kennington hasn't.[2]

There is to be quite a do over here soon — 45 minutes of Radio France (even including 5 from the insignificant author)[3] and more articles.

And there were extracts in Illustrated from Lawrence's C.O. at Uxbridge.[4] How sickening journalism is! The full letter from Squadron-Commander Breese was an admirable picture of the disgust of a regular officer for the abnormal creature wished on him. L. was constantly "on the mat" at Uxbridge as "consistently dirty," "insubordinate" "refusal to obey order re kit," "persistently late on parade." His Flight-Commander and Segt reported he was bone lazy! Such a pity it was not given entire; but journalism is an accursed thing. It has to flatter the mental laziness of the lowest, and has no integrity.

More later. Weather not so bad here, but I've bronchitis again.

Ever yours,
RICHARD ALDINGTON

1 See above, letter 52; RA did not accept the invitation. Custot is not to be confused with Jacques Cousteau, who instituted the Oceanographic Center at Monaco.

2 Rob Lyle; see below, letter 80.

3 RA did not participate in the program; Alister Kershaw spoke in his behalf.

4 G. F. Breese "The Storm over Lawrence" 26 Feb 1955. Breese's remarks first appeared in the Daily Express 28 Jan 1955.

79

3 March 1955   Montpellier

MY DEAR BIRD,

I made a slip in replying to Hart in Telegraph — overlooked a few words in the Official History. But I have used it to try to get the debate away from the petty points of opinion to the wider things the Bureau never mentions — I have suggested that if the telegrams Lawrence speaks of in the Erzerum – Kut business could be produced that would be real proof. But do they exist? I very much doubt it, though there may have been a wire from Cairo to London and reply over L. being sent to Kut. If L. in his Cairo office had indeed this occult influence to secure an arranged surrender of Erzerum to the Russians, what a pity he never used it on behalf of our own armies fighting so much nearer! 1

The bicycle episode is another of these trifling affairs, but surely it is up to Garnett to explain how if Nuffield gave up making bikes before 1900 (as Garnett states that Nuffield told him) when Lawrence was 10–11, the same Nuffield sat waiting for a cheque in 1905 when L. was 15? And could the 12-yr bike be used by the 18-yr rider of 180 miles a day? As a matter of fact "before 1900" means 1899 at latest when Lawrence was only 10–11, and it is surely incredible that he was able to instruct Nuffield in building cycles at that age.2

But I can't deal with all these trifles, and had better keep quiet. Only I would greatly like to know if any evidence does exist for that Erzerum story.

The latest figure is 32,169, but as Collins just points out a lot of these are "export" to Dominions and we don't know how they will go there. The book appeared in Canada on the 19th, but there were an infinite number of articles and letters about Lawrence pre-publication! It had not reached the smaller towns of Transvaal on the 21st, when a letter was written to me hoping it would be out soon. And of course it has not reached Australia and New Zealand. I don't ever remember to have seen on Heinemann and other accounts any "returns" from over-seas — I should have thought the transport made any speculative sales prohibitive. But perhaps in this case Collins agreed in case of a sudden run. I don't quite understand the situation. I infer that the English sales have been knocked down by the tremendous anti-me press. It is surprising that it continues to sell at all after that. Do you know I have had nearly 200 cuttings, about 75% at least hostile and even ferocious? There are more than half of them from periodicals I didn't know exist, and not one with a genuine historical approach. Deplorable. But if I get it back from Kershaw I must send you a glorious one from one small Welsh paper, run for dissenting, very left-wing, very Welsh independence people. The author deals pretty sharply with my imperialist snobbery in passing over Lawrence's Welsh ancestry so lightly — there are many in Wales who remember his grandfather, Lawrence *bach*.[3]

Yes, I think you have hit off the attitude of the "upper-class" reviewers. They can't deny what I say, but for some reason they dislike me so much they've got to "take a swipe at me"? Why, I wonder? Talking of which — I was amazed on Tuesday to get a BBC cable asking to use in England calling the Continent the free-verse epilogue to Death of a Hero. Now that is 25 years old, and I think this is the first time it was ever quoted. No doubt it is rather tame and obvious, but I don't think even now I could read it aloud without breaking down.

Have you ever realised that the article Guerrilla in the 1929 Ency. Brit. is signed TEL, but is not an original contribution? It is simply L's Army Quarterly self-glorifying stuff a little edited by Hart! There is no acknowledge to A.Q. so far as I can see, or to 7 Ps., for part of it appeared there also.[4] Now surely this is a case of rather delicate literary ethics? I thought E.B. articles were supposed to be original? And isn't it a trifle self-centred to omit all mention of all other guerrillas to concentrate entirely on Lawrence and "the Arabs?" Has this ever been noticed, do you think? Hart was "Military Editor" so presumably got permission to use an edited reprint. But it's odd.

Some queer things have occurred in the DNB in the past owing to the editors being Catholics. When Charles Waterton died, a whimsical but detailed Life was put out by a Protestant, Dr Hobson.[5] As soon as Waterton was dead the bigoted family had refused to see Hobson. They gave Waterton's Autobiography to be edited by a Catholic convert Dr (Sir) Norman Moore, who in the Romish way cut out without mentioning it all references to Hobson.[6] When Hobson died [7] Moore wrote a brief life for the D.N.B., denying the truth of Hobson's book and his intimacy with Waterton, and asserting that a second edition of Hobson's life had been issued correcting the first. I have both, and Hobson withdrew nothing that I can see. But, when my life of Waterton came out the TLS tried to kill it by saying I had been wrong in quoting Hobson against Moore, and as authority used that very D.N.B. article which the writer (surely a Jesuit?) must have known was written by Moore himself! [8] It is like Churchill finding proof of the truth of Lawrence's Egyptian assertion in Lawrence's own letters. The "pay-off" as the Americans say was that Price-Jones refused a letter of correction from me, and Moore's son took advantage of an admittedly ambiguous phrase about the two *medical* rivals to write a smug reproof to me for "imputing medical rivalry" since Hobson died when Moore was still a student.[9] The phrase meant of course the "rivalry of the two medical men as biographers," but I wasn't allowed to state that either. Now here is an odd mix-up, don't you think? On top of the R.C. intrigue over two generations or more, we have the DNB vilifying an innocent old eccentric, and the TLS treating me with an unfairness which in France would bring an action for damages from the Société des Ecrivains.

So the chance of my being asked to correct Storrs for the DNB is minus zero. I did the DHLawrence for them in the 1930s, and more than one English reviewer picked on that article as utterly unworthy of the D.N.B.! It may have been bad, but was it as bad as all that? And surely some of this severity over TEL is due rather to dislike for me than love for Lawrence — e.g. Nicolson.[10] Did you notice in Truth a letter before Lyle's signed something Green? [11] On the whole it maintained that the Bureau have not in any way answered my facts, but it began with a hymn of hate against my "petulance" and "vindictiveness." Well, I suppose we are often quite unaware of our own faults, but I don't and didn't feel guilty of those crimes.

Unquestionably Balzac was an admirer of Scott, and always held him up to young novelists as a model. The long-windedness of Scott evidently didn't distress his contemporaries, for he had enormous continuing sales. Balzac has a much more vivid and authentic world, but I think he is even more diffuse. It is surely the great trouble with many novels. I marvel how Macaulay could enjoy Richardson so intensely, and I've never been able to read Mlle de Scudéry and d'Urfé even in selections. But I don't think I'm a novel-reader really. For instance I like The Antiquary,[12] although I know it's a silly missing heir story and the hero and heroine are bores, simply because I admire the skill with which the old man's out of the way learning is maintained and made amusing, and also the Scotch characters. I think the chapter where the old women gossips at the postoffice are trying to read the girl's letter through the envelope is admirably done, and the final touch of telling the poor girl there's nothing for her (so that they can go on spying) is superb irony. It was Balzac's misfortune to live a contemporary of Victor Hugo, the greatest master of falsity in literature. Whether by contagion or not Balzac has a good deal of Hugo's pretentiousness and theatricality. In knowledge of human beings and the whole novelistic bag of tricks he is infinitely Hugo's superior. But what a blunder that pseudo-Alsacian Jew accent of Nuncingen is in type.[13] Still Balzac was a great novelist.

I have never read Claudel with any pleasure, and I feel he wrote for a type of French Catholic intellectual who hardly has any equivalents in England outside the circle of T. S. Eliot. Often I don't know what he means. And even more often I don't care. The one book of his I liked was Connaissance de l'Est [14] which I thought very interesting, unlike his plays. But I am hopelessly out of touch with modern French highbrow literature, which just annoys without stimulating me. And how they have the nerve to insult Anatole France as fifth-rate I don't know. This view is not shared by the French public, for A.F. reprints are everywhere, whereas the effort to revive Zola as social realism seems to have failed — I judge simply from the shop displays and the increasing number of titles. Yet I don't think any young French professor would dare to admire him.

I have had another bout of bronchitis — went out too soon. Excuse this long scrawl.

Yours ever,
RICHARD ALDINGTON

P.S. I am contemplating a few sketches of dubious characters under the title "Frauds or Not Frauds?" which should not be too strenuous, and be a breaking-in for an eventual full length biography.[15] (The delays and anxieties of this TEL have wasted a lot of time.) What do you think of the T. J. Wise "forgeries" and piracies? I can't see that he made so much money out of these frauds — nothing much compared with his oil business or his legitimate deals in books. The money made by sales of the frauds is not known, but a great number seem to have gone eventually to Gorfin for about 300 pounds — not much for a man who left 120,000, and a Library which the B.M. bought for 60,000. The ethics of the thing are indefensible of course, and Shaw's theory that Wise "did it as a joke" won't bear scrutiny — he shouldn't have taken money if that was the case. The argument seems to be that Wise got money from these frauds when he needed it badly to buy up genuine book bargains which afterwards brought huge profits, and that his supposed "discoveries" gave him authority as a book expert which enabled him to buy up valuable items. It is disconcerting to find Gosse so closely mixed up, but I am a little surprised Wise imposed on him so completely.[16]

[1] Reference to whatever part Lawrence played in 1916 in an attempt to reduce the Turkish siege of the British Army at Kut by bribing Khalil Pasha, to whom a sum of £2 million was offered. Lawrence's participation arose, he told Liddell Hart, from an earlier success, also in 1916, in arranging the surrender of Erzerum to the Russian Army of the Caucasus (See *Letters of T. E. Lawrence* 203). RA's attempt to get the debate away from the "petty points of opinion" (*Daily Telegraph* 21 and 24 Feb 1955) was in reply to "Lawrence and His Arabs Help to Allenby Invaluable," a letter signed by Liddell Hart in the *Daily Telegraph* 12 Feb 1955. Liddell Hart objected to the derogatory opinions of Lawrence expressed by Major-General Lord Burnham and General Sir George Barrow, also in the *Daily Telegraph* (5 and 10 Feb 1955). Numerous letters about T. E. Lawrence and RA's book on him appeared in the *Telegraph*, including another by Liddell Hart (26 Feb 1955).

[2] Reference to various statements that Lawrence travelled in France in 1906 and subsequent years on a special bicycle built by Lord Nuffield, then Mr Morris of Oxford, according to a design he had worked out with Lawrence (RA *Lawrence of Arabia* 59). David Garnett reported Morris's statement that his firm stopped making bicycles before 1900 (*Letters of T. E. Lawrence*, 44 n 2).

[3] The Welsh newspaper has not been identified.

[4] See above, letter 10. See also "The Evolution of a Revolt" *The Army Quarterly* Oct 1920. The article on guerrilla warfare is composed from *Seven Pillars*.

[5] *Charles Waterton: His Home, Habits, and Handiwork* (1866). Hobson maintained that he showed this book, in manuscript, to Waterton and that Waterton approved, but it is contended that many of the anecdotes in the book are false and Waterton's letters altered.

[6] *Wanderings in South America, The North-west of The United States and The Antilles, in The Years 1812, 1816, 1820 & 1824 . . . by Charles Waterton, Including a Memoir of The Author by Norman Moore, M.D. . . .* (1887).

[7] 1868.

[8] See "Odd Man In" *TLS* 26 Aug 1949.

[9] Letter signed Alan Moore in *TLS* 2 Sept 1949.

[10] See Harold Nicolson "The Lawrence Legend" *The Observer* 30 Jan 1955 where Nicolson remarks, after exposing his own distaste for Lawrence, "As I turned the acid pages of this wearisome book, one wish arose within me to defend Lawrence against so mean an enemy."

[11] Leonard Green in *Truth* 25 Feb 1955.

[12] By Sir Walter Scott (1816).

[13] See *La Maison Nunçigen* (1838); *Père Goriot* (1834–35); *Splendeurs et misères des courtisanes* (1838–47); *Cesar Birotteau* (1838).

[14] First series (1900); second series (1907).

[15] *Frauds*, published by William Heinemann in 1957.

[16] Thomas James Wise manufactured more than fifty "pre-first" editions and pirated the works of a number of nineteenth-century authors. In the sale of these forgeries Wise was closely associated with Edmund Gosse, as well as H. Buxton Forman. Herbert E. Gorfin, Wise's clerk and agent, was chief distributor of the forgeries.

80

MY DEAR BIRD,

I enclose carbon copy of a letter from a F.O. official.[1] I have of course accepted, and have a card from Sark saying his narrative will come by next boat. An ambassador's report of what the King said should be interesting.[2]

I enclose a carbon of a diatribe about TEL published in Australia by Major-General-and-Senator Rankin.[3] This is being used by Lyle in a counter-blast to that would-be ferocious article of Hart in the London Mag.[4] Lyle completely squashed Kennington,[5] and though Hart is more impudent I think he will follow.

I have sent Randolph Churchill a very polite letter showing that his father sponsored a lie when he signed that letter to Liddell Hart. You see, the old man forgot and Hart didn't know that through Storrs I sent Churchill the Lawrence statements about "Egypt"; and Hart drafted a letter which C. signed, saying that when C. said "certainly unfounded" he didn't know L. had claimed it in letters, but as he did C. believes it!!! My information was sent in Jan 1951. The Hart – Churchill letter was signed in 1954. I daresay they'll think up an escape, but it's an awkward one for the honest little fellows, don't you think?[6]

I also enclose a first list of possible Frauds and not Frauds — the difficulty being to get away from mere history text-book stuff. I think you are too kind about Wise. I have read the books by Pollard and Carter[7] and by Partington;[8] and Wise was guilty. So I think were Richard Clay (printers), Buxton Forman, Shorter, and possibly even Gosse. Wise "forged" or produced "suspect" 54 different pamphlets according to P. and Carter, and Partington adds 24 more. When you realise that his "10 or 12 copies" were often as much as ten times as many and that some of them ran up as high as £200 in sales! I wrote to the B.M. about him, and they are very severe, though of course they bought his library for £60,000 — after he had got the kudos of saying he would "give" it to the nation! Get Pollard and Carter, and you will see what a racket it was. Forman, Shorter, and Gosse all left very valuable libraries collected by Wise's help, and they "innocently"(?) supported all the forgeries. I have seen so much of the innocent dupe in this TEL business that I am prepared to believe they may have been dupes in the Wise affair. But . . . Read the evidence, and I fear you may have to suspect Gosse either of complicity or extreme credulity and stupidity. I find that even William Allingham had the right date about the E.B.B. sonnets, so how *could* Gosse have been deceived? It must have been common talk in literary London. But examine the evidence. I have written my little essay, but will correct anything if you disagree.

Do you know about Dr Chambers (C. 1780) and his "Celestial Bed" which he rented at £100 a night to couples with guarantee of wonderful offspring![9] His clients are said to have included half the nobility and gentry — which accounts for a good deal, don't you think? I must get or try to get full data about him.

Did you know that A. R. Wallace (evolution) believed firmly in the Cock Lane Ghost?[10] I wish I could drag in that really remarkable and most scholarly article of Myers, in which he makes out a striking case for the thesis that the oracles were in fact spiritualist communications![11] Until I read Myers the thought had never come to me. But were not the Pythian priestess and the rest actually what we should call mediums? I shall be most grateful for your instruction in this. We need not believe in the objective reality of the "messages" of course; merely in the subjective self-deception. How, as one grows older, one sees the value, the necessity of a national Church! Men's guesses and fantasies about the unknown must somehow be captured and canalised. I am more and more in favour of the C. of E., especially since living in America, where religion is a business — the best clergyman is he who can raise the most funds! I find this entry in a brief diary kept during a trip from Hollywood to Jamaica in 1945. April 24th: "This place, Yuma, Arizona, is a great place for hasty marriages. The USA Gretna Green "Mecca of Marriages" advertises weddings at any time of day or night in huge letters stating: 'Licenses procured. Dressing rooms. Dignified service by Rev R. L. Roberts.' Another huge notice says the sheriff can marry, loans wedding gowns and can rent bridal chambers!" Work upon that, as Dekker says. It seems to me that the most hardened atheist (myself if you like!) could hardly applaud that. Why bother to "marry"? It makes continental adultery a gay and honest affair. Especially when you know that Reno, Nevada, will undo the "marriage" in three weeks for so many 1000 dollars. Am I becoming smug? Check me, if so. [. . .]

I have air-mailed your news of the Eastwood memorial to Frieda Lawrence, and have adapted the Johnson – Chesterfield letter for her to reply to them. Eastwood is too late.[12] The pictures and most of the interesting MSS are in USA and stay there! Tom Thumb after the Giant — mine are rapidly going there too! But England will have all Raymond Mortimer, Lawrence, Nicolson and Montagu of Beaulieu.

Mistral advances slowly — about half done. I suggest in my script that Mireille is not in the least "epic" but a modern and versified Daphnis and Chloe.[13] The great difference — or one of them — is that Mistral's "risticities" are first-hand observation and those of Longus paraphrases of pastoral poets. Has anybody tried to restore the poems from his cribs? Impossible, I suppose, but no more so than many papyri.

Are you not disgusted with American war-mongering?[14] But for them and Churchill we could have peace. Ever yours,

RICHARD ALDINGTON

Can you get me a statement from the R.A.F. man[15] about L. in India?

1 The letter runs: "Sark via Guernsey, 14.3.55. Dear Mr Aldington, Sir H. Rumbold, under whom I served in Berlin, returned one day from London where he had had an audience of Geo V. The King had just seen Lawrence and was so upset that he remained silent for what seemed an age. He apologised and told R that L. had just declined an Honour and how insulting L. had been. If you are interested, I shall jot down R's story as he told it to me at the time. I told Harold Nicolson this story when he was writing the King's Life but he made no use of it so if it's of any interest to you it's yours but I don't want the bother of typing it for fun. Yours sincerely (Signed) T. F. Breen." The reference is to Lawrence's refusal of a decoration, the C.B., or the return of it. For Breen's full account see Phillip Knightley and Colin Simpson *The Secret Lives of Lawrence of Arabia* (1969) 136–37.

2 The letter has not been located.

3 In the Melbourne *Argus* 2 Mar 1955. It runs in part: "Lawrence was without question one of the greatest imposters of the 1914–18 War. . . . The contribution made by the Arab forces under Lawrence to the desert campaign was negligible. Ask any Light Horse men who served in the desert. The Arabs were craven in the face of any real opposition, preferring to skulk behind the battle, waiting to lay waste towns captured by our organized forces. Their barbaric slaughter of wounded and helpless prisoners and senseless destruction were sickening to

any civilized man. If Lawrence was not a sadist, at least he made no attempt to control the primitive savagery of the Arab rabble at his heels bought by Foreign Office gold. . . . Shortly after the entry into Damascus by the 4th Light Horse Regiment . . . my regiment was called out to prevent the looting and slaughter in which Lawrence's Arabs were indulging. I had my Sgt-Major Robertson set up a Hotchkiss machine-gun covering Jemal Pasha Avenue, where some of the worst incidents were happening, with orders to shoot any Arabs who refused to desist. Lawrence, theatrically garbed in the silken garments and gold-threaded head-dress of an Arab Shareef, haughtily complained that my troops were shooting his Arabs. I threatened to shoot him if he didn't attempt to control them. When I think of what the Shari-fians did in Damascus and other towns I am sometimes sorry I did not shoot. The men who really did something towards organising the Arabs were Colonel Newcombe and Major Joyce, two fine British Army officers, and Jaffa Pasha, afterwards a powerful force in Iraq, who were in the Hejaz long before Lawrence ever appeared."

4 See Basil Liddell Hart "T. E. Lawrence, Aldington and the Truth" *London Magazine* Apr 1955. Rob Lyle replied to Liddell Hart in a letter published in *London Magazine* June 1955.

5 In *Truth* 25 Feb and 11 and 18 Mar 1955. Kennington reviewed RA's book on Lawrence in *Truth* 4 Feb 1955.

6 Refers to T. E. Lawrence's statement that he was offered the post of High Commissioner for Egypt (see RA *T. E. Lawrence* 381–85; see also Liddell Hart "T. E. Lawrence, Aldington and the Truth" *London Magazine* Apr 1955).

7 *An Enquiry into the Nature of Certain Nineteenth Century Pamphlets* (1934).

8 *Thomas J. Wise in the Original Cloth* (1947).

9 It was Dr Graham who offered the Celestial Bed.

10 Mysterious noises heard at 33 Cock Lane, Smithfield, London, supposedly connected with the uncovering of a crime were attributed to the Cock Lane ghost. In 1762 the noises were found to be the work of the William Parsons family.

11 Frederick Myers *Miracles* (1831).

12 The Council of Eastwood, Nottinghamshire, where D. H. Lawrence was born, was planning as a memorial to him, a recreation center and swimming pool.

13 1859; see RA *Introduction to Mistral* (1956) 76–78.

14 The United States, expecting the Chinese Communists to begin a campaign to capture Matsu and Quemoy, were weighing all-out defense including the use of atomic weapons. France's Premier Edgar Faure, on March 30, had said the "great powers" should intervene to avoid war, and by that date President Eisenhower had begun to deprecate "war talk."

15 Summel; see above, letter 10.

81

26 April 1955   *Montpellier*

MY DEAR BIRD,

In one of your letters you wrote that it was a pity I said in my book that the Mint would never be published because &c. How about verifying quotations? What I said was: "The book will never be publicly issued intact, and, even if it were, would probably disappoint most readers except those determined to worship everything 'T.E.' did." 1

I call that prophetic. It hasn't been "publicly issued intact" but expurgated with 1000 privately-printed copies for smut-fanciers.2 One of these, rather tardily, has been confiscated as "obscene" by the Milwaukee Customs, and I sincerely hope the movement will spread. It is amazing that Cape got away with it as he did, but of course he has official protection. If other Customs officers in USA make the same move it should help me.

In France the Mint has been a real failure. [. . .] The translator is a Montpellier professor,[3] and yet not one copy has been on display in any bookshop, although they all had mine.

Ever yours,
RICHARD ALDINGTON

[1] RA *Lawrence of Arabia* 364.
[2] In the latter part of 1927, possibly at Christmas, T. E. Lawrence gave Edward Garnett a notebook containing what was substantially *The Mint*. Garnett had one or more typescripts made and thus later supplied the text for a few copies printed by Doubleday, Doran & Co., New York, in 1936. Meanwhile, in the last months of his life, Lawrence made revisions and corrections on a typescript recopied, with some changes, from Garnett's. From the corrected typescript Jonathan Cape issued an edition of 2000 copies in 1955.
[3] Étiemble.

82

28 April 1955 *Montpellier*

MY DEAR BIRD,

I am undergoing my annual spring-cleaning — i.e. a month on the water-waggon and a modest diet. Depressing at first, but after the first week worth it. Lent was surely a very wise institution in our fore-fathers. It might be better for the nation if we all kept it rather strictly, though not with the absurd persecutions we read of in Voltaire!

The Midi Libre at last came out with a review of the Mint which was translated by a professor on the Faculty here. The reviewer is another much more distinguished professor, who dismisses the Mint as completely uninteresting — "everyone in France has done military service!"[1] And Garnett's absurd remark about the horror of it and being greater than Dostoevsky is dismissed as fatuous — which I think it is.[2] Going into town later I looked once more for copies of La Matrice in the vitrines, but not one. What pleased me greatly is that two or three shops had replaced *my* book in the window! [. . .]

I have been reading a very interesting article about the Australian bower-birds and their irrepressible habits of stealing bright objects for their bowers. Query: Were these contracted from the earliest settlers in New South Wales? I have also been re-reading Darwin's Beagle[3] and Bates's Amazon.[4] What excellent books they are. Filled with most interesting observations, though Darwin is pretty smug about British superiority. (I suppose that with his income he had no idea what poverty meant.) For a good travel book a writer must have real interests and real knowledge and some purpose. I can get along with J. A. Symonds on Italy[5] (with some crabs) because he has a genuine purpose, as Darwin and Bates had their quite different purposes. But the mere "travel book" seems to me a bore. I even rather sniff at Slocum, the first solitary sailor round the world — it was a yankee stunt, and without any real object. Slocum has one good joke. In his little sailing boat he was passed by the US battleship Oregon, dipped flags, and got an admiral's signal that there was war with Spain, adding "Have you seen any Spanish warships?" Slocum answered "No," and then ran up the signal: "Let us keep together for mutual protection."[6]

Thank you very much for the notes on my "frauds." I really ought to be at the B.M., but I can't face colds and bronchitis in the spring. I haven't read the Howell book,[7] though I have wondered about him. Somewhere or other I have a photograph of Ruskin and Rossetti arm in arm in a garden, with a third rather truculent looking person gazing at them. I have an idea this must be Howell. What an enormous distance off 1855 seems! An utterly different world.

When you say Violet Hunt was "detested by the author," I infer you mean Helen Angeli and not Gosse? Violet Hunt was gifted and amusing, but a fearful gossip. Ford Hueffer used to mimic her thus. The phone rings; Violet picks it up: "Oh, how *are* you, Lady St Helier? What? *What?* I said you had a baby before you were married? Oh no, I said that about dear Lady Bainbridge." She told me the story of how her affair with Ford began, and I think truthfully. She'd known him for years, went to see him in his English Review office, found him plunged in misery — no money, review had to go. She thought he looked like a miserable child, and gave him a kiss and told him to cheer up. This inflamed his passions, and he insisted on being in love with her. Then she fell in love with him. Then [there] was all the ténébreuse affaire (which I never understood) of Ford's phoney divorce in Germany [8] and bigamous marriage with Violet! He got that publicised by a bit of stupid magazine publicity which brought a libel action from his real wife. Then he fell in love with someone else,[9] and joined the army! At that time the F.O. were paying him to do rather silly anti-German books and me to act as his secretary.[10] Violet used to walk me round Kensington Gardens going over their affair endlessly. She was 51 but still coquettish. One day she paused in the midst of her recriminations, smiled archly and said: "It was here I used to meet Andrew Lang — by permission of his wife!" There was a Pre-Raphaelite portrait of her as a young woman at South Lodge, and if it resembled her she must have been beautiful. No wonder Oscar was smitten. I don't think people gossip like that now — for one thing they haven't the wit and invention. [. . .]

What a passion for the aesthetes exists! I have been comparing my Heinemann account for 6 months ending 31/12/54 with 6 months ending 31/12/53. In '53 Religion of Beauty sold 4 copies in England, exported 19: total 23. In '54, same book: 8 copies England, export 15, total 23! Walter Pater: '53, England 2, export 16, total 18; '54, England 6, export 23, total 29. Getting on! I am not going to "write for" England any more. As a start I am making my next long book a foreigner, and signing up with an American publisher and the usual foreign languages. England can have American sheets. Or nothing! Still I must keep my word with the Frauds book for Heinemann. Perhaps I could get out of it. [. . .]

What humbug that Eliot speech [11] — the English dearly love a Fraud.

Ever yours,
RICHARD ALDINGTON

The £ is falling steadily once more — anything seriously wrong?

[1] A review by Emile Bouvier in *Le Midi-Libre* 27 Apr 1955.

[2] See extract from a letter from Garnett to Lawrence 20 May 1928 and Lawrence's reply 14 June 1928, in *Letters of T. E. Lawrence* 610–11.

[3] *Journal of Researches into the Geology and Natural History of the Various Countries Visited by H. M. S. Beagle* (1839).

[4] *The Naturalist on the Amazons* (1863).

[5] Probably *Sketches in Italy and Greece* (1874).

[6] Joshua Slocum *Sailing Alone Around the World* (1900) 264.

7 Charles Augustus Howell is the subject of Helen Rossetti's Angeli's *Pre-Raphaelite Twilight* (1954).

8 Ford — or Hueffer, as he then was — had married Elsie Martindale on 17 May 1894. In the autumn of 1911, after spending more than a year in Germany, Ford joined Violet Hunt on a visit to a seaside resort in Belgium. There they were interviewed for two English publications the *Daily Mail* and *The Throne*. Subsequent articles referred to Violet Hunt as Mrs Ford Madox Hueffer and Elsie, the first Mrs Hueffer, sued both periodicals. The *Daily Mail* apologized, but *The Throne* contested and the case went in Mrs Elsie Hueffer's favour after considerable notoriety for Ford.

9 Stella Benson.

10 *When Blood Is Their Argument* (1915) and *Between St. Dennis and St. George* (1915). For both books, written in 1913–14, RA, Alec Randall, and possibly others acted as researchers.

11 Possibly T. S. Eliot's *The Three Voices of Poetry*, a lecture delivered 19 Nov 1953 at the annual meeting of the Book League in London and published in 1954.

83

4 May 1955 *Montpellier*

MY DEAR BIRD,

Forgive another letter so soon.

Do you think you could persuade that RAF man you mentioned either to write me a letter or to make a signed statement about L. in India? [1] In view of the probability that Hart will pursue this vendetta to the bitter end I must collect as much evidence as possible. Try to get this, will you?

I think the Campbell mentioned by the Rev. E. C. Tippetts may be Major-General Walter Campbell. Military Ops., [2] which is often vague, mentions his name in the summary (Vol 2. pp 300–1) describing the administration of occupied territory, and says he used trains returning to Egypt to carry Palestine goods and so earn Egyptian currency. But this Campbell was D.A.Q.G. and so may have been O.C. puffers anyway. Yet I think he may be the man, and have used the word "commissioner" not as a title but to describe his functions as one of the deputies appointed by Allenby to administer the country.

If you read the two books on Wise, the Enquiry by Pollard and Carter, and the Life by Partington, I think you'll find Wise more guilty than you think, and even Gosse suspect. Oddly enough it seems that Sir Theodore Cook was one of the two first to suspect Wise. He was joint editor of the complete Ruskin, and proved decisively by collation that two of Wise's reprints of Ruskin items could not possibly be firsts. [3] But these proofs were lost in the footnotes to a 40 vol edition, which naturally was not read in the high state of English scholarship! The booksellers Pollard and Carter discovered them and made them known. Interesting to come on Cook again. The high standards of scholarship shown by Cook and his associate is in striking contrast to all that Wise – Gosse set, and should be highly gratifying to Wadham men. One of the most disquieting aspects of the Wise "forgeries" (I wrote the Brit Mus and they insist on "forgeries"!) is that all of them were printed by Richard Clay, who destroyed all their letters and ledgers in 1911. Why? Strangeways and Walden [4] told Cook in 1903 that they had all their ledgers since 1845 — 58 years. Clay's London manager who took all Wise's orders over a period of at least 20 years without ever putting the firm's name on the work died in 1929, before the "enquiry" began.

Ever yours,
RICHARD ALDINGTON

[1] T. Summel (see above, letters 10 and 80) made no such statement. He had conditionally offered information about T. E. Lawrence to Bird. Bird, having little reliance in the information, decided to have no dealings with Summel.

[2] *Military Operations, Egypt and Palestine. From the Outbreak of War with Germany to June, 1917* (2 vols 1928–30). Tippetts's remarks on Campbell have not been traced; Bird believes they appeared in some periodical or newspaper published in the city of Oxford.

[3] Not Theodore Cook but E. T. Cook, with Alexander Wedderburn, edited Ruskin's *Works* (39 Vols 1903–12); see xii 514, 561–68; xvii 491 n; xxxvii 721–24 *et passim*.

[4] British firm of printers.

84

9 *May 1955*   *Montpellier*

MY DEAR BIRD,

Your account of the Richards – Curtis letters in Listener pleases me.[1] I must point out that the Trotsky – Lenin story was originally told by Namier, and there is no mention of the butler detecting any humour in it.[2] (I wonder if Curtis and Richards ever read "Friends" carefully? Certainly Churchill, Storrs, Amery, and David Lloyd didn't!) Curtis is quite in the Bureau tradition. He says that Hogarth made Lawrence's acquaintance at the Bodleian by looking over his shoulder and seeing that L. was reading Arabic.[3] Yet at the Cairo Conference Lawrence could not read the telegrams in Arabic; he could not read a letter from Jaafar sent to him in England; and when Graves stated that L. could read classic Arabic poetry, L. commented: "Not one blinking word!"

Do you realise that in their reviews Hart, Graves and Garnett either made gross blunders or perjured themselves?[4] Graves's statement that soon after the war he saw a letter from S.A. to L., and that S.A. was a woman is really the limit. In *1938* when G. published "TEL to his Biographer RG," Graves asserted that *he did not know* who S.A. was, but reported the belief that it was Dahoum! Now in 1955 he "recollects" this woman story and publishes it to try to convict me of falsehood![5] Churchill (foolishly signing a letter drawn up by Hart) has pretty nearly perjured himself too. I can only say that the memory of the Lawrence Bureau (especially when ex-post-facto) is as remarkable as that of the hero himself. How is it that NONE of these bigger people ever mentioned Egypt until I brought it up? Richards couples it with "India"![6] But none of the bigger guns including Churchill mentions it. Pah. What a case which has to be so supported.

I share your apprehensions about the commercial-financial future of G.B. With our inadequate home-production of food, our absence of almost any raw materials but coal, the loss of two-thirds of the Empire, a standard of living derived from the days when we were the wealthiest nation, and intensive competition — what an outlook! And it seems to me utter folly and vanity to go in for A- and H-bombs and all the rest of the military squandering. Much as I hate "austerity" and wish it could be abandoned, I see no other way out. Poor people can't afford luxuries. Everybody could make a start by voluntarily (but not ostentatiously) ceasing to smoke American tobacco, to patronise American films (two big deficits), to buy unnecessary American goods of any kind. The government daren't stop buying from America, but the people can. I can't understand why we have to buy America's surplus food, when we can now get it from France, or at least quite a lot. I think myself the Conservatives want to get in, if only because of the love of power; and they may think they can handle the situation better.

What amazes me is the smug and contemptuous attitude to France in our papers. True, the political set-up is deplorable, though the lobbies are no worse than in USA; but economically the recovery is almost spectacular. In 1946 when I returned, meat was almost non-existent; in the first quarter of this year nearly 80,000 tons were exported, and it is of course ration-free here and not frozen! That Mondragon-Bolene water-power electric affair is nearly as powerful as the much-boasted TVA, and it is only one. New oil wells are coming in at intervals, and I believe this year the oil in France will run well over 50,000 tons, not to mention vast quantities of natural gas. There is a surplus of coal, though its quality is not high. And there is a small export surplus nearly every month without counting any invisible exports. And not so long ago one of our countrymen told me condescendingly that "of course" the French envy England its wealth! Some wealth, some envy! But I wish I could see some way out for us. But what?

I am working on Mistral now, which would be a nice foil to TEL, but Heinemann want to postpone, and bring out the Frauds. The difficulty is getting America to touch Mistral, for he stands for everything they want to destroy. I have an American offer to do d'Annunzio and Heinemann are willing, while Mondadori [7] will co-operate. This I shall accept if terms are reasonable. But the comparison with TEL is inevitable. But what a change for me to have the Duse instead of Dahoum and the "too beautiful ones" of the bodyguard! (Aptly named.) Perhaps it would be better to do Mistral first, but everything I do will be hooted down, sneered at or ignored in England; and I am switching everything back to America.

Apropos Mistral. I should much like to see that Nostradamus article,[8] as Mistral half-believed in N. who was born in St Rémy and lived and died at Salon. Mistral's peasant mother so much believed in Nostradamus that she wanted to christen her son with that name, but neither the priest nor the mairie would accept it! I can't understand the priest — surely it is simply Nôtre Dame dog-latinised in the masculine? (And I fear we must give up the "Marius" of Marseille as a memory of the great Roman — it may possibly date from the Revolution, but is now the Marseille mothers' transfer of Maria to their sons.) There is a strong streak of superstition in Mistral, partly as a matter of loyalty to his neighbours, partly as a matter of "poèsie" but partly genuine.

Two Mistral queries. M. convinced himself that Dante got the idea of Malebolge from the Vallée de l'Enfer near les Baux. Now is there any evidence that Dante ever visited Arles apart from the celebrated lines:

"Si come ad' Arli ove Rodano stagna . . .

Fanno i sepolcri tutt' il loco varo."?

True the Rhone then did "stagna" near Arles because the levees were not built until the first decade of the 18th century, one of the worst blunders of Louis XIV's engineers. But the Aliscamps was then intact, and must have been almost if not quite the most famous burying ground in Christendom. Dante could easily have heard of it. As for Malebolge I am now pretty well convinced by the evidence Briffaut quotes in that excellent book on the Troubadours [9] that Dante swiped the geography (or cosmography) of his poem from the Arabs, particularly from Mohammed's Dream.[10] Mistral relies on the fact that D. mentions rocks (!) and asserts that the word "balze" is derived from "Baux." These are surely the fantasies of local patriotism.

Can you find anything about St Clair, whose legend is unknown to every curé and schoolmaster I ask. St Clair is very répandu in these parts, and has a chapel to himself in the Cathedral at Albi. St Clair (where I used to live) is named from the cell of a hermit from a local Carthusian monastery, now in ruins of course — but the name I think comes not from the hermit but from the pre-existing saint. Before the Revolution St Clair was the patron saint of tailors and sempstresses (also Sainte Claire and Ste Luce) and (naturally) of the makers of lantern-glasses. Incidentally, "Crispin Crispian" were still the patrons of shoemakers.

Can you also tell me anything about St Médard (8 June) and how it is he is connected with that weird story (Mireio Bk 5) of the spirits of the drowned rising from the Rhone and wandering along the banks with lights in their hands, looking for "a good deed" or "an act of faith" in the living? They were allowed this one night, in the year, and when they had collected "a bouquet" of such good deeds might be received by St Peter. The drowned presumably cannot receive unction and absolution and hence are damned, but the humanity of the people imagined this way out. Is there any classical precedent for the Manes appearing with lights? Curiously enough the now disused church of St Honorat in the Aliscamps has an open tower which was not a belfry but a "lanterne," a beacon of the dead. (Derived from whence?) Light may thus have become associated with the dead. Legend has it that Christ in person appeared to bless the Aliscamps, or rather the Apostles who evangelised Arles. It is no small tribute to the power of paganism in Arles that its extirpation required no less than seven of the disciples — Maximin, Eutropius (hopelessly confounded with the local St Tropez), Saturnin, Martial, Sergius, Fronton (who became Bishop of Périgueux!) just as the others became respectively bishops of Aix, Orange, Toulouse, Limoges, and Narbonne! [11]

But I can find nothing about St Clair and St Médard, though the latter is in the ordinary French calendar to this day.

At this moment I receive by the post an invitation (as a Soci of the Félibre) to attend the bravade de St Tropez on the 29th, when a Court of Love will be held under the presidence of la Rèino dou Felibrige e dou Capoulié!!! I am tempted to go, but the bravade itself is fearfully noisy, with incessant firing of shot-guns and fire-crackers "religiously popped." There is a banquet, but the eloquence at these banquets is endless, and as I know Provençal very poorly by ear I miss a lot.

I am feeling horribly smug at having reached the 15th day of my fast, but intend to persist until friends turn up on the 26th. I must be careful not to get drunk. A month's complete abstinence makes one as susceptible as a lad.

I have been reading about Titus Oates. If I formed an Oates Bureau I should begin by hammering on the fact that he was received by William III, given a present of 500 pounds and a pension. Now would a great man like William of Orange have supported Oates if the charges against him had not been horrible calumnies? Of course there was a Popish Plot. Of course Sir E. Godfrey was murdered by the Papists. Of course those condemned to death were guilty. Who condemned Oates? The infamous Jeffreys. Do you pretend to know better than Allenby III — I mean William III? Out, rogue!

Adieu! Lovely weather here. I saw a hoopoe in the public gardens.

Ever yours,
RICHARD ALDINGTON

¹ Vyvyan Richards's letter (*The Listener* 21 Apr 1955) protested statements about T. E. Lawrence, which L. P. Hartley made in " 'The Mint': A Failed Masterpiece" *The Listener* 14 Apr 1955. Lionel Curtis's letter (5 May 1955) corrected details of Richards's letter.

² That is, Lawrence's and Namier's having themselves announced at Lionel Curtis's wedding reception as Lenin and Trotsky. See *T. E. Lawrence by His Friends* 226. The "Richards – Curtis letters" both refer to the incident.

³ See *T. E. Lawrence by His Friends* 258.

⁴ See above, letter 80, Robert Graves "Lawrence Vindicated" *New Republic* 21 Mar 1955; David Garnett "Lawrence in the Dock" *The New Statesman and Nation* 5 Feb 1955.

⁵ *T. E. Lawrence to His Biographer Robert Graves* 16–18; see also Robert Graves "T. E. Lawrence and the Riddle of 'S.A.' " *Saturday Review* 15 June 1963; see above, letter 11 n 1.

⁶ *Portrait of T. E. Lawrence* (1963) 193.

⁷ Mondadori (Edizioni Scolastiche) of Milan, Italian publishers.

⁸ It has not been identified.

⁹ Robert Briffaut *Les Troubadours et le sentiment romanesque* 1945.

¹⁰ RA refers to an account of Mohammed's journey to heaven written by ibn-'Arabi (1165–1240). See also Ángel González Palencia *Influencia de la civilización árabe* (1931) 56.

¹¹ Included with this letter are notes about St Médard which run:
St Médard and the souls of those drowned in the Rhône, rising up that night, each with a light, they seek their "good works and acts of faith."

Mistral has no note on this, and I cannot find that St Médard was even known in Provence. His name does not figure among the lists of saints revered by the various Guilds and trades.

In a collection of brief lives of Bishops and Archbishops of Arles his name occurs under Nothon, who is supposed to have held the See from 828 to 831. Here it is stated that the revolt of the sons of Louis le Débonnaire compelled the king to do penance in the monastery of St Médard. (Anachronism here, surely?) The first recorded bishop of Arles is no earlier than 250, and he was a heretic — Marcien — said to have been excommunicated by Pope Stephen I. St Césaire was the first Archbishop, 1st half of 6th century. Some of these prelates had strange names. Under Charlemagne lived Archbishop Elifant. Circa 985 came Annon, succeeded by Pons!

Quasimodo (first Sunday after Easter) anciently in Provence was a "Fête des Morts," said to be of pagan origin. In the Middle Ages a coin ("obol") was buried with the dead in the Aliscamps. Said to exist even today. Aromatics were placed in the coffin, a statue of the B.V.M., and a bottle of wine. It was "unlucky" to marry in May, "month of the dead."

An old song says that at Toussaint, the dead rise, each with a light. Food was put out for them. Ditto at Xmas.

Fires were lighted in Provence, not only for Xmas and the feast of St J.-B. but for Epiphany. Fires also for St Vincent on 22nd Jan.

Around the 25th March nut-shells, containing burning pitch, were launched on rivers.

On Candlemass Day was the fête of "new fire."

May was the "month of souls," a dangerous epoch.

Mamert, bishop of Vienne, and Césair of Arles, instituted during the three days before Ascension a procession of relics in boats on the Rhône. Suppressed in 1493 as too dangerous, they were continued on land.

On St John's Eve, many bon-fires and processions. At Arles the place in front of St Trophime was illuminated with lighted tar-barrels. The people of Aix carried torches to the summit of Mont Sainte-Victoire.

A fire and Water fête celebrated the baptism of Christ.

At Monaco the feast of St Dévote, fires were lighted everywhere, and nowadays a boat is burned on the shore.

Perhaps Mistral put these together, but I still don't despair of finding the story.

8₅

13 May 1955   *Montpellier*

MY DEAR BIRD,

Collins, amused that V. Richards had at last spoken, sent me the Listener letters. Is there any nation in the world which so busies itself publicly with idiotic trifles? Pre-war I used to be amazed at the pedantic rot in the correspondence columns of the Observer and S. Times. Even so, Mr Curtis hasn't got it quite right. The anecdote appeared originally in that monument of heroism TEL by his Friends, and the heart-shaking facts were communicated by Lewis Namier, who (rightly) insisted on being called Trotsky as Trotsky was a Jew. There is no question of the butler detecting this exquisite jest, but the sensitive Namier was "embarrassed." [1] Beaumarchais said Ce qui ne vaut pas la peine d'être dit, aujourd'hui on le chante — and nowadays what is too silly to be said is related to TELawrence.

What a lot of American PH. Ds. will be earned by theses on such important points. How many Guggenheim "scholars" will approach Europe with their $2500 to clear up Lawrence mysteries which in my ignorance and European lack of background I have left unsolved!

Authorship is really encouraged by modern governments. Recently I got so fed up with the frustration by Americans of all attempts to collect the Japanese money due me that I gave it to a young Jap professor who wanted to get married.[2] Now I learn that owing to the fact that my pre-Hitler German publisher lives and works from Leipzig, the East German govt. forbids the transfer of (let me see, yes . . .) DM. 6,567, due for a reprint of Death of a Hero in German.[3] Now, I was suppressed (and, I have been told, honoured by burning) by the Nazis; and now the Marxists nationalise my poor little property. England and USA bleed me white with taxes. In fact only France and Italy behave nicely. Yesterday I had from Mondalori his (three months late!) royalty accounts on old books, and the Italian Govt took only Lit. 4,728 on Lit. 157,598. But why should they take anything? If they buy pork or popguns do they make the foreign exporter pay Italian income tax? [. . .] Why should authors alone (apparently) be so treated? I'll tell you — it is all due to the American Senate and the American hatred of "highbrows." Other governments have adopted it (the yanks began pre-1914) allegedly in retaliation, actually because authors don't protest, and can't strike or do any damage.

I think I shall become an Anarchist and join Sir Herbert Read! [4]

Interesting about the Memnon statue. A. H. Sayce in his Reminiscences (a great favourite of mine) relates that at considerable hazard he climbed up the statue to verify a tale told by the Arabs to the effect that the sound was due to a loose stone inside the body. Sayce found that when the statue was re-erected after the earthquake the loose pieces had been patched together.[5] Sayce does not offer any theory about the alleged sound. A legend, I should think.

Did you ever happen to look at a book of mine on Charles Waterton? [6] A most amiable and entertaining person of astounding credulity in some respects (anything connected with Catholicism) though most sensible in others. He firmly believed in the miracle of San Gennaro's blood, and in fact went to Naples mainly for the purpose of seeing it. The (non-Catholic) guide books tell us that during the occupation by the French Revolutionary army, the blood refused to liquify for hours, but the miracle occurred shortly after the French General announced he would shoot every priest in the church if it didn't! I am naturally interested in the problem of credulity since Waterton and the dupes of TEL. We seem to be peculiarly liable to be taken in by frauds. (The English dearly love a Fraud!) Or is it that we like detecting them after falling for them, and thus getting it both ways? Since reading up Titus Oates I am not surprised by the abuse of me in England. The first persons who ventured to disbelieve in Oates were committed to prison — either by Scroggs or Jeffreys! And if you will read the account in Philip Sergeant's "Liars and Fakers" [7] (the Cantab Hist is mealy-mouthed and face-saving) you will see that the line of defence of the Lawrence Bureau (i.e. how is it so many great persons believed in L. and only Mr A. disbelieves?) could more easily white-wash Oates than Lawrence. Oates had the Commons, the City, and many of the Lords, plus all the non-conformists and some even of the Church [8] on his side. True, he was eventually condemned for perjury — but only by the infamous Jeffreys! And Macaulay's hero, William III, received him, paid his debts and gave him a pension. Now, Shaw tried hard to get L. a pension from Baldwin and from Ramsay MacDonald — and failed in both cases! So Oates had the greater official backing. What a theme for Plutarch in the parallel!

Of course very old people do get neglected, especially when they survive a great chasm like the war of '14–18. Ford was certainly good-natured, very kind to young people, hospitable, extravagant. Violet, as I remember, was rather "near," but then she may have been economising to pay Ford's debts. He was extremely annoyed that she fed us largely on stewed rabbit, and served ginger beer instead of the Rhine wine he loved! But I think her gossiping made many enemies, and the scandal cut off most social callers. Why, I remember Kensington smothered with posters: "Violet Hunt in Box," "Famous Authoress Sued for Libel" and then "Violet Hunt Loses." In 1913 (I think it was, certainly pre-war) that was hard to survive.[9] Her parties were nearly all made up of Ford's Bohemian friends and very few loyalists among the respectable. Lady Byron I remember there, but was she "respectable"? I was too naif to know or ask. And it was a great honour when H. G. Wells appeared — with whose wife, I wonder? I forget.

Try to find my Saints. I must back to Mistral. Still such a refreshment after the fetid Colonel!

Ever yours,
RICHARD ALDINGTON

P.S. I am threatened with an "Old Boys" [10] dinner at the Savoy — and "unaccustomed as I am to public speaking" I am asked to usurp the place of guest of honour! What next?

How quickly a feeble joke gets round! You know how in France to-day the only law universally obeyed is that which closes down everything — but everything — from 12 to 2 for lunch. Well, some little time back I was driving with some friends, one of whom is French, and arrived back in Montpellier at the fatal hour — the streets a pandemonium of bikes, vélo-moteurs, Vespas, Lambrettas, small and big cars, buses, all hastening away from work — the traffic cops having already knocked off exactly at noon! In idle mood I said to my French friend (blaspheming Hugo):

"C'était l'heure tranquille où les lions vont boire." Believe it or not, this feeble jest appeared yesterday in the local paper as an original by the writer. How one is frustrated of one's well-earned fame! Perhaps it was an "independent discovery," like all these Russian and American scientific discoveries of things we had believed found by English, German, French or Italian scientists.

1 See above, letter 84 n 2.
2 Morikimi Negata of Kobe City University of Foreign Studies.
3 Paul List Verlag first published a German edition in 1930.
4 Probably a reference to Read's *Poetry and Anarchism* (1938) or *The Philosophy of Anarchism* (1940).
5 1923 p 231.
6 *The Strange Life of Charles Waterton, 1782–1865* (1949).
7 1926 pp 13–131.
8 Such as Israel Tonge, an Anglican clergyman, who assisted Oates in his early plots.
9 In 1911; see above, letter 82 n 8.
10 RA's school was Dover College.

86

18 May 1955   *Montpellier*

MY DEAR BIRD,

Thank you very much for the information about St Médard. It is curious that the tradition you find is of water from the sky, and the tradition here of "waters under the earth" and ghosts rising with lights. His early date is all in favour of your identification, for this was clearly an early centre of Christianity. As to the lanterns at St Honorat — I think it very probable that like those you mention in England it was also a lighthouse. Arles was a great port in the Moyen Age — much safer than Marseille because some distance up a river, like London — and I think that 1000 years ago the mouth of the Grand Rhône was probably some miles nearer the town. It was in the spirit of the age to associate works of public utility with religion — as for example making a saint of the engineer who built the Pont d'Avignon. By the way, do you know why it is unrepaired? A dispute between the Pope and Louis XIV! How typical of our own dear governments.

St Clarus of Vienne — 7th cent. — sounds very hopeful. Probably that is my man. I must tease the librarian here and get a look at the Acta Sanctorum. *Why* was he so popular? But then why did our St Gilles get to Seven Dials? He ought to be the patron of the SPCA. If they put themselves under him they would make much progress in Catholic countries. The facade of St Gilles is wonderful, in spite of mutilation, but even so not comparable with that entry to heaven at Sant' Iago da Compostella, which is utterly intact, still keeps many traces of colour, and is the work of a great Frank genius, Mateo. What an ignoble epoch we are in comparison!

Wandering along the roads here in a little car, and stopping, I realise why the French King was entitled "Most Christian" — there is no country which still has so many place names of saints, and that in spite of the revolutions. There is a tiny hamlet near here named Ste Eulalie, who was martyred at Barcelona, with whom we were once one people. On one of the few towers of the ramparts which Richelieu (may Allah reject him) destroyed, is an inscription in langue d'oc of this century recording the loyal regret of the citizens for Marie de Montpellier and Jaime d'Aragon, "our lords."

The cathedral of Albi was founded in 1277 — very new for down here, and after the infamous crusade. There must surely have been an earlier one? I have two books on Albi, but they are superficial. And of course unfair and mendacious. I cannot think of a viler major crime in history than the self-styled Albigensian "Crusade," [1] and were I another Dante I would place in fiery furnaces those filthy brigands Simon de Montfort and "Saint" Louis the Frantsimang! They are still execrated here, along with the "abominable" Foquet of Marseille. But I would not for the world touch the religion of the people here — it and it alone saves them from the appalling vulgarity and evil of industrial "culture complex."

In the delayed voting for 12 communes of the Hérault (on strike because people won't buy their bad wine) the communist vote dropped from 24,000 to 17,000. But it is still far too high. [. . .]

Talking of which — have you read "Honours for Sale" by Gerald Macmillan (Richards), a life of Maundy Gregory? If not, get it, and learn why the world jeers at English titles. [2] A companion piece to Lawrence.

Apropos, Some people think I should reply to the Bureau, but the majority are against. I think, with A.C.S., that "silence is most noble to the end." If I am wrong, the Guggenheim Foundation will prove it with a bevy of Ph.Ds. If right, why should I add to what is said? I am a pioneer. Much will come out to modify, perhaps contradict things which now look certain; but I think that ten or a dozen theses in the next twenty or thirty years will not only make me a back number, but show me up as too kind to him. He is one of the nastiest sods in a sodomitical "Society." Apropos which — Maundy Gregory was another!

I have no right to be talking about Mistral. He is a good poet, a very fine man, and the very soul of the Midi. He is a life study. My only excuse is that I am a little less ignorant than the average reader of the Daily Mail, but what does that signify? Such people won't want to learn even the little I can tell. A strange world we live in. I like to hear about persons and places I don't know. But apropos the Colonel I get letters, especially from USA, the gist of which is: "I am not interested in TEL so why should I read your book, for I know nothing about him?"

Did you happen to see in a recent N. Statesman an article on DHL by Muggeridge? [3] What a lamentable exhibition of British stupidity and that esprit de Londres which wearies me (at least) by its inability to recognize its superiors. I I wish I could write French. I would never more worry with the islanders.

You have snow and a general election. How I understand the hermits of old time. Especially since I am clearing my work table and keep turning up forgotten press cuttings. They — inasmuch as they exist, and not because of what they say — make me doubt myself. One should not get into that world. All I can plead is that it is Lawrence's world, into which I unhappily strayed in all innocence. I heartily wish I had never had anything to do with him and his "friends" — the body-lice of England.

Adieu! Tell me of saints, particularly if you can clear up this strange and impressive tradition of the drowned rising with lights on St Médard's day.

Ever yours,
RICHARD ALDINGTON

[1] Proclaimed 1208 by Pope Innocent III.

[2] 1955. The book exposes Gregory's confidence tricks in pretending to get the new war millionaires and the unduly ambitious on the Honours Lists during the period immediately after 1918. Lloyd George, England's Prime Minister, 1916–22, was thought to be implicated but he was eventually absolved of all guilt.

[3] "Lawrence's *Sons and Lovers*" 23 Apr 1955.

8 7

MY DEAR BIRD,

It is wrong and disgraceful and I shouldn't feel this way, but I am a little pleased that Berenson pulled a boner over that Francia.[1] Now, I have loved pictures for at least 45 years and know most of the galleries of Europe, particularly those of England, France and Italy; and I have long been annoyed by Berenson's interference with attributions, which are surely unimportant? If the actual painter is uncertain, then surely the right label is e.g. Venetian school, Unknown, 16th cent.? But I go to the Accademia, at the age of 20, and find a picture labelled "Giorgione" or "Palma Vecchio" or "Tiziano Vecelli." I come back years later and find it labelled "Loreo Lotto" (a painter almost unknown in my youth) or "Amico di Gentile" or some such tripe. Ten years later it is something else, which American millionaires happen to be buying. Why not leave them as they are? Or label them "Amico di Bernardo"? In Florence one sees a "school" picture, probably a fraud, somewhere between Botticelli and Filippino Lippi; and Berenson changes the "Amico" every few years to please the American market. Whoops for the Francia! Vive Koetser! [2] A chi t'e morto to Berenson! Merde to him. Why can't we enjoy European pictures in our way without his officious mis-namings? Let the Americans paint some pictures for a change.

Did you some time back see that most gratifying expression of French "resistance" to yank autocracy? A collection of "moddun Amurrican paintings" was sent to Paris "under official auspices" for Paris to admire, and a jury of distinguished French painters was lassooed to hang them. They unanimously decided that the moddun Amurrican paintings were incompetent daubs, and refused to hang them! Rage in Washington (D.C.); orders to French Govt.; paintings hung; "exposition" boycotted by all but yanks and Brits! Vive La France. Merde to Berenson!

Thank you very much for the tip about the Pope-Henessey book.[3] I must get it at once. I had the quote from Mme Darmesteter = A. Mary F. Robinson = Mme Duclaux.; and am all in favour of her. (A Miss Robinson, her octogenarian sister, sent me the sweetest and kindest letter about Religion of Beauty — about the only fan letter I received. I have it somewhere. She felt — dear lady! — that people today are not as responsive to Beauty as "we were" in the 1890s. I'll tell the world.) I'm glad I sponsored that failure. It cost me two or three hundred pounds I can't afford, annoyed Heinemanns, was unanimously conspué by the reviewers headed by Sir H. Nicolson (I think), R. Mortimer &c. And I feel proud of it. Considering that two-thirds of the contents are by Oxonians it seems rather a nice answer to Rowse's accusation that I am anti-Oxford and anti-don (anti-donkey, as I suggested!) I was longing to say that my most valued helper and adviser over the TEL &c had been a Wadham don, but respected your tranquillity and safety. You might have been assassinated by a delegation from All Souls.

Your St Clarus sounds very likely — but how did he get to the Midi? By the same road as our St Gilles got to St Giles. I am getting to be very fond of that Catholic Europe of the 6th-12th centuries. There were defects and crimes (are we so perfect?) but they saved civilisation, saved "humanity" in every sense. St Gilles was a S.P.C.A. man (you know the story)[4] and I believe now unorthodox, according to a ruling of Leo XIII (a nasty man) but I like St Gilles. They say he is buried at St Gilles. What does it matter? He lives in our hearts. Tell me more about St Clarus — how did he get to Albi and Lavandou? In spite of de Quincey's theory about the proof of a true philosopher, I am sorry he was murdered. I prefer my saints to be confessors and virgins — such as the beautiful (but murdered) Unde-camilliax. How did she get such a strange name? Do you like the cathedral at Cologne? I'm not crazy about it. Aachen was nicer, but I believe "we" bombed it. Was their silly war worth a thousandth part of the damage they did? Of course it wasn't. The destruction in Florence is a wound that won't heal. And I daren't think of Rimini and fifty other loved places. Tout passe — but one doesn't want to see it murdered by vile Americans and Boches.

I don't think Symonds saw the Camargue. Of course he is quoting Dante about the stagnant Rhone,[5] but I doubt if he really went to the Saintes Maries and the Camargue and saw how the river now rushes. Inverted commas would have saved him. Like the pious sons of Noah, let us supply them. I like Symonds. He seems to have been a congenital bugger, but fought what he thought was a sin to the very point of insanity — saved by the devotion of a wife who can't have been so happy about it! I like them both for that. And J.A.S. loved Greek, Italian and English poetry — wherefore much is forgiven him. Who cares now? Do you think Eliot and Connolly and Laurie Lee and Auntie Jane Cobley of the BBC really care, *really* care, I mean, for poetry which is not by them or friends, and is just "poetry"?

Yes, Mistral was wrong about Dante and Les Baux.[6] I'm sure he was. The evidence for even the Paris journey of Dante is pretty thin. And of course, you are entirely right — there are plenty of rocks in the Appenines and Alps. Mistral had the failings of a regionalist — who might be defined as a patriot without chauvinism and without common sense.

I am so pleased you liked my Waterton. I really loved the man in spite of his faults — and who hasn't faults? They were due mainly to his Jesuit teachers and a too ardent temperament. But to spend ten thousand gold pounds on a wall to protect wild birds — noble. And to arrange for converse between his pigs and comfort for his cows! If there is a Heaven I am sure he is there, rat-catcher and foumart-destroyer to St Peter! And do you remember how the blessing of the animals at Sant' Antonio seemed to him "replete with wisdom"?

All thanks for your letter with its knowledge and wisdom. I am for ever in debt to you.

Ever,

RICHARD ALDINGTON

[1] On 14 May 1955 The National Gallery, London, reported the painting *The Virgin and Child with an Angel* attributed to Francia, a forgery. The painting, verified by Berenson, had come to the National Gallery in 1924 under the Mond bequest. Dr Ludwig Mond had bought it in Rome in 1893.

[2] Leonard Koetser, London art dealer, first challenged the authenticity of the National Gallery's *The Virgin and Child with an Angel* attributed to Francia after purchasing what he maintained was the original at a Christie sale in 1954. See the London *Times* 13 Dec 1954.

[3] Probably Una Pope-Hennessey *Charles Dickens* (1945).

[4] See below, letter 91.

[5] See above, letter 84.

[6] See above, letter 84.

88

MY DEAR BIRD,

These alternating and simultaneous Anglo-French holidays are rather a trial since they cause such delays in receiving and answering letters. Indeed, since the war "doing business" with business men has become an exasperation, owing to their affecting the delays of the bureaucracy they served or disserved during the war. Add to this, for one who lives abroad, the maddening and uncertain delays of "exchange controls" . . . !

I heard yesterday from a small publisher in New York that he is interested in doing a cheap edition of the Eliot – Pound lecture.[1] I hope my agent can arrange it. The English publisher was here over Pentecôte, and says he not only disposed of a good few copies in USA but well over 30 in Japan! How do you account for that? He (Sims) is now considering the Housman and Yeats from the same course.[2] Looking over them I found with amazement that I had quoted 7 Ps. with Housman's remark on it, taking TEL then at his own valuation.[3] If the lecture is published the Bureau will of course accuse me of having fabricated it ex post facto, though I was able to lend Sims the original 1930–40 script. I suspected Housman even then was a disciple of Vergil's second eclogue, but I never dreamed such a thing of Lawrence — who now seems to me infinitely worse than Housman.

There is to be yet another TEL debate over the French wireless on Friday next, a propos this book of Villars.[4] My publisher Georges Roditi is taking part, and I am sending him some ammunition. How weary I am of the Colonel!

Do you think the Sinclair family derived their name from the Saint? If so, how and what? I wish there were more accessible books on the saints. Living down here and motoring about I see such interesting and numerous relics of their influence, and understand why the King of France was "Most Christian." The Saints were necessary to revive the spirit of religion which tended constantly to die away or at any rate languish under the too worldly clergy. If the Reformation had succeeded in France, would the Revolution have been so bitterly destructive?

I know nothing of theology, beyond the N.T. which can hardly be so called. Does the C. of E. accept the 6th of the Gospel according to St John as canonical? If so, how do we evade transubstantiation, which there seems to my feeble mind plainly asserted? If it was not a "hard saying" why did so many of the disciples "walk no more with him"?

Most interesting to see how the Church slowly and tactfully de-barbarises popular superstition. The cult of Ste Sara by the gipsies has had a great uplift since 1935 when she joined the Saintes Maries in the semi-annual landing from the sea — the "char naval" which Bênoit insists is of great antiquity. Three years ago the gipsies were pinning on the statue in the semi-crypt offerings of handkerchiefs, photographs of themselves and cheap jewellery. Next year the handkerchiefs were ranged on strings beside the clothed statue; then the photographs were put beside it in a glass-fronted box; and now the statue has nothing on it, and even the necklaces &c are in the box. Dignity is saved, and the barbarity of the material gifts gently rebuked. I suppose that the Bishops are right to discourage the offering of ex-voto paintings of accidents where the Saintes Maries intervened? I regret this, for the paintings sometimes have a rare quality of naive sincerity. Alas, at the Revolution scores of them were burned, along with books, hymnals, vestments and so forth.

Nostradamus — how interesting. Of course down here we know all about that execution of Montmorency at Toulouse,[5] and execrate the memory of Richelieu the "franchiman" who destroyed Montpellier, Les Baux, Sommières, and so many other places. I suspect he left Carcassonne in a worse state than Viollet le Duc's admirable restorations lead one to think.

How apathetic some people are nowadays! I tried to interest English visitors in the fact that Augustine was consecrated in St Trophime of Arles before starting for England,[6] and they seemed never to have heard of him. You must come down here and drive round with me and muse over these sites. I find that the ancient chapel of St Croix at Montmajour was also a "lanterne des morts" like St Honorat. But I believe that in the 12th century lighthouses may have been needed for the successors of the utricularii. It is rather baffling to learn that fires were also lighted on the Tour Magne at Nîmes, which must have been a trophy like La Turbie originally. Montmajour was founded by a pious and wealthy lady, Teucelind, who died 2nd Sept 977. Her grave-stone vanished at the Revolution, but was later found in a garden, where it still is! I wonder why the Alyscamps at Arles and the environs of Montmajour were such sacred places that burial in one or other was so much valued? In the 19th and 20th centuries most of the Alyscamps were turned into shunting yards for the PLM railway, and almost all the tombs and graves at Montmajour were wrecked. I suppose those of the old kings and comtes de Provence were wrecked in the 1790s.

Is it not interesting that both Caesar and Constantine seem to have liked Arles so much? The alleged palace of Constantine is on the bank of the Rhône in a mistral-swept situation. Is it possible that the mistral was then less ferocious? Or did it blow the mosquitos and hence the malaria from the legions? But after all the Romans brought the malaria here as they did wherever they went.

I hope the strikes will soon be over. They don't help much.

Ever yours,
RICHARD ALDINGTON

P.S. There is a new Victor Hugo anthology just out [7] — the humorous, witty passages. I must get it. He was a great man — too big for his boots.

---

[1] The edition was not published.

[2] *A. E. Housman and W. B. Yeats: Two Lectures* published at Peacocks Press in 1955 in an edition of 360 copies. These lectures were part of a series delivered at Columbia University about 1938.

[3] See *A. E. Housman and W. B. Yeats* 7–8.

[4] Jean Béraud-Villars *Le Colonel Lawrence, ou, La Recherche de l'absolu* (1955).

[5] In 1642 Henri II, Duke de Montmorency, was executed for his part in a conspiracy of Gaston d'Orléans against Richelieu.

[6] In 597.

[7] *Victor Hugo s'amuse* ed Christiane Bayet.

89

4 June 1955   *Montpellier*

MY DEAR BIRD,

Curious how a trifle torments one. I cannot find the exact place of that battle between Charles Martel and the Saracens, but it was certainly Moussais-la-bataille, and not far from Poitiers. This as you say was in 732, and the invasion of the Midi was four years later. Whether the Poitiers raid was undertaken by the Saracens as allies of the Midi or not, I can't discover; but the feeling one gets is that the real enemy was not the Saracen but the Frank. Surely the "crime" for which the whole Midi was so brutally obliterated by Simon de Montfort (Earl of Leicester!) and his vile ruffians was simply that they were too wealthy, too cultured and too friendly with the Saracens? [1] Did you know that the church in Carcassonne citadel has an engraved stone to the memory of the Simon de Montfort [2] slain at the seige of Toulouse? Yet he was certainly buried somewhere in the north. I don't quite understand what happened. Perhaps he was temporarily interred in Carcassonne after the attack on Toulouse, and later moved.

. . . I have found it! Moussais-la-Bataille is on the right bank of the Clain, about 7 km from Châtellerault, and 22 from Poitiers. Huge mounds known as the Tombelle du Cheneau and the Fosse au Roi are thought to mark the collective graves of the Saracen leaders. I don't know why the English history books say "Tours." They were 75 klms south. It must have been a horrible slaughter. Perhaps they were drunk. Mohamed was quite right to forbid all drink to his followers. They can't stand it.

That Catholic "niaiserie," yes indeed. Due to the Jesuits? I remember long ago visiting an old friend with a wife and four young children. He had 'verted. And the way those otherwise delightful English children canted about "dear Lord Jesus" and kissed the hand of a filthy Franciscan monk revolted me! [3]

In haste!
RICHARD ALDINGTON

[1] Commencing in 1248.
[2] Father of the Simon de Montfort named above.
[3] The family has not been identified.

90

11 June 1955   *Montpellier*

MY DEAR BIRD,

The spectacle of a Fellow of All Souls personally advertising the Daily Mail is certainly staggering; but I expect he is hard up.[1] Many intellectuals are at present, owing to the enormous cost of material living, the long degradation of the war and post-war in terms of lowered material standards, and the unfair incidence of a confiscatory taxation. You mentioned the bankruptcy of Vyvyan Holland. The Wilde copyright came to an end in 1950, but if Oscar had cheated the people by selling them deleterious patent medecins and had invested his gains, the profits could go on indefinitely. Yet what property is so completely the creation of its owner as literary property? And the meanness of official England to all artists and writers is staggering. Do you know that they will not grant even the piffling little pensions they give without a means test! The English governing class and its hangers-on have always hated the independent writer and artist. Why, our literary history is largely a tale of the persecution of talents and the reward of official boot-licking. Perhaps Rowse has a wife and a sick child. But if he is really in residence at All Souls I should have thought the other Fellows would have indicated displeasure at such a breach of academic decorum.

There was yet another 45 mins on the radio (Paris) last night, but I didn't listen. This was to launch a book by one Béraud-Villars which the Bureau hopes will displace mine. You may guess its veracity when I tell you he asserts that Brémond's book [2] criticises only Lawrence's political policy, not his "heroism" and military exploits! This was repeated by Henriot in Le Monde,[3] and I am trying to get some quotations from Brémond printed. The difficulty is that the newspapers are all dishonest and simply refuse to print an answer. Under French law I believe even a foreigner has the "droit de réponse," but if the paper refuses one has to prosecute and that is too expensive. I must see what Amiot-Dumont will do. It is all such a bore, especially as Collins have now involved me publicly with Liddell Hart . . . I loathe controversy.

I don't think there is any evidence that Gregory did secret service work. According to Gerald Macmillan, Gregory put out one of his TELawrence tales: "He told his friends that he had offered his services to the Senior British Naval Officer at Dieppe and was being employed on mine detection work. This seems a highly improbably story." [4] Of course he was interned by the Germans. With a temperament and education utterly different from those of TEL, Gregory had the same propensity for spinning self-glorifying tales, many of which were believed though he had not TEL's intense cunning. But what tales would not TEL have told if he had had a gold cigarette case actually given him and inscribed by the King of Greece? Surely in a private interview the King would have offered to make TEL Prime Minister, and of course have been turned down — the tale itself not being told until the King was dead!

Interesting that the Communist party vote increased. But it is very small in England. Here they are about the largest single party, with the Socialists next, since the Gaullistes have slipped badly. The Communist vote dropped at the last election, but is still very high. I am told that malcontents of all sorts vote Communist, not because they agree with or know anything about the Party, but because it ranks as the extreme Left! It should be the extreme Right, as it stands for dictatorship. One of the many blunders Eisenhower made as C.-in-C. here was handing over collaborationist newspapers to "resistance workers" who were frequently fanatical Communists. People went on taking the same local paper and thought Communism was the policy of France. At elections the Communists here seem to have more funds advertising, hiring halls and electioneering generally than all the others put together!

I got a heavy batch of letters from England yesterday, so hope the troubles are ending.[5] The comforting thing here is that the only people who seem united are the Poujadistes,[6] and they are very recent and not political — yet. They are perfectly right in their protest against taxation which was mostly Communist-socialist in origin, and intentionally tries to crush out the individual and the one-man business — as in my opinion the English do also.

Your Theodore Cook news is most interesting. When the railway strike is really over, I shall get my friend Dibben to look for some of these titles. Peter Russell (to whom I gave your address) says that Cook's "Curves of Life" [7] is a remarkable book. Strange that we can afford to let such a man drop out entirely — while retaining Rowse! I suppose the combination of sport, journalism, scholarship and travel is too much.

I wish I could find some informed book on the topic of Saints, not from a sectarian or even theological point of view, but as history and psychology. Why did people *need* Saints? I suppose it was partly a transfer of pagan polytheism and partly arose unconsciously from visits paid to graves of relatives and martyrs. I must confess that at times in Italy I have felt it was too much a cult of old bones and rags and rather silly stories. I forget where I was when a priest showed me what looked like a large turkey-bone and asserted it was part of the arm of St Thomas Aquinas. It had attached a beautifully written Latin text said to be a Papal guarantee of authenticity. It would surely have interested Eliot? But the Saints as they live in the imagination of the people, especially down here, are interesting and touching. Do you know about St Gent or Gens? The first remarkable point about him is that he apparently never existed as a human being, and I think is not recognized by the Church. He is a rain-maker, and used to be honoured by a torchlight procession carrying his image. I've got a bit about him in my Mistral book — which, by the way, is depressingly bad and must be re-written, although already over-due.

Have you heard Billie Graham? He is now finding the Parisians a little harder to deal with than Londoners. But he has some success.

Ever yours,
RICHARD ALDINGTON

1 A. L. Rowse; the circumstances to which RA refers have not been clarified.

2 *Le Hedjaz dans la Guerre Mondiale* (1931); see above, letter 88 n 4.

3 For his weekly column "La Vie Littéraire" on 8 June 1955, Henriot's subject was "Un portrait français du colonel Lawrence."

4 See *Honours for Sale* 213.

5 A railway strike in England.

6 Small businessmen and farmers organized by Pierre Poujade in the Union for the Defense of Tradesmen to resist taxation.

7 1914.

91

14 June 1955   *Montpellier*

MY DEAR BIRD,

Excuse another letter so soon, but this morning I was looking up a book for information on London, and apropos the parish of St Giles came on Butler's account of this saint, which differs considerably from that told here.[1] Butler's account is pointless, and he is indeed in error if he speaks of the *French* king. Our story is that St G. came from Athens to Marseille and Arles, where he performed various miracles. He then established himself as a hermit near the ruins of Heraclea (now identified with the modern town of St Gilles by local enthusiasts) where he lived on roots and the milk of a doe. This doe was hunted by

"Flavius Wamba," King of the Visigoths, fled to St G. for protection, and was killed by a shaft from the king which also pierced the hand of St G., who prayed that the wound might never heal. He told his life story to the remorseful King who gave him lands and "all that is necessary for constructing an abbey," including perhaps the undoubtedly classical columns worked into the present façade. Later, St G. went to Rome, and then to Orléans, this time to the Frankish King, Charles Martel, whose confession he received — doubtless of his atrocious and barbarous violence in the Midi; and while the saint was saying mass an angel brought him a piece of parchment with the King's pardon signed by God.

Note first the laborious effort to exculpate Charles Martel from his crimes against the Midi by asserting that he was absolved by so popular a local saint. But the Midi will never forgive Charles Martel, any more than it will forgive Folquet of Marseille, Simon de Montfort, the Black Prince or Richelieu, or the commanders of Louis XIV who brutalised the country. History in French schools is falsified by making Charles Martel invade the South to expel the Saracens. On the contrary, our story is that Provence and Languedoc though nominally ceded to the Franks by the Visigoths had recovered their independence: and the Saracens were called in by the *patrices* or local rulers in an effort to stem the Frankish invasion which utterly ruined Nîmes and Maguelonne. It would be interesting to know when the St Gilles – Charles Martel story was invented.

Note also the protection of animals and wild things, which comes up as late as Francis of Assisi and Anthony of Padua. The early and mediaeval Church was therefore not in favour of cruelty to animals. It was the fussing of somebody (Acton perhaps?) for Leo XIII to patronise the SPCA which led to the stern pronouncement that "man owes no duties to the lower animals and it is heretical to teach that he does." It takes the mind of an Englishman, impenetrable by logic, to think otherwise. If man did indeed owe duties to the lower animals then the first of them would be not to murder them for food, and for everyone to become vegetarians. I look for this to be the doctrine of the Church in about a century when over-population and the exhaustion of sea, land and air, will have exterminated practically everything but man and the insects and their parasites. Meanwhile, the present doctrine is logically water-tight, and good Catholics will continue to torture animals with a clear conscience.

I think I must have Chatterton in my literary Frauds. Is there a good modern book which traces the chronology of the forgeries, and attempts some analysis of motive? I am taking the provisional view that Chatterton was misled by the success of Bishop Percy and Macpherson. Percy was not a fraud, of course, but a very lax editor. Nobody can dogmatise about Macpherson now even if he knows Gaelic, but I question whether he was so much a fraud and forger as the English said. I think he just went a step or two ahead of the practice which Percy soon afterwards indulged in with applause.

I don't like this strike situation in England,[2] and we are obviously working up for a serious clash here. There are constant over-crowded meetings of the mdidle classes protesting violently against over-taxation, waste of public money, and unfair social security laws. At the same time I have cuttings of a threatened series of strikes by the PTT and other government services (paid from taxes!), partial strikes in the mines (ditto) the profound discontent of the peasants, the closing of textile factories with unemployment in Valenciennes and Colmar. The success of Bidault's dirty intrigue against Mendès-France was a misfortune. He at least had a programme to deal with this situation which he foresaw, and on which he is making desperate last minute speeches. The present govt. is simply holding office and obeying the big financial and commercial interests. You would be horrified if you saw how patent alcohols (Ricard and so forth) are almost forced on the workers here, while the govt. takes partial action but refuses to take the really drastic steps Mendès-France wanted. This is the most temperate part of France from the sheer alcoholic point of view except in Marseille where they drink that filthy pastis. Brittany and Normandy and Paris are the drunken areas. But the beets from which these immense quantities of alcohol are made have a govt. subsidy, voted in 1916 because the alcohol was then needed for explosives! No govt. has dared to crush the financial interests thus created.

What drives me mad is that when I try to explain this to English visitors they listen vaguely and then say in that condescending way of theirs: "Ooh, but we have a beet subsidy in England too, didn't you know?" Damn the fools, that's a sugar subsidy (which we have here too) but the crime is the *alcohol* subsidy for beets. God knows I'm no teetotaler but Mendès-France is wholly right on that point.

Don't you think Eden has mismanaged this strike badly? My friend Dibben who is a traffic manager (and madly overworked in consequence of the strike) says the men have a genuine grievance!

Ever yours,
RICHARD ALDINGTON

1 Alban Butler *The Lives of the . . . Principal Saints* (1756–59).
2 A month-long newspaper strike, in full effect by March 31, followed by a railway strike.

92

19 June 1955 *Montpellier*

MY DEAR BIRD,

I had to speak this morning in my Mistral book of the Ste-Baume, Mary Magdalene and St Maximin. I discovered that Barras and Freron at the Revolution destroyed everything in the cave-chapel, and renamed the site "Thermopyles"! What strange imbeciles fanatics are. I am glad to say the peasants won, and it is still on the Ordnance Map of the 4th Republic "Grotte de la Sainte Baume." (In Provençal baumo = cave.)

The eve of Corpus Christi is an idea, but I don't quite see how or why the miracle of Bolsena links up with the drowned in the Rhône? The miracle was a blunder, anyway, as the scientists have proved with the scarlet fungus in wheat. It is well to have these things arranged. When I visited the shrine of St Andrew at Amalfi, the sacristan was more and more distressed at my disappointment in finding none of the holy oil sweating from the tomb. At last, scenting bakscheesh I fear, he said consolingly: "Never mind, Signore, come again to-morrow — we're expecting a miracle then."

I had no idea that Witiza – Benedict influenced England so much. Aniane is sadly fallen. The church, which must have been a superb and gorgeous example of Romanesque, was much damaged by the Huguenots, and had to be rebuilt about 1718. In a side-chapel near the chancel are two inscribed marble plaques detailing St Benedict's achievements — put up, needless to say, during the Vichy régime, which I begin to think is the only good home govt France has had for decades. (This pinchbeck republic is a travesty of the real France.) The monastic part of Aniane (also 18th cent) is now — horresco — a reformatory, and therefore difficult to visit. More is preserved at Gellone, now St Guilhem le Désert, and they still claim they have the piece of the True Cross given in 800 to Charlemagne by Zaccharias, and passed on by Charlemagne to his cousin Count Guilhem Court-Nez when he founded Gellone and became a monk. Aniane and Gellone had relapsed badly by the 11th century, and had become a nest of forgers — I have a few notes on them in my Frauds MS. I don't think it was considered much of a crime then — there are no forgers among Dante's Falsifiers — and in fact rather meritorious if it was done A.M.D.G. or to increase the patrimony of a monastery. Forgery is a mercantile crime.

I hear there is a very good fairly recent book on the murder of Sir Edmund by John Dickson Carr.[1] I sent for it, but of course the strike held up all books, and even letters are still uncertain. My traffic-manager friend said they hoped to get straight by about Monday the 20th![2] I think Eden behaved like a fool over the whole matter, which might never have occurred but for his attempt to put the workingman in his place.[3] If the British Govt could be persuaded to use for other purposes some of the 1500 millions sterling it wastes annually on ineffective military preparations, the country could be eventually solvent. The decision to make H-bombs was one of the silliest sacrifices to conceit and chauvinism ever heard of. For a second-rate power to make them is inviting annihilation, as Edgar Faure pointed out when refusing to allow France to be dragged along that stupid path.

My old friend Alec Randall is now at Geneva and says he may look me up. If he does, I'll turn St Clair on to him. He knows a lot of the Catholic prelates, so might be able to help us.

Did you happen to look at the letters in the Listener for the 16th? The page was sent me, as I was mentioned; but what struck me greatly was a letter from Seltman about the status of women in Greece, apropos some remarks of Harold Nicolson.[4] Now if not a practitioner among the belated followers of Socratic behaviour he is certainly an ardent supporter, and Seltman's letter rang like a rebuke to me. I may be wrong. I hope I'm right for I'm rather tired of waging a single-handed fight among the outrageous abuse of the sect. I don't want to be pharasaic or compound for sins I am inclined to by damning those I have no mind to, but I do think it is a deplorable phenomenon in English upper class life, and very bad for art and literature. Wilde did immense harm by giving the government and lawyers of the day their chance to discredit art and letters. You know I admire Oscar's work and wit, but he was a damned nuisance.

One of the American reporters who came to see me here had never heard of TEL, but started reading 7 Pillars on the way down. He asked me with a sneer why I was writing about such an obvious fairy! Rather hard on me, I thought.

I didn't know about the Housman note-books,[5] but of course Americans delight in anything which seems to discredit an Englishman, and have no sense of honour or scruples whatever.

Giorgione of course is a battlefield. Did you see there was to have been a legal fight over the authenticity of the Vermeers, only the millionaire died.[6] The actual author has pretty well proved he forged them in Cagnes. I ought to have this, but the thing is too close — Heinemann would have kittens about libel. They are even rather shy of Wise, though approving in the English way a feeble pun of mine to the effect that it is a Wise script which knows its own father.

Ever yours,
RICHARD ALDINGTON

1 *The Murder of Sir Edmund Godfrey* (1936).

2 See above, letter 90. RA's friend was Bill Dibben.

3 Eden had become Prime Minister, following Churchill's resignation 6 Apr 1955.

4 Seltman had recently completed *Women in Antiquity* (1956).

5 See *The Manuscript Poems of A. E. Housman: Eight Hundred Lines of Hitherto Uncollected Verse from the Author's Notebooks* ed Tom Burns Haber (1955). Following directions in his brother's will, Laurence Housman had published from four notebooks the poems he had considered worthy of publication, but instead of destroying all others, he had cut from the notebooks leaves containing unpublished matter on both sides. Then erasing or scoring in ink or pencil everything not already published, Laurence Housman pasted the remaining leaves and parts of leaves onto large sheets so as to expose only the poems he or A. E. Housman had previously published. These sheets then passed by gift from an American purchaser to the Library of Congress, and from there Haber recovered the still unpublished lines. The publication involved two questions, whether Laurence Housman had surrendered copyright and the ethics of such publication in view of A. E. Housman's directions.

6 On 12 July 1945, while under arrest at the Hague for collaboration with the Nazis, H. A. van Meergeren, a long-time expatriate Dutch artist, said he had painted a number of canvases generally accepted as works of the seventeenth-century painters Pieter de Hoogh and Jan Vermeer. After careful investigation, van Meergeren's confession was accepted as true. In confirmation Dr P. B. Coremans, who had analyzed all questionable canvasses, published his findings in *Van Meergeren's Faked Vermeers and De Hooghs: A Scientific Examination* (1949). Jean de Coen, a Belgian expert, dissented in *Return to the Truth*. On the basis of de Coen's dissent, Daniel-Georges van Beuningen, a Dutch collector who owned a supposititious Vermeer, *The Last Supper*, claimed damages of 100,000 Belgian francs from Coremans and demanded a retraction. Van Beuningen died on the day the trial was due in court, 2 June 1955.

93

3 July 1955   *Montpellier*

MY DEAR BIRD,

Real mid-summer. When the maid brings my breakfast she bids me note that the cigales announce a hot day. Strange how silly some of those late Greek epigrams are. You remember those (too hot to look them up) where a string breaks on a lyre, and the cicada jumps on it and fills the place? Well, it's not one note, it's two — jig-jag, jig-jag — I can hear them sawing away madly now. I suppose those are Byzantine efforts. What happens to the human mind that it suffers these eclipses? Don't you feel those late Greeks — people like Athenaeus and Diogenes Laërtius for example — were terribly inferior? And except for Longus, those late novelists are punk. Aren't we going the same way, compared with our glorious past? Or is this the esprit chagrin of old age?

I have just done a 7000-words article on Wainewright (a "probable" for my frauds book) which I hope may undo some of the harm Wilde did by making him an aesthete-hero.[1] He wasn't. He was vile. And, though I can't prove it, I am sure those London Mag articles of Vinkboons, Weathercock &c., were (a) self-advertising in the Wilde greenery-yallery fashion, and (b) advertisements of the bric-a-brac and prints and etchings which Wainewright dealt with for his living.[2] Lamb was so drunk in those days he noticed nothing. There has been a great deal of exact knowledge turned up since Wilde's essay. But the Tasmania 10 years are practically unknown. It appears that English families have in many cases contrived that the dossiers of their Australian black-sheep shall not be there! The Wainewright family got his destroyed. Pity. But Wilde's picture of him with a studio in Hobart and *paradis artificiels* must go — he was a hospital orderly on 3rd class wages (!) and when he did besot himself with opium, a patient for 2½ years. Some of his recently published drawings made there are highly erotic.[3] Published in a book by DHLawrence they would ensure prison sentences for all concerned; but are all right in a book about one of the vilest and most heartless poisoners in our history. We have many faults as a people, but that beastliness of Wainewright is very rare. It is disgusting to make him a hero. If I can get the thing published it will be interesting to see if Wainewright has as big a following as TELawrence. I shouldn't wonder.

Nice that Oxford has done Corbet.[4] When will they get down to work and issue my Corpus of British Poets [5] on India paper, which Cambridge turned down with such a sneer when I proposed it? Some time back I saw that fellow Hopkins in Paris. I don't think he really cares about English poetry. I doubt if any of them does. It is a matter of keeping up with the cliques and common rooms. And yet what a marvellous literature we have! Have you seen the Vinaver Malory? [6] I can't see it's such an improvement. Can you?

I am now on the literary "frauds" — mainly Macpherson, Chatterton and Ireland, with Wise as finisher. By the way, apropos that E.B.B. forgery, I discovered my Critical Kit-Kats under two inches of dust, and Gosse in 1896 is firm that he got the story of the sonnets from R.B. as a sacred trust! [7] And yet Allingham's Diary has the true story.[8] I can't believe Gosse wrote a deliberate lie — it would be so silly. The only explanation is that R.B. got fed up with questioning, and handed out this story, forgetting that he had left the true story in letters and in confidences to other people. What a damn silly thing to do. But those Victorians had such guilty consciences they were terrified of anything coming out. In Hallam Tennyson's Life [9] (not nearly as bad as Sam Butler says!) there is a tale of Alfred's immense approval of an old lady who had years of most interesting letters from some famous person and who, hearing that such letters were published, rushed to burn them, screeching: "They were written to *me*, not to the Public!" I think the great Alf and the old lady were wrong. After she was dead the letters belonged to the English people, not to her. And she had no right to destroy them. What do you say? Suppose Morris had given you a copy of his Chaucer — as he gave one to Yeats — would you destroy it? The analogy is incomplete. But after our death, if people are interested, why shouldn't they know the truth about everyone — and not only about Pepys and Boswell?

I'll ask for that Chatterton book.[10] What I want is some scholarly guidance on the probable dates of the forgeries. [. . .]

The story of St Gilles I sent you is taken from a pamphlet by the Curé, so the anachronisms are not surprising. The interest of all this to me is partly the poetic imagination involved, but chiefly the fact that these fantastic stories are still part of peoples' lives. Of course the Socialists are rapidly killing them. Clemenceau in his young days, in spite of Mistral, got the festival of the Tarasque suppressed! It was obviously necessary that popular credulity should be turned from old legends to the promises of Radical politicians. I must remember to get that story into my Mistral, which book, by the way, is going to anger Heinemann to such an extent they may repudiate their agreement. Not a concession to low-browism. Not one "popular" (i.e. moronic) touch. Well, if I starve, 'tis the destiny of Grub Street, which must hold itself a peg above Fleet Street.

That "invasion" of the Arabs against Charles Martel was a raid, and they probably came as allies of the Midi.[11] I have unluckily mislaid the Michelin map, or I could give you the exact reference of the mound which is said to mark the graves of the slain Saracens. I'm almost sure it is nearer Poitiers than Tours. I'll look it up. It is a place called Moussés-les-Bataille or some such name.

Ever yours,
RICHARD ALDINGTON

[1] "Pen, Pencil, and Poison" *Fortnightly Review* Jan 1889.

[2] Wainewright contributed essays on the arts to the *London Magazine* in the period 1820–23 under the pseudonyms Egomet Bonmot and Janus Weathercock. In 1826 he published *Some Passages in the Life of Egomet Bonmot.*

[3] In Jonathan Curling *Janus Weathercock* (1938).

[4] *Poems of Richard Corbet* ed J. A. N. Bennett and H. R. Trevor-Roper (1955).

[5] The book was not issued.

[6] Eugène Vinaver *Malory* (1929).

[7] "The Sonnets from The Portuguese" in *Critical Kit-Kats* 1–3.

[8] See William Allingham *Diary* ed. A. Allingham and D. Radford (1907) 380.

[9] Hallam Lord Tennyson *Alfred Lord Tennyson, a Memoir* (2 v 1897).

[10] E. H. W. Meyerstein *Life of Chatterton* (1930).

[11] The battle near Tours or Poitier in 732 when Charles Martel halted the Moslem invasion of Europe by defeating the Arabs of Spain who were led by Abdu-r-Rahman or Abd-el-Rahman, governor of Spain.

94

7 July 1955   *Montpellier*

MY DEAR BIRD,

Yesterday I drove my daughter over to Carcassonne for her birthday trip. For a very modest sum in the new town they gave us hors d'œuvre, turbot, cassoulet (for me), chicken (for her), and choice of cheese or ice-cream. A carafe of wine was 70 francs, quite good. I can't understand why people think Italy cheaper, where one is cheated all along the road. The old Cité is really wonderful. Now I have had the privilege of being able to visit it often, I realise what a great thing Viollet le Duc did there.[1] One does get the feeling — perhaps a bit factitious — of a great mediaeval fortress. But I *think* it is Bloomsbury Intellectual snobbery to affect to despise Carcassonne (as Ezra Pound does); because it does bring the past alive. It may be only an "object lesson," but I am glad to try and learn.

We could not help noticing that most of the cars of bathers on that wonderful stretch of sands (at least 13 miles) between Agde and Sète were GERMAN. That the most noisy tourists able to buy expensive souvenirs in the Cité were ITALIAN. That on the road GB was conspicuous by absence. Which raised a debate between us as to whether the "finest hour" of an old dipsomaniac clown making an obscene gesture had really been economically or otherwise profitable to our country?

Yes, I know Surtees; and the highbrows used to try to pretend he is better than Dickens, which is rot. It is huntin' stuff; but I personally don't think as good as Lever. The Irish are not such coarse brutes.

I wish I had finished the Mistral, and I wish it had some merit! At the moment I have done about 40,000 words, and have said most of what I can say about him, and have got only to 1868! I have to cover the rest of his work in about 25,000; and try hard not to repeat myself. The great merit of Mistral to me is one which the highbrows will think a defect. Mistral wrote one long narrative poem and several short ones which really touched *the people,* and yet the poets and critics of the time had to admit they were first rate. Poetry to-day is worthless, because it is neither fashionable nor popular. It is a languid diversion of affected intellectuals. May it perish! Mistral was a man, and for sixty years he fought to save his people from the vulgar degradation of machinery. He failed in the end, of course. It was a noble failure, and should inspire those who are working to undermine the machine-age and its parasites and slaves. There is no hope of success, but I must fail without compromise. It is the consolation of my life that my daughter admires Rostand's Cyrano,[2] and agrees that I am the same sort of ass.

I despise Richards and Ogden as pedants and corrupters of language and literature. Basic English![3] Basic charlatanism and self-seeking. We would not die in those men's company. Basic English would kill English literature.

The Saints, yes, I agree about the barbarity of the people, but prefer it sometimes to the barbarity of the prelates. What you say about the "need for a father-figure" is true enough, but doesn't nearly cover it. Living in an area where the Saints are still so near and real, where there are so many, where places-names are so often "St so-and-so," I feel their reality in the life of the people. I think the great Saints are those — such as Benedict, Bernard, Dominic, Francis, Ignatius — who renewed religious feeling. In Protestant countries a Saint is unorthodox and founds a new sect — Wesley, Booth, whose true religious inspiration I can't doubt though I can't share. This Billy Graham is perhaps another? But the Church either persecutes or absorbs. It is still the Great Showman. Annually there are more pilgrims to Lourdes than to Mecca. Do England's thoughts on religion matter? It is not a religious country.

There has been a terrific forest fire in the Var, starting very close to Gustave Cohen's summer house there. Really, the insanity of town people is beyond belief. The fire started (it is said) from the garden of a hotel, which was cleaning up for the season, and started burning leaves — in July! Of course, there weren't any dead leaves, but some fool servant from Paris or Marseille started burning rubbish of some sort, and set fire to the landscape. It is forbidden to light fires in that area in summer, and above all during a mistral. But no! jackanapes knew better. And if he is a member of a trade union, they won't dare give him a prison sentence. Meanwhile that beautiful woodland area is destroyed, and will never recover, because there is "no money" for such silly things as trees. I must learn not to care, and rather rejoice in the fact that I have often enjoyed what nobody will ever again enjoy. Still, I'm afraid Gustave's garden may be burned out, and that's no fun for a man so crippled he can only move in a wheeled chair. I have express-lettered for news, but can't hear yet.

The moronisation of "literature" proceeds apace. The English publishers are rapidly following the Americans, and insisting that books must be "popular" and not "academic." By "popular" they mean journalism in book-form; by "academic" anything reasonably accurate and informed and written with a regard for grammar and syntax. "Their finest hour!" What next!

Yours sincerely,
RICHARD ALDINGTON

¹ That is in restoring the town walls of Carcassonne.
² 1898.
³ A simplified basic vocabulary of 850 words conceived by I. A. Richards and Charles K. Ogden.

95

9 July 1955   *Montpellier*

MY DEAR BIRD,

According to the local guide-book (but you know how dangerous they are) the body of Simon de Montfort was first buried under the inscribed stone at Carcassonne, and later transferred to Montfort-l'Amaury. I wish I had thought to copy the inscription for you on Wednesday when we were there. I took an inner road which avoids all the Germans, Italians and Americans hurtling down the main road to their dear friend, Franco, and has the additional merit of going through Cabestang. We passed a rather ancient-looking obelisk on which I noticed only part of an inscription "Carcas — sonne." My daughter formed the interesting theory that it marks the spot where Charlemagne was standing when they came to him and said: "Sir, Carcas te sonne"!

Talking of which — did I ask if you have read the Morton book on Belloc? Now, I like and admire Belloc, and certainly do not subscribe to the veracious Colonel's definition of him as "vile" (because he was hetero, loved wine and France, and was a hard-working professional author?) but I can't subscribe to the proposition that two historical passages quoted by Morton are "secure in the treasury of English literature." Now, the poetic Charlemagne of course has a beard, but historical Charlemagne was clean-shaved like most of the Roman emperors. So I pedantically object in a *historical* purple patch about the French monarchy to Charlemagne appearing with a "long white beard tangled like an undergrowth." ¹ Nor do I see why the steps of the Merovingians under the vaults of the Thermae were necessarily "slow." Why? And the second masterpiece has a plural subject with a singular verb. One does not find such slips in Gibbon. All the same Belloc was a good man, a much better man than, say, Jean Cocteau or T. S. Eliot. I am sorry to learn that Belloc was "unhappy and disappointed." I wonder what he expected? Surely, if a man can live, even frugally, by the unnecessary and comparatively pleasant means of writing books, he has little to complain of? I think he was most unfairly treated by his inferiors, who tried to rob him of his living. But, again, what else did he expect? What porridge had John Keats?

Send me what you can on Chatterton, will you, please? I have just done Macpherson, and want to lead up to Wise, via Chatterton and Ireland. I take the view that Lady Wardlaw and Bruce and the ingenious Dr Harrington were blameless enough; that forgery in literature was then a venial sin; that Macpherson was not so very guilty, not much more than Dr Percy; but that Chatterton was, for he did try to deceive Horry Wappul,² and the Rowley poems were really "literary forgeries." As for Ireland and Wise, they were damned crooks. Tell me, would you and other good men from that great University be offended and annoyed if I concluded:

"Oxford, which expelled Shelley with ignominy, and did nothing to save Chatterton from starvation, made T. J. Wise an Honorary Fellow of one of its Colleges. How right Homer is: 'Never do the immortal gods fail to know one another when they meet.'"

I humbly submit myself to your judgment. I think the "crack" deserved. If you think otherwise, it shall come out. But only in the name of Justice and of reverence for a great seat of learning — no "expediency." "Command me," as Mr Bob Sawyer's friend said when he offered to pitch into the landlord or go and groan on the stairs.

I started a bit about Surtees, because Bonamy Dobree and other Criterion[3] (save the mark!) geniuses tried to persuade me that Jorrocks[4] etc. is better than Dickens. Rot. Dickens is a vulgar, middle-class, inferior Shakespeare, but he is almost the only writer we have who can be compared with Shakespeare. Surtees was good enough, but nobody compared with Dickens. As to the cockney sportsman — it was simply flattery of British class snobbery. The cockney couldn't afford "a shoot," he went out and blazed away (damn him) on common land at anything from sea-gulls to linnets. The "satirists" didn't care about *that*. What they hated was the vulgar fellows intruding on their exclusive domain of "sport." Now, note the greatness of Dickens. He was commissioned (a poor journalist) to make fun of these "cockneys" in the snob spirit which Thackeray would have done so splendidly, as he did in his contributions to Cruikshank's Comic Almanack[5] and to the Book of Snobs.[6] (With Thackeray a "snob" means a "cad.") He, Thackeray, was the snob snobissimo. But Dickens! In two wags of a duck's tail he emancipates himself, out of the cockney sportsman creates Mr Winkle (on whom be Prayer and Peace) and all that immortal gathering — second only to Shakespeare, and DAMN Miss Austen and Mrs Woolf! Think of Mr Smangle. Think of the Nupkins family. Think of that immortal party chez Bob Sawyer I have referred to. By the bye, I think Dickens got his "Weller" name from someone in the employ of the Thrales, just as he got his "Snodgrass" from a despatch of the Duke, who in reporting the capture of St Sebastian gravely commends the "gallant conduct" of "Major Snodgrass and his gallant Portuguese." I don't think even Shakespeare could have done better than to make our Mr Snodgrass out of that — remember his beginning to take off his coat and announcing he was going to begin? Why can't we praise our great men and stop boosting pretentious phonies? What's the matter with the "critics"?

"What are they feared on, fools, 'od rot 'em?
Were the last words of Higginbottom."

Ever yours,
A. HIGGINBOTTOM

P.S. I see from what you say that I am forestalled on the topic of Wainewright.[7] Can't be helped. Pereant qui nostra . . . Heinemann will have kittens when they see this book. They expect something "popular" and will get a dollop of pedantry such as will oblige them to call in Professor Namier — as I learn Collins did with my TEL. What next!

[1] J. B. Morton *Hilaire Belloc, a Memoir* (1955) 146–47.

[2] That is Horace Walpole, to whom Chatterton sent a history of painting purported to have been written by a 15th-century monk Thomas Rowley.

[3] The periodical edited by T. S. Eliot with the early financial support of Lady Rothermere. The first number (which contained the first printing of *The Waste Land*) appeared without Eliot's name as editor in Oct 1922.

[4] Sporting grocer created by Surtees.

[5] See above, letter 53.

[6] First published in *Punch* (1846–47) as "The Snobs of England"; republished (1848) as *Book of Snobs*.

[7] R. Crossland *Wainewright in Tasmania* (1954).

96

18 *July 1955*   *Montpellier*

MY DEAR BIRD,

This Crossland book is rather a nuisance, as I sent off my "Wainewright" only last week! Reviews are nearly always inaccurate, but I doubt if this book adds much to Jonathan Curling's book,[1] which was the real pioneer, and added much to knowledge of the Tasmanian period. Curling discovered and published the only known portrait (self-portrait) of Wainewright which makes him look like a vicious snake! He also published a number of W.'s Tasmanian drawings, three of them very erotic — D.H.L. would have been jailed for publishing them. One mistake — which must be the reviewer's and not Crossland's — is saying that W. was a ticket-of-leave man. Curling reproduces the official document refuting it. What happened was that W. was to some extent favoured. He spent only a year in that pre-view of Buchenwald, the English Convicts' station in Tasmania. He then worked as hospital orderly on "third class wages" and somehow contrived to get enough opium to make himself a patient for $2\frac{1}{2}$ years. The doctors favoured him, and he was allowed to visit houses and make sketches or give drawing lessons, but always attended by a warder. As a convict he could not sign his name even to his own drawings. (I didn't know that. Did you?) And there is evidence that a doctor took him to Sydney, and that W. made a sketch of the harbour. I don't know what is meant by saying he wasn't a poisoner. The evidence is crushing, although of course W. was never indicted for murder, owing to the more than G.P. stupidity of the doctor. I disagree about W.'s talents. His sketches are better than his essays,[2] which I think are affected, self-advertising, and possibly meant to advertise his secret trade in antiques. He certainly dealt secretly in etchings and engravings, and cheated some of his friends by selling them copies of Marc Antonio as originals.[3] I really think he was a 4-letter man.

I am on the literary Frauds now, and wonder if I dare ask the favour of your reading the script? It would be a great help. I begin by showing that "apocrypha" are usually quite innocent — it is not the fault of the author that his work is wrongly labelled. Then I point out that in the Dark and Middle Ages forgery was practically a prerogative of the Church, instancing the Donation, and (my own private interest in) the amazing contest of forgery down here between such really sacred centres as Aniane and Gellone (St Guilhem). I then come to our own (and the Scots') 18th century batch, and feel very inclined to exonerate Macpherson and to a great extent Chatterton. But Ireland (whom I've done) seems to me a vulgarian and a real forger. "Vortigern" [4] is really beyond a joke, and so too Shakespeare's "Confession of Faith" about which Dr Joseph Warton (amazement!) made such a silly statement.[5] Perhaps he didn't. I have left a loophole. I can't believe the headmaster of a great Public School (and T. Warton's relative!) could have been such as ass.

I have only to insert Chatterton, for I am waiting to receive the book you mention.[6] Dibben confirms that it is the best book on C. but adds that he has been trying to find a copy not too madly expensive. There is a great demand, and it is hard to find. I thought it is still in print? [. . .]

As to Oxford — you have been so kind to me . . . but why should I not be unfair to "Oxford"? Except for you, has it ever in 40 years been fair to me? Undergraduates, yes, but that is another story.

I wish I admired C's poetry more. I have asked Dibben to get a modern edition. Those I have are old. But I see very little merit, and even the remarks of Ker (a great scholar) don't convince me. How can you possibly rank them between, say, Gray on the one hand, and Byron on the other? Or Collins and Keats? They all have glorious things, but what the hell has Chatterton done? "Oh drop the briny tear with me."

Did I tell you? I wrote to Noel Sharp — a friend — at the B.M , trying to get Wise let off forgery. But "in no wise." The librarians and bibliographers are still furious with him. But I do think that the "hoax" excuse has worn very thin. [. . .]

Belloc . . . Morton, who after all knew him well, says definitely "Belloc was an unhappy and a disappointed man." [7] His unhappiness, it seems, came from the death of his wife in 1912. His disappointment from his failure as a writer — he had to produce and over-produce, until his brain collapsed, in order to live, though he lived a little extravagantly — spending about a tenth, I mean, of what a moderately successful stock-broker spends, but obviously unpardonable luxury in a mere highbrow. His R.C.ism is a bore, and so is Morton's. But Belloc was somebody. And Chesterton's parodies, particularly of Yeats, are masterly. If you learn the Yeats one by heart, and repeat it gravely to the earnest phonies and know-all-dicks, asking them: "Who do you think that is?" they fall, hook, line and sinker! I've done it a dozen times. "YEATS" And then one shows the book, and sits back. And the Swinburne is good too.

Of course the depreciation of Swinburne is rot, but then the trouble of these war-fret years is the power of groups of sham intellectuals, who haven't read (where would they find time?) and simply parrot somebody like Tom Eliot (who I know reads damn little) or Leavis or Richards. Much of the early Swinburne is glorious, though I wish he didn't take his metres so much from Thomas Haynes Bayly. Some of those plays are remarkable, not only Atalanta,[8] but the Mary Stuart trilogy; [9] and there is a very fine verse in Tristram of Lyonesse.[10] But when he ceased to intoxicate himself with wine, women and song (under Watts's [11] supervision) he got drunk on words, and that was a pity. You know Heinemann admired him so much he bought all the copyrights for 5000 gold pounds, plus 900 to that cheat Wise who pretended he had bought rights he hadn't bought. I always tease Frere by telling him (what I think is the truth) that Swinburne will come into fame once more when his copyright expires, in the 1960s.

Dickens, again, suffers from being talked about and not read. Hard Times [12] and Bleak House [13] are excellent, but his summits are Pickwick [14] and Copperfield.[15] There are good things everywhere, and I am delighted by the Boz Sketches [16] and by other minor work. What warmth of feeling, what generosity of affection towards the dispossessed, there are in that sketch of the Christmas with the nine (is it?) poor travellers in the alms-house? He was far too well-off to need to do it for "copy," and it was noble for a man with children to give up his Xmas like that. Dickens is the real old England which the pseudo-highbrow hangers-on have made shoddy. But it will survive them. I sometimes catch myself thinking we ought to be a republic. A sham monarchy treated with sham flattery and real contempt makes social shams of us all. One of the little events which sent me into permanent self-exile many years ago . . I was waiting (with fitting humility) in the luxurious outer room of the sapphic editresses of Vogue, circa 1925–26,[17] and a girl came in timidly, — she was "a lady" — trying to sell photographs of celebrities. Miss Todd sent her secretary — the girl was obviously poor. And that secretary. "Noo, we don't want them," "Noo, we couldn't possibly use them." "Noo — ooh — yes, I can give you a guinea for that — they're kite good people." Vogue is American of course, but there was a separate English edition to cater for our snobbery. You'll say I exaggerate. But I thought of that poor girl's guinea when I learned that they gave Nancy Cunard thirty or thereabouts for some snob tripe, and her not very aristocratic name.[18]

I am having much Mistral trouble at the moment, mainly from realising more and more painfully how ignorant I am. The Mistral literature both in French and Provençal is appalling in bulk and detail, yet there is no collection of letters, and all these learned books are issued with no index, so you can imagine the chore either of making notes or hunting. Then I have tried to persuade H'mann to bolster my trashy book with a new version of M's magnificent Moun Espelido [19] — and of course come up against the blank wall of publisher's ignorance and formulas for success. But they have a Morton's fork line of argument which annoys me. If I want to write about Mistral, they say: "But nobody has *heard* of Mistral," and if I want to write about Wainewright, they say: "But *everybody* has heard about Wainewright." Of course what they want is another Willie Maugham and another Graham Greene and another Noel Coward.

Yes, my daughter's birthday is the 6th July, and Count Potocki de Montalk who has now, (for reasons which are not clear to me) promoted himself King of Poland, threatens her horoscope. I shall of course keep it to myself. I do not see how he can be King of a country which does not and never did recognise royal descent, though of course he is a genuine Potocki and therefore I suppose eligible for election when Moscow restores the Polish monarchy — a remote contingency.

We had a thunderstorm here on the 14, which spoiled all the set-pieces for the fireworks. Much concern in the leftist press — the French citizen no longer puts out a flag on the 14. There wasn't one I could see in M'pellier except on public buildings. Also the dancing in the streets has virtually ended. The 4ième is very unpopular, and events in Maroc don't help. But as some keen-sighted cynic remarked: "La République gouverne mal; mais se défend bien." It is quite true. And anyway it is the Departments of the Administration which rule. The Ponts et Chaussés still carry on Colbert's orders, and pay no attention to these ephemeral politicians. Have you noticed in Paris that the fleur de lys still stand und steht over the Palais de Justice and the Mint? Madame Coty [20] inhabits the town house of Mme de Pompadour . .

The cicadas are jig-jagging away like mad. I am quite unconvinced by the "scientific" explanation that this perpetual noise (during sunlit hours) is to attract the females. I don't believe it. My daughter, who is an expert at capturing them, shows me how you can make them sing by a slight pressure, really a warmth. I think it possible that the sun gives the impulse. Whether there is a "practical" outcome I know not. How the world has been degraded by utilitarian theories. Why does the nightingale sing? Why has the bee-eater dazzling colours, and the hoopoe that crest and barred wings? I have never forgiven my old friend H. G. Wells for writing that flowers are "sexual advertisements."

Ever yours,
RICHARD ALDINGTON

[1] See above, letter 93 n 3.

[2] 1880.

[3] In 1506, in Venice, Marc Antonio or Marcantonio Raimondi counterfeited in copperplate Dürer's *Life of the Virgin* and *Little Passion*, appending the counterfeited signature of Dürer. The German artist complained to the Senate of Venice.

[4] *Vortigern and Rowena*, a play which Ireland wrote and foisted on the public as by Shakespeare. Richard Brindsley Sheridan produced it — unsuccessfully — at Drury Lane in 1796.

[5] The *Profession of Faith* is another forgery which Warton, headmaster of Winchester, saw in Feb 1795 on exhibition at the home of Ireland's father in Norfolk Street, London. Warton declared about it, "We have very fine things in our Church Service, and our Litany abounds with beauties; but here is a man has distanced us all!"

[6] See above, letter 93 n 10.

[7] Morton *Hilaire Belloc* 120.

[8] *Atalanta in Calydon* (1865).

[9] *Chastelard* (1865); *Bothwell, a Tragedy* (1874); *Mary Stuart* (1881).

[10] 1881.

[11] That is Watts-Dunton under whose supervision and in whose home Swinburne lived from 1879 until his death.

[12] 1854.

[13] 1852–53.

[14] 1836–37.

[15] 1849–50.

[16] 1836–37.

[17] In 1926, two articles by RA appeared in British *Vogue*, "Light Novelists of the Eighteenth Century" in June and "How They Did It an Hundred Years Ago; The Hairy Jeaune-France of Romantic Paris Who Worshipped Byron," in August.

[18] Nancy Cunard and RA had once had a close relationship. For a time she so enchanted him that he slept with beads around his neck which she had worn around hers. That occurred during the autumn of 1928, when RA was at Port Cros with Dorothy Yorke (Arabella), Bright Patmore, and the D. H. Lawrences. Later, with Mrs Patmore, RA visited Nancy Cunard at her home at Reanville, north of Paris. Three of his books were published at Miss Cunard's Hours Press: *Hark The Herald* (1928); *The Eaten Heart* (1929); and *Last Straws* (1930). Also in 1930, he helped her award a £10 prize to Samuel Beckett for "The best poem on Time" in a competition at the Hours Press. By 1932 RA's regard for her had changed. That year he published a cruel short story about Nancy in *Soft Answers* called "Now Lies She There," a piece which he and Derek Patmore turned into the play *Life of a Lady* (1936). The estrangement between Miss Cunard and RA was sharpened by her outrage at the depiction of Norman Douglas in *Pinorman* (1954), a book which she privately called "sewage" and "a mess of lies" and publicly attacked in *Time and Tide* (see above, letter 60, n 9). When Nancy Cunard was invited to contribute to the memorial volume *Richard Aldington: An Intimate Portrait*, she refused.

[19] *Moun Espelido: memori e raconte* (1906).

[20] That is, the wife of France's president.

97

20 July 1955   *Montpellier*

MY DEAR BIRD,

We are swamped with indignant Helvetians flying from Geneva, which they say has been made uninhabitable by the fantastic "security" exigencies of the Americans and Russians.[1] Certainly, the French newspapers are jeering at them as far as they dare. Have you had the story of the Swiss soldier who fired at a presumed assassin, thereby turning out about half an Army Corps, only to find it was — a hedgehog! But for American arrogance, ignorance and suspicion, I believe we could have peace. Of course, both the Russians and Chinese do appalling things to individuals, but don't we? We've had a very bad press here — at least Ll-George[2] has — over Ruth Ellis.[3] They — the French — didn't quote it, but they came near to the Kaiser's "cold-hearted haberdashers!"

We are all wrong about St Medard and Corpus Christi. C.C. is a moveable feast — first Thursday after Holy Trinity, which depends on Whitsun, which depends on Easter! But why St Medard? Mystery. [. . .]

Much oppressive heat here, but a soft mistral this morning has chased off the thunder and cooled the air.

The complications of life are appalling! I have done about two-thirds of my Mistral book, and have been making enquiries about "permissions" to quote. I learn from Maître Julian, who is a Majoral of the Félibrige by the way, that the poems are vested in the "Estate"; the Memoirs in Plon; the Armana Provençau pieces in Grasset[4] and the heirs of Devoluy; and the Letters in Maître Julian himself! Apparently the use of photos of the Museon Arlaten depends on the Council of the Félibrige which runs the Museum! What a bore!

More later!

Ever yours,
RICHARD ALDINGTON

[1] A conference of the Big Four Heads of Government (Eisenhower, Faure, Eden, and Bulganin) began in Geneva on Monday, 18 July 1955.
[2] That is, Gwilym Lloyd-George, Home Secretary.
[3] The execution by hanging of Ruth Ellis for murder on 13 July 1955 prompted a strong, well-organized protest against capital punishment.
[4] Plon and Grasset are French publishing houses.

98

27 July 1955   *Montpellier*

MY DEAR BIRD,

I am glad there is another Englishman who feels more or less as I do about that Ruth Ellis affair, which haunts me in the waking hours of the night. There seems a cold brutality about it which surely is alien to our character, which is fundamentally humane? Such irony — a young woman with two children executed by order of a young woman with two children! [1] I do not know this Mrs Waters of the French journalist who is supposed to have cut up her elderly neighbour who bored her, and yet got reprieved! I thought the Rosenberg case [2] in USA was heart-breaking, but this is worse. I think you are right. Better have no death penalty. The horrid *pedantry* and inhumanity of the English Law are really alien to the people, though obviously not to the governing class and lawyers. Do you remember that speech of Kaiser Wilhelm, which gave so much offence, directed against "the cold-hearted haberdashers on the Thames?" I begin to think they're just that.

Surely if we had warm hearts Wilde's Ballad of Reading Gaol [3] should have abolished hanging long ago?

I must do the Chatterton with what material I have. Dibben (who gets me books) has gone off on holiday without sending those I asked for. Everybody goes on holiday except the unhappy "pen-pusher." I am trying to get Frere (of Heinemann) to let me do a new translation of Mistral's "Moun Espelido," a book so wholesome and fresh after all these years I think it might do good. Of course, the mere suspicion of something "academic" (as they call anything civilised) frightens him, and he does the brave British thing of postponing until he gets back! Why can't Englishmen be frank and open as they used to be, and not always side-step and lie? I assure you that in my dealings now I always or nearly always find this shirking of issues. If F. doesn't want to publish the Mistral, why the hell can't he say so honestly? I don't care. There are other publishers. But they do the dog in the manger until one gets furious!

I believe myself that Simon de Montfort may have been temporarily buried at St Nazaire, Carcassonne, and then the body moved north when the disturbed conditions of the country allowed. The monument in Carcassonne is, appropriately, a slab of blood-red marble. I will copy the inscription for you when I am next there.

Recently an opera on the theme of the Albigenses was produced at Nîmes in the Roman amphitheatre, but it seems to have been ill-received. [4] Somebody wrote an English novel about it recently, I think, but it failed. [5] That "crusade" [6] is one of the great crimes of history, worse I think than the sack of Rome in 1527. The barbarous cruelty and brutality are so horrible that I hate to think of it. Hundreds upon hundreds of entirely innocent and delicately-bred women, stripped naked, paraded before an army, and burned alive while priests and saints jeered at their shrieks. Montfort's sack of Béziers — every man, woman and child murdered — and the treachery, the broken oaths, by which he got hold of Carcassonne! If that is Christianity, heaven preserve us from it!

I am glad you are enjoying Dickens. He is one of our greatest writers, and the "highbrows" have done untold harm by sneering at him. Believe me, I have been jeered at myself in the T.L.S. merely because I quoted Dickens with approval and reverence.

I am asked to give some talks (in Frensshe of Stratforde-atte-Bowe) on English poets for the Regional Radio. [7] I'm going to risk the ridicule. There is too little attention paid to poets in these Iron-hauser times.

Gustave (Cohen) is trying for the Académie Française this autumn. I doubt he'll make it, for the Catholics will black-ball a Jew though he is a "convert." [8]

Did you know that Mistral translated Genesis into Provençal?[9] And but for the intervention of the Bishop of Montpellier (Cardinal de Cabrières) would have been censured by Rome as he omitted to get the obligatory Nihil Obstat and Imprimatur? I agree with Coulton — the Church of Rome was and is totalitarian.

You are most kind. I will send the script of the Literary Frauds when I have added the Chatterton.

Here is the transcript of a letter just in from Los Angeles:

"You have the wrong title on your new and filthy book — it should have been "HATE." Why didn't you mention who it was that paid you to write the miserable thing you call a book just for the purpose of smearing the name of a *good* man, and a genuine and real Englishman? You are just a dirty RAT and if we never see your name on another book it will be too soon. S. R. McAlary."

By their friends ye shall know them!

Ever yours,

RICHARD ALDINGTON

[1] RA refers to the Queen, who had only two children in 1955.

[2] In March 1951 Julius and Ethel Rosenberg had been found guilty of conspiring to give atomic information to Russia during the Second World War. Because their activity was in wartime, the death sentence, according to U. S. law, was mandatory. Despite world-wide protest and all legal appeals, the Rosenbergs were executed 19 June 1953.

[3] 1898.

[4] *Les Albigeois*, adapted by Raymond Hermantier from the play by Maurice Clavel and Jacques Panigel; music was by Georges Delerue. The opera was presented first on 2 and 3 July 1955.

[5] A trilogy by Hannah P. Closs consisting of *High Are the Mountains* (1945); *And Sombre the Valleys* (1949); and *The Silent Tarn* (1955).

[6] See above, letter 86.

[7] A series of fourteen programs entitled "Conversations with Richard Aldington" broadcast from Montpellier once every two weeks. Conceived and directed by Jacques Temple, the series commenced on 8 Nov 1955. The subjects discussed were:

1. Boyhood; literary beginnings; A. E. Housman; the creation of Imagism with H. D. (Hilda Doolittle) and Pound; sojourn in Italy.

2. *The Egoist*; W. S. Blunt.

3. Yeats, Roy Campbell, and Joyce; Imagism and Symbolism; W. C. Williams, Hemingway, Wallace Stevens, and Marianne Moore.

4. H. D. and her account of Pound at St Elizabeth's Hospital; literary essays of Aldington's father; life in London on the eve of the war of 1914.

5. D. H. Lawrence and F. S. Flint; the war of 1914; Wilfred Owen.

6. The war of 1914; Henry Williamson, Carl Fallas, Peguy, Apollinaire, and Blaise Cendrars.

7. France at war; demobilisation; Aldington's debut with the *Times Literary Supplement*; sojourn in Berkshire.

8. Sojourn at La Vigie de Port-Cros; *Death of a Hero*; Frieda and D. H. Lawrence; Joyce, Proust, and Amy Lowell.

9. Lawrence and the intelligentsia.

10. Lawrence's debut; *The English Review*; *Lady Chatterley*.

11. Lawrence and his prophetic vision; Norman Douglas.

12. *L'Affaire* Maurice Magnus; Pino Orioli.

13. Orioli.

14. World reception of *Death of a Hero*.

[8] Cohen was not elected.

[9] 1910. See RA *Introduction to Mistral* 7, 163.

99

13 *August 1955*   *Montpellier*

MY DEAR BIRD,

Monday is Assumption, and this week-end is usually the most murderous in motor accidents of the whole year in France — the B.V.M. on the 14th-15th Aug. getting a larger human holocaust than Marianne on the 14th-15th July. I am longing to get about a bit again (my car has been under repair) but I am NOT going out on the roads until this blutbad is ended. Really! this frenzy for speed! And it attacks everyone. A few days ago a man from near Strasbourg in a car laden with baggage, his wife and four children, was frenziedly trying to get to Lourdes *in one day* (!) and ran into a policeman (father of five children) riding a bike in the same direction, and killed him. The bike was flattened *from the rear*! He must have been going 80–90 miles an hour. Why?

My daughter is away "faisant du camping" at St Clair (the elusive St Clair, whose name, I have just found, is given to a hill 180 metres high in the Corbières. Why?) near Lavandou (which is, alas, the wash place and not the lavender place) and I want to spend a little time there, and then perhaps nip over the "causse de things such as the Grimaldi skeletons at Monte Carlo.) We have a nice little pre-history museum at Les Matelles (itself a gem of mediaeval "bastide" architecture) and I want to spend a little time there, and then perhaps nip over the "causse de la Selle" to St Guilhem. That lovely site is becoming "touristy" I fear. But they can't spoil it for a long time. A curious custom in the church there which may interest you. The valley is much subject to severe thunder-storms coming off the Cevennes; and the Church *says* it still has the piece of True Cross given to Charlemagne by the priest Zaccharias in Rome circa Xmas 800; and by l'Empereur given to his cousin Guilhem on demobilisation. Well, they make tiny little "pains" about the size of a boy's marble, stick them together in the shape of a cross, and sell them to you as protection against lightning. Had you ever heard of this? Is there any pagan precedent? I always buy them for English and American visitors I take out there, to watch their embarrassment. I think the Catholics suffer most. Apropos, a friend of mine returning to Australia via USA, sent me a card of the St Guilhem cloisters in the Metropolitan.[1] They are less elaborate than my memory of them.

I must tell you that your views about the Simon de Montfort stone in Carcassonne are correct, and I was (as usual) mis-led by the local guide. I remembered I have Viollet-le-Duc's excellent little book on his restorations. He says that the inscription is a forgery (Wise? or Ireland?) and that nobody could tell him how the stone got there, i.e. into St Nazaire. But as he found it there, he felt he ought to leave it *in situ*, while denouncing it. The story of the temporary inhumation of the infamous one is therefore yet another of the innumerable legends evolved by the mythopoeic Midi. J. A. Symonds laments its disappearance (i.e. of the mythopaeic faculty), he should have stayed longer here.

It is possible that Mistral did invent that St Médard story, which is told with great skill and imagination (in book five of Mirèio), and he has no note on it. Unfortunately I haven't a copy of the Trèsor dou Félibrige [2] (it costs at least 25,000 francs, and no bookseller has a copy) which probably has the legend. I should think he heard the story as a lad on one of those winter evenings he tells about when the villagers grouped round a single candle, and each told a tale or related a legend. How much better than going to the pictures!

Yesterday I finished the draft of my Mistral, though I think I must add a short winding-up chapter. I must spend the week-end reading and correcting. Do hope it doesn't have to be re-written. I think of calling it: "QU'ES ACÒ, FREDERI MISTRAL?" with the title-page motto: "Nous avons toujours fait route avec les pauvres. Il faut rester avec eux." Which was Mistral's reply when Mariéton promised him a safe seat in the Chambre des Députés.[3] No doubt Heinemann will fight hard against title and motto, and if I save them, the press will have a fine time sneering; but I feel like standing by both. In the first place the contemporary English don't know anything much about Mistral, and certainly can't read modern langue d'oc, which is devilish difficult. Second, that "going with the people" seems to me one of Mistral's supreme virtues. What the hell is the good of poetry which is meant only for a few highbrows, and is unintelligible to "people?" Surely it can only be a sterile diversion of mandarins. They call Provençal a patois — the Tresor contains 100,000 words! Some patois.

I feel Macbethy about this Mistral script of mine — "look on it again I dare not." I realise my ignorance, and that I ought not to have undertaken so difficult a job. All I can hope is that I have avoided too many blunders, and that I may induce a few people to learn Provençal. What hideous asses these esperanto and Basic English people are! Varied speech is among man's greatest glories — no language should be lost — it is the creation of a people — and to reduce it to a series of truncated grunts for socialised man is an outrage. Ogden and Richards should be publicly castrated — if indeed the operation is possible with such eunuchs of the spirit. What's the matter with the world that it admires only phoneys?

You are quite right about Pétain &c. Do you remember that smack of Roy Campbell's at the Auden–Spender–Lewis crowd when they called him a "talking bronco?"

> "But for the Channel and the Bronco few.
> You would have been collaborators too." [4]

Some of the best laws passed in modern France were Pétain's — laws everybody knew were needed, but the deputies dare not pass. The Americans make me sick. Somebody had to accept responsibility for defeat, and Pétain did it with great dignity and patriotism. Where was America in June 1940? What did Roosevelt do to help in the calamity and crash of a falling empire? He instructed his ambassador to lay a lily on the altar of Jeanne d'Arc at Domrémy! Et merde à Monsieur Roosevelt! The English at least did something, and their resistance was heroic. You know the Americans insist that there was no merit in it, since Hitler never intended to invade. If so, why did he waste all those planes on "softening up?" It's a damned awkward thing to invade England with the Fleet intact, as it was. Damn the Americans. I wish I could get the alleged "documents" they produce, for I suspect they forged them. But we are so subservient to America (partly through necessity, partly through Churchill's idiocy) that we dare not repel such a calumny. Churchill and his "gentleman's agreements" with USA — what is the good of making gentleman's agreements with people who aren't gentlemen? And didn't Churchill know Roosevelt and Stalin treated him and his "archaic empire" as a joke? And don't you think that — if those Yalta minutes are correct and not American forgeries — that Churchill shows up as a yahoo? [5]

There is an immense amount of French Folklore literature, but the difficulty is to get at it. The Germans simply looted France of books, and they have never been returned. In their idiot way they burned all libraries belonging to learned Jews — including Gustave Cohen's unique collection of Mediaeval French. Any excuse to destroy. The full wickedness of that war and this "peace" has never been even partly exposed. Why was that invasion of Provence undertaken, with its destruction of unique places like Arles and Tarascon and Toulon &c? There was no military purpose, beyond getting decorations for generals. The obvious way to recover the Mediterranean ports was not by attacking (with casualties) the fort-defended coasts, but from the interior. The Americans smashed everything on Port Cros, including the old Vauban fort and many lovely trees; and I have asked scores of people who were on the coast at the time about it. They all say there was not a German on the island. They had been withdrawn long before as they knew the attack was coming. Why this frenzy of destruction of beautiful things? Don't the "industrialists" destroy fast enough?

I don't think it is now believed that MADAME [6] was poisoned. Saint-Simon of course had to have the sensational and criminal version — what an editor of the Daily Express was lost in him. But I read somewhere — can't remember where — a very convincing doctor's essay which showed the poor thing died of appendicitis, made suddenly acute by the glass of cold chicory water.

I think the Jesuits ill-deserve their reputation for Machiavellian skill and foresight. I think they were fanatical fools. Their advice to Louis about the Revocation de l'Edit de Nantes was entirely wrong,[7] and was the beginning of the French Revolution. Their advice to James II was idiotic.[8] They can't have known either the French or English people. It was the Jesuits who made France anti-clerical. They ought never to have been reconstituted. Strange — last night I was looking over Chateaubriand's Memoirs, and came on the section where he visits Charles X and Henri V in exile at Prague.[9] When he — a Catholic! author of the Génie du Christianisme [10] — learns that Henri has been given a Jesuit tutor, he reflects: "Ces paroles me firent frémir . . . Que, dans l'état actuel de la société en France, l'idée de mettre un disciple de Loyola auprès de Henri V fût seulement entrée dans la tête de Charles X, il y avait de quoi désespérer de la race." (Des Bourbons.)

Are we (I mean England) going to have a good harvest at long last? Did you know that as an exporter of cereals France is now fourth — after USA, Canada, and Argentina, but in front of Australia? And this year, if all goes on as well as now, it will be third and maybe second! What folly it was in us to allow uncontrolled industrial expansion with consequent over-population! I don't know whether the English papers are discussing it, but the pound is very weak again, and "des malheurs" are feared when the autumn payments come along. The moment a political area reaches the state when it MUST import food in exchange for industrial products, it is doomed. It is self-evident; given intelligent treatment, the earth is inexhaustible in food; but not in metals and minerals. And we have to face the competition of those ghastly Germans and Nips! I honestly think the only way out is to petition Congress to take over England as the 50th state of the union. Free trade with America, free entry of superfluous population there, would save us. But would the Americans be such fools as to agree? Of course they wouldn't. What have we to offer? We might stuff Churchill for the N. Y. Natural History Museum, and hire out Margaret to Hollywood, and sell Windsor to be transported stone by stone and re-erected on Jones Beach as a hawt-dawg stand . . . me ché!

Ever yours,
RICHARD ALDINGTON

1 Presented by John D. Rockefeller Jr in 1925; see above, letter 14.

2 Mistral's dictionary of Provençal, published in 1885.

3 See RA *Introduction to Mistral* 198.

4 See "Talking Bronco" in the book of the same name, 1946. RA misquotes; the second line runs, "They would have been 'Collaborators' too!"

5 Complete text of the agreements of the Yalta Conference, held 4–11 Feb 1945, was published in 1947.

6 That is, Henrietta of England who married Philippe, Duke d'Orléans, brother of Louis XIV. In his behalf she negotiated the secret Treaty of Dover (1670) with her brother Charles II. When she died shortly thereafter, having returned to France, her husband was rumored to have poisoned her.

7 Promulgated by Henry IV of France in 1598 and revoked by Louis XIV in 1685.

8 Possibly a reference to James's abrogation of The Test Act and other acts designed to force Catholicism on England.

9 *Memoirs d'outre-tombe* (1849–50) Livre Trente-Huitième. The visit occurred in late May 1833.

10 1802.

I O O

18 August 1955   *Montpellier*

MY DEAR BIRD,

The Mistral book is finished at last, except — there is always an exception — for the tedious task of noting all quotations, and getting "clearance" from the legal trustees of the Mistral estate. I noticed that the 16th was St Roch's day, and as he is an authentic saint of Montpellier, I have dated my book "St Roch's day," and if it gets published I shall be accused of some misdemeanour by the reviewers for using it. I can't find that St R. did anything much except have a sore leg and go to Rome and back on foot — not a very awful task.

I think this book is another mistake. It has taken far too long and falls between two stools in that it is neither "academic" nor "popular." I have sent off a copy for "the American market" but doubt it will be published there,[1] and though I have a contract with Heinemann, publishers break contracts with impunity nowadays. They won't like my title "Qu'es aco, Frederi Mistral?" or the denunciation of machine-mania and exploitation of the people for money and bullying of the people by bureaucrats. Finally, as Frere at this moment is spending his holiday at a villa in Cap Ferrat, he won't on his return like either the description of the Côte d'Azur as "Paris-sur-Méditerranée" or the motto I have chosen from Mistral: "Nous avons fait route avec les pauvres. Il faut rester avec eux."

But, really, that area is becoming a scandal. On Monday there was a night-club affair at Monte-Carlo to hear Lollobrigida sing! (She is a lovely girl, but she can't sing, and now the Americans have got hold of her they are going to exploit, vulgarise and destroy her as they did Greta Garbo.) Anyway, an ecstatic report in the Figaro reveals that 1200 people were present ("des grands noms, des fortunes, des vedettes, des princes" — talk of British snobbery after that!) and that each paid 15,000 francs for the dinner, champagne extra (certainly 2000) — so that about £20,000 must have been spent. Of course, like all these things, it is disguised as "for charitable purposes" (polio, in this case) but consider the thoughts and feelings of a French workman or small rentier or retraité on reading that — 15,000 is more than a fortnight's living to them! It is obvious that the polio fund is a mere excuse for a plutocratic feast. That area is fast becoming the paradise of every vulgarian in the "free" world. Do you know some cheap woman's paper here advertises a new serial by Graham Greene, to include "all the delights of a honeymoon at Monte Carlo!" I always thought he was an exploiter of vulgar people, but that "caps owt" as the Lincoln man said on reading the Northern Farmer.

My book-buyer[2] has ceased to write or send, so I suppose that the holiday spirit has whipped him off, or he is gone a hunting or perchance he sleepeth. Anyway, for lack of that Chatterton book I am held up on that brief section of the Literary Frauds essay. I had hoped to get it to you long ago. I think I must do it from the two books I have and use your letter to correct any blunders. And then turn to the Tichborne case.[3] The crux there is surely Lady T. and the fact that she was French? Otherwise the first letter from Orton would have betrayed him — no gentleman, however ill-educated, writes or speaks in that style. "Your beloved son" indeed, instead of "your loving son." What a real blackguard Orton was. How do such people get so large a following? Fellow feeling, I suppose.

I begin to feel that even down here I live in a nest of historical forgeries! After the shock of Viollet le Duc's remarks about the Montfort slab,[4] comes the shock of two forged inscriptions and a mystery one in Arles! The Musée Lapidaire has a "Roman" monument inscribed: D M / Calpur / niae / Cai Marii / Cons Filiae / piissimae / Cimbror / victrici. Surely this is a fraud? Had Marius a daughter, Calpurnia?[5] Even if he had, can she be described as "conqueress" of the Cimbri? And why the Cimbri, since Marius destroyed the Teutones in Provence?[6] Sir Theodore Cook doesn't quote it in his otherwise complete collection of Roman epitaphs of Arles, and it certainly existed in his day.

There is no need to point out the anachronisms in the following which was found cut in stone inside the entrance to Notre-Dame de la Major in Arles:

"Anno creati orbis 4414. Christi nati 453. Pontificatus Leonis princi magni 14. Valentiniani et Martiniani impp. III. Opilione et Vicomelo romanorum coss. Méravée Francorum regis V Ravenio Arelat. Episcopo 8 Ides julii dedicata est basilica haec Sanctae Maria Majoris hujus Arelatensis civitatis in praesentia 34 episcoporum quii ibidem tertium Arelatense concilium celebraverunt."

Unluckily, the original seems lost, and the inscription is only known from a 17th cent. transcription. There seems no record of when it was put up or by whom. But are the Montfort, Calpurnia and this inscription from the same hand? Some late Renaissance joker? And if you want a cross-word puzzle here is a genuine one from St Trophime. Labande (de l'Institut, no local guide) says it is probably

11th cent. It was partly mutilated in the 17th century when they put up an organ-loft. I have bracketed lost letters with a dot for each:

TE(. . . .)VM ROMA GEMINA DE LUCE MAGISTRA
RO(. . . . .)VS S(. . . . .) ADERIT VELUD INCOLA IOSEP
OL(. . . .)NT(. . . .) LOETEO CONTULIT ORCHO

I can make nothing of it. Notice that the initials of the first words in each line, the middle words (which in the original are aligned) and the last three letters make: TRO(phimus) GAL(liarum) APO(stolus). I can't think that a coincidence, and it is surely consonant with the rather childish mediaeval mind? I shall be much interested if you can tell me a meaning for the whole inscription, which task the good Labande dexterously side-steps! What can it mean? The cathedral was originally dedicated to St Stephen, and the lapidation occurs as a scene in the famous carved portal. The relics of Trophime were brought from the Aliscamps circa 972, whereafter the name was changed. St T. was taken back to the Aliscamps in 1078, but again returned in 1152. (I infer rival religious orders contending for these valuable relics.) There is a Carolingian ivory oliphant in the Treasury — perhaps it is Roland's.

Ever yours,
RICHARD ALDINGTON

[1] Published in America by Southern Illinois University Press in 1960. See below, letter 138.
[2] Bill Dibben.
[3] Roger Tichborne, heir to the Tichborne estates, sailed from Rio de Janeiro in 1854 in a ship which was lost at sea. Arthur Orton presented himself as Roger Tichborne, but in a famous trial of 1871–72 his claim was disallowed. Orton was then tried for perjury and imprisoned.
[4] See above, letter 99.
[5] See below, letter 101.
[6] At Aix in 102 B.C.; Marius defeated the Cimbri at Vercelli (northwest Italy).

I O I

16 September 1955   *Montpellier*

MY DEAR BIRD,

Your references to no text of Swinburne and the Oxford Corbett awaken in me the memory of a cherished *dada*. More than 20 years ago I formed a plan for an India paper edition of a Corpus of English poets and dramatic poets, well edited, and so arranged that people could buy any volume singly while public libraries bought the set as it progressed. The idea was to provide the texts in a small material format to meet modern conditions. C.P. Snow was so interested he took me to see one of the Syndics of the Cantab Press, who received it in a typically British way, hardly listened, and asked sneeringly if I were prepared to subsidise it. Now, if the English care for their literature as the French do, there is no need for a subsidy. The idea evidently got to France, and Gallimard started the éditions de la Pléiade which are very successful. I have the whole of Ronsard in 2 quite small vols, and Balzac in 10;[1] Three vols of St Simon are out, and we shall eventually get the lot:[2] Ce caquetage de tabourets as Chateaubriand wickedly but cleverly called it. Our glory is our poetry, and it is unknown to the people. Think what it would be if we could have all the best of our poetry and drama in about 50 vols at two pounds each. Of course the thing shouldn't start with unsaleable Beowulfs, but with Elizabethans and Romantics, and gradually expand. Just think how nice it would be to have a volume of our pre-Romantics, then all the "Lakkers" (as they call them here) in one volume or two (alas that dear Southey is so voluminous and uninspired) and then Byron, Shelley, Keats in one vol. There would have to be anthologies, but abundant. Well, it is a dream. We spend 1500 millions a year on the most inefficient armed forces in Europe, an expenditure which can mean nothing but money for armament firms and their innumerable machine-minders, and we cannot afford 100,000 to launch our greatest achievement on contemporaries and posterity. (Oxford ought to do it.) Amazing what can be got into those India paper vols. I have all Rabelais in one, and all Montaigne in another.[3] Why is Anatomy Burton only available second hand in that rotten edition of Chattos?[4] Surely Sir T. Browne in one vol might conduce to settling the Near East, for in tones of incomparable gravity and eloquence we should all be told that Jews do NOT stink. . . .

Heinemann used to do a very good Swinburne in 2 vols[5] (I think the dubious Gosse edited) but I daresay they leave it out of print to find paper for Graham Greene and Baxter. I would send you mine, but alas! my daughter as an infant crawled to the shelves and before she could be stopped tore out some pages of Thalassius with eldritch laughter. Evidently a disciple of Buchanan[6] and opponent of the fleshly school. But if, in spite of that wound — so painful to a scholar — you would like it, say so, and it flies north at once. I have Swinburne almost complete in firsts. I revere the man, he was a great poet; and not the least of his achievements is the fact that he survived the affectionate care of Jowett. Bothwell[7] may be heavy, as Oscar complained, but it is a great achievement. Yet who reads it?

I am sure the Calpurnia epitaph is a fraud. I did not know the Pliny story.[8] It is surely one of the many echoes of Iphigeneia? I don't think a Roman general could murder his daughter without being charged with murder. Surely the laws of the great republic forbade human sacrifice? Must have. Captives of course were slaughtered ad lib, but surely not a Roman citizen? I look for your interpretation of the St Trophime inscription.

My Literary Frauds is all waiting to be sent to you, but I have only two copies, and my agent has not yet acknowledged receipt of the other. The posts are uncertain. I am vexed by the loss of Brémond and a corrected copy of the French TEL which have disappeared in the posts. Talking of TEL the German and American editions are due in Oct.[9] Do you know Professor Baumgartner of Basel? In the Neue Zuricher Zeitung he has written a perfect article on Der Fall T.E.L., which rejoices me.[10] He is the first real scholar to review the book, and I could ask nothing better. Gustave Cohen has also done a nice article, but nothing like so "magistral." He is innocently sending it to the New York Times, which is an annexe of Liddell Hart. But as Gustave will almost certainly be elected to the Académie Française in November, it won't be so easy to refuse him.[11]

I am weighed upon by MSS. A youngish man sends me an excellent study of Vivant Denon with a less excellent translation of Point de Lendemain,[12] which is being published by the Richards Press, without the study. Can I get the study published? Well, can I? Can anyone? Does anyone in England care about Denon?

Then another man sends me a brilliant but certainly erotic novel about modern Sydney which amuses me greatly.[13] He says the English publishers reject it because of the love scenes. I am tempted to say: "Make your heroines into boys, and it will sell forever."

My daughter and I drove over to lunch with Gustave at Prats de Mollo in the Pyrenees (450 klms there and back!) and he had found for us a delightful little restaurant far up the valley of the Tech, which gave us such raw ham and charcuterie de montagne as I have never tasted, with trout and then little open tarts with field mushrooms sautés. I am no friend to vin rosé, which is the refuge of those who don't know wines, but there was a local rosé among the wines which we agreed is truly remarkable, better than many Tavel which are apt to be too dry. Alas, and you are in eggs-and-bacon and high-tea Land! You really must come down here, and see some of these remarkable Languedoc places and try a few of our local wines and dishes. Well, I will not boast. The best dinner and wines I ever had were given me by Charles Whibley at the United Universities in company with Tom Eliot.[14] The U.U. had a Meursault Goutte d'Or such as I have never found since. What a funny nose Whibley had, but he was a good man and loved literature. He did not like me, but then he had never before dined with a genuine ranker of the British Expeditionary Force!

Ever yours,
RICHARD ALDINGTON

[1] 1938; 1935–37.

[2] 1947–61.

[3] 1934 and 1933.

[4] 1924.

[5] Heinemann published Swinburne in 20 volumes edited by Gosse and T. J. Wise, 1925–27.

[6] After some literary fencing between Robert Williams Buchanan and both Swinburne and W. M. Rossetti, Buchanan, writing under the name Thomas Maitland, severely attacked Dante Gabriel Rossetti and the Pre-Raphaelites in the *Contemporary Review* Oct 1871 with the article "The Fleshly School of Poetry."

[7] See above, letter 96 n 9.

[8] See above, letter 100; the reference to Pliny has not been traced.

[9] Rinn of Munich published in Germany and Henry Regnery, in the USA.

[10] In the issue numbered 2126 for 1955.

[11] Cohen was not elected to the Académie Française (see above, letter 98) and his article ("Affaire Aldington contre Lawrence d'Arabie" *Hommes et Monde* Mar 1956) was not published in the New York *Times*.

[12] 1777. No record of a translation published by the Richards Press has been located. The translator is unknown.

[13] The author has not been identified.

[14] For RA's account of the dinner see *Life for Life's Sake* 220–21.

102

18 October 1955   *Montpellier*

MY DEAR BIRD,

It is always delightful to have your letters; and at the moment I have quite a lot of "news" interesting to me anyway! First, my excellent friend Bill Dibben has discovered an old bookseller who is going out of business and is selling off odd Loebs very cheap. Thus I am getting odd vols (which Bill says he can complete) of Strabo, Philostratus, Diodorus, elder Pliny, Aulus Gellius, Cicero's Letters, Apollodorus, Manetho, and another set of the Anth Graeca to replace my old one which was damaged in a Florida hurricane.[1] This is wealth! If only I could get the leisure to give my last years to such books. I had been reading Strabo in the Guarini 15th century Latin reprinted in Lyon about 1550. It is a comfort to have the text and a scholarly crib for one so weak as I. This is an occasion when one sings a Te Deum privily. I am paying only 2/– each and already have 24. Hush!

I am deep in the Tichborne – Orton affair, the excellent Bill having found me 8 folio vols of Law Reports of the perjury case with Kenealy's idiotic notes, for 15/– including postage! Of course it needs a book, and my poor essay cannot but be a feeble affair. Difficult to know how to handle it. Perhaps wrongly, I am not doing it as a "Trial" but exposing Orton as I tell the story. What an idiot he was to make that lying charge against Lady Radcliffe,[2] and Kenealy must have been crazy. Even if "the Claimant" had had a case, Kenealy would have lost it for him. I read his memoirs and an apologia for him by his daughter, Arabella.[3] The man was a crazy Irishman delirious with vanity and evidently a vile temper. Did you know that in the very year he married he was jailed for cruelty to a natural child by another woman? What next! I am trying to persuade my friend Kershaw to do a book on the subject, but he is very discouraged because the publishers won't take his Guillotine book to which he gave three years of research. They say it is not "popular" enough![4]

I muse much about Jowett. Of course, as you suggest, he tried to imitate Johnson; and we have had more suitable literary figures for imitation. His gifts, I think, were social and practical. He was an admirable head of a College, but that took up so much time, he had little left for self-improvement. I have his Plato at my bedside, and can't take kindly to it. I can always hear Swinburne's shrill voice from the inner room: "Another howler, Master!" And Jowett, closing the door to cut off the visitor of whom ACS was unconscious: "Thank you, Algernon." A bit of a phoney perhaps? Why did he urge Swinburne to go down without taking a degree? Did he dread scandal? Or a blaze of academic glory for ACS? I still think highly of the best of Swinburne in spite of current depreciation and the strange verbal flatulence of his later years. But every artist is entitled to be judged on his best, and Swinburne at his best is very fine indeed. [. . .]

In my view Swinburne would have been one of our greatest poets if he had lived in a less stupid era or with a few people of his own calibre. I am no friend to Wise, though, for publishing those flagellation pieces.[5] We need to know the weakness, but not to pay Wise for publishing the deplorable results. I have almost a complete run of Swinburne firsts — Bill got me Atalanta for 6d![6] (He got me a first of Christmas Eve and Easter Day for 1/– last month.)[7] The only Swinburne first hard to find is 1st Poems and Ballads.[8] [. . .]

I have a letter from two lads at Keble who want to revolt against what they call "the unintelligible nonsense that appears in the so-called literary journals."[9] This sounds very healthy, and I write to-day promising all support and the contribution they ask for. We must get away from this damned nonsense of Pound –

Eliotismus – Audenism. I know America well, and we have nothing to learn from them, nothing. "England ne'er shall rue . . ." I hope you will be kind to these lads if they apply to you. Strange it should come from Keble.

I have found a French interpretation of the St Trophime [10] inscription which runs: Terrarum Roma Gemina de Luce Magistra Ros missus semper aderit velut incola Joseph Olim contrito Laeteo contulit orcho. On which the gloss runs: La double Rome maîtresse de la terre sera toujours une rosée envoyée du ciel telle que le colon Joseph a portée dans le monde après avoir vaincu l'infernal orcus. Notes: (1) Rome called Gemina because of Rome – Constantinople as capitals; (2) Rome mistress of the world; (3) Ros said to = religion? (4) Missus de Luce — sent from the abode of light; (5) Jesus is called "incola" because he is a "colon" in this world, as Joseph in Egypt; (6) Lethe and Orchus mean Hell. "Pretty i' th' Mantuan!" but are they true?

My "Mistral" is accepted, mainly I believe because the American publisher of TEL has advertised in the New Yorker,[11] which is fame. Vincent Sheean very insulting in H–Tribune [12] — doubtless fears an investigation into "Inside Europe." [13] N. Y. Times says I am tedious, pedantic and flat-footed.[14] Frere (Heinemann) thinks they would not advertise in N. Yorker (very expensive) unless the book were "moving." All I know is subscription was only 3500. The Atlantic Monthly promises a "feature" article in Nov. German edition due any day now. But of course no news from Buenos Ayres. What rot it all is. I can't sympathise much with Cape, because he handicapped truth by refusing me the right to quote. If the Lawrences are so disinterested, why do they try so hard to protect their material interests?

Ever yours,
RICHARD ALDINGTON

[1] On 7 Oct 1941; see above, letter 35.

[2] Orton, posing as Tichborne, charged that he had seduced his cousin Catherine Doughty, later Lady Radcliffe, before departing on his crucial journey, 1852, and that, being pregnant, she had urged him to marry her. The charge was false and was so proved. See RA *Frauds* 119–20, 124–25. Kenealy was Orton's lawyer.

[3] *Memoirs of E. V. Kenealy, LL.D. by His Daughter Arabella Kenealy* (1908).

[4] *A History of the Guillotine* published by Calder in 1958.

[5] Possibly a reference to two poems, "Arthur's Flogging" and "Reginald's Flogging" and a prose piece, "A Boy's First Flogging at Birchminster," all contained in *The Whippingham Papers*, all unsigned, and all attributed to Swinburne. The British Museum's copy shows no publisher or date of publication, although the Museum dates its copy as 1887.

[6] 1865.

[7] Browning (1850).

[8] 1866.

[9] The Keble men have not been identified.

[10] See above, letter 100.

[11] 1 Oct 1955.

[12] 25 Sept 1955.

[13] By John Gunther, 1936.

[14] See Carlos Baker "A Hero Challenged" *New York Times Book Review* 2 Oct 1955.

103

11 November 1955 *Montpellier*

MY DEAR BIRD,

I've had rather a scare over Mistral. Although I had a contract and Frere had written he was publishing in the spring, what is known as a contretemps arose. In an evil moment Frere handed the book to one of his "editors" whose job of course is to pick out entertaining novels, who know as much about Mistral as I do about the Talmud. They reported it as "heavy going for the uninitiated." Now as my stated object is to write only for the "uninitiated" while confessing that I am simply not up to the standard of the real scholars, this was what Euphues called "a cooling card." However, after some correspondence, all is well, and the book has gone to the printer. Do anything you can for it when it comes out, for I fear old Frere will drop money on it, which is a shame. Nobody else would have done the book.

The Battle of the Bastard [1] now rages in USA, where the usual blasts have come from H–Tribune and N. Y. Times,[2] but I am told the Atlantic Monthly [3] has come out mildly for me. I am very pleased at a letter from William Yale, who is professor of History at Durham, New Hampshire, and writes that he is reviewing for the Annals of the Historical Society of America.[4] He is one of the very few Americans acquainted with the Middle East, and was a delegate at the 1919 "Peace" Conference. I think this is the first time the book has been treated by a competent historian. I am eager to read what he says.

I fear that living thus far away I tend to be very self-centered. Please try to forgive me. It has been very disconcerting for a humble "man-of-letters" to be splashed by the mud of TEL's publicity chariot. However, the Bureau have decided that I am now forgotten, so all is well.

I am exulting in my Loebs — 45 to date, and I hear there may be more. It is really an "aubaine." I have been reading Cicero's Letters in the night watches. Would not the world have benefitted if he had supported Caesar in that first triumvirate? Surely that was the moment for the few decent men to get together, and stand against the awful corruption?

I am also reading for the first time Pliny Senior — there is the source of half of the world's unnnatural history.

My Tichborne – Orton is now done, about 15,000 words — a poor affair, but the subject needs a book, and I can't ask Frere for that. Well, I have read those 8 vols twice, and I'm hanged if I can see any comedy in it. I have given some attention to Kenealy, who seems to have been a scholar, and was unhappily a political and sectarian fanatic. I read his daughter's book about him, and felt sympathy, though of course his conduct was inexcusable.[5]

Storrs was one of the least malevolent of the Bureau, but he was a poseur. I think his love of "culture" was genuine, but oh dear, he invited me to call on him (C. 1930) and told me most condescendingly how he read Dante every morning from a folio on a lectern (which he displayed) and so on, while he very kindly told me who Dante was, in case I should be embarrassed. He was allowed pre-publication to see all refs to himself in the TEL. The only point he queried successfully was about his part in the St Paul's bust.[6] He denied he had any, yet I could have sworn the Times reported him as a prime mover.

Much as I dislike agreeing with Leavis, I think there is much to be said for his preference for Rainbow, and Women in Love.[7] Of course, a cockney provincial like him could not possibly understand the overseas books. He is wrong about St Mawr,[8] I think. It is too full of personal spite and vengeance to be a great book. I wonder if Leavis realises that L. was one of those very personal writers whose books cannot be correctly understood and evaluated without an intimate knowledge of his life and the emotional circumstances in which they were produced. St Mawr is a "vengeance" book, so is Aaron's Rod,[9] and much of Women in Love. I am a character in some of the Aaron's Rod scenes, and know how vividly L. caught aspects of what went on, and also how utterly he was mistaken, and how perverse sometimes. He draws a wonderful and sinister sketch of "Josephine," the Paris-educated vamp, with snake-like tongue flickering in and out. Alas, poor Josephine! She arrived at my rooms before the Ls. and complained that her lips were badly chapped by an east wind! My wife gave her some feminine cream, which didn't work.[10] I think this is typical of L's fault in working up a fearfully wrong inference from a rightly observed fact. Of course, it is legitimate enough in fiction. Does Leavis say how much of St Mawr is animated by L's bitter hostility to Mabel Dodge Luhan and to Murry? I don't agree with you about Leavis. I think he is a mere parasite, incapable of understanding art as he is of making it.

Gissing of course is one of the many heart-breaks in life. With a tenth the money and "influence" which go to the careers of so many mere place-hunters, he might have done so much. I have gone over a good deal of his trail as recorded in "By the Ionian Sea," [11] and of course it is navrant. There is so little remaining, and so much that is repulsive. Croton is a ghastly place, and Sapri a misery. The country is all ruin, malaria and squalor. I never saw such filth as at Spezzano Albanese, for example. Castrovillari is the one decent place. He would have learnt so much more if he had given the time to further explorations of Rome and Naples.

I think the Paris art dealers are so cluttered up with unsold masterpieces of "modern" art that no new genius will be allowed for a long time. The whole Ecole de Paris is a manufactured vogue, and supported mainly by art snobbery. Whenever Picasso comes up for sale he has to be bought in secretly by Rosenberg, and the "price," doubled or trebled, advertised in the French press. It's a racket. But nobody has the courage to say so. I leave that crusade to someone else!

I am doing a series of interviews on modern Anglo-American Poetry for the wireless here.[12] My daughter deplores my accent! I hope to boost the Anglo at the expense of the American. No doubt I shall be punished for that.

Ever
RICHARD ALDINGTON

[1] That is, T. E. Lawrence.

[2] See above, letter 102 n 12 and n 13.

[3] See C. J. Rollo "Book With a Past" *Atlantic Monthly* May 1955. Liddell Hart reviewed RA's book on Lawrence in the Nov 1955 issue.

[4] Yale's review appeared in *The Annals of The American Academy of Political and Social Science* Sept 1956.

[5] See above, letter 102.

[6] In the brochure soliciting contributions, Storrs's name does not appear as a member of the committee appointed to deal with the memorial to Lawrence in St Paul's.

[7] See F. R. Leavis *D. H. Lawrence, Novelist* (1956) 5. Leavis's book was first published in 1953. *The Rainbow* was published in 1915 and *Women in Love,* in 1920.

8 1925.

9 1922.

10 Robert Cunningham in *Aaron's Rod* is meant for RA and Josephine Ford in the same book is Dorothy Yorke, called Arabella. H. D., RA's wife, appears as Julia Cunningham.

11 1901.

12 See above, letter 98 n 7.

104

20 November 1955   *Montpellier*

MY DEAR BIRD,

I forget if I mentioned that every fortnight I do a literary "interview" over the regional wireless here with my friend Temple. I discovered yesterday that he intends to bring up the question we once discussed by letter about Medora, and the child down here who became a nun. Now considering the infinite insults about French immorality and decadence in the English papers it is natural that the French should want to publicise this. Can you give me a briefing on the facts of Medora as acknowledged in England, particularly the financial help? It seems quite certain from local archives that (a) she married the batman of a French colonel who was an agricultural labourer, (b) that he looked after her and her child by — what was that fellow's name? — and that the Byron – Leigh family gave her and the child nothing.¹ It is a squalid story. I thought of staging an immediate counter-attack:

"Mais Médora était-elle vraiment la fille de Lord Byron et d'Augusta? C'est vrai, Médora l'a dit, et probablement l'a cru. Mais comment prouver le fait? Guillaume Apollinaire se disait fils de l'évêque de Monaco, mais est-ce un fait prouvé?"

What do you think? Is that too much of a "tu quoque?" I fear Medora is a very black little ewe, but of course the French are interested in trying to show (a) the incestuous origin, (b) the alleged meanness of the families.

What has all this to do with literature? [. . .]

Your remark about the present price of Loebs being high interested me. Do you realise 15/– is quite uneconomic and could not be maintained so low but for the Loeb subsidy ² and the fact that the established demand and the large purchase of sheets by Harvard University enable large editions to be printed? The larger the impression the less the printing cost of the individual volume. But if the books were unsubsidised and had to take the conditions imposed on the contemporary author, the price would have to be about 35/– to 40/–. The paper pound is now worth about 4/6 in terms of gold. People complain of the high price of books, but it is in fact too low, and the publishers are at their wit's end. A novel ought to be at least 20/–, and the public can't or won't pay it. The collapse of Simpkin Marshal has been another heavy blow to the "better" type of book which had a small continuous sale. The publishers are naturally rejecting everything but books which look like being best-sellers. It is disheartening. What chance can there be for young writers to-day unless they have inherited an income?

I have done another of my "frauds" — Psalmanazar. I take the view, which I think has been neglected, that the Memoirs are probably as false and hypocritical in their way as the Description.[3] I particularly take him up on the subject of the Rev W. Innes, who is accepted by everyone as a scoundrel and an accomplice. I think he was a dupe. I don't think that any man in holy orders — even in the 1700s — would have been promoted as Innes was if he had been guilty of what Psalmanazar claims he was, simply to shield himself. There was no such enormous kudos in converting a "Formosan" from the Jesuits that it could excuse such drunkenness and debauchery on the part of Innes that he was allegedly turned out of his lodgings in London (!) and in spite of that scandal get him promoted Chaplain-General to the Forces in Portugal. A C.-G. now ranks as a Major-General and holds a commission, and presumably is recommended by his Bishop and investigated by the Secretary for War. Surely Innes's disappointed rivals would have raised a fearful outcry if he had been such a scandal to the Church? And when he came back from the front he was given good benefices and made a D.D. All that is proved against him is that he prefaced a theological treatise by someone else without stating the author's name — which might quite well be the printer's fault.[4] I think the "repentant" part of Psalmanazar's life [5] was pure Tartuffe. He was a laudanum-addict (7–8 fluid ounces a day!) and the inertia was counted as Christian virtue, eked out by his love of talking theology and (doubtless) many pious expressions. He took old Johnson in completely.[6] Imagine respecting as a saint and one worthy to be a bishop, a self-confessed impostor and liar, a swindler, an obvious hypocrite and a drug-addict!

But I fear the book is no good. I haven't the "write-up" journalist touch which is almost indispensible now, and then I try never to go beyond facts or reasonable inferences which, as the reviewers always remind me, is "dull!" No doubt, after Orwell and the spate of sensational "war" books which disgust me by their exaggerations and the dreadful attitude of winning by any trick and vileness. What does it profit a nation to win a war and lose its own soul?

Ever yours,
RICHARD ALDINGTON

[1] See above, letters 64 and 66. Possibly in the second program on November 22, when W. S. Blunt was discussed.

[2] That is, from James Loeb.

[3] 1764 and 1704. See RA's "George Psalmanazar" in *Frauds* 46 *et passim*.

[4] *An Enquiry into the Original of Moral Virtue* (1728) actually written by Dr Alexander Campbell but published as by Dr William Innes, with his preface.

[5] Stated in Psalmanazar's *Memoirs*.

[6] Dr Samuel Johnson admired Psalmanazer immensely; they sat together many hours in an ale house in Old Street, London and Johnson said that he wished the end of life might resemble that of Psalmanazar in its "purity and devotion."

105

3 *December 1955*   *Montpellier*

MY DEAR BIRD,

By a coincidence your letter arrives on the day I make my third broadcast with F. J. Temple — or rather I record and it is broadcast on Tuesday. Your information is of the utmost service. I entirely agree that the Medora episode has nothing to do with literature, but it is necessary to try and tell the truth about this repulsive subject which is very much in the literary news down here. In a very humble way I am publicly representing English literature on the air here, and I want if possible to get the facts clear. Can you give me the date of Medora's birth, and place, if known?

I can't help feeling there is some confusion of Medora's daughter Marie with some other legitimate Marie Leigh, probably a daughter of one of Augusta's children. If the wife of the Bishop of Ontario had been "married for some years" to him in 1899, then it was a strangely belated marriage, for in 1894 Marie daughter of Medora was already 60! I think the French must be right, and that the real Marie did go into a convent somewhere near St Affrique. I will ask Temple this afternoon if he can get proof from the regional archives.[1] Élie is certainly known, and I'll find out about him. The information you send clears the family to some extent, but they evidently didn't look after the girl.[2] She should never have been allowed to stay with the Trevannions, and the family should have given her a decent allowance doled out weekly by some trustworthy person and arranged under a deed which forbade her raising money on the expectation. This is difficult but I think it can be done, legally I mean.

Is it known when the wife of the Bishop of Ontario died?

A curious little question of fact comes up this afternoon. James Joyce's Portrait of the Artist was published as a serial in a little periodical called the Egoist pre-1914, of which I was "literary editor." [3] Temple has discovered an article by Stuart Gilbert in which S.G. says that The Portrait was printed in America and imported in sheets which were destroyed by the police. I don't think so, though I think I was in the Army when the Portrait came out in book form.[4] Gilbert must have mixed it up with Ulysses — the Egoist edition (also in my absence) was partly destroyed by the New York Customs, and 500 of the Paris edition by the English Customs.[5] It is curious because Gilbert knew Joyce much better than I, was indeed one of the Exagminators round his Factification.[6] Did you ever see that "Exagmination?" I wondered that a man of Joyce's real eminence not only encouraged but devised it. The only good thing was a parody of his Finnigans Wake jargon beginning "Dear Mr Shame's Choice," which was so good I always think Joyce wrote it himself.[7] He is strangely out of the literary news at present, killed I suppose by too much American admiration and above all imitation. I recollect Frere telling me circa 1930–5 that 50% of the new novels then coming in were poor imitations of Ulysses. The firm had decided henceforth to reject all such without reading them. At the same time I learned that during that financial year the firm had paid out over £1500 for reading fees of unsolicited MSS — after a preliminary weeding out by the staff. At 2 to 3 guineas a time (the fee then) this would imply 500 to 750 MSS. Only 2 were eventually published and both lost money! I then asked how they got their books, and was told partly by agents, partly by other authors, and partly by the partners picking out new writers in literary or other mags. I believe Charles Prentice picked Huxley for Chattos on the strength of some very early magazine piece.

Storrs, and now Curtis. I did not know about the Colonial Office, but all that comes to me tends to show that much of the unscrupulous blackguarding of me in the press at home and abroad has official support.[8] Did you know that the author of that illiterate "answer" to me in USA, "The Desert and the Stars,"[9] is one Florence Armitage who is regularly in the employment of the British Information Service in New York? I begin to feel I stumbled in all innocence on deeper intrigues than I suspected. You will have noted that this Govt is still carrying on the Arab Bureau intrigues in the Mid East, and as usual against France. I think there'll be a local war there soon, and we shall be backing the Arabs by the side of the Russians! I can never understand why all this energy, money and military force is turned on the barren Mid East, while fertile and still undeveloped Africa is neglected or allowed to slip into the hands of the Boer Govt in Sth Africa. Is there some distant and fallacious hope of "reconquering" India and Burma from these bases?

I wonder if you saw that my friend Gustave Cohen withdrew along with others from the contest against Carcopino at the Académie? Carcopino was minister for education at Vichy, but escaped at the post-war trials as he had been deported (to Dachau, I think) by the Germans. But Gustave is a grand mutilé de 1914, Commandeur de la L. D'H. à titre militaire, and though a hopeless cripple a partisan of de Gaulle from June 1940. The merit of the two as scholars is about even. However, the Royalist – Pétain group now carries all before it at the Institut, and Gustave hadn't a chance. He is very sore about it. There is a large pro-Pétain book just out, purporting to be written by a Judge of the High Court here.[10] I think the Left made a mistake in imprisoning the old man and in refusing burial with his soldiers at Verdun. Gustave won't hear of it — "France should have resisted to the end." But how could it with a defeated and surrendering army and a bolting civilian population? Hitler would have been delighted for a chance to harry and destroy and torture, and above all to smash Paris.

The political situation here is very confused. Faure has betrayed his party,[11] who wanted the electoral reform before the elections. By acting thus, Faure has secured the return of all these extremely dishonest politicians and himself. Herriot and Mendés-France have kicked him out of the Radical Socialist party. People look grave, and for the first time the word "revolution" crops up in conversation. But what is the good of revolting *against*? A nation must revolt *for*, otherwise it is a futile waste. I suppose we are to blame as usual. Suppose Boney had established his dynasty?

Ever yours,
RICHARD ALDINGTON

When & where do the Lovelaces say Medora *died*?

[1] John Travers Lewis, Bishop of Ontario from 1871, had no connection with Marie, daughter of Medora Leigh. Marie's vows were taken at the Convent of the Nativity at Saint-German-en-Laye. See above, letters 64 and 66.

[2] That is, Medora Leigh.

[3] The *Egoist* ran the first chapter of *The Portrait of the Artist* in its issue of 2 Feb 1914 and the last in that of 1 Sept 1915. RA was named assistant editor of the *Egoist* in Jan 1914; he was replaced in 1916 by H. D. and then by T. S. Eliot.

[4] Dec 1916 in the U.S.A. and Feb 1917 in England from American sheets. None was destroyed by police. RA had been conscripted and called into service on 24 June 1916. For Stuart Gilbert's article see "L'Ambiance Latine de l'art de James Joyce" *Fontaine* (1944) a special issue (Nos 37–40) devoted to "Aspects de la littérature anglaise de 1918 à 1940." *Fontaine* was published in Algiers.

⁵ The second edition and first English edition of *Ulysses* (Oct 1922) was published for the Egoist Press by John Rodker, Paris; of this edition of 2000 copies, 500 were seized and burned by the United States government. In Jan 1923, Rodker published a second English edition of 500 copies; of these about 497 copies were confiscated by the English customs authorities at Folkstone.

⁶ *Our Exagmination Round His Factification for Incamination of Work in Progress* by Samuel Beckett, Marcel Brion, Frank Budgen, Stuart Gilbert, Eugene Jolas, Victor Llona, Robert McAlmon, Thomas McGreevy, Elliot Paul, John Rodker, Robert Sage, William Carlos Williams. With letters of protest by G. V. L. Slingsby and Vladimir Dixon (1929).

⁷ It is generally accepted that the letters of protest are by Joyce.

⁸ See above, letters 59 n 15 and 60.

⁹ 1955.

¹⁰ Louis Noguères *Le Veritable procès du Maréchal Pétain* (1955).

¹¹ The Radical-Socialist party excluded Faure early in 1956, and as a member of the Rassemblement des gauches Républicaines (R.G.R.), he served as Minister of Finance in Pflimlin's cabinet in 1958.

106

15 December 1955   *Montpellier*

MY DEAR BIRD,

Your two last letters will enable me to stand up to the cross-examination over Medora &c on the radio. This week I have kept to other subjects. Can you let me know if I am right in saying that Mrs Trevannion (Georgiana Leigh) was Augusta's sister-in-law, i.e. a sister of Colonel Leigh? ¹ And do the Lovelaces give any explanation of why they made no financial provision for Marie or for Elie? I suppose there was still some of the old feeling of getting rid of the bastard and still more the bastard's children with virtuous brutality. There is a quite dreadful passage somewhere in Pepys about a suspected natural daughter of his brother — Pepys's sole concern is to get rid of the child as cheaply as possible, knowing she must either die or if she grew up be exploited as a slave.

I am glad you share my suspicions about Psalmanazar's Memoirs. One point I have stressed in my little sketch is the improbability that the Rev. W. Innes was the utter cheat and impudent debauchee P. says he was. Of course there are bad parsons, but it seems unlikely Innes would so put himself into P.'s power by knowingly sponsoring such a fraud. I think he was duped like the Bishop of London, the Archbishop, and apparently some of the Ch. Church dons. Moreover, if Innes had really been publicly turned out of London lodgings for drunkenness and consorting with street women, is it possible that his Bishop would have persuaded the War Office to send Innes to Portugal as Chaplain-General to the Forces? [. . .] I think P. lied in his "repentance" as much as he did in his "imposture." He was admittedly a Tartuffe at first, and so he remained. Johnson was nearly always wrong in these real life affairs. He was wrong about Savage, wrong about Lauder, brutal to Macpherson and very much in the wrong, and I think he was wrong about Psalmanazar.

I am on Maundy Gregory now, with Bottomley to come. I am a little abashed and amazed to find Churchill is unmistakeably connected with both. I can never forget that as a private soldier in the line in 1916–17 I was forbidden to receive my copy of Massingham's Nation, while John Bull ² was practically forced on the other tommies, whose niaiserie and stupidity fed me up with the "workers" for life. I don't think such gullible fools should be allowed to vote — they are a danger to civilisation. And to think that in the midst of the 1914–18 War, the Clydeside was ready to imperil the armies and the safety of England by a strike,[3] which was only averted when the Govt humbled itself to beg Bottomley's intervention!

The news you give of that pro-Lawrence "clique" is most interesting. They are stooping to some very low tricks, such as placing vile articles by Hart in USA,[4] and sending letters to the American and Canadian papers refuting statements I have never made! There was one such in the Montreal Star recently, replied to very well by a Mrs Alison Palmer who seems to know my books very well.[5] The line is to represent me as an illiterate and inaccurate novelist animated by vile envy of the great and good man. On the other side, Hommes et Mondes have announced for Jan 1st "Aldington Contre Colonel Lawrence: par Gustave Cohen." [6] This will infuriate the Bureau, as it goes a good deal further than I do in denouncing the Prince of Mecca. My German agent is trying to place it in Germany, where the book has just appeared. There are two good quotes in the blurb, both from Zürich, which the Bureau overlooked as unimportant, so the reviews there at any rate have been free from this really shameless animus. Gustave's article refused everywhere in London.

Curious the passions aroused. That little review "Nine" [7] is apparently not going to appear at all, since the editor and the printer-impresario will neither of them yield — the editor insisting on defending me, and the printer refusing to print a word in my defence! [. . .] Further, Kershaw knows a man called Lismore (I think) whose father-in-law was a Wing-Commander in the RAF, and after a bitter quarrel with Harold Nicolson over my book Lismore and N. are no longer even on speaking terms! I am sorry about this, but it is often true that people get most worked up over unimportant differences. What does it matter now that the Prince of Mecca was a fraud? Except, I suppose, for some reflected discredit on the F.O., which would explain Nicolson's anger. He was so cross that he abused me for a sentence about Lowell Thomas which N. thought was meant for the Prince.[8] They were just hunting for offence.

I laughed over the Lowell Thomas and Cinerama, especially when it explodes to six times its former size, which is just what L.T. did with the Prince.

I doubt if Pino reprinted Norman's limiteds. What Pino did tell me is that he and Norman after dinner would get out a dozen or so unsold copies in which N. would write personal dedications to well-known friends deceased; and then send them to Sotheby. Those Lungarnos [9] didn't sell so well. Also, I feel sure the Joyces [10] were burned, for I heard so much about it at the time, and Miss Weaver's distress was genuine. I think the numbers are easily explained on the grounds that the copies sent to England and burned were not numbered in exact sequence, but were taken from different sections of the total printed. Or, in reprinting it is just possible that false firsts were off-printed, a dangerous thing to do, for a skilled printer-bibliophile would detect it at once. There are "false firsts" of Surtees which my friend Dibben tells me are rather hard to detect until you know the signs, and they are often sold to inexperienced antiquarian booksellers by crooks.

Ever yours

RICHARD ALDINGTON

[1] RA was mistaken; see above, letter 64 n 3.

[2] Because it was Bottomley's periodical (founded in 1906) and because it was extremely jingoistic. In its first comment on the imminent 1914–18 war, *John Bull* came out strongly against British intervention with the headline "To Hell with Serbia!" In the next issue, it changed front and thereafter was rabidly chauvinistic. Bottomley was not included in *Frauds*.

[3] That is, the shipbuilders at Britain's main shipbuilding center. Bottomley, owing to his oratorical powers and the jingoism of his editorials in *John Bull*, had enormous influence on the masses.

[4] See "T. E. Lawrence: Man or Myth" *Atlantic Monthly* Nov 1955.

[5] Nothing which answers RA's description here has been found in the Montreal *Star*. On either 9 Jan 1956 or 21 Jan 1956 (these letters are two versions of the same argument), RA wrote a long letter to the editor of the Montreal *Gazette* to emphasize the veracity of his book on Lawrence and to protest statements made in the *Gazette* about it. On 1 Feb 1956, he wrote again in answer to the question "How far was T. E. Lawrence . . . a truthful man especially about himself and his alleged achievements?" (Southern Illinois). Mrs Palmer can supply no information about this incident or about her letter, which has not been located. Both the *Gazette* and the Montreal *Star* had reviewed RA's book on 19 Feb 1955.

[6] "Affaire Aldington contre Lawrence d'Arabie" appeared in the March issue.

[7] Edited by Peter Russell.

[8] See above, letter 76.

[9] Series of books by English authors published by Pino Orioli from 14 Lungarno delle Grazie, Florence; RA's *Stepping Heavenward* was number 7 in the series.

[10] See above, letter 105.

107

3 January 1956   *Montpellier*

MY DEAR BIRD,

Many thanks indeed for the additional Medora information. I think the query down here about the provision for Medora, Marie and Elie arises from the French feeling for "la famille," and its responsibilities. If Medora was his lordship's daughter, then their notion is that the Byrons were as responsible for her and her offspring as the Leighs. They know nothing about the deed,[1] which in fact does not seem to have benefited either of M's two children in France. Two difficulties arise. One is that the Lovelaces are dead set on proving his lordship a scoundrel and Annabella a much-wronged woman, as no doubt she was — one of those virtuously oppressive women who in France are usually murdered by their exasperated husbands or lovers. And then the information about Marie and Elie down here is rather vague. My friend Temple, who runs the wireless station here, suggests that we might make a day-trip to St Affrique and make the mayor turn up any records he has. If we could get any definite information about Marie and Elie it would make the discussion a little less futile. I wonder if Augusta was really as depraved and silly as the Lovelaces claim? There is no squabble like a family squabble, especially when money is involved. One cause of moral indignation down here is that they imagine that all these "milors" were far richer than they actually were. I remember meeting a Lady Byron chez Violet Hunt pre-1914, and my impression is that she and her husband were really poor — living at Hampton Court perhaps? I don't remember.

Norman's statement about Capri Materials (in Late Harvest) is to the effect that the original edition consisted of 100 copies on blue paper imported at enormous cost and with consummate taste from Czechoslovakia.[2] The cheaper edition, still signed and numbered, was limited to 525 "of which" 500 were for sale. I have number 466 signed by both Norman and Pino. They may quite well have pretended that two or three of the original blue paper edition were special copies. I don't think they printed more copies than those numbered, for the simple reason that the 500 were a long time selling out; and printing extra copies if and when they did sell out would be too expensive. But I feel sure Pino was (for once) telling truth when he said that Norman would write phoney dedications to defunct or imaginary friends either in unsold copies or in second-hand copies bought up cheaply by Pino. There must have been a lot of N.D. stuff in Firenze in the 1930s — copies given or bought there and left behind for some reason. Norman was very much neglected by nearly all the English until in his old age and under stress of war he was allowed to come back to London. Then Graham Greene & co, who had probably never read him before, discovered he was a "genius" and started the preposterous absurdity of remoulding him into a Grand Old Man,[3] in which he was joined by Miss Cunard, Monty Mackenzie,[4] and such hangers-on as D.M. Low, Davis, young Cecil Woolf and so on. It is so damned absurd, and could only happen in a completely provincial (intellectually) country like England. Willie King and Graham Greene didn't know Norman in his active days, and certainly have only "glanced at" his books. Greene's assertion that Norman was "kind to the poor" of the Naples area is one of the most stupid lies or blunders ever penned — in Looking Back, Norman exults in his having "swindled them more than they swindled me." [5]

Except for a couple of days of very heavy rains early in December we have had a very warm and mild and sunny winter so far. It may change at any time, but we hear that disconsolate ski-ers in the mountains have been picking daisies and primroses instead of sliding over snow as they expected. I hear from friends in Lourdes (themselves ski-ers) that the snowfalls in the Pyrenees have been grossly exaggerated in the interests of the winter resorts and their trade. There have been falls, but the reports omitted to state that they were light and melted very quickly! The world we live in.

Nothing can be found about Psalmanazar in the Midi because his true name is unknown. He must have had a church (probably Jesuit) education, since his knowledge of theology was good, and some of his absurd stories about the "Formosans" clearly come from Pliny's Natural History. An English contemporary thought P. came from Languedoc because he had "the accent of Gascony" — which is like saying someone was a Yorkshireman because he had a Lancashire accent. I don't believe anyone in England in the 18th century had any accurate knowledge of the langue d'oc and its dialects, and an ignorant Englishman could easily mistake langue d'oc for Languedoc. Judging by P's prowess as a spinner of tall yarns and his love of mystification, he was more likely to come from Marseille. Indeed in my sketch I suggest that his real name should have been "Marius de Marseille." His fooling the English was an enormous galéjade. [. . .] As to Johnson, whatever his virtues and abilities, he was the slave of his prejudices and bad temper, plus the vanity of the pedant. It was Boswell's genius as a literary reporter which immortalised Johnson. I think, if you reflect, that the reputation of "a great man" is often given to someone who is advertised into notoriety, often self-advertised. Beau Brummel was once "a great man" (he was certainly an impudently witty one) so were Dizzy and Oscar, so are the bogus Prince of Mecca and Winston Churchill. They all strike me as more interesting than Johnson, who did nothing in particular but utter some bullying bons mots on the tritest topics, e.g. Scottish poverty, "vile Whiggism" and so forth.

I am still on Gregory, hope to finish this week. Then Bottomley, for whom I have this epigraph:

"Beer, beef, business, bibles, bull-dogs, battleships, buggery, bishops, Bottomley, bunkum, blackmail, bankruptcy." James Joyce, *amplified*. Heinemann won't like that. [. . .]

Ever yours,
R.A.

¹ A Deed of Appointment, possibly executed about 1839, whereby Medora was to receive £3000 on the deaths of her mother, Mrs Leigh, and Lady Byron. Medora obtained possession of the deed in 1842 through a suit against Mrs Leigh. See above, letter 64 n 3.

² *Capri Materials for A Description of the Island* (1930; No 3 in the Lugarno Series). Douglas states that the blue *cloth* used for binding was imported from Czechoslovakia; see *Late Harvest* (1946) 17.

³ Nancy Cunard's book on Douglas is called *Grand Man* (1954); Miss Cunard and Douglas returned to England together by way of Portugal, Curaçao, and Bermuda.

⁴ *Capri* is dedicated to Mackenzie.

⁵ (1933) 212.

108

25 January 1956   *Montpellier*

MY DEAR BIRD,

My (Catholic) almanack tells me to-day is the Conversion of St Paul. How do they know? I suppose it is a merely conventional date settled by some Council.

Living in a Poujade stronghold I must say I think he and his movement have been misrepresented by the foreign press at the bidding of the money powers in Paris. I can speak only from those I know here, who are neither fascist nor anti-Semite. Their dislike of Mendès-France is that of people who live by growing wine for a rabid T.-T.! Poujadism has been growing in the Midi for two years, and it is a protest of the small one-man business and professional men of France against the crushing between the Syndicats and the big Paris "interests." In cases I know, the income of a shop-keeper after payment of taxes is less than that of the more highly-paid "workers," and yet the shopkeeper has to contribute by taxes towards the Social Security from which he gets nothing. He has to pay in full for himself and family for doctor, drugs, holiday, and various other benefits they get free. They get a pension at 60 — if he hasn't saved, he starves. I daresay Poujade is ignorant — he is only a bookseller — but so was Wat Tyler. I have an article on Poujadism coming out in Feb in the travel mag "Courier." ¹ It is hopelessly out of date, as it was written 6 months ago. If the fools had used it in Dec or even Jan, it would have been news. Now it merely looks as if I'm copying others. I can only add that in my experience at least 90% of the individual business people in Montpellier are Poujadistes. But there may be more sinister persons "behind the movement" of which I (and the Montpêllérains) know nothing. [. . .]

Yes, I have the poetry vol of Papyri.[2] It is most tantalising, as you say. Have the disturbed conditions meant the abandonment of all further search? Is the site at Oxyrrhynchus exhausted? I noticed the other day that some French archaeologists claim a sensational discovery of "documents" left by the Essenes in a cave beyond Jordan.[3] I feel a little sceptical, especially since the Glozel scandal[4] in France and the doubt cast on some of the "pre-historic" cave paintings. However, the Essenes may be genuine; but I wish they had been classical Greek.

The Casement cuttings — for which many thanks — are indeed interesting.[5] It is clearly a bitter injustice to hang a man for treason partly because he possesses a homosexual diary. In this house I have the Mint and 7 Pillars — which I hope don't make me guilty of the sin of Sodom. Showing the diary to Page[6] &c. was an appeal to prejudice, particularly strong in Americans. However authentic, it was not evidence in the charge against Casement. As I understand, Casement had thrown off allegiance to England with the outbreak of the Irish revolt. Ireland was his country, and therefore he was not a traitor but a prisoner of war. This argument would have much weight with Americans, whose country passed through exactly the same phase. By July 1916 America was becoming almost essential to our survival. Hence the need to influence Page. I think the diary may be genuine IF it is true that it reveals Casement's life so accurately as is claimed. But that is an ex-parte statement. Who can tell without (a) a close knowledge of Casement's exterior life and (b) the original diary? You are quite right — Basil Thomson was framed by his own police after he retired on a Hyde Park charge and jailed.[7] I always supposed it was departmental jealousy. The English police are notoriously intrigant and vindictive. Somewhere among my books I have a volume of "aesthete" poetry with his name written in it.

I have just finished the "Frauds," but without Bottomley. Having included Maundy Gregory and Wise, I felt that the inclusion of Bottomley would look like pressing it too hard. There is no doubt that from the time of James I on the English have been one of the most gullible peoples in history. I was surprised to find that Thomas Seccombe (formerly Lecturer in English at Sandhurst and a great hero in the T.L.S. of my day) is most shockingly inaccurate about Oates.[8] A woman called Jane Lane is excellent and most documentée, but she gives one much trouble by not discriminating evidence — i.e. she takes genuine testimony on the same basis as the scurrilous assertions of the party pamphleteers.[9] Muddiman's theory, as developed by Carr,[10] that Godfrey was really murdered out of private revenge by that homicidal maniac, Lord Pembroke, seems rather likely. Pembroke was related to Shaftesbury, and he could easily have been egged on to kill Godfrey without a hint why. This left Shaftesbury perfectly clear.

Heinemann are still coughing over Mistral, and I can see they intend to hold it up — as if it will be more saleable six months hence than now! There is a militant philistinism in the English which I used to take for granted but which now surprises me as I've forgotten it, and it hardly exists in France. The English "business" type and most working men really hate literature, poetry, art, knowledge. Heinemann really hate Mistral simply because he is a poet who isn't in their list of "live authors."

I have been reading Churchill — Charles — once more. He is certainly the best of Dryden's followers, and his satires being based on real life are still (to me) very readable. Here again I find myself disagreeing with Johnson who refused to see the poet because he hated the vile Whig. 18th century coarseness sometimes is very effective, as e.g. the actor:

> The monarch quits his throne, and condescends
> Humbly to court the favor of his friends;
> For pity's sake tells undeserved mishaps,
>   And, their applause to gain, recounts his claps!

Ever yours,
RICHARD ALDINGTON

1 "Poujade."

2 The first of two proposed volumes of *Greek Literary Papyri*, published as a Loeb Classic.

3 A later discovery of Dead Sea Scrolls, the first having been made in 1947.

4 At Glozel, in 1924, a peasant allegedly discovered a sort of trench made of vitrified bricks; and subsequently investigators found in it polished axes, a variety of implements and, most important, unusual ceramics, *vases à masque*, and bricks covered with marks which might have been alphabetical writing. These objects created a sensation, and they were variously interpreted — relics of a pagan Gallic sorcerer of the third century, artifacts of the neolithic period, frauds. After much controversy and scientific evaluation, the last explanation prevailed.

5 See Admiral Sir W. M. James "The Mystery of a Diary" *Spectator* 23 Dec 1955 and rejoinders in *Spectator* 13 and 20 Jan 1956.

6 As recounted in James's article; Page was U.S. ambassador to Great Britain, 1913–18.

7 In 1926.

8 See Thomas Seccombe "Titus Oates, Perjurer (1649–1705)" in *Lives of Twelve Bad Men: Original Studies of Eminent Scoundrels by Various Hands*, ed Thomas Seccombe (1894) 95–154.

9 *Titus Oates* (1949). Jane Lane is a pseudonym for Elaine Kidner Dakers.

10 In *The Murder of Sir Edmund Godfrey* (1936); see *The Bloody Assizes* ed Joseph George Muddiman (1929).

109

16 February 1956   *Montpellier*

MY DEAR BIRD,

Indeed we have caught the cold here this year. In Montpellier, one of the least afflicted places, the thermometre has been down to − 17.9° centigrade! The agricultural damage in France is enormous. Over a million hectares of cereals are said to be destroyed, all the vegetables, flowers &c are lost, some fruit trees, many vines from the Italian to the Spanish frontier. There cannot be a live mimosa, eucalyptus or orange tree left in France. Along the Riviera each department has losses running into two or three milliards. Vegetables and seeds are to be imported, but meanwhile the speculator and the profiteer have it all their own way. And those fools in the Palais Bourbon go on playing their silly farce. There is a genuine revolutionary feeling here and in N. Africa, and the French will not put up with being fleeced by governments playing the old Parliamentary tricks as apparently the English will. There was very nearly a serious riot in Beaucaire a few days back (hardly reported at all) when the Tax Commissioner and the gendarmes took the furniture and even beds from the house of an artisan who couldn't pay his taxes, leaving bare walls and floors in this weather! Luckily the Préfet had the sense to telephone and call it off, or there would have been bloodshed. It is the bitter resentment against taxation of the "small man" which lies behind Poujadisme, and Poujade is right. Do you know, the man who runs this little pension has to pay in addition to everything else in the way of taxes direct and indirect a license of 200,000 francs a year? He showed me the demand note. In addition his drink license is 40,000 francs. It is ridiculous. The governments will have to cut down on their absurd armaments and make State-owned industries and Social Security economically sound. The railways here alone were 60 milliards in debt last year, partly for electrification but partly because the over-staffing for political motives means that pensions are payable to the absurd number of nearly 400,000, while anyone related to a railwayman, or so pretending, travels for about 20% of the fare. They all get free doctors and almost free drugs. A carpenter, a market-gardener, a small vine-grower, a shopkeeper, all the numerous one-man businesses get none of these benefits and are sold up to pay for others to get them! Monsieur Michaud [1] spends half his time trying to keep this large garden in order as he can't afford to hire a casual laborer at 1500 francs a day. He made it quite nice, and they have taxed him 20,000 francs extra on his chiffre d'affaires for the garden — it is this year ranked as a signe extérieur de richesse! Of course the plot is obvious — capitalists and socialists, as in England, play into each others' hands to crush the middle class and increase the proletariate. The socialist wants them for his revolution and the capitalist for his "pool of unemployed labor." However France can't quite reach the cynical absurdity of making the honest proletarian ex-leader into a belted Earl.[2] I'd belt him!

No, the French don't claim the discovery of those Essene documents, and if I gave you that impression the truth was not in me.[3] They are merely sceptical about their authenticity and value. The summary of the first scroll as reported here seemed a mere hash of Biblical topics of the usual Jewish kind.

The Evening Standard had a note on the coming "Mistral," [4] very kind of them; and there is a possibility that parts of it may be serialised in a travel magazine called "Courier." [5] I hope so, for even a small payment would make the thing less of a financial loss to me, and might even cheer up the drooping heart of Heinemann who are certain of failure. I optimistically believe that there may be a few thousand of the public not quite such low-brow scoffers as modern publishing theory (and practice) insists they are. Books are now classified on the American plan into "academic" and "popular." Everything that isn't aimed at the mass of circulating-library morons is "academic." Did I tell this joke? One of the syndicated reviews of L'Imposteur in USA wound up by saying that as I had not taken the slightest trouble to make the book "a popular biography" it would have no effect. By the very same post came a letter from my Australian friend Geoffrey Dutton (late of Magdalen by the way) who is completing a biography of Colonel Light who laid out Adelaide. Dutton sent his script to one of the University professors (who rather fancies himself as a Leavis of the Antipodes) and got back a letter of disapproval — instead of "making a definitive book" Dutton has merely turned out the usual "popular biography like Aldington's Wellington and Lawrence of Arabia." So I'm a literary Poujadist, it seems, to be liquidated by both camps!

My dear friend, I've let myself in for a ghastly job with the book on RLS.[6] The "lives" creep with humbug and then "debunking," while on re-reading I cannot imagine why I ever admired his books. He seems to have written boys' books for men, and men's books for boys. And I find my taste utterly different from that of public and pundits. Treasure Island is a machine-made B.O.P. serial[7] and not too well done, whereas the Amateur Emigrant[8] seems to me most honourable in its effort to touch the lives of the poor and to tell the truth about them. I admire him for that. The life of Fleeming Jenkin[9] is dull but thorough and honest. Prince Otto[10] is imitation Meredith (and I think RLS must have read Duke Carl of Rosenmold)[11] but it is streets beyond the imitation Scott of the Master of Ballantrae.[12] What do you think of the tale about his wanting to marry the prostitute? Rather in the lad's favour, I think, if true. But is it true? Do you remember Buckle's[13] terrific swipe at the effect of Knoxism on Scotland? I thought I might begin with that, reminding readers that the appalling "austerity" lasted well into the 19th century, and that with "Cummy" and his equally Calvinistic father[14] poor RLS had much to endure and may be forgiven much. Still, I ought to have read further before accepting the job. What a lot has been written about Stevenson! Would he be admired anywhere but in the Yankosachsen world? I find practically nothing about him in other languages. Did you know that when RLS (without permission) dedicated a book to Paul Bourget, it was met by contemptuous silence?[15] Did he really think that the Black Arrow[16] and Dr Jekyll[17] put him on a level with the author of Impressions d'Italie?[18]

Yes I dislike Shaw. I will try to explain later. He is a great pamphleteer, but a very stupid man, I think.

Ever yours,
RICHARD ALDINGTON

[1] That is, the keeper of the pension Les Rosiers.
[2] That is, Lloyd George, created first Earl Lloyd-George of Dwyfor in 1945.
[3] See above, letter 108.
[4] The note has not been found.
[5] It was not; see below, letters 110 and 111.
[6] *Portrait of a Rebel* (1957).
[7] 1882; that is, a *Boy's Own Paper* serial.
[8] First published in volume iii of the Edinburgh edition of collected works, 1894–98.
[9] Prefixed to *Papers of Fleeming Jenkin* (2 vols 1887).
[10] 1885.
[11] The subject of one of Walter Pater's *Imaginary Portraits* (1887).
[12] 1889.
[13] Henry Thomas Buckle *History of Civilization in England* (1857, 1861).
[14] Thomas Stevenson; "Cummy" was Alison Cunningham, R. L. Stevenson's nurse.
[15] *Across the Plains with Other Memories and Essays* (1892).
[16] 1888.
[17] *The Strange Case of Dr. Jekyll and Mr. Hyde* (1886).
[18] Gustave Charpentier, 1890; the second part is dedicated to Bourget.

IIO

19 February 1956   *Montpellier*

MY DEAR BIRD,

I appeal to you, as I am baffled by a seemingly simple enquiry from a correspondent who has been reading Saintsbury on "Prose," [1] finds him rather absurd,
and asks what are the best books on English prose? The enquirer is himself a writer,
so it is not the enquiry of an idle or uninstructed person. As a stop-gap I am
sending Arthur Galton's "English Prose," [2] though I think its scholarship constantly
drops into pedantry both in choice of examples and in the false exactitude of contemporary spelling when spelling was a chaos. Quoting old authors in the "original spelling" is simply a Sitwellian formula for receiving a D. Litt., D. Litt.,
D. Litt., from a dazzled provincial university. I have a great respect for Canon
Beeching and handle his Milton reverently, [3] but he doesn't convince me. Compared with him I know nothing about Milton, which is perhaps why I prefer
Milton in modernized spelling, though I like to keep the "pernicious heighth." In
my childhood the Kentish peasantry always said "heighth" and not "height." It
must be the true English word.

I fear Heinemann are coughing over some of my impertinences in "Frauds." I
venture to say that the last native King of England died with his house carls,
fighting the intruder at Hastings. I also say that to a native ear, the names of
Lambert Simnel, Perkin Warbeck, and Wilburg sound more English than Plan-
tagenet, Orange Nassau or *even* Saxe-Cobourg-Gotha. [. . .]

"Pain, pain ever, for ever" or, more moderately, "still bad luck." The editor of
a popular "mag" called "Courier" by a mystery I cannot explain knows Provençal
and quotes it (the mediaeval) correctly and to the point. He was strongly inclined
to use parts of my "Mistral" as a serial — surely the oddest serial in the history of
"mags"? — but I think that even if the absurdity of the idea had not dawned on
him by now, the project is killed by the lock-out of the printers. 8000 of them
demand a minimum of 12 pounds a week — about five million sterling a year!
Can so small an industry pay so much and live? I am lucky if I get 10 guineas for
one article out of five. What is printing for? Well, thank goodness I am able to
discourage a few young men and women from taking up writing as a trade. I
direct them to advertising, reporting or suicide, as more favourable careers.

The cold has killed almost all the wild life in the Camargue. The bulls and
horses are mostly saved, but over 1000 dead flamingoes have been picked up,
and the frozen étangs are littered with teal, wild duck, coots, snipe &c, frozen
or starved to death. I wonder if the beavers have gone too. If so, the last of those
in western Europe are gone, and the species is extinct. A calamity. Something
should have been done to feed the birds in the Vaccarès, but such ideas never
occur to the French. Nor did it occur to me that they would fail to do so, for
otherwise I should have raised hell, and tried to get something done. L'esprit
de l'escalier. What a damn fool I am — I should have realised they would let
"Nature take its course." Roman Catholicism teaches that "man owes no duties to
the lower animals" and it is one of the Church's lessons which all accept without
query. Cruelty to animals thus becomes a religious duty most religiously performed.

I foresee my RLS doomed to failure. Travels with a Donkey [4] seems to me a charming book with many original observations, and Weir of Hermiston [5] not much better than many another Mudie's [6] failure. Gosse's Father and Son [7] puts a similar situation, taken from life, infinitely better and more touchingly.

My daughter has just refused a suggestion for the opening of a school essay on the English Romantics:

"All true aristocracies are classical. Romanticism only arrives when a wealthy bourgeoisie apes a departed aristocracy. That is why England, and not Germany or France, is the real birth-place of Romanticism. 1688." This, she says, does not include Rousseau; and I say: "So what? Rousseau was not a Romantic — he was a cad." And she says: "You want me to get zero for my essay?" So there we parted.

Ever yours,
RICHARD ALDINGTON

[1] *History of English Prose Rhythm* (1912). RA's correspondent was W. Somerset Maugham; see below, letter 111.
[2] *English Prose, from Maundevile to Thackeray* (1888).
[3] John Milton *Poetical Works* ed H. C. Beeching (1938).
[4] 1879.
[5] Left unfinished but published in 1896.
[6] A well-known London bookshop which operated a lending library.
[7] 1907.

III

1 March 1956   *Montpellier*

MY DEAR BIRD,

I have sent three of your titles on to Maugham, but what he wants are books dealing with the "problem of style" from the point of view of the writer. I wonder if any exist. I sent WSM my own copy of Galton. He rejects Saintsbury. So where are we?

RLS is a horrible problem. I have more and more the feeling that his grandfather was greater than he. The "Account" of the building of the Bell Rock is first class,[1] and I am struck, on re-reading, by the deference of Sir Walter in his Journal of that voyage.[2]

It is going to be difficult to keep cool about that marriage. I *suspect* Fanny [3] had a touch of the tar-brush, half an octoroon, which explains much. Why in the name of Aphrodite and the Nine Muses, a man of 29 marries to make himself a step-grandfather baffles me. I have uneasy wonderings. The parallel with DHL is unavoidable, though the publisher doesn't want it, because it is almost entirely in favour of DHL, who was damned by the Brit public for doing exactly what they blessed RLS for doing.

There was one person who damned the Black Arrow and that was Fanny. She wanted him to go on writing that Wrecker and Wrong Box trash with Lloyd.[4]

I ought not to have undertaken the job, but I had not read Stevenson for so long I hadn't realised the situation. For the rest, I agree wholly with you. But remember his friends and family killed The Amateur Emigrant (a most honest piece of observation) and the "critics" all boost those phoney novels against Travels With a Donkey.

Courier has gone silent, but they have not abandoned the serialising of Mistral. There are parts which could be used with illustrations as "local colour," but so far as I have heard the printers lock-out is not ended. I do not think there is the slightest chance for "Mistral" in England. The reports of the travellers are wholly unfavourable, and if Frere were not an old friend it would never be published. The "Dam Busters" [5] and that sort of thing are what the public want.

Spring here at last, but wind *always* a mistral. It becomes almost a madness. I must rush to post — will write again — meanwhile any titles on "prose" most welcome.

Of course, the "feature" of this decade is the break-up of France and England. A more stupid government than that of England could hardly be imagined if the French were not there. I think the jig is up for both of them, but they don't yet know it. Possibly France may be saved to some extent by agriculture but I can't see any hope for England unless the USA will take it over as the 51st State, and they don't take over bankruptcy! The situation is much worse than the newspapers say. Alas, and alas and alas. But there is nothing we can do.

Ever yours,
RICHARD ALDINGTON

P.S. Yes, there is something we can — and I do — do. Stop smoking American tobacco. Stop going to American films. Never buy anything American. If everybody did that, England would be solvent. It's the fags and the pitchers that cost the money — and the armaments, against which we ought to agitate daily. The whole thing is a capitalist's racket. But the workers are just as bad — they will give up nothing for the common good.

[1] Robert Stevenson, who commenced building the Bell Rock Lighthouse in 1807; see Stevenson's *An Account of the Bell Rock Lighthouse* . . . (1824).

[2] Commencing under the date 29 July 1814, Scott's diary of the voyage was first published in John Gibson Lockhart's *Memoirs of the Life of Sir Walter Scott, Bart* (6 vols 1838).

[3] That is, Mrs Fanny Osbourne, whom Robert Louis Stevenson married in 1880.

[4] Stevenson wrote *The Wrong Box* (1889), *The Wrecker* (1892), and *Ebb Tide* (1894) in collaboration with his step-son Lloyd Osbourne.

[5] See above, letter 22 n 6.

112

14 March 1956   *Montpellier*

MY DEAR BIRD,

It is most kind of you to send the names of the Prose books. Lucas [1] sounds the most hopeful, but none of these authors has ever done anything much in the way of creative prose. It is evidently not a subject of much interest. I suppose Henry James wrote about it, but his prose is so bad it would only be admired by the worst highbrows.

My raciste views on Fanny are based on the following. If she had been Indian she would have said so — there is no prejudice against that in USA. She said vaguely she was part "Moorish." Therefore there was some sort of admitted "coloured strain." If you will look at the photographs of "Belle"² you will see at once that she is negroid. Lloyd does not, so probably looked like his father, a rather brutal yankee type. Like most Americans Fanny was a little "fanciful" about her ancestors. Thus among her female ancestors was a Mildred Cook; promoted to rank as "a near relative of Captain Cook."

Lloyd went on as a novelist, and died in Calif about 1947. They sold Vailima as soon as they could, and Fanny also lived and died in California (1914). They got most of RLS's estate. Mrs T. Stevenson inherited most of the old man's money, and as she returned to Scotland as soon as RLS was buried, I hope she had sense enough to leave it to Scots. They owed something to his cousin Katherine de Mattos, for Fanny certainly got hold of the plot of the story of Katherine's in a dubious way. Henley was right.³

The French papers have not been very complimentary to England of late, as you may imagine, and a lot has been written about the underground opposition of England to France in the M/East since 1918. They remember that Glubb was with the British troops who threw the French officials out of Syria ten years ago. I could only get hold of the D. Mail, and its rancourous rage because of Glubb was a remarkable display.⁴ They have a certain amount of nationalist conceit, I think, and when they are kicked therein are much annoyed! Why we had to plagiarise Hussein by deporting Makarios is a query.⁵ But when Sir Lee Stack was murdered, Allenby as H.C. of Egypt plagiarised Mussolini by imposing the same terms as M. had imposed on Albania.⁶

The great excuse for our meddling in Arabia is oil. There is certainly oil in Irak,⁷ but is there any in Jordania? And it doesn't seem very intelligent to quarrel with Ibn Saud,⁸ and other sheiks who do control oil, for the sake of one who doesn't. Mad or not, Hussein will support England just as long as it suits his book, and no longer. Is he worth 10 million a year? When we have such difficulty in meeting overseas payments?

I think that unquestionably there is grave danger of a slump, which is already starting in USA. They are madly searching for outlets for that immense over-production of consumer goods. Here in France they have staged a huge show of such things, and are offering them entirely on credit. You pay nothing, take away a refrigerator, a washing machine, a vacuum cleaner, any one of their 50 or more gadgets, and pay so much a month. The thing is a flop. The Americans overlooked the fact that French incomes are far below American and that there is infinite taxation on the middle classes. The average French family can't afford such things, and don't particularly want a lot of them.

I forgot to tell you, I think, that Heinemann have definitely decided to issue a new edition of my Anthology,⁹ the 30,000 being now sold out. They propose to improve the "production" and a Book Club will take 3000 copies to start with. I am hoping that Viking may take some for America. There is of course very little for me in this, although the high printers' wages, bookbinders' wages, and cost of paper means the price to the public must go up from 15/– to 30/–! Who can afford that? The middle-brow is being driven off the market. You will get some idea of the position when I tell you that on the sale to the Book Club I get threepence a copy!

The Religion of Beauty, on the other hand, is remaindered — yet there were some interesting things in it, I thought. I sent a copy to Maugham. Curiously enough he singled out for praise the A. Symons on Dowson which you enjoyed! [10]

They have not yet started to set Mistral, which has been with the printers since November. But there was a long ca' canny followed by a lockout, and as the publishers kindly say, there is consequently a large back-log and the more important books must come first. Have a look at H'manns' spring list! Yet they still do a few books not wholly money-making. It won't last. Frere is 60, and when he goes, they will be wholly "modern" and "popular."

This winter is nerve-racking. The worst I ever knew, though M'pellier has been one of the least touched. There is snow again all over Italy and along the Riviera as far as Marseille. Here we have had N., N.N.W. (mistral) or N.N.E. winds since the 2nd Feb. There is a cold mistral to-day, and we should be in summer clothes.

I am sorry to hear you have been ill, but it is the same report I get from other friends, not only in England but in Switzerland. My friend Dibben had bronchitis very badly, and has been hors de combat for weeks. This cold and illness on top of the war in N. Africa makes the French very gloomy — no wonder.

My daughter has just rushed in from the Lycée [11] exclaiming: "Well, in spite of what you say, daddy I like Diderot!" At lunch I must try to find out what.

Stevenson goes very slowly — I don't really like him enough, and what I like are the unpopular things. Oh dear, and the publishers are always urging me to be "popular!"

Ever yours,

RICHARD ALDINGTON

---

1 F. L. Lucas *Style* (1955).

2 Isabelle Osbourne, daughter by her first marriage of Mrs Robert Louis Stevenson.

3 The plot of Fanny Stevenson's "The Nixie," first published in *Scribner's Magazine* Mar 1888, was originated by Katherine de Mattos. She tried to place her version of the story with the help of W. E. Henley. When she was unsuccessful, Katherine turned the idea over to Fanny who altered it for her own purposes. After "The Nixie" appeared, Henley, in a letter to Stevenson, accused Fanny of using not only Katherine's plot but her "phrasery & imagery, parallel incidents — que sais-je."

4 Because King Hussein of Jordan had dismissed Glubb Pasha from his post as commander of the Arab Legion. See the *Daily Mail* 1, 2, and 5 Mar 1956 *et passim*.

5 That is, deporting Makarios from Cyprus on Mar 9 as Hussein had deported Glubb to Cyprus on Mar 2.

6 Stack, sidar and governor general of the Sudan, was killed at Cairo on 19 Nov 1924; Mussolini invaded Albania in 1939. In the Egyptian crisis, the British occupied the customs at Alexandria and demanded the withdrawal of all Egyptian forces from the Sudan, a condition which Egypt rejected. Mussolini had demanded from Albania a customs union and the installation of an Italian garrison in Albania. When these and other demands were rejected, Mussolini had invaded Albania.

7 Ruled in 1956 by Feisal II.

8 Actually Saud, King of Saudi Arabia, who succeeded his father Ibn Saud.

9 *Poetry of the English Speaking World* first issued by Heinemann in 1947.

10 Pp 264–77.

11 Catherine Aldington attended the Lycée de Jeunes Filles de Montpellier.

113

13 April 1956   *Montpellier*

MY DEAR BIRD,

I am very glad that you approve professor Cohen's article. He sends me to-day a letter from Marc Brimont (sécretaire général du gouvernement d'Algérie) in which Brimont says:

"J'avoue n'avoir jamais subi — combattant, puis homme du bled par la suite — le poids du prestige de Lawrence. Je me méfiais un peu du mirage orientale, des mensonges de ces pays de sable et de pierre morte, et le déguisement lui-même de l'acteur, dont j'ignorais les masculines et stériles amours, me laissait déviner l'ésthete, facile sous l'aventurier masqué. Le courageux et érudit Aldington a trouvé l'assentiment Français de votre plume et la caution de votre authorité. Vous rendez à la Vérité sa couleur et son pittoresque, sa substance historique et son fil conducteur. Nous dirons tout cela dans 'Afrique' de cette fin de semestre, le prochain numéro étant sous presse active, avec votre beau message et un sommaire aussi éclectique que robuste." [1]

Is there any English equivalent for "homme du bled"? Having spent a couple of months in N. Africa I know roughly what it means, but how translate it? Anyway I shall be interested to see what "Afrique" says.

I was a little surprised to find that Moscow News for April has an article by Mikhail Urnov (qui ça?) entitled "Richard Aldington and his Books." I must say that although they dislike my coldness to Marxism the article is much more polite and incidentally far better documented than any in England — there is none of Rowse's insolent "who is Mr R.A.?" Apropos Lawrence, Urnov says: "Here again the theme was not the author's but was suggested to him. However the "national hero" of the colonialists did not receive the expected eulogies. In the words of the author himself "the national hero turned out at least half a fraud."

The verbal exactness of that quote suggests that Urnov must have the book. Possibly if I held out hopes of conversion — strongly hinted at in this article — I might have it translated.

I hope you won't think me self-important if I add that I wish some English voice could be added to these foreigners. Because I criticised Douglas and Lawrence and also the British war party, and satirise laughingly some national absurdities, it doesn't mean I am "anti-English" as Rowse asserts. One thing I can say about the British intellectuals, which is that they are moral cowards. They won't risk their popularity to defend the truth. I have letters here from at least two important British writers. If they said in public what they write privately they would be abused by Hart and the Bureau, but they would shake public opinion in my favour. But it is easier and more paying to allow me to stand alone and take the brunt of the battle. (By the way, I must send you the German reviews — some are quite interesting.) I must exempt Rob Lyle from this sweeping condemnation for he fought loyally and bravely. Roy Campbell wrote most amusing things but so violent that he must have known they wouldn't be published. [2]

Have you any textual corrections for the Anthology? I must correct the "Vache" in the gloss to Chaucer; and I think there are blunders in the text of the bailey beareth the bell and in Binyon on the dead heroes. [3] I must get these off at once, as I think Heinemann are already setting now the lock-out is ended. I should have liked to revise, and this was at first suggested by Frere — who wanted to include Australians for sales reasons! Luckily I was spared a battle there by still more imperative sales reasons. The cost of setting &c is now so high that the new edition is only possible because a book club will take I forget how many 1000 copies on which I get a royalty of only threepence! This allows a subsidy for the ordinary edition (I know not how many) on which I receive 10%

Religion of Beauty was killed by the brutal ignorance and stupidity of "literary editors" who handed it over to hacks to kill. There was not one favourable review. Anyway Heinemann didn't believe in it, and cut down the selections as well as omitting the bibliography and index. No doubt, before long the subject will be taken up by someone who is persona grata and "the period will be revived." It is an interesting episode in the long history of English literature and will have to be dealt with sooner or later. I am glad you liked MacCurdy. He is still alive — 84 — and though his Leonardo books [4] were a great success he cannot find a publisher for his recent work, and I have utterly failed too on his behalf. I think you can take it as settled that the recent exaction of the printers unions have pretty well killed for good any sort of free-lance and experimental and "cultural" writing unless subsidised. I have before me a printers' estimate (29/3/56) for a book catalogue of 18 pages and cover, in 8 point Bembo, wire-stitched, 1000 copies. The price is £86.10.0. or roughly 1/8 a copy! How can a small second-hand bookseller afford such prices? That would have been the cost of 1000 copies of professor Cohen's article, and of course we have abandoned it, as also the printing of my remaining American lectures [5] — spat on incidentally by Hugh Fausset in the Man. Guardian! [6] Well, it's no loss, but I feel very sorry for young men trying to start.

I hear — via Germany! — that Heinemann have announced Mistral in their spring list which they have not deigned to send me. I was told that there would be no interest anywhere in the subject, but the book is already enquired after from Germany and USA; so if it doesn't appear in those countries the fault will be with me, not with Mistral. This cast-iron philistinism of the British publisher to-day is really tiresome. What they don't know isn't knowledge, and there is a lot they don't know. You will think me ridiculous, but I really believe they would rather lose money on a bad book than make it on a good book. What is to be done with a national mentality almost wholly conditioned by journalism? Go to Monaco and shout for "Grace and Ray?" [7] There are protests here against that vulgar display.

Hardy later. I must think over what you say.

Weather still dull and demnition damp.

Ever yours,
Richard Aldington

P.S. Like DHL, I think England owes me an apology!

<hr>

[1] See the trimestrial article to which Brimont contributed or which he wrote entirely, "La Vie des livres," in the issue of *Afrique* (published by the Association of Algerian Writers) for the third trimester, 1956. The relevant paragraph runs: "Il n'est pas de paranthèse blanche pour GUSTAVE COHEN. Dans 'L'AFFAIRE ALDINGTON CONTRE LAWRENCE D'ARABIE' (Extrait de 'Hommes et Mondes,' Mars 1956, tirage à part) il prend parti en angliciste informé et homme de sens contre Lawrence 'ce Falstaff, ce fieffé menteur, ce comediante dont l'Angleterre s'est plu a faire son héros.' Le portrait d'Aldington, écrivain de vaste culture, celui de

Lawrence dans ses sinuosités équivoques, le rappel historique et le théâtre oriental sont traités avec un mouvement de vie irrésistible."

2 See above, letter 77 n 4.

3 "For the Fallen."

4 See above letter 27 n 9.

5 Those on D. H. Lawrence, H. D. (Hilda Doolittle), and Osbert, Edith, and Sacheverell Sitwell.

6 Fausset's comment has not been found.

7 Grace Kelly, the American actress arrived in Monaco on 12 Apr 1956 for her wedding to Prince Rainier III. The wedding ceremony was scheduled for Apr 18 and 19.

114

8 May 1956   *Montpellier*

MY DEAR BIRD,

I thought a lot about Hardy after your letter, but did not go to the extent of re-reading him. I get on better with his poetry than with his novels, mainly because though I write (or have written) novels, I don't much care for them to read. Poetry, biography, essays, but seldom novels. I have to toil through H's novels, but not his poems, though the latter are too numerous. And his constant commonplaces about death put me off — they are so very simplistes. The fact is we know death is inevitable, but beyond that know nothing about it. So why not leave it at that?

I enclose a letter which followed Professor Cohen's article, but they misprinted the general Cousse as Gousse, whih suggests the noble family of Gousse d'Ail.[1] The author is a full Colonel, regular, late G.S.O. one, of the Etat Major, I believe.[2] I am dismayed by his most courteous letter wishing to call on me to discuss Arabian affairs — I expect he is an Arabic scholar. *He* will be dismayed when he finds that in spite of a promotion to 2nd Lieut sur le champ de bataille, my real rank is the same as TELawrence's — full private.

> Alas, what perils do environ
> The man who meddles with — a British hero! [. . .]

I would send you the Moscow News but the [literary] agent[3] has it [. . .] The book which "best-sold" was Death of a Hero.[4] Later with their lack of humour they took up, serialised and issued in book form, a novel called "Very Heaven."[5] This was an attempt to present sympathetically the case for young men growing up in the slump of the 1930s, who found no place for themselves in society, and turned to communism. You know how many undergrads in those days thought they were communists. Well, bright Moscow thought this meant I had seen the light, and were most disappointed when I resisted their blandishments and asked merely to be paid for my books. I think they said they owed me about 3000 pounds — and actually sent about 12.

Apropos, the blot on your letter reminds me of something. A young man in Prague, (who *will* write me as "Maître" in spite of my protests)[6] puts a seal on each of his letters, having warned me through a Greek friend in Dieppe or some such place that letters without the seal may be forgeries! Does not this trifle give you goose-flesh? What have these people done to human life and decency? Frog-men, no doubt.

The periodical boycott against me has been slightly broken in Australia. An article worth about 20 English guineas was accepted, published, and paid — 3 Australian guineas.[7] Sales of my back books in England brought about 12 pounds on last accounts instead of about 200. Religion of Beauty shows one copy for G.B. and 14 export. It is hopeless. I have a new agent in USA,[8] and must "write for" them and let England go. What absurd vanity and jingoism this Lawrence cult implies.

I wish I knew about Mistral's date, but the whole publishing schedule is upset by the 3 months printers lock-out. Heinemann have announced it, and have agreed that my blurb shall take the place of their ignorant assertions. The fact is the commercial publishers really hate "literature" and I believe would rather lose money on a bad book than make it on a good one. Mistral is such a lovely poet and so attractive a personality. But they hate him at sight. Amazing. H'mann warn me not to go after "exotics" but to remember that readers are interested in people like themselves. Which lends a terrific impact to the fact that they welcome the "frauds" as enthusiastically as they dislike Mistral!! What are we to infer? By the way I think I have got them to accept for the frauds my title: "Hot Livers and Cold Purses." I dare not raise the question, but I have an uneasy feeling they think the phrase is mine.

Do you ever see a small review called "Nine," published Tunbridge Wells by one Peter Russell? The April number (just out!) has a very nice article by Lyle on the topic.[9] He is very restrained, and would make the Bureau ashamed if they were capable of such an emotion. It is strange that the British can't or won't see that the violence and abuse of the Lawrence faction must hide guilty consciences and a bad cause. As Lyle points out, if the book is as dull, false and malevolent as they say, why bother to notice it? [. . .]

I stagger on with RLS, with little satisfaction. It is a worked-out subject. "Tout a été dit." The publisher will not like my view, i.e. that his best books are the neglected ones, and his worst the popular ones he wrote under prods from his father and wife. Why did he marry that ghastly woman? I am just finishing an Inland Voyage,[10] and want to say that the "view of life" in it influenced the English bohemian for over half a century. [. . .]

A nightingale is singing in the garden, by day. Down here they seldom sing by night, and seem to me infinitely inferior to those in England. But I think you don't often see our huppes. 200 flamingoes have survived!

Ever,

RICHARD ALDINGTON

[1] That is, clove of garlic.

[2] André Garteiser, whose letter in *Hommes et Monde*, May 1956, "À propos du Colonel Lawrence," is a response to Gustave Cohen's "L'Affaire Aldington contre Lawrence d'Arabie" in the Mar 1956 issue. Garteiser explains that he knew T. E. Lawrence through General Cousse — who is designated as Gousse throughout — and that Cohen's defense of RA and RA's book on Lawrence is wholly justified.

[3] Mrs Rosica Colin, London.

[4] 1929; first published in Russia in 1932.

[5] 1937; see the first issue of *Internatsional'naja Literatura* (1938). *Very Heaven* appeared in Russia in book form in 1939.

[6] The young man can not be identified.

[7] The only article by RA published in Australia in the late 1950s which has been traced is "Australian Revaluation: An Introduction to Frederic Manning" in *Australian Letters* June 1959. Since *Australian Letters* did not commence publication until June 1957, apparently RA refers here to another article.

[8] Ann Elmo.

[9] "Lawrence, Aldington, and Some Critics."

[10] 1878.

115

21 May 1956   *Montpellier*

My dear Bird,

Forgive another letter so soon, but I see I have not responded to your remarks on RLS, which looks as if I were being "cagey," which I detest. I fear that I am missing an opportunity here, from lack of leisure to visit Edinburgh, Monterey &c to read unpublished documents and letters. I should have looked up the California stuff while I was living there.

Of course there is a Stevenson myth — thanks be, others have said it before me! — but there is an anti-Stevenson myth. Example, he is much censured for wanting to marry the Highland prostitute, Kate Drummond.[1] Harsh things have been written. But, in the first place, I don't find this fact proved, but merely possible. And, as I have said in my text, if it were true, all the more honour to a romantic young man who was thus nearer St John than writers who throw the first mud.

I have taken religion as about the most important fact in his life, the key to his fearful struggle with his father, and his revolt from Scotland to bohemia. Cummy I take to be an evil genius, who should have been instantly dismissed for terrifying the little boy with her sensational Covenanters, ghosts, body-snatchers, and so forth. I'm sure she looked after the child devotedly, and I'm equally sure she caused him untold terrors and suffering, and very nearly ruined him.

I am now on the very difficult and ill-documented early Fanny period in Grez and Paris and even London. Of course Fanny was a yankee Mom, but she had more common sense than the absurd and self-centered fools round Louis in G.B. I'm sure Henley loved him, but I'm equally sure he had no idea of RLS's sensitive spirit, frail body, and menaced lungs. Fanny as mistress saw the peril long before the parents, who relied on the opinion of Sir Andrew Clark.

It seems to me that in re-action from the whitewashing and suppressio veri of Graham Balfour [2] et Cie, the more recent biographers exaggerate the wickedness of his behaviour with Fanny in France. "Make love to a married woman." say they, "Fie! what next?" I can't prove she was his mistress, though I'm sure she was; but the point is he loved her, she trusted him, and went through hell to meet his trust. I quite agree with J. A. Symonds in feeling it was creditable to them both.[3] What they went through must have been very painful, and that old fool in Edinburgh,[4] sitting on his money-bags and Shorter Catechism, has much to answer for.

A woman writer (Doris Dalgish) sneers at RLS for becoming a step-grandfather at marriage.[5] As a matter of fact, it was only potential, for Belle married only a few weeks before her mother re-married. I have her on my conscience, and I think RLS had, for I suspect that she sacrificed herself for the sake of her mother and Lloyd. She realised they couldn't all three hang on RLS's neck. But Joe Strong looks an awful bounder in his photographs, and she divorced him in Samoa when there was enough money to justify it. I think RLS realised this later — hence his particular care of Belle and her boy.[6]

On the writing side I find that the non-fictional RLS takes me first, but that may be because of my dislike of novels. Jekyll and Hyde ("J. and H."!) I can take as a rather obvious parable, although J. is as bad as H., and RLS misses the whole point of an evil life. Individual evil like Hyde's chiefly harms him. The real evil man is the man of collective evil — the newspaper owner who spreads lies to increase his money, the politician who becomes a hero on the wars which wreck his country, the bishop who is reputed saintly for an amendment to a law which wrecks thousands of lives, the journalist who (like Edgar Wallace) prolongs a war by sending a false despatch.[7] Those and those like them are the evil man, and RLS's Hyde is a mere buffoon in comparison.

Did Fanny kill him by over-working him? I think very likely she did. You have to live in America to understand the materialistic ruthlessness of the average Mom, and Fanny was an over-average Mom. It was essential that Louis should make at least 1000 dollars a year more every year, in order to show the world (of Indiana) that he was a success. That absurd Vailima chore is typically American, but Fanny thirsted for "considération" and thus she acquired it. Probably the grief of her life was that, after he made his first money success, Louis wouldn't settle down in a fine ten thousand dollar Spanish-type adobe house in Santa Barbara — to which she retired as a widow.

Poor RLS. The Table of Affinities says we may not marry our mothers, but that is what he always wanted to do, and very nearly achieved by marrying Fanny. We thus gained Treasure Island, The Wrong Box and the Black Arrow, and lost — what?

It is not good to be a literary artist in England, and infinitely worse in Scotland.

Of course I am writing another failure, but that can't be helped.

Apropos St Médard — you remember our researches? — have I mentioned that the change in the Julian calender must have moved him from May to June? I still don't see why he presides over the flame-like ghosts from the Rhône, and my questions on the subject to my brother Félibres are evaded with a skill which would have made Cicero envious. The fact is they don't know. If I ever get any money again I must buy the Acta Sanctorum,[8] and spend my days and nights on them. The importance of the saints in the *popular* history of Europe is never recognised. I don't think England was ever as pious as France, judging by place names, traditions &c, which accounts for the violence of the 1st Revolution. What a stupid work Acton's Cambridge History [9] is — it deals with nothing but wars from the point of view of GHQ and cabinet meetings, — there is nothing about the people. He contrives to write a history of the reign of George I, without one word about the mug-house riots which convulsed London.[10] If the Whigs had been defeated in those street battles England would have gone Jacobite. Would not a People's

History of England be interesting? J. R. Green tried, but was not very successful.[11]

[. . .]

Adieu!

Ever yours,
RICHARD ALDINGTON

[1] Not proven; see RA *Portrait of a Rebel* (1957) 47.

[2] See *The Life of Robert Louis Stevenson* (1901).

[3] John Addington Symonds *Letters and Papers* ed Horatio F. Brown (1923) 111.

[4] That is, Robert Louis Stevenson's father.

[5] See *Presbyterian Pirate: A Portrait of Stevenson* (1937) 206.

[6] Austin Strong.

[7] Probably Wallace's inadequately substantiated report of Boer atrocities (the shooting to death of wounded British soldiers) at Vlakfontein. An angry dispute involving the *Daily Mail*, Wallace's paper, the War Office, and the House of Commons followed.

[8] The great hagiographical collection first conceived by Heribert Rosweyde (1569–1629) and started early in the seventeenth century by the Jesuit Father John van Bolland (1596–1665), who edited the first volume.

[9] Although Acton planned the entire work, he wrote only the opening chapter of the first volume of the *Cambridge History* (1899–1912).

[10] Riots in favour of James Stuart, the Pretender and son of James II, after the return of the Whigs to power in the election of 1715. One result was the passage of the Riot Act, still in force.

[11] See *Short History of the English People* (1874) expanded into the four volume *History of the English People* (1877–80).

116

26 May 1956   *Montpellier*

MY DEAR BIRD,

Have you seen the N. Statesman review of Armitage's book?[1] I haven't, but a friend in Paris refers to it, and reports that the reviewer refers to the attempts of the Bureau to kill my book, and "adds that all but fans must recognise after reading your book that Lawrence was a phoney." You will remember that K. Martin gave the book to D. Garnett, although the said Martin promised a friend of mine (Bill Dibben) that if I sent French translation and proofs (which I did) they should be reviewed by a "historian not a friend of Lawrence!" Can you imagine such mean perfidy? This palinode is not good enough. I did not of course expect a favourable review, but I was promised an impartial review — and the little squirt handed me over to Garnett![2]

I have sent an order for a dozen copies of Nine with Lyle's review, but of course in the fearful incompetence of modern England they haven't been sent. I'll send you a copy as soon as they arrive. Campbell has a brilliant parody of Doughty's Dawn in Britain,[3] which is as good as anything since Calverley.

Your comments (and advice) on the Moscow News will be valued. I replied, in a letter revised and approved by Professor Cohen, which I hope was right. I feel that, however humble, we must do anything we can to promote peace, but not be duped into their propaganda traps. They have not condescended to notice me since 1939, and I think it a little cheeky on their part to think I can be beckoned over by an article. I do hope you agree.

I had an advance copy of Fanny's journal,[4] and was relieved to find that the "hideous scandals' were not more than the reasonable criticisms of any wife to any husband. I hope I haven't played down his early amours too much. I notice L. Osbourne speaks of his (RLS's) being involved with many women.[5] I sent the first 5 chapters to my New York agent, and received a very encouraging report. She thinks she can get a contract on these alone. I hope so. England is a very poor proposition nowadays.[6]

I believe it is still confidential news, but Penguin are going to issue a second half million DHLawrences — ten titles, and have asked me to provide introductions for six of them.[7] They are including Lady C.[8] What can one say except that it was a generous blunder? It may have advertised him, but I think it did his real reputation much harm. Apropos, the film here was a flop. I blame Frieda for it to a great extent. She urged him to write the book, and then to publish it, when I am almost sure he realised it was a mistake. He should have left it for posthumous publication.

Symonds was indeed very good on RLS — most perceptive. I wish he said more in his notes and diary.[9] Perhaps he did, and Brown cut them out in fear of Fanny and Lloyd. How our literary history is falsified by that law of libel, and the passion for idealising the "deceased." The Stevenson myth is almost as fantastic as the TEL myth, except that RLS was very gifted, very charming if wayward, and though a terrific egoist, a really good man au fond — whereas TEL was corrupt from the core. Do you know the bitter fact that contemporary England is now known in USA and the dominions as "Oscar Wildes' Revenge?" or "'Colonel' Lawrence's Heirloom." You cannot imagine the damage to our reputation done by that immense clique of sodomites who control so much of our intellectual life, and flaunt themselves apparently with approval of the populace. Amazing! It is a very great scandal outside England and does us immense harm.

When I get some leisure again I must re-tackle Hardy and George Eliot. I feel I ought to admire them, but the Baalam's ass of my flesh won't respond. And how I agree about Dickens! Of course he is our greatest since Shakespeare, and diminished only because he lived in a diminished time. And yes, he was a poet. I was rereading the Boz sketches the other night, and thinking just that — a great if clumsy poet. Compare a scene like the party at Bob Sawyer's in Pickwick, with all the wonderful touches, culminating in the loyal friend who offered to go and groan on the landlady's staircase, with the miseries of Tess and Maggie Tulliver! Dickens is the very heart of the good, real England, and I love him for it. Mrs Gamp and old Bill Barley — England!

I am not against RLS. He is fundamentally sound, or as Dr Johnson would say "had a bottom of good sense." I like him, but how stupid of Graham Balfour and the rest of them to try to make him a Fifeshire Galahad when he was nothing of the sort. Still we must give Hardy and, especially, George Eliot their due. I feel I have never done justice to her, but I've never been able to "click," as I do always and instantaneously with the excellent Dickens. Of course Esther Summerson (e.g.) is awful, but if you read Bleak House as something like a parody of genius of the great British melodrama — having a child out of wedlock — it is wonderful. I like Inspector Bucket too — he jostles Holmes in one's heart.

My daughter and I lunched last Thursday at the "artists' restaurant" in Sète. They gave us a curious pie of anchovies and black olives for dessert, then conger eel, and then (to my joy) small cuttle-fish stuffed as Athenaeus describes them. We had a white wine, and liked the place much, though the view is spoiled by a new house. Still, we could see the Mediterranean, dreaming deeper blue as the sun passed the meridian. When are you coming this way? There is much for you to see.

We must have another look at the Camargue soon, and let you know. The 200 flamingoes are certain — I have seen them. Quantities of other birds, but I saw no avocets this year, and the egrets are certainly much reduced. I think the olives will not be restored for a generation, if ever. It is a great disaster. We shall have to live on that disgusting pea-nut oil. You must come down, and have a genuine bouillabaisse at the Saintes Maries, and, another day, a genuine Chateauneuf du Pape on the spot — a very different wine from the dreadful commercial imitation. And you must see the church at St Guilhem le Desert. Adieu!

Ever yours,
RICHARD ALDINGTON

1 5 May 1956.
2 That is, for a review in *The New Statesman and Nation*, see above, letter 84 n 4.
3 1906.
4 Fanny Stevenson and Robert Louis Stevenson *Our Samoan Adventure; with a Three-year Diary by Mrs. Stevenson* ed Charles Neider (1955, U.S.A.). RA's advance copy was from the English edition (1956).
5 No such statement has been found in Osbourne's *An Intimate Portrait of R.L.S.* (1924).
6 RA's book on Stevenson was published only in England.
7 No record of such introductions has been found.
8 1928; the Penguin Books' edition appeared in 1960. RA did not write an introduction to it.
9 See above, letter 115 n 3.

117

15 June 1956   *Montpellier*

MY DEAR BIRD,

I wish I had sent you my copy of the Moscow News. Since then they have printed my "cautious" letter of thanks as a "box story."[1] I did not send it in until I had Professor Cohen's approval. I have wondered since if I might send them a series of modestly phrased letters trying to explain our differences, and to resolve them. But who am I? They speak for a great government, and I for an obscure writer. I do so agree that we should do everything to help this détente, and I rage against the folly of idiots like Dulles and the criminal American lobbeys for war.[2] The German-Americans are determined on war to avenge the fatherland, simply because they don't realise what they'd get if they started!

Get hold of a new book, Geoffrey Dutton's "Africa in Black and White" (Chapman and Hall) which I think will interest you, and also give you a more cheerful view of Roy. He lives in Portugal, not Spain. I no more accept his Catholicism than his bull-killing, but I can tell you that he is one of the most warm-hearted and generous men I ever met, keeps the table in a roar. And he is a very great poet, certainly our greatest satirist since Byron.

> I kiss his dirty shoe, and from heart string
> I love the lovely bully.

Yes, it is going to be hard to defend Lady C., and how much I wish he had never written it, let alone published it in such a foolish way.[3] You are quite right, it has done him infinite harm with good men and women who otherwise would have found much pleasure in his work. Lady C. is so unintelligent, especially for DHL. "Obscenity" is an emotional judgment, particularly in words. You can't destroy that by trying to use them decently. They were low words in 1928 and are low words in 1956 and they can't be changed. [. . .]

I battle daily with the problems of RLS, trying hard (but unsuccessfully) to reconcile obviously honest but conflicting testimonies. I have my suspicions of Fanny. And then suspicions of myself, thinking I may be prejudiced. Henley was such a good chap and loved RLS, and she bust it up. But then Henley was such a bull in a china shop, and didn't realise how exquisitely frail and sensitive RLS was. But then Fanny was such a go-getter and gold-digger. I wish you would look at a photo of the Vailima crew opposite page 192 of Elwin's RLS.[4] Deduct 6 Samoans who are "attendant lords," one with an axe. Then we have RLS's mother [5] in a widow's cap with a scowling Scottish maid at her feet; Lloyd with folded arms standing between her and RLS, the only one of the party who looks normal. Then Fanny and Belle with arrogant American faces, and the boy Strong. What was the urge, the need to acquire all this tail of Duniwassels (excuse Southron spelling) and flog himself to death to support them? It is almost Sir Walter over again.[6] On the other hand, though Scotland was (I am sure) RLS' best inspirer, he would have died by 35 if he had stayed there. To my way of thinking, he wasted magnificent gifts on producing pot-boilers to keep all that crowd of parasites. His father disinherited him (except for 3000) because he disagreed with RLS's religious views. Thomas Stevenson was a most unfortunate influence, and yet a most well-meaning one!

I have Ella d'Arcy's stories [7] somewhere in the Keynote Series — so charming the best of them with the Beardsley covers.[8] I will go through my books — they are in double file and let you know. Vincent O'Sullivan was in Paris when I heard of him. I will look up what I have, and let you know.

I venture to send you a letter received to-day from Montevideo. I have replied at length. It — the letter — is perhaps a first answer to those who, defending Lawrence, say I am "anti-Oxford." [9] [. . .]

Thank you for the cutting from the Observer, but where was Philip Toynbee when the guns were rolling? [10] The English intellectuals didn't come out of that fracas very well. They fled while the battle was on, leaving me to hold the breach alone; and now are cautiously cashing in. I am told the New Statesman has also done so.[11] I suppose it is because I eventually stepped into the blood-bath of the Somme that I find Orwell contemptible. I don't think he ever cried because his rifle had become too hot to fire.

Did I tell you that my French-bred daughter innocently asked me why the newspaper photographs of the royal family always or almost always showed them on horses or with horses? "My dear," I said, "It is the secret of the great British Constitution — the only way to preserve a stable dynasty."

> Always yours,
> RICHARD ALDINGTON

P.S. We are on the verge of the Baccalauréat exams — first rate in English and French literature, good in biology, but weak in physics and maths. Ora pro nobis!

Did you have to be finger-printed as a potential Ormskirk murderer? [12] What next!!

1 Michael Urnov "Richard Aldington and His Books" in *News: A Soviet Review of World Events* Apr 1956 (see above, letter 113) elicited RA's reply in the *News* May 1956.

2 Dulles emphasized preparedness for "massive retaliation" in case of attack.

3 That is, D. H. Lawrence's *Lady Chatterley's Lover*; it was printed by the Tipografia Giuntina for Lawrence, who sent order forms to friends in England, France, and America. These, in turn, distributed the book. RA stated that he sold "about 400 copies of Lady Chatterley in Berks when it was suppressed, and the police couldn't think where the hell they were coming from!" See RA to Rob Lyle, Montpellier 18 Sept 1954 (Berg).

4 Malcolm Elwin *The Strange Case of Robert Louis Stevenson* (1950).

5 Mrs Thomas (Margaret Isabella Balfour) Stevenson.

6 Heavily in debt from the purchase of Abbotsford in 1812 and the failure of the Ballantyne publishing house in 1825, Scott ruined his health by incessant writing in order to meet his obligations.

7 *Monochromes* (1895).

8 A series published by Elkin Mathews and John Lane, associates in the Bodley Head. The name of the series originated with the success of George Egerton's *Keynotes*, 1893; for it, Beardsley designed the title-page and cover which had on it a key ornamented with the author's initials. Thereafter Mathews and Lane published thirty-four novels in the Keynotes series. Beardsley designed covers for twenty-one of these and keys for fifteen.

9 From a young man named Mourigan. The letter is lost.

10 See Philip Toynbee "John Buchan" *The Observer* 10 June 1956, where Toynbee compares Buchan's fictional character Sandy Arbuthnot and T. E. Lawrence. Toynbee's remarks run in part: "Since it is chronologically impossible that Sandy was based on Lawrence I supposed that Lawrence had built his myth on the model of Sandy. In a sense the parallel is extraordinarily close. Two brilliant English intellectuals of slight build and feminine personality who dressed up as Arabs in order to lead Arab revolts against the Turks! Yet Lawrence, with all his complexities, vanities and dishonesties, signally failed to achieve the heroic clarity of his original. Every real man who tries to live a myth is doomed to get his Aldington, while Sandy forever eludes the grasping fingers of the debunker."

11 Perhaps the letter signed by Paul Johnson in the *New Statesman* 5 May 1956.

12 All males living in the vicinity of Ormskirk, Lancashire, as Bird does, were fingerprinted after two old women, sisters who were keepers of a small sweets shop and money lenders, were battered to death together with their dog. Neighbors who heard cries for help failed to respond. The murders remain unsolved.

118

29 July 1956   *Montpellier*

MY DEAR BIRD,

Always so pleasant to hear from you!

Perhaps you will like to see the second letter from the young man in Montevideo. As you will see, I advised him to get Pater's complete works and to study them chronologically. In my last letter, which went off yesterday, I urged him to translate anything of Pater he found attractive and to try to place the translations in literary reviews. Are there any in Uruguay? I hope you agree that a young man like this should be encouraged.[1]

RLS is completed. One script has gone to London; and the duplicate is wrapped up, waiting to go to USA as soon as I hear script One is safe. I wish I could have discussed some of the evidence and problems with you. Perhaps unwisely, I have stressed the influence of Scottish Calvinism on RLS, both positive and negative. I think he really believed in predestination, which explains Fanny. He would never have been "received" by Society ladies.[2] Do you not know that he had a very bad reputation from his affairs with low-class women? Both Baxter and Henley told Steuart that there was a free fight at Swanston in 1879 between two of RLS's women (one named Margaret Stevenson!) and his father kicked him out of the house?[3] Penniless Henley took him in and nursed him. It has not been easy to deal with this and more than this, I assure you.

After finishing, a few days back, I re-read all Henley's poems, with renewed admiration. What a pity it is that our public taste is formed by pedantic effeminates of the Eliot – Auden – Leavis type, so that a whole man such as Henley is utterly detested and misrepresented by them. Strange, too, that the anthologies give some of Henley's less successful efforts. I don't like that "I was a king in Babylon" at all.[4] On the other hand, Henley — the uneducated! — was the only one who handled those difficult forms with skill and originality. I don't say he is up to the standard of Banville, still less of Villon, but he is the only Englishman who could really make poems in those forms. Dobson and Gosse are nowhere, and Lang is only good when jesting — the cricket ballade is A.I.[5] Poor RLS didn't exist there.

If you have any influence with university presses can you put up some protest against the scandalous fact that the letters of RLS exist only in Colvin's dishonest and milk-and-water versions?[6] What is needed is a Complete Letters in full text (including all in Edinburgh and collections) with the replies from Henley, Mrs Sitwell, Colvin, Lang, Baxter, Bob Stevenson, his parents, Fanny, Lloyd — wherever they exist. How contemptible England is in its treatment of its great men! In France a fascinating correspondence like this would have been published long ago by the Académie. But Oxford and Collins enjoy their Bible monopolies, and let such things slide. The only editor is the American, Furnas, who certainly knows more about RLS than anyone living. Unluckily he is a journalist, and, as I discovered to my distaste, as complete a master of the suggestio falsi and suppressio veri as the Times itself. His treatment of the row over Fanny's stealing the story from Katherine de Mattos is, I think, worthy of the Lawrence Bureau.[7] Still, if we had the text of ALL those letters, his annotations and preface wouldn't matter much so long as the text was exact. Colvin is dreadful. But I waste energy. Who can be such a fool as to think England will take its writers seriously?

No, my dear friend, you are wrong about Arlen. I knew him well. His one financial success was the Green Hat,[8] and from that he saved 90,000 pounds. He was a shrewd Armenian and a great friend of Beaverbrook, and increased his fortune by clever switches. He got back into sterling before the great American slump; and switched from sterling back to dollars pre-1939 when he went to live in USA. I visited him in his Cannes house (which he sold at a profit) about 1931; and I should say it was worth quite 40,000 dollars. The sum you saw was simply the amount he kept in England for his rare visits. Poor fellow, he died of cancer of the lungs. I liked him. However, I have already (figuratively) wept on Maugham's shoulder about him, so won't afflict you also.

Bernard Docker is a disgrace, and it is an indication of British fiscal corruption that he and his like have been protected so long by their political friends.[9] The filthy bad manners and arrogance of the Dockers down here have made them so unpopular that I trust they'll never come to Monaco again. Rainier loathes them. He is quite a decent fellow, and a great lover of literature and oceanic biology. [. . .] Out of his not too excessive privy purse Rainier annually gives a prize of 1000 pounds to a living author. What do the British Royal Family do? Give it to the horse's arse, don't they?

I hope you join me in 3 cheers for Nasser, who has most cleverly called the British bluff.[10] I am longing to hear the reports of what Sir Anthony's own followers say about it. Fine to make Margaret curtsey to Feisal of Irak [11] — "O Kate, nice customs curtsey to great kings"! — but those London fools have never realised that the Hashemite dynasties [12] are "foreigners" and exist only by virtue of British arms, and Nuri Said in Baghdad. They think in terms of temporary rulers, not of permanent peoples. And in all this fracas not 5% of all the Arabs in the world but are on Nasser's side — only Neguib and his personal enemies are against him. However, unless Russia backs him 100%, his hubris will destroy him. But I should not be human if I did not rejoice exceedingly in this new humiliation of the Lawrence Bureau in all its branches!

Ever yours,
RICHARD ALDINGTON

P.S. By way of change from RLS I am re-reading Marino and the very rare volume of Marinisti edited by Croce.[13] Have you ever read the Adone? I always mean to, and always get stuck. Symonds says he read it in 3 days. This is as bad as Ronsard and his Iliad! But how lovely Italian is, how lovely!

[1] See above, letter 117.

[2] Not proved. See John A. Steuart *The Cap of Youth* 271–72.

[3] John A. Steuart *Robert Louis Stevenson: A Critical Biography* (2 vols 1924) I 272. See J. C. Furnas *Voyage to Windward* (1951) 46, 464–65, where Steuart's evidence is questioned; see also RA *Portrait of a Rebel* 104.

[4] Henley's poem which has as refrain for the first stanza:
> I was a King in Babylon
> And you were a Christian slave.

[5] Lang wrote a number of poems on cricket. RA may refer to "Ballade of Cricket" in *Ballades and Verses Vain* (1884). The opening lines of the poem run:
> The burden of hard hitting: slog away!
> Here shalt thou score a "five" and there a "four,"
> And then upon thy bat shalt lean, and say,
> That thou art in for an uncommon score.

[6] *Letters of Robert Louis Stevenson* ed Sidney Colvin (1899 and 1911).

[7] See Furnas *Voyage to Windward* 284 *et passim*.

[8] 1925.

[9] Docker, on May 31, was removed as chairman and managing director of the Birmingham Small Arms Co, possibly owing to the extravagant expense account of his wife Lady Norah Docker, which included a gold-plated Rolls Royce, and a plan to add her brother to the company's board. In mid-June Docker took his fight to recover his position to the public by buying time on British Commercial TV. Docker was not successful in his efforts.

[10] On 26 July 1956, in reprisal for withdrawal of a promised Anglo-American loan for construction of the Aswan High Dam, Nasser nationalized the Suez Canal Company, forcing British troops to leave.

11 Feisal II was educated at Harrow. Following his assumption of the rule of Iraq on 2 May 1953 (his sixteenth birthday), Feisal returned to England for holidays, each of about a month's duration, on 19 Sept 1954 and 14 Sept 1955. He had visited London earlier, that is in 1951.
12 Twentieth-century Arab descendants, direct or collateral, of the prophet Mohammed, his daughter Fatima and her husband Ali, and their son Hassan. Of this family were Feisal I of Iraq and Abdullah of Jordan, both sons of Husein ibn Ali, emir of Mecca and king of the Hejaz.
13 *Poesie varie* ed Benedetto Croce (1913).

119

11 September 1956   *Montpellier*

MY DEAR BIRD,

I have just discovered that the index to my Cambridge Hist of Literature has the entry:

"Goose, Edmund."

Have you ever looked at the Loeb edition of Oppian, edited by Mair of Edinburgh?[1] It is indeed a monument of scholarship, and the introduction a most formidable piece of Scotch pedantry.

It was most kind of you to trouble to send me your notes on the RLS letters at Edinburgh. The letter from Henley about Fanny and the stolen story has been printed almost entire.[2] I think myself that the "Confidential" was added by Henley after he found he had given away so much of his secret life in a moment of depression. The short piece about Fanny was put in almost at random. Katherine didn't know Henley had written. But the letter exploded the whole Fanny against Henley and the "Shepherd's Bush crowd" situation of mutual suspicion and dislike. And all Fanny's American insolence and conceit came out. She bullied RLS into writing those letters to Henley and Baxter, and the unpardonable one to Katherine. RLS didn't want to break with Henley, but Fanny insisted on an "apology" which Henley naturally refused to make. So poor Katherine was made the scapegoat.[3]

Yes, I read Steuart, and concluded that he accepted too readily local hostile gossip. But unless Steuart lied deliberately he had the authority of Baxter and Henley for the story of the two women fighting at Swanston in 1879.[4] Certainly Fanny was then on the scene and he hoped to marry her, but that wouldn't stop him having other affairs.

The letter from Bush St (Feb 1880) to Baxter has also been printed.[5] It was intentionally dismal about Fanny, for Baxter was meant to show these letters to the parents. What Fanny's "fits" were I know not, whether mere faintings or epilepsy as some suggest. I think they were largely imaginary like the statement that she had "only a year to live." She lived in fact 34 years more! What RLS was trying to do via Baxter was to work on his parents so that (a) they would agree to his marrying Fanny, and (b) give him a larger allowance. This Baxter most skilfully obtained for him.

I shan't put it in the book, I think, but the obvious reason why RLS did not write any letters to Fanny when they were separated was fear that Sam Osbourne might intercept one, and be able to sue Louis in the divorce court. The RLS excuse that he had told Fanny all she needed to know is an excuse worthy of T. E. Lawrence! How easily one is taken in. As a matter of fact, Sam Osbourne behaved very well, even magnanimously — in reward for which he has been mercilessly abused and calumniated by the Stevensonians! They even invented a wholly imaginary scene between Fanny and Sam's disappointed second wife, in which the latter is made to abuse him! David should have said: All hero-worshippers are liars.[6]

The cutting about the Lawrences in the Aldington house in London in 1917 is far more accurate than such things usually are. I suspect it was written by P. C. Trotter. However it makes too splendid a tale, for we had only a floor of the house. And I was not present when the homeless Ls were taken in by H.D. I was then, disguised as a Gaulish chieftain, engaged in rallying the local tribes in Artois and Picardy, particularly in and about the mine craters on Hill 70. It strikes me as prophetic that I was nearly killed in Hart's crater! Got a dent in the tin hat which impressed even the Sergeant-Major. When I suddenly got leave the Ls had to move, but they came every day for meals and parties.[7]

The new edition of Poetry of the English-Speaking World is supposed to come out on the 17th. I asked Heinemann for an advance copy, but if sent it has vanished into the French Customs. The Mistral is "probably" due out on the 29th Oct. Why they had to be so slow I don't know, except that they loathe literature. I saw Gustave on Saturday, deep in the Mistral proofs and saying the book is "inspired and inspiring." I suspect it will fall into the hands of Orr, the Scotch pedant who has ruined the recent meetings of the Félibres and the French by his omniscient intrusions. The Americans won't touch the book.[8] "Who," they say, "was Mistral?" As the book is designed to answer that question in words of one syllable it seems an inadequate motive for refusal. On the other hand Evans in London write very nicely about the RLS, and even hope for "a very considerable public." They are reckoning without their literary gangsters who will never allow anything signed by me to succeed. Evans thought they had a winner in my Waterton, and it was simply murdered by the reviewers led by the Times Litt Supp,[9] which lied about it and knew they lied; and refused to publish my letters of rebuttal. I warned Collins time and again about the Lawrence, but they wouldn't believe me, and took no steps to influence or buy publicity. They allowed the Lawrence Bureau to hand out the ten pound notes to the indigent reviewers.

I have a strong intuition that you will be my only genuine reader for Mistral in England. But then you really do care for poetry, and you are willing to be indulgent to faults. Probably I shall do Mistral more harm than good in England. He should have been taken up by someone really competent — say, Raymond Mortimer or Richard Church or Peterborough. I would send you the page proofs, but the index is not completed, and anyway I have only the one set. A copy shall come to you as soon as available.

Your letter raises many interesting points about RLS, but as my views on them are given in the book I won't trouble you with them.

I very much want to get away for a few days, but my daughter has to sit again for the "Bac" exams this week, and next week a very dear English friend is coming to see me, and thereafter seems too far ahead to plan.

Ever yours,
RICHARD ALDINGTON

P.S. Do look at the photograph of Colvin in his Memories and Notes.[10] I am trying to get Evans to use it in the book.

[1] *Cynegetica and Halieutica* with English translation by A. W. Mair (1928).

[2] See Furnas *Voyage to Windward* 285–86; see also RA *Portrait of a Rebel* 192.

[3] See above, letter 112 n 3.

[4] See above, letter 118 n 3.

[5] In *Stevenson's Letters to Charles Baxter* eds De Lancey Ferguson and Marshall Waingrow (1956) 76–77; see RA, *Portrait of a Rebel* 118.

[6] King David, in whom Stevenson was interested early in his career.

[7] The "Aldington house in London" in 1917 was at 3 Mecklenburgh Square where RA and his wife Hilda Doolittle (H.D.) had a set of rooms. In October 1917, when the D. H. Lawrences were ordered to leave Cornwall on suspicion of spying, H.D. offered them the rooms. To do so, she had to ask Dorothy Yorke to vacate them. Miss Yorke (Arabella) moved to other rooms hired by John Cournos in the same house. He was in Russia at the time.

[8] See above, letter 100 n 1.

[9] *The Strange Life of Charles Waterton* (1949); see "Odd Man In" *TLS* 26 Aug 1949.

[10] *Memories & Notes of Persons and Places: 1852–1912* (1921).

I 20

30 September 1956   *Montpellier*

MY DEAR BIRD,

The same reliable friend who tipped me off long before the public announcement that Rattigan was doing a "hero" film of the bogus prince of Mecca sends another piece of news. They are naturally not announcing it, but Rattigan and his backers have decided (although his script is done) that owing to events in the Middle East the making of the film will have to be dropped! [1] I am told that after he had got some way Rattigan *did* read my book, and complained that it made his task much more difficult! I don't know whether the abandonment is permanent or temporary. No doubt in the incoherent whirligig of power politics the "Arabs" may again turn up as our bosom pals, and "atheist agnostic France" once more spewed forth by the virtuous haberdashers by the Thames. But for the time being the prince of Mecca as a screen hero is out! [. . .]

At last, publishing (so far as I am concerned) is recovering from the disastrous effects of the long printers' strike in the early part of the year. I seem to have been living in proofs. Apparently no public notice was taken of it, but the new (and in format much improved) edition of my 1000-page Poetry of the English-Speaking World was published on the 17th. [. . .]

At the present moment I am trying desperately by cable and letter to persuade Heinemann to change the wrapper of the Mistral book. Professor Cohen has written a most generous letter of appreciation with permission to quote. I want them to cut out from the back of the wrapper a mere perfunctory list of some of my books and substitute part of this letter which is excellent on Mistral and very kind to me. Whether I shall succeed I don't know.[2] They held up the book for 12 months because they had never heard of Mistral and don't much care about poets, particularly foreigners, and then held up the proofs of the wrapper so long that the accompanying letter said: "If you have any corrections or comments to make could you let me have them quickly as we shall soon be going to press"!!!! The insolence of that after holding the book up for a year! However, publication after so many postponements is now put as Oct 29th. Meanwhile, they have killed the book by raising the price (for 200 pages) to 25/–. I suppose the booksellers' orders are very poor.

Now I am on the proofs of the Frauds book, which is supposed to come out in February; but who knows? The great difficulty with that book is that it falls between two publics. The educated will know it all beforehand, and the others will not have the least idea what it is about. This is the complaint from America too. How does it happen that this gap exists?

Have the English papers had any news of this beatification of H.D. in America? [3] She has been fêted and flattered at Yale where they have on show a whole series of her books, MSS, photographs and so forth. The papers have carried most fulsome reviews of her "Tribute to Freud." [4] And she writes me that she will probably move to New England!! Yale needs an American poet to set against Harvard, and no doubt they will build a "shrine." The trouble is that her good work is far too good for this kind of ballyhoo.

That seems the extent of my news, except that my daughter failed at her Baccalauréat, and the vintage is late this year but far better in quantity and quality than had been predicted.

Why doesn't England have a revolution? About time, isn't it? I dreamed last night I was part of a band of revolutionaries attacking Whitehall! What next?

Ever yours,
RICHARD ALDINGTON

[1] Robert Bolt wrote the screenplay for the film about Lawrence, produced by Horizon Pictures (G.B.), Ltd, London, 1962. Rattigan's play about Lawrence, *Ross*, was staged first in 1960.
[2] He did; see below, letter 121.
[3] H.D. had recently given her papers to Yale University.
[4] 1956; praised largely for its poetical prose.

121

19 October 1956   *Montpellier*

MY DEAR BIRD,

I long to hear your comment on the enclosed letter which I have copied for you.[1] The writer, I infer, is Headmaster in a South London school (dreadful martyrdom for a cultured man!) and it is remarkable that he is not a Lawrence–hero–worshipper.

The Garrod remarks on Keats leave me toiling stupidly in the rear.[2] That casement ope at night To let the warm love in never suggested a moth to me, but "a maid at" the "window," that "out a maid Never departed more"; but you can attribute that to my immoral Continental associations. A moth, forsooth!

And of course the song is of the nightingale species not of the individual bird. It is perhaps over-refining to see this hinted at in the "no hungry *generations* tread thee down."

Among the many (too many!) literary battles of my life, one of the most unexpected was having to battle for Keats against the New York followers of Eliot in 1942. I did not realise that beauty is so much hated. The critic of The New Yorker (a female poet, omitted from my anthology, whose name I have forgotten) asserted with extreme virulence that Keats is an inferior poet, and that in any case I had chosen all his worst and left out anything good.[3] The publishers, who had been pleased by my selection, wrote courteously to ask if she would let them know what the choice should have been; to which she replied curtly that she "hadn't time"! Or, I suspect, knowledge.

Henley did cling to Stevenson, and you will see that one of his most affectionate poems about RLS is dated the very month of the quarrel.[4] I can't think that what Fanny did was a small thing, though I may be swayed by nationalist prejudices. What she did was in fact thieving, and she tried to bluff it out by bullying a helpless invalid husband and writing insolent letters to Baxter. You are right about the pornography, which I believe still exists. Why they had to write such stuff I can't imagine — reaction against super-puritanism perhaps. Henley had the damning evidence, and after the row RLS tried to get it back on the grounds that its non-destruction would be harmful to Lloyd!!! The tragedy of Henley's life was the death of his little daughter, Margaret.[5] He never got over that. Otherwise I think him a cheerful though noisy, boisterous and tactless person. Have you read Connell's book on him? [6] It is a useful antidote to the too pro-RLS school. [. . .]

Well, I managed by dint of cabling and persisting to get Professor Cohen's praise on to the Mistral wrapper. I hope you will try to excuse me with the plea that it is partly for Mistral. But the "set" against me is so strong that something of the kind is needed to make reviewers look again. I suppose the bookseller you mention is Blackwell? [7] Professor Cohen mentioned it, but I have not seen it. However, the 25/– is what they call "the kiss of death." [8] [. . .] The only hopeful note I have is that Macmillan of New York have asked to see it; but I have no hopes.[9]

As to the reviews — there is a formidable Scotch pedant and philologist at Edinburgh named Orr, and I suspect he will be employed by the Times to kill the book, though I make perfectly clear that it is offered only as the work of a semi-ignorant amateur. Heinemann have dodged the TLS by publishing on Monday 29th, which means Sunday 28th, but perhaps the Times will "give a lead" of denigration on Saturday. I do not expect any response or any credit or any sales.

If you get the Mistral you will see that I rather deplore the existence of Maurras.[10] I was interested to learn this morning from one of Maître Maurice Chauvet's learned articles in the Midi Libre, that the name "Maurras" almost always implies descent from a North African.[11] That explains much.

Apropos, I had a moment of embarrassment when I was at Hollywood. Another "writer" named Pagano told me his grandfather had emigrated from the Salerno area, and could I say anything of the family? Well, the man looked exactly like a well-washed North African, and the name "Pagano" suggested descent from one or other of Frederick II's "Saracen" bodyguard who were settled near Salerno. Strange how the racial type persists as much as the negro I think. It is still visible here to me, and I see Chauvet finds it so also. The piratical razzia with raping of women etc went on here until France occupied Algeria in 1830.

The international scene is depressing, and though the French Socialist government has done much better than was expected,, they have still failed to deal with the gross and impudent profiteering which so vilely exploits the poor here. Yves Farge in 1947 suggested that the only remedy would be to shoot the profiteers and I'm not sure he wasn't right. But governments seem utterly helpless before them. Mendès-France tackled the alcohol scandal, but the "interests" hurled him from power and he has been out ever since. How fantastic the situation, this example will show — in August the excellent tomatoes of the Arles – Cavaillon area fell to 3 francs a kilo wholesale. They were 20 frcs here, but still 120 in Paris and the north! Transport and legitimate profit can surely not justify a multiplication of 40 of the original price!

Do you see that USA is trying to bring international pressure to bear to stop the high tax (100,000 francs) on the big luxury cars rated over 16 h.p. here? True, many of them are American, but all belonging to US civil or military personnel are exempt. The tax is aimed at the gross profiteers — and America is willing to make an international incident to defend them! Angels and Burgesses of God defend us!

Ever yours,
RICHARD ALDINGTON

1 The letter, written from London on 10 Oct 1956 and signed R. A. King, runs: "I have just finished reading your biography of T. E. Lawrence. Having read your opinions on the hero-worship of Lawrence I am sure you will be interested to hear a very recent perpetration of the myth. Under the title 'Tiger of the Sands' he appears in a comic strip in 'Express,' a 'super colour weekly' a copy of which I was fortunate enough to confiscate from one of my third form. As number 6 in a series called 'The bold and the brave' Lawrence shares covers with Rex Reene, Jet Morgan, Slick and Nick, and Red Devil Dean. In the issue that I have Lawrence, tight-lipped, jutting chin, is attacking the Aleppo – Medina railway line 'with which the Turks were trying to control Arabia.' The Arabs call him 'el Orrens' and he is prone to thinking in small clouds. Fortunately the caption does not say it is a true story or, indeed, that Lawrence ever existed. Perhaps this particular one never did."

2 H. W. Garrod *Keats* (1926).

3 Louise Bogan, reviewing *Viking Book of Poetry of The English-Speaking World* in *The New Yorker* 18 Oct 1941. Selections from Keats in RA's anthology include seventeen poems or parts of poems (p 768–94).

4 That is, the quarrel arising from Fanny Stevenson's short story "The Nixie" and the origin of its plot with Katherine de Mattos; see above, letter 112 n 3. The Henley poem may be "De Amicitia," first published in the *Scots Observer* 6 Apr 1889; see also the poem written after Stevenson's death, which runs in part:

> O, Death and Time, they chime and chime,
>   Like bells at sunset falling! —
> They end the song, they right the wrong,
>   They set the old echoes calling:
> For Death and Time bring on the prime
>   Of God's own chosen weather,
> And we lie in the peace of the Great Release
>   As once in the grass together.

5 1894; the child had not had her sixth birthday.

6 John Connell, *W. E. Henley*, n.d. [1949].

7 That is, a bookseller who had recommended RA's *Introduction to Mistral*.

8 The cost of RA's *Introduction to Mistral*.

9 Macmillan did not publish. See above, letter 100 n 1.

10 See pp 142–43 and 200.

11 See below, letter 124 n 7.

122

23 October 1956   *Montpellier*

MY DEAR BIRD,

Forgive another letter so soon, but . . .

Can you tell me the name of the bookseller you spoke of who recommended my Mistral book?

I am translating Mistral's Moun Espelido (with little hopes of publication) and find Provençal as he uses it a most expressive but difficult tongue. He quotes a Latin inscription over the entrance of the originally Augustinian monastery of Saint Michel de Frigolet:

"Ecce elongavi fugiens et manis in solitudine, quoniam vidi iniquitatem et contradictionem in civitate. Haec requies mea in saeculum saeculi; his habitabo, quoniam elegi eam."

This is easy enough to translate literally, but is this not quoted from the Bible? The first half phrase is in the Psalms, I think, though I can't find it.[1] I don't want to make a fool of myself by putting into modern English what is actually in the Bible.

Have you any idea what the boys' games of coupe-tête and cheval fondu may be? My daughter disclaims any knowledge of them and the French have naturally no idea of the English names. The Provençal names are sauto-chin and cavaleto. I may say that Mistral's knowledge of farm life and implements and of wild flowers and birds has involved a lot of dictionary and text-book searches.

Professor Cohen is anxious for a reprint of my translation of that XVth century Mystery of the Nativity in the dialect of Liège, which he discovered among the MSS at Chantilly. There is of course not the slightest chance, but I can't make him see it; so I have written to Sir Stanley Unwin (who published it) and can send on his refusal.[2]

An unsold packet of the first edition of my Images of War[3] has turned up, but as the poems take the view that war is destructive, debasing and inhuman, and not "our finest hour" I fear they will have to be pulped. I have been reading the English papers again in this period of unrest everywhere and am interested by the continuing flood of books on British heroes — the supply seems inexhaustible.

Do you note how the elections in Amman went?[4] What happens now?

Ever yours,
RICHARD ALDINGTON

---

[1] Bird has written in the margin: "Psalms CXXXII."

[2] *The Mystery of the Nativity, translated from the Liègeois of the XV Century,* published by George Allen and Unwin Ltd (1924).

[3] 1919.

[4] Election, Oct 21, for members of the Jordanian parliament. Anti-Western forces were victorious and many of the new deputies favoured ending the London defense tie.

123

30 October 1956   *Montpellier*

MY DEAR BIRD,

Thank you very much for the references to the Psalms. I suspected that origin, but I don't know them as you do. From the point of view of this translation it does not matter whether the quotation is from a cento made by Saint Augustine or whether the monks of St Michel made it. The essential was to avoid the absurdity of making a modern version of Biblical texts. The mistakes you mention are my typing errors. Thank you very much for this help.

I think you are right, too, about the cheval fondu, though professor Cohen says it has not been used in his time. Coupe-tête, he says, baffles him entirely. He suggests looking up J. J. Jusserand's Sports et Jeux,[1] but though this might have a description, it would not give the English equivalent! [. . .]

A local poetry magazine, half Provençal, half French, called Marsyas, has this little jest:

Bilinguisme
Churchill est *fat* en anglais,
Eden est *fat* en français.

Only too unhappily true. What sort of a mess has he led us into now? Did you see that Sir Somebody at the United Nations only two weeks ago fatuously boasted of our alliance with Jordania — an invented country now in alliance with Nasser![2] Which side are we on? Here is another legacy of TEL and the strange F.O. and C.O. infatuation for the Hashemites.

You are right about the depression of RLS after that Fanny – Henley – Katherine row, in which I think Fanny was mostly to blame and acted with vile American conceit and vindictiveness. I haven't said so in the book, but I think the desperate venture of spending 2000 pounds on chartering a yacht was designed to get away from the miseries of that situation. It may have had more to do with RLS's exile in the South Seas than we realise. Here again Fanny behaved like a fool. They could have got passages on trading schooners for a fraction of the cost and she apparently was swindled by the San Francisco millionaire while omitting to have an inspection by Lloyd's. In consequence the yank Captain "discovered" at the appropriate moment that the masts had dry-rot, and they took three of the six months to repair (at RLS's expense!) while the family almost starved in Tahiti.[3] I can't forgive the Balfours and Colvins and Gosses for building up this myth of Fanny the perfect wife, when she was a damned nuisance, and one more case of a man wanting to marry his mother.

All thanks for your help.

Ever yours,
RICHARD ALDINGTON

[1] *Les Sports et jeux d'exercice dans l'ancienne France* (1901); see above, letter 122.
[2] Sir Pierson Dixon, on 20 Oct 1956, remarking on the dispute between Jordan and Israel arising from border clashes, said that Jordan had Britain's "sympathy and commendation."
[3] The schooner yacht *Casco* owned by Dr Henry Merritt of San Francisco; the captain was A. H. Otis. The *Casco* sailed 28 June 1888 and eventually landed the Stevensons at Samoa.

124

MY DEAR BIRD,

I too read those pages in Connell's book and resented them. It is monstrous to suggest that the affection of two decent men such as RLS and Henley had any of this sickly "homosexuality" now fashionable.[1] I have heard the suggestion that the affection between Tennyson and Hallam was "homo" — and that from creatures who most obviously were! It is a great pity that there can't be a more wholesome outlook on this perversion — neither persecuting, as with the unfortunate Oscar Wilde, nor cultivating, as the sect and its numerous supporters now do. Anyway, I don't for one moment believe it of RLS and Henley, and nobody who has been a private soldier or worked in comradeship with "common" men will ever confound the two.

Your letter-date (5th) shows me that no reviews of Mistral occurred in the Sunday papers as would normally be the case. I was prepared for this. After the denigration comes the boycott. The idea is to crush me into obscurity and poverty. Do remember that, whatever their merits, Norman Douglas and T. E. Lawrence were and are both heroes of the homosexuals, and themselves particularly impudent practitioners and preachers. And remember that such is British moral courage and love of fair play that nobody, literally nobody, has dared to stand up for me on that issue.

I had not seen these remarks about Wise, but I knew that he did "mend and complete" books with pages from defective copies. Do you mean to say he stole pages from books in the B.M.?[2] Apropos Wise — I hear from Tony Burt (the "Londoner's Diary")[3] that he had just received for review a copy of a compendious book on Frauds just issued by Faber's under the title The Great Deception.[4] He thinks this will kill my book, and I daresay he is right. That comes of Heinemann's holding up scripts for a year because they are afraid of the pro-Lawrence press. So more work is probably wasted.

The Suez business looks a much bigger mess here than your letter indicates. The bleak facts seem to be these. The 50-years rivalry with France for the Moyen Orient has destroyed the power and prestige of both without helping England. American greed is determined to use any means short of open war to control ALL the petrol of that area as their own supplies dwindle. The U.N. is a fraud, a mere rubber-stamp for USA and USSR. The Anglo-French action may have been unwise,[5] but I don't know what else we could have done. But what are the results? The canal is blocked for 3 months; the pipe-lines are cut; Ibn Saud of course comes in and boycotts oil for England-France; Nasser is still there; USSR threaten us with atomic attack; the occupation of the canal was so stupidly delayed by the tactics of that idiot Montgomery (applied by a pupil)[6] that we have not occupied the whole area, and face a 63–1 vote from the U.N. to get out at once! If a U.N. "police" force of 197 Swedes and 300 Danes moves in, the Arabs will have it all their own way, and can choose whether they sell their oil to the USA or USSR.

I cut out for you and send an article on the "Moors" from our little local paper, the Midi Libre.[7] You will excuse its shortcomings, and not expect it to conform to the high standards of English scholarship. But I thought it quite interesting in its amateurish way.

I did not know that the Principal of Somerville is the grand-daughter of J.A.S., though I knew Margaret married Vaughan of Harrow, wasn't it? I'm afraid that I don't particularly approve of "intellectuals" starting agitations over matters of foreign policy about which they can know nothing but what they read in the newspapers and pick up from gossip.[8] They might be better employed in helping some of the victims of the Welfare State. For instance, does Mme Vaughan know or care that John Gawsworth (for years the brains and energy of the Poetry Society) is starving in a Maida Vale cellar? Does she know or care that Carl Fallas, who has written three or four beautifully constructed novels, is dying in poverty and despair in Amersham, supported by the charity of his two sons-in-law? And so on.

Thank you very much for the information about the boys' games. This must be true, and leap-frog and Hay-cockalorum would explain why my daughter knew nothing about them — for neither is played by girls![9] I find the translation of Moun Espelido a difficult but fascinating task, Provençal as used by Mistral is so much racier than modern French. But of course it is a waste of time.

I fear I am rather depressed, but the Suez situation seems to me much more explosive and dangerous than English complacency and self-importance can realise. I think the USSR may intervene, and in force. Then what happens? If only England can get out of this scrape and learn the salutary lesson that it is only a second-rate power. . . . We have a possible though not very prosperous future as something between Spain and Holland, but this pretence of military might and every Englishman a hero is fatal folly. A really peaceful and sensible policy from 1945 would have saved us. But Churchill and Eden have to be famous and give us our finest hours. 19th century ideas — Victoria is dead. I agree with the man who said this Suez business is "Sir A. playing at red-coats and fuzzy-wuzzies."

Forgive me, but who is so despised and fretful as the disillusioned patriot?

Ever yours,
RICHARD ALDINGTON

[1] See Connell *W. E. Henley* 68–70.

[2] He did.

[3] In the *Evening Standard*.

[4] Alexander Klein *Grand Deception*, first published in USA, 1955.

[5] That is, the attempt to regain control of the Suez Canal by force.

[6] General Sir Charles Keightley, former Commander-in-Chief of British Middle East Land Forces, had been named commander of the Anglo-French forces on Oct 31.

[7] Pierre Guilhem [Maurice Chauvet] "Survivances mauresques" *Midi-Libre* 18 Oct 1956. See above, letter 121.

[8] A letter to the London *Times* (3 Nov 1956) signed by Miss Janet Maria Vaughan (later Dame Janet Vaughan) and sixteen others associated with Oxford University protested against the "action of her Majesty's Government in launching an attack against Egypt in defiance of the United Nations, against the principles of international morality, and in violation of the dictates of common prudence." The letter urged Great Britain and France to cease hostilities and to do everything possible to check fighting between Israel and Egypt.

[9] See above, letter 122 and letter 123 n 1.

125

26 November 1956   *Montpellier*

MY DEAR BIRD,

I am greatly obliged to you for the additional information about Wise, which I was just in time to add to the proofs as a brief footnote. I wonder who was the B.M. accomplice — or accomplices? Did it happen under Richard Garnett or his successor? [1] In my text I point out that the general manager of Clays must have been an accomplice, and the libel lawyer let it pass. To my surprise, he also passed the list of high table guests (including Churchill and Winterton) at the Maundy Gregory "Eve of the Derby" dinner; and I state that I disbelieve Macmillan's assertion that they didn't know what Gregory made his money by and that he was really paying for their dinner. Among the guests at other tables were two big newspaper proprietors — and you can't tell me they didn't know all about Gregory! [2]

Talking of which my agent writes: "I have sent a proof copy of FRAUDS to the Kemsley Press." Coals to Newcastle?

In the hope that it may interest you I send along a privately printed essay on Jowett by my octogenarian friend Edward MacCurdy. There are some aspects of Jowett which leave one repelled. The most conspicuous in these memories is the occasion when J. asks some of his students to meet four V.I.P.s and then makes no effort to see that the two sets of guests mingle! [3] I wonder if such blatant rudeness could occur outside England? No wonder J. told the lads that if they didn't learn good manners at home they never would! As to his sermons, do you remember the anecdote of the University Bedell who said: "I've listened to every University sermon for fifty years and, thank God, I'm still a Christian!" You will know MacCurdy's excellent work on Leonardo [4] and perhaps remember an essay by him in the Religion of Beauty.[5] I have tried hard to get publication for his unpublished work and re-issue of his two books of essays,[6] but they are everywhere rejected. As MacC. is a Balliol man I suggested he might try the Oxford Press on his own; but he reported they returned the script at once, and evidently hadn't read it. The book was a set of studies in the literature of several modern countries under the title "The Kindly Tradition." [7] Luckily MacC. has private means, but he told me part of his money is in Canal shares, so that looks unhopeful.

Your description of the plight of Fallas and Gawsworth as "comparative poverty" is side-stepping the issue. The poverty is complete and absolute, and they would starve but for private charity. So would Mrs R. A. Taylor if she didn't get a charity pension from some historical society. The Welfare State does nothing. A lifetime of intellectual work doesn't count with them.

Apropos the Canal — did you see a remark of Winston's to the effect that if "we" had not intervened there would be "chaos" in the Mid East and "our prestige" would be gone? A more hopeless chaos can hardly be imagined, I should say, for a maximum of harm has been done with a minimum of achievement. And by way of "prestige" the P.M. runs away to Jamaica! Is he going to resign "on grounds of health?" [8] He ought to. Surely it doesn't mean a general election? It seems to me a long time since England has been so completely divided.

Perhaps because I'm the victim I can't wholly share your view about the Listener — many thanks for sending it. I should say it is a typical instance of bad reviewing, combining incompetence and presumption, ignorance and pedantry, misrepresentation and bad faith! A reviewer is a literary reporter, and his first duty is to describe what a book is, not what it isn't; his next is to find out what the author's intention was and to try to determine whether it has been attained or not. When a quotation from the book is made it should be made honestly and not (as here) truncated of essential words. (This is a favourite trick of English highbrows, who are not interested in truth, but in trying to make a score.) Elementary integrity in the reviewer would not have concealed the fact that in the opening chapter I say the book is "not for the few who know all about Mistral, but for these others who have scarcely heard of him . . ." Fat lot of good an academic thesis would be to them! The sneer about folk-lore is ignorant. All Mistral's long poems and many of the short ones and a great deal of his voluminous prose are deliberately concerned with what highbrows call "folk," i.e. the traditions, customs, beliefs, way of life of a people, in a word "Provence." Take that away, and what is left of Mistral? The suggestion that nothing is said about the language is a lie, as a reference to the index would have shown. And the objection to my giving my own experience of Provence, of the Félibrige, of the survival or not of ancient beliefs and crafts, is sheer impertinence. I have a perfect right to interest my readers by my experience, above all since I say (what this honest gentleman conceals) that one of my declared objects is "the joint exploration of Provence and of Mistral" — how can that be done without a guide? Of course the book is "untidy," just as the life of a poet and life itself are untidy compared with the symmetry of bureaucratic pigeon-holes or an academic morgue. One reason Mistral is neglected is because he has been the prey of philologists and pedantic thesis-writers. And how this dreary little highbrow resents the suggestion that poetry should be "social, festive and popular, not the mysterious vaticination of grimly aloof solitaries" — which in his ignorance he attributes to me, though for a century just that has been the principle of Mistral and the Félibres! *He* would like to keep Mistral for himself and a few other pedants, instead of trying to share. . . . And finally the thing is malicious, because it entirely conceals the attraction of the book in order to stop people from reading it.[9]

I have been wondering whether some publisher might be induced to issue a series of popular but accurate and scholarly handbooks on the saints of Western Europe, say, Italy, France, Spain and England to start with? It is a stupendous task, especially the critical one of trying to disentangle biography from legend — but of course legends should be included. Mistral's St Gent, for instance, is a most interesting saint, but never existed. Look at the legend of St Gilles, and how it spread. But I suppose the orthodox would be furious, and the rest of the world totally indifferent. Machinery has killed interest in humanity.

Ever yours,
RICHARD ALDINGTON

[1] Garnett's successor, George Knottesford Fortescue, who became Keeper of Printed Books at the British Museum in 1899. See RA *Frauds* 238. Fortescue was not involved with Wise.

[2] See RA *Frauds* 170–01, where he refers to the Derby Eve Dinner, 2 June 1931.

[3] No copy of MacCurdy's essay has been traced. In a letter to RA dated 17 Nov 1956, Mac-Curdy wrote, "I am having a few copies printed by a letterhead printer of a paper I wrote

many years ago on Jowett and I thought I would like to send one of them to you" (Southern Illinois).

4 See above, letter 113 n 4.

5 Pp 330–41 (a selection from *Roses of Paestum*, 1900).

6 *Roses of Paestum* and *Essays in Fresco* (1912).

7 Still unpublished.

8 Eden spent a holiday of about three weeks in Jamaica, returning Dec 14. He resigned as Prime Minister 9 Jan 1957 because of serious illness.

9 See the anonymous review in *The Listener* 15 Nov 1956.

126

28 December 1956   *Montpellier*

MY DEAR BIRD,

How beautiful that Verrocchio head! I don't think I ever saw it before. It does suggest the early Leonardo, don't you think? And I have found nothing for you yet! The choice here is between Woolworth, purely Catholic, and the Ecole de Paris.¹ I get so sick of seeing the Ecole de Paris that I could rest with satisfaction on the Royal Academy of 1875. They have made painting a set of empty futile tricks of colour-matching or contrasting.

I am pleased you liked MacCurdy's note on the great Jowett. I have that life by Campbell and somebody in 2 vols,² which contains many of the defects and few of the virtues of the Victorian biography. The hints one gets in J. A. Symonds are much more interesting and lively.³ Strange you mention Sheppard of King's whom I once met.⁴ I thought him a silly poseur and quite a vile pederast who should never have been allowed to have any authority over young men.

I venture to pass on to you another of MacCurdy's essays, this time of "the Gaelic," which I find very attractive.⁵ Astonishing that he is forced to reproduce such work at his own expense. What is the matter with us that there is apparently no periodical who will publish him?

The year 1956 will be memorable to me as the year in which elderly ladies fell down and broke bones. H.D. is still in hospital in Zürich with her broken hip, and a few days before Xmas Madame Gustave Cohen had exactly the same accident in her Paris studio. Now I hear by grape-vine and Indian smoke signals that Dame E.S. slipped on the marble floors of Montegufoni et se cassait la gueule. This last is supposed to be a secret, so hush. I also hear that the great American specialist who has made such sensational treatments of Parkinson's has refused to treat Osbert! I wonder why.

Obviously that review of my Mistral was the work of the bureaucrat-intellectual who is killing all that is genuine and spontaneous in literature.⁶ My book is not addressed to them, and specifically says so. And I am not concerned to give lecture-room formulae of Mistral, but to give my own experience of the poet and the country which made him, in which I have lived for years. However, let it go. The cockneys are so superior, they know everything, so let the book die. Nobody bothers to read it, anyway!

What do you think of this? You may recollect an article in that Moscow paper? I now have a very courteous letter in faultless English from the same person informing me that my "early novels" are to be reprinted in Russia, and asking certain biographical and other questions.[7] This is more embarrassing than agreeable. I don't want to have the police suddenly arriving (as the F.B.I. did on me in Hollywood apropos Ezra)[8] to call on me to show cause why I should not be arrested for corresponding &c with the enemy. But as an immediate reply was apparently wanted and everybody is "away" I hadn't time to consult, so frankly answered the questions. Much the same bureaucratic-intellectual nonsense, such as: When I wrote XYZ was I not "influenced" by Meredith's Egoist[9] and did I not intend to shew that anarchistic tendencies must inevitably lead to so-and-so? In fact I hadn't at that time read The Egoist and "anarchistic tendencies" had never entered my head. Can't they see that one is interested by human beings and their action and reaction on each other, and the tears and laughter and rage of it all?

If it is not too much trouble could you send me the titles &c of the Catholic books on saints, and the Baring-Gould?[10] I must try to wash off a little of my immense ignorance. I feel so frustrated when every day I come on Saints about whom I know *nothing*. I like Baring-Gould. For a tourist his book on the Midi is very good.

I spent Christmas alone — my daughter gone ski-ing in Vorarlberg — and twice read the galley proofs of my 80,000 words on RLS. I think I shall again be conspué by the bureaucrats, for I have tried to explain the *life* of RLS (and I insist a "biography" means a life not a literary criticism) on the basis of his revolt against the rigid Calvinism of his father and the Philistinism of Edinburgh, and of his enormous blunder in marrying that vulgar American woman. (Lloyd was all right, a very decent man, and evidently much preferred RLS to 'Mom.') Of course it is not all as simple as that, but the RLS myth is to some extent as big a lie as the TEL myth. The real RLS was a much nicer person than the myth created by the cockney journalists and Colvin–Gosse–Balfour–Fanny. Henley was right to be angry, but he too had the cockney outlook, and could not see that the world is wide and all of it interesting. I believe RLS was more important than the modern highbrows will concede. Of course the highbrows are often frauds — they give off lofty opinions about subjects they haven't studied.

Now I come to your cold, which is distressing to hear about. And I hope you are now better. Strange that with all the alleged "progress" of medical science, we are still left to suffer from these maladies. I picked up a chest cold myself through going round the churches to look at the "Presepii," about the best thing they do. The Carmelite Fathers are said to have a very fine one, but I've not seen it. Anyway; a chest cold with me usually means bronchitis. However, as I was worst on Xmas Day I thought I wouldn't disturb the doctors on duty — with the result that I am today (28th) almost well without any treatment whatever. Reminds one of Molière, who by the way picked up his Femmes Savantes[11] in Montpellier.

I feel I must add my most grateful thanks for your letters, which cheer me up and help me to keep in touch with the real mind of England.

Ever yours,
RICHARD ALDINGTON

[1] References throughout this paragraph are to picture postcards.

[2] E. Abbot and L. Campbell *The Life and Letters of Benjamin Jowett* (2 vols 1897).

[3] *Letters and Papers* 40–41, 123, 143 *et passim*.

[4] See above, letter 77.

[5] No copy of MacCurdy's essay has been traced. In a letter to RA dated 10 Dec 1955, Mac-Curdy wrote, "The Gaelic Book has found a form of lodgment for itself — the long studies are in course of being read before the meetings of the Gaelic Society of Inverness and may some day appear in their transactions. That is not what I looked and hoped for when I began 'Gaelic Hours' but they seem to like having them without me to read them. Some half dozen are too short for the purpose and of the shortest of all I have had some copies printed to serve as a Christmas greeting and I am sending you one with this letter. It is a rather nice story I think" (Southern Illinois).

[6] See above, letter 125 n 9.

[7] Mikhail Urnov; see above, letter 113.

[8] During World War II, when Pound was active in Italy on behalf of the Fascists.

[9] 1879.

[10] *Curious Myths of the Middle Ages* (1866–68).

[11] 1672.

127

18 January 1957   *Montpellier*

MY DEAR BIRD,

[. . .] I gave up in disgust and despair the attempt to find you any but Ecole de Paris or usual Louvre stuff here, and fall back on these humble local postcards which I hope may interest you. The reliquary at St Guilhem le Désert is said to contain the portion of the True Cross given to Charlemagne in Rome in 800 by the priest Zaccharias, and given by Charlemagne to Count Guilhem au Court Nez when he retired to his monastery. I fear the tale is more pretty than true. The other represents the curious machinery for lowering the relics of Mary Salome from the roof chapel over the apse of the Saintes Maries into the nave during the annual pilgrimage.

When you see the church and the site, the custom becomes understandable. The church is a fortress with enormously thick walls, and must have been exposed to attack by Nasser's predecessors at any moment. The monks and garrison evidently retired to the roof and the relics were kept there permanently for safety. France was only freed from raids by North African pirates when after centuries of provocation the conquest of Algeria was begun in 1830. Really, Eisenhower and his plan to diddle his allies at the behest of American Oil Cos make one sick.

It is useless to ask the Russians for payment. They immediately try to draw one into some form of communist propaganda, and if that is refused, no payment. On the other hand American publishers take advantage of their "laws" to issue unpaid editions of any book which has not been set up and published there within 5 weeks of English publication. I have been robbed of thousands of dollars that way — and of course the authorised edition being more expensive doesn't sell a copy. Curse them.

Of course your friend can't get a copy of Mistral. The cockney literary Camorra have taken care of that — Sodom and Camorra!

You surprise me when you speak of the low standards of education in Jowett's time. I should have thought it high. Where now would you find a Prime Minister (Gladstone), a Poet Laureate (Tennyson), a successful doctor (Dr Symonds) able to discuss points in Homer as they did circa 1860? Of course a lot of wealthy young men went through the universities on their fathers' incomes and a cricket bat, but that left the way open to the scholars.

In much haste but always with thanks but for your kindness and encouragement.

Ever yours,
RICHARD ALDINGTON

128

3 February 1957   *Montpellier*

MY DEAR BIRD,

I am trying to translate Cohen's La Grande Clarté du Moyen Age,[1] which he is most anxious to see in English. I am so much in his debt that I do it gladly if without much hope, though I am pulling wires with a view to blackmailing Yale (where he had a visitor's chair) into doing it. The USA have behaved so vilely to France (not to mention us!) that they owe some slight compensation.

There are one or two points which he has agreed shall be submitted to your decision. How do you translate "l'Amour Courtois?" G.C. thinks "Courtly Love." I have "Chivalric Love." He says "chivalric" suggests fighting, which it does in French, but does it with us? I say "Courtly Love" suggests not the high-flown devotion of the moth for the star but the kind of love which went on at the Court of Charles II.

In describing Stonehenge, he speaks of the circle as made up of "menhirs." I say that in English "menhir" means a single stone like those remaining at Avebury and in the Carnac avenues. The Stonehenge stones are "trilithons," I say. He says "trilithons" is pedantic. I think "menhirs" inaccurate. What do you decide?

This erudite prose is very hard to translate with accuracy and lucidity — there are so many subordinate clauses and parentheses. It is easy in French because of the case endings; but a lot of rearrangement is needed to keep subject, predicate and object quite clear.

These scholars are amusing with their footnote compliments to one another — which I have suggested relegating to the appendix. Gustave extricated himself with great skill from one difficult situation. He was a close friend (and I think pupil) of Jeanroy who of course was proved completely wrong on the subject of the Arabic influence on early Provençal poetry. The charming way Gustave deals with that arouses my admiration — he should perhaps have been at the Quai d'Orsay? He tells the truth but without anything which could offend le vieux Maitre.

I think, though, he is unfair to W. P. Ker, and I wonder if he has read Ker's Dark Ages.[2] Gustave wants to call his book The Bright Ages, in opposition. But he defines his period as "from the Chanson de Roland to Jeanne d'Arc." Surely Ker's book covers the period from the fall of the Empire to Charlemagne? If I remember rightly the book was part of a series, and was followed by one on the Moyen Age. Or does Ker come down to the first Crusade?

Am I not right in objecting to Alucin as *ninth* century?[3] He just lived into the ninth century, but all his work was done in the eighth, wasn't it? You might as well call Meredith a twentieth century author since he lived until 1909 or thereabouts.

You will laugh at my latest job, which is to write for a Paris medical paper (in French) an article on L'Enfant abandonné dans la littérature anglaise![4] I am going to give them Savage and Dickens, with some remarks on Captain Coram and — though it is not strictly relevant — a quote from Dickens's admirable speech on behalf of the Gt. Ormonde St hospital. I fear I must bring in Bleak House Joe. I am trying to find the sketch of the (tear-producing) situation where he found a little girl doing washing to provide for herself and orphan brother and sister.

Apropos Dickens and the blacking factory — did you ever hear the story that some German got a Ph.D. with a thesis on Die Schwester von Mealy Potatoes? If not true, it ought to be.

That Times article seems to have done some good.[5] I had to renew my passport last week, and applied humbly for the usual areas. To my amazement I received a long endorsement I have never seen before which (subject to military permits where needed) gives me the entrée to all countries in the world! I have sent H.M.'s Consul-General my most humble thanks, and wonder whether to plan Tibet, Uruguay or the Antarctic. Perhaps on the whole I should do best to stay in France, but I think the endorsement was kindly meant.

Have you seen the violent and (I think) mean and cowardly attack on Ezra Pound in the Herald-Tribune for the 2nd Feb? It is typical American journalistic bullying and spite against all authors, artists and culture. The accusation is that a certain Kasper has been fomenting racial hatred in the Southern States (having lived two years in the Southern States I can definitely assert no outside influence was needed to provoke racial hatred) and this Kasper is a friend of Pound's. The utterly mean insinuation is made that as a 71-year old patient in captivity Pound has, so to speak, founded the Ku Klux Klan, and therefore should be deprived of the letters and visitors who alleviate his hard lot. Really, when it comes to skunks, the Americans are I-T, it. I have been restraining myself from writing violent letters of protest, as I feel sure Pound's American friends (plus the newly-married)[6] will come to the rescue more effectively than I.

Ever yours,
RICHARD ALDINGTON

[1] 1943.
[2] 1904.
[3] Alcuin's dates are 735 to 804.
[4] *Problèmes* Mar-Apr 1957.
[5] Possibly "Richard Yea and Nay" by Oliver Edwards in the London *Times* 3 Jan 1957.
[6] That is, Mr and Mrs T. S. Eliot, married on 10 Jan 1957.

129

24 February 1957   *Montpellier*

My dear Bird,

Yes, the relics of Ste Marie Salome are errant; but that is nothing to St Marie Magdalene who was simultaneously buried at St Maximin and Vézelay. I enclose with this a photograph of the interior of the Saintes Maries. You will see a light burns before the opening in the apse which leads to the chapel of the relics. If you look carefully above the first row of pews on the right, you will see the crozier-shaped iron hook from which the large reliquary is suspended when lowered from the opening. The small crypt under the altar (similar to that at St Honorat, Arles, and at Mont-Majour) is now the shrine of the gipsy Saint. Up till two years ago the dress of the Saint's statue was covered with pinned-on handkerchiefs, letters, and snapshots of devotees! The clergy have now succeeded in having the offerings put into a large glass case beside the saint. I have a theory that for the gipsy offering of a handkerchief to be really acceptable it must have been stolen, but my daughter accuses me of cynicism.

Thank you for your help over the Grande Clarté troubles. I doubt my translation will ever be published, for preliminary reports from both USA and England are most discouraging.[1] Still, Gustave has set his heart on an English translation; and I'll do the best I can, if only because he was about the only historian of international status who had the guts to stand up for the truth over TEL. Moreover, he has translated the Luxembourg, and mirabile dictu persuaded La Table Ronde to publish it in July.[2] Indefatigable in a difficult cause, he is now about to attack A Fool i' th' Forest. How will it look in French, I wonder?[3]

Well, I managed to finish the Enfants Abandonnés,[4] with some help from my daughter in "idiotismes." I find writing French very tiring, mainly I suppose because I don't really know it. I often regret that in 1919 when I was demobilised I did not at once establish myself in France and try to make myself a French writer. The English don't like me, and never will. But it is too late now, and I must console myself with such praise as I get from Italy and Russia. I find the Russians stole four of my novels pre-1939, and are proposing to re-publish.[5] With the brutal cynicism of a bourgeois capitalist I have asked for their terms. This may put an end to it, but even a pirated Russian reprint might be useful if that authorised the Czechs to reprint. I had a much bigger public in Tchecoslovakia (not to mention Russia) than in England. My last book there before the communist putsch subscribed 50,000.[6] I have a friend in London, a publisher, who pays many 1000s a year to Prague printers, so that if, if, if . . . I could in short transfer Czech royalties to him.[7] How noble a spirit is man!

Have you ever heard of the "International Institute of Arts and Letters" centred in Zürich and (or rather but) sending out its communications from the German side of the Bodensee — cheaper postage. They invite me to become a member, so that for a modest annual fee of ten pounds I may put after my name the letters F.I.A.L. Fellow of the International Institute of Arts and Letters — or as James Joyce put it in Ulysses "Kiss My Royal Irish Arse."

Among recent elections I find:

Marc Chagall, FIAL (Vence France)

Rene Clair, FIAL (Neuilly — chic mais cher!)

Andre Dunoyer de Segonzac, FIAL (Paris)

Thomas S. Eliot, FIAL (London, Eng.)

Lion Feuchtwanger, FIAL (Pacific Palisades, Calif.)

Graham Greene, FIAL (London)

Aldous Huxley, FIAL (Los Angeles)

Daphne du Maurier, FIAL (Menabilly, Par, Cornwall)

Raymond Piper, FIAL (Belfast)

Namba Roy, FIAL (Jamaica BWI)

William Saroyan, FIAL (Malibu, Calif — très chic, très cher)

Thornton Wilder, FIAL (Hamden, Conn.) [. . .]

What is this racket? I think it must be an American swindle, since practically the only clear advantage (if it is one) to members is "To register their biographical data in the International Scientific Information Service (ISIS)." I am almost sure I had a rather similar offer from Chicago, but without the chi-chi of the FIAL. I took no notice and was cut off with a quarter.

Could we not found the Order of the Gold Brick and sell it to the same people at 25 quid a throw? I could easily persuade my friend the King of Poland (Montalk) to give his accolade for a fiver. If we could find 100 suckers we could do very well. We could give Montalk 500, take 1000 each, and buy some books. I don't think the Inland Revenue could chase us. We'd say it was a new form of football pool.

Your revelation of a projected marriage between Strachey and Virginia Woolf staggers me.[8] The marriage of two whats? They were both gifted, and I rather liked Virginia, but she was so self-conscious she made me unhappy.

The air is really warm, and a small lizard is running on the sun-warmed stone of my balcony. Yet my daughter tells me the snow is still deep on the Cevennes and even on Mont Aigoual. Still, on consulting the map I find that Mont Aigoual is higher than Ben Nevis, so the fact is less surprising. But here it is spring, and my gratitude is immeasurable. Last night the bats were out, and — come to think of it — the first swallows should be here, unless Nasser has nationalised them all.

All good wishes, and all thanks for your unfailing kindness,

RICHARD ALDINGTON

---

[1] See above, letter 128; it was not published.

[2] It appeared in the *Table ronde* Oct 1957.

[3] It was not published in French.

[4] See above, letter 128.

[5] Pre-1939, Russian translations included *Death of a Hero* (1932); *The Colonel's Daughter* (1935); *All Men Are Enemies* (1937); and *Very Heaven* in the first issue (1938) of *Internatsional'naja Literatura*. *All Men Are Enemies* was reissued in 1959 and *Death of a Hero* in 1961.

[6] *The Romance of Casanova* (1946).

[7] Possibly Paul Hamlyn of Spring Books.

[8] On 17 Feb 1909 Strachey proposed to Virginia Stephen, who accepted him. Both realised the unsuitability of such a marriage and both retreated from it. See Virginia Woolf and Lytton Strachey *Letters* eds Leonard Woolf and James Strachey (1956) 32.

130

19 May 1957   *Montpellier*

MY DEAR BIRD,

I hope the enclosed may amuse you.[1] Bouvier is professor of French literature here, and as a sideline "does" the articles on modern literature for the local Midi Libre in which "Deux Anniversaires" appeared today. I thought it amusingly satirical, especially for a local paper in the uncultured Midi.

I have been wretchedly ill for a long time, and was knocked back just as I was recovering by the death of Roy Campbell.[2] It is a great loss to me.

How are you? I hope you have recovered from the winter and that you are not affected by the explosions of H-bombs, which I strongly suspect are more dangerous than the various official and interested parties will admit.

One has to lie low at the moment, the English being less than the dust beneath the Gallic chariot-wheel on account of the final Macmillan submission to Nasser.[3] Is that what he means by "England's greatness"?

We seem to live here in a perpetual economic, social and political *crise*. It is strange that people so amiable and intelligent as the French should govern themselves so badly.

I picked up in a friend's house a copy of Mr Untermeyer's new anthology of "Ribaldry." The extracts from Candide were of course taken from my translation, without my name or permission or payment. Of course there are pirated editions without my name, but it is a curious tribute to American scholars to note that they *never* come on a copy of the editions which do bear my name.[4] The translation of course is copyright in all countries (including Canada) outside the USA. Unluckily book-piracy turns out to be a misdemeanour, and one's only remedy is to launch the police on some quite innocent bookseller. Strange that the two most unscrupulous thieves of European books are the USA and USSR.

Talking of which, I have been receiving the most amiable letters from members of the "Writers Union" in Moscow, in perfect English. (I suppose they have British communists who do the translation?) They speak of reprinting some of the four novels of mine they stole entre les guerres, and recently suggested a selection of my short stories from Roads to Glory and Soft Answers.[5] For this they say they will pay. Amazement! But no doubt it will be the usual blocked roubles. There is a certain irony in my appearing as a writer of short stories in the land of Chekhov and Gorki, seeing that the British intelligentsia long ago daffed them to oblivion.

Such an affliction — we have to move,[6] and my books weigh at least a ton and a half, and finding a place in these modern utopias is difficult. On top of which, my daughter has to face the Bachot again in June. This year she has won 1st prize for both English and French, which must be rather rare for an English girl in a French Lycée. I thought the professor who marked her French paper and gave her top marks was open minded. The topic was to contrast the ideas and personalities of Rousseau and Voltaire. Without having ever read Landor, she excogitated a dialogue of the dead and staged it outside the Institut on the Quais. There was an awkward moment for Voltaire when the news-boy came along, crying "France-Soir, Paris-Presse!" with news of another H-bomb explosion. He got out of it (rather unfairly I thought) by dragging in the Last Judgment. A pedantic examiner might easily have got cross, and given a zero for irreverence.

Let me have a line when you are at leisure.

Ever yours,
RICHARD ALDINGTON

They have put on the stone over Roy's grave the lines he was always quoting from the Canadian Boat Song: [7]

> From the lone shieling in the misty island
> Oceans divide us and the waste of seas,
> But still the blood is strong, the heart is Highland
> And we in dreams behold the Hebrides.

Perfect over a Scot in exile, don't you think?

[1] The enclosure is apparently lost.

[2] On 24 Apr 1957, as the result of an automobile accident. On 23 May 1957, from Montpellier, RA wrote to John Atkins about Campbell: "The death of my most dear Roy Campbell has broken my heart and scattered any sense I had left. He was the last of the poets. . . . Put all you have on Campbell. He is the last of the great ones" (Texas).

[3] Great Britain had agreed to release sterling for payment of British shipping tolls through the Suez Canal. Egypt had named a delegation to start negotiations on May 23 with Britain for the resumption of economic relations, and both nations regarded these arrangements as a prelude to the resumption of full diplomatic relations.

[4] See *Treasury of Ribaldry* (1956) 343–54. See also above, letter 54 n 3.

[5] *Farewell to Memories* (1961). Hanna Tshekoldina made the translation into Russian.

[6] To Maison Sallé, Sury en Vaux, Cher; see below, letter 131 n 1.

[7] Despite various conjectures, the author has not been established.

131

2 January 1958 [1]   *Maison Sallé,* [2] *Sury en Vaux, Cher*

MY DEAR BIRD,

Very glad indeed to hear from you, though sorry to hear of your ill health. I can make but a poor report myself. On the credit side I am installed in my friends' cottage here, but my daughter could not find a Paris vacancy until too late and has to spend this academic year at Montpellier, which defeats the main purpose of coming so far north. And now I have again fallen ill, and have to stop all work on books for some months. I hope to get permission to do some articles for America.

Wonder of wonders — I not only received official telegrams of congrats on my last birthday from USSR, but a few weeks ago was stunned to learn that they had lodged 360 pounds sterling to my credit in Paris. After an enormous amount of fencing with suspicious officials Barclays succeeded in getting this transferred to my francs account. I correspond with a member of the Union of Writers [3] (appalling thought to dwell on) and enclose his New Year card for you to see. It is interesting, isn't it?

As to the trip there — quite apart from the fact that I am too ill to go to Paris let alone Moscow, I have to consider America. They are beginning to forgive my lèse-majesté to Lowell Thomas and Lawrence by republishing my Decameron and Candide and re-issuing my Anthology. There is even a chance that they may follow the Four Square republication of Death of a Hero with an American soft-cover. [4] But if I went to Moscow I should be completely wiped off, as artists were here after the "liberation" if they had "made the journey to Berlin." In spite of which I am tempted to go, so perhaps it is as well I just can't.

You will not have heard but the English-speaking broadcasts from USSR and a Tass despatch have repeatedly said the publication of English books is to increase, "especially Somerset Maugham, J. B. Priestley and Richard Aldington." This appeared in the D. Worker and one or two provincial papers and (mirabile dictu) in the E. Standard; [5] but the remainder of the press either did not carry it or left out the third name. They are doing Hero in *English* for advanced students [6] (I pity them with all that slang and those colloquialisms) and a selection of the stories from Roads to Glory and Soft Answers. [7] As those stories were conspués by practically every "critic of standing" in England it is a great and real consolation to have them accepted with enthusiasm in the land of Chekhov. They are using all S. Answers except Nobody's Baby, for they discovered that Charlemagne Cox *might* be Ezra Pound, though I shouldn't myself consider the likeness a flattering one.

Apropos — poor Ezra is really off the rocker, perhaps a result of all these years in an asylum. His last letter asked me in a most cryptic style to write a letter to the Times (!) seemingly to link E.P. with Romain Rolland! I give this merely as a conjectural reading. I sent the letter to H.D., who has known him for 50 years and can see a hint of meaning when all other means fail. She returned the letter along with his last to her, asking if I can explain *that* — which of course I can't. But I notice that Ezra's name is constantly cited by "the critics" as one of the five greatest writers &c. I wonder if they know the real situation. Poor Ezra — he was extremely attractive and amusing round about 1912. [8] It is a sad déchéance.

Have you heard about the Sweeniad, the amusing skit on TSEliot by Victor Purcell, the Cambridge historian! It was issued privately and I had a copy, but it is now to appear publicly and with his name in USA and England. [9] The private edition was signed "Myra Buttle." I am glad he acknowledged the book at once, and did not hide behind a pseudonym. I wonder what the reply of the Sweenians will be? The first seemingly was a curt notification to Purcell from Elton to say that P. will not be required as an examiner when his present contract ends in *1960*. Why give such very long notice?

We are doing here a Hommage à Roy Campbell, which should be out in time for Easter — I'll send a copy. [10] These are merely personal reminiscences. I think the English have allowed themselves to be biased critically because (like so many from the outside world) he didn't think much of them. His wild life poems are superb, and his master in satire, and almost his only rival, is Dryden. That he punched the heads of some of the numerous pederasts of the BBC does not trouble me. His religion was genuine, not the phoney pose of an arriviste, like Eliot's. I loved the man.

I do hope you will regain health and find 1958 a more congenial year than 1957. For myself I have been so long in and out of health I hardly know what to think. My right arm, among other woes, is affected and often painful as well as nearly useless. However, it turns out not to be any form of paralysis, but neuralgic or nervous — part of the general condition of overwork and worry. But, as the peasants say, le coffre est solide, and I still hope to lead one or two more forlorn literary hopes before I am silent.

With all good wishes
Yours assuredly,
RICHARD ALDINGTON

P.S. Did you receive the paper-back edition of TEL [11] and the off-print of Professor Cohen's translation of Luxembourg? [12] [. . .]

---

[1] This is the only extant letter which RA wrote to Bird in 1958. Bird thinks there were more, but he cannot account for them or their loss, partly because he was ill in late 1957 and 1958. There were very likely only a few more for that reason and because, in 1958, RA was also ill and unhappy. Roy Campbell's death in April 1957 (see above, letter 130) had disturbed him grievously, his removal from Montpellier to Maison Sallé upset his habits and left him too much alone, and his health began to decline. In August he reported his "health news" as "not good," but he declared he could expect little else at the age of sixty-five. "Strictly speaking," RA added, "it would be a benefit if we were all poisoned at 60" (RA to Edward Nehls, Maison Sallé 24 Aug 1957 [Texas]). He was sick and dispirited throughout much of 1957 and seriously ill at the end of that year and the beginning of 1958. On 24 Jan 1958 he wrote to Michael Harrison: "Damn it, I have been ill again, and have a Quack's ukase ordering 'complete rest' for some months. I have compromised by dropping work on Balzac [a full length book, never completed], but keeping up small things, articles and so forth. It is a fearful nuisance, but after about three weeks of rest, I do feel better. My right arm went all wonky — I thought it was rheumatism or sciatica or even a touch of Ikery, but no. Merely a symptom of 'complete nervous exhaustion.' And I must say that under this régime of idleness the arm is already much better. In any case, I've written too many books. Place aux jeunes! As Ezra said . . .

> 'There'll come better men after us
> Who will remember — will they not?
> The noble deeds that we forget.' " (Texas)

The next month, February, RA told John Atkins, "I can hardly hold my head up. *Damn* old age and its beastly feebleness" (Texas). Even in April he reported that, owing to illness and weariness "everything seemed an impossible effort" (RA to Edward Nehls, Maison Sallé 26 Apr 1958 [Texas]). Only in late June did RA begin to improve, and he was busy by then preparing the foreward for the third volume of *D. H. Lawrence: A Composite Biography* ed Edward Nehls (1959). His work was delayed by an attack in July of "pseudo-angina pectoris" (RA to Edward Nehls, Maison Sallé, 13 July 1958 [Texas]), but he managed to get off his introduction (see below, letter 133) and doggedly to keep alive his interest in his work. These circumstances were not conducive to an active correspondence; thus they partially explain the scarcity of letters after May 1957. Once its regularity was broken, it was inevitable that the exchange between two men who had never met should be a desultory one even though it was maintained until a few weeks before RA's death.

[2] A tiny village in the neighborhood of Sancerre, where Alister Kershaw has a holiday house. In it RA lived, with frequent excursions to Sancerre and occasional ones elsewhere, until his death.

[3] Mikhail Urnov.

[4] The *Decameron* was reissued (1957) as No 1 in the Masterpieces of World Literature Series. *Candide*, illustrated by Rockwell Kent, was reissued in 1959. A revised *Viking Book of World Poetry* was published in 1958 as a mid-century edition in two volumes. The Four Square Books' edition of *Death of a Hero*, a paper-book, was published in England in 1958, but no paper edition came out in the U.S.A.

[5] These references have not been found; see below, letter 137 n 10.

[6] Brought out by Foreign Language Publishing House, Moscow, in 1958.

[7] See above, letter 130.

[8] See above, letter 2 n 12.

[9] *Sweeniad* (1957) was published only as by Myra Buttle, Purcell's pseudonym, as were his two later satires, *Toynbee in Elysium; A Fantasy in One Act* (1959) and *Bitches Brew; or, The Plot against Bertrand Russell* (1960).

[10] *Hommage à Roy Campbell* was published 10 Dec 1958.

[11] Four Square Books (1958).

[12] In *Table Ronde* Oct 1957; see above, letter 129.

132

5 *August 1959*   *Maison Sallé*

MY DEAR BIRD,

I was delighted to have a letter from you. Unhappily it arrived while I was away at a medical centre [1] "under observation and treatment," which latter has to be continued indefinitely, at least for some months. After nearly 2 months I can't say I feel much better, but I am warned it will be a long job.

I have often thought of you, and hope indeed that all is well with you. [. . .]

I am not able to do any original work, but I have a "job" which will need attention, and your aid will be most valuable. Circa 1944 the USA office of Enc. Britt asked me to do an Anthology of Poetry of Western World in translation — Huxley doing the Essays, and Singer the Science etc. Absurdly pretentious, of course, but I thought that owing to war it would never appear in Europe. Now after nearly 14 years of delay they propose to publish,[2] but I have got a few months in which to revise. If it is not abusing your good-nature, I should much like to consult you on the various problems, and particularly on any good translations since 1939.

I must stop. Will write again.

Ever yours,
R. A.

[1] In Montpellier; see below, letter 133.
[2] The anthology was not published.

133

12 *September 1959*   *chez Alister Kershaw, Sury en Vaux, Cher*

MY DEAR BIRD,

A friend in Montpellier lent his flat to my daughter and me for July.[1] It was hot, and unluckily I had to spend most of my time at the medical centre, both dentistry and "nervous diseases." The fact is my disagreeable symptoms are mainly upsets of metabolism due to age (I am 67) plus the annoyances of life. I take the dragées and ampoules prescribed, without much improvement, but still a little. I should enjoy the truly marvellous weather up here more if I were in better health, but the days are so beautiful one wonders why they occur only once in a decade. They remind me of the summer of 1921. The vintage this year should be superb in quality, though lack of rain will (the peasants say) limit quantity.

My daughter has now a diploma from the Académie de Montpellier raising her to the "grade" of Bachelier en Philosophie, avec la mention "assez bien," which only means marks 10% above pass. Thank goodness all that is over. Now we have the worse problem of finding a not too uncongenial and badly-paid job. Since I left the Midi (fin Juillet) she has been living with another girl in a Cabane de Gardian of the Camargue, acting as supernumerary gardian to a manadier, and so getting plenty of riding every day. With a motor-bike she was able to go swimming daily, and do the marketing. I expect her here next week, and she then goes

to Switzerland to consult one of these alleged experts in "orientation" who is supposed to be a wizard in suggesting careers. I am rather sceptical, but the expenses
are being met by an old friend of mine who takes an interest in the girl,[2] and no
harm can be done.

The little events of an author's life today ought to provide much hilarity for a
scholar like yourself. [. . .] You will scarcely believe this — Mrs Macy, relict of
the late proprietor of Macy's Store, Fifth Avnoo, is continuing her husband's hobby
of printing limited editions.[3] I was invited to contribute an introduction to a translation of Eugénie Grandet.[4] Now, after generations of critics and scholars what
remains to be said about that book which might be new and also true? I could do
nothing but summarise the facts, mention that Balzac's uncle was guillotined for
murder, and sprinkle a few mild jests. All's well that ends well — the article was
received with mild praise and a "check" for a hundred pounds, not bad for 2000
words. Following that I did another introduction, this time to a collection of photographs of Rome, for a London firm.[5] The photographs struck me as amateurish,
so I wrote a rather learned discourse on the theme of "the ruines of Rome'" and
the building of new Romes from the same, ranging from the obelisk of Tuthmosis
outside the Lateran and the Niger Lapis, to Borromini and the costume of the
Campagna in 1850. Only when I had finished it did I realise that it was less an
introduction to the book as it is than to the book as it ought to be.

I am now on two other tasks. There is a proposal from N.Y. to cash in on the
immense new publicity given DHLawrence by the judgement of the Supreme
Court [6] by issuing a selection of his poems, to include those Pansies which yelped
in a melancholy way over the prosecution of Lady C. and the pictures.[7] It seems
I shall never get free from that man, for I had to do the introduction to VOL 3 of
that immense Composite Biography issued by Wisconsin University [8] — and I
believe it is being reprinted this autumn in some Lawrence miscellany edited by
Professor Moore.[9]

The other is the anthology I think I mentioned to be published by the Encyclopaedia Britannica — which is of course Americana. They were to do it in 1946
but the efficiency of modern publishers held up the script (and that of other books
in the series) until now. They mysteriously want it "revised and brought up to
date," and with publishers that means "anyone who has been written about and
gossiped about lately." My script ranges from Ancient Egypt, through Babylon-
Assyria, Israel, Greece (to the 6th cent A.D.) Rome, mediaeval and Renaissance
Latin (down to Vincent Bourne), Provençal, French, Italian, Spanish, Portuguese,
German, a sprinkle of Icelandic, Danish, old Celtic, then England and USA. This
will run to nearly 600 closely printed pages, and heavy fees for copyright translations. Now, to set some limit and to avoid both many extra fees and also the yelps
of the disappointed I excluded all living authors in any language. You will see
at once what an enormous flood of mediocrity is let loose if this salutary barrier is
thrown down. I have written to the "editors" pointing this out, and trying to persuade them to uphold me. BUT of course I am trying to include any good translations which have appeared since 1945, and also any English-American poets who
have died since then. Thus, I could use Campbell as poet and translator, Dylan
Thomas as poet, but Day Lewis only as translator. I can include Valéry, but not
Perse or Cocteau or Aragon.

Can you give me any help here? I have inserted some of Rieu's Homer, but in close proximity to Sam Butler,[10] who did that sort of thing first and better. It is simply taking the novel of the Iliad and Odyssey while omitting the poetry. I have looked over the Prince of Mecca's version,[11] and it just won't do. I was too kind to it.

The greatest problem about this anthology of translations (for I think the Anglo-American at the end a mistake, but the publisher insists) is that though one can easily track new versions of the Big Pieces like the Iliad and the Commedia, the more interesting lyric pieces are hidden away in periodicals, books of verse, essays, literary histories and so forth. I am particularly short of good translations from the German, and have had to include many which are of poor quality. Anyway, if you can think of any good translations you have approved since 1945 I shall be most obliged. I can get the books either through the London Library, or my agent can buy them. I have until Xmas to revise, but with such a huge script and such an immense area, the difficulties are baffling. Of course, it is a typically American pretentiousness — but the proposal as first made was Poetry of the *World* (!) on the lines of Mr van Doren [12] and other genii of the sort.

What I dread is that the E.B. will do to this book what Viking did to the new edition of my English anthology — i.e. insist on stuffing the end with a mass of mediocre stuff by people who will be forgotten in a decade but who have friends among the fashionable reviewers. Even in the first version, the American edition had about 15 poems (which I cut from the English edition in 1946) which Viking then insisted on and which they mostly cut themselves in 1958!! [13] This subservience to the newspaper and its opinions is ignominious and exasperating.

In the course of this revision I have managed to catch George Saintsbury bending. Footnotes to Philip Ayres in vol 2 of the Minor Carolines [14] highly praise two of his poems as original contributions to Eng. poetry. Both are translations — one from Girolamo Preti and the other from Claudio Achilini — followers of Marino, of course. This raises an interesting query. If translations from two minor Italians are thought by Our Omniscient Critic to be important contributions to English poetry, how good is the despised Italian poetry which can show hundreds of poems as good or better? I happened to recognise these two as I own Benedetto Croce's "exceedingly scarce" (bookseller's note) Poeti Marinisti, which was not published when G.S. wrote. Still, there were many editions of both poets in the Seicento, and I am certain the Bodleian must have some of them. There were at least ten editions of Preti. Of course, I say nothing about this — am merely giving the poems, and hoping that some incautious follower of G.S. will reproach me for printing English originals as Italian translations.

Did I tell you that the Russians have been paying me about 350,000 francs annually? They re-issued the Hero in Russian and then in English with Russian notes (I observe there is a Russian commentary on "strike me muckin' pink" — I wonder how they explained it?), also a Russian collection of the short stories in Roads to Glory and Soft Answers (omitting any which criticise the working class) and now they are going to reprint All Men in Russian. December or January, they say.[15] Meanwhile the Czechs put on a play derived from my Casanova novel,[16] and paid two guineas for each performance. And now I hear that Very Heaven is to appear in Bulgarian [17] and part of All Men in Japanese.[18] Considering these works are sedulously kept out of print in England and that my friends tell me they are perpetually teased to lend copies of these books, the question arises: Who censors contemporary English books? A friend in London says that he has had weary traipses trying to get second-hand copies of Portrait of a Genius and Wellington, both of which cost him more second hand than the original published price. My agent had much difficulty in finding even a second rate publisher to issue my Decameron — which has been selling in USA steadily for 30 years.[19] The whole English edition of 10,000 sold out on publication day, and the publisher was so utterly unprepared that it took him 3 months to print a second impression. That sounds incredible, but it's true. The 4 Square books have now sold out nearly 40,000 of the Prince of Mecca and 30,000 of Hero. Landsborough [20] was all set to put others back into print — something intervened, and silence. Ditto another publisher who had agreed by letter to re-issue All Men and Wellington — just about to draw agreement, something intervened, and silence.[21] Ah well.

I hope you are in good health, and able to enjoy walks and books, without which life would be a desert. I am pretty shaky on my pins, but a little French Renault 4 CV takes me about. I am not surprised the Americans are buying small French cars. Pre-1939 I always had Americans, and spent fortunes in repairs and petrol. I have had this Renault 6 years — few repairs, and it still runs nearly 20 klms to the litre. By starting early I can do the 600 klms from here to Montpellier in a day, and for much less than a third-class ticket. No wonder a married man with two or three children insists on a car. Why must the railway be so dear? They are putting up fares and freights yet again, and trying to stop people buying cars by huge sales tax and the most expensive petrol in the world. 66 cents of every dollar one spends on French petrol are tax!

When my daughter comes — and if the fine weather holds — I must run her over to Vézelay. It wasn't touched in the late shambles, and I haven't been there since 1936. [. . .]

Ever yours,
RICHARD ALDINGTON

[1] Jacques Temple.

[2] Bryher.

[3] Mrs Macy was the widow of George Macy, publisher, and in no way connected with R. & H. Macy, the department store controlled by the Strauss family.

[4] Published, 1962, by The Heritage Press in a translation by Ellen Marriage and with illustrations by René ben Sussan and an introduction by RA.

[5] Rome: A Book of Photographs published by Spring Books (1960). Richard Magowan made the photographs.

[6] On 21 July 1959 the Federal Court, with Judge Frederick van Pelt Bryan on the bench, ruled Lady Chatterley's Lover not obscene and thereby upset a U. S. Post Office decision of June 11 that the Grove Press's edition was "obscene and non-mailable." Owing to the Federal Court ruling, both the book and 20,000 circulars of Readers' Subscription, Inc announcing Grove's publication, seized on April 30, were released for mailing at noon on July 22.

[7] Because of threats of police raids, English booksellers were reluctant to stock copies of Lady Chatterley's Lover in the summer of 1928, the year of its publication. (See above, letter 117 n 3). In late Dec 1928 the novel was suppressed in London. Because of the action against Lady Chatterley, two typescripts of Pansies (1929) which Lawrence sent from Bandol in early 1929 to his London agent Curtis Brown, were seized by postal authorities on orders from the home office. Action against the showing of Lawrence's paintings came later. On 5 July 1929 the police raided an exhibition of the paintings in the Maddox Street Gallery and confiscated thirteen pictures which were subsequently returned to Frieda (Mrs D. H. Lawrence). RA's

statement that *Pansies* "yelped" may refer to Frieda Lawrence's description of the poems as "real Doggerel." RA did not prepare the selection of Lawrence's poems mentioned here.

8 RA was invited to write the introduction to this volume after indicating that he was hurt when its editor Edward Nehls asked Aldous Huxley to introduce the second volume with the explanation to RA that "there wasn't time" for him to do it. RA composed his introduction in the summer of 1958, finishing it in the latter part of July despite ill health (see above, letter 131 n 2).

9 *A D. H. Lawrence Miscellany* edited by Harry T. Moore (1959). That same year the introduction was used also as a review of Nehl's composite biography in *The European*, a London literary periodical.

10 Rieu's translation of *The Odyssey* was published in 1907; Butler's *Iliad* appeared in 1898 and his *Odyssey* in 1900.

11 A translation of the *Odyssey* (1932).

12 *Anthology of World Poetry* (1928).

13 The mid-century edition; see above, letter 110.

14 "On a Fair Beggar" and "Lydia Distracted"; see Saintsbury's introduction to Ayres's poems, p 266.

15 December 1959.

16 On Czechoslovak radio.

17 No Bulgarian translation has been located.

18 Part I, with notes in Japanese, for use as a text book, 1960.

19 Since 1930. Reissued in 1957 by Elek Books Ltd.

20 That is, Four Square Books. RA's were two of the first four books selected by Landsborough for publication by Four Square. About the book on Lawrence and RA, Landsborough said, "Richard began his research on the over-blown Lawrence, found Lawrence's character highly irritating and conceived a real dislike of L. His book was tinged with . . . malice? That's what the critics said of him. I don't think it was. Richard, a true writer, got carried away with his subject. His was quite the best, most accurate portrait of Lawrence published to that date (and since, in my opinion . . .). He could have expressed it differently. It would not have been as good a book. And what a beautiful writer Richard was. When he used words they fitted together with a harmony not found in many writers" (see Gordon Landsborough to MJB, Hampton, Middlesex, 26 Mar 1971).

21 Possibly Elek Books.

134

21 October 1959   *Maison Sallé*

MY DEAR BIRD,

Just a swift one in answer to yours of the 16th . . . The labour-of-Sisyphus anthology for the Encyclopaedia is almost finished. It is called Poems of the Western World, contains over 1200 items, which run to at least 900 printed pages, and so must unhappily appear in 2 vols. (I wanted India paper, but the format of the series forbids.) It is in two sections: Mediterranean and North Atlantic, as follows:

Ancient Egyptian, Vth Dynasty to XXIInd.	38 items
Sumerian Babylonian, Assyrian — Epic of Creation to Prayer of Asurpanipal	7 items
Greek, Homer to Agathias	175 items
Latin, Lucretius to Vincent Bourne	155 items
Classical Provençal, Guilhem to Rudel	12 items
Italian, Guinicelli to d'Annunzio	178 items
Spanish, El Cid to Lorca	80 items

Portuguese, King Diniz to Junqueiro	26 items
French, Roland to Valéry Larbaud	176 items
Geran, Nibelungenlied to Werfel	70 items
Old Irish, Welsh, Breton	18 items
Old Danish, Icelandic	8 items
Old, Middle, Modern English	180 plus
USA	37 plus

I have had to bar all dramatic poetry (alas) and all living poets — inclusion would mean another volume. At the moment, I am expanding English and American — finding to my distress about 3 English to each American (what nonsense the latter often are) since this is an American publication, and I must try to compliment my hosts. I have sent out SOS for German lyrics — and of course get nothing but Heine and Rilke. I am qualifying to write a sarcastic note, on the lines of Housman's introduction to his Manilius,[1] on the ignorance of modern intellectuals supposedly devoted to European poetry. The same names and even poems of Baudelaire, Rilke, Lorca, Rimbaud, Juan de la Cruz, Verlaine and Cocteau (still living) repeat endlessly! Go a little outside those chewed-over personalities of the avant-garde, and there is a blank gaze and a dropped jaw.

I am heinously pressed for time, as this huge script (over 1600 typed pages) must go off to US before the Xmas parcel rush. I still have to fill up the Yankosachsen sections, and retouch others. As you don't know what I've got it is impossible for you to make suggestions specifically. But it would help if you could answer the following:

(1) Egyptian chronology — is there any agreement yet? Can one put roughly a date in centuries BC for the V Dynasty?

(2) Can you suggest and, if possible, send text of translation of one or two of those poems Venantius Fortunatus wrote for Saint Radegunde? I am not including such things as Pange lingua and Vexilla Regis as too liturgical. I have had to lean heavily on H. Waddell and Jack Lindsay for "dark ages" Latin,[2] as there seems no one else who is readable. For Boethius I am using Chaucer, "I.T." (Loeb) and Lindsay.[3]

(3) Can you lend me The Dove's Neck-Ring by A. R. Nykl[4] (professor of Oriental Languages at Chicago) which is transcription and translation of the extant poems of Mohammed Ali Ahmed ibn-Hazm al-Andalousi. I have Nykl's edition (edited and translated in Spanish) of the Cancionero of Ibn Kuzman.[5] These are obviously the type of Hispano-Arabic poems from which Provence derived metres, themes and point of view, especially the cult of the "amor de lohn." You will find this ably summarised in Robert Briffault's Les Troubadours.[6] But, one mustn't go too far — the Duc Guilhem frequently uses the rhythm of the Pervigilium.[7] Further, Asin Palacios and Gonzalez Palencia "show cause" to believe that Dante lifted a great deal from Latin translations of Moslem voyages to the next world — particularly from Al-Arabi.[8]

I can only devote a paragraph or so to this fascinating topic, but I want to be accurate. The London Library haven't The Dove's Neck-Ring, and Foyle[9] have advertised for it without result

I should perhaps interject that nine-tenths of my work was done in USA, with their magnificent library service at my disposal through the University of California.

(4) Modern Americans. I have from birthdate 1869 on — Amy Lowell, Vachel Lindsay, E. L. Masters, Wallace Stevens, Elinor Wylie, E. St V. Millay, Hart Crane. I don't like H. Crane but they think he is wonderful. Is William Carlos Williams still living? Any others?

Personal news is that my daughter got her second part of the Baccalauréat with mention Assez Bien. After her holidays she was interviewed by two psychology experts in orientation, who reported her as gifted, probably for creative writing (alas) and recommended 3 years at the University of Paris. Through the generosity of a friend she will have an ample subsidy for 3 years,[10] and is already "inscribed" for the course of Sciences Politiques. It is a great weight off what is jestingly referred to as my mind.

I am doing a short book on DHL for publication direct in German, and probably a selection of his verse for USA [11] — the latter is practically settled but no contract. University of Wisconsin will issue Mistral, and thus make up for Heinemann's dropping the book.[12] [. . .] So I can cock a snook at the BBC, New Statesman and all the rest of them. They won't get *me* down.

All thanks for your interest in the anthology.

RICHARD ALDINGTON

[1] 1903–30; an abridged edition was issued in 1932.

[2] *Mediaeval Latin Lyrics* (1924) translated by Waddell and *Mediaeval Latin Poets* (1936) translated by Lindsay.

[3] Chaucer's translation, made before 1382, was published by Caxton at Westminster in 1480; reedited, 1868, by Richard Morris for Early English Text Society. For the Loeb edition see *Five Books of Philosophical Comfort . . . Newly Translated Out of Latine . . .* [by I.T.] revised by H. F. Stewart in *The Theological Tractates . . .* (1936) See also Jack Lindsay *Song of a Falling World* (1948).

[4] Ali Ahmad Ibn Hazm *A Book Containing the Risāla Known as The Dove's Neckring, about Love and Lovers* ed A. R. Nykl (1931). Bird sent this as well as translations of the poems by Venantius Fortunatus.

[5] 1933.

[6] *Les Troubadours et le sentiment romanesque*; see above, letter 84 n 9.

[7] *Pervigilium Veneris*, author unknown, c. 2nd century.

[8] González Palencia *Influencia de la civilización árabe; discursos leídos ante la academia de la historia . . .* ; see 67–84 for "discurso de don Miguel Asín Palacios." See also González Palencia *El Islam y Occidente . . .* prologo de don Miguel Asín Palacios (1931) and Asín Palacios *La escatologia musulmana en La Divina comedia* (1943).

[9] The bookshop in Charing Cross Road, London.

[10] Bryher.

[11] *D. H. Lawrence in Selbstzeugnissen und Bilddokumenten* (1961); the selection of poetry was not published.

[12] The University of Wisconsin did not issue *Mistral*; see above, letter 100 n 1.

135

5 November 1959 Maison Sallé

MY DEAR BIRD,

Gunpowder Treason — and I have just finished re-typing the Anglo-American table of contents. I think this about completes the job, except that I must rewrite the Introduction, and may have one or two last minute changes. But to all intents and purposes the mighty chore is over, and very thankful I am. The amount of work involved is far in excess of any possible reward, as I made a very bad financial bargain (as usual) and there is no chance of any book with my name being reviewed fairly or even with common courtesy. No matter — 'tis not in mortals to command success . . .

If you could send me Nykl's Hispano-Arabic Poetry (1946) I shall be grateful. It is evidently the book I need since the Dove's Neck-Ring is unobtainable. I need the information only for the Introduction — I simply can't expand an already over-packed book with probably mediocre versions of Arabic poems.

I can't understand why Eliot and other Dante-friends try to minimise and even to deny the Arab sources of the Commedia. Dante's was an encyclopaedic mind. He included in his survey Christian culture, the pre-Christian culture of antiquity (what little of it he knew) and a good deal of the great alien culture of his time. Why not? Where's the harm? Some of what he took over is perhaps not strictly orthodox from the viewpoint of the Holy Office — but does that matter to us? So far as I know the Commedia has never been condemned on doctrinal grounds, though I believe it ought to be if the H.O. were consistent. I think Siger of Brabant died while under the ban of the Church and lo! the poet pops him into Paradise with loud encomiums..

The Egyptian date. I kick off with the so-called Cannibal Hymn, which is nothing of the sort — it's a pyramid text from the tomb of Unas,[1] last king of the Vth dynasty. What date do they give him now? I have reckoned it at approx B.C. 2500; but please let me know if they've changed it again. I ought to revise all that opening with the new Cantab Ancient Hist — but you will understand that with a work on this scale there is sometimes as much as 20 years between the earliest compilations and the latest. But one can't go on revising and bringing up to date for ever. As one section is revised another grows out of date. [. . .]

Yes, I have E. A. Robinson — not *very* good. Frost and Williams are both living. This ban against still living poets is most salutary. The present day favours the building-up of a number of mediocrities as "great figures," who soon subside when the personal boost is gone. Dylan Thomas is very small beer compared with Campbell. I have used two Campbell poems — the Skull, and the Clock — which have hitherto been carefully boycotted. Thomas is Dowson and De la Mare à la mode — Campbell's passion and virtuosity make him a formidable customer. Thomas reads like a little boy beside him — worse, a little girl.

What do you say to the Charles van Doren scandal?[2] Perhaps inevitably, that "literary family" are among the ardent American supporters of the Prince of Mecca. A fellow feeling perhaps. It is amusing to note that a man who is discharged by his university as unfit to teach is at once taken on by the fashionable "Leisure"[3] as literary critic — evidently one American activity which does not demand integrity. [. . .]

How is your health? You don't say. I am being urged to consult yet another specialist, though I would rather stay peacefully here.

All thanks for your help and encouragement.

Ever yours,
RICHARD ALDINGTON

1 The source of RA's text has not been established.

2 On Nov 2, Van Doren admitted to the House Special Subcommittee on Legislative Oversight that for "Twenty-one," a television quiz game produced by Barry & Enright and televised by NBC, he had been coached before his television appearances. His confession admitted perjury, inasmuch as he had denied such complicity before a Federal Grand Jury in January. He had also denied it during the House Subcommittee's investigation into the validity of "The $64 Challenge" and "The $64 Question" as well as "Twenty-one." It became clear that other contestants in these quiz games were coached or provided questions and answers; but Van Doren, who had won $129,000 on "Twenty-one," received particular publicity owing to the intellectual prominence of his family. His resignation as Assistant Professor of English at Columbia University had been accepted on Nov 2.

3 Van Doren was Book Editor of *Leisure*, scheduled to appear for the first time on 12 Nov 1959. In fact, *Leisure* published four issues in 1960 and expired.

136

17 November 1959   *Maison Sallé*

My dear Bird,

I was about to start off "tetelstai," but remembered that this would indeed be profanity! I had better say Tenella kallinke.

THE DAMNED ANTHOLOGY IS FINISHED!

It fills, crams, five large folders, plus an introduction of about 5000 words, and 56 pages of Contents. It goes off this afternoon in three large parcels, registered, and then, as the cockney soldiers used to say in the trenches after a strafe "I reckon we can 'ave a spit and a dror." [. . .]

The date of publication I can't give you. The script has to follow channels as complicated as the army. First to my London agent; then to the London branch of the Encyclopaedia Britannica; then to the head office in Chicago. The book will run over 900 pages I think, in 2 vols, boxed. The setting will take time — then I must have proofs, read carefully, and return. I should think the earliest date will be autumn of 1960.

I hope you will not accuse me of hybris when I say that on this occasion I make no acknowledgements. The conception of the book is mine, and at least 99% of its contents are "all my own work." It has been a labour of years, without one penny of subsidy from outside and hardly a word of anything but sneers except from you, for an anthologist's fee of 1500 pounds which leaves me badly out of pocket. Well, mustn't grumble. Most luckily the book is based on USA, where I feel sure it will be well received. So the jeers of the British reviewers or their silence won't matter.

Next week, not "obleeged by hunger" but "by request of friends" who can no longer be denied I am going to Suisse to be looked at by a medical specialist. I have no particular hopes of this, for there is no known cure for the universal disease of Anni Domini. But these kind people are footing the bill, and it would be most ungracious to refuse. I am going to drive in my ancient 4 CV, and on the way back hope to "do a bit of Kultur." I should like to see Cluny and Vézelay again — saying farewell — and perhaps Dijon, though the damage done the churches there by the revolutionaries makes it painful. But there are lovely things in that museum housed in the ducal palace. I am not so frightfully keen on the église de Brou, although it is a wonderful piece of work. And I go through Autun. Have you ever visited Bibracte, the great Gaulish stronghold on the hill not far from there? It has a most overwhelming "atmosphere" and ambiente of the distant past — more even than St Aldhem's head and church fifty years ago. It is 25 years since I was at Bibracte, and I daresay it is now a dumping ground for picknickers — sardine tins, orange peel, eggshells etc. as Wayland Smith's Cave on the Icknield Way was the last time I visited it — leaving more in anger than in sorrow.

My next job is to do a Taschenbuch on D. H. Lawrence for a German publisher — to appear first and only in German.[1] This will be easy enough, but I'd like to have the proofs of the new collection of DHL's letters coming from the University Press of Southern Illinois.[2] Professor Moore tells me the book will double in size the original Huxley Letters.[3] Also, to my great relief, two or three of the letters to me (stolen 1930 with a lot of others interesting for their literary history of 1912–29) have turned up at Sotheby's. I shall not prosecute, of course, for the essential thing is that they shall be preserved; and any threat of prosecution might lead to the destruction of those not yet sold. The deed-box containing these documents had the correspondence when at Pound's request I tried to raise an income of 10 pound annual subscriptions to enable Eliot to leave Lloyds Bank. I got about 150 a year — but as anyone but Pound would have foreseen Eliot naturally refused.[4]

Forgive all this — reaction on the lifting of a load which made me think so often of the millstone of the N.T.

Ever yours,
RICHARD ALDINGTON

---

[1] See above, letter 134.

[2] 1962.

[3] That is, *The Letters of D. H. Lawrence* ed Aldous Huxley (1932).

[4] RA refers to the plan originated by Ezra Pound to solicit lifetime donations of £10 a year from each of 30 donors to enable T. S. Eliot to leave his post in Lloyd's Bank and devote his entire time to literature ("I don't want him to write anything but poetry," Pound, who had already seen *The Waste Land*, late 1922, declared). The three original donors were Pound, May Sinclair, and RA. Natalie Barney, whose contribution was $50, named the plan "Bel Esprit." In the spring and summer of 1922, Pound wrote a series of letters to RA about the "Bel Esprit" plan (Texas). These letters evaluated the scheme, devised ways to put it into effect and encouraged or bullied RA to cooperate. On 12 March 1922 Pound wrote from Paris:

> Now Faunus, it is distinctly not good, nor yet pleasing to Zeus our father that the Conductor of the Dead work in a bank. That you know, even as I know it.
>
> Also Hermes our brother is too near unto death for the matter to be trifled with. Between us we must brain some putrid usurer, or milk so[me] she-cow of the occident (dry uddered and bitter of teat, . . .)
>
> Nothing is any good save a regular subsidy, of I take [it] at least £300 a year.

On that point Pound was adamant, repeating it three times in one way or another in that same letter, though he conceded that when Eliot had had time to rest and increase his own earnings, "The subscribers cd. reduce themselves to twenty (beginning with the poorest, and thereby shifting the burthen from us onto the lured-in plutes) . . ." Pound had already told RA in an earlier letter from Paris, "When its the ploots as pays it shd mean regular sub; when T. ceases to need it, it wd. devolve on some other worthy head." Pound went on, "You may not see any other worthy at the moment, but there'll be another 'jeune' before it is wholly self-propelling."

In answer to RA's objection that the scheme smacked of charity — and Eliot later took the same attitude — Pound wrote that his "formula" was the "employment of credit to increase production; in this case to augment the quality rather than the quantity." And he added in a letter also from Paris, dated 16 Mar 1922: "There is no affront to his bloody pride. Only people who want his poetry, and who are willing to pay for IT are in on this deal. There is NO question of his being an object of charity. We are restarting civilization, and have devised a new modus of making art and lit. possible." The letters are filled with instructions as to who will help in the scheme (Alfred Kreymborg, Pound's "belle-mere," Walter Fowler, Robert McAlmon, "The Asre-Hole-brook Jackasson," Lady Ottoline Morrell, John Quinn, Amy Lowell, Harriet Weaver) and who will not (the Sitwells whom Pound called "mutts" and Lady Rothermere, whom he called "Bothermere").

The "Bel Esprit" plan came to nothing. Despite their awareness that what all men hate is not "POESY" but literature, that men prefer not to feed "on larks tongues only" but "beller for tripe and onions," Pound and RA persisted. Pound maintained that Eliot's working in the bank was "the greatest waste in contemporary letters" and that "it's gotterbee stopped" and RA secured a number of subscriptions. But Eliot, who left Lloyd's bank anyway to edit a new periodical subsidized by Lady Rothermere, *The Criterion*, found their efforts belittling, undignified, humiliating. And they came to an end.

137

20 December 1959

Maison Sallé

MY DEAR BIRD,

It is a great encouragement to have your very kind letter about the Encyclopaedia anthology. For obvious reasons the genuine reader is becoming rather scarce. A wealthy and elderly woman I met in Zürich told me that even 20 years ago she had 18 persons to whom she regularly gave or lent books knowing they would be read — now there remain 3. My one hope is that in spite of the hardship they inflict on authors the "decent" pocketbooks may create a new race of reader. A Nottingham postman [1] with whom I correspond (he is of course interested in DHLawrence) says he has collected about 1000 books, but is considered very eccentric for so doing, the more so since he hasn't either TV or radio, and regularly practises the violin.

As to the bibliography [2] — it must be as Allah or rather the E.B. wills. I have provided the materials, since at the foot of each poem I marked its source. But you must consider that the cost of producing such a book is much more than double what it would have been in 1939, while the "public" insists on having books as cheaply as possible. (Much as they insist on having cheap food while paying any price for machine products.) The fees for copyright translations and poems will run into thousands of dollars. There ought to be index of originals, index of translators, index of first lines, and bibliography. Can they afford these? In a book which must now run to over 900 printed pages?

My own view was and is that the inclusion of Old Testament extracts was a mistake. Everybody in USA and England has a Bible; such extracts must be inadequate, and moreover ignore all the later Hebrew poetry, which is not inconsiderable, I am told by a Rabbi friend. [3] The inclusion of Anglo-American poetry is an even greater blunder, for it occupies much space yet must appear inadequate. The saving of space would have enabled me to be less scrappy in the translated portion which is the raison d'être of the whole book. But I was over-ruled by the publisher, and as this is a commissioned book I could not stand out. Fortunately, I was able to stand out against the admission of living originals (not translators) for that would have made the book impossibly bulky while involving me in all the coterie feuds I try hard to avoid.

I expect nothing for all my years of work, except a good deal of carping. There are obvious weaknesses, which a scholar will understand, but unluckily reviewers are seldom scholars. The work is so extensive that parts of it are already 20 years out of date — but while one catches up on one section, all the others are getting older! The most interesting translations are not catalogued — one has to hunt them down in literary histories, books of archaeology, memoirs, literary essays, periodicals, and books of poetry. Thus, I have included (and mention in my introduction) Milton's version of the Pyrrha ode, Crashaw's of a Catullus poem, Byron's of a passage from Petrarch's Africa, Matthew Arnold's of that mime of Theocritus, Meredith's of Mistral's horses of the Camargue (though Campbell did it far better — but in the case of Nonnus which was attempted by Mrs Browning (!) I "preferred the scholarship of Dr Rowse to the poetry of the lady." Another difficulty is that reviewers, so often being unsuccessful minor poets, will accept no verse translations not by contemporaries. But it so happens that earlier versions are better or that contemporaries, being very sheep-like in admiring the same few models, have not provided any versions — though of course this fact will be ignored. Further, as every copyright version must be paid (at least 15 dollars plus 2 guineas) I had to use 19th century or earlier versions often, even if contemporaries existed. So I can only let it go, and hope that the E.B. will not make too much of a mess of it, or be too vulgar in their publicity. Luckily, my agent got a clause which enables me to bar anything too vulgar or inaccurate. The state of affairs in England is such that Heinemann could present my late friend Gustave Cohen (then senior Professor Emeritus of the Sorbonne) as of "the Institut Delphique" which was a private affair for improving Franco-German relations but happened to be on the notepaper his secretary used in writing to them. Elek gloatingly insist on the pornographic aspects of Boccaccio as "sophisticated," which is exactly what they are not — being mostly "folk" or local Tuscan or Provençal tales. (A version of the Lamporecchio tale is told of himself by William IX of Aquitane.) [. . .]

Alas, no sooner am I free from the unprofitable (in a money sense) labours of the anthology, but a new yoke is put on my neck owing to the absurd and indecent fuss about Lady Chatterley in the USA.[4] Against the grain I have had to do an article for Encounter defending the book against the not always unfounded but obviously personally envious remarks of Katherine Ann Porter.[5] Then there is to be a big revival in Germany — the publisher wants a 30,000 words handbook, and also appoints me his adviser, which means a lot of work and thought. I have managed to evade introducing a new French pocketbook on him, but I dread the mails! They have raked up two or three old literary articles of mine in USA to republish. How absurd and distasteful is this making "news" out of some event which has nothing to do with literary merit. Think of the fuss about Ezra! If he had been torn in pieces by wild communists that would not make the Cantos one whit more intelligible.

There is much more real contact between the French and the Arabs than between the British and the Arabs, in spite of the British sentimentality about Arab Sheiks, the prince of Mecca etc. There are over a million Europeans in Algeria, many of them French; and there are at least 50,000 French refugees from the liberal govern-ments of Bourguiba and the king of Morocco.⁶ Not far from Marseille a new town to house 5000 of these tyrannous colonialists is being built. These things bring peoples closer in touch if not in friendship. It is easy for the Americans to be friendly with the Arabs — they know nothing whatever about them, and their main contact is the petrol-cash nexus.

Talking of poor translations from the Arabic, I have lately gone over again Burton's versions of the poems in the Nights.⁷ They are usually poor and some-times quite atrocious. His method is to try to copy servilely metrical structure, rhymes, puns, allusions, in a jargon so uncouth that the essential meaning of the poem is often quite obscured. They are much better and in my opinion more poetic in the French prose of Mardrus.

Apropos this — here is a tiny but not wholly insignificant instance of the "official boycott" on me. The UNESCO people issued a report on the translations of living British authors — Maugham 65, Priestley 50, Greene 40 — some such figures, but certainly no more. I counted up mine — 55, and I am not mentioned! Why? The Times and other papers used a Tass report (which I got in full from a French paper) citing me along with Maugham and Priestley as the three authors of England regularly paid by the USSR. This is true, but the English papers omitted my name — why? They did cite my name in another Tass report, on Eng. books in Russian but put me at the bottom linked with an avowed communist.⁸ Inciden-tally — since the Times won't publish the news — I hear from Mr Urnov at the Moscow Commissary of Foreign Literature that they are issuing (1) All Men Are Enemies in Jan 1960; (2) a new translation of Death of a Hero with an intro-duction by Urnov and a letter from me, also in 1960; (3) a selection of the stories in Soft Answers and Roads to Glory, in 1960, and (4) Urnov has strongly urged an English edition of the stories, to go alongside the Moscow English edition of Hero, and writes that the suggestion has been well received. The payments of course are ex gratia, as USSR and Imperial Russia were not signatories of the Berne Convention, and it is 250 pounds a year for British authors. I asked a friend of mine in UNESCO to try to find out from the Russians there — why 250, neither more nor less? But they were too cagey. Incidentally, this friend (a woman)⁹ says that not only are the Russians extremely good at their jobs but easily the hand-somest men in the whole show!

Forgive this unseemly boasting, but with the hostile British press suppressing (pun intended) anything in my favour, I feel I have a right to expatiate, and at least give the facts to a few friends. I think I might add that the new Russian History of English Literature gives me a whole chapter, and altogether allots me about 40 pages [. . .]

Christmas seems too degraded into "a conspiracy of tradesmen" (as old GBS rightly said) for one to be able to send any but strictly limited wishes! Still, this does bring my warmest good wishes, and grateful thanks for your help, and for your very kind letter about the woeful anthology.

Ever yours,
RICHARD ALDINGTON

¹ He has not been identified.
² That is, for the projected anthology.

3 Slonimsky.

4 See above, letter 133 n 6.

5 See Porter's "A Wreath for the Gamekeeper" in the Feb 1960 issue; RA's reply, "A Wreath for Lawrence?" appeared in April.

6 Mohammed V.

7 1885–88.

8 RA's exact references have not been found. His remarks arose from these circumstances. In London on 1 Dec 1959 Russia and Great Britain signed a cultural agreement. The next day the London *Times* carried the editorial "Getting to Know Each Other," which regretted that book publication was not included in the agreement. On Dec 4, Zhukov, Chairman of U.S.S.R. State Committee for Cultural Relations with Foreign Countries, replied to the editorial in a letter to the *Times*. Entitled "Anglo-Soviet Contacts Part That Books Can Play," the letter mentioned among other authors, Maugham, Priestley, Graham Greene, Sean O'Casey, Katherine Mansfield, and RA. A number of other letters to the *Times* on the same subject appeared in subsequent issues, ending on 10 Dec 1959.

9 Mrs Alister (Sheila) Kershaw.

138

4 March 1960   *Maison Sallé*

My dear Bird,

Under separate cover I send you a copy of a book "What *is* Wisdom?" by Cyril Upton,[1] on which I should much like to have your opinion. I do not know Upton personally, although I saw him at the Mistral Centenary banquet at Avignon in 1954. He is a Soci dou Felibrige, and adviser to them on all English-language activities dealing with Mistral. I heard, but cannot assert, that Upton was at one period Riviera correspondent for the Times. He must know the Orient pretty well, and he is a friend of Purcell who was a civil servant in the far East and now lectures at Cambridge. Upton must be a man of some means since he has a villa in Monaco as well as an address in Aix-en-Provence, of whose Académie he is a member.

His book impressed me, but then it is easy to be impressed on topics out of one's range. If you can spare time to look through the book, I should much like to know if you think I should recommend it to one of the university presses in America.

What an absurd epoch we live in. The decision of the Supreme Court, holding that Lady Chatterley is not obscene, has resulted in a quite fantastic DHL boom. It was already considerable, but it is now immense, simply because of newspaper twaddle about him. [. . .] After allowing Lawrence's books to remain out of print for 25 years the Viking Press of N.Y. are re-issuing them, and using the Introductions I did for the Penguins and Heinemann.[2] Last week I sent a preface to Seghers in Paris for a pocketbook he is issuing on DHL,[3] and with many groans I am trying to turn out a similar book for Rowolt in Hamburg,[4] who plans a big revival, including the new complete Letters which Moore is editing.[5] [. . .]

The E.B. eventually sent their cheque for the anthology, which of course implies definite acceptance; but they expressed no opinion, and have sent no proofs, though of course that will take a long time with so large a book.

The University Press of Southern Illinois at last sends announcements of the Mistral, but the list merely says "spring" without a definite date. The university blurb writer needs to brush up on it, for he writes of Mistral as French (not Provençal) and thinks Montpellier is in Provence.

My most interesting literary news, however, comes from Moscow. I am informed that they printed 20,000 copies of Death of a Hero in English, and have just issued in Russian 225,000 copies of All Men — perhaps I sent you a transcript of Urnov's letter? [6] I forget. [. . .]

I hope you managed to get through the winter without serious illness. The winter here has been mild, though rather too damp of late. Of course there is still time for more cold and even snow, if the wind changes.

An unexpected annoyance has dropped on me. In this remote cottage and at my age it is impossible to get on without a small car for shopping, and meeting visitors at the Cosne station — 12 kilometres. I have had a British license for 30 years, which automatically gave one the right to an annual International. I have held licences in USA, Italy, and Jamaica, but never in France. Suddenly the Ministry of Transport announces that British subjects domiciled abroad will no longer be allowed International licences — real bureaucracy in action! Consequently I had to go to Bourges and make application to pass a driving test, if you please. Driving almost every day I ought to be able to do it easily, but experience is by no means the same thing as knowing their Code de la Route, which has some sound points but is insanely complicated and over-detailed in others. There are sometimes two different road signs for the same thing; sometimes one sign is used to mean two different things; sometimes a sign means one thing in a built-up area and another on the open road! Ah well.

Ever yours,
RICHARD ALDINGTON

[1] *What is Wisdom? The World's Oldest Question Posed in the Light of Contemporary Perplexity* (1959).

[2] Viking published no such editions of Lawrence.

[3] *D. H. Lawrence: L'Œuvre et la vie* by F.-J. Temple.

[4] See above, letter 134.

[5] Rowolt did not publish Lawrence's letters.

[6] The letter written from Moscow on 28 Jan 1960 runs:
Your novel All Men Are Enemies has just been published in Russian translation and is very warmly received here. As I passed the bookshops on Pushkin's Street the other day I saw it myself — copies of your book being unpacked and disappear at once among an eager throng of booklovers. If you saw it, I thought, you would be moved and inspired. I want to congratulate you on that occasion and shake your hand in friendship.

M. URNOV

139

9 April 1960 *Maison Sallé*

MY DEAR BIRD,

I am deeply grateful to you for your brilliant analysis of Upton's book,[1] which points out to me aspects of it I had never suspected. I am a terre à terre person, with absolutely no mystic experience whatsoever, but I never deny that it (the mystic experience) may be real to others. So, in trying to be fair, I became too easily impressionable. And then, I have no training in philosophy. I was carried away by the fact that the "popular" books of to-day are in general so depraved and hysterical, and this seemed at least to be concerned with great issues. Where shall we end up, if the Americans continue to command the servile obedience of our governments? [. . .]

I wish I hadn't given my word to [write a "pocketbook" on D. H. Lawrence for Rowolt of Hamburg], for I am sick of DHL and sick of writing. I shall do no more.

I hope you will not condemn me when I say that I believe the Americans hoped to establish a world hegemony, and that the Russians have defeated it. Moreover, I believe that all this talk about War from Russia is simply the propaganda of the Pentagon and the American armaments-capitalists. And I do not say this for interested reasons, since the Russians have not paid me for my last book, though I know they have paid such deserving persons as Maugham, Priestley, and Graham Greene. I think of sending my correspondent in the USSR Union of Writers a text from Holy Writ: "To him that hath shall be given, and from him that hath not . . . xx." [. . .]

I managed to pass the driving test, but I was cheated by the examiner, to whom I gave the 1500 francs needed for the certificate. I found out at the Mairie [2] that he did not pay the money over to the Préfecture, but pocketed it. Of course, I have paid again, filled with respect for the integrity of bureaucracies. The license hasn't yet reached the Maire here — a very kind and good wine-growing peasant.

Do not lose touch with me. I am old and solitary, and your letters are always most welcome. My daughter does not neglect me, but she is now in the Institut de Sciences Politiques in Paris, and the work is very hard. So we meet only on holidays.

All good and kind thoughts to you,

RICHARD ALDINGTON

[1] See above, letter 138.
[2] Of Sury en Vaux.

                                          140

16 April 1960   *Maison Sallé*

MY DEAR BIRD,

Many thanks for your good letter which I was very glad to have, though sad to find that you can't approve of Upton's book.[1] It struck me as the work of a sincere and well-read man with whom I don't always agree, but whose view is in praiseworthy opposition to the dreadful "go-getting" of the modern world. After all, the USSR and the USA are sisters under their skin, with nothing to offer the world but propaganda, machinery, and destruction. It doesn't seem to me to matter whether the profiteers call themselves business executives or party members — it comes to the same thing, other people do the work, and they have the privileges, the datchas, etc.

I have been whirled about a good deal lately. With some Australian friends [2] I motored first to Zürich (to see H.D. whose novel Bid Me To Live,[3] is obviously booked to be a SUCCESS in USA) and then through a bit of southern Bavaria via Schaffhausen to Rottweil. I liked two Barok churches in Rottweil, one of which had a great set of 17th century processional lanterns on poles with painted coloured decorations — very pleasant. Then to Strasbourg — that wonderful Cathedral! — and to Colmar, where we spent a morning in the Unter den Linden Museum with the superb Grunwald paintings — "discovered" if I mistake not, by Huysmans. We ran south, spending a night at Bourg en Bresse, and a morning in the Eglise de Brou, which I had not seen since 1929. Much of the old convent has been renovated, turned into a regional museum, and thrown open to the public. I had not known that so late as the 16th century the canton of Vaud formed part of the duchy of Burgundy. All that area, north-west Suisse, south Bavaria, Alsace, Bourgogne even, are neither really French nor German. They should be federated into an independent state, with Suisse and the Pays Bas. Lorraine I feel is French, malgré le Général.[4]

After returning here, I had to go again to Zürich to pick up my daughter, and we motored back last week. After crowded and industrialised Suisse, country France is so beautiful. I think that from the frontier on we saw nothing horrible but the new skyscrapers of Dijon and petrol stations. The country was rich with wild flowers and fruit trees in full bloom. We reached Vézelay a little before eight, and the last 100 klms was made through a sleeping land, villages already closed down for the night, — so simple and laborious still is the life of the genuine French agricultural population. I thought of the absurd Anglo-Saxon journalists who ignorantly denounce France on the little they know — i.e. the restaurants, night clubs, strip-teases, Folies Bergères etc of Paris, which are mostly for foreigners.

The wild flowers this spring have been wonderful. I have never seen such sheets of anemones, cow-slips, ox-slips and primroses.

My daughter is spending Easter in her favourite haunt the Camargue, with another girl in a cabane de gardian. On Wednesday, she wrote, they were going over to see Lawrence Durrell and his wife; on Thursday they were going to ride all day; on Friday they were going to church at Li Santo; and on Saturday and Sunday there was the corrida. She wants to buy or rent a stone cottage in or near Maussane, which is close to the Moulin de Daudet. I must say I feel a nostalgie du Midi, though here one is better protected from the hordes of ignorant and noisy tourists.

Ever yours,
RICHARD ALDINGTON

[1] See above, letters 138 and 139.
[2] Mr and Mrs Geoffrey Dutton.
[3] 1960.
[4] That is, General de Gaulle.

141

14 May 1960   *Maison Sallé*

MY DEAR BIRD,

It was cheering to have your letter, since I have been feeling very miserable about the situation created by those Washington war-mongers. I think they have deliberately destroyed the chances of an understanding, partly from imperialist ambition, partly because too many persons in USA make huge profits out of cold war and are ignorant enough to suppose they might survive a sub-atomic war, and partly because the détente was largely started by England. Espionage goes on from both sides, and the Russians profit by their immense and secret fifth column. But a photographic flight is a violation of territory, hence an act of war, and it was insultingly staged on the 1st May.[1] What would the Americans say if a Soviet spy plane were shot down 500 kilometres from Washington on the 4th July? The Russians are very susceptible to insult, and this was a real slap in the face when they were (or seemed to me) trying to be friendly. K.[2] is not so almighty as it pleases the press to pretend, and, as the launchers of the attack well knew, the event places him right in the hands of the Soviet war party. Notice he is to be accompanied by Malinovsky,[3] while Vershinin cancels his visit to US.[4] It has put us back in the evil days of mutual suspicion and hatred; and one can only hope that in their rage with one another they don't start firing missiles.

I sometimes fear that there is no hope of Pater's letters turning up, but that they have been destroyed in accordance with the exaggerated Victorian susceptibility about "the sacredness of private life" from which modern psychology has rid us. I think it is Tennyson who commends an old lady who, on hearing that some private letters had been published, rushed upstairs and destroyed a whole trunkfull of letters to her from various important persons, screaming: "they were written to me, not to the public." But surely this is an excess of the possessive urge, and after the deaths of writers and recipient how could publication matter? while she doesn't reflect on the pleasure and possible instruction she withheld from posterity.

The taschenbuch on DHL went off to Hamburg on Thursday, and now that duty to Lawrence's memory is performed I don't expect to intrude on the public again.[5] One must not make rash statements on such future contingencies, but I have no intention of writing more if I can avoid it. I have refused four contracts already this year, and an offer of 2500 dollars to write an article for that infamous sheet, the Saturday Evening Post. I should be glad to earn 2500 dollars honestly but not by the kind of writing the SEP wants.

It is quite a mistake to suppose there is any interest in my books in England or even USA except for the translations (i.e. Boccaccio, Candide, Laclos,[6] which I suspect are sold as pornography, not as literature) and the "paperbacks" of Hero and TEL.[7] My sales are nearly all in foreign translations, and even the English copies are mainly sold abroad. Most of my books are out of print, and those still in print are simply the fag-end of editions which will never be re-issued. Some belated accounts from Heinemann received yesterday will give you the "picture." From June 1957 to June 1959 Religion of Beauty sold 28 copies, of which 19 were export; Pater sold 57, of which 35 were export; Portrait of a Genius, But . . . sold 322, of which 226 were export. All my novels, stories, biographies, essays, poems are out of print — except of course in foreign translations, on which I live. If the Anglo-American public really wanted to read me their enquiries for the books would soon stimulate reprinting.

I'd like to query the phrase about "standard of living is so high" in England now. Surely what you really mean is that the standard of *expense* or "spending" is so high. All this rushing about in cars and bikes, buying houses, washing-machines,

TV, refrigerators, radio, gramophone, transistor, cigarettes, etc. etc. is really rather "low," since it is done mostly on tick, and is accompanied by an almost total absence either of literary culture or the traditional culture which still lingers among the remote peasantry here. (The children of my neighbour Maxime have never been to the films, and he and his wife not for the past five years. Yet they can all sing, play the old tunes on the vieille and modern accordion, and dance bourrées — perfectly charming all of them.) Modern "civilisation," I think, is a cynical conspiracy to foist machines and machine products on the people, in order to profit utterly unscrupulous yahoo bosses, who through newspapers, films, comics, pulp, and all the ersatz "culture," including jazz, intentionally keep the people silly and vulgar. Inflation easily gives the spending money, though a time of reckoning always comes to inflation. But, there, I am a crank about this.

I think there can be no question but that you are right about the date of the Raleigh poem. I have never seen any question raised about the authenticity of the Bible story. The most scholarly and accurate of modern editors of our poetry is Norman Ault; and he merely notes: "The Prerogative of Parliaments 1628. (Poem written on the eve of his execution, 1618.)" [8] Thus, the picture [9] could not have been painted prior to 1618, and very probably not before 1628. Considering the situation, I should think that no painter would dare to show sympathy for Raleigh while Our Royal Solomon lived; and should guess the epoch, then, as Charles I. The only defence of the expert I can see is that the picture might have been painted in the 16th century, and the scroll added much later.

Since I got rid of my last literary incubus, I have been looking into Sir William Dampier's History of Science,[10] and am surprised to find how very high he rates Leonardo's achievements as scientist — among the highest. Mrs Taylor, who knows no more about Science than I do, rather scouts L's achievements — seems to despise him because although apples were falling every autumn he did not immediately produce the theory of gravitation. Dampier seems to put him almost with Archimedes and Galileo. I must re-read MacCurdy's translation of the Note Books,[11] which I have. End of page!

All good wishes,
RICHARD ALDINGTON

1 On May 5 Khrushchev had announced that, four days earlier, a U.S. plane, a U-2, had invaded Soviet territory and been shot down near Sverdlovsk. The pilot was Francis Gary Powers. The U.S. called it a weather observation plane strayed off-course at the Turkish-Soviet border. On May 7, Khrushchev revealed that Powers had admitted CIA connections and his mission, photo-reconnaissance. Powers was eventually sentenced to a ten year prison term as a spy.

2 Khrushchev.

3 To a Big-Four Conference in Paris.

4 A ten-day tour with nine other Soviet Air Force officers.

5 See above, letter 134.

6 1930, 1927, and 1924.

7 See above, letter 133.

8 RA refers to the poem "Even such is Time" found in Raleigh's Bible at his death. For Ault's statement cited here, see *Elizabethan Lyrics* ed Norman Ault (1925). The second edition (1928) vii and 536, n 481*a*, authenticates 1618 as the date of Raleigh's poem.

9 RA is commenting here on Bird's account of a portrait belonging to the Weld-Blundell estate exhibited at Liverpool's Walker Art Gallery. It was described as the portrait of an unknown

subject by Sister W. Relyes. Noting the poem "Even such is Time" on a scroll painted as part of the portrait, Bird had concluded it was one of Raleigh and discounted the attribution.

10 *Readings in the Literature of Science; Being Extracts from the Writings of Men of Science* eds Sir William Cecil Dampier and M. D. Dampier (1959).

11 See above, letter 113.

142

18 *November 1960*   *Maison Salle*

MY DEAR BIRD,

It is a great pleasure to have a letter from you again. I have been occupied with the difficulties arising from the fact that my daughter could not endure Paris or the Institut de Sciences Politiques, and wanted to transfer to the Faculté des Lettres at Aix-en-Provence. I got recommendations to various people including the Rector of Aix, Rostaign (who is now Capoulié of the Félibrige, of which I am an honorary Soci) but in spite of many kind words, we are still entangled in the coils of all-conquering Bureaucracy. The Paris students Union stole (in order to alter and sell) the original of her Baccalauréat certificate, which she should not have let them have. Montpellier refuses to issue another, though she is entitled to a decorative "parchemin," which are years in arrear, it seems. Paris refuses to transmit her dossier to Aix. And even Somerset House took 5 weeks to produce a birth certificate, though every detail was precisely given. However, she is attending lectures, and I suppose will eventually be properly registered. There are so many students and the staff of professors is so small and over-worked that she has to pay for a correspondence course.

I was three weeks in the Midi, came back on the 4th, and intend to go south again soon, and if possible to take my daughter to Rome for Xmas.[1] I don't look forward to the City as it is now — motorised and Americanised — but one must do the best one can.

The big anthology has not yet appeared in proof, though I sent my enormous script in twelve months ago. Back in the summer I enquired why the delay? and was told haughtily that my book is part of a series, that all the scripts are not in, and that the E.B. do not intend to start even asking permissions until all are in, "otherwise we should be involved in extra work." Recently I received from a London address a ballyhoo about the "series" — no names of literary editors yet mentioned — coupled with some absurd American trick for indexing all knowledge in a book. It is infuriating, but what can one do? I noticed that one of the directors or "editors" of this affair is Adlai Stevenson, who must indeed be hard up.

A similar annoyance has arisen with the German publisher Rowohlt, who wanted to cash in on the Lady C. uproar. I agreed to do him a 35,000 paperback on DHL, and to let him re-issue paperback of Death of a Hero.[2] For a time he was most obsequious, and then when he got my script of DHL in May (two days ahead of fixed date) he stopped writing, and I don't know if the thing is out or not.

So, although my health at last is very much better, I am sticking to my determination not to write any more. It is not worth while. And anyway, I've done enough.

If the Anglo-American are interested in my books, then why not re-issue them, as the Russians, Czechs, Italians etc. are doing?

Did you happen to see Colonel Meinertzhagen's Middle East Diary, 1917 to 1956 (Cresset Press, 1959)? Most people never heard of it, since it was apparently boycotted. It has some deadly stuff on TEL (who claimed M. as one of his best friends) including a 2-page vindication of my book.[3] I sent this to Times and N. Y. Times, pointing out that I have been vilified for what I said, and here is TEL's best friend emphatically agreeing that my book is "true." Haley sent a "friendly" letter brushing it aside; N. Y. Times said it is their rule never to publish letters except on matters they have dealt with — as if they are not now publishing pro-Prince of Mecca propaganda put out by Anthony Nutting, who is acting as paid publicity man for the Marlon Brando film of 7 Pillars! So I added more evidence, and sent the lot with the Times' two letters to a friend on the Writers Union in Moscow. Promptly came a reply that their "Literary Gazette" would have an article giving, or summarising, this evidence "in mid-November." One of Meinertzhagen's diary entries, which I sent, is pretty damning to Churchill, whom M. blames severely for his absurd "hero-worship" of TEL. By the way, Meinertzhagen was Chief Political Officer in Palestine, and then for two years shared a room with TEL at the Colonial Office. There has also been a long article, published in two sections, by some academic periodical in Japan — defending me, according to the author, a Professor Megata, but of course I can't read one character. The success of Rattigan's "Ross"[4] shows how completely the British are determined to support the myth. I shall do nothing more about it.

I think you overlook the main factor in the Lady C. case. Lawrence was a very poor man. Lane[5] could afford to hand out 10,000 pounds in "costs" to the lawyers, and with that douceur they were content to let him have a verdict. The witnesses for the defence were mainly the type of person who 32 years ago would have bitterly condemned the book, and joined in the man-hunt of Lawrence. I remember the day in November 1928 when we read the Lady C. reviews from England, and Lawrence grew so angry that next day he had a haemorrhage. It is surely typical of the British attitude to poets — Byron, Shelley, Keats, Lawrence — that they are hounded down in their lifetime, and when to the horror of the hounders the victim turns out to have been a great writer — in whom there is actually MONEY — they turn round and cringe to his "memory." Much good that does the handful of dust under that chapel in the Rockies.[6]

I hope all goes well with you, and above all that you have not lost your interest in literature.

Every good wish to you,

RICHARD ALDINGTON

[1] A holiday planned with Michael and Helen Harald. Owing to involvement with Sir Oswald Mosley, Michael Harald was prevented from going to Rome.

[2] *Death of a Hero* was not reissued. The book on D. H. Lawrence, published in 1961, is *David Herbert Lawrence in Selbstzeugnissen und Bilddokumenten*; see below, letter 145.

[3] See *Middle East Diary* under the date 20 Nov 1955. It runs, in part: "Richard Aldington has just published a book exploding the Lawrence Myth. It is a venomous book but true. Lawrence was the victim of his own desire for publicity but I blame the so-called Lawrence Bureau for pushing him into such an impossible position — men like Lowell Thomas, Storrs, and his own family. There are also men like Lloyd George, Winston Churchill, Allenby and Wavell who helped erect the myth and made the most extravagant claims for Lawrence's military genius.

Lawrence had great charm, great ability, and was in many ways a genius; he used all these virtues for deception. Not one single one of the men mentioned above had any first-hand knowledge from Lawrence himself and from what he spread about, knowing it to be either false or exaggerated. Comparing him with Napoleon and Hannibal is just nonsense for Lawrence never commanded anything but a looting rabble of murderous Arab levies, he took part in no major military operation, and his desert exploits had not the slightest bearing on Allenby's campaign. In his own words, his was a 'side-show of a side-show.'"

4 The stage play in which Alec Guiness played Ross (T. E. Lawrence).

5 Sir Alan Lane, managing director of Penguin Books, who issued an authorized, unexpurgated *Lady Chatterley's Lover* on 16 Aug 1960 in 12 copies. These were handed to the police, and the question of the book's obscenity became a test case of England's new law in respect to obscenity, effective in 1959. In a six day trial which ended Nov 2 the court declared the book not obscene and on 10 Nov 1960 Lane was allowed to release the book to the public. The trial cost Penguin Books about $28,000.

6 That is, D. H. Lawrence.

143

3 *January 1961*   *Maison Sallé*

MY DEAR BIRD,

The Rome introduction *was* longer, much longer.[1] I was so much annoyed by its being slashed to bits by a half-educated "editor" that I planned to send it out as a Xmas card, and paid an amateur printer in these parts to run off 100 copies or so.[2] Alas, as you will see, he made a mess of it; and by way of rounding out his task, went off for his holiday and dumped on me the sheets unfolded and unstitched! I have done the best I can, and you must throw it away after looking through it. From a title-page I have cut his advertising of a work I disapprove.

My good-humour over this fiasco was deepened by the next packet I opened — advance copy of the DHL pocketbook I did for Rowohlt. Snappy newspaper headlines have been substituted (without my consent) for my sober, I, II, III etc. Russell's photo is marked "Sir Bertrand Russell." Pino is labelled "Reggie Turner" and Reggie "Orioli." "Young" photos are given of such beauties as Edward Garnett and JMM,[3] while the once beautiful Lady Cynthia[4] is shown as an old woman. Finally, again without my consent, the book is ended with a set of "opinions" about DHL, including those of my dislike — Spender and Simone de Beauvoir, not to mention Russell. In the bibliog Nehls's composite biography[5] becomes "compositive." Hell.

Against this I must tell you that owing to good friends of mine in Moscow the Russian Literary Gazette ran an article on TEL, Rattigan, the film, quoting Meinertzhagen, and also letters from Haley and the N. Y. Times to me evading publication of the Meinertzhagen piece.[6] This is being translated into English, and I'll send you a copy. The only fly there is that soon after the Lit. Gaz. published a poem by Mr Lumumba, who is not one of my white-headed boys, though doubtless much calumniated by the bourgeois press.

The German DHL will come to you when I get my extra copies. Did you see F. J. Temple's book in French with my intro?[7] Latter was penned long before the new Lady C. rumpus, and I found with satisfaction that I had kicked off by repudiating Lady C. as one of DHL's best books. Two million — a scandal, which almost makes one sympathize with the wowsers, Dr. Fisher, Dame Edith, etc. I venture to say that not one in a 1000 was bought as literature — but as pornography. Durrell, who in some ways is a man of genius, almost starved on his poems and excellent travel books, but now that he has tapped the Alexandria "sex" theme,[8] he is opulent. As a feeble and obscure protest I have allowed the cancelled passages of Hero to be restored in the pending re-issues in Russian, Polish, Czech, and German, but not in English.

Well, that's enough about that.

In spite of the yanks, the traffic, and the noise, I found Rome wonderful, and did wish I could have stayed on. But lectures start at the University here to-day, and I couldn't let Catherine return alone. I simply *wallowed* in the most 1875 aestheticism — Pater and I would have walked arm-in-arm — and was thoroughly happy. I thought the Church music and singing greatly improved — the American influence perhaps, for the church music in N. Y. is excellent — and rejoiced to hear Mass sung by a Cardinal on Xmas day in S. M. Maggiore. The Santa Culla in its lovely Renaissance shrine of crystal with gold putti was on the altar.

Have you been in the Vatican Pinacoteca? The collection of Italian Primitives is much finer than of old — best in the world, I should think. There is a lovely Sir Thomas Lawrence (that name again!) portrait of our late dread sovereign leige, G.R. IV, in a sumptuous costume (with a sword) probably of his own devising — he obliterates the Popes and Cardinals in the room. I found I like Raphael more, and Angelo a little less than of old — but the Pietà and the Moise are still marvellous. Capella Sistina looked faded. I looked with interest at the S. Pietro monument to Paul III, on which M-Angelo, with superb irony, placed naked statues of Giulia Farnese and her pimping mother-in-law,[9] to whom of course the Farnese owed their power. Alas, some prudish Pope put tin nightgowns on them, after sticking fig-leaves on all the statues in the Vatican galleries.

Pater's fortune — I didn't know. Mrs Rachel Taylor misled me on that, saying she felt sure he could not have worked so disinterestedly and also supported his sisters unless some money had been left. Perhaps it went to the girls?

In the garden of the hotel Rivoli, where we stayed, was the small sarcophagus of Terentius Verus, who lived VI years, IV months and II days, inscribed by his father, also Terentius Verus, and his mother, of the Caecillia gens — now used to grow geraniums. Pulvis et umbra . . .

I must humbly confess that I'm not a Great Expectations fan. Pickwick, Copperfield, Bleak House, Nickleby, Twist, almost all the Boz and other sketches — but not the detestable Italian and American — Chuzzlewit, though, but not particularly Tale of 2 Cities [10] — so false . . . But he is one of our greatest, and always to be defended against the Eliots and such-like denigrators. Pound is the silliest.

All thanks for your card and kind letter and good wishes. May all be well in 1961 for you.

Ever yours,
RICHARD ALDINGTON

[1] That is, the introduction to *Rome: A Book of Photographs* (1960).

[2] A *Tourist's Rome* printed by Count Potocki; see above letter 133, below letters 144 and 145.

[3] John Middleton Murry.

[4] Lady Cynthia Asquith.

[5] See above, letters 131 n 2 and 133.

[6] D. Zhantieva "Unmasking A False Hero" *Literaturnia Gazeta* 3 Dec 1960.

[7] See above, letter 138 n 3.

[8] In *Justine* (1957); *Balthazar,* and *Mountolive* (1958); and *Clea* (1960); published as *The Alexandria Quartet* (1962).

[9] Adriana de Mila.

[10] 1860–1, 1837, 1849–50, 1852–3, 1838–9, 1837–8, 1836–7, 1843–4, 1859.

144

12 February 1961   *Maison Sallé*

MY DEAR BIRD,

I am back in Sury, after more than two months of delightful vagabondage with Catherine in Aix and the Camargue, with the fortnight in Rome. Of course I had to celebrate it with a second "go" of bronchitis, so that I am still barking in a wearisome way night and day like an idiotic dog. But the mild weather helps very much. I see with concern that the weekly influenza mortality in England has passed the 1000. This may be newspaper sensationalism. There are always elderly casualities from respiratory diseases in winter, and — well, we know sadly what journalism is.

Why does one learn so often just a bit too late? You will remember that in the little Rome piece I mentioned Leo X's emerald eye-glass, copied from Nero.[1] After the thing was in the infamous print of the local genius I came on a letter of Ariosto from Rome when he was sent as envoy to Leo by the duke of Ferrara.[2] It is dated the 7th April 1513, and Ariosto says that he would not have believed it if he had not seen it himself, but that since he has come to be Pope, Giovanni has abandoned his eye-glass [3] — and all the courtiers pretend to be short-sighted! It is one up to H.B.[4] that he felt an eye-glass was incompatible with the decorum exacted of a Pope.

We saw the Manger on Xmas Day in S. M. Maggiore, though not so closely as I did on Xmas Eve 1923. The châsse of crystal and gold Cupids is lovely. No, San Stefano delle Carrozze is still there — close to S.M. in Cosmedin, but only 19 of the original 20 columns are there.

I think the "stones" of Rome carried to build other cathedrals were not all marble, though Lanciani makes it sound so.[5] Possibly as Rome had little to export but Peter's pence, out-going ships carried stones and marbles as ballast. This would account for Pisa, Salerno and Amalfi, and even Lucca and Westminster were on rivers accessible to ships. Orvieto is the problem. They would have to be carried by ox-cart. I've never read Dean Stanley's book on the Abbey,[6] and know not who would be able to tell us about the foreign stones used. They would mostly be used as rubble packing for walls and piers, as in S. Pietro, I think.

I enclose the Russian Literary Gazette article,[7] which pleases me. After a whole year I have at last got hold of the excellent article in the Gazette de Lausanne,[8] which I had failed to find because it was erroneously reported as being in the Journal de Genève. The author, Miss or Mrs Thérèse Lavauden is now a school-mistress at Roedean! I must write to her, but don't quite know what to say. I made a translation to send to los yanquis, who never know anything. The original has gone to Paris with enquiries about photostats. Unluckily the form of the lit supp to the Gaz de Laus. is that of a newspaper, and as the article occupies the better part of 4 long columns on page I, and thirds of two columns within, the technical problem of photostating is considerable. If my friends in Paris can't get this done, I must send you a carbon of my translation, with apologies.

My Russian publisher, Mr Puzikov, head of the State Fiction Publications, sends me a magnificent fur cap, and asks for a photograph. When I can get to Cosne, I must have it done. As they have in the press a new version of Hero, and a collection of stories, I daresay they can use it in their literary mags. The questionnaire they sent was most conscientious and intelligent — a complete contrast to the money-making Rowohlt. Considering that they are outside the Berne convention, I find it pleasant that they asked my permission to move the story Farewell to Memories from the last place in Roads to Glory to the first. I put it last because I like to finish with a sprint, instead of a Wyndham Lewis flop; but they are quite right — it is the best of the lot. I shouldn't say so, but if the yanko-saxons were not warmongering imbeciles they would have recognised it.

I think they (USSR) are so scared of Ezra that they are leaving out Nobody's Baby,[9] though even he could scarcely say it is a panegyric. You will have seen that the Writers Union (my friends) are starting a new press agency, supplementing Tass. The D. Tel. reporting, omitted the "Writers Union," and said it was "a rival." Really, one's contempt for the capitalist press grows daily. Anyway, from the very warm-hearted and (I am sure) sincere letters I get from Mikhail Urnov and Mrs Zhantieva, I infer that the writers are very far from toe-ing the Party Line, but have to go cautiously — and we must help them. They want peace and culture. What do the Beaver, the Rother,[10] the yanquis want, but Cold War and more Money For Them?

True, at one time Lord Byron was too fat, but he starved himself relentlessly back to beauty. Do you not remember his first dinner with Sam Rogers and Moore? He refused all delicacies, asked for biscuits and soda water, and when those failed dined on potatoes in vinegar? He was wrong about the potatoes. The British, as usual, are idiotic about Byron. Not even Shakespeare had so immense an influence — from Petersburg to Lisbon to Philadelphia to Buenos Ayres. And he was a man of noble charity and generosity — which his denigrators were not.

The battle of DHL is won, and now I find myself in the position of trying to explain to BBC and other exploiters and cashers-in that I have nothing more to say. As long as the battle lasted I was there, and now leave with all wounds in front. They can now slobber over him and Frieda all they want, but without me.

With all good wishes,

Ever yours,
RICHARD ALDINGTON

---

1 See above, letter 133 n 5.

2 Alfonso d'Este I.

3 Pope Leo III's baptismal name was Giovanni de'Medici.

4 Horatio Brown.

5 Lanciani wrote numerous books about Rome, but RA probably refers to *Ancient Rome in the Light of Recent Discoveries* (1888).

6 *Memorials of Westminister Abbey* (1865).

7 See above, letter 143.

8 Miss Lavauden published two articles in the *Gazette de Lausanne* in 1960: "La Musique dans l'oeuvre de Fantin Latour" and "Au-dessus de la mêlée." RA probably refers to the latter.

9 The satire of Pound in *Soft Answers*; see above, letter 2 n 12.

10 That is, Beaverbrook and Rothermere.

145

6 July 1961   *Maison Sallé*

MY DEAR BIRD,

Unless a letter has been lost I have not heard from you since November of last year, and hope that this does not mean illness or other troubles. Let me have a word.

Did I send you the pamphlet I had privately printed (or rather misprinted) in France — A Tourist's Rome, and the booklet on DHL I wrote for publication in German? The latter is well illustrated with photographs, but has some omissions which I could have supplied if the publisher had condescended to consult me. It is typical of the contemporary publisher's impudence that Rowohlt [. . .] announced the book in the German press as the work of their "editor" Kurt Kusenberg, without mentioning my name! [1] The German notices were disappointing, all by mere journalists who knew nothing about DHL but what they gained from the book. If there are any real German critics they're not interested in DHL. Yet, Burns apart, he is the one great working class "genius" we have produced, and worthy someone's attention. Rowohlt, on my exhortation, are now bringing out Twilight in Italy, Sea and Sardinia, Mornings in Mexico, and Etruscan Places,[2] which are surely greater artistic achievements than Lady C. I am now trying to persuade them to issue a book of DHL's shorter travel sketches — most of them in Phoenix [3] or in the Selected Essays I did for Penguin.[4] Even more important, I am trying hard to induce my friends of the USSR Writers Union to start re-issuing DHL, who seemingly was banned some time during the Stalin régime — heaven knows why, perhaps Russell's rot about DHL being a Nazi. I may be biassed by their friendliness to me, but my impression is that the Russian writers and publishers are far more "liberal" than the capitalist press asserts. The country is not such a rigid C.P. monolith as our journalists proclaim. I was looking over All Men Are Enemies, and wondering how the devil it got by, unless indeed they made cuts. I think it one up to USSR that foreign books for translation are chosen by the *writers* and not by the *publishers*, and apparently the money earned by Soviet writers goes to them rather than to the intermediaries. Urnov is a critic and historian of English literature, yet he has a nice flat in Moscow, a datcha on the Black Sea, and apparently is allowed to write much as he likes. I have kind letters from other Russians, and can't believe they are false. A human touch — their publishers are as incompetent and dilatory as our own. The volume of my short stories scheduled for January, appeared in late May! [5] Urnov says it practically sold out on publication. Considering that our highbrows dismissed both books as negligible I feel some satisfaction in finding them accepted 30 years later by the countrymen of Tolstoy and Chekov.

I have good news from other fronts. The USA is certainly coming round again. I have lately signed agreements for large "paperback" editions in USA of my Decameron and the Life of DHL, and my agent is negotiating for two others about which she is hopeful.[6] I have done articles on Mistral and the bogus prince of Mecca (the latter uncompromising) for a new edition of Collier's Encyclopaedia; a 3000 words article on Wellington for Americana; and have just had an invitation to do a new Pater for the Britannica. The Americana editor liked the Wellington, and hinted at further orders. [. . .] And there are other developments in other countries. I think my plan should be to concentrate on them, particularly USSR and USA, and leave our countrymen to brood over their bad temper aroused in defence of such Galahads as Norman Douglas and T. E. Lawrence. It will be interesting to see what happens when the great American film of TEL appears, with the "good taste" (according to its publicity agent, Anthony Nutting) of "a screen showing 500 Turkish corpses."

I spent Xmas in Rome with my daughter, and had a magical 6 weeks in Venice in April-May.[7] After these French fields, it was an immense stimulus to live once more with the arts again. I must try to do a little piece on Venice for a few private friends. Do you know about Gabriele Bella? There are about 50 pictures of his in the Palazzo Querini-Stampalia — which very few people visit. They have practically no aesthetic value, but as "documents" of Venetian life and episodes in the 18th century are truly fascinating. No photographs obtainable, but I hope to return to Venice later with a friend who is an expert photographer (amateur, and not Mr Armstrong-Jones) and to take the whole lot. I spent hours with them. Also, poor dear Ruskin was too prejudiced. The 16th, 17th and 18th centuries produced marvels in Venice. I revelled in the super-Barocco of the Scalzi and the Gesuati. The angels on the façade of the latter hold real incense-burners, which sway and clatter in the breeze. I often lunched at the Locanda Montin on the Zattere, in the garden, listening to the blackbirds and a nightingale. It is certainly the restaurant described by J. A. Symonds. When one gets away from the Americans, even my primitive spoken Italian secured a warm and friendly welcome.

My daughter has just taken her Propédeutique at Aix-en-Provence. I don't know what the English equivalent is. She has her first and second Baccalauréat, and this is the last University exam on general topics — which incidentally I couldn't have passed. She had to do an English translation of a difficult passage from Maupassant with dissertation; a long dissertation on a passage from Supervielle; and another on the Marché Commun. She now proposes to specialise in practical psychology, and the exams will be less exacting. As a University man you will understand why the 1st and 2nd Bac and the Propédeutique are made so severe, to eliminate students who have no real gifts, who don't know what to do with themselves, whose parents can afford to keep them at the university. Now, it will be all solid training.

Forgive all this egotism, and do give me news of yourself. You "hide your life" as carefully as Pater himself! I am glad of the chance to do him justice in the Encyclo.

Yours sincerely,
RICHARD ALDINGTON

¹ Because he was editor of Rowohlt's monographs, "Klassiker der Literatur und der Wissenschaft," of which RA's book on Lawrence was no. 51. See above, letter 142.

² 1963 (in one volume).

³ *Phoenix: The Posthumous Papers of D. H. Lawrence* ed with an Introduction by Edward D. McDonald (1936).

⁴ 1950.

⁵ See above, letter 130 n 5.

⁶ See below, letter 147.

⁷ See RA's letter to John Gawsworth, written from Sury on 11 Mar 1961 (a Saturday): "I leave here on Monday for the south of France en route to Venice where I expect to be for a few weeks, having a literary job which can only be done there" (Texas).

146

11 August 1961   *Maison Sallé*

MY DEAR BIRD,

If I left a letter from you unanswered it was a bad oversight, since I greatly value your views and comments. I thought also I had sent the Taschenbuch on DHL. A copy comes to you under separate cover. [. . .] It seems clear that Rowohlt cannot be in touch with real German criticism, for not one article was worth the paper it was printed on. The reverse happened in France to the Introduction I wrote to F. J. Temple's excellent book on DHL.¹ I sent a torpedo through the French "legende" of DHL, and nearly all the reviews had the decency to admit the fact. The one exception was somebody sucking up to Malraux, greatly indignant that I brushed aside that superb genius with the rest. I read Malraux's introduction to the French Lady C.² — a very good essay on erotic literature which might have prefaced anything from Aristophanes to Henry Miller, but showed no real knowledge of DHL. They all dogmatise about him without having really read him. You are quite right, he is *the* genius, and in comparison Hemingway and Greene are journeymen. Lawrence never wrote for a market; they did. "Not I, but the wind that blows through me . . ." He meant the Hagion Pneuma of course.

Apropos which in one of my novels — forget which — a careful publisher's reader changed it for me to Hag*ia* Pneuma. Another turned Goya's Los Desastres into Desastros. Thus are we served by the omniscient gents who preside over publishing.

I am delighted by your enthusiasm for Venice, and much obliged by the Bella references, which will be useful if I ever get back to the Querini palace with my photographing Australian professor.³ But really I know too little about Venetian history and art to venture anything but a little personal "A Tourist's Venice" and perhaps something on Bella if I can discover something about him.⁴ The brief remarks I have seen stress the pictures of public ceremonies, and the usual reference to "costume" comes I infer from the article of Mazzarotto you list.⁵ What interested me is the series of popular fêtes and celebrations. The ritual fist-fight on a bridge recalls the annual fight over Osiris, but no doubt it is a pure coincidence. After all our own countrymen had plenty of fist-fights over nothing in particular, but the Venetian one seems to have been an annual ritual. I suppose the Corso delle Cortegiane was a race of harlots? And who were the Solaciere who raced with the Ballottine? Bella is not always contemporary — he has an imagined

"Entrance of Henri III in 1574." And his pictures of the Ten in council must surely be as imaginary as would be a picture of the British Cabinet.

I have looked longingly at the outside of the Palazzo Labia, but never dared to present myself, having no credentials, not even a visiting card. The room at the Rezzonico is wonderful. And I am fascinated by the "Pagliacci" frescoes from Villa Zianigo. Wandering one day from S. Stae towards the Zattere I came on the Scuola dei Carmini, which I'd never seen before, and was quite conquered by the very mondaines Virtues and Vices of Tiepolo. The custode, a sulky fellow smoking a pipe (!) yielded to the seduction of cento lire, and reluctantly produced some not very good photographs. I can appreciate these and other Venetian splendours, but I am too ignorant to write about them, except perhaps for a very few indulgent friends.

Pater may have avoided Venice because he felt it had been taken over by Ruskin and by his contemporary Symonds. Ruskin really loved Venice, and I was pleased to see that acknowledged on the plaque to his memory on the Zattere pensione. But he was terribly at ease on Zion, and mis-directed by the sectarian hybris of his otherwise admirable parents. In the Stones [6] he denounces Renaissance and still more Barocco art as "popery." But surely "popery" was more of a menace in the days of Hildebrand and Innocent III, than under the amiable scholars of the Settecento or even the pagan simonists of the Renaissance? I don't think the Renaissance Popes wanted to overthrow the Ancient Faith — even Leo X — or Alexander VI. They had the nostalgic longing to reconcile Christianity with the Ancient Religions. It can't be done, but I feel tender towards the attempt.

As you justly say, Symonds was nearer to us. But he "profited" (as the French say) by what Ruskin achieved, and at the same time was far more open-minded. I like J.A.S., and only wish that some of the statues of the divinised Marcus Aurelius didn't betray some of the same weakness and angst in their features. But I like to follow in his footsteps, and like to think that the Locanda Montin is the place he describes so charmingly. There is another garden restaurant near the Salute, but I didn't go to it since it advertises too blatantly, and so suggested Americans to my suspicious mind. I lunched at the locanda at Torcello, a charming setting and good food, but the minimum menu is 3000 lire — too much for the likes of us — and tables were "Reserved for Harry's New York Bar visitors" who, alas, turned up. If you want to see over-wealthy Americans at their worst, look at the enclosed from the Figaro on Monte Carlo.[7] Is it any wonder that so much of the Midi votes communist? I also enclose the latest Figaro on the prince of Mecca, but I daresay it is in full blast in England.[8] This is the first European notice I have seen which admits the complicity of Nutting. While the US papers were booming him like a new soap, none of the European notices I saw mentioned him. And they claim that the Political Establishment has no control of the "press"!

It is so kind of you to enliven my solitude with your learning and appreciation of the things which mean so much to me. The "not-my-cup-of-tea" school seems to reign in London!

Ever yours,
RICHARD ALDINGTON

[1] See above, letter 138 n 3.
[2] 1932.
[3] Geoffrey Dutton.

[4] Bird suggested that RA write some such book.

[5] Possibly in *Le Feste veneziane. I Giochi popolari, le ceremonie religiose e di governo* by Bianca Mazzarotto Tamassia (1961).

[6] *Stones of Venice* (1861–63).

[7] 8 Aug 1961.

[8] That is, Anthony Nutting *Lawrence of Arabia* (1961). For the article in *Figaro*, see the issue of 10 Aug 1961.

147

5 February 1962   *Hotel de Sévigné, Aix en Provence, B. du R.*

MY DEAR BIRD,

Please try to forgive me for omitting the usual greetings. I am only just recovering from another severe attack of bronchitis, and everything is an effort. Besides, in spite of its tradition, its university, and its Law Courts, Aix is rather a philistine town. (There is not a text of Shakespeare to be bought here!) I shall try to send you something of interest later, especially if I go to Venice in the spring; which may be.

The school of Verocchio picture is charming, and certainly (if one may judge from a reproduction) genuine. My sister[1] sent me a Sth Kensington terracotta (15th cent) which looks like della Robbia school influenced by Verocchio or even Leonardo. A clever modern Italian forgery? Remember that "Etruscan tomb" the B.M. displayed so proudly? It was far too elegant to be genuine, which the B.M. at last had to admit. Recently, the Metropolitan has admitted its polychrome "Etruscan warriors" are forgeries — I thought so the moment I first saw them in 1935. And now you tell me of the doubts about Evans.[2] Last year I got from the London Library a couple of recent books on Crete, and noticed the authors were rather severely critical. Should archaeologists "restore" so freely to attract visitors? I haven't seen the recent work at Pompeii, but the Director[3] (just retired) there seems to have rebuilt the ruins to please himself. Which doesn't console me for the barbarity of the Americans in shelling the place.

I shall try to get hold of Horatio Brown,[4] as you suggest, but, the secondhand shops now in these regions either cater for American libraries or have nothing but rubbish. Perhaps my London bookseller may find it. Meanwhile, Lawrence Durrell (who lives near Nimes) picked up and gave me a French translation of P. Molmenti's Private Life of the Venetians.[5] Many interesting details, including a long description of the visit of Henri III. He was king of Poland, and passed through Venice on his way back to France when unexpected deaths made him king of France. The scenes must have been of great splendour.

You never tell me anything about yourself. Have you a chair at Liverpool? Or are you a private philosopher?[6] Forgive my ignorance — I am so out of touch with England.

Yes, people sent me cuttings about Nutting's book,[7] and even the extract in The S. Times where he displayed his ignorance by insinuating I had concocted a letter from TEL which exists in the B.M. Library.[8] The S.T. refused a letter from an American scholar pointing out Nutting's blunder.[9] Instead they published a communication (Liddell Hart under a pseudonym) containing the preposterous lie that "Lawrence always wanted the truth" and sneering at me as "scrappy," while quoting the exact words of the letter.[10] I was "scrappy" because the Lawrence Trust forbade me to quote literally (or rather verbatim) so I was forced to give the information in paraphrase, which in fact was made (as in other cases) by a solicitor. If the Lawrences "want the truth" why did they forbid me to quote his works and essential letters? An American scholar (Dr. Weintraub of Pennsylvania) is writing a thesis on Lawrence and GBS.[11] When he arrived at the Bodleian he was refused all access to the Lawrence papers "by order of Sir A. W. Lawrence." Why?

But you are mistaken in thinking there is no public interest in TEL. "Ross" is still running in London, and has been well received on Broadway, though it was laughed off the Paris stage. Sam Spiegel (Bridge of Kwai)[12] is just completing a sensational "Lawrence the hero" film,[13] for which Nutting has been acting as hired publicity man in the USA. Strange to say, this has increased my sales. [. .] Moreover, the Americans, after saying "there is no interest in TEL in America" are suddenly alerted by the film pre-publicity. Crowell-Collier have just issued my DHL as a paperback. In Feb. there will be a paperback Decameron in the USA,[14] and a hardback reprint of Cyrano de Bergerac.[15] Folio Book Society London (also in Feb) will re-issue an illustrated Laclos.[16] Paperbacks of that and of my own books are under consideration in N.Y. and London. And the Russians have backed me most generously. The Establishment effort to discredit and suppress me has thus failed, though of course they did much temporary harm. "Sir, no man was ever written down except by himself." So I have stopped writing! Let them reprint the old stuff if they like. I shall do no more.

I'll try to send you copies of any reprints which I think you might like to turn over. But the meanness of the contemporary publisher now extends to the author's free copies. They send one, instead of the old-time six (Eng.) or ten (USA). In the modern book racket the least important and least-paid person concerned is the author.

I intend to stay on here (though hotel and restaurants are too dear) until milder weather allows me to return to the more economical conditions of Sury. Another attack of bronchitis might turn to pneumonia, which is not advisable in a solitude with only a few over-worked peasants as neighbours. And I don't want to trouble my daughter, who has a very difficult Psychology Course at the University here.

All good wishes for 1962.[17]

Yours ever,
RICHARD ALDINGTON

[1] Mrs Margery Gilbert.

[2] Evans's findings in respect to a Minoan civilization, based on his excavations at Crete, were sharply questioned with the deciphering of two scripts, Linear B by Michael Ventris in 1953 and Linear A by Cyrus Gordon in 1961.

[3] Dr M. Della Corte.

[4] One of Brown's four books on Venice: *Venetian Studies* (1887); *Venice, an Historical Sketch* (1893); *In and Around Venice* (1905); *Studies in the History of Venice* (1907).

[5] *La Vie privée à Venise depuis les premiers temps jusqu'à la chute de la Republique* (1882).

[6] A private philosopher. Bird is actually a critic, a dramatist, an educator who writes and lectures; see above, Introduction.

7 See above, letter 146 n 8; the book was widely reviewed.

8 In the issue of 15 Oct 1961.

9 Stanley Weintraub.

10 No such letter has been found. A letter headed "Lawrence's Confessions" and signed by K. J. Fielding appeared in *The Sunday Times* for 17 Sept 1961; it comments on the fact that the British Museum had mislaid a letter from Lawrence to Mrs Shaw.

11 Subsequently published as *Private Shaw and Public Shaw* (1962).

12 *The Bridge on the River Kwai*, the film in which Alec Guiness played the leading rôle.

13 The film *Lawrence of Arabia*, for which Mike Wilson prepared one script and Robert Bolt, another. David Garnett was retained as a consultant, but nothing he suggested was used. (See Garnett to B. H. Liddell-Hart, Hilton, Huntington 5 and 11 Jan 1963 [Texas]). The film was released late in 1962 with Peter O'Toole playing the part of Lawrence.

14 No record of such publication has been located.

15 RA's translation of *Voyages to the Moon and the Sun*, re-issued by Orion Press, 1962.

16 That is with wood-engravings by Raymond Hawthorn. RA's translation with a foreword by Harry Levin also appeared in the United States in 1962 as a Signet Classic, a paperback.

17 This last letter which RA wrote to Bird is dated less than six months before his death. On 23 June 1962 RA and his daughter arrived in Russia for a three week's stay as the guest of the Soviet Writers' Union. There on July 8, his seventieth birthday was celebrated with flowers, telegrams, and a warm encomium. It was a satisfying visit, but it left him exhausted. Once back in Sury, RA did not recover his energy and, on the morning of 27 July 1962, having gone to fetch his mail, he fell ill and sank to the doorstep of his home with a heart attack. His neighbors, the Gueneaus, helped him into the house, but he died before the day was done.

Index and Biographical Glossary

THE INDEX, limited to names of persons (and one bull) and titles of literary works, refers to the introduction with an I and to the letters by number. The biographical glossary attempts to provide information about everyone mentioned by name in the text of the letters. Owing to editorial insufficiency or to the fact that a few of those mentioned failed to attain enough prominence to leave an accessible record and that others, once well known, have fallen into oblivion, the glossary lacks some biographies. Any person whose name occurs only in the notes is listed without a biography.

Aaron's Rod (D. H. Lawrence) 14, 103
Abbaye De Montmajour, L' (Benoit) 18
Abbot, E. 126
Abd-ul-Aziz 7
Abdullah ibn al Hussein (1882–1950), the sherif of Mecca's second son whom T. E. Lawrence first met at Jiddah in 1916. Abdullah lost Hejaz, ruled from 1916 by his father Husein ibn Ali, to Ibn Saud in 1924. Abdullah was named first emir of Jordan in 1923 and then king of Jordan in 1946. He led the British-trained Arab Legion, the most efficient fighting unit in the Arab world, against Israel in 1948. Abdullah died by assassination on 20 July 1951. 14, 17, 21, 41, 118
Abdu-r-Rahman 93
Abercrombie, Lascelles (1881–1938), English poet, playwright, and theorist of poetry. What he considered his masterpiece, "The Sale of St. Thomas," a verse drama, appeared in the first volume of *Georgian Poetry: 1911–1912.* 36
Abu Nuwas (d. ca. 810), Arabic poet 28
Achilini, Claudio (1574–1640), Italian lawyer and poet 133
Account of the Bell Rock Lighthouse, An (Stevenson) 111
Acta Sanctorum (ed Van Bolland) 115
Acton, John Emerich Edward Dahlberg Acton, 1st baron (1834–1902), English historian, a noted liberal and Roman Catholic, Acton wrote *History of Freedom* (1907). 91, 115
Across the Plains with Other Memories and Essays (Stevenson) 109
Addison, Joseph (1672–1719), English writer whose essays contributed much to the success of Richard Steele's *Tatler* and *Spectator* 53
Adenauer, Konrad (1876–1967), German statesman known as "Der Alte." Adenauer urged German reunification through free elections and insisted on Western European cooperation and, with France's de Gaulle, a Europe independent of the U.S. 48
Adone (Marino) 15, 69, 118

Adventures of a Bookseller (Orioli) 25
Africa in Black and White (Dutton) 117
Aga Khan (1877–1957), Indian leader and hereditary head of the Mohammedan Ismali sect, famed for his wealth 67
Agathias (fl. 6th c.) called *"la Scolastique,"* a Byzantine author who wrote a history of Justinian and a book of poems and epigrams 134
Aglaura (Suckling) 47, 48, 50
Ahmed, Sheik (ca. 1897–1917), nicknamed Dahoum meaning "Darkness," whom T. E. Lawrence first encountered in 1912 at Carchemish where Dahoum was the "donkey boy." Lawrence taught him photography and in 1913 took him and Sheik Hamoudi, foreman of the dig, to Oxford; they were lodged in Lawrence's cottage in the garden of the Lawrence home on Polstead Road. Dahoum died of typhus at Damascus in November 1917. According to some opinion, Lawrence's chief motive for the "Arab affair" was Dahoum. See the letter to G. J. Kidston, [Oxford], 15 Nov 1919, in which Lawrence explained his motives "in order of strength," listing first a personal one: "I liked a particular Arab very much, and I thought that freedom for the race would be an acceptable present." Some writers have identified Dahoum as that Arab. 11, 19, 84
Aicard, Jean 14
Akenside, Mark (1721–70), English physician and writer best known for *The Pleasures of Imagination* (1744) and a number of poems 57
Albany, Countess of 14
Alcestis (tr RA) 64, 65, 66, 67
Alcuin or Albinus (735–804), English theologian, man of letters who wrote prose and poetry, and coadjutor of Charlemagne in educational reforms. Owing to his connection with Charlemagne, whom he met at Parma in 781, Alcuin settled on the Continent. He eventually was named Bishop of Tours. 128

[295]

Walter Scott in his books. His wife was Catherine Carswell. 3, 70

Carswell, John Patrick (1918–   ), son of Catherine and Donald Carswell, edited his mother's autobiographical *Lying Awake* (1950). To celebrate his birth, D. H. Lawrence wrote "War-Baby," a poem first published in the *English Review* (June 1918). 3

Carter, John Waynflete (1905–   ), English bookman, bibliographer, and writer on bibliographical matters 80

Casement, Roger David (1864–1916), Irish patriot as well as a member of the British Consular service. While on the Continent, Casement attempted to arrange German aid for the Irish Rebellion of 1916. When he returned to Ireland in a German submarine, he was captured, taken to England for trial, and hanged for treason. In 1959, his diaries were released for publication, and in 1965 Casement's body was sent to Dublin for a hero's burial. 8, 73, 108

Castries, Charles Eugène Gabriel de la Croix, marquis de (1727–1801) *maréchal de France*, a position achieved in 1783 after a long and successful army career which commenced in 1739. Named *Minister de la Marine* (1780), in 1786 he published *Le Code Castries*, a summary of his ordinances and rules as minister. At the start of the Revolution, Castries was governor of Flanders and Hainaut. He emigrated in 1791, finding refuge with the Duke of Brunswick, his former adversary at the battle of Clostercamp in 1760. Although Castries later returned to France, he spent his last months with Brunswick. 27

Castries, Claire-Clémence-Henriette de Maillé, duchesse de (b. 1797), was still the marquise de Castries when she first wrote to Balzac in October 1831 and thus began an ardent romance, at least on his part. By then she had already participated in one notorious love affair. In 1822, her marriage a failure, the duchesse had fallen deeply in love with Victor von Metternich, son of the Austrian chancellor. By him, she bore a son Roger, Baron von Aldenburg. In 1829, her lover died of consumption. Aged about 34 when she wrote to Balzac and hardly able to walk owing to injuries in a riding accident, she was noted for her charm and the beauty of her red hair and white skin. She revealed to him the exclusive elegance of the Faubourg St Germain and involved him with the legitimists, led by her uncle the duc de Fitz-James. Balzac pursued her passionately, but in late 1832, en route to Italy with her and her uncle, Balzac brought matters to a head at Geneva and parted from

her. She served as model for the fictitious duchesse de Langeais in the novel of that name. 27

Catullus, Gaius Valerius (87–ca. 54 BC), Roman poet and epigrammatist, born at Verona. His country home was at Sirmio on the Lake of Garda, the Sirmione of Tennyson's "Frater, ave atque vale." 19, 137

Caxton, William (ca. 1421–91), first English printer who learned his craft at Cologne and then printed the first book in English at Bruges in 1475. Caxton was also a translator and author of prologues and epilogues. 27, 134

Cendrars, Blaise (1887–1961), pseud of the French-Swiss writer Frederic Sauser 98

Cervantes Saavedra, Miguel de 77

Césair of Arles 84

Césaire, St 84

César Birotteau (Balzac) 79

Chabaneau, Camille (fl. late 19th c.), philologian and historian who collaborated on a history of Languedoc and on *La Revue des langues romanes* 63

Chagall, Mark (1889–   ), Russian painter who has lived mainly in France since 1910 129

Chalmers, Alexander (1759–1834), biographer, miscellaneous writer, publisher (with George Robinson of Paternoster Row), and prolific editor of, among many others, Fielding's *Works*, Warton's *Essays*, Gibbon's *History*, and the works of Shakespeare, Bolingbroke, and Johnson. Born in Scotland, Chalmers lived in London from 1777. 55, 59, 60, 61, 63

Chamberlain, Arthur Neville (1869–1940), British statesman who was twice chancellor of the exchequer (1923, 1931–37) and prime minister (1937–40). He became the symbol of appeasement as British signatory of the Munich Pact in 1938. When war began in 1939, Chamberlain was still in office, but opposition following the British debacle when Germany invaded Norway in 1940 forced him to resign. 20

Chambord, Henri Charles Ferdinand Marie Dieudonné, count de (1820–83), grandson of Charles X of France and claimant to the French throne; known to legitimists as Henri V. Except for his mother's efforts to overthrow Louis Philippe in 1832 and his own half-hearted move in 1871, nothing was done to gain the throne for Chambord. 62, 99

Champion, Honoré (1846–1913), French publisher and bookseller with a special interest in linguistics. Champion established the scholarly periodicals *Romania* and *Revue des bibliothèques*. 28

Lollobrigida, Gina, continued

in 1949 by Howard Hughes for RKO. Her first film made in the U.S. was *Solomon and Sheba* (1959), although a number of her films had already been exhibited. With her husband Dr Drago Milko Skofic and their son, she moved to Canada in 1960. 100

Longus (fl. ca. 2nd c. AD), possibly the author of *Daphnis and Chloe* 19, 80, 93

Looking Back (Douglas) 63, 107

Lorca, Federico Garcia *see* Garcia Lorca, Federico

Lost Girl, The (D. H. Lawrence) 14

Lotto, Lorenzo (ca. 1480–1556), Venetian painter 87

Louis le Debonnaire or Louis the Pious 16, 84

Louis IX (1214–70), member of the Capetian dynasty of France and king from 1226, starting his reign under the regency of his mother, Blanche of Castille. His rule of France was marked by the establishment of relative peace, real prosperity, and progress. Most of the great Gothic cathedrals of France and Sainte-Chapelle in Paris were built during his reign. In 1927, he was canonized as Saint Louis. 86

Louis XIV (1638–1715), king of France (1643–1715), called "roi soleil" and "the Great" 84, 86, 91, 99

Love and the Luxembourg see *Dream in the Luxembourg, A*

"Love Lives Beyond the Tomb" (Clare) 55

"Love Will Find Out the Way" 55

Love's Martyr (Chester) 61

Lovelace, Augusta Ada Byron, countess of (1816–52), daughter of the poet Byron, born after his departure from England. The first wife of Baron King, who was created first earl of Lovelace in 1838, she was the mother of two sons and a daughter. 64, 66, 105, 106, 107

Low, David Morrice (1890–   ), English school master (Marlborough, Westminster, Kelvinside Academy), lecturer at King's College, London, literary editor and writer. Low was an admirer of Charles Prentice and thus objected to his inclusion in RA's *Pinorman*. 25, 51, 52, 61, 63, 68, 107

Lowell, Amy (1874–1925), American poet who associated herself with the first Imagist anthology (1914), to which RA was a major contributor. Thereafter she sponsored other anthologies, but none was as important as the Imagists'. Her editorial method with it (allowing each poet to select his own contributions) caused a break with Ezra Pound, who had put the Imagist movement together, according to his own statement, from five poems by RA, "five by H.D. and one by

Bill Williams." Pound sometimes referred to Miss Lowell as the "fat bitch of Boston." 3, 98, 134, 136

Lowell, James Russell (1819–91), American poet, essayist, and minister to London (1880–85), where he did much to increase respect for American learning and literature. His *Democracy and Other Addresses* (1887) contains speeches made in England. 1, 43

Lowenfels, Walter 68

Lucas, Frank Laurence (1894–1967), fellow and lecturer of King's College, Cambridge; University Reader in English. His numerous publications include scholarly comments, translations from French and Greek, anthologies, a novel, plays, and poems. T. E. Lawrence described Lucas as an "exquisite" Cambridge don. 2, 112

Luce, Clare Booth (1903–   ), American editor and playwright, representative from Connecticut from 1943 to 1947, and U. S. ambassador to Italy from 1953 to 1957 48

Luce or Lucy, St (fl. 4th c.), a martyr under Diocletian 84

Lucian (fl. 2nd c.), Greek prose writer who was born in Syria and lived in Rome and Egypt. Most characteristic of his almost 80 works are his *Dialogues*, satirizing ancient mythology and contemporary philosophy. His wit, distrust of extravagance, and distaste for fraud make him especially appealing to the modern spirit. Lucian's *True History* may have influenced T. E. Lawrence (his brother thought it did) in its interpretation of the doctrines of the Cynics: "abstention from honour and power with their attendant temptations, and satisfaction with the simple life of the righteous poor." 19

Lucretius (ca. 99–ca 55 BC), Roman poet known for his *De Rerum Natura* 72, 134

Luhan, Mabel Dodge (1879–1962), American writer whose fourth and last husband, married in 1923, was Antonio Lujan, a Navaho Indian. They were intimately associated with D. H. Lawrence during his stays at Taos, New Mexico. Among Mrs Luhan's works are *Lorenzo in Taos* (1932); *Intimate Memories* (1933–37); *Winter in Taos*, and *Taos and its Artists* (1948). 25, 70, 103

Lumumba, Patrice Emergy (1925–61), Congolese nationalist who participated in winning independence from Belgium. Named first prime minister of the Republic of the Congo, Lumumba was dismissed when the army mutinied in 1960, placed under house arrest, and then taken to Katanga where he was killed. 143

Lustra (Pound) 18

Luna, Countess de 64

"Lydia Distracted" (Ayres) 133

Montmorency, Henry II, duke de (1595–1642), admiral and marshal of France and governor of Languedoc. He fought in the religious and foreign wars of Louis XIII, but in 1642 he joined the conspiracy against Richelieu led by Gaston d'Orleans and after capture at Castelnaudry was executed. 88

Moore, G. E. 24

Moore, Alan 79

Moore, Harry T. (ca. 1908–   ), professor of English at Southern Illinois University, whose numerous works include *The Intelligent Heart: The Story of D. H. Lawrence,* (1954) and editions of Lawrence's *Sex Literature and Censorship* (1953) and *The Collected Letters of D. H. Lawrence* (1962). Moore is currently at work on an edition of selected letters of RA. 24, 133, 136

Moore, Marianne (1887–1972), American poet. Her first publication was in *The Egoist,* of which RA was an editor. Miss Moore published several volumes of poetry, winning the Pulitzer Prize in 1951 with her *Collected Poems.* She also published a number of essays, some collected in *Predilections.* From 1925 to 1929, she edited the prestigious literary review *The Dial.* 98

Moore, Sir Norman (1847–1923), 1st bart., created 1919; distinguished British physician long connected with St Bartholomew's Hospital, of which he wrote a history. Moore published several medical treatises, 459 lives written for the *DNB,* and a *Life of Charles Waterton* (1871). 79

Moore, Thomas (1779–1852), Irish poet whose *Irish Melodies* (1808–34) included the well-loved poems "Believe Me If All Those Endearing Young Charms" and "Oft in the Stilly Night." Moore was a friend of Byron, and his biographer. 55, 64, 144

Mordaunt, Charles, 3rd earl of Peterborough (1658–1735), British admiral, general diplomatist, patron of men of letters and science, and friend of such writers as Pope and Swift. Peterborough also wrote poetry, which was published in *The Universal Journal* (1724). 55, 119

More Trivia (Smith) 28

Morgan, Sulwen 64

Mornings in Mexico (D. H. Lawrence) 14, 18, 61, 145

Morrell, Lady Ottoline 24, 136
  Ottoline: The Early Memoirs of . . . (ed Gathorne-Hardy) 24

Morris, Richard 134

Morris, William (1834–96), English poet, craftsman, and socialist, educated at Oxford. Morris found inspiration in the Middle Ages for his furniture, tapestries, and wallpaper as well as for his poems and prose romances.

Among these are *A Dream of John Ball* (1888) and *The House of the Wolfings* (1889). Morris's final proect was the Kelmscott Press. He was T. E. Lawrence's favorite author. About Morris, Lawrence said, "Morris was a great poet; and I'd rather have written the Well at the World's End or The Roots of the Mountain or John Ball or The Hollow Land than anything of the 19th century except War and Peace or Moby Dick. . . ." 7, 19, 31, 55, 58, 59, 93

Mortimer, Raymond (1895–   ), English writer who is currently a reviewer for the London *Sunday Times* 80, 119

Morton, John Cameron Andrien Bingham Michael (1893–   ), English journalist who, since 1924, has been "Beachcomber" of the *Daily Express.* His publications are numerous, including biography, travel books, poetry, short stories, and essays. 95, 96

Mosley, Sir Oswald 142

Mossadegh, Mohammed (1880–1967), Iranian statesman. He nationalized the British-owned oil industry of Iran in 1951, a step which led to a diplomatic break with Britain and economic difficulties. His popularity, however, was a threat to the Shah, and Mossadegh was tried and imprisoned. He had a superabundance of tears, which he caused to flow freely in any difficulty. 17, 33

Moun Espelido (Mistral) 96, 98, 122, 124

Mountolive (Durrell) 143

Mourigan 117

Moving Along (Orioli) 25

Muddiman, Joseph George (b. ca. 1862), wrote *A History of English Journalism . . .* (1908) and *The King's Journalist, 1659–1689* (1923); and edited or helped edit books having to do with state trials in England 108

Muggeridge, Malcolm (1903–   ), English editor variously on the staffs of *Manchester Guardian* (for which he was also corespondent in Moscow 1932–33), *Calcutta Statesman, Evening Standard, Daily Telegraph* (for which he was also correspondent in Washington 1946–47), and *Punch.* He was rector of Edinburgh University 1967–68. His publications include a life of Samuel Butler (1936) and the English edition of Ciano's papers (1948). 77, 86

Muallaquat 19

Munro, Hugh Andrew Johnstone (1819–85), Scottish Classical scholar and compiler of a particularly notable edition of Lucretius 6

Murray, George Gilbert Aimé (1866–1957), British Classicist and translator of Greek drama 24

Murry, John Middleton (1889–1957), English critic, editor, biographer. Murry was the husband of Katherine Mansfield (1888–

1895 and returned to Newport on 27 June 1898. His account of the voyage is in *Sailing Alone around the World* (1900). Slocum sailed again on the *Spray* on 14 Nov 1909 and was never heard of again. 82

Slonimsky, Harry (b. 1884), Polish American philosopher, professor at the Jewish Institute of Religion. He and RA first met in London in 1911 at one of T. E. Hulme's "Tuesday evenings," when Slonimsky had recently completed his education with a degree of doctor of philosophy at Marburg. RA, aged 19, was much impressed with Slonimsky's arguments against Hulme's Bergsonian faith. Slonimsky and RA continued their friendship, meeting later in Paris and New York. Slonimsky was author of *Heraklit and Parmenides* (1912), issued in part as his inaugural dissertation at Marburg. 29, 137

Smart, Christopher (1722–71), English poet chiefly notable for his *Song to David* (1763). Boswell gives an account of a discussion of Smart's madness between Dr Johnson and Dr Burney. 58

"Smile" (D. H. Lawrence) 70

Smith, Alexander (1830–67), Scottish lace-pattern designer turned poet, who published *A Life Drama* (1853), sonnets on the Crimean War jointly with S. T. Dobell, and other poems, as well as two volumes of prose essays 59

Smith, Arthur Lionel (1850–1924), English historian, master of Balliol (1916–24) and author of *Church and State in the Middle Ages* (1913). Smith devoted much time and interest to the education of working-class people. 3
Arthur Lionel Smith . . . ; A Biography and Some Reminiscences by His Wife 3, 5

Smith, Mrs Arthur Lionel (Alice Elizabeth Strutt) 3, 5

Smith, C. H. *see* Harcourt-Smith, Sir Cecil

Smith, F. T. (ca. 1897–   ), after many years in charge of the editorial department of Wm. Collins Sons & Co, Ltd, publishers, was named editorial director in 1952. Smith retained that post until his retirement in 1962. 46, 49, 60

Smith, John Thomas (1766–1833), keeper of drawings and prints at the British Museum and author of two books, *Nollekens and His Times* (1828) and *A Book for a Rainy Day, or, Recollections of the Events of the Years 1766–1833* (1845) 54

Smith, Logan Pearsall (1865–1946), biographer and essayist, who settled in England with his parents, famous in America as Evangelical Quaker preachers. Smith attended Haverford College and Harvard University in America and, after his removal to England, Oxford University, where he obtained a second class in *literae humanores* in 1891. His best-known work, *Trivia*, when it appeared in 1902, attracted even among his friends, little more than "angry contempt." Among his friends were Benjamin Jowett, Robert Bridges, Bernard Berenson, Desmond MacCarthy, and, for a time, Bertrand Russell. 1, 28

Smith, Sydney 75

Smith, Wayland *see* Wayland the Smith

Snow, Charles Percy, Baron Snow of Leicester (1905–   ), English physicist, government official, and writer of essays and of the series of novels *Strangers and Brothers* (1951–64). In 1964–66 Snow was Parliamentary secretary to the ministry of technology. He was made a peer in 1964. 56, 101

Soane, Sir John 35

Soft Answers (RA) 2, 6, 29, 96, 130, 131, 133, 137, 144

Some Diversions of a Man of Letters (Gosse) 29

Some Passages in the Life of Egomet Bonmot (Wainewright) 93

Son of Woman (Murry) 62

Song of a Falling World (Lindsay) 134

Sonnets from the Portuguese (Elizabeth Barrett Browning) 80

"Sonnets from the Portuguese, The" (Gosse) 93

"Sohrab and Rustum" (Arnold) 69

South Wind (Douglas) 23

Southey, Robert (1774–1843), English poet and historian. In 1803 he joined Wordsworth and Coleridge in the Lake District. Ten years later, Southey was named poet laureate. 101

Spalding, Percy (b. ca. 1860), son of H. B. Spalding, paper merchant. Spalding joined Chatto & Windus in 1876 and continued until 1926 with that firm. 36

Speed (Bird) 2

Spender, Stephen (1909–   ), English writer, especially of poetry and literary criticism 99, 143

Spenser, Edmund (ca. 1552–1599), English poet best known for *The Faerie Queene* (1590, 1596) 43, 55, 72

Spiegel, Samuel P. (1904–   ), Austrian born motion-picture producer who came to the United States in 1939 and in 1948 organized Horizon Pictures Inc, of which he is president. Among his pictures are *The African Queen, On the Waterfront, The Strange One, Suddenly Last Summer, Lawrence of Arabia*, and *The Bridge on the River Kwai*. 147